Economic Transition in China
Long-Run Growth and Short-Run Fluctuations

Series on Chinese Economics Research
(ISSN: 2251-1644)

Series Editors: Yang Mu *(Lee Kuan Yew School of Public Policies, NUS)*
Fan Gang *(Peking University, China)*

Published:

Vol. 1: China's State-Owned Enterprises: Nature, Performance and Reform
by Sheng Hong and Zhao Nong

Vol. 2: Food Security and Farm Land Protection in China
by Mao Yushi, Zhao Nong and Yang Xiaojing

Vol. 3: The Micro-Analysis of Regional Economy in China:
A Perspective of Firm Relocation
by Wei Houkai, Wang Yeqiang and Bai Mei

Vol. 4: The China Dream and the China Path
by Zhou Tianyong

Vol. 5: Beyond Demographic Dividends
by Cai Fang

Vol. 6: People's Livelihood in Contemporary China:
Changes, Challenges and Prospects
edited by Li Peilin

Vol. 7: New Paradigm for Interpreting the Chinese Economy:
Theories, Challenges and Opportunities
by Justin Lin Yifu

Vol. 8: Economic Transition in China:
Long-Run Growth and Short-Run Fluctuations
by Yuan Zhigang

Series on Chinese Economics Research – Vol. 8

Economic Transition in China
Long-Run Growth and Short-Run Fluctuations

Editor

Zhigang YUAN
Fudan University, China

World Scientific

NEW JERSEY · LONDON · SINGAPORE · BEIJING · SHANGHAI · HONG KONG · TAIPEI · CHENNAI

Published by

World Scientific Publishing Co. Pte. Ltd.
5 Toh Tuck Link, Singapore 596224
USA office: 27 Warren Street, Suite 401-402, Hackensack, NJ 07601
UK office: 57 Shelton Street, Covent Garden, London WC2H 9HE

Library of Congress Cataloging-in-Publication Data
Economic transition in China : long-run growth and short-run fluctuations / [edited] by Zhigang Yuan.
    pages cm. -- (World scientific series on Chinese economics research, ISSN 2251-1644 ; vol. 8)
    ISBN 978-9814569972
    1. Economic development--China. 2. China--Economic policy--1976–2000. 3. China--Economic policy--2000–   I. Yuan, Zhigang, 1958–
    HC427.95.E34128 2014
    330.951--dc23
                                                          2014003538

British Library Cataloguing-in-Publication Data
A catalogue record for this book is available from the British Library.

Copyright © 2014 by World Scientific Publishing Co. Pte. Ltd.

All rights reserved. This book, or parts thereof, may not be reproduced in any form or by any means, electronic or mechanical, including photocopying, recording or any information storage and retrieval system now known or to be invented, without written permission from the publisher.

For photocopying of material in this volume, please pay a copying fee through the Copyright Clearance Center, Inc., 222 Rosewood Drive, Danvers, MA 01923, USA. In this case permission to photocopy is not required from the publisher.

In-House Editors: Dong Lixi/Sutha Surenddar

Typeset by Stallion Press
Email: enquiries@stallionpress.com

Printed in Singapore

Contents

Acknowledgement xi
List of Tables xiii
List of Figures xix

Chapter 1 **China's Economic Growth Under Globalization** 1
Zhigang Yuan and Yuxin Yu
  1. The Opportunities of China's Economic Development Brought by Globalization 2
  2. The Change in the Driving Force of China's Economic Development Since Reform and Opening Up 5
  3. Problems and their Influences in the Current Stage of China's Economic Development . . . 16
  4. Development Strategy of Sustainable Growth in Chinese Economy 32
  5. Conclusion 38
  References 39

Chapter 2 **Potential Economic Growth of China in Transition** 41
Zhigang Yuan and Yuxin Yu
  1. Introduction 41
  2. History and Stages of the Chinese Economy Since 1978 43
  3. Trends of Potential Economic Growth Rate in China 45

	4. Conclusions and Policy Implications	66
	References	68
Chapter 3	**Is China's Export Really Special? Perspective from Trade in Value Added**	**71**
	Changyuan Luo and Jiajun Xu	
	1. Introduction	72
	2. Theoretical Considerations	76
	3. Data	83
	4. The Domestic Value Added of China's Exports	86
	5. The Difference in Domestic Value Added of Exports Between China and Other Countries	92
	6. China's Trade Balance in Value Added	103
	7. Conclusions and Policy Implications	106
	References	109
Chapter 4	**The Consumption Issue in the Long-term Growth and Short-term Fluctuations**	**111**
	Zhigang Yuan and Can Rao	
	1. Introduction	111
	2. Consumption in Long-Term Economic Growth and Short-Term Economic Fluctuations	114
	3. Characteristics of and Change in Chinese Residents' Consumption Behavior	117
	4. The Causes of China's Under-Consumption Problem	129
	5. Consumption Improvement: Factor Market Reform and Equal Public Goods Supply	138
	References	145
Chapter 5	**The Political Economy of Chinese Reform**	**147**
	Zhe Yang	
	1. Introduction	147
	2. Review of System Researches on China's Reform	149

	3. The Theory Construction of Chinese Characteristic Market Economy	153
	4. Chinese Characteristic Market and Government	157
	5. The Prospect of the Reforms	166
	References	171
Chapter 6	**Whither Federalism, Chinese Style**	**175**
	Yongqin Wang	
	1. Introduction	175
	2. Incentives Facing Local Governments in the Chinese Style Federalism	177
	3. Costs of Chinese Style Federalism: Perverse Incentives	180
	4. Costs of the Chinese Style Federalism	183
	5. Reforming Federalism, Chinese Style	200
	References	206
Chapter 7	**Financial Reform: Opportunity and Challenge to China's Future Growth**	**211**
	Zhigang Yuan and Jingwen Yu	
	1. Introduction	211
	2. Evolution of China's Financial System	213
	3. Chinese Economic Growth: Role of Finance	217
	4. Economic Growth Through Further Financial Reform	227
	5. Future Path of Financial Reform	240
	References	242
Chapter 8	**China's Urbanization: Past, Present, and Future**	**245**
	Hao Zheng	
	1. The Basic Facts of China's Urbanization	246
	2. China's Urban System	254
	3. The Opportunity and Challenge of the New Urbanization	262
	References	274

Chapter 9   China's Real Estate Market Development   277
Yuan Wang

1. Introduction 277
2. Development and Tendency: A Closer Look at China's Real Estate Market 278
3. The Real Estate Market and Economic Growth   305
4. Real Estate Policies 315
References 318

Chapter 10   Fiscal System and Local Government Behavior   321
Shengyan Xu and Wancong Li

1. Introduction 321
2. Evolution of China's Fiscal System and the "Tax-Sharing" Reform 322
3. Changes in Local Governments' Incentives .. 334
4. Formation and Impact of Land-Based Finance   341
References 355

Chapter 11   The Demographic Factors in the Chinese Economy   357
Qin Chen

1. Introduction 357
2. Demographic Change in China 358
3. China's Demographic Changes Impact on the Economy 377
4. The Impact of Demographic Changes in Other Aspects of Economic Development 388
5. Conclusion 390
References 391

Chapter 12   The Labor Market in China   395
Qin Chen

1. The Urbanization of Labor 396
2. The Speed of Rural–Urban Migrants, and the Composition of Urbanization 403

	3. The Scale and Structure of Rural–Urban Migration	409
	4. The Education and Wage in the Labor Market	416
	5. Conclusion	424
	References	425
Chapter 13	**Social Justice and Intergenerational Income Mobility**	**427**
	Lin Chen	
	1. Introduction	427
	2. The Importance of Enhancing Social Mobility	429
	3. The Intergenerational Income Mobility in China	432
	4. The Estimation Bias in the Calculation of IIE in China	436
	5. The Mechanism of the Intergenerational Income Mobility in China	440
	6. The Public Policies for Enhancing Intergenerational Income Mobility	456
	References	458
Chapter 14	**Further Development of Urbanization and the Policy Research on the Rural Migrant Workers Granted Urban Citizenship**	**463**
	Jing Tan	
	1. Introduction	463
	2. China's "Two Steps of Urbanization" and Its History	464
	3. The Characteristics of Rural Labor Force Migration in China	471
	4. The Institutional Barriers and Costs for Citizenization of Rural Migrant Workers	476
	References	498
Index		**501**

Acknowledgement

We gratefully acknowledge the financial supports by 985 Project at Fudan University (Project No. 2011SHKXZD003), Social Science Foundation of China (Project No. 12&ZD074) and Translation Project of the Shanghai Chinese Humanities and Social Sciences Academic Boutique.

List of Tables

Table 2-1	Incomes of China, South Korea, and Japan in the transition period (current international $).	44
Table 2-2	Savings rates of different countries (%).	59
Table 2-3	Shares of expenditures on education and medical and healthcare in GDP (%).	60
Table 2-4	Regression results.	63
Table 2-5	TFP growth, output growth, and the contribution of TFP before 1978.	64
Table 2-6	TFP growth, output growth, and the contribution of TFP after 1978.	64
Table 2-7	TFP growth rate of Japan in its transitional years (%).	65
Table 3-1	Comparison of TiVA and trade in the traditional method.	84
Table 3-2	Domestic value added at the sectorial level (%).	87
Table 3-3	The change in value added ratio of China's exports and its decomposition (%).	91
Table 3-4	Cross-country comparison of domestic value added of gross exports (%).	93
Table 3-5	Difference in domestic value added between China and the United States (%): all sectors.	96
Table 3-6	Difference in domestic value added between China and Germany (%): all sectors.	98
Table 3-7	Difference in domestic value added between China and Brazil (%): all sectors.	100

xiv List of Tables

Table 3-8	Difference in domestic value added between China and South Korea (%): all sectors.	102
Table 3-9	China's trade balance with trading partners (million US$).	105
Table 5-1	Profit and loss of the SOEs nationwide (1990–1998).	162
Table 6-1	Main indicators of all state-owned and non-state-owned industrial enterprises grossing more than 100 million yuan size in 2009.	195
Table 7-1	External wealth of China (million US$).	224
Table 7-2	External wealth of the United States (million US$).	225
Table 7-3	China's financial development in 2010 (Billion US$).	227
Table 7-4	Variable definitions and sources.	233
Table 7-5	Descriptive statistics.	234
Table 7-6	Financial repression regression results (estimated on OECD sample).	235
Table 7-7	Financial repression gap and economic development.	236
Table 8-1	China's administrative division (1980–2010).	247
Table 8-2	Japan's county-level administrative division.	248
Table 8-3	China's urban population (1970–2010).	252
Table 8-4	Chenery model and China's facts.	253
Table 8-5	Cities more than 1 Million population taking up the countries' proportion (%).	255
Table 8-6	The urban scale distribution of China (2000–2010).	259
Table 8-7	The distribution of urban scale.	260
Table 8-8	The comparison of Atlanta and Barcelona.	270
Table 8-9	Water resources of the first tier area in 2011 (billion cubic meters).	273
Table 9-1	A retrospect on China's real estate market development since 1979.	280
Table 9-2	Statistical characteristics of real estate development in eastern, middle, and western China.	288
Table 9-3	General situation of the banks' real estate fund products.	304
Table 9-4	Private equity investment (billion yuan).	304
Table 11-1	Fertility difference between rural and urban areas.	365

Table 11-2	Change of maternal education from 1990 to 2010.	372
Table 11-3	Age structure in China from 2010 to 2100.	378
Table 11-4	Model Parameters for pension simulation.	380
Table 11-5	China's future trend in GDP and labor productivity.	382
Table 11-6	Simulation scenarios.	385
Table 12-1	Types of domiciles and their urban–rural character.	400
Table 12-2	Population by types of resident and original location (migrated in last 5 years).	401
Table 12-3	Population out of their domicile by types of resident and domicile.	402
Table 12-4	The composition of 2010 urban population (10 and older).	404
Table 12-5	Rural–Urban migrants out of their domicile in 2000 and 2010 (million).	405
Table 12-6	The structure of increasing urban population.	408
Table 12-7	Comparison of the age structure of migrants in urban areas with/without agricultural *hukou*.	409
Table 12-8	Share of rural–urban migrants in urban region, by age group.	412
Table 12-9	Share of rural–urban migrants out of rural region, by age group.	414
Table 12-10	Proportion of workers living in rural regions working off-farm.	415
Table 12-11	Returns to education, 1988 to 2011.	419
Table 12-12	Comparison of the education structure of rural–urban migrants or migrants from township/villager's committee of Town.	420
Table 12-13	Rural–urban migrants and rural residents by each education level (thousands).	421
Table 13-1	Descriptive statistics for the time trend.	434
Table 13-2	Descriptive statistics for the measurement error.	438
Table 13-3	Reliability ratio for the persistent transitory income bias ($\lambda^{AR(1)}$).	439
Table 13-4	Reliability ratio for the life cycle bias in father's income ($\lambda^{LCY,FATHER}$).	440

xvi List of Tables

Table 13-5	Reliability ratio for the life cycle bias in children's income ($\lambda^{LCY,CHILD}$).	440
Table 13-6	IIE estimation for different countries.	441
Table 13-7	Descriptive statistics for the mechanisms.	447
Table 13-8	Human capital and intergenerational income mobility.	449
Table 13-9	Social capital and intergenerational income mobility.	450
Table 13-10	Housing assets and intergenerational income mobility.	451
Table 13-11	Living area and offspring income in urban areas.	452
Table 13-12	Financial assets and intergenerational income mobility.	453
Table 13-13	Land assets and intergenerational income mobility.	454
Table 13-14	Different income sources and children's income in rural areas.	455
Table 13-15	Public expenditures and intergenerational income mobility.	456
Table 14-1	The payment rate of urban employees' basic Social Insurance and Urban Housing Fund in China.	478
Table 14-2	The social welfare differences between workers with and without Shanghai *Hukou* in the urban labor market.	480
Table 14-3	The basic labor social insurances conditions across nations.	481
Table 14-4	The economic situation of rural migrant workers' families in Beijing, Shanghai, and Guangzhou in 2012.	482
Table 14-5	The ratio of rural migrant workers who participate in the "Five Social Insurances and Urban Housing Fund" in several investigations.	484
Table 14-6	The scale and proportion of students with urban *hukou* in vocational schools.	485
Table 14-7	The scale and sources of fund of vocational schools.	486
Table 14-8	The situation of average rent in the rural migrant workers' families in Beijing Shanghai and Guangzhou in 2012.	487
Table 14-9	Different studies relating to the citizenization costs of rural migrant workers.	490

Table 14-10	The social security costs for the rural migrant worker.	492
Table 14-11	The education costs for the migrant children.	494
Table 14-12	Total costs of citizenization of the rural migrant worker.	495

List of Figures

Figure 1-1	Net inflow of FDI (BoP, current US$).	3
Figure 1-2	FDI inflows' share of GDP.	4
Figure 1-3	Three main industries' share of GDP before and after reform and opening up.	6
Figure 1-4	Three main industries' share of GDP since the 1980s.	8
Figure 1-5	The total sum of profits of SOEs and non-SOEs beyond designated size.	11
Figure 1-6	Total import and export volume.	12
Figure 1-7	Total import and export volume's share of GDP.	12
Figure 1-8	Actual use of foreign capital.	13
Figure 1-9	The share of primary and industrial products in total exports.	14
Figure 2-1	Capital allocation distortions in China.	50
Figure 2-2	Household savings rate.	53
Figure 2-3	Household income growth.	55
Figure 2-4	TFP growth rates.	64
Figure 4-1	International comparison of consumption growth rate.	115
Figure 4-2	Growth rate of final consumption, gross capital formation and net export.	115
Figure 4-3	The numbers of car ownership and GDP per capita.	117
Figure 4-4	The change of average propensity to consume in urban area.	119
Figure 4-5	Final consumption and residents' consumption.	122

Figure 4-6-1	The amount and growth rate of retail sales of consumer goods.	122
Figure 4-6-2	The monthly change of wholesale and retail & accommodation and catering.	123
Figure 4-7-1	The change of consumption structure in urban area.	124
Figure 4-7-2	The change of consumption structure in rural area.	124
Figure 4-8	Annual change in the number and growth rate of car production.	125
Figure 4-9	The comparison of China's consumption ratio with the developed countries.	127
Figure 4-10	Comparison of China's consumption ratio with Asian countries.	128
Figure 4-11	The gap of consumption expenditure between urban and rural areas.	131
Figure 4-12	The comparison of consumption structure in urban and rural area.	131
Figure 4-13	Number of major durable goods per hundred families in urban and rural areas.	132
Figure 4-14	China's Gini index (2003–2012).	133
Figure 4-15	Comparison of the disposable income of urban and rural residents.	134
Figure 4-16	House price and family planning policy.	137
Figure 6-1	Proportion of national income made up by labor income.	185
Figure 6-2	Growth of real GDP and inflation (1986–2009).	190
Figure 6-3	Proportion of fixed asset investment and household consumption in GDP (1970–2009).	190
Figure 6-4	Retail price index and real interest rate for saving in China from Feb 1989 to Sep 2007.	191
Figure 6-5	People employed by urban businesses according to ownership (1978–2009).	194
Figure 6-6	The proportion of China's trade surplus to GDP (1985–2008).	197
Figure 6-7	Micro-foundation of China's macro economy.	199
Figure 7-1	Sequence of interest rate liberalization and bank crisis.	212

Figure 7-2	Consumption per capita in China (yuan).	214
Figure 7-3	Technical efficiency between SOEs and non-SOEs.	220
Figure 7-4	Deposit interest rate and GDP growth rate (China).	221
Figure 7-5	Deposit interest rate and GDP growth rate (US).	222
Figure 7-6	Ratio of dividend to market valuation.	222
Figure 7-7	Financial repression and economic performance in China.	228
Figure 7-8	Quantile coefficients of financial repression for Log real GDP per capita.	229
Figure 7-9	Quantile coefficients of financial repression gap for Log real GDP per capita.	237
Figure 7-10	Financial repression gap (China vs. World Average).	238
Figure 7-11	Optimal financial repression in China.	238
Figure 8-1	Definition of China's urban population in the fifth census.	251
Figure 8-2	Countries' urbanization ratio and per capita GNI.	253
Figure 8-3	China's urbanization ratio and industrialization ratio (1960–2010).	254
Figure 8-4	The proportion of construction industry taking up the secondary industry.	262
Figure 8-5	China's major provinces' crop acreage.	264
Figure 8-6	China's major provinces' rice acreage and yield.	264
Figure 8-7	China's major provinces' wheat acreage and yield.	265
Figure 8-8	Major nations' rice acreage and yield.	266
Figure 8-9	Major nations' wheat acreage and yield.	266
Figure 8-10	Major nations' per capita arable land and fertilizer usage.	267
Figure 8-11	China's major provinces crop acreage.	268
Figure 8-12	The world's major national road network and rail network density (2009).	269
Figure 8-13	Major cities subway operator mileage and planning.	271
Figure 9-1	Real estate development and economic growth during 1978–2010.	279
Figure 9-2	Land sales through public auction during 2003–2010.	283

xxii   List of Figures

Figure 9-3	Price index of land and housing during 1998–2009 (compared to the previous year, which takes the value of 100).	283
Figure 9-4	Land revenue during 2003–2010.	284
Figure 9-5	The growth rate of land supply volume and housing price during 2000–2010.	284
Figure 9-6	Land use pattern during 2003–2008 (land supply for free for specific use is excluded).	285
Figure 9-7	Land supply from government and land finished construction during 2003–2008.	286
Figure 9-8	Housing prices in eastern, middle, and western China during 1998–2011.	288
Figure 9-9	Contribution of real estate sector to GDP during 1998–2011 in different regions.	289
Figure 9-10	The year-in-year growth rate of real estate investment during 1998–2011 in different regions.	289
Figure 9-11	Real estate investment elasticity during 1999–2011 in different regions (Real estate investment elasticity = growth rate of real estate investment/growth rate of GDP).	290
Figure 9-12	The real estate self-financing ratio during 1999–2011 in different regions.	291
Figure 9-13	The ratio of sales area to built-up area of commercial housing during 2004–2011 in different regions.	291
Figure 9-14	The ratio of purchased land area to developed land area during 1999–2009 in different regions.	292
Figure 9-15	The growth rate of the areas of commercial housings for sale during 2008–2010 in different regions.	292
Figure 9-16	The housing price for residential estate during 1998–2011.	294
Figure 9-17	The housing price index and rent index for residential estate during 1998–2009 (compared to the previous year who takes the value of 100).	294
Figure 9-18	Investment growth rate of residential estate during 1998–2011.	295

Figure 9-19	The ratio of sales area to built-up area of residential estate during 1998–2010.	296
Figure 9-20	The growth rate of the areas of residential estate for sale during 2000–2010.	296
Figure 9-21	Investment growth rate of commercial estate during the period 1998–2011.	298
Figure 9-22	Commercial estate price during 1997–2011.	299
Figure 9-23	The ratio of sales area to built-up area of commercial estate during 1998–2010.	299
Figure 9-24	Funding sources of real estate enterprises during the period 1997–2011.	301
Figure 9-25	Average duration and return of the collective capital trust during 2003–2011.	302
Figure 9-26	The issued scale of real estate collective capital trust during 2003–2011.	303
Figure 9-27	Real estate loans during 2005–2011 (billion yuan).	305
Figure 9-28	Real estate investment and economic fluctuation during the period 1996–2011 (Data in this table are calculated at current year).	306
Figure 9-29	Real estate and economic growth during the period 1979–2011 (Data in this table are calculated at current year).	307
Figure 9-30	Urban expansion and urban population growth during the period 1998–2010.	308
Figure 9-31	Urbanization and housing price during the period 1998–2011.	309
Figure 9-32	Urbanization and sales area of housing during the period 1998–2011.	309
Figure 9-33	Real estate taxation during the period 2000–2011.	310
Figure 9-34	Relationship between land, urbanization, real estate market, and economic growth.	310
Figure 9-35	Mortgage on one unit of land and revenue generated by one unit of land during the period 2003–2010.	311
Figure 9-36	Real deposit interest rate of China vs. the United States during the period 1980–2010.	313

List of Figures

Figure 9-37	Housing price to income ratio during the period 1998–2011 (for a family of three people with the area of residence being 90 m²).	314
Figure 9-38	1998–2012 House price and real estate policies.	316
Figure 10-1	Growth rate of national fiscal revenue and GDP (%), 1978–2011.	327
Figure 10-2	National fiscal revenue to GDP ratio (%), 1978–2011.	327
Figure 10-3	Central and local fiscal revenue structure (%), 1978–2011.	330
Figure 10-4	Central and local fiscal expenditure structure (%), 1978–2011.	331
Figure 10-5	Local fiscal revenue and expenditure gap, 1978–2011.	332
Figure 10-6	Central tax return and local fiscal deficit, 1999–2012.	333
Figure 10-7	National infrastructure stock growth rate (in constant prices).	339
Figure 10-8	Land leasehold revenue and local fiscal revenue, 1999–2011.	342
Figure 10-9	Land leasehold revenue and land mortgage loans.	343
Figure 11-1	Birth rate and mortality rate of China (0.1%).	359
Figure 11-2	The population age structure of 4 censuses from 1982 to 2010.	360
Figure 11-3	Fertility rate of women of childbearing age fertility rate of 4 censuses (number of births/1,000 persons).	361
Figure 11-4	Difference in number of children between Han and Minority.	363
Figure 11-5	Fertility difference between Han and minorities by education and cohort.	364
Figure 11-6	Fertility difference between rural and urban women by education and cohort.	366
Figure 11-7	East Asian fertility levels over the years.	367
Figure 11-8	The percentage of reductions in fertility from 1990 to 2010.	370
Figure 11-9	Average education level of women and change of fertility rate of 358 prefecture-level cities.	371
Figure 11-10	Effect of changes in years of education on fertility — quintile regression.	372

List of Figures   xxv

Figure 11-11	Changes of fertility of 2010 and 2030.	373
Figure 11-12	Simulation and census data of total population and age structure of 2010.	375
Figure 11-13	Total population change under various fertility rate scenarios.	376
Figure 11-14	The ratio of balance gap to nominal GDP under four scenarios.	385
Figure 11-15	The ratio of accumulated deficit to GDP in 2010 under four scenarios.	386
Figure 11-16	The subsidies of urban and rural residents pension system subsidies from 2010 to 2030.	388
Figure 12-1	The structure of *hukou* migrants.	407
Figure 12-2	The structure of migrants with agricultural *hukou*.	410
Figure 12-3	Age structure of migrants with agricultural *hukou* (%).	411
Figure 12-4	Share of rural–urban migrants in urban region, by age group.	413
Figure 12-5	Share of rural–urban migrants out of rural region, by age group.	414
Figure 12-6	Population with agricultural *hukou*: 2000 and 2010.	415
Figure 12-7	Education distributions in 1990 and 2010.	417
Figure 12-8	Education distribution across age (Census 2010).	418
Figure 12-9	Rural–urban migrants by education level.	421
Figure 12-10	Monthly wage of first job in Shanghai, proportion relative to 2000.	422
Figure 12-11	Monthly wage of first job in Beijing, proportion relative to 2000.	423
Figure 12-12	Monthly wage of first job in Guangzhou, proportion relative to 2000.	424
Figure 13-1	The trend of IIE in China (1988–2005, total).	434
Figure 13-2	The trend of IIE in China (1988–2005, high- and low-income group).	435
Figure 14-1	Urbanization rate, the proportion of non-agricultural household registration, the proportion of agricultural output, non-agricultural employment proportion, and industrialization rate over the years.	469

Figure 14-2	The arc elasticity of GDP per capita to UPE and the arc elasticity of GDP per capita to NHE over the years.	470
Figure 14-3	The scale of rural migrant workers and local rural workers from 2008.	472
Figure 14-4	The differences of pension fund received per capita and spent per capita of urban employees' basic endowment insurance between SOEs and NSEs (1999–2010).	479

Chapter 1

China's Economic Growth Under Globalization[1]

Zhigang Yuan

School of Economics, Fudan University

Yuxin Yu

School of Economics, Shanghai International Studies University

In the past 30 years, China has achieved average annual growth of 9%, which is considered to be China's economic miracle. China's economic development is achieved by exploiting the economic potential of internal factors in a favorable external environment. The economic globalization process brought opportunities and development spaces for China since the 1980s. Chinese policy makers have seized the favorable strategic development period. Therefore, China's economic growth miracle is also a process of China's economic integration into the global economic system. The global perspective is required to understand China's economic development process and the reforming orientation in the future.

Since reform and opening up, the Chinese economy went through the rural reform of the rural land contract system, the rise of township enterprises and the expansion of rural industrialization, reform of state-owned enterprises (SOEs) in the urban area, and the complete integration into economic globalization characterized by its accession to the

---

[1] The research is supported by the program of young teachers' innovation group in Shanghai International Studies University. Program code: 2011114012; the planned program in Shanghai International Studies University. Program code: 2012114045.

WTO. Economic globalization promotes China's economic growth. With the participation of China's elements in the global industrial value chains of multinational corporations, the characteristics of economic globalization have been embedded in all aspects of the Chinese economy. China's economic development strategy cannot be separated from globalization, its regional imbalances in development, and the history of the planned system. China's sustainable economic development requires both top-layer design and market exploration, including the improvement of its bilateral relations with other countries, the change of the relations between the government and the market, and efficiency-oriented reforms of the factor market. With all these reforms, China's sustainable economic growth will be achieved.

1. THE OPPORTUNITIES OF CHINA'S ECONOMIC DEVELOPMENT BROUGHT BY GLOBALIZATION

China's economic miracle is achieved by its globalization strategy. The appearance of a global communication system in the 1970s marked the beginning of mutual contact in human society. At the same time, the world entered the era of globalization. Since the early 1980s, the rapid development of transportation and information technology has resulted in significantly decreasing costs of communication and transportation (Frankel, 2000).[2] The change in the factor endowment structure due to the aging society and the increased competition in the domestic market encourage multinational corporations to seek to exploit comparative advantages around the world. Meanwhile, market-oriented allocation of resources is gradually becoming more prevalent, which provides a favorable external environment, thus contributing to the implementation of China's reform and opening-up policy.

This round of economic globalization is promoted by the industrial value chain layout of multinational corporations in developed economies, which pursue global competitiveness and profits. China becomes the most important undertaker of industrial transfers because of its comparative advantages and abundant labor resources.

---

[2]Frankel, J. A. (2000). *Globalization of the Economy.* NBER Working Paper, No. 7858. August.

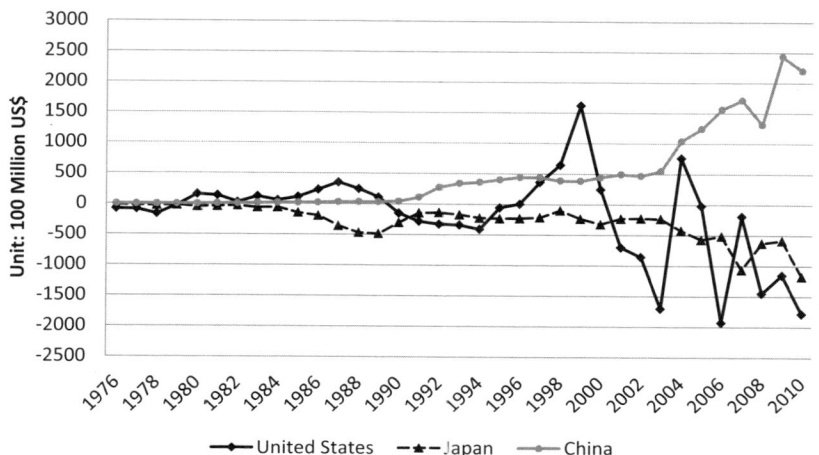

Figure 1-1: Net inflow of FDI (BoP, current US$).
Source: World Bank database.

The advanced economies dominate global foreign direct investment (FDI), and these global industries flow out from developed countries (see Figure 1-1). Naturally, it can be observed that these countries are mostly net FDI outflow countries since the 1980s, such as the United States and Japan. Developing countries are home to corresponding industries, and China is one of the prominent representatives. According to data from the United States, Japan, and China, net FDI flows were very small before the mid-1980s. In terms of the United States, the US economic stimulus plans have attracted some FDI inflows before the 1990s. Subsequently, net external investment appeared in the United States in the mid-1990s with the rise of its information technology. However, as the network technology bubble burst, the US FDI outflows, which represent external net investment, remain larger than the FDI inflows, despite the rebound of FDI inflows due to the Iraq War and the events of 9/11.

Since the mid-1980s, Japan's FDI rose sharply, as the investment growth of the four dragons (Hong Kong, South Korea, Taiwan and Singapore) in Asia and China. Since then, Japan has been a net outward investor, and there is a substantial growth trend of FDI outflow over the last 10 years.

In China's case, it is clear that, since the reform and opening up in the 1980s, net FDI inflows continue to increase. Except for the occasional two years of lagging behind the United States, China has always had the largest net inflows of FDI, which shows that China is the most important undertaker of industrial transfers in globalization and the industrial basis of the largest import and export industry in the world. The developed countries naturally open their markets to China, while transferring their industries to China at the same time, which offers a ready-made market space for China's industrial development. The large international market offers great opportunities for optimal allocation of production factors in China and maintains a relatively long period of the high-speed development of China's economy.

Global industry transfer is a strong external driving force of the transition of China's economic structure and China's economic growth. Net FDI inflows continued to increase since the 1980s, which accounted for the highest proportion of GDP over 5% (see Figure 1-2). Even in the 1990s when the share of net inflows of FDI in GDP was declining, FDI was still playing a crucial role in promoting China's economic development. Without the entry of these internationally competitive investors, the allocation efficiency of China's economic development would decline. Therefore, FDI, which integrates China's economy into the global industrial value chain, is an essential factor and cannot be ignored in the economic growth of China. In particular, the spillover effects of FDI have a positive impact on the

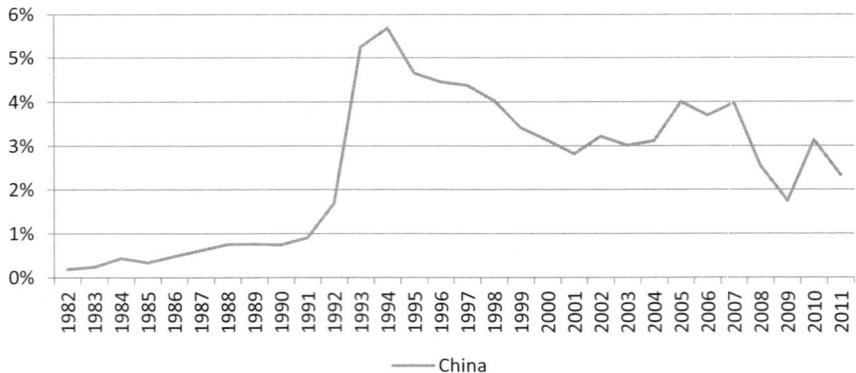

Figure 1-2: FDI inflows' share of GDP.

Source: World Bank database.

efficiency of the allocation of economic factors in China (Geng Qiang and Shen Kunrong, 2001).[3]

2. THE CHANGE IN THE DRIVING FORCE OF CHINA'S ECONOMIC DEVELOPMENT SINCE REFORM AND OPENING UP

As an internal driving force for China's economic growth, the institutional change due to reform and opening up since 1978 promoted economic development, and started China's high-speed economic growth for more than 30 years. As Deng Xiaoping said, China's economic reform is "touching the stones and gradually moving forward." At different stages of development, the obstacles of economic development are different, and the goal of the reform is also different at each stage. Therefore, China's main drivers of economic growth in the past 30 years are not the same at different stages of development.

From the perspective of the main driving force of China's economic growth, the 30 years of China's economic miracle can be divided into four stages: rural land reform, rural industrialization, urban reform, and joining the WTO.

2.1 Stage 1: Rural Land Reform

The first stage of China's initial economic reform started from the third plenary session of the 11th Communist Party of China (CPC) (1978–1984) the focus of which was in rural areas. Specifically, rural land reform eliminated the people's commune system, restored the country regime, and introduced the household contract responsibility system, which has inspired farmers' production enthusiasm, which made a real breakthrough of the reform process. This stage accelerated the pace of agricultural development, and average annual growth of agricultural output rose from 2.7% to 6.2%

---

[3] Sheng Kunrong and Ge Qiang (2001). FDI, technology spillover and endogenous economic growth: The empirical analysis and econometric test on China data. *China Political Science* 5.

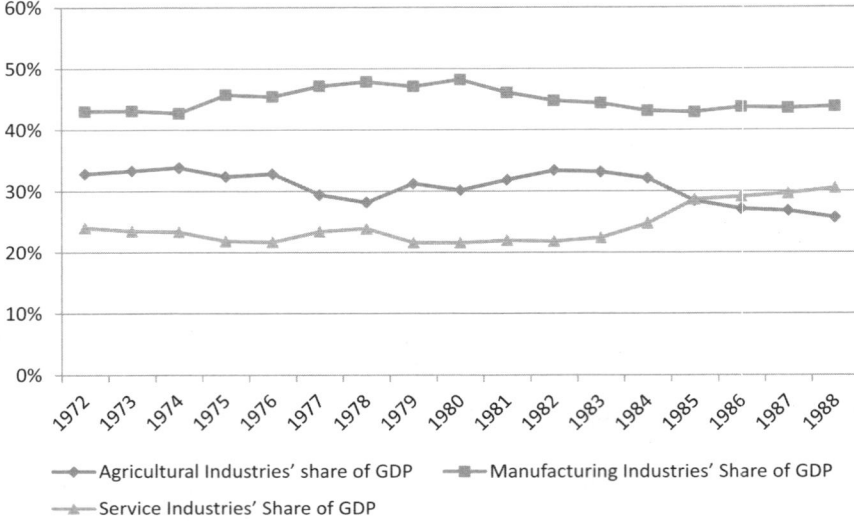

Figure 1-3: Three main industries' share of GDP before and after reform and opening up.
Source: CEIC databases.

(Gao Shangquan, 1991).[4] The agricultural sector's share of GDP in the period had a significant rebound (see Figure 1-3).

Rural productivity enhancement resulted from the change of land-use patterns due to the rural household contract responsibility system. The shift from collective focus to the family-farm model motivated farmers' enthusiasm for agricultural production and liberated rural labor forces. Therefore, this period of economic growth was mainly driven by the systematic reform of rural land use. Because the added value of land production is much smaller than modern industrial production, the primary driving force of economic growth gradually became weak after several years of rapid development of agriculture. In order to further boost economic growth considering policy obstacles, China started the policy of "leaving the land but not the country," which means the transfer of agricultural labor to non-agricultural labor within the rural areas. The policy started the reform of

---

[4]Gao Shangquan (1991). The achievement of China's reform in economic system in the 1980s. *Enterprise Management* 1: 11–13.

rural township enterprises, and the Chinese economy entered the second stage of economic reforms.

2.2 Stage 2: Rural Industrialization

The second stage of China's economic reforms is the industrialization in rural areas (1985–1991). Along with the gradual dissolution of the people's commune, the original social enterprises officially changed their name to "township enterprises" in 1984, and local township governments inherited the management of enterprises. In order to further promote China's economic reform and ease the impact of shortages on economic development, the central government started rural industrialization and actively promoted the development of township enterprises.

Township enterprises used the large market demands and production shortages left from the planned economy, and produced higher-profit products in the market. Tight market conditions ensured the efficiency and growth of township enterprises, which spurred their rapid expansion. From 1985 to 1994, the township enterprises' share of national industrial output went up from 14.6% to 30.45% (Yan Yuming, 2011).[5]

The development of township enterprises promoted China's economic growth in the manufacturing industry. There was a marked rise in the manufacturing industry's proportion of the GDP in the late 1980s. At that time, FDI's share of GDP was less than 1% because reforms in the city were difficult and SOEs lacked flexible mechanisms. The phenomenon provided a relatively good environment for the development of the rural township enterprises, which became the major driving force of China's rapid economic growth and industrial development at that time (Zhang Weiyin and Su Shuhe, 1998).[6]

Township enterprises entered the stage of rapid development from 1984 to 1991, and the township enterprises' number, their share of GDP, and industrial production increased sharply. By 1991, the gross output value of township enterprises in China reached 1,162.2 billion yuan, absorbing

---

[5]Yan Yuming (2011). A Survey on the reasons of transformation of enterprises. *China Foreign Trade* 11: 2–4, 22.

[6]Zhang Weiyin and Su Shuhe (1998). Interregional competition and privatization of China's SOEs. *Economics Research* 12: 13–22.

Figure 1-4: Three main industries' share of GDP since the 1980s.
Source: CEIC databases.

96.14 million of the labor force, which accounted for 22.3% of the total rural labor force. In contrast, in 1983, the township enterprises' output value was 101.683 billion yuan and absorbed 32.35 million of the labor force, which accounted for 9.4% of the total rural labor force (*The Yearbook of Chinese Township Enterprises*).[7] There was a huge improvement of township enterprises in job creation over this period in both absolute and relative terms. In the 1990s, the ability of township enterprises to absorb labor force slowed down and there was even absolute reduction of jobs in occasional years, which means that in the latter part of the second stage of the reform and opening up, the ability of township enterprises to absorb labor continued to weaken and there was a decline in the driving force of economic growth from township enterprises.

There is a wide difference between the market mechanism of township enterprises and the firms in the planned system. The market adjusts the supply and demand of the township enterprises' products. The labor

---

[7] *The Yearbook of Chinese Township Enterprises (1989–1999)*. China Agriculture Press.

market and distribution system are both flexible, and rely on the market to allocate resources. The township enterprises improved the efficiency of resource allocation. Because of the labor-intensive production, while township enterprises gained labor absorption and market adaptability, the problem of production blindness and instability also appeared. In some ways, labor productivity is generally lower in the township enterprises. Therefore, once the SOEs in the city are reformed, the technical, market, and capital advantages of the SOEs in the city put the township enterprises at a disadvantage. The township enterprises gradually declined with the deepening of reform of the SOEs in the city.

Although township enterprises are no longer the main driving force of China's economic growth, it is undeniable that they played a crucial role in China's economic development at this stage. Township enterprises' active role in China's economic reform and growth process includes the following: (1) The market-oriented operation mode of township enterprises has promoted the spreading of market awareness, and became the actively educational model at that time; (2) From the perspective of politics, township enterprises played the role of a mediator between state-owned economy and private economy, which effectively mitigated the shock of "privatization" on the national economy, thereby reducing the political costs of China's marketization and ensured smooth transition of China's economic system; (3) The development of township enterprises has promoted urban reforms, provided experience for the transformation of enterprises in the city, and therefore created favorable conditions for the reform in the next stage.

With the changing market environment and the deepening of reform in the city, the development of township enterprises slowed and gradually retired from the stage of history. Then, urban reform fully began, and China's economy gained a new driving force of growth.

2.3 Stage 3: The Start and Deepening of Urban Reform

As early as in October 1984, the CPC's 12th Central Committee adopted "the CPC Central Committee decision on the reform of the economic system." These programmatic documents show that China began reform in its urban areas. Deng Xiaoping's "South tour speeches" and the convening of the CPC 14th Central Committee marking China's market-oriented economic system completely determine the establishment of a modern enterprise system, which started from the reform of SOEs and the financial system. It is the stage of starting and deepening the reform of the city (1992–2002), which highlights the reform of SOEs. Through the reform of SOEs, the urban market increased the efficiency of resource distribution and enhanced the competitiveness of urban enterprises, and therefore, the dominant role of township enterprises is changed in the industrialization process.

China's reform of SOEs used a progressive reform thought, reforming the less difficult field before the hard ones, allowing local pilots before universal implementation, changing the competitive industries before the monopoly ones, and adjusting the assignment of power within the planned system before institutional innovations. During the preliminary exploration stage from 1978 to 1992, the main direction of SOE was "decentralization," which expanded the autonomous right and improved SOE efficiency through the contract system, producing lump sum profit and transferring profit collection to taxation. These measures expanded enterprises' full right to independent operation, and increased the efficiency of SOEs. However, these measures cannot be the fundamental solutions of SOEs' market adaptability problem. Therefore, the institutional innovation of SOEs started in 1992 through the transformation of property structure, establishing the modern enterprise system, guiding SOE to become independent legal and market competition subjects, which have "clear property rights, separation of duties and responsibilities, separation of enterprises from administration and scientific management" (Sheng Feng, 2012).[8]

In the stage of deepening city reform, China's driving force of economic growth came from two sources. The first is the optimization of the SOE operating mechanism that improved the operation efficiency of SOEs (Groves et al., 1994; Bai Zhongen et al., 2006),[9] which enhanced China's economic growth. The second source is the privatization of SOEs. It strengthened

---

[8] Sheng Feng (2012). Productivity, innovation and SOEs reform: The empirical analysis on data of micro-level enterprises. *Industrial Economics Research* 4: 37–46.

[9] Groves, T., Hong, Y., John, M., and Barry, N. (1994). Autonomy and incentives in Chinese state enterprises. *Quarterly Journal of Economics* 109: 183–209. Bai Chongen, Lu Jiangyong, and Tao Zhingang (2006). The empirical research on effects of SOEs reform. *Economics Research* 8: 4–13.

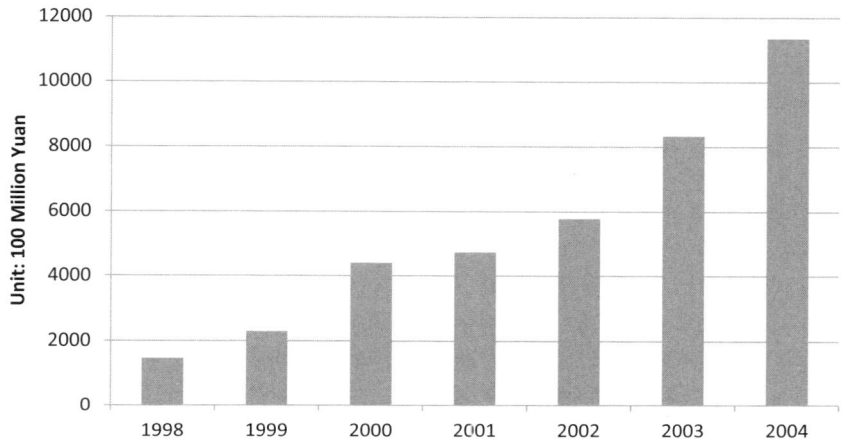

Figure 1-5: The total sum of profits of SOEs and non-SOEs beyond designated size.
Source: NBS.

the market power of resource allocation and promoted economic growth efficiently (Zhang Weiyin and Su Shuhe, 1998).[10]

Figure 1-5 shows the profits' growth trend of SOEs and large-scale non-state-owned industrial enterprises below, the urban reform was successful since 1998. Industrial enterprise profit increasingly rose, while the increase of profit reached a new stage since 2002, which was over 800 billion yuan. The growth since 2002 is a result of China's joining the WTO, which brought China's comparative advantage into full play.

2.4 Stage 4: China's Economic Growth After Joining the WTO

On December 11, 2001, China formally joined the WTO, and the Chinese economy participated in economic globalization more actively. Both in terms of the absolute amount of the total import and export and the total import and export share of GDP, joining the WTO was a landmark event. China's import and export volume exceeded 5 trillion yuan (see Figure 1-6), while the total import and export share of GDP is more than

---

[10]Zhang Weiyin and Su Shuhe (1998). Interregional competition and privatization of China's SOEs. *Economics Research* 12: 13–22.

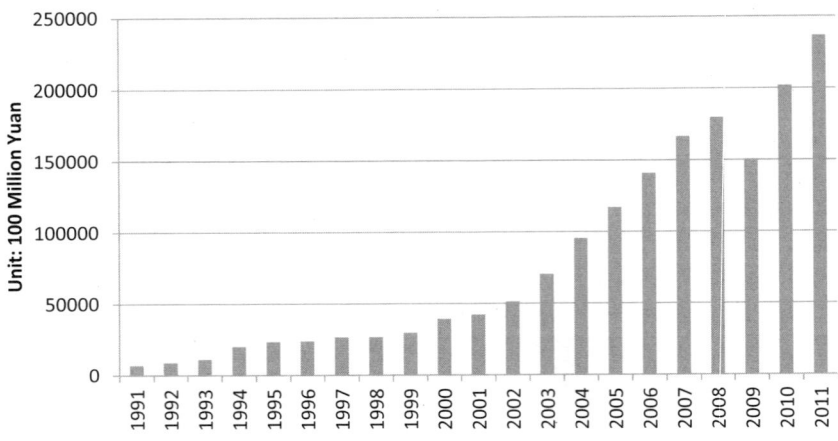

Figure 1-6: Total import and export volume.

Source: NBS database.

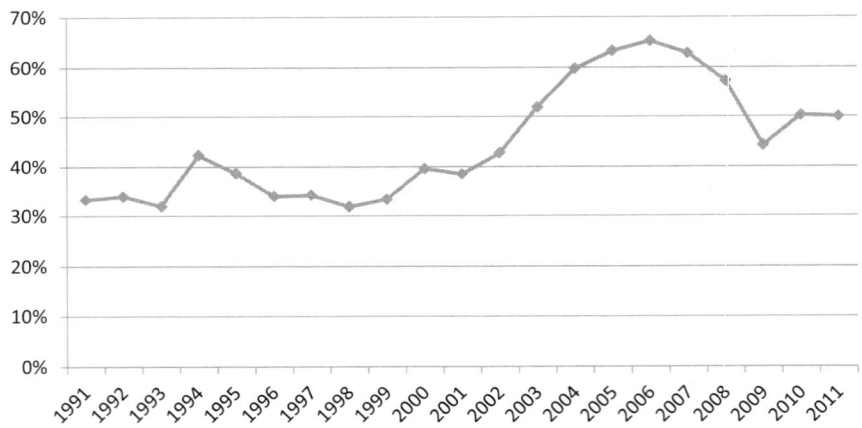

Figure 1-7: Total import and export volume's share of GDP.

Source: NBS database.

50%, reaching 51.3% in 2003 (see Figure 1-7). External demand became China's economically most important driving force, and the openness of the Chinese economy is unprecedented.

Due to the accession to the WTO, reductions of tariff levels and non-tariff barriers improved China's foreign trade environment, and brought rapid growth in import and export volumes (see Figures 1-6 and 1-7). From

1996 to 2001, the total amount of import and export commodities rose from US$289.88 billion to US$509.65 billion, extending by 75.8% with an average annual growth rate of 9.86%. In contrast, from 2001 to 2006, the total amount of import and export commodities rose from US$509.65 billion to US$1.7607 trillion, extending by 146% with an average annual growth rate of 22.95%.[11] Foreign demand has become an important engine of economic growth in China.

In addition, there is a more rapid development of China's actual utilization of foreign investment. The actually utilized foreign capital reached US$116.1 billion by 2011 (see Figure 1-8). After joining the WTO, the field of FDI was expanded, and FDI structure changed from the agricultural sector and traditional manufacturing industries to the tertiary sector and high-tech industries. Some services in the tertiary industry, such as finance, insurance, real estate, and commerce, became hotspots for international direct investment, playing a positive role in China's industrial structure upgrading and comparative advantage exploitation.

China's foreign-funded enterprises promote the export of China's manufacturing goods, and boost the comparative advantage of labor-intensive

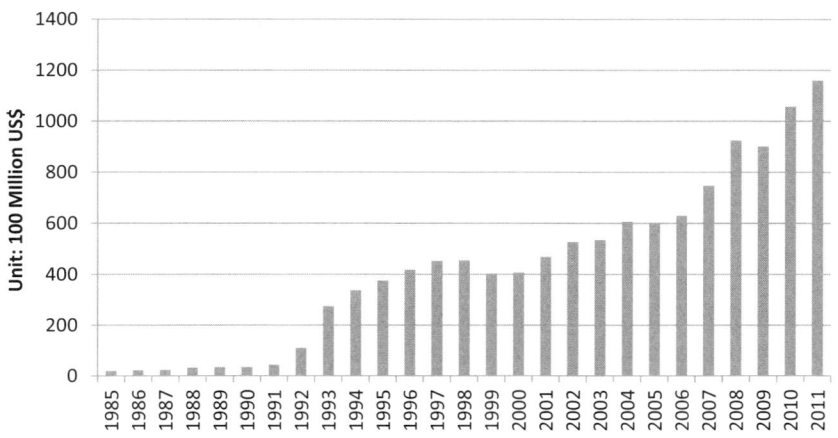

Figure 1-8: Actual use of foreign capital.

Source: NBS database.

---

[11] *Data Source*: NBS.

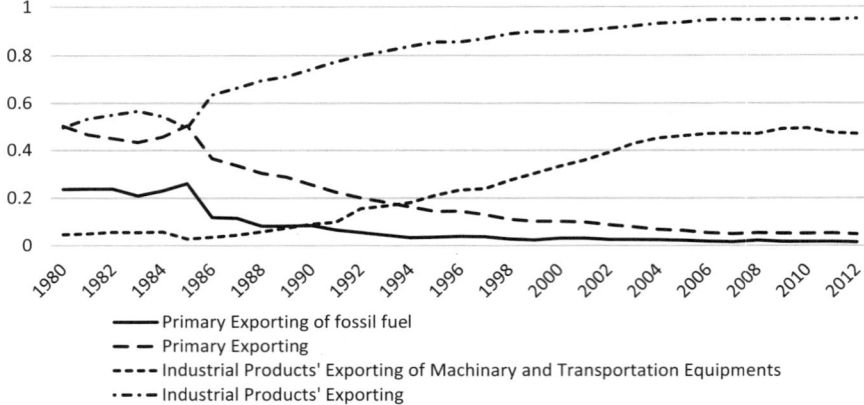

Figure 1-9: The share of primary and industrial products in total exports.
Source: CEIC databases.

products. China's active participation in the capital and technology-intensive industries gradually weakens its comparative disadvantage in these products (Song Jing, 2005).[12] This is represented by the rise in the share of exports in manufacturing, and China's exports of machinery and transport equipment's share increased to 23.58% in 2008 (see Figure 1-9). While optimizing the economic structure, China's economy gradually walks into the global value chain of multinational corporations.

After joining the WTO, reform of SOEs has been accelerated. The introduction of foreign strategic investors changes the SOE business models dramatically in the financial sector, and thereby strengthens the market allocation of resources and results in considerable development of SOEs and private enterprises.

With the improvement of China's economic growth and income levels, Chinese household consumption is also an important aspect of China's economic growth. Housing needs and home appliances upgrading stimulates the domestic demand-led economic growth in China. Furthermore, it is to be noted that the investment role of real estate is the most spectacular in the past 10 years. With the support of financial credit, China's real

---

[12] Song Jing (2005). The impact of FDI on China's industrial upgrading: The analysis in the perspective of foreign trade. *International Trade Issue* 4: 82–86.

estate market has developed rapidly and increased the consumers' housing demand. Meanwhile, investment in domestic cement, steel, and other real estate-related industries is expanding. The reliance on land finance encourages the local government, fueling the bubble of real estate. The investment in real estate and infrastructure also became the most important driving force of China's economic growth after joining the WTO, and hardened the structural change of China's development in the future.

After joining the WTO, China's economic growth relied on both external demand and domestic investments. In this process, the upgrading of Chinese household consumption also has a crucial role that cannot be ignored, which mainly includes housing consumption.

2.5 Summary

In different stages of China's economic growth, we can see the different driving forces of China's development. It also shows that there are different principal conflicts at each stage of China's growth during the 30 years from reform and opening up, in which the government plays a very important role.

Reform and opening up started from rural reform, which actually laid the foundation for urban reform. The success of China's reform and opening up resulted from the positive role of the Chinese government, which chose the correct economic reform path in line with its actual development conditions. First, the initial reform started in rural areas and selection of the agricultural sector reflects political rationality. China's large rural population means only stability in rural areas can create the appropriate space for further reform, which was achieved by the rural reform; second, before the reform, China failed to solve the food supply problem, and according to the basic law of economics, individuals who try to solve the "clothing" "living," and "transportation" problem have to solve the "food" problem first. Therefore, rural reform as the beginning meets the basic laws and principles of economics, and this is also the starting point of successful economic growth. Furthermore, the reform was carried out under the planned economy system, and the interest group in the city was too big. Reforms from the rural areas avoided the challenge from the interest group of urban residents because rural residents lack political leadership and also made it easy to make policy changes. So, even after completion of the reform of agricultural production, economic industrialization of town and township enterprises in China is also a very smart choice.

Through the development of township enterprises, market power, which can allocate resources efficiently, grows. The market's importance in the economy increases. Decision makers used the dual track system to gradually coordinate and balance plans and markets. The space that plans exited was filled by the markets and created the market condition for promoting urban reform naturally. SOE reform cannot be separated from the favorable market environment created by the township enterprises. Due to the market-oriented urban reforms, a large number of state-owned resources were used efficiently. The privatization of SOEs and the establishment of a modern enterprise system in SOEs greatly contributed to the development of a market mechanism as an engine for economic growth. Joining the WTO has enhanced China's market business philosophy and the market environment, and further promoted international market development, the competitive power of Chinese enterprises, and China's comparative advantages. The demand effect of economic growth also accelerated the upgrading of the industrial structure in China. China's economy was transformed from the industrial system dominated by textile and other light industries to electric and heavy equipment industries, and the manufacturing sector was promoted effectively in global competitiveness. Growth of real estate demand, which boosts China's rapid economic growth, forms the difficult conditions faced by the Chinese economy now, hindering the new driving force of China's economy and producing potential problems in the future.

3. PROBLEMS AND THEIR INFLUENCES IN THE CURRENT STAGE OF CHINA'S ECONOMIC DEVELOPMENT

China's economy maintained rapid growth over the past 30 years under different driving forces. However, due to the sharp decline in external demand under the financial crisis, economic structural problems hindering economic sustainable growth in China are increasingly prominent and noticeable. Whether the Chinese economy will continue to maintain a high growth rate attracts the world's attention. Deep understanding of the strategic role and impact of China's economic problems at the current stage is required. We will discuss some important strategic issues of China's sustainable economic growth from the perspective of China's economic development, analyze the impacts of these structural problems on sustainable economic growth, and explore its causes and mechanisms, so as to provide guidance for regulations. Specifically, the analysis mainly includes the following two aspects: the first is the analysis from the perspective of China's foreign relations, and the second is the analysis from the perspective of China's own economy, which includes the relationship between the government and the market, structural problems of economic development such as the issues of urbanization, industrialization, and the aging problem, and environmental costs of economic development.

3.1 The Challenge of an Export-Driven Growth Strategy After the Financial Crisis

From the perspective of the external economic environment's impact on China's economic growth, China's external environment for development changed significantly after the subprime crisis. China has faced challenges of unsustainable economic development using an export-led growth strategy. After joining the WTO, China's export growth was impressive, but at the same time, it also brings China more trade frictions than any other country. From 2003 to September 2012, China suffered 758 cases of foreign trade remedy investigations, valuing US$68.4 billion. China has gone through 17 consecutive years with more anti-dumping investigations than any other country in the world, and 6 consecutive years as the world's highest anti-subsidy investigation receiver.[13] Due to the subprime crisis, the Chinese economy cannot maintain its high-speed growth relying on the export and processing business, which imports foreign capital, technology, management, raw materials, and semi-finished products, and exports the final goods to foreign markets. Export-driven economic growth is not sustainable in this situation.

The main feature of China's old economic external model was fully using the comparative advantage of labor at the cost of price distortion

---

[13] *Data Source*: Ministry of Commerce, PRC. http://www.mofcom.gov.cn/aarticle/ae/ai/201211/20121108423879.html.

of land, natural resources, and environment (low price), and stagnation of factor market development. The local government directly participates in economic activities as an important player, who invests and introduces external funding. Driven by the profit-oriented operation of international capital, factors of global production are distributed efficiently in China, the manufacturing sector develops quickly, and the capacity of commodity production increases sharply. Production has to be export-oriented due to insufficient domestic demand, which is caused by low labor income. Because of the seriously dual structure of the Chinese economy, both the opportunity cost of labor in the agricultural sector and manufacturing sector's wages are low. The *hukou* (Household Registration System in China) restrictions, the inconsistency of industrialization and urbanization, and the lack of social security and social welfare for migrant workers tend to lower labor costs, eventually leading to insufficient demand. This process in fact means that millions of Chinese workers are combined with sophisticated global production factors (capital, technology, management, brand, and intellectual) and form the Chinese manufacturing base, maintaining China's more than 30 years of economy growth in the way of intensive development.

The financial crisis in 2008 is an important turning point of globalization, which also changed the external environment of China's economic development. First, the globalization's main driving mechanism was changing. Both developed and developing countries took advantage of their endowment structure, grew fast, and shared the gains of globalization. On the one hand, developed countries restructure the industrial chain of transnational corporates, enhance the high-end and high-tech industry development, and expand the service industry. As a result, productivity increases and the added value of the industry chain rises. Further development of financial innovation increases the added value and profits of the finance sector. On the other hand, emerging economies take advantage of low-cost advantages and huge market capacity, gaining rapid economic growth. However, this phenomenon of globalization led to imbalances in the global economy: first, the unequal distribution of the gains of globalization toward capital or other monopoly elements (technology innovation, knowledge, management, and brand) results in the imbalance of global aggregate demand and supply, and accumulates trade surpluses and deficits in the world and causes global overcapacity. The excessive development of the financial sector in developed countries is necessary to maintain the balance of aggregate supply and demand through the extension of debt chain and asset bubble creation to digest the global supply. The financial crisis in 2008 showed that this globalization model is unsustainable. The debt crisis continues to spread in western developed countries, and the external economic recovery driving growth in emerging economies is impossible in the near future. Second, the low-end manufacturing sector in developed countries disappears, which causes unemployment of unskilled workers and widens income gaps and class division. The middle class of Western society is increasingly polarized, while the aging problem worsens. The welfare level cannot be maintained and trade protectionism recurs. Once the internal differentiation of the middle class in developed countries appears, their political polarization is also inevitable. The United States and other developed countries find it more difficult to agree on a global strategy and provide the public goods for the development of globalization in the future. Therefore, the problem of lack of global governance is increasingly serious.

China's non-balanced participation in globalization is reflected in the income distribution formed by low-price competition, which is difficult to maintain a large domestic market, and economic growth depends on the external market. Trade surplus changes into foreign exchange reserves, which are invested in the US financial markets with low return and cause large welfare losses due to quantitative easing. Meanwhile, China's demographic dividend starts to decline and the demographic structure changes. Land and environmental factors have become increasingly scarce. Investment projects cannot be completed without considering the interest rates and by lowering prices as in the past. However, the shortage of labor, land, and environment, and the aging of the population mean that this factor price cannot participate in the construction of global industrial value chains of transnational corporations at a low cost. The future development of China's economy is becoming increasingly unsustainable. Therefore, China's economic development in the future must adopt factor market reforms to gradually realize a change in the mode of foreign trade. A proactive open strategy should be adopted to confront the new situation of economic globalization and changes in the domestic factor endowments. Meanwhile, China's sustainable growth requires accelerating the transformation of foreign economic development policy, advancing the opening up toward optimizing the economic structure, and realizing efficiency-oriented changes.

3.2 The Problems and Challenges of Reasonable Definition of the Relationship Between the Government and the Market

During the process of China's economic development, the adjustment of the relationship between the government and the market is a very significant aspect. The government played an important role in the reform for the past 30 years. At the beginning of the reform and opening up, through the institutional reform of the rural land, the government stimulated the production efficiency of the primary industry. Then, the Chinese government gradually established the market mechanism through developing the price mechanism in the commodities market. Finally, the rationalization of the price signals efficiently released the initiative of Chinese economic entities. After 1990, China has gone through the reform of SOEs and the reform of the real estate market as well as the reform of the fiscal and taxation systems. The government on the one hand helps the original SOEs to improve their efficiency, and helps to foster and rapidly develop the credit market driven by the real estate market. On the other hand, the Chinese government efficiently releases the local governments' initiatives to jointly promote economic growth. Thus, after the accession to the WTO, China's economy gives full play to its comparative advantage to combine China's abundant labor resources and foreign capital. Nowadays, China has become a successful part of the global industry value chain built by the multinational companies, which therefore drives and maintains a long-term "Golden Growth." To a large extent, the success of China's economic growth is due to the price distortion of factor markets by the government, such as the price of labor and the price of capital, as well as the environmental cost factors distorted under the control of the government's "visible hand." For all the above, China becomes the "world factory." However, with the changes in China's economic structure, the growth driven by the distortion of the price of factor markets cannot be sustained. In order to fundamentally change the relationship between the government and the market and to develop the impetus that drives China's economy more sustainably, there are three challenges that must be addressed. The first is the reasonable definition of the boundaries of the government and the market; the second is the balance of the administrative authority and the fiscal authority between the central government and local governments; and the third is equal rights of the SOEs and private enterprises.

3.2.1 The problems of reasonable definition of the boundaries of the government and the market

China's reform and opening up originates in the period of the comprehensive planned economy. The economic resources are originally allocated by the central government. The market mechanisms are gradually introduced into the operation of China's economy through the implementation of the reform and opening up policy, while the governmental control over the economic resources is still extremely powerful. The financial system especially, whose major part is the state-owned banks, always makes the influence of governmental control over the allocation of resources prominent.

At the beginning of the reform, the construction and investment of the infrastructure in the early stages of China's economic development benefited from the strong governmental control over the resources. This control became an important guarantee of China's strong and powerful economic growth. However, after 30 years of growth, the expansion of the total scale of economy and the enhancing complexity of economic relations happens. The negative effects of government allocation of resources are increasingly evident. The patterns of competition as well as the right of resource allocation between the government and the market have a profound impact on the organisms and the structure of China's economic development that therefore help to form the over-reliance on government control. This kind of distortion of economic incentives leads to a lack of sustainability of economic growth momentum. And corruptions caused by the above reasons also lead to an increase in the transaction costs of economic operation. It becomes increasingly important to rationalize the relationship between the government and the market. At present, the Chinese government is facing the biggest challenge to promote transformation of the government services function. Moreover, it is difficult to eliminate the excessive interference and influence of the "visible hand" of the government on the "invisible hand" of the market.

Fortunately, the Chinese government began to steadily promote the super ministry reform on March 10, 2013, promoting transformation of the government functions. The Chinese central government has issued the scheme of the institutional reform and function transformation of the State Council. With the implementation of this scheme, the number of the departments at the ministerial level under the state council will be reduced to four, in which two organs composing the State Council are revoked, while the increase and decrease in the amount of the vice-ministerial level departments are offsetting each other. After the reform, in addition to the General Office of the State Council, the State Council is set up by 25 sectors.[14] Focusing on the transformation of the government functions, the super ministry reform changes the situation of omission, offside, and dislocation of the government functions and tries to deal with the long-term doubt about the incorrect positioning of government functions. For now, the reform program is trying to solve the absence of government functions of social services. And the reform also makes efforts to encourage the government to take on the necessary responsibilities, such as environmental protection, food security, and social security. Also, this reform is intended to eliminate the offside problem of government functions, that is, excessive intervention in the market behavior resulting in price distortion, as well as rationalization of the role of the government departments dislocation in order to avoid the phenomenon of scramble for the profitable and prevarication of the profitless in the field of the fuzzy division of responsibilities.

If the rationalization of the relationship between the government and the market is carried out by the way of efficient transformation of government functions, the market mechanism will take a greater role in improving the efficiency of resource allocation. Moreover, the motivation of market entities will be greatly enhanced, and thus, China's economic vitality and innovation will be strengthened. All these combine to give sustainable impetus to China's economic growth.

---

[14] http://www.xinhuanet.com/.

3.2.2 The balance of the administrative authority and the fiscal authority between the central government and local governments

In order to promote the successful implementation of the above reform and to achieve the aims, it is needed to make the necessary supporting reforms in the political system. In this supporting system, a very important aspect is to create a balance of the administrative authority and the fiscal authority between the central government and local governments. The tax sharing system reform in 1994 did not make adjustments to the expenditure and responsibilities of the central government and local governments. The expenditure function of the local governments continuously takes the pattern of the 1980s, leading to the expenditure functions incurred by the central government being passed onto local governments. Since the local governments have different expense preferences, they tend to lower the expenditure efficiency. That is why excessive government control distorts the price of economic factors. Therefore, actually, the balance of the administrative authority and the fiscal authority between the central government and local governments is also part of the relationship between the government and the market. Since the reform and opening up, the local governments play a very important role (Wang Yongqin et al., 2007),[15] and it is essential for China's economic growth to make adjustments and take control of the local governments' behaviors.

In the current system, for the local government, first the pattern of competition between local governments is a kind of "GDP Championship" that promotes increasing regional development. But this competition also brings about issues such as "local protectionism" and "redundant construction," thus resulting in some consequences such as the interregional blockade and severe fragmentation in the product market and factor markets, impediment of further labor and capital flow to the big cities, severe industrial isomorphism across different areas, and excessive competition between cities and waste of resources. Second, under the influence of land-based finance, local governments start to carry out the campaign of city construction

---

[15] Wang Yongqin et al. (2007). On China's development model: The costs and benefits of China's decentralization approach to transition *Economic Research Journal* 1: 4–16.

and expansion, resulting in homogeneity of industrial structure and lack of motivation of independent industrial development, as well as the low efficiency of urban land use. Third, mass constructive investment from the government brings about severe local debt. Until the end of 2010, the local governments' debt balance is a total of 10.7 trillion yuan. Included in this, the debt that the government bears the responsibility to repay is 6.7 trillion, accounting for 63% of the fiscal revenue of local governments. In addition to the contingent debt that the local governments bear the guarantee obligation for, totally, the debt ratio is up to 85%.[16] Moreover, the debt repayment of local governments casts over-reliance on land revenue, and thus, the falling house prices will affect the solvency of local governments. Therefore, local governments need some kind of transition from land-based finance to land-based taxation and from the economic constructors to the public goods providers.

The transformation of the local governments' function is based on the balance of the administrative authority and the fiscal authority between the central government and local governments. For example, with the devolvement of the fiscal authority from the central government upon the local governments, the administrative authority of the local governments could be balanced with the fiscal authority. Thus, the initiative of all levels' governments will be efficiently mobilized. In the meantime, it is needed to avoid the situation of "disorder after devolvement." Therefore, it is important to stress the supervision of the National People's Congress, the people's congresses at all levels, social populace, and public opinions. All the above should accelerate the pace of the political restructuring in order to realize a balance of the administrative authority and the fiscal authority between the central government and local governments.

3.2.3 Equal rights of the SOEs and private enterprises

Another aspect of the relationship between the government and the market is the equality of the relationship between the SOEs and private enterprises. In fact, the solution to this problem depends on the solution to the first two

---

[16]Website of National Audit Office of the People's Republic of China, http://www.audit.gov.cn.

problems, because unequal position of the SOEs and private enterprises in market competition stems from two aspects. First, relying on the power of administrative monopoly, the SOEs possess exploitation status over other economic entities. Second, relying on the dominant position of the bank credit system led by the state-owned banks and financing facilities of the capital market, the SOEs gain the advantages of capital expansion. Both of the two points are shaped by the excessive intervention of governments in the market resources' allocation. Thus, to solve the problem of the equal competitive relationship between the SOEs and private enterprises, it is needed to transition government functions and let go of administrative monopoly of the industries. Once the dominance of market mechanisms in resource allocation is achieved, the capital and other price signals are straightened out. Then, it will be possible to better stimulate the vitality and momentum of economic entities, to promote market competition, to improve the efficiency of the allocation of state-owned capital, to expand the space for the development of the private economy, and thus enhance the sustainable growth of the Chinese economy.

3.3 The Problems and Challenges Resulting from the Asynchrony of Urbanization, Industrialization, and Aging of Population

The asynchrony of urbanization, industrialization, and aging of population mainly refers to the phenomenon of urbanization behind the industrialization and urbanization in advance of aging of population. The asynchrony results in the "aging before getting rich" and the start to the drying up of the labor factor comparative advantage. This will have a major impact on the structural imbalances of China's economy and optimized allocative efficiency of factors, causing rising costs of China's economy and the increasing lack of growth momentum.

3.3.1 The causes and effects of China's urbanization behind industrialization

From the experiences of developed countries, urbanization and industrialization have coordinated with each other. On the one hand, industrialization renders a guarantee with employment supply for the urbanization of rural population, and the concentration process of production from industrialization will inevitably bring about the concentration of the labor factor, thus contributing to the development of urbanization. On the other hand, the development of urbanization will bring about the intensive use of factors including the labor factor and the congregation of all kinds of production factors to cities and towns, so as to promote optimal allocation of economic resources, to increase employment and to expand the market, and to make further development of industrialization.

By 2011, China's urbanization rate reached 51.27%,[17] while the proportion of the secondary industry of GDP in China's economy in 1995 was more than 52%.[18] This indicates that the development of China's industrialization is much faster than the development of urbanization. The level of urbanization is far behind that of industrialization, for several reasons: First, ever since the early stage of industrialization beginning in the late 1970s, the population scale of rural and agricultural workers is very large and the urbanization rate has a very low starting point. Second, the policy orientation of China's economic development also acts as a very important effect. China adopted a catching-up industrialization strategy of giving priority to heavy industry and distorted the price of capital to promote economic development. This strategy also results in industrialization ahead of urbanization. Third, since 1980, China has a long-term implementation of urbanization policies of "strict control of major cities, proper development of medium-sized cities, and vigorous development of small towns" and rural industrialization policies of "shift from farming to other trades within the rural area and work in the plant without entering into the city." These policies are a serious impediment to the general development of urbanization. The fourth is the imperfection of China's land system, due to which land urbanization is faster than population urbanization in the development of the realty industry. So China's urbanization development lags far behind industrialization (Chen Jiagui *et al.*, 2012).[19]

---

[17]China Association of Mayors (2012). *Annual Report on Urban Development of China (2011)*. China City Press.
[18]Website of National Bureau of Statistics of the People's Republic of China, http://www.stats.gov.cn.
[19]Chen Jiagui *et al.* (2012). *Report on the Progress of Industrialization in China (1995–2010)*. Social Science Literature Publishing House.

Since urbanization development is lagging behind industrialization, it is not conducive to the optimization of the economic structure. Also, it will bring a series of internal contradictions in social stability and economic sustainability. For now, it has become a prominent issue to restrict China's economic development, and it mainly shows in four aspects: First, urbanization's lag behind industrialization inhibits the growth of domestic demand and industrial upgrading. Due to the differences in income levels and consumption levels between urban and rural, urbanization's lag has led to low income, low proportion of consumer groups, inhibition of the growth of domestic consumer demand, and a dent in economic growth sustainability. Second, due to urbanization's lag behind industrialization, the demand structure upgrades slowly. The elimination of backward production capacity and changes in extensive industrial growth mode are both affected during the industrialization process of China's economy. Furthermore, because of urbanization's lag behind industrialization, the use of economic factors is not highly intensive and urbanization takes the route of flattening development. The two reasons combine to greatly inhibit the rapid development of the tertiary industry with a significantly lower proportion of the service industry and hinder the marketization of the service sector and the growth of the demand for services. Third, urbanization's lag reduces the opportunities for the rural surplus workers to access urban employment and makes it hard for the rural migrants to integrate into the urban development. Thus, the efficiency of urbanization is affected, the urban–rural income gap is widening, and agricultural modernization is hindered, and even the city slums are likely to be formed. Therefore, the sustainability of urban development is dented. Fourth, urbanization's lag goes against the accumulation of human capital. As for the educational facilities and levels of education in rural areas, they are all far less than those in urban areas. So, the differences between rural and urban areas cast a negative impact on the effective increase in skilled Chinese labor, the efficient use of factors, and economic development. And finally, these will make the economy lack social innovation, and inhibit deepening and restructuring industrialization.

As a result, urbanization's lag behind industrialization in China results in the increasingly severe imbalanced challenges in urban and rural structure and industrial structure. And therefore, it is necessary to solve the problems of rural land capitalization and facilitate the residencization of rural migrant workers, choosing a sustained and efficient pattern of urbanization, so that the Chinese could address the challenges of imbalance in urban and rural structure, as well as define property rights, that is, make clear the definition of the rural land usufruct. Also, it is necessary to attract the advanced production factors to actively enter rural areas and promote the accelerated development of agricultural modernization. It could also be critical to fulfill the industry transfer and transformation by the principle of comparative advantage, improve the capability of independent innovation, upgrade the industry value chain, and promote the development of China's tertiary industry in the context of globalization. And last, the permanent goal is to realize the optimization of industrial structure, render the foundation of industry support to urbanization, and achieve the coordinated development of urbanization and industrialization.

3.3.2 The causes and effects of the untimely arrival of aging of population

In 2011, the proportion of population over 65 years accounted for 9.1% of the total population.[20] According to the United Nations, in 2000, China was an aging society.[21] Compared to the developed countries, which are already aging societies, China has become a society that is aging before getting rich. This situation increases the difficulty for China to solve the aging problem from the economic level. The untimely arrival of aging of population in China has an adverse and far-reaching impact on economic development now.

Aging of the Chinese society arrives before proper economic development, and it comes at a rapid pace. Also, the aging comes with other prominent features, such as large elderly population and aged or hyper-aged problems. This kind of situation is caused by many factors, and the two critical and direct ones are sharp and significant decline in fertility and

---

[20] Website of National Bureau of Statistics of the People's Republic of China, http://www.stats.gov.cn.

[21] Website of National Bureau of Statistics of the People's Republic of China, http://www.stats.gov.cn.

mortality (life expectancy increases). And from the institutional perspective, aging is due to decades' implementation of China's family planning policy. With the family planning policy in the late 1980s, a sharp decline in the fertility rate speeds up the arrival of the aging society. If this is not appropriately adjusted in a short time, the proportion of the elderly population will continue to grow in the foreseeable future. Then undoubtedly, the degree of aging will be further increased. Due to the rapid socioeconomic development, improved living standards, disease control, improved health conditions, and so on, the life expectancy has also been substantially increased, which is a natural process in socioeconomic progress. Therefore, the principle reason for China's untimely arrival of aging is the family planning policy.

And in terms of economy, China's untimely aging poses many challenges to economic development. First, aging has a significant effect on the scale and structure of labor supply. And this prematurely weakens China's comparative advantages in the global industrial chain. Especially with the incompleteness of the reform in the *hukou* system and the land system, aging will further affect the development and upgrading of Chinese industrial structure and hinder the competitive strength in the global chain. Therefore, it cannot be sustainable to rely on the labor-scale-driven pattern, and an efficiency-driven pattern needs to be pursued. Second, the untimely arrival of aging also affects the demand structure. And with the aging process, the society needs relevant investment in the aging service industry. As a result, investments in other fields, which can promote the innovation and economic development more rapidly, will be decreased. For the Chinese economy, lacking long-term development momentum, investment in the aging service industry will inevitably hamper development. Third, aging also poses challenges to the entire pension insurance system. The current system is a combination of historical arrangement and the current situation. However, it cannot tackle the problem of untimely arrival of aging. Thus, this problem needs to be solved through reform and measures such as lowering the contribution rate, reducing pension levels, postponing the retirement age, and expanding the pension funds' investment channels. Fourth, aging problems will deplete savings, lower the level of savings, and furthermore decrease the investment level; this will inevitably inhibit the potential of China's economic growth.

3.4 The Environmental Costs Problem in Economic Development

The high-speed growth of China's economy is mainly due to the extensive growth style in the past 30 years. Increasing the input but not raising the productivity achieves long-term growth. However, the environmental costs increase sharply due to this growth style, and damage China's sustainable growth in the future.

China is a country with relatively poor natural resources in terms of ownership per capita, and the resource constraint limits economic and social development. The importance of resources in the information age relatively drops, but land, water, forest, minerals, and oil resource are still the material foundation of economic development. China's field size is only one-third of the world's average. The cultivated land area per capita of some coastal provinces and cities is less than 0.8 square meters, which is below the world's warning line. The water resource per capita in China is equal to one-fourth of the world's average in 2003. There exists shortage of water supply in 400 cities and water is urgently needed in 100 cities among China's 600 cities (Qu Haohui, 2003).[22] In recent years, the external dependence on foreign energy rose significantly, and the degree of the external dependency on oil rose from 32% to 57% in the past 10 years. China has become the biggest consumer of energy (China State Council Information Office, 2012).[23] The vast consumption of energy causes serious damage to China's environment and challenges China's sustainable development.

China's resource endowment is not abundant, and use efficiency is lower when compared with developed countries. The environmental costs of economic development are higher than other countries. Zen Xianyin (2004)[24] has measured that the environmental pollution and degradation problem is extremely serious in China. The economic cost's share of GDP is about 5.5% to 9.8% in China, while the corresponding value is 4.5% in India, 3.3% in Mexico, and 2% in Indonesia. This shows that the environmental costs of economic development in China are high, even if compared

---

[22] Qu Haohui (2003). Vice Minister of Ministry of Water Resources.
[23] China's State Council Information Office (2012). *China's Energy Policy*. White Paper.
[24] Zen Xianyin (2004). Environmental Management for a New Road to Industrialization. *Resource and Environment Economics Progress* Series 2.

with the developing countries. The Environmental and Planning Institute in the Ministry of Environmental Protection,[25] following the United Nations' system of integrated environmental and economic accounting, believes that the ecological cost of environmental degradation is 1,538.95 billion yuan, which was 3.5% of GDP in 2010. The costs of environmental degradation are 1,103.28 billion yuan, which is 2.51% of GDP, and increased 132.26 billion yuan compared with the previous year. The growth rate of the environmental degradation's cost is 13.7%. The cost of ecological damage (forest, wetland, and mineral) is 441.7 billion yuan, which is 1.01% of GDP. The Green GDP accounting of the Environmental and Planning Institute in the Ministry of Environmental Protection in seven consecutive years (2004–2010) shows that China is still at the stage of rising environmental costs. The costs of environmental degradation have risen from 511.82 billion yuan in 2004 to 1,103.28 billion yuan in 2010, and increased by 115%. The estimated costs of management (the expenditure to manage the pollution according to the contemporary technology and pollution level) have increased from 287.44 billion yuan in 2004 to 558.93 billion yuan in 2010, and increased by 94.5%. All of these facts show the environmental deterioration along with the economic development in contemporary China.

Therefore, sustainable economic development has to be environment-friendly in modern China. China has to start the reform of energy prices and distribute the resources efficiently. Only through changing the resource-using method, promoting the technological innovation, and reducing the environmental costs, can China's sustainable growth be gained in the future.

3.5 Summary

China has become a middle-income country through reform and development in the past 30 years. However, China will confront an increasing number of challenges in the future. First, the export-driven growth is not reliable due to the rebalance of the global economy after the financial crisis. China's development in the future has to depend on the internal rise of consumption power, due to the changes in the external environment of China's

---

[25]Environmental and Planning Institute of the Ministry of Environmental Protection. *Environmental and Economic Accounting Report 2010 (Public Version)*.

development and transition of China's comparative advantages. Second, the government-led development is unstable and inefficient along with the rise of market power. The problems of government failure and market absence can be corrected through redefining the government's role, harmonizing the relation between local governments and the central government, and equalizing the market status of private enterprises and SOEs. Meanwhile, factor market reform has to be started to solve the structural problem that is related to the distortion in the land, labor, and financial markets. Finally, the reform of resource prices is required to distribute the resources efficiently in order to decrease the environmental costs in economic development.

4. DEVELOPMENT STRATEGY OF SUSTAINABLE GROWTH IN CHINESE ECONOMY

As China became a middle-income country, the Chinese economy has faced a lot of challenges. If the structural imbalances led by these challenges cannot be solved effectively, then China's future economic growth will not be sustainable. Therefore, further reform through which the Chinese economy could be rebalanced will attract more attention. How to reform to help the Chinese economy step into a sustainable growth path becomes more important?

4.1 Principles for Chinese Economic Reform

The transformation characteristics and the structural imbalances of the Chinese economy that become outstanding because of the middle-income trap faced by China and the influence of the subprime crisis after 2007 affect economic efficiency at the micro level.

4.1.1 Debate on Chinese economy reform

At present, the debate on the Chinese economy reform is fierce. Overall, there are three opinions about the future path of the Chinese economy reform.

As for the first opinion, Chinese economic reform should take a top-down strategy, emphasizing an overall roadmap for further reform. The institutional problem should be taken into consideration for sustainable economic growth primarily, which is the basis for bottom-up reform. Moreover, the specific reform that could solve the institutional problem should be classified, and thus be formulated for each field, such as the financial sector, fiscal sector, and so forth. The most urgent reform should be recognized after screening the above sub-field reforms. Therefore, an overall roadmap is formulated.

As for the second opinion, Chinese economic reform should take a bottom-up strategy. The top-down strategy is not feasible mainly because there is a contradiction between the market-oriented reform and the government-oriented reform. The market-oriented reform means that the individual in the market is the dominating, while the government-oriented reform emphasized by the top-down strategy will make China go back to the era of a planning economy, reinforcing the power of government in the economy. Besides, the top-down strategy needs more information; however, collecting and manipulating the information is quite difficult. Furthermore, as an economy system, most structural problems in China are closely associated with other problems, and thus, it is hard for us to distinguish which kind of structural problem is the most important. Therefore, the top-down strategy seems reasonable; however, it is difficult to implement.

Next, the top-down strategy and the bottom-up strategy should be combined to solve problems during the process of Chinese economic reform. On the one hand, the reform should proceed through searching the key field for the reform. On the other hand, the government and the market should focus on different fields. For example, the market should be the main force in allocating the resource while the government should formulate the regulations and laws for the fair market environment, which could contribute to the structural adjustment, scientific innovation, social harmony, and the raising of living standards. However, what is the most important field in the reform is still a question; and there is no specific guideline for the combination of top-down strategy and bottom-up strategy.

4.1.2 The choice of the Chinese economy reform path

Chinese economic reform should take globalization into consideration. China's economy has integrated into the global economy, which is the basic historical background. Meanwhile, in the context of Chinese economic reform, importance also needs to be attached to the regional imbalance in the Chinese economy and the history of central planning economy in China. These three elements determine the feasible and effective reform strategy in China.

Because globalization is beyond the control of the Chinese central government and the regional imbalance in China adds more difficulties in government decisions, the top-down reform strategy seems undesirable. Additionally, the history of a central planning economy in China generates lots of interest groups in the state-owned sector, which adds obstacles to the reform, and thus makes market-oriented reform more difficult to implement. Therefore, the combination of top-down strategy and bottom-up strategy could be more realistic and easier to implement.

However, how to combine the top-down strategy and the bottom-up strategy requires more deliberate thinking. First, the globalization force, which imposes an external restriction for Chinese economic reform, cannot be neglected. The regional imbalance and the history of central planning economy in China impose an internal restriction on Chinese economic reform. These restrictions determine the limitations of top-down strategy and bottom-up strategy. Second, because there is an overflow effect of reform, we cannot ignore the influence of reform in one field on the others. This will add more uncertainty to the effect of the reform. As a result, only the top-down strategy or bottom-up strategy could not solve the coordinated problem in this context. Third, the relation between the government and the market is one of the most important aspects in Chinese economic reform. The top-down strategy could be used to restrict the role of the government while the bottom-up strategy could be used to activate the market. This will alleviate the negative influence of the reform on the national economy, provide room for revising the reform policies, and make the reform more feasible.

4.2 Thinking on the Reform Path

The principle of Chinese economic reform should guarantee a fair competition environment under the guidance of market efficiency. Further reform in China cannot deviate from the principle of market efficiency. Otherwise, the misallocation of resources could lead to an unsustainable growth path for the Chinese economy. Moreover, basic social security could not be based on sacrificing the economic efficiency. Under the background of globalization, competition comes from all over the world, which implies that resources should be allocated globally by efficiency; the Chinese economy cannot depart from such a law for development.

4.2.1 Thinking on the reform of foreign relations

One aim of the reform is to solve the unsustainable problem of an export-oriented economy. Therefore, how to balance foreign relations becomes one of the most important strategic issues.

At present, a multilateral trade agreement is hard to achieve among countries. The new pattern of globalization is regional integration. The Chinese position in the global production value chain determines that the export-oriented economy could be changed in the short term. The multinational corporation in developed countries dominates the global production value chain. Therefore, China cannot obtain enough discourse power in the international economic engagement. This situation makes China take part in globalization for further development with more difficulty through multilateral trade agreements. Additionally, bilateral trade agreements become more frequent in the world. China should take advantage of these bilateral trade agreements to obtain more opportunities to develop and change the present foreign trade pattern.

There are several advantages of bilateral agreements for China. First, the influence of the trade conflict will be reduced. There is great competition between the export products of China and the products of the multinational corporations in developed countries, which is harmfully affecting the normal international association of China through the multilateral mechanism. By contrast, the bilateral agreement will be easier to make between one country and another. This will promote market integration and liberalization, and reduce the rate of dispute or increase the efficiency of settling the dispute. Furthermore, the diversification of export trade will be facilitated.

Second, the rights of China in multilateral negotiation will be guaranteed. The countries that have close relationships with China will be grouped together through the bilateral agreement. This will offset the disadvantages of China in the global production value chain. As a result, the external development environment of China will be improved. Moreover, the coordinated mechanism is more flexible in bilateral agreements. The market size and the advantages in the manufacturing sector in China could be fully utilized, achieving sustainable economic growth.

Third, the dispute in multilateral agreements will be solved effectively and its negative impact on export and outward direct investment will be reduced. The "Walk Out" strategy will be achieved more easily through bilateral agreements. The environment of investment in foreign countries will be improved. Therefore, Chinese enterprises could utilize the comparative advantages from other countries to provide another driving force for sustainable economic growth in China. The core competitiveness of Chinese enterprises will be strengthened, and thus, these enterprises will fully participate in the process of international specialization.

Fourth, the benefits of Chinese enterprises will be effectively protected in bilateral agreements. The international risk for the "Walk Out" strategy will be reduced and the hostile environment in the local market will be improved.

Under the present situation, bilateralism is the main pattern in Chinese foreign relations. The comparative advantages of the Chinese economy will be fully utilized through bilateral agreements. The capacity of utilizing the foreign resources and foreign markets will be enhanced, and the room left for "Walk Out" strategy will be enlarged. The international environment for the operation of Chinese enterprises will be improved finally. Specifically, the bilateral association between China and developed countries should focus on the technology market, high skilled labor market, product market, and the development of innovation environment. The bilateral association between China and developing countries should focus on the reciprocity of both the factor market and the product market. The more effective utilization of Chinese factors will be achieved through exploring the comparative advantages between China and the others.

4.2.2 Thinking on the domestic reform

As for domestic reform, the primary task of Chinese economic reform is the transformation of government functions. The public service function should be clear for both the central government and local government. Specifically, the transformation of local government should be pushed forward, transforming from an economic builder to the provider of public service. Generally speaking, the government should provide institutional guarantees and legal protection for the operation of enterprises, and finally the long-run economic growth.

Factor market reform is the key field for Chinese economic reform, through which the problems caused by the structural imbalance will be solved and the efficiency of resource allocation will be improved. Capital market reform should be the most important one among factor market reforms including the capital market, the labor market, and the land market. There is a lot of government intervention in the capital market, which will lead to the inefficiency of the capital resource. Therefore, the resource allocation is not satisfied with the principle of efficiency. Correspondingly, the economic structural imbalance is strengthened, which generates great challenges to the sustainable economic growth in China. As the economy develops, the efficiency of the capital market becomes more important. As a result, the upgrade of the economic development is also the process of capitalization of economic resource. The efficiency of capital price signal will determine the capitalization of other factors as well as the utilization efficiency. Therefore, the capital reform is the precondition for the other reforms.

Land market reform is the second most important reform. The rapid economic growth of China in the last 10 years relies on the prosperity of the real estate market. However, such a driving force becomes unsustainable gradually and also inflicts a negative influence on economic structural imbalance. In order to promote the development of the real estate market, the local government depends too much on the land-based fiscal mode, which seriously interrupts the economic operation. The role played by the government in the economy distorts the resource allocation, and thus decreases efficiency. The land market reform should focus on the capitalization of land, which could be another driving force for economic growth.

The reform of the household registration system could be one important sub-field reform of the labor market. The household registration system restricts the free mobility of the labor force, which will distort the labor allocation. Meanwhile, the influence of family planning policy on the labor market structure should be taken seriously. The demographic changes caused by the family planning policy lead to the decrease of the labor force, which inflicts harmful impact on the economic growth. Moreover, the human capital investment should be emphasized. On the one hand, the efficiency of human capital investment should be raised. On the other hand, the institution arrangement should be formulated to stimulate the motive of the individual to invest in human capital.

4.3 Summary

The choice of development strategy for sustainable economic growth in China should take globalization as a background and attach importance to the regional imbalance in the Chinese economy and the history of a central planning economy in China. The restriction of the historical condition decides the basic principle for Chinese economic reform, which is a combination of top-down strategy and bottom-up strategy. Specifically, on foreign relations, China should focus more on bilateral relations, through which the comparative advantages of the Chinese economy could be totally fulfilled. This will enhance the capacity in utilizing the foreign resource and also the foreign market, and thus be helpful for the "Walk Out" strategy. On domestic reform, the sustainable growth of the Chinese economy should rely on the reform of the factor markets. This will optimize allocation efficiency, and thus provide a positive motive for individuals. The quality and the sustainability of economic growth depend on capital market reform, land market reform, and labor market reform. Besides, the transformation of government functions is also an important aspect for China's future economic growth.

5. Conclusion

The globalization process in China, starting from the 1980s, brings opportunities and dynamism for China's economic development. Global industry transfer, promoted by transnational corporations, accelerates China's industrialization and has achieved the rapid growth of China's economic miracle during the past 30 years.

China's incremental reform maintains the social stability under the dramatic changes in China's economic structure. The driving force of China's economic development in different periods has changed in the process of reforms from the responsibility system of land contract to joining the WTO. There are four stages of China's economic growth. The first stage is driven by the agricultural development due to rural reform; the second stage is driven by the township enterprises reform in rural industrialization; the third stage is driven by the reform of SOEs and development of private enterprises; and the final stage is driven by the consumption upgrading after joining the WTO. Due to the imbalance of national development, the external environment of economic growth changes sharply. The development costs caused by an unhealthy relation between governments and markets gradually emerge. The structural imbalance of urbanization, industrialization, and aging, and environmental costs increase the pains of China's economic growth. The driving force of economic development is increasingly weak.

Therefore, reform aimed at removing the obstacles that hinder China's sustainable development is necessary to maintain China's long-term growth. Due to the constraints of real-world conditions, the combination of top-level design and market-oriented exploration should be considered as the fundamental principles of economic development and reform. On the one hand, China should base on bilateralism as the main mode of international relations, and take advantage of China's comparative advantage, resources, and markets overseas to receive adequate external driving force of China's long-term growth. On the other hand, secured by the transformation of the government's role, factor market reform, which is led by capital market reform and followed by land and labor markets reform, is necessary to maintain China's sustainable development in the future.

REFERENCES

China Association of Mayors (2012). *Annual Report on Urban Development of China (2011)*. China City Press.

Sheng Feng (2012). Productivity, innovation and SOEs reform: The empirical analysis on data of micro-level enterprises. *Industrial Economics Research* 4: 37–46.

Song Jing (2005). The impact of FDI on China's industrial upgrading: The analysis in the perspective of foreign trade. *International Trade Issue* 4: 82–86.

Yan Yuming (2011). A survey on the reasons of transformation of enterprises. *China Foreign Trade* 11: 2–4, 22.

Zhang Weiyin and Su Shuhe (1998). Interregional competition and privatization of China's SOEs. *Economics Research* 12: 13–22.

Zen Xianyin (2004). *Environmental Management for a New Road to Industrialization*. Resource and Environment Economics Progress Series 2.

Chapter 2

Potential Economic Growth of China in Transition

Zhigang Yuan
School of Economics, Fudan University

Yuxin Yu
School of Economics, Shanghai International Studies University

With the Chinese economy stepping into a transition period, its growth trend has become the topic of related researches. The potential economic growth rate of China is studied in this chapter based on production functions. We find that sources of economic growth, including labor supply, capital accumulation, and total factor productivity (TFP) growth, all tend to decline in the near future. It is likely that potential economic growth rate in China will fall significantly. To escape the "middle-income trap," structural adjustments of the Chinese economy should be made. Factor markets, including the capital market and land market, should be reformed so that institutional barriers that compress consumption can be eliminated and new liquidity can be injected into the Chinese economy. Besides, human capital investment should be further encouraged so that TFP growth can be promoted.

1. INTRODUCTION

The Chinese economy has been growing rapidly since 1978. The average GDP growth rate after 1978 is 9.9%, and the 10.6% average annual growth rate in the most recent decade (2001–2011) is even more spectacular. Years of rapid growth have made China the world's second largest economy in 2010 and the country holding the highest foreign exchange reserves. In 2011, GDP per capita in China exceeded US$5,000, making it a middle-income nation. China's rapid economic growth in the past was sustained by its high potential growth rate. Therefore, China is able to become a "well-off society" in such a short period of time.

Becoming a middle-income nation has also brought China some new challenges, one of which is the most widely known "middle-income trap." Whether the Chinese economy can keep on growing rapidly is essential for escaping the "middle-income trap," and it is the potential growth rate that matters for sustaining future economic growth. Studying changes in the long-run potential growth rate will enable us to predict China's future economic growth more scientifically and provide us a theoretical basis for figuring out China's strategy to escape the "middle-income trap."

Generally speaking, there are two ways to study a country's potential economic growth rate. One method implements time-series filter analyses on real outputs (Institute of Economics, Chinese Academy of Social Sciences, 2005, 2006; Zhang, 2005), while the other makes estimations based on production functions (Shen, 1999; He, 2004; Guo and Jia, 2004; etc.) The first method is relatively easier to implement because it is based on actual output data. Moreover, very few other factors need to be taken into account. However, as the Chinese economy steps into a transition period, factors that used to sustain economic growth may change. Growth in labor supply may be slower; capital accumulation rate may fall; room for technology progress as a "late developer" may be narrowed; and the transition from a manufacturing-oriented economic development strategy to a service-oriented strategy may lower TFP growth rate. Therefore, predictions of future economic growth made by past data are not reliable. Besides, influences of supply-side factors on potential economic growth are also neglected in the first method. As for the second method, though estimation procedures might be more complicated, supply-side factors and technology progress are included in analyses (Guo and Jia, 2004). So, it is more credible to use estimations based on production functions to analyze potential economic growth rate in transitional China.

However, changes in the economic structure of China may add complications to the analysis of its potential economic growth rate. Results from different studies differ a lot. For example, Li *et al.* (2005) believes that the potential economic growth rate in China is around 7%, while estimations from Guo and Jia (2004) find it to be 9.56%. Estimations of potential output growth rates using different methods are compared in Gao and Liang (2005). Results show that potential output growth rates differ significantly when different methods are adopted. This is because data on production factors are usually difficult to obtain and accurately estimate. For example, estimations of capital stock have always been one of the great difficulties in these studies. In the face of data limitations, instead of implementing "accurate" estimations of the potential economic growth rate, we will analyze its tendency based on production functions in this paper. Tendency analysis is preferred in this study not only because estimations based on production functions are more credible as the economic environment is subject to change in the transition period, but also because inaccuracies resulting from data limitations and influences of short-term fluctuations can be avoided.

2. HISTORY AND STAGES OF THE CHINESE ECONOMY SINCE 1978

2.1 Economic History of China since 1978

The growth miracle of China started from 1978 when the reform and open policy was implemented. Land reforms and the subsequent rise in the living standards of rural China also acted as a prelude to the Chinese miracle. With increases in the rural income level, trade in the agricultural products market was activated. However, in the meantime, the urban economy was still restricted by the planned economy system. The development of township and village enterprises (TVEs) facilitated economic growth by means of industrialization with Chinese characteristics; therefore, shortages of goods in the planned economy were relieved. Meanwhile, with the development of TVEs, the Chinese began to realize the advantages of the market economy, and reforms in the urban sector were then encouraged. Reforms focusing on the state-owned enterprises (SOEs) implemented by the Chinese government led by Zhu Rongji afterwards not only promoted growth of the private sector, but also further encouraged opening up and globalization of the Chinese economy. Reforms in the urban sector activated the use of existing assets, and shortage of goods became history in China. With China's entry into the WTO in 2001, the market began to play an even more important role. As a result, production factors, especially the labor force, are more integrated into the global industry chain dominated by multinational companies, and China has become the "world factory." Meanwhile, with the boom of the real estate market, urbanization is promoted. With upgrades of consumption, manufacturing industries also upgraded from light manufacturing industry which focuses on food processing and textiles, to heavy manufacturing industry, because consumption demands for home appliances, automobiles, and real estate were higher. Economic growth in China is thus sustained, and a new era of the Chinese economy is about to come.

2.2 Current Stage of the Chinese Economy

Different stages in economic development are usually distinguished by different income levels. Countries are thus divided into three categories, including low-income countries, middle-income countries, and high-income countries. China became one of the middle-income countries in 2011 when its GDP per capita exceeded US$5,000. It is now growing to become a high-income country.

The World Bank uses GDP per capita valued at purchasing power parities (PPPs) (Current International $) to evaluate a country's income level. According to data from the World Bank, (see Table 2-1) GDP per capita in China was 4,761 and 5,568 current international dollars in 2007 and 2008, respectively. GDP per capita in South Korea was 4,951 and 5,655 current international dollars in 1987 and 1988, and 4,590 and 4,250 current international dollars in Japan in 1968 and 1969. Therefore, using GDP (PPP) per capita as a standard, the development stage of China in 2007 corresponds to 1988 South Korea and 1969 Japan. The years of 1988 and 1969 were the

Table 2-1: Incomes of China, South Korea, and Japan in the transition period (current international $).

	China		South Korea		Japan	
	2007	2008	1987	1988	1968	1969
GDP per capita	4,761	5,568	4,951	5,655	4,590	5,250

Source: The World Bank.

transitional years for South Korea and Japan. Economic structures changed significantly in the transition period, so it will be difficult to predict future economic growth based on past data in transitional years. As a result, in this study, we will use data from Japan and South Korea in their transitional years as a benchmark to evaluate the potential economic growth rate of China.

3. TRENDS OF POTENTIAL ECONOMIC GROWTH RATE IN CHINA

Labor supply, capital accumulation, and increase in TFP are sources of economic growth in standard production functions. Analyzing trends of potential economic growth rate in China from these sources will not only enable us to evaluate the quality of growth of China since 1978, but will also provide us evidence on the sustainability of economic growth. Thus, the question of how likely China will be able to escape the "middle-income trap" can be answered.

3.1 Labor Supply

Labor supply is usually evaluated from perspectives of quantity, quality, and structure. The positive influence of labor supply on potential economic growth is usually referred to as "demographic dividends" in the literature.

On demographic dividends, no consensus has yet been reached about its magnitude, duration, or influences. For example, Cai and Wang (1999) believe that labor supply contributed 23.71% to economic growth, while Wang and Mason (2006) believe its contribution to be 15%. Cai et al. (2005) find that decreases in the dependency ratio as a result of changes in the age structure raised the growth rate of GDP per capita by 2.3% points, contributing 25% to GDP per capita growth in the same period. In spite of the different conclusions reached in the above studies, the fact that demographic dividends in China are dying out cannot be concealed. Changes in the age structure of the population imply that the contribution of labor supply to potential economic growth will undoubtedly decline. Predictions from Cai (2009) show that working age population (those aged from 15 to 64) will cease to increase around 2015. Meanwhile, the share of the population aged 65 and above will rise to 9.6% in 2015. The dependency ratio will reach its turning point by then, after which it will stop decreasing but begin to increase instead. Predictions from the United Nations also show that working age population in China will peak in 2015, with its total being 0.998 billion. These results imply that the contribution of demographic dividends will gradually die out.

The Research Group on China's Economic Growth and Macroeconomic Stability (2007) found that in the Chinese labor market, the "horizontal effect" has begun to decrease and the "vertical effect" has emerged. Therefore, long-run economic growth in China cannot depend on demographic dividends any longer. Instead, endogenous economic growth based on knowledge and technology should be encouraged. However, human capital investment in China is inefficient due to many institutional reasons, so its role in economic growth is constrained.

In the face of these labor supply changes, potential economic growth will be greatly constrained if China does not reform its education system or enhance its human capital investment efficiency.

3.2 Capital Accumulation

Capital accumulation contributes to economic growth in two ways. The first is from the perspective of efficiency. Capital investment will improve the allocation efficiency of capital, leading to efficiency gains of the whole economy. The second is from the quantity perspective. Capital investment increases the quantity of production inputs, and thus promotes economic growth.

3.2.1 Contribution of capital accumulation: The efficiency perspective

As capital investments can improve the allocation efficiency of capital, capital accumulation is able to facilitate potential economic growth. By studying capital allocation distortions across different industries, we will try to reveal the rule of distortions and its changes in this section. Then, we will compare China's experience with South Korea and Japan in their transitional periods in order to show the possible positive influences of improvements in capital allocation efficiency on the potential economic growth rate.

(1) Capital Allocation Distortions in China

According to the principle of equalizing marginal returns to capital, if there are distortions in capital allocations, returns to capital will be unequal across different industries. Conversely, if capital is allocated efficiently, its returns will tend to be equal (Wurgler, 2005).

Baumol and Bradford (1970) were the first to estimate returns to capital by regressing output on capital using data from the United States. However, results based on regressions may suffer from missing variable bias (Brealey *et al.*, 1976; McFetridge, 1978; etc.). Besides, regression analyses are generally based on input and output data at fixed prices. More recently, scholars began to use input and output data at market prices, instead of fixed prices, to estimate returns to capital. One example is Mueller and Reardon (1993). Besides, early studies generally estimate returns to capital in the capital market only. It is not until Mueller and Yurtoglu (2000) and Gugler *et al.* (2003, 2004) that the whole economy's returns to capital are estimated. However, these two studies still suffer from the representativeness of their research subjects. In situations when the capital market is underdeveloped and there is not sufficient market competition, results from these studies may be unreliable.

Bai *et al.* (2006) estimate returns to capital of the whole economy using macroeconomic data of China in the period 1978–2005. Time variations can be observed when macroeconomic data is used to estimate capital returns, which cannot be done using the regression method because it only estimates the average return over a given period of time. However, estimations based on macroeconomic data tell us nothing about resource allocation efficiency. Therefore, distortions in resource allocations and their changes are not revealed when this method is used.

Costs of capital data in all industries are needed when one wants to estimate capital allocations distortions. However, data quality is still a great concern when macroeconomic data is used to estimate capital prices. Estimating capital allocation distortions might be difficult if credible data on capital price and capital returns are not available.

To overcome the above difficulties, in this study, we will project capital returns in different industries to one variable whose data could be more easily and credibly obtained. Variations in this variable are then studied to illustrate changes in capital allocation distortions. Generally speaking, capital prices are equal to the expected returns to capital. Therefore, changes in expected returns and changes in prices are two sides of one coin. Changes in capital allocation distortions can thus be revealed by studying changes in expected capital return differences across different industries.

Statistically, changes in capital stock are usually much larger than changes in capital prices. Therefore, in order to study capital allocation distortions, we need to project price differences of capital to changes in capital stock so that changes in capital stock can be used to represent capital allocation distortions. Assuming that investors make investment decisions according to the expected returns to capital, we get the investment Equation (2-1):

$$I = \alpha(R - r)K. \tag{2-1}$$

As capital accumulation is determined by investment and depreciation rate, capital accumulates as follows:

$$\dot{K} = I - \delta K \tag{2-2}$$

where $\dot{K}$ represents changes in capital stock, I is investment, δ is depreciation rate, and K represents capital stock.

Combining Equations (2-1) and (2-2), we get Equation (2-3) on the relationship between capital returns and changes in capital stock.

$$\frac{\dot{K}}{K} = \frac{I}{K} - \delta \Rightarrow R = \frac{(g_K + \delta)}{\alpha} + r \tag{2-3}$$

g_K in Equation (2-3) is the growth rate of capital stock. Equation (2-3) shows that capital allocation distortions between two different industries, that is, differences in their capital returns, can be expressed as differences in changes in the two industries' capital stocks. As a simplification, assume that α and δ are the same across different industries. Then, capital allocation distortions in two industries can be expressed as follows:

$$R_1 - R_2 = \frac{g_{K_1} - g_{K_2}}{\alpha}. \tag{2-4}$$

Equation (2-4) reveals a linear relationship between return differences of two industries and their differences in capital accumulation growth rates. Therefore, the speed of convergence of capital accumulation between two industries can be used to reflect capital return differences between two industries. Furthermore, changes in capital allocation distortions can be revealed. When there is no distortion in capital allocations, Equation (2-4) should equal 0.

Taking squares of both sides of Equation (2-4), we get Equation (2-5). Squared terms of return differences can still be used to represent allocation distortions, and the sign of return differences is no longer a concern in squared terms.

$$(R_1 - R_2)^2 = \frac{(g_{K_1} - g_{K_2})^2}{\alpha^2}. \tag{2-5}$$

Based on Equation (2-5), we can use data on capital stock of the three main sectors to compute their capital allocation distortions. Capital stock is usually computed using the perpetual method in literature, and the capital stock data used in this study are from Li (2010).

(2) Capital Allocation Distortions: Estimates

According to Equation (2-5), capital allocation distortions across different sectors can be calculated. Figure 2-1 shows that distortions were the lowest in 1996 and were the highest in 2003. Before 2002, capital allocation distortions between the secondary industry and tertiary industry and distortions between the primary industry and secondary industry are two major sources of aggregate capital allocation distortions. This is mainly because development policies during this period gave priority to the development of secondary industry and thus resulted in over-investments in this sector. After 2003, distortions are mainly from distortions of the primary sector with the two other sectors. The more modernized secondary and tertiary sectors are more marketized. As a result, distortions between the secondary and the service sector are alleviated greatly. However, the agriculture sector has not yet been completely modernized. So, capital is allocated inefficiently between the primary sector and the other sectors under such dualistic structure.

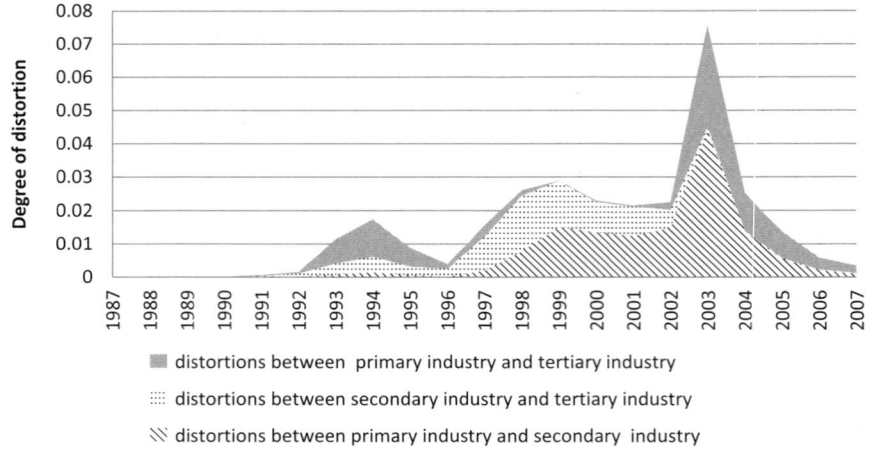

Figure 2-1: Capital allocation distortions in China.

Besides, from Figure 2-1, we find that distortions peaked in 2003 and gradually decline afterward, implying that the influence of capital allocation distortions on the Chinese economy is disappearing. This, on the other hand, implies that economic growth will benefit less from industrial restructuring in the future. "Structural bonus" will no longer play an important role in economic growth. Our finding is consistent with Gan and Zheng (2009), who estimate influences of industrial restructuring on productivity growth using the shift-share method. They also find structural bonus to be insignificant in capital allocations.

Experience from Japan and South Korea shows the share of the primary sector will continue to decline after transition. The share of the secondary sector will also fall, while the tertiary sector will become more and more important. Structural changes of the three sectors are mostly results of changes of the secondary and tertiary sector, which means that after transition, structural adjustments of the whole economy will be primarily from the secondary and the tertiary sector. With increases in income per capita after transition, consumption structure will also change. Individuals will have higher demand for service goods. The development of the tertiary sector will thus be promoted, and it will become the dominant sector of the economy. Therefore, the room for motivating economic growth by alleviating capital allocation distortions will be further limited.

It is confirmed in our analyses that after 30 years of marketization, structural bonus is no longer important, and there is very limited room for China to promote growth by increasing capital allocation efficiencies across different sectors. Therefore, the influence of capital accumulation on potential economic growth rate will not be from increasing allocation efficiencies, but largely from how fast capital can accumulate — in other words, the savings rate in China.

3.2.2 Contribution of capital accumulation: The quantity perspective

Results in Section 3.2.1 show that quantity is now the most important perspective to evaluate the influence of capital accumulation on economic growth in China. Capital accumulation of one country is fundamentally determined by its savings rate, and is determined jointly by savings rates of households, enterprises, and the government. The savings rate in China has always been relatively high. It is not only higher than most high-income and middle-income countries, but is also higher than the world average.

According to data from the flow of funds accounts in *China Statistical Yearbooks*, savings rates in different sectors vary a lot. Both government and corporate savings rates began to increase around 2000, while the household savings rate fell to some extent. The share of household savings in total savings is also decreasing, while the share of corporate savings keeps increasing. The share of government savings increases as well. Rises in corporate and government savings are the primary reason for the rapid growth of China's aggregate savings rate. As determinants of savings rate in different sectors differ, it is necessary to analyze different sectors separately so that trends of the future savings rate in China could be revealed.

(1) Household Savings

The household savings rate is determined by households' inter-temporal optimal consumption decisions. According to Barro and Sala-i-Martin

(1995),[1] when the production function is Cobb–Douglas, that is, $f(k) = Ak^\alpha$, and consumption function is CIES, the equilibrium savings rate can be solved as follows:

$$s^* = \alpha(x + n + \delta)/(\rho + \theta x + \delta) \tag{2-6}$$

where s^* is equilibrium savings rate; α is the output elasticity of capital per capita in production; x is technology growth rate; n is population growth rate; δ is depreciation rate; ρ is time preference, and θ is the inter-temporal elasticity of substitution.

Equation (2-6) shows that when the elasticity of capital in the production function increases, or in other words, returns to capital are higher, the household savings rate will increase. Higher technology growth rate, higher ρ, or higher inter-temporal elasticity of substitution brings down savings rate, while more rapid population growth brings the savings rate up.

The household savings rate is primarily determined by substitution effects and income effects. Substitution effects influence the savings rate because households have incentives to smooth consumption over different periods. Higher household income and higher inter-temporal elasticity of substitution will lead to higher household savings. Income effects will influence household savings because when household income in the current period is higher, disparities between current income and permanent income are smaller. As a result, households' incentives to smooth consumption will be lower, which will in turn raise the savings rate.

Based on the fact that China is in its transition period and there are many uncertainties, we find it most important to focus on household income, interest rate, inflation rate, and income distribution to explain the trend of the savings rate in China.

The household savings rate in China gradually increased after 1978 when household income rose (see Figure 2-2). It peaked in 1997 at 44.9% and gradually declined afterwards. In 2002, the household savings rate in China was only 12.4%. China's entry into the WTO enhanced its integration with the global economy. Globalization and booms in the real estate market both raised the household savings rate. However, more recently, the

---

[1] Barro, R.J. and Sala-i-Martin, X. (1995). *Economic Growth*, McGraw-Hill, New York.

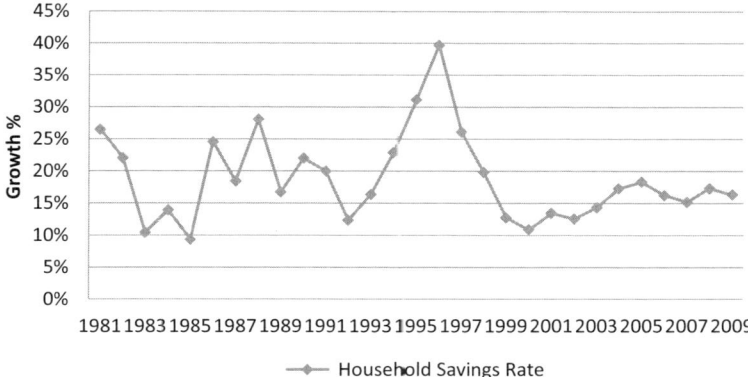

Figure 2-2: Household savings rate.

household savings rate has begun to fall again. Our analyses below will show that it is very likely that the household savings rate will decrease in the future.

Household income will affect the household savings rate directly because with increase in disposable income, households' incentives to save are higher. Besides, households with higher income growth rate will have better expectations of future economic growth, and therefore will be more motivated to save.

Both Japan and South Korea experienced declines in the savings rate after transition. The 15-year-average savings rate after the transition years was around 4%. Average savings rate in China in the period 1981–2009 was 5.84%. With increases in capital accumulation, declines in savings rate in China are inevitable. The interest rate of deposits is equal to capital returns. Therefore, its influence on the savings rate corresponds to the influence of α on the savings rate in Equation (2-5) and is positively correlated in Equation (2-6). So, with declines in the interest rate, the household savings rate in China will fall.

Inflation influences the savings rate through income effects. With increases in the inflation rate, real income falls, and the savings rate will decline correspondingly. Shocked by the oil crisis in 1973, the inflation rate in Japan soared afterwards. Similarly, the inflation rate in South Korea also rose when South Korea was influenced by the 1997 Asian financial crisis. However, apart from these shocks, inflation rates in Japan and South Korea tended to decline generally when outliers are excluded from analysis. Average 15-year inflation rates after the transition years of Japan and South Korea were 5.7% and 5%, respectively. In China, the average inflation rate in the period 1981–2009 was approximately 4.3%. As a result of structural inflation in the transition period, the inflation rate in China in 15 years may rise by 0.7 to 1.4% points. Therefore, the rising inflation rate will tend to bring down the household savings rate in the future.

The household savings rate can be influenced by income distributions as well. Though no consensus has been reached on the exact value of the Gini coefficient in China, it is widely accepted that income inequality in China is higher than in many other developed countries. Income inequality in Japan and South Korea is among the lowest in developed countries. The Gini coefficient in Japan was 0.25 in 1993. It was 0.32 in South Korea in 1998. Meanwhile, the average Gini coefficient of all developed countries is 0.32. Therefore, with economic development and increases in labor income share in China, the Gini coefficient will tend to decline in the future. However, the influence of income distribution on the savings rate is quite limited. So, a declining Gini coefficient may contribute to a rise in the savings rate only to a very small extent.

Population growth plays an important role in the household savings rate. Equation (2-6) shows that population growth will have positive effects on the savings rate. Besides, age structure of the population is also important. With increases in the age dependency ratio, the savings rate tends to fall because the old have lower ability to save. In 2007, the age dependency ratio in China was 12.86%. According to the estimates in Du *et al.* (2005), the age dependency ratio in China will be 26.3% in 2020. With the dependency ratio rising by approximately 13.5% points in the transition period, the savings rate in China will tend to decline. Both the one-child policy and income rises will exert negative influences on the fertility rate in China, and such negative influences will not be reversed in the transition period. As a result, even from the perspective of population structure, the household savings rate in China will tend to decline.

Based on the above analyses and comparisons with experiences from Japan and South Korea, the household savings rate in China will decline

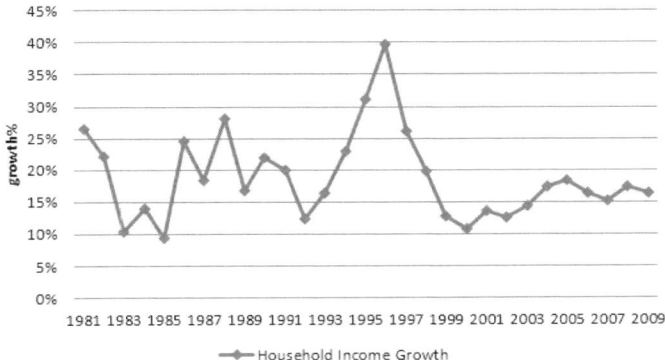

Figure 2-3: Household income growth.

to about 13–14%. As a result, the capital accumulation rate will fall in the future.

The average household income growth rate since 1978 is 18.8%, which is very high compared with other countries (see Figure 2-3). However, as household income becomes higher, its growth rate will tend to decline. Household income growth rate in recent years averaged around 16%, which is lower than the average growth rate since 1978. Therefore, it is likely that income growth rate will further decline in the future, and such declines will have negative influences on the household savings rate. What Japan and South Korea experienced after their economic and political transitions can be taken as benchmarks. After 1969, the 15-year average income growth rate of Japan was merely 3.7%. The average of South Korea after 1988 was 5.5%. Comparison studies show that the household income growth rate of China is likely to fall significantly in the future. Therefore, the household savings rate is unlikely to remain at a high level.

(2) Corporate Savings

Corporate savings refers to undistributed profits of firms with inventory value and capital deprecation adjusted. The corporate savings rate is the ratio of corporate savings over national disposable income. Data from flow of funds accounts in *China Statistical Yearbooks* show that the corporate savings rate in China increased from 11.73% in 1992 to 21.6% in 2008. Average corporate savings rate in the period was 17.53%, which is higher than many other countries. The rising corporate savings rate has become one of the most important sources of a rising national savings rate.

Corporate savings is equal to the firms' first distribution incomes plus redistribution incomes. As the relationship between the first distribution and redistribution is fairly stable, changes in corporate savings can be revealed even only if the first distribution income is analyzed. From the perspective of first distribution, firm income is equal to value added excluding labor income, net property income, and the net taxes on production. Therefore, increases in firm income from the first distribution are either from its more rapid increases in revenues or from the fact that value added grows faster than the growth of labor income, net property income, and the net taxes on production. Firm data shows that after 2003, value added increased much faster than labor income, net property income, and the net taxes on production. Though growth of value added has slowed down due to the subprime crisis, firm profitability still grows significantly recently. Besides, increases in firm income from the first distribution imply that firms have benefited greatly from low labor cost and capital cost in recent years.

As the most important determinants of corporate savings, labor income share decreased from 44.62% in 1992 to 35.78% in 2008. Net property income also fell from its highest in 1996 at 9.48% to 2.2% in 2008, while net taxes on production stayed around 20%. As a result, firm income from the first distribution has been increasing since 2000 and reached 39.77% in 2008.

Therefore, low labor income and declining property income share are two major sources of rising corporate savings in China. On the one hand, labor remuneration has been declining. For example, labor productivity in China is one-seventh of the labor productivity in South Korea. However, the wage level in China is only one-thirteenth of that in South Korea. On the other hand, capital cost has been kept at a disequilibrium low level, leading to declining property income share. Low capital cost encourages firm investments, and thus raises corporate savings.

Influences of the above two factors are further strengthened by other structural factors in China. For example, apart from finance firms and a few of the listed firms, SOEs never pay out dividends. With rapid economic growth and marketization, profits of SOEs increased significantly by restructuring and transferring their social responsibilities to the government. This is especially the case in many monopolistic SOEs, who instead of paying out dividends to all citizens, retain almost all of their revenues for investment, leading to a huge amount of corporate savings. For private firms, constrained by limited bank loans, they have to save for future investment. Besides, for income tax considerations, private firms do not have incentives to pay out dividends either. As a result, the savings rate of private firms is also high.

Industrial structure distortions in China are also responsible for the high corporate savings rate. The share of manufacturing industry in GDP in China is overly high. Due to the development strategy biased to the heavy industry, the share of heavy industries in all industries in China is also too high. However, heavy industries are generally more capital intensive. As a result, firm incomes are more distributed to capital instead of labor, further pushing up the corporate savings rate.

Besides, the economy's over-dependence on exports raises the corporate savings rate as well. Policies encouraging exports and attracting foreign direct investment (FDI) have motivated firms to invest. As China is becoming more open to the outside world, returns to investment gradually rise. Firms' incentives to invest are further encouraged by the low capital cost and labor cost. Therefore, as more FDI is utilized by firms, firms also save more. The corporate savings rate becomes even higher in this situation.

To sum up, the high corporate savings rate in China is primarily from distortions in the factor market, including distortions in the labor market and capital market. Distortions in the factor market compress labor and capital cost, which in turn encourages firm investments. With reforms in the labor market and the capital market, the corporate savings rate will decline correspondingly.

(3) Government Savings

Government savings is the difference between government revenue and government consumption expenditure. Government savings is not only determined by government revenues during a period, but is also related to government expenditure structures. Recurrent revenue, including tax revenue and non-tax revenue, and capital revenue are two components of government revenue. In 2009, government revenue amounted to 7,629.99

billion RMB, including the 6,851.83 billion recurrent revenue and 778.16 billion capital revenue. High government revenue indicates that government interventions into economic activities are strong in China.

Since 2000, the share of government savings in total national savings has kept increasing. The rising share of government savings can be explained by the following three reasons. First, with the more rapid growth of tax revenues and land sale revenues, government disposable income rises significantly. Second, government investment expenditures have kept increasing rapidly, while consumption expenditures on education, medical and healthcare, and social safety net increase only a little. Third, government intervention into economic activities has become stronger recently, raising the government's propensity to save.

Kuijs (2005) finds that the government savings rate increased in China because the Chinese government supported the development of SOEs by ways of "capital transfer." But this finding is problematic because capital transfers fell greatly after 2003, and capital accumulation, or in other words government investment, was much higher than capital transfers were in the meantime. The implementation of active fiscal policies after 1997 raised both government expenditure and its growth rate. However, consumption expenditures on education, medical and healthcare, and social security increased fairly slowly. As two most important factors influencing government savings rate, capital accumulation and consumption expenditures account for about 60% of government disposable income. Therefore, changes in the government savings rate depend on changes in capital accumulation and consumption expenditures a lot.

The high government savings rate in China is mostly the result of the state-led economic development strategy. It is also the case in South Korea whose development strategy is state-led as well. Actually, the government savings rate in South Korea is even higher than in China (He and Cao, 2005). Based on the high government savings rate, investments led by the government are also high. However, government-led investments are inefficient and non-sustainable. Therefore, reducing inefficient government investments depends crucially on reducing the government savings rate. The share of capital expenditures in total government expenditures is generally lower than 5% in many developed countries such as the United States. Therefore, for the Chinese government to transform its role in economic

Table 2-2: Savings rates of different countries (%).

	1996				
	China	France	Germany	Japan	South Korea
Government savings rate	5	0	−1	3	10
National savings rate	40	17	20	30	35
	2007				
	China	France	Germany	Japan	South Korea
Government savings rate	9	1	2	0	11
National savings rate	51	19	24	26	29

Sources: Data for China is from *China Statistical Yearbooks* and the authors' calculations; Data for countries other than China is from Qiao and Zhu (2009).

development, it is essential to cut back its investment expenditures. Compared with the fact that capital expenditures account for 5–10% in total government expenditures in the United Kingdom, France, and Germany, if the Chinese government is able to cut back its share of capital expenditure from over 20% to 5–10%, there is still much room for consumption expenditures to rise (see Table 2-2).

Compared with other developed countries, shares of expenditures on education and medical and healthcare in GDP in China are lower. They are even lower than shares in India, indicating that government consumption expenditures in China are too low. The government savings rate is influenced by consumption expenditures greatly. Increase in the share of government consumption expenditures can bring down the government savings rate a lot. Currently in China, the share of government consumption expenditures in GDP is about 11% (see Table 2-3). It is expected to be raised by 10% points in the future. Therefore, based on 2008 data, government consumption expenditures will increase by 2.1 trillion RMB, which will further bring down the government savings rate to around 1.6%, a level that is comparable to India. Since there are still a lot of economic resources being controlled by the Chinese government, economic development will continue to be influenced by the government in the near future. As a result, the actual government savings rate might be higher than the estimated 1.6% level, and will be at around 5%. But still, the 5% savings rate will be about 3% points lower than the savings rate in 2008.

Table 2-3: Shares of expenditures on education and medical and healthcare in GDP (%).

Country	Education	Medical and healthcare
Australia	4.8	6.4
Japan	3.7	6.4
South Korea	4.6	2.8
New Zealand	6.9	6.3
China	2.9	1.1
India	3.3	1.2

Source: Data for China is for the year of 2009, while data for other countries are for the year of 2004 from Zhang (2006).

To sum up, the national savings rate in China will be around 29.4–34% in the future, implying that the investment rate will also be between 29.4% and 34%. The present capital-output ratio in China is about 6.5%, while it is around 3.5% in developed countries. Assume that the capital-output ratio in China will decline to 4 or 5. When the depreciation rate is taken as 11%, we can calculate the contribution of capital accumulation to potential economic growth rate according to the following equation:

Contribution = (Savings Rate − Depreciation Rate)/Capital-output Ratio

Calculations show that the contribution of capital accumulation to potential economic growth rate will be 3.7% to 5.7%, or around 4.6% when averages are taken. The average contribution of capital accumulation in China in the period 2001–2009 was 5.5%. Therefore, it will fall by 0.9% points in the future, or even 1.8% at its highest.

3.3 TFP

3.3.1 Theoretical model

In this section, we will analyze the influence of TFP on potential economic growth rate using the production function. Changes in TFP growth rate will be studied and international comparisons will be made.

In the literature, TFP is usually studied using the Solow production function. For example, Wang (2000), Young (2003), and OECD (2005) all applied the Solow production function to estimate changes in TFP in China.

In this study, we will use the same method as in Young (2003) and Zhang and Shi (2003). Assume that output in China is determined by the following production function, which has constant returns to capital and labor:

$$Y = F(K, L, t) \qquad (2\text{-}7)$$

where K is capital input, L denotes labor input, and t is a time variable. Differentiating 2.6 with respect to t leads to Equation (2-8):

$$\frac{dY}{Y} = \left(\frac{F_K K}{Y}\right)\frac{dK}{K} + \left(\frac{F_L L}{Y}\right)\frac{dL}{L} + \frac{F_t}{Y}dt \qquad (2\text{-}8)$$

where F_i denotes derivatives of output to capital or labor. By rearranging Equation (2-8), the growth rate of TFP can be expressed as follows:

$$\begin{aligned} TFP\ growth &= \frac{dY}{Y} - \theta_K \frac{dK}{K} - \theta_L \frac{dL}{L} \\ &= \theta_K \left(\frac{dY}{Y} - \frac{dK}{K}\right) - \theta_L \left(\frac{dY}{Y} - \frac{dL}{L}\right) \end{aligned} \qquad (2\text{-}9)$$

θ_K and θ_L in Equation (2-9) are output elasticities of capital and labor, respectively. They also represent shares of capital income and labor income in total output. To study changes in TFP in China, assume that the production function is Cobb–Douglas:

$$Y_t = A_0 e^{\alpha_1 t} K^{\alpha_K} L^{\alpha_L} \qquad (2\text{-}10)$$

where α_K and α_L are output elasticities of capital and labor. Besides, inclusion of subscript t implies that the production function is subject to change across different periods. Taking Logs on both sides of Equation (2-10), we have Equation (2-11), which can be applied to regression analysis.

$$\ln Y = \ln A_0 + \alpha_t t + \alpha_K \ln K_t + \alpha_L \ln L_t. \qquad (2\text{-}11)$$

Regressions based on Equation (2-11) can provide us estimates of α_K and α_L. By normalization, we have:

$$\alpha_K^* = \alpha_K/(\alpha_K + \alpha_L),\ \alpha_L^* = \alpha_L/(\alpha_K + \alpha_L). \qquad (2\text{-}12)$$

TFP can thus be defined as:

$$TFP_t = \frac{Y_t}{K_t^{\alpha_K^*} L_t^{\alpha_L^*}}. \tag{2-13}$$

3.3.2 Data

Estimations of TFP and its growth rate need time series data on output, capital input, and labor input, that is, Y_t, K_t, and L_t in the model. Generally, GDP or GNP at constant prices is used to measure output. Data on GDP and GNP are available from *China Statistical Yearbooks*, and we use GDP data based on the prices in 1990 to measure outputs in this study. Its unit is 100 million RMB. Labor input is measured as the number of employed persons in various years, and the unit of labor is 10,000. Measures on capital stock are based on previous studies, including He (1992) and Zhang (2005). The measuring unit of capital stock is 100 million RMB.

The perpetual method is usually adopted to estimate capital stock. Capital stock data in the period 1978–1998 used in this study is from Zhang and Shi (2003), and data in the period 1999–2009 are calculated using the whole country's total investment in fixed assets data based on Equation (2-14) developed in Zhang (2005) and Shan (2008):

$$K_t = \frac{I_t}{P_t} - \delta K_{t-1} \tag{2-14}$$

I_t in Equation (2-14) is the country's total investment in fixed assets, P_t is the price index of fixed asset investment, and δ denotes depreciation rate. The depreciation rate in this study is taken to be 10.96%. Data on I_t and P_t are from *China Statistical Yearbooks*.

3.3.3 Regression results

The following econometric model is used in our regressions.

$$\ln Y = \ln A_0 + \alpha_t t + \alpha_K \ln K_t + \alpha_L \ln L_t. \tag{2-15}$$

As we find time variable t insignificant in Result (1), it is excluded from Regression (2). Regression results are displayed in Table 2-4.

Regression results show that both labor and capital stock have significantly positive effects on output, and the goodness of fit in both regressions

Table 2-4: Regression results.

Variables	(1) ln Y	(2) ln Y
ln L_t	0.496**	0.658***
	(0.230)	(0.0713)
ln K_t	0.603**	0.768***
	(0.222)	(0.0155)
t	0.0208	
	(0.0279)	
Constant	1.256	−1.110***
	(3.199)	(0.319)
Observations	32	32
R-squared	0.999	0.999
F Statistics	7338.94	11180.61
Prob > F	0	0
D-W Statistic	1.659	1.731

*** $p < 0.01$, ** $p < 0.05$, * $p < 0.1$
Note: Standard errors in parentheses.

is very high. However, the time variable is not significant in Result (1), so Result (2) is preferred. From Result (2), estimates of α_K and α_L are obtained, equaling 0.768 and 0.658, respectively. By normalization, we get estimates of α_K^* and α_L^*, which are 0.539 and 0.461 respectively. Our results are consistent with findings in OECD (2005), in which the estimates of α_K^* and α_L^* are 0.53 and 0.47.

Using Equation (2-13), we obtain estimates of TFP growth rate (Figure 2-4).

As is shown in Figure 2-4, except for years 1989 and 1990, TFP has always been growing in China since 1978. Declines in TFP in 1989 and 1999 might be the result of deflationary policies implemented in the late 1980s and early 1990s.

The contribution of TFP growth to output growth in China changed significantly before and after reform and open door policies were implemented (Tables 2-5 and 2-6).

Comparisons of Tables 2-5 and 2-6 show that TFP growth rate varies a lot before 1978. After 1978, TFP grew significantly. The average growth rate of TFP in the period 1979–2009 was 2.9%, contributing 29.3% to total

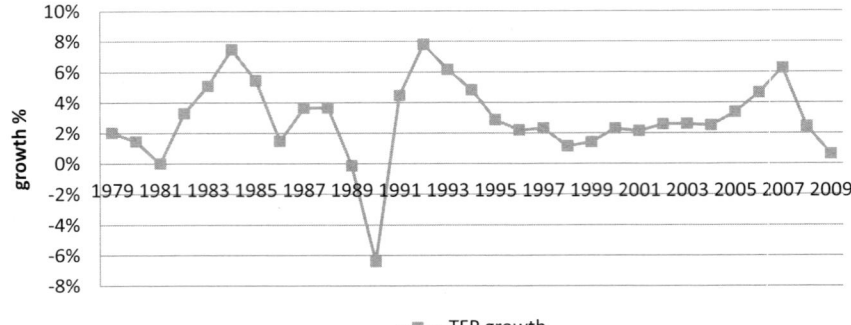

Figure 2-4: TFP growth rates.

Table 2-5: TFP growth, output growth, and the contribution of TFP before 1978.

	1953–1959	1960–1962	1963–1970	1971–1976
TFP growth rate	1.5%	−15.2%	4.2%	−1.3%
Output growth rate	10.8%	−11.9%	9.9%	4.6%
Contribution of TFP growth to output growth	13.6%	−127.7%	42.5%	−27.8%

Source: Zhang and Shi (2003).

Table 2-6: TFP growth, output growth, and the contribution of TFP after 1978.

	1979–1989	1990–1999	2000–2009	1979–2009
TFP growth rate	3.0%	2.7%	2.9%	2.9%
Output growth rate	9.6%	10.0%	10.3%	9.9%
Contribution of TFP growth to output growth	31.8%	27%	28.2%	29.3%

output growth, implying that TFP growth in China did benefit a lot from economic reforms.

The average TFP growth rate in 1979–1989 was around 3.0%, contributing 31.8% to output growth. The growth rate and contribution of TFP in the period 1990–1999 were 2.7% and 27%, respectively. In the period 2000–2009, TFP grew by 2.9% annually on average and contributed 28.2% to output growth. TFP growth made great contributions to output growth in all periods after 1978. Compared with results in Zhang and Shi (2003), who studied TFP growth before 1978, our results show that the Chinese economy benefits greatly from market-oriented reforms after 1978.

However, it is also revealed in Figure 2-4 that TFP growth rate declined significantly after 2007. So, there is still a possibility that TFP growth rate may vary to a greater extent in the future. In Section 3.3.4, we will try to predict future trends of TFP growth in China based on experience from Japan in its transition period.

3.3.4 Future trends of TFP growth: Predictions based on experience from Japan

The TFP growth rate in Japan has been estimated in many studies. In this paper, estimates from Jorgenson and Gollop (1992) are used. TFP growth rates in Japan in its transition period are displayed in Table 2-7.

Table 2-7 shows that TFP growth rates were relatively lower in years when the Japanese economy suffered from external shocks such as the "oil crisis" in the 1970s. Similarly, estimates of the TFP growth rate in China also declined significantly after the subprime crisis.

The global economy was negatively shocked by the oil crisis in the 1970s. As a result, the TFP growth rate in Japan during the period decreased significantly due to declines in external demand. Based on analyses of the global environment and the current stage of the Chinese economy, we

Table 2-7: TFP growth rate of Japan in its transitional years (%).

Year	Japan
1960–1965	1.478
1965–1970	1.946
1970–1973	0.686
1973–1975	1.481
1980–1985	0.469

Source: Jorgenson and Gollop (1992).

believe that the situation in China after the subprime crisis is similar to the Japanese economy after the oil crisis. The TFP growth rate in Japan fell by 65% after the oil crisis. Similarly in China, the TFP growth rate fell by 62% after the subprime crisis, from 6.3% in 2006 to 2.4% in 2007. Therefore, we find it reasonable to use changes in the TFP growth rate in Japan after the oil crisis as a benchmark.

The TFP growth rate in Japan after the oil crisis was only about 76% of the rate before the crisis. The 10-year average TFP growth rate after the crisis was only 24% of the 10-year average before the crisis. The average TFP growth rate in China is 2.9%. If we use the Japanese experience as a benchmark, average TFP growth rate in China in 5–10 years after the subprime crisis will be around 2%. It will further fall to around 0.7% ten years later. Therefore, falls in the TFP growth rate may bring down the potential economic growth rate of the Chinese economy by 0.9–2.2% points.

4. CONCLUSIONS AND POLICY IMPLICATIONS

Analyses in this paper show that as sources of economic growth, labor supply, capital supply, and TFP growth rate all tend to decrease in the future. Therefore, potential economic growth rate in China tends to decline. However, escaping the "middle-income trap" requires the Chinese economy to grow at a relatively high and stable rate in the next 20 years. Therefore, structural reforms are needed to sustain economic growth. Specifically, the following policies can be implemented to enhance the potential economic growth rate in China.

First, investment in education should be encouraged. Both the quality and quantity of human capital should be increased, and a platform that promotes communication between universities and industries should be set up. It is quite natural for a developing country like China to have fewer opportunities to learn from developed countries, or in other words to lose their advantages as a late comer. Therefore, investments in science and technology and innovation should be encouraged. There are usually gaps between university researches and industrial production. It is essential to eliminate communication barriers so that education and researches can promote economic growth more directly. Besides, intellectual property should also be protected so that innovation can be encouraged.

Second, the tax system should be improved to bring down corporate savings and the social security system should be improved to encourage household consumption. The system of value added taxes needs to be further improved, and changes in tax policies should encourage industrial upgrading so that productivity and resource allocation efficiency can be enhanced. When the time is right, social security taxes can be imposed because only when the social security fund has stable and sustainable income can it truly provide security and benefits to households. Under a better social security system, households will save less and consume more. Economic growth will benefit greatly from larger domestic demand afterwards.

Third, the government's role in economic development should be changed. Instead of being a government that relies heavily on investment to promote economic growth, the Chinese government should focus more on public services. The government should spend more on public goods such as education, healthcare, and social security. If so, not only can capital expenditure be brought down, the uncertainty of household expectations will be lower as well. Thus, households will have fewer incentives to save for precautionary purposes. Besides, based on experience from the United States and Japan, firms with higher risks or firms in important industries need to be subsidized.

Fourth, the financial system should be reformed and the development of the capital market should be encouraged. We need to promote the marketization of interest rates. Interest rates should be based on the base rate set by the central bank and should be determined by demand and supply in the capital market. The financial sector should be more competitive so that financial resources can be allocated more efficiently. But still, the capital market should be regulated because investors will not have confidence in a financial market that is not in order. Besides, the government should try to increase capital supply and adjust the existing structure of capital stock so that capital is utilized more efficiently.

Finally, land market reforms can become a new way of liquidity injection for the Chinese economy. Capitalization of rural land will not only improve the allocation efficiency of land, but also increase the property income of farmers so that urban–rural disparity can be narrowed. Lower income inequality will boost domestic demand in the long run. Besides, with the capitalization of land, farmers will have the funds to go to cities, and urbanization can thus be further encouraged.

REFERENCES

Bai, Chong-En, Hsieh, Chang-Tai and Qian, Yingyi (2006). The Return to Capital in China. *Brookings Papers on Economic Activity*, Vol. 2.

Brealey, R., Hodges, S. and Capron, D. (1976). The return on alternative sources of finance. *Review of Economics and Statistics*, 58(4): 469–477.

Baumol, William J. and David F. Bradford (1970). Optimal departures from marginal cost pricing. *The American Economic Review*, 60(3): 265–283.

Cai, Fang (2009). China's future demographic dividend: Digging new source of economic growth. *Chinese Journal of Population Science*, 1: 2–10.

China's Economic Growth and Macroeconomic Stability (2007). The effects of labor supply and economic growth path transition. *Economic Research Journal*, 10: 4–16.

Du, Peng, Qu, Zhenwu and Wei Chen (2005). Trends of population aging in China in one hundred years. *Population Research*, 1: 90–93.

Guo, Qingwang and Jia, Junxue (2004). Estimating potential output and the output gap in China. *Economic Research Journal*, 5: 14–18.

Gao, Tiemei and Liang, Yunfang (2005). Cyclical fluctuations and appropriate economic growth of China. *Economic Perspectives*, 8: 37–43.

Gan, Chunhui and Ruogu Zheng (2009). A study on industrial structure evolution and productivity growth since the reform and opening up: Testing the structure-bones hypothesis in China from 1978 to 2007. *China Industrial Economics*, 2: 55–65.

He, Juhuang (1992). Estimations on fixed asset net values. *The Journal of Quantitative & Technical Economics*, 12.

He, Xinhua (2004). Potential Economic Growth Rate in China Based on Production Functions. *Statistical Studies of the World Economy*, Vol. 1.

He, X. and Cao Y. (2005). Analyzing the high saving rate in China. *Research on Economics and Statistics*, 10: 13–29.

Jorgenson, Dale W. and Frank M. Gollop. (1992). Productivity growth in US agriculture: A postwar perspective. *American Journal of Agricultural Economics*, 74(3): 745–750.

Kuijs, L. (2005). How Will China's Saving-Investment Balance Evolve? *World Bank China Research Paper*.

Li, Shantong, Hou, Yongzhi, Liu, Yunzhong and Jianwu He (2005). An analysis of China's economic growth potential and perspective. *Management World*, 9: 7–27.

Li, R. (2010). The measure of capital stock in three major industries of China. *The Journal of Hainan University*, 2: 47–52.

McFetridge, D. (1978). The efficiency implications of earnings retentions. *Review of Economics and Statistics*, 60(2): 218–224.

Mueller, D. and Reardon, E. (1993). Rates of return on corporate investment. *Southern Economic Journal*, 60(2): 430–453.

Mueller, D. and Yurtoglu, B. (2000). Country legal environments and corporate investment performance. *German Economic Review*, 1(2): 187–220.

Shen, L. (1999). Trends in potential economic growth rate in China. *The Journal of Quantitative & Technical Economics*, 12: 21–26.

Wang, Feng and Andrew Mason (2006). The demographic factor in China's transition. *Chinese Journal of Population Science*, 3: 2–18.

Wurgler, J. (2005). Financial markets and the allocation of capital. *Journal of Financial Economics*, 58(1–2): 187–214.

Young, Alwyn (2003). Gold into base metals: Productivity growth in the People's Republic of China during the reform period. *Journal of Political Economy*, 111(6): 1220–1261.

Zhang, Hongwu (2005). Output gaps and an estimation of potential economic growth rate in china. *Economic Perspectives*, 7: 44–49.

Zhang, J. and Shi, S. (2003). The change in China's TFP: 1952–1998. *World Economic Reform*, 2: 17–24.

Chapter 3

Is China's Export Really Special? Perspective from Trade in Value Added

Changyuan Luo
Institute of World Economy, Fudan University

Jiajun Xu
St Antony's College, Oxford University

In the context of accelerating development of vertical integration, the global value chain has turned up a "fragmentation" trend. There are few products produced by a single country; on the contrary, number of countries as suppliers of value added participate in the creation of value. However, trade statistics did not keep up with the evolution of international division of labor, which leads to information distortion. In particular, China, as a country posted in the "terminal link" of value chain, is overestimated in the global trading system under the traditional measure. In order to reflect more accurately the current situation of international division of labor as well as the position of a country in the international trading system, a value-added measure may be more desirable. This chapter based on this perspective tries to have a new view on China's exporting development.

As for the theoretical interpretation of trade in value added (TiVA), Johnson and Noguera (2012) put forward an indicative analytical framework. Its core idea is that the essence that Country B imported a product (it may be for final demand or intermediate input) from Country A reflects the output transfer from Country A to Country B. In order to calculate the figure, we have to deduct the intermediate inputs from other countries including Country A. Taking China's reality into account, we developed the framework and focused on domestic value added and bilateral trade balance on the background of vertical integration in East Asia. Then, combining the database of "global TiVA" lately released by the OECD/WTO, we conducted an empirical study on China's export and drew three main conclusions:

Since 2005, China's total domestic value added share of gross exports has increased from 64% to 71% in 2009. We decomposed the change of value added ratio from an industrial perspective, and the result showed that the rise of value added within an industry (called intra-industry effect) was the main reason for the total change during this period. In contrast, the changes in export structure have become an obstacle to increase in value added ratio.

The ranking of China's value added ratio has climbed from the global lower–middle to the middle level since 2005. The representative developed countries, such as the United States, Japan, and the UK, and representative resource-intensive countries, like Brazil, Russia, Indonesia, and South Africa, maintain high value added ratio worldwide. Germany was a special case, as its ratio was just a little higher than China's. The ratio of South Korea was always lower than that of China. After decomposition of the gaps of domestic value added of exports between China and representative countries, we found the key factor leading to the gap came from the gap within an industry.

If calculated under value added measure, we found that China's trade surpluses with the United States and EU27 dropped dramatically while its trade deficits with Germany and South Korea decreased to a different degree. In 2009, the trade surpluses with the United States fell while both South Korea and Japan increased their trade surpluses to the United States at the same time, which reflected the fact that vertical integration developed in East Asia.

1. INTRODUCTION

Since the outbreak of the global financial crisis in 2007, the world economy has witnessed profound changes, which were the turndown of traditional economic powers as well as the increasing advancement of emerging countries. A similar situation happened in international trade. "North–North Trade" (trade between developed countries) has gradually been replaced by "South–South Trade" (trade between developing countries) and "South–North Trade" (trade between developing countries and developed ones) due to gradual improvement of economic strength in developing countries (Hanson 2012). In this context, China's international trade position changed dramatically. Its trade volume once ranked it No. 29 in the world in 1978, while in 2009, the ranking jumped to No. 2. Meanwhile, the export scale climbed to No. 1 from the original No. 31 in the world. The prosperity of China's international trade boosted the free flow of products and factors throughout the world, whereas it led to certain shocks on the current division system, which increased the induced trade frictions gradually. According to the data issued by Antidumping publishing, in 2011 China has confronted up to 49 cases of anti-dumping investigation. The total number, accumulated to 853, in the preceding 16 years China has the most anti-dumping case in progress, three times higher than that against South Korea where the second most cases of investigation happened with 284 cases. The circumstances of China's international trade seemed to deteriorate further in recent years. A study from Bown (2011) showed that 40% of global trade protections focused on China after the financial crisis. Both developed and developing countries were more likely to treat China as the target of trade protections.

The expansion of export scale may be a reason for trade protection, but another indispensable one is the export structure's upgrade. The largest share of export products was textiles in 1986 in China, while 10 years later machinery and transport equipment has occupied the first place, and recently digital products have become the "new favorite" (Lu et al., 2013). The fast change in China's export structure garnered attention from the world's famous economists. Rodrik (2006) pointed out the complexity of China's export product was excess of the due level of its current developing stage. Additionally, Schott (2008) found that the overlapping degree of export structure between China and OECD countries became increasingly high, which meant that in international trade, China not only became the rival of developing countries but also put competitive pressure on middle-income or even developed countries. As a result, trade protection happened in many areas.

However, the upgrade of both size and structure in China's exports do not result in side-effects on other countries inevitably. Among studies on the global influence of China's exports, there was no solid evidence to hold the view that China's exports were the main factor leading to the shrinking of others' exports, the decrease of export prices, and the deterioration of income allocation so far (Eichengreen and Tong, 2006; Jenkins and Edwards, 2006; Gaulier *et al.*, 2007; Fu *et al.*, 2009; Autor *et al.*, 2011). On the contrary, other papers demonstrated that it was the competitive pressure from China's exports that promoted related countries' technical progress and drove these economies to upgrade their industry structure (Iacovone *et al.*, 2010; Bloom *et al.*, 2011; Luo and Zhang, 2012). Consequently, the matter for trade protection against China may not lie in quick change in export size and structure, but reflect the game among different interest groups that launched trade protection. Another factor was that as the special terms of the WTO for China were about to expire, before the introduction of new ones, many countries took measures about trade protection against China (Bown, 2011).

Some other studies argued that China's exports were not very special, so it was irrational to criticize China. Xu (2007) pointed out that although the complexity of China's export seemed a bit high on the overall developing level, it was reasonable on the premise that the exports mainly concentrated on coastal provinces, which were at a high level of economic development. So it was not as special as Rodrik (2006) and Schott (2008) thought. He also believed that for similar kinds of products, the ones made in China had a low quality, which could not affect its developed counterparts directly. Domestic content was another important argument. Many studies thought if the fact that processing trade occupied a large proportion in gross exports of China was ignored, it would seriously overestimate domestic value added of gross exports as well as the influence on other countries (Koopman *et al.*, 2008; Zhang *et al.*, 2012). Inspired by this view, this chapter started from a similar point of view. In particular, we will use trade in a value added framework to test the trends of China's exports, which matched the trend of current development in international division.

WTO Secretary General Lamy mentioned the iPhone example in his paper called "'Made in China' Tells Us Little about Global Trade" in January 2011. According to traditional trade statistics, China had a US$1.9 billion surplus with the United States on iPhone trade. However, if calculated under a value added measure, the number was only US$73 million. Linden *et al.* (2007) shared a similar case in their report named "Who Captures Value in a Global Innovation Network? The Case of Apple's iPod." The retail price for an iPod was US$299, while the factory price was US$150. When an iPod was shipped from China to the United States, the trade deficits were about US$150 with shipping fees. Whereas there were just a few dollars added from labor-related input during assembly process in China. That was to say, if measured under value added measure, the trade was another situation. They pointed out if the iPod assembly factories moved to the United States, the imbalance from iPod trade would vanish. But the US trade deficits on an iPod would still exist between the United States and parts suppliers. These two examples reflect an important fact that in the era of integration, each country is a link of the value chain, which creates corresponding value added.

From the OECD/WTO's point of view, a product integrates intermediate goods from various countries and industries before it enters the market. And TiVA is defined to trace all sources of value added for a final commodity. The OECD/WTO demonstrated the significance of TiVA from three aspects: first, TiVA can indicate a country's position in the world's value chain, as well as job and growth opportunities through its participation in international division of labor. Second, the value added method can measure bilateral trade better. Although it causes no changes to a country's whole trade balance, it has an effect on the allocation of trade balance between partner countries. The results calculated under the traditional measure overestimate the role of countries in the terminal link of the value chain, but underestimate that of countries in middle parts. Third, TiVA shows a totally different view on policies. For instance, Country C exports a product for US$90 to Country A, then Country A processes it and exports it to Country B for US$100, and Country B processes it again and exports it back to Country C for US$110. Depending on the traditional measure, Country C generates a US$110 trade deficit for Country B; thus, the former will take trade protection measures against the latter. However, in fact the biggest victims of trade protection are those departments and manufacturers in Country C that serve Country A with intermediate goods in accordance with a value added calculation. As a result, countries following a "beggar thy neighbor" trade policy will beggar themselves at last.

Corresponding to the context, we will use the value-added trade framework to conduct empirical analysis of China's exports, and specifically discuss the following questions: The domestic value added of gross exports and its changes; the differences between China and other countries on TiVA and the reasons; compared with the traditional measure, the changes in bilateral trade balance in a value added calculation. Our study has three innovative points as below: first, unlike the former studies on China's international trade based on a traditional measure, we use the latest data of world TiVA published by the OECD/WTO to conduct research, which can be more accurate to present China's position in the global trade system. Second, combined with the expansion of representative papers, we will put forward an analytical framework that is able to capture the stylized facts of China's TiVA. Third, within the perspective of inter-factory and intra-factory effects, we will explore the reasons for changes of domestic value added of exports and make comparisons between China and other countries on this category relying on the decomposition method.

This chapter will include the following sectors: In Section 2, based on the expansion of representative papers we will put forward an analytical framework of China's TiVA; then we will introduce the data applied in the paper in Section 3; we will hold an empirical analysis for China's export based on value added method in the following three sections.

2. THEORETICAL CONSIDERATIONS

With the degree of vertical integration deepening, the world goes into an era of TiVA. In the division of labor system, there are few products made and exported from a single country. On the contrary, before a kind of product enters the market, many countries are involved in the creation of value. The evolution of international division of labor indicates two important changes: on the one hand, the world is moving from "made in China" to "made in the world." Though China is still playing the role of the "workshop of the world," it only shows that many "terminal" steps of manufacturing are done in China. On the other hand, the world is now stepping from

"Trade in Goods" times to "Trade in Tasks" times. Under this pattern of trade, the exchanges between countries are "tasks" rather than products, where tasks are "exchanges" among different links of the industry chain (IDE-JETRO and WTO, 2011). However, as the TiVA rises, the traditional statistical methods are still popular, which makes it difficult to understand the facts of international trade. Facing this dilemma, the WTO launched a project called "World Trade in Value-added Index" on March 15, 2012. As a result of the research, the WTO and OECD published a report of TiVA on January 16, 2013.

In order to understand the TiVA, we put forward an analytical framework here, combined with the combing and expanding to the representative papers. In existing studies, there are two papers related to TiVA. One is about factor content of trade. For example, based on input–output tables of multi-regions, Trefler and Zhu (2010) tracked the transnational flows of intermediate goods and used this information to calculate the factor content of intermediate and final goods, but they did not calculate the added value of exports. The other one is about domestic content of trade. Hummels et al. (2001) calculated the domestic content of exports in OECD countries. But the hypothesis that imports are completely consumed as the final goods was too strict. The actual situation may be as follows: Country A first exports intermediate goods to Country B, Country B processes them into finished products, and then sells them back to Country A or exports to other countries. In the recent research of Johnson and Noguera (2012), they relaxed the hypothesis of Hummels et al. (2001) and put forward an analytical framework to calculate the TiVA. The framework generally includes two steps: Step 1, using the international input–output tables to calculate the transnational output transfer; Step 2, combining transnational output transfer and input–output coefficient to compute domestic value added of exports. Next, we will expand this framework and build the theoretical foundation to discuss China's TiVA. Our contribution is to put the actual "scenarios" of China's participation in international vertical division into the framework, and to give a method of calculating the domestic value added share of gross exports, the bilateral trade volume, and the trade balance in the value added.

Johnson and Noguera (2012) assumed that the output was used for two purposes: One was final demand (c), the other one was the intermediate input of other products. Accordingly, the Equation (3-1) is established:

$$y_i(s) = \sum_j c_{ij}(s) + \sum_j \sum_t m_{ij}(s, t), \qquad (3\text{-}1)$$

In the equation, i and j represent the producer and destination of the products, s and t stand for the industries, and m means the output of industry s, which became the intermediate goods of industry t. Assume that $\alpha(s, t)$ is the proportion of the intermediate goods from s used by t in the output of t, then we had:

$$\alpha_{ij}(s, t) = m_{ij}(s, t)/y_j(t). \qquad (3\text{-}2)$$

Put Equation (3-2) into Equation (3-1), we get:

$$y_i(s) = \sum_j c_{ij}(s) + \sum_j \sum_t \alpha_{ij}(s, t) \cdot y_j(t). \qquad (3\text{-}3)$$

If there are N countries and N industries (this is a key assumption, one industry for one country), then we have:

$$A \equiv \begin{pmatrix} \alpha_{11} & \alpha_{12} & \cdots & \alpha_{1N} \\ \alpha_{21} & \alpha_{22} & \cdots & \alpha_{2N} \\ \vdots & \vdots & & \vdots \\ \alpha_{N1} & \alpha_{N2} & \cdots & \alpha_{NN} \end{pmatrix}, \quad y \equiv \begin{pmatrix} y_1 \\ y_2 \\ \vdots \\ y_N \end{pmatrix}, \quad c_j \equiv \begin{pmatrix} c_{1j} \\ c_{2j} \\ \vdots \\ c_{Nj} \end{pmatrix}$$

Based on these matrixes, we can put Equation (3-3) as the following:

$$y = \sum_j c_j + Ay. \qquad (3\text{-}4)$$

Equations (3-1)–(3-4) are the cornerstone of this framework. In order to discuss the TiVA of China, we consider a situation close to the reality. Assume that the United States (state 1), China (state 2), and South Korea (state 3) comprise a world, the United States and South Korea export intermediates to China respectively, China exports final goods to the United States, and there is no direct trade between the United States and South Korea. (In the article by Johnson and Noguera (2012), this was called "three countries, each country an industry" model). Corresponding to this situation, based on Equation (3-4) we can get:

$$\begin{pmatrix} y_1 \\ y_2 \\ y_3 \end{pmatrix} = \begin{pmatrix} c_{11} \\ c_{21} + c_{22} \\ c_{33} \end{pmatrix} + \begin{pmatrix} \alpha_{11} & \alpha_{12} & 0 \\ 0 & \alpha_{22} & 0 \\ 0 & \alpha_{32} & \alpha_{33} \end{pmatrix} \begin{pmatrix} y_1 \\ y_2 \\ y_3 \end{pmatrix}. \tag{3-5}$$

According to this equation, we can get the output of the United States, China, and South Korea in turn:

$$y_1 = \underbrace{\frac{1}{1-\alpha_{11}} \cdot c_{11}}_{y_{11}} + \underbrace{\frac{1}{1-\alpha_{11}} \cdot \frac{\alpha_{12}}{1-\alpha_{22}} \cdot c_{21} + \frac{1}{1-\alpha_{11}} \cdot \frac{\alpha_{12}}{1-\alpha_{22}} \cdot c_{22}}_{y_{12}}, \tag{3-6}$$

$$y_2 = \underbrace{\frac{1}{1-\alpha_{22}} \cdot c_{21}}_{y_{21}} + \underbrace{\frac{1}{1-\alpha_{22}} \cdot c_{22}}_{y_{22}}, \tag{3-7}$$

$$y_3 = \underbrace{\frac{1}{1-\alpha_{33}} \cdot \frac{\alpha_{32}}{1-\alpha_{22}} \cdot c_{21}}_{y_{31}} + \underbrace{\frac{1}{1-\alpha_{33}} \cdot \frac{\alpha_{32}}{1-\alpha_{22}} \cdot c_{22}}_{y_{32}} + \underbrace{\frac{1}{1-\alpha_{33}} \cdot c_{33}}_{y_{33}}. \tag{3-8}$$

In Equation (3-6), y_{11} is the output that the United States must provide to meet its own demands, y_{12} is the output that the United States must provide to meet China's demands, which is the output the United States needs to transfer to China. In the output the United States transfers to China, the added value equals:

$$va_{12} = (1 - \alpha_{11} - \alpha_{21} - \alpha_{31})y_{12} = \frac{\alpha_{12}}{1-\alpha_{22}} \cdot c_{22}. \tag{3-9}$$

In Equation (3-7), y_{11} and y_{12} are the output that China must provide to meet the demands of the United States and itself. In the output China transfers to the United States, the added value equals:

$$va_{21} = (1 - \alpha_{12} - \alpha_{22} - \alpha_{32})y_{21}$$
$$= c_{21} - \frac{\alpha_{12}}{1-\alpha_{22}} \cdot c_{21} - \frac{\alpha_{32}}{1-\alpha_{22}} \cdot c_{21}. \tag{3-10}$$

In Equation (3-8), y_{31}, y_{32}, and y_{33} are the output South Korea must provide to meet the demands of the United States, China, and itself. In the output

South Korea transfers to the United States, the added value equals:

$$va_{31} = (1 - \alpha_{13} - \alpha_{23} - \alpha_{33})y_{31} = \frac{\alpha_{32}}{1 - \alpha_{22}} \cdot c_{21}. \qquad (3\text{-}11)$$

In the output South Korea transfers to China, the added value equals:

$$va_{32} = (1 - \alpha_{13} - \alpha_{23} - \alpha_{33})y_{32} = \frac{\alpha_{32}}{1 - \alpha_{22}} \cdot c_{22}. \qquad (3\text{-}12)$$

For the convenience of the following discussion, we also need to calculate the trade volume in the traditional method. Look at the exports from the United States to China:

$$ex_{12} = c_{12} + \alpha_{12}y_2 = \frac{\alpha_{12}}{1 - \alpha_{22}} \cdot c_{21} + \frac{\alpha_{12}}{1 - \alpha_{22}} \cdot c_{22}. \qquad (3\text{-}13)$$

The exports from China to the United States:

$$ex_{21} = c_{21} + \alpha_{21}y_1 = c_{21}. \qquad (3\text{-}14)$$

The exports from South Korea to the United States:

$$ex_{31} = c_{31} + \alpha_{31}y_1 = 0. \qquad (3\text{-}15)$$

The exports from South Korea to China:

$$ex_{32} = c_{32} + \alpha_{32}y_2 = \frac{\alpha_{32}}{1 - \alpha_{22}} \cdot c_{21} + \frac{\alpha_{32}}{1 - \alpha_{22}} \cdot c_{22}. \qquad (3\text{-}16)$$

Based on Equations (3-9)–(3-16), we can discuss three questions. First, the value added export ratio. Second, the differences between value-added and traditional methods in the calculation of bilateral trade balance. Third, the differences between the two methods in the calculation of bilateral trade volume.

From Equations (3-10) and (3-14), we can get the value added export ratio of China to the United States:

$$DVA_{21} = va_{21}/ex_{21} = 1 - \frac{\alpha_{12} + \alpha_{32}}{1 - \alpha_{22}}. \qquad (3\text{-}17)$$

Obviously, as the exports from China to the United States include the products from the United States and South Korea (α_{12} and α_{32}), the value added export ratio of China to the United States is less than 1.

According to Equations (3-9) and (3-10), we can get the trade balance of China to the United States calculated in value added:

$$va\_tb_{21} = va_{21} - va_{12}$$
$$= \left(c_{21} - \frac{\alpha_{12}}{1 - \alpha_{22}} \cdot c_{21} - \frac{\alpha_{32}}{1 - \alpha_{22}} \cdot c_{21} \right) - \frac{\alpha_{12}}{1 - \alpha_{22}} \cdot c_{22}. \quad (3\text{-}18)$$

And according to Equations (3-13) and (3-14), we can get the trade balance of China to the United States calculated in the traditional method:

$$tb_{21} = ex_{21} - ex_{12} = c_{21} - \left(\frac{\alpha_{12}}{1 - \alpha_{22}} \cdot c_{21} + \frac{\alpha_{12}}{1 - \alpha_{22}} \cdot c_{22} \right). \quad (3\text{-}19)$$

Comparing Equations (3-18) and (3-19), we can find that the trade balance of China to the United States reduces by $\frac{\alpha_{32}}{1-\alpha_{22}} \cdot c_{21}$ when calculating in value added. Calculated in the traditional method, the exports from China to the United States also include the indirect product output from South Korea to the United States.

From Equation (3-11), we can get the trade balance of South Korea to the United States calculated in value added:

$$va\_tb_{31} = va_{31} - va_{13} = \frac{\alpha_{32}}{1 - \alpha_{22}} \cdot c_{21}. \quad (3\text{-}20)$$

As we can see, although there is no direct trade between South Korea and the United States, according to value-added, South Korea has trade surplus to the United States indicated by Equation (3-20).

According to Equation (3-12), we can get the trade deficits between China and South Korea calculated in value added:

$$va\_tb_{23} = va_{23} - va_{32} = -\frac{\alpha_{32}}{1 - \alpha_{22}} c_{22}. \quad (3\text{-}21)$$

And according to Equation (3-16), we can get the trade deficits between China and South Korea calculated in the traditional method:

$$tb_{23} = ex_{23} - ex_{32} = -\frac{\alpha_{32}}{1 - \alpha_{22}} \cdot c_{21} - \frac{\alpha_{32}}{1 - \alpha_{22}} \cdot c_{22}. \quad (3\text{-}22)$$

Comparing Equations (3-21) and (3-22), we can find that the trade deficits reduce by $\frac{\alpha_{32}}{1-\alpha_{22}} \cdot c_{21}$ when calculating in value added, because the exports from South Korea to China in the traditional method also include the indirect product output from South Korea to the United States.

Then, we look at the total trade volume comprised by the United States, China, and South Korea, in the traditional method:

$$t_{123} = \underbrace{\underbrace{\frac{\alpha_{12}}{1-\alpha_{22}}c_{21} + \frac{\alpha_{12}}{1-\alpha_{22}}c_{22}}_{\text{exports from US to China}} + \underbrace{c_{21}}_{\text{exports from China to US}}}_{\text{trade volume between China and US}}$$

$$+ \underbrace{\underbrace{0}_{\text{exports from South Korea to US}} + \underbrace{0}_{\text{exports from US to South Korea}}}_{\text{trade volume between South Korea and US}}$$

$$+ \underbrace{\underbrace{\frac{\alpha_{32}}{1-\alpha_{22}}c_{21} + \frac{\alpha_{32}}{1-\alpha_{22}}c_{22}}_{\text{exports from South Korea to China}} + \underbrace{0}_{\text{exports from China to South Korea}}}_{\text{trade volume between South Korea and China}}. \quad (3\text{-}23)$$

In value-added:

$$va_{123} = \underbrace{\underbrace{\frac{\alpha_{12}}{1-\alpha_{22}}c_{22}}_{\text{exports from US to China}} + \underbrace{c_{21} - \frac{\alpha_{12}}{1-\alpha_{22}}c_{21} - \frac{\alpha_{32}}{1-\alpha_{22}}c_{21}}_{\text{exports from China to US}}}_{\text{trade volume between China and US}}$$

$$+ \underbrace{\underbrace{\frac{\alpha_{32}}{1-\alpha_{22}}c_{21}}_{\text{exports from South Korea to US}} + \underbrace{0}_{\text{exports from US to South Korea}}}_{\text{trade volume between South Korea and US}}$$

$$+ \underbrace{\underbrace{\frac{\alpha_{32}}{1-\alpha_{22}}c_{22}}_{\text{exports from South Korea to China}} + \underbrace{0}_{\text{exports from China to South Korea}}}_{\text{trade volume between South Korea and China}}. \quad (3\text{-}24)$$

Comparing Equations (3-23) and (3-24), we can find that the trade volume calculated in the traditional method is $\frac{2\alpha_{12}+\alpha_{32}}{1-\alpha_{22}} \cdot c_{21}$ higher than that of the value added. The reason is that in the traditional method, intermediates trade has been double counted. Hanson (2012) pointed out that in the era of vertical integration, due to the double counting of intermediate goods the traditional method overestimated the real size of global trade.

Through the analysis above, for the special "scene" discussed here (namely, the United States and South Korea export intermediate goods to China, and China processes them into final goods and exports to the United States), we draw three conclusions (Table 3-1). First, in the value added method, the exports from the United States to China, from China to the United States, and from South Korea to China decline at the same time, while there are actual exports from South Korea to the United States. Second, under the added value, the trade surpluses between China and the United States decline, the trade deficits between China and South Korea reduce, but there are trade surpluses between South Korea and the United States. Third, in value added, the trilateral trade volume of the United States, China, and South Korea declines.

3. DATA

On the empirical research of TiVA, the global trade analytical project in Purdue University provides a set of available data (GTAP7.1). It is a blend of the macro data and the international balance data of the World Bank and the International Monetary Fund and the commodity trade data and the input–output data based on different nations of the United Nations, including 94 countries, 19 regions, and 57 departments (18 agricultural and resource departments, 24 manufacturing departments, and 15 service departments). Johnson and Noguera (2012) made a significant empirical analysis on the TiVA from an international view with this set of data, but in terms of our focus, this study has two weaknesses. First, they only have data for 2004, but the expansion of China's exports happened after 2004. It is necessary to use new data to analyze. Second, they study the TiVA from the perspective of international trade, but do not analyze China exclusively. The changes of China's domestic value added of exports and the differences in this index between China and other representative countries are scarcely mentioned, either. Therefore, we will use the global TiVA data released by

84 Economic Transition in China

Table 3-1: Comparison of TiVA and trade in the traditional method.

Trade		Traditional method	Value added
Trade between China and the US	Exports from China to the US	c_{21}	$c_{21} - \dfrac{\alpha_{12}}{1-\alpha_{22}} \cdot c_{21} - \dfrac{\alpha_{32}}{1-\alpha_{22}} \cdot c_{21}$
	Exports from the US to China	$\dfrac{\alpha_{12}}{1-\alpha_{22}} \cdot c_{21} + \dfrac{\alpha_{12}}{1-\alpha_{22}} \cdot c_{22}$	$\dfrac{\alpha_{12}}{1-\alpha_{22}} \cdot c_{22}$
	The bilateral trade balance	$c_{21} - \left(\dfrac{\alpha_{12}}{1-\alpha_{22}} \cdot c_{21} + \dfrac{\alpha_{12}}{1-\alpha_{22}} \cdot c_{22} \right)$	$\left(c_{21} - \dfrac{\alpha_{12}}{1-\alpha_{22}} \cdot c_{21} - \dfrac{\alpha_{32}}{1-\alpha_{22}} \cdot c_{21} \right) - \dfrac{\alpha_{12}}{1-\alpha_{22}} \cdot c_{22}$
Trade between China and South Korea	Exports from China to South Korea	0	0
	Exports from South Korea to China	$\dfrac{\alpha_{32}}{1-\alpha_{22}} \cdot c_{21} + \dfrac{\alpha_{32}}{1-\alpha_{22}} \cdot c_{22}$	$\dfrac{\alpha_{32}}{1-\alpha_{22}} \cdot c_{22}$
	The bilateral trade balance	$-\dfrac{\alpha_{32}}{1-\alpha_{22}} \cdot c_{21} - \dfrac{\alpha_{32}}{1-\alpha_{22}} \cdot c_{22}$	$\dfrac{\alpha_{32}}{1-\alpha_{22}} \cdot c_{22} - \dfrac{\alpha_{32}}{1-\alpha_{22}} \cdot c_{21}$
Trade between South Korea and the US	Exports from South Korea to the US	0	0
	Exports from the US to South Korea	0	$\dfrac{\alpha_{32}}{1-\alpha_{22}} \cdot c_{21}$
Total trade of these three countries		$\dfrac{\alpha_{12}}{1-\alpha_{22}} c_{21} + \dfrac{\alpha_{12}}{1-\alpha_{22}} c_{22} + c_{21}$ $+ \dfrac{\alpha_{32}}{1-\alpha_{22}} c_{21} + \dfrac{\alpha_{32}}{1-\alpha_{22}} c_{22}$	$\dfrac{\alpha_{12}}{1-\alpha_{22}} c_{22} + c_{21} - \dfrac{\alpha_{12}}{1-\alpha_{22}} c_{21}$ $+ \dfrac{\alpha_{32}}{1-\alpha_{22}} c_{22}$

Note: Summary according to Equations (3-9)–(3-24).

the OECD/WTO on January 16, 2013, to conduct an empirical analysis that makes up for the inadequacy of these two aspects.

The data of TiVA released by the OECD/WTO is based on the international input–output tables and bilateral trade data provided by OECD. Among these, the input–output table covers 34 OECD countries, as well as 15 non-OECD countries and regions, including Argentina, Brazil, China Mainland, Taiwan, Cyprus, India, Indonesia, Latvia, Lithuania, Malta, Romania, Russia, South Africa, Thailand, and Vietnam. Bilateral trade data covers all OECD countries and 31 other countries and regions, including Albania, Argentina, Bosnia, Brazil, Brunei, Bulgaria, Cambodia, China Mainland, Taiwan, Croatia, Cyprus, Hong Kong, India, Indonesia, Latvia, Lithuania, Macedonia, Malaysia, Malta, Moldova, Montenegro, the Philippines, Romania, Russia, Saudi Arabia, Serbia, Montenegro, Singapore, South Africa, Thailand, and Vietnam. Based on the information on TiVA database, we can trace the global production networks and supply chains. In the data released this time, 34 OECD countries and 6 non-OECD countries, Brazil, Russia, India, Indonesia, China, and South Africa, are covered, and the aggregated data of 27 members of the European Union (EU) and other countries in the world is contained, including agriculture, mining, nine manufacturing departments and seven service departments, in 2005, 2008, and 2009.

Next, combining TiVA data we will make an empirical analysis of China's exports from the perspective of value added and specifically discuss three questions. First, the domestic value added of China's exports and its changes. Second, the differences of the domestic value added between China and other representative countries and the reasons. Third, the differences between the value-added measure trade balance and the traditional measure trade balance. Before the empirical analysis, we will first give an illustration for the composition of value added. Under normal circumstances, value added includes three parts. The first part is the direct domestic value added that is provided by an industry for its own exports. The second part is the indirect domestic value added, the value added of the domestic upstream industry contained in the exports of an industry. The third part is re-imported domestic value added, which means that the exports are processed into intermediate goods and then the intermediate goods are imported back as the intermediate inputs of other exports.

86 *Economic Transition in China*

4. THE DOMESTIC VALUE ADDED OF CHINA'S EXPORTS

In this section, we will inspect the domestic value added of China's exports from the overall and industry level, and dig into the changes of the domestic value added of exports from the aspects of the export structure and the intra-industrial value added of exports.

4.1 The Change of the Domestic Value Added of China's Exports

According to the information provided by TiVA, in 2009, China's GDP reached US$5.07 trillion and the exports were US$1.39 trillion, sharing 27.48% of GDP. According to the same data source (see Table 3-2), in 2009, domestic value added was US$995.7 billion with a proportion of 71.47% in gross exports. To be specific, the direct domestic value added was US$298.6 billion, accounting for 21.43% of China's exports; the indirect domestic value added reached US$669.5 billion and the ratio was 21.43%; the re-imported domestic value added was US$27.6 billion and the ratio was 1.98%. In 2008, China's GDP reached US$4.55 trillion and the exports were US$1.58 trillion, which occupied 34.76% of GDP. According to the same data source, in 2008, domestic value added was US$1.08 trillion with 68.05% of gross exports. Specifically, the direct domestic value added was US$334.8 billion, accounting for 21.18% of China's exports; the indirect domestic value added was US$709.5 billion and the ratio was 44.87%; the re-imported domestic value added reached US$31.7 billion and the ratio was 2%. In 2005, China's GDP reached US$2.29 trillion and the exports were US$836.5 billion, sharing 36.49% of GDP. According to the same data source, in 2005, domestic value added was US$534.5 billion in China's exports with a proportion of 63.9% in gross exports. Specifically, the direct domestic value added was US$173.9 billion, sharing 20.79% of China's exports; the indirect domestic value added reached US$350.6 billion and the ratio was 41.91%; the re-imported domestic value added was US$10 billion with 1.2% of exports.

The data of the three years revealed that the scale of exports reduced by 30–40% calculated under the value added measure, which corresponded to the theoretical analysis. What interested us most was that the domestic value

Table 3-2: Domestic value added at the sectorial level (%).

Year	2009		2008		2005	
Industry	Export ratio	Domestic value added	Export ratio	Domestic value added	Export ratio	Domestic value added
All industries	**100.00**	**71.47**	**100.00**	**68.05**	**100.00**	**63.90**
Agriculture	**0.90**	**84.92**	**0.98**	**82.49**	**1.03**	**81.58**
Mining	**0.65**	**68.77**	**0.87**	**70.77**	**0.80**	**67.63**
Manufacture	**88.74**	**62.40**	**88.97**	**59.64**	**89.35**	**56.10**
Food industry	2.24	81.46	2.38	79.49	2.23	77.40
Textiles and clothing industry	15.72	85.17	15.35	83.04	15.02	80.94
Wood and paper industry	2.54	71.07	2.29	67.14	2.29	63.69
Chemical industry	9.12	63.61	10.27	61.59	10.47	58.39
Metal product industry	7.91	70.30	9.02	67.22	9.28	63.37
Machinery	7.69	70.32	8.76	67.64	8.86	64.31
Electrical equipment industry	33.51	62.49	30.16	57.37	30.51	51.14
Transport equipment industry	3.59	70.54	4.02	67.93	4.00	64.49
Other manufacturing industries	6.41	80.16	6.71	76.15	6.67	73.03
Service industry	**9.72**	**60.63**	**9.18**	**57.80**	**8.82**	**54.42**
Public utility	0.08	65.51	0.08	63.25	0.07	64.37
Construction industry	0.24	58.40	0.27	52.09	0.26	48.28
Wholesale and retail industry	4.14	91.58	3.79	89.58	3.46	87.50
Transportation industry	1.79	75.45	1.83	72.66	2.01	70.94
Financial industry	0.11	91.17	0.06	89.02	0.06	87.22
Commercial service	2.75	70.89	2.64	61.86	2.52	56.28
Other services	0.60	78.58	0.52	74.74	0.45	72.12

Data Source: OECD/WTO TiVA database and calculated by the author.

added of China's gross exports climbed from 63.9% in 2005 to 71.47% in 2009. However, further demonstration was needed to judge whether this change was a trend or temporary. Relying on Equation (3-17), we inferred that the increase of domestic value added of gross exports was likely to be related to the decrease of the use of importing intermediate goods. To examine this, with the information of the UN commodity trade database (UNCOMTRADE) and World Development Indicators Database (WDI), we found that the intermediate imports share of GDP has decreased from 23.57% in 2005 to 16.94% in 2009, which seemed to be evidence for the argument of "trend change." However, since China joined the WTO in 2001, the intermediate goods' imports share of GDP once soared from 14.98% to 23.57% in 2005, which implied that, in terms of intermediate goods imports, year 2005 was a turning point. Interestingly, in China, the rapid expansion of trade surplus began in 2005, and how Cui and Syed (2007) explained this was due to the improvement of the production capacity of intermediate goods itself, China reduced dependence on imports of intermediate goods. Luo and Zhang (2012) also pointed out that on account of the advancement of intermediate goods production, China reduced the amount of intermediate goods imports from ASEAN, but increased the intermediate goods exports to the latter. These researches tended to illustrate that the rise of China's value added export ratio has a basis, but without data for a longer time span, it would be difficult to make an accurate forecast for the future trend. Especially during the period from 2005 to 2009, the biggest drop of intermediate goods' imports ratio happened in years 2008 and 2009, during which China was facing the shock of the global financial crisis. Due to the shrinking of the external market demand, China's exports, especially processing trade, were severely hindered. Based on the logic of "import for export," imports (especially intermediate goods ones) were naturally negatively affected. Therefore, it was difficult to conclude that the decrease in the share of intermediate goods imported during this period and the increase in the value added export ratio was a trend. In fact, with the rebound of China's economy in 2010, intermediate goods' imports share of GDP gained momentum again, and whether it would lead to the reduction of the value added export ratio or not, was still unclear due to data unavailability.

4.2 The Differences of Domestic Value Added of Gross Exports Across Industries

According to the data provided by TiVA, we also paid attention to the differences of domestic value added of gross exports across industries (see Table 3-2). In 2009, ranking the industries depending on the ratios from high to low, the top eight industries included wholesale and retail, finance and insurance, textiles and clothing, agriculture, food, other manufacturing, and other services and transportation, and the construction industry came last. The industries from second to fifth from the bottom were electronic equipment, chemical industry, public utility, and mining. In manufacturing industry, the order from high to low was textiles and clothing, food, other manufacturing, wood and paper, transport equipment, machinery, metal product, chemical industry, and electrical equipment. Among service industries, the order was wholesale and retail, financial and insurance, other services, commercial services, public utility, and construction industry. The ranks in 2008 and 2005 were the same as that in 2009.

As can be seen from the table, agriculture, mining, manufacturing, and service industry had obvious distinctions in domestic value added of gross exports. Among them, the domestic value added of exports in manufacture and service was respectively the weighted average of the figures of industries they covered. In 2009, ranking the value added export ratio from high to low, the order was agriculture, mining, manufacturing, and service industry, and the ranks in 2008 and 2005 were alike. The differences of domestic value added of exports across industries may be related to the different ways of participating in international trade across industries (Johnson and Noguera, 2012). For example, in China, the direct export of financial products was a minor part, but the input from financial departments were contained in many other exported products, thus the value added ratio of financial exports would be high calculated under the value added method.

4.3 The Driving Force of the Change in Domestic Value Added

The changes in domestic value added of gross exports have two causes. In the first place, domestic value added of gross exports varies by industries,

90 Economic Transition in China

and the changes in export industry structure will result in the changes in the value added export, which is called the inter-industry effect. Second, the change of value added of intra-industrial exports, even if the export industry structure remains stable, will also lead to changes in the total domestic value added of gross exports, and we call this the intra-industry effect. Based on this idea, we decompose the changes in domestic value added of gross exports as follows:

$$VA_t - VA_t(exsh_{ybase}) = \sum_j VA_{jt} \cdot (exsh_{jt} - exsh_{j,ybase}), \quad (3\text{-}25)$$

$$VA_t(exsh_{ybase}) - VA_{ybase} = \sum_j (VA_{jt} - VA_{j,ybase}) \cdot exsh_{j,ybase}.$$

$$(3\text{-}26)$$

In Equations (3-25) and (3-26), j means the 18 industries in the sample; t is the year, 2008 or 2009; $ybase$ stands for the base year, which may be 2005 or 2008; VA measures domestic value added of gross exports; $exsh$ represents the industry's proportion in the whole export. Equations (3-25) and (3-26) respectively indicate the inter-industry effect and the intra-industry effect, and the sum of these two effects was the total effect. Based on this method, we respectively calculated the two effects in 2008 compared to 2005, 2009 compared to 2005, 2009 compared to 2008, and the results can be seen in Table 3-3.

Table 3-3 inferred that compared with 2005, in 2008, value added export ratio increased by 4.15%. The intra-industry effect and the inter-industry effect accounted for 3.98% and 0.18%, respectively. This result had two implications: the first one was the changes of both export industry structure and domestic value added of intra-industry gross exports were factors pushing domestic value added of gross exports to rise; the other one was that the intra-industry effect occupied the absolute dominant position, which meant the increase of domestic value added of intra-industry gross exports was the most crucial factor causing the increase of the total value added of exports. We could also see from Table 3-3 that in 2008, compared with year 2005, within the three components of value added, the indirect domestic value added increased by 2.96%, which was much higher than the increase of direct domestic value added and re-imported domestic value added. This

Table 3-3: The change in value added ratio of China's exports and its decomposition (%).

The change and its decomposition	Change in 2005–2008	Change in 2005–2009	Change in 2008–2009
Total changes	4.15	7.57	3.42
Intra-industry effect	3.98	7.50	3.51
Inter-industry effect	0.18	0.08	−0.09
Direct domestic value added	0.39	0.64	0.25
Intra-industry effect	0.27	0.65	0.39
Inter-industry effect	0.12	−0.01	−0.13
Indirect domestic value added	2.96	6.14	3.18
Intra-industry effect	2.88	6.17	3.27
Inter-industry effect	0.08	−0.02	−0.08
Re-imported domestic value added	0.8	0.78	−0.02
Intra-industry effect	0.82	0.68	−0.14
Inter-industry effect	−0.02	0.11	0.12

Data Source: OECD/WTO TiVA database and author's calculation by Equations (3-25) and (3-26).

indicated that the improvement of domestic value added of gross exports could be mostly attributed to the increase of the value added that export products gained from domestic upstream industries. Similar to the decomposition above, we also made a corresponding analysis of the changes in the three components of value added. Generally speaking, in this period, the rise of intra-industrial indirect value added (at 2.88%) made the greatest contribution to the whole increase, that was to say, the increase of intra-industry value added obtained from domestic upstream industry was the most critical factor in the increase of domestic value added of exports in 2008.

We followed the analysis above to decompose the changes of domestic value added of exports for 2005 to 2009 and 2008 to 2009, and the result was similar. In general, since 2005, the major driving force for the rise of the total domestic value added of gross exports was from the domestic intra-industry value added exports, especially the indirect intra-industry one. From the time dimension, the changes of the export structure were increasingly not conducive to the improvement of local value added exports, because the proportion of local high value added agriculture, mining, and manufacturing in the total exports declined while that of low value added local services exports rose.

5. THE DIFFERENCE IN DOMESTIC VALUE ADDED OF EXPORTS BETWEEN CHINA AND OTHER COUNTRIES

In this section, we will concentrate on the gaps on domestic value added of exports between China and typical countries, and then discuss the relevant reasons in terms of both export structure and intra-industrial value added of exports.

5.1 Cross-Country Difference in Domestic Value Added of Exports

The international differences on domestic value added of exports can be seen in Table 3-4. China's global ranking has improved from a lower level to a moderate one (showed by not only mean but also median) during the period from 2005 to 2009. Additionally, other information could be obtained as below: first of all, resource-intensive countries, such as Russia, Brazil, and Australia, maintained a high domestic value added share of gross exports at 85% or above. Then the value added export ratios of three typical developed countries as well as major exports, which were the United States, Japan, and the UK, were also in the forefront at over 80%. Third, as the second largest exporter, Germany was significantly different from other developed countries with approximately 75%, which was in the middle level and a narrow gap from China. Fourth, among the BRIC countries, China had the lowest value added export ratio, and its gap with India was the least one. Fifth, Mexico and South Korea were two representative countries. The figures of Mexico and China were closest in developing countries. In terms of South Korea, as an export-oriented country and East Asian economy, its value added ratio was even lower than China's. Sixth, the lowest ratios were from the small economies in the EU.

It can be seen from Table 3-4 that there was no tight link between domestic value added of exports and economic development level. Johnson and Noguera (2012) explained that domestic value added of exports generated two opposite effects to the economic development. For one thing,

Table 3-4: Cross-country comparison of domestic value added of gross exports (%).

2009	Domestic value added	2008	Domestic value added	2005	Domestic value added
Russia	92.8	Russia	90.98	Russia	90.42
Other countries	92.18	Other countries	90.24	US	88.28
Brazil	91.41	Brazil	89.1	Brazil	87.98
US	88.61	Australia	86.86	Australia	87.67
Australia	87.56	Norway	85.79	Japan	86.58
Norway	85.65	US	85.24	Norway	86.48
Indonesia	85.42	Indonesia	81.63	Other countries	86.42
Japan	85.07	UK	81.59	UK	83.49
South Africa	83.07	Japan	80.59	South Africa	82.47
UK	83.03	Chile	78.84	Chile	82.24
Italy	82.08	Italy	78.47	Indonesia	81.85
Chile	81.44	Canada	78.26	Turkey	79.89
Spain	81.12	Spain	77.23	India	79.83
New Zealand	80.78	New Zealand	76.99	New Zealand	79.22
Canada	79.11	South Africa	76.66	Italy	75.83
Turkey	78.93	India	75.09	Greece	75.55
Greece	77.41	Greece	74.21	Germany	75.27
India	76.55	Turkey	73.78	France	74.75
Austria	75.62	Germany	73.51	Spain	74.04
Germany	74.62	France	72.14	Canada	73.76
France	74.27	Poland	69.73	Portugal	73.18
Poland	72.2	Mexico	68.08	Holland	70.12
China	71.47	China	68.05	Denmark	69.54
Denmark	69.5	Denmark	67.87	Sweden	69.06
Switzerland	69.46	Switzerland	67.08	Poland	68.8
Slovenia	69.44	Austria	66.95	Switzerland	68.58
Mexico	68.67	Sweden	66.03	Austria	68.11
Portugal	68.41	Slovenia	64.99	Mexico	67.88
Israel	67.99	Holland	64.76	Finland	67.47
Belgium	67.98	Finland	64.46	China	63.9
Sweden	67.75	Portugal	64.16	South Korea	63.53
Finland	67.68	Iceland	62.97	Slovenia	62.71
Iceland	66.33	Belgium	62.25	Israel	61.26
Holland	66.1	Israel	62.04	Chech	60.19
Estonia	64.53	Chech	61.29	Iceland	58.78
Chech	61.34	Ireland	60.97	Belgium	58.64
South Korea	60.4	Estonia	58.3	Ireland	53.77

(*Continued*)

Table 3-4: (Continued)

2009	Domestic value added	2008	Domestic value added	2005	Domestic value added
Ireland	59.65	South Korea	56.46	Slovakia	52.12
Hungary	59.25	Hungary	54.73	Hungary	51.42
Slovakia	55.15	Slovakia	51.29	Estonia	48.95
Luxembourg	39.44	Luxembourg	38.6	Luxembourg	40.35

Data Source: OECD/WTO TiVA database.

with the improvement of economic development, the export structure of a country would be biased to the manufacturing sector, but domestic value added share of manufacturing exports was lower than agriculture's and resource products' (Table 3-2 showed the same situation in China), which meant the development of the economy resulted in downward pressure on domestic value added of gross exports; for another thing, the main products of developed countries in the manufacturing industry were those with high value added ratio, while the developing counterparts focused on low value added ones.

5.2 The Difference in Domestic Value Added of Exports Between China and Other Countries

Just as what we do to decompose the changes of domestic value added of China's exports, we can also decompose the difference in domestic value added of exports between China and other countries. We choose the United States, Germany, Brazil, and South Korea as representative countries to compare with China.[1] As for the decomposition method, taking difference between the United States and China as an example, the following formula

---

[1] We cannot make a comparison between Russia, India and China due to lack of data. We also examined the differences in domestic value added of manufacturing exports from China to the United States, Germany, Brazil, and South Korea, the results were the same as the gross exports'. For reasons of space, we did not list them in this chapter. If you are interested, please contact the author.

was available:

$$VA_{cht} - VA_{ust} = \sum_{j} exsh_{usjt} \cdot (VA_{chjt} - VA_{usjt})$$
$$+ \sum_{j} VA_{usjt} \cdot (exsh_{usjt} - exsh_{chjt}). \quad (3\text{-}27)$$

In Equation (3-27): j means the same as in earlier equations; t stands for years 2005, 2008, and 2009, respectively; ch means China while us stands for the United States (if other countries, just replace us); VA and $exch$ have the same meaning as before. The first and second items in the right-hand side of Equation (3-27) represent intra-industrial effect and inter-industrial effect, respectively.

First, we will discuss the situations in China and the United States. We choose the United States because of its strong export competitiveness, high domestic value added, and tight trading relationship with China. The result shown in Table 3-5 indicates clearly that: first of all, the value added ratio of China has been lower than that of the United States with a gradual decreasing range since 2005. Then, according to the decomposition, it is proved that both gap from export structure (inter-industry effect) and gap from domestic value added within an industry (intra-industry effect) are responsible for the lower ratio in China. In addition, the intra-industry effect is in a dominant position (-14.17% in 2009), which is the main reason for the distinction between two countries, but the proportion of the inter-industry effect was increasing all the time. Finally, specifically, among the three components of value added in exports, we can also find that difference of direct value added (-27.63% in 2009) is the main cause of the different ratios. After further decomposition, it can be seen that gap from domestic value added within an industry (-17.73% in 2009) is the most important factor resulting in the distinct gross ratios.

Germany is another country that should be given attention. As the second largest exporter, it is just in the middle level of the global value added ratio that is far from developed countries like the United States, Japan, and the UK in spite of strong competitiveness in manufacturing. The gap between China and Germany, which gets smaller and smaller, is much less than that between China and the United States (see Table 3-6).

96 *Economic Transition in China*

Table 3-5: Difference in domestic value added between China and the United States (%): all sectors.[2]

Year	Difference of value added	Decomposition of the difference		Difference of value added composition			
2009	−17.14	Intra-industry effect	−14.71	Direct value added	−27.63	Intra-industry effect	−17.73
						Inter-industry effect	−9.90
				Indirect value added	9.03	Intra-industry effect	2.51
						Inter-industry effect	6.53
		Inter-industry effect	−2.43	Re-imported value added	1.45	Intra-industry effect	0.51
						Inter-industry effect	0.94
2008	−17.19	Intra-industry effect	−15.14	Direct value added	−23.45	Intra-industry effect	−14.81
						Inter-industry effect	−8.65
				Indirect value added	4.90	Intra-industry effect	−0.87
		Inter-industry effect	−2.05			Inter-industry effect	5.77

(*Continued*)

---

[2]We also examined the differences in domestic value added of manufacturing exports from China to the United States, Germany, Brazil, and South Korea: the results were the same as the gross exports'. For reasons of space, we did not list them in this chapter. If you are interested, please contact the author.

Table 3-5: (*Continued*)

Year	Difference of value added	Decomposition of the difference		Difference of value added composition			
				Re-imported value added	1.36	Intra-industry effect	0.54
						Inter-industry effect	0.82
2005	−24.38	Intra-industry effect	−21.79	Direct value added	−26.57	Intra-industry effect	−18.27
						Inter-industry effect	−8.28
				Indirect value added	1.66	Intra-industry effect	−3.67
		Inter-industry effect	−2.60			Inter-industry effect	5.32
				Re-imported value added	0.53	Intra-industry effect	0.17
						Inter-industry effect	0.36

Data Source: OECD/WTO TiVA database and author's calculation by Equation (3-27).

Similarly, the key factor to the different ratios is value added of exports within an industry. However, in terms of China, unlike what happens with the United States, the driving force of the gap change with Germany gradually becomes export structure. In addition, as for the main reason after decomposition, the situation with Germany shares the same result as the United States.

Brazil and China belong to the BRIC countries, but Brazil has a higher value added ratio. Based on our study, the ratio gap narrows down since 2005 (see Table 3-7). Although it is mainly caused by value added within an industry, the Chinese figures not only export industrial structure but

Table 3-6: Difference in domestic value added between China and Germany (%): all sectors.

Year	Difference of value added	Decomposition of the difference		Difference of value added composition			
2009	−3.15	Intra-industry effect	−3.22	Direct value added	−13.51	Intra-industry effect	−9.13
						Inter-industry effect	−4.37
				Indirect value added	9.2	Intra-industry effect	5.59
		Inter-industry effect	0.08			Inter-industry effect	3.61
				Re-imported value added	1.15	Intra-industry effect	0.32
						Inter-industry effect	0.83
2008	−5.46	Intra-industry effect	−5.43	Direct value added	−13.22	Intra-industry effect	−9.59
						Inter-industry effect	−3.64
				Indirect value added	6.73	Intra-industry effect	3.85
		Inter-industry effect	−0.03			Inter-industry effect	2.87
				Re-imported value added	1.04	Intra-industry effect	0.31
						Inter-industry effect	0.74

(*Continued*)

Table 3-6: (Continued)

Year	Difference of value added	Decomposition of the difference		Difference of value added composition			
2005	−11.37	Intra-industry effect	−11.06	Direct value added	−17.07	Intra-industry effect	−13.73
						Inter-industry effect	−3.34
				Indirect value added	5.62	Intra-industry effect	2.92
		Inter-industry effect	−0.32			Inter-industry effect	2.69
				Re-imported value added	0.08	Intra-industry effect	−0.25
						Inter-industry effect	0.33

Data Source: The same as in Table 3-5.

also intra-industry domestic value added have improved compared with Brazil. After making comparison with the two situations above, we found the unique feature of the situation between China and Brazil was a relative high effect (−3.41% in 2009) from the different export structure, because there are considerable exports from agriculture and resource industries in Brazil, while the main reason for the gap ratio in three situations lies in direct value added (−20.02% in 2009), which is the same as the former two situations. In addition, if decomposing the direct value added, we find the intra-industry effect and the intra-industry effect are equivalent (−9.45% and −10.57% in 2009, respectively).

There are many similarities between South Korea and China, including the fact that both are East Asian economies, and important exporting countries characterized by high reliance on external markets as well as a high degree of economic integration. Our analysis can be seen in Table 3-8: since 2005, China's domestic value added share of gross exports has always been

Table 3-7: Difference in domestic value added between China and Brazil (%): all sectors.

Year	Difference of value added	Decomposition of the difference		Difference of value added composition			
2009	−19.94	Intra-industry effect	−16.53	Direct value added	−20.02	Intra-industry effect	−9.45
						Inter-industry effect	−10.57
				Indirect value added	−1.86	Intra-industry effect	−7.68
		Inter-industry effect	−3.41			Inter-industry effect	5.83
				Re-imported value added	1.94	Intra-industry effect	0.60
						Inter-industry effect	1.34
2008	−21.05	Intra-industry effect	−17.32	Direct value added	−20.3	Intra-industry effect	−10.51
						Inter-industry effect	−9.80
				Indirect value added	−2.68	Intra-industry effect	−7.49
		Inter-industry effect	−3.73			Inter-industry effect	4.81
				Re-imported value added	1.94	Intra-industry effect	0.68
						Inter-industry effect	1.25

(*Continued*)

Table 3-7: (*Continued*)

Year	Difference of value added	Decomposition of the difference		Difference of value added composition			
2005	−24.08	Intra-industry effect	−19.58	Direct value added	−16.36	Intra-industry effect	−8.94
						Inter-industry effect	−7.42
				Indirect value added	−8.84	Intra-industry effect	−11.17
		Inter-industry effect	−4.50			Inter-industry effect	2.33
				Re-imported value added	1.12	Intra-industry effect	0.53
						Inter-industry effect	0.59

Data Source: The same as in Table 3-5.

higher than South Korea's, which may amplify in the future. According to our decomposition, the main factor is from the intra-industry gap (9.09% in 2009). After further decomposition, we can draw the conclusion that the most important explanation to the phenomenon is indirect gap in value added (15.22% in 2009), which contains the intra-industrial one (11.19% in 2009), the greatest effects.

To sum up, there are two points concluded: on the one hand, as for the total domestic value added share of gross exports, there is still a long way to go for China to keep up with other leaders because of the gap in an identical industry; on the other hand, the ratio gap between China and other countries seems a downtrend as the ratio gap in the same industry gradually decreased. However, as we mentioned in Section 4, it is difficult to draw the conclusion that China's value added of gross exports during the period from 2005 to 2009 presents an upward trend without further demonstration.

Table 3-8: Difference in domestic value added between China and South Korea (%): all sectors.

Year	Difference of value added	Decomposition of the difference		Difference of value added composition			
2009	11.07	Intra-industry effect	9.09	Direct value added	−5.32	Intra-industry effect	−3.16
						Inter-industry effect	−2.16
				Indirect value added	15.22	Intra-industry effect	11.19
		Inter-industry effect	1.98			Inter-industry effect	4.03
				Re-imported value added	1.16	Intra-industry effect	1.07
						Inter-industry effect	0.10
2008	11.59	Intra-industry effect	9.57	Direct value added	−5.32	Intra-industry effect	−3.04
						Inter-industry effect	−2.29
				Indirect value added	15.74	Intra-industry effect	11.55
		Inter-industry effect	2.02			Inter-industry effect	4.19
				Re-imported value added	1.17	Intra-industry effect	1.06
						Inter-industry effect	0.12

(*Continued*)

Table 3-8: (Continued)

Year	Difference of value added	Decomposition of the difference				Difference of value added composition		
2005	0.37	Intra-industry effect	−1.72	Direct value added	−9.05	Intra-industry effect	−7.41
						Inter-industry effect	1.64
				Indirect value added	9.11	Intra-industry effect	5.36
		Inter-industry effect	2.07			Inter-industry effect	3.74
				Re-imported value added	0.31	Intra-industry effect	0.33
						Inter-industry effect	−0.03

Data Source: The same as in Table 3-5.

6. CHINA'S TRADE BALANCE IN VALUE ADDED

In this section, we will discuss the trade balance in value added and its gap with the traditional method. Different methods lead to a similar trade balance in a country but different bilateral trade balance.

6.1 China's Trade Balance in Value Added

According to TiVA data, if counted by value added, China's international trade in 2009 is shown below: the trade surplus with the United States was US$131.3 billion, accounting for 48% of total surplus; the figure to EU27 was US$30.2 billion with 11% of all. Among the five largest EU countries, trade with the UK, France, Spain, and Italy all presented a surplus while that with Germany was the opposite situation, a US$15.7 billion deficit, which was the largest in all trading partners. In addition, similar to Germany, China kept trade deficits with Japan as well as South Korea with which China had a deficit of US$10.4 billion, just lower than Germany's. The countries China kept trade surpluses with also included Mexico, India, Turkey, Russia, and South Africa while those that had a surplus with China were Indonesia and Brazil.

During the period from 2005 to 2009, depending on the value added measure, we found in developed countries China shifted from surpluses to deficits with Japan but retained trade deficits with South Korea as well as Germany, which seemed an upward trend, while in developing countries, China kept trade deficits with Brazil with the increasing trend. But the trade with Russia altered from deficits to surpluses, so did India, which may rise in the future.

6.2 Difference of Trade Balance in Two Methods

In theory, we have proved from data that there were huge differences calculated under these two measures (see Table 3-9). In 2009, the trade surpluses to the United States fell by US$45.1 billion, occupying 25% of traditional trade surpluses. And surpluses with the EU decreased by US$11.9 billion, which was just 28% of traditional calculation, and situations for the UK were US$5.1 billion and 25%, respectively. As for other typical partners, deficits with Germany dropped by US$10.4 billion, 40% of the alternative measure. Statistics with Japan were US$12.4 billion and 86% and those with South Korea were US$46.5 billion and 81%. In the developing partners, deficits' decrease with Brazil was US$3.9 billion, accounting for 45% of the other method. The trade surpluses with India rose dramatically but trade with Russia changed from deficits to surpluses. However, trade with Indonesia was opposite to Russia's and surpluses with South Africa also reduced.

In 2008, the trade surpluses to the United States, the EU, and the UK dropped by 27%, 22%, and 23%, respectively. In other developed countries, the trade position with Japan, which was deficits originally, reversed. Trade deficits with Germany and South Korea presented an observable reduction by 65% and 99%, respectively. In developing countries, trade deficits with Brazil decreased by 56% but trade surpluses with Russia increased. The situation with India, which was a minor deficit, became surplus. However, trade surpluses with Indonesia and South Africa both fell.

Table 3-9: China's trade balance with trading partners (million US$).

2009	Difference of two methods	2008	Difference of two methods	2005	Difference of two methods
US	−45,114.4	US	−61,180.3	US	−46,991.7
Mexico	−14,813.8	EU27	−19,006.2	EU27	−25,310.5
EU27	−11,904.7	Mexico	−12,424.4	Mexico	−6,614.6
UK	−5,090.9	UK	−6,243.2	UK	−5,639.7
France	−2,622.6	Turkey	−2,994.9	France	−3,942.4
Spain	−2,046.8	Spain	−2,877.7	Spain	−3,750.8
Turkey	−1,987.1	France	−2,539.4	Italy	−2,544.2
Other Countries	−1,135.1	Italy	−2,407.5	Indonesia	−2,279.8
Italy	−1,021.7	South Africa	−2,292.4	Turkey	−1,555.9
Indonesia	−863.4	Indonesia	−961.8	Japan	−1,480.6
South Africa	−448.5	Russia	2,565.8	South Africa	−630.6
India	3,720.6	Brazil	3,338.3	Germany	333.6
Russia	3,744	India	4,767.4	Brazil	656.3
Brazil	3,992.9	Austria	6,029.4	Austria	1,937.7
Austria	6,208.9	Germany	11,856.6	India	2,041.8
Germany	10,374.6	Other Countries	19,274.9	Russia	7,689.7
Japan	12,439.6	Japan	21,220.4	South Korea	37,302.3
South Korea	46,452.6	South Korea	47,396.8	Other Countries	42,142.9

Notes: 1. *Data Source*: OECD/WTO TiVA database; 2. Difference of two methods = trade balance in value added − trade balance in traditional method.

In 2005, the trade surpluses to the United States, EU27, and the UK dropped by 31%, 50%, and 35%, respectively. In other developed partners, trade deficits with Germany and trade surpluses with Japan and South Korea all fell by 5.2%, 28%, and 74%, respectively. In developing countries, figures of trade deficits with Brazil, Russia, and India fell by 24%, 40%, and 50%, separately. However, trade surpluses with Indonesia and South Africa decreased.

According to the results of different years, after using value added measure, trade surpluses with the United States and EU27 dropped by a quarter or even a half, so did trade deficits with Germany and South Korea. Combining the analysis in the Section 2, we can see that the reason for the decline of surpluses with the United States and EU27 under the value added measure was that there were other intermediate inputs from other countries (especially East Asia like South Korea and Japan) when Chinese products were exported. Similarly, it is rational to understand the fact that deficits reduced with Germany and South Korea as intermediate goods imported there were exported to other countries as final products. As far as China goes, we should pay attention to the effect of East Asian integration on trade value added. Take 2009 as an example: although trade surpluses with the United States dropped under the value added measure, Japan and South Korea increased trade surpluses with the United States by US$13.4 billion and US$7.86 billion, respectively. As we said in the section on theoretical framework, Japan and South Korea exported intermediate goods to China, and then China exported them to the United States and EU27 after processing. Relying on the division system, Japan and South Korea finished exporting to the United States and EU27 indirectly through China.

7. CONCLUSIONS AND POLICY IMPLICATIONS

In the context of accelerating development of vertical integration, the global value chain has turned up a "fragmentation" trend. There are few products produced by a single country; on the contrary, number of countries as suppliers of value added participate in the creation of value. However, trade statistics did not keep up with the evolution of international division of labor, which led to information distortion. In particular, China, as a country posted in the "terminal link" of the value chain, is overestimated in the global trading system under the traditional measure. In order to be more accurate in reflecting the current situation of international division of labor as well as the position of a country in the international trading system, the value added measure may be more desirable. This chapter based on this perspective tries to have a new view on China's export development.

As for the theoretical interpretation of TiVA, Johnson and Noguera (2012) put forward an indicative analytical framework. Its core idea is that the essence that Country B imported a product (it may be for final demand or intermediate input) from Country A reflects the output transfer from Country A to Country B. In order to calculate the figure, we have to deduct the intermediate inputs from other countries including Country A. Taking China's reality into account, we developed the framework and focused on domestic value added and bilateral trade balance against the background of vertical integration in East Asia. Then, combining the database of "global

TiVA" lately released by the OECD/WTO, we conducted an empirical study on China's exports and drew three main conclusions:

To begin with, since 2005, China's total domestic value added share of gross exports has increased from 64% to 71% in 2009. We decomposed the change of value added ratio from an industrial perspective, and the result showed the rise of value added within an industry (called intra-industry effect) was the main reason for the total change during this period. In contrast, the changes in export structure have become the obstacle to the increase of value added ratio. With the development of the economy, agriculture and resource-intensive industries, characterized by high value added, are gradually replaced by low value-added industries. Consequently, the total domestic value added of gross exports was under downward pressure.

In addition, the ranking of China's value added ratio has climbed from the global lower–middle to the middle level since 2005. The representative developed countries, such as the United States, Japan, and the UK, and representative resource-intensive countries, like Brazil, Russia, Indonesia, and South Africa, maintained high value added ratios worldwide. Germany was a special case as its ratio was just a bit higher than China's. The ratio of South Korea was always lower than that of China. After decomposition of the gaps of domestic value added of exports between China and representative countries, we found the key factor leading to the gap came from the gap within an industry. The further study on value-added components demonstrated that the most significant factor that was responsible for the gap between China and the United States lay in direct intra-industrial gap of value added, while the critical explanation for the case of China and South Korea was indirect intra-industrial gap of value added.

And finally, if calculated under the value added measure, we found China's trade surpluses with the United States and EU27 dropped dramatically while its trade deficits with Germany and South Korea decreased to a different degree. In 2009, the trade surpluses with the United States fell while both South Korea and Japan increased their trade surpluses to the United States at the same time, which reflected the fact that vertical integration developed in East Asia. South Korea and Japan, exporting intermediate goods to China, succeeded in occupying the United States market indirectly through the process of China's exports to the United States with final goods.

Three points are necessary to mention in terms of the conclusion. First, the sample we used showed that China's domestic value added is gradually increasing, but it is still too early to infer it as a tendency change. Since 2005 the trend of the proportion of China's intermediate goods' imports on GDP has shifted from increase to decrease, and the largest decline happened in 2008 and 2009. On the one hand, according to relevant data and studies China's capacity to provide intermediate goods itself has improved. The reliance on intermediate goods' imports gradually reduced, so the increase in the value added ratio is sustainable. On the other hand, as China has suffered the most severe shock from the global financial crisis in 2008 and 2009, exports of processing exports have confronted huge side-effects, which impeded imports of intermediate goods directly. As a result, the increase in domestic value added of exports is temporary. Due to data unavailability, it is difficult to draw a conclusion in the two explanations.

Second, if the rise in value added is not temporary, according to our study, in order to improve the domestic value added of exports we should enhance the intra-industrial domestic value added instead of promoting change in the export structure artificially. The fact that the rise in intra-industrial domestic value added is the most important driving force to the rise of total value added ratio can be seen from both the change of China's domestic value added of exports and the gaps between China and other countries in the domestic value added.

Finally, as far as the domestic value added ratio is concerned, although the United States and Germany are located in different positions, China can learn from both. What China can acquire from the United States includes two main points: one is to improve the direct value added inside the industry. China should improve its industrial level in R&D and design, encourage corporations to develop from the bottom of the "smile curve" to both ends to enhance the ability to create value added; the other is to promote the integration of the domestic market. Forming a hierarchical division of labor in China can create internal circumstances for enhanced domestic value added. Germany's case tells us that first, we should strengthen expertise in manufacturing so that we can shape strong competitiveness in processing area; second, we should promote market integration with neighboring countries and take advantage of the natural vertical division of labor.

REFERENCES

Autor, D., David Dorn and Gordon Hanson (2011). *The China Syndrome: Local Labor Market Effects of Import Competition in the United States.* Working Paper.

Bloom, N., Mirko Draca and John Van Reenen (2011). *Trade Induced Technical Change? The Impact of Chinese Imports on Innovation, IT and Productivity.* NBER Working Paper No. 16717.

Bown, Chad (2011). Taking stock of antidumping, safeguards and countervailing duties, 1990–2009. *The World Economy*, 34(12): 1955–1998.

Eichengreen, B. and Tong, H. (2006). Fear of China. *Journal of Asian Economics*, 17(2): 226–240.

Fu, Xiaolan, Kaplinsky, R. and Zhang, Jing (2009). *The Impact of China's Exports on Global Manufacturing Prices.* SLPTMD Working Paper Series, No. 032.

Gaulier, G., Francoise Lemoine and Deniz Ünal-Kesenci. (2007). China's emergence and the reorganization of trade flows in Asia. *China Economic Review*, 18(3): 209–243.

Hanson, G. (2012). The rise of middle kingdoms: Emerging economies in global trade. *Journal of Economic Perspectives*, 26(2): 41–64.

Hummels, D., Jun Ishii and Kei-Mu Yi (2001). The nature and growth of vertical specialization in world trade. *Journal of International Economics*, 54(1): 75–96.

Iacovone, L., Wolfgang Keller and Ferdinand Rauch (2010). *Import Competition and Domestic Response: New Evidence from Mexico*, Working Paper.

IDE-JETRO and WTO (2011). Trade Patterns and Global Value Chains in East Asia: From Trade in Goods to Trade in Tasks, Working Paper, IDE-JETRO and WTO.

Jenkins, R. and Edwards, C. (2006). The economic impacts of China and India on Sub-Saharan Africa: Trends and prospects. *Journal of Asian Economics*, 17(2): 207–225.

Johnson, R. and Noguera, G. (2012). Accounting for intermediates: Production sharing and trade in value added. *Journal of International Economics*, 86(2): 224–236.

Koopman, R., Wang, Zhi and Wei, Shang-jin (2008). *How much Chinese Exports Is Really Made in China — Assessing Foreign and Domestic Value-added in Gross Exports.* NBER Working Paper No. 14109.

Linden, Greg, Kraemer, Kenneth and Dedrick, Jason (2007). Who Captures Value in a Global Innovation System? The case of Apple's iPod. Unpublished Manuscript, Personal Computing Industry Center, UC Irvine.

Lu, M., Chen, Zhao, Wang, Yongqin, Zhang, Yan, Zhang, Yuan and Luo, Changyuan (2013). *China's Economic Development: Institutions, Growth and Imbalances.* UK: Edward Elgar Publishing Ltd.

Luo, C. and Zhang, J. (2012). Innovation spillover effect of export expansion in China (In Chinese). *Social Science in China*, 11: 57–80.

Rodrik, D. (2006). What's so special about China's exports? *China & World Economy*, 14(5): 1–19.

Schott, P. K. (2008). The relative sophistication of Chinese exports. *Economic Policy*, 23(53): 5–49.

Trefler, D. and Zhu, S. C. (2010). The structure of factor content predictions. *Journal of International Economics*, 82(2): 195–207.

Xu, B. (2007). Measuring China's Export Sophistication, Working Paper, China Europe International Business School.

Zhang, J., Tang, Dongbo and Zhan, Yubo (2012). Foreign value-added in China's manufactured exports: Implications for China's trade balance. *China & World Economy*, 20(1): 27–48.

Chapter 4

The Consumption Issue in the Long-term Growth and Short-term Fluctuations

Zhigang Yuan
School of Economics, Fudan University

Can Rao
School of Economics, Fudan University

1. INTRODUCTION

In recent years, the well-known scenario is that China has sustained rapid economic growth during the past 30 years. Cheap labor is used in the manufacturing sectors and produces huge trade surplus. Under the financial crisis, China has started as much as 4 trillion yuan of fiscal stimulus package and maintains a relatively low level of government debt. However, we hardly see consumption's contribution to economic development in the past 30 years of China's economic takeoff. From 2000 to 2011, China's ultimate consumption's share of GDP has dropped from 62.3% to 49.1%. The economic growth is investment-driven but not consumption-oriented. Meanwhile, China's society is increasingly focused on the quality of economic development, rather than the speed of economic growth. Only healthy consumption demand can bring structural upgrading of economic development and maintain the sustainable growth of China's economy. Furthermore, the oversaving problem, caused by insufficient consumption, breeds a large trade surplus and foreign assets, also resulting in international imbalance of payments. In this sense, China's consumption is not just a domestic economic issue.

In order to explore current consumption, it is necessary to understand the historical transitions of Chinese residents' consumption behavior. Putting the Oriental culture aside, Chinese residents' consumption decisions are no different from any other country in the world. The theories of individuals' consumption decisions are applicable to analyze Chinese residents' consumption behavior. But China has a transition process from a planned economy to a market economy, causing significant and profound changes in Chinese residents' consumption behavior. Generally speaking, in the early days of reform and opening up, China's economic reform started a gradual liberalization of markets. The consumption market boomed in the 1980s because of the innovation of the dual track system of prices. In 1988, China's government decided to push forward the reform of prices, which led to severe inflation and caused the failure of complete price liberalization, which finally completed in the 1990s.[1] Until then, China was in the phase of releasing consumption potential. The insufficient consumption problem started from the late 1990s. After the Asian financial crisis, China entered a deflationary period, and consumption insufficiency has aroused wide concern. For achieving a soft landing after the crisis, China's government continued deepening the reform and opening up. Benefiting from the state-owned enterprises, the housing market reforms, and joining the WTO, China's annual GDP growth rate remained at 7%. However, a series of institutional voids made the under-consumption problem increasingly serious. Meanwhile, China's over-investment problem is increasingly highlighted, worsening after the 2000s (Il Houng Lee *et al.*, 2012).[2] Facing the 2008 financial crisis, the Chinese government formulated a 4-trillion-yuan fiscal stimulus plan. This program has boosted the economy immediately, while also causing excessive investment in China and worsening the insufficient consumption problem. The report of the 18th National Congress of the Communist Party of China (CPC) also emphasized that the Chinese Communist Party aims "to expand domestic demand, release consumption potential, maintain rational growth of investment, and expand

---

[1] Ezra, Feivel Vogel (2013). *Deng Xiaoping and the Transformation of China*. Life, Reading, Joint Publishing.
[2] Il Houng Lee, Murtaza Syed and Liu Xueyan (2012). *Is China Over-Investment and Does It Matter?* IMF Working Paper No. wp12277.

the domestic market."³ It shows the important role of consumption in China's economic development and the government's concerns regarding insufficient consumption.

Consumer behavior changes with the evolution of China's economic system and the role of government. People always make optimal decisions in a given economic system. As a result, reshaping Chinese residents' consumption behavior and encouraging consumption require further reform of the current economic system. Therefore, the question now is how the economic system causes an under-consumption problem in contemporary China. We believe that, first of all, the dual structure of urban and rural areas causes the fragmentation of consumption patterns. Due to incomplete urbanization and the household registration system, urban and rural residents receive an absolutely different goods market, social security system, and income level, which are resulting in the gap of consumption level and structure between the rural and urban residents. Second, unequal income distribution contributes to the under-consumption problem. The gap between the rich and poor in China widened significantly in recent years. Due to the lack of a middle class and unequal income distribution, Chinese residents' consumption behavior cannot maintain sustainable economic growth and promote structural transformation. Finally, the changes in the population structure are also crucial to the insufficient consumption problem. In 2012, China experienced an absolute decline in the number of working-age population. China is showing a trend of aging society. Consumption smoothing incentives and the rise of the elderly's legacy will increase the savings. Before the actual arrival of the aging society, China's consumption level will continue declining.

This chapter is divided into four sections: Section 2 discusses consumption in China's long-term economic growth and short-term economic fluctuations; Section 3 describes the characteristics and changes of residents' consumption behavior in China; Section 4 analyzes the factors causing the under-consumption problem in contemporary China; Section 5 clarifies the

---

³Hu's Report at the 18th National Congress of the Communist Party of China (CPC) (2012). *March Firmly on the Path of Socialism with Chinese Characteristics and Strive to Complete the Construction of Well-off Society in all Respects* (Yuan, Zhigang (1996)).

crucial importance of factor market reforms and equal public goods supply in raising consumption in the future.

2. CONSUMPTION IN LONG-TERM ECONOMIC GROWTH AND SHORT-TERM ECONOMIC FLUCTUATIONS

Understanding the role of consumption in China's economy is necessary to further explore China's consumption problem, and propose appropriate advice. We will analyze consumption by dividing it into China's consumption in short-term fluctuations and long-term growth.

2.1 Consumption in Short-Term Economic Fluctuations

From the perspective of short-term economic fluctuation, a country's gross national product in the short term equals the sum of consumption, investment, government purchases, and net exports. It is well known that China's development was investment-driven during the past 30 years of reform and opening up, and exports of textiles and manufacturing products are contributing to China's large trade surplus. However, the phenomenon does not mean that consumption is unimportant and can be ignored in China's short-term economic fluctuations.

China has ranked third in its amount of final consumption expenditure in 2011, following the United States and Japan. In 2012, China's total retail sales of consumer goods reached 2.07 trillion yuan, which included 1.84 trillion yuan of retail sales and 0.23 trillion yuan of food and beverages. China's average annual growth rate of final consumption expenditure was 11.31% from 1978 to 2011, while the United States' average annual growth rate of final consumption expenditure was only 6.06% (Figure 4-1). Furthermore, China's average annual growth of final consumption expenditure and gross domestic product are approximately the same (Figure 4-2). China's average annual GDP growth rate was 12.15% from 1978 to 2011, which was close to the growth rate of final consumption. It can be said that in terms of both total amount and growth rate, China's consumption is becoming increasingly important and experienced a rapid development in recent years.

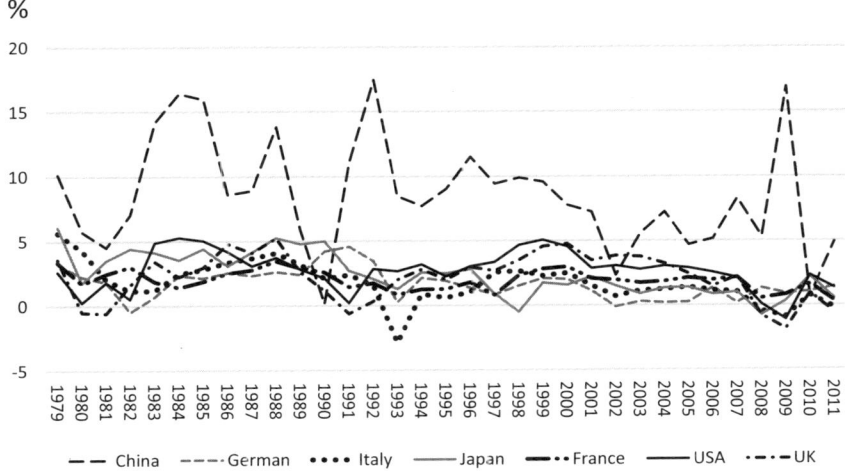

Figure 4-1: International comparison of consumption growth rate.
Source: World Bank WDI.

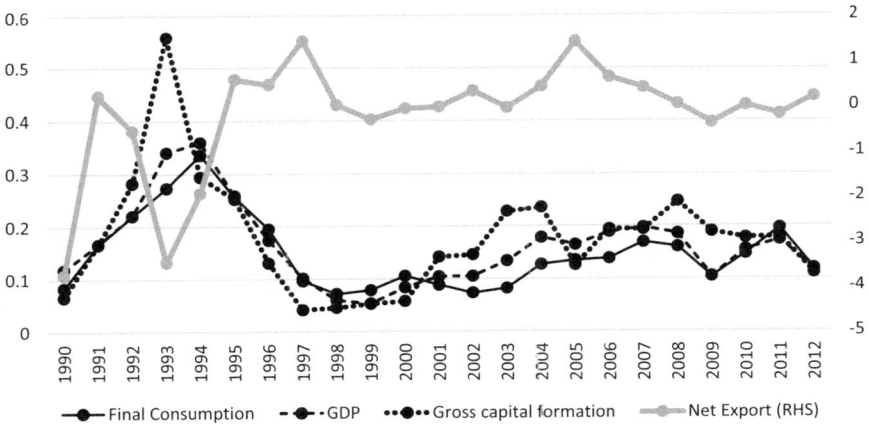

Figure 4-2: Growth rate of final consumption, gross capital formation and net export.
Source: NBS, CEIC databases.

Investment rather than consumption plays a more important role in China's short-term economic growth in recent years. The ultimate contribution of gross capital formation to GDP growth is almost always greater than the ultimate contribution of consumption to GDP growth from 2002 to 2010. Investment-driven economic growth is unsustainable, which is not only worsening the problem of investment inefficiency, but also accumulating huge local governments' debts. Meanwhile, China's insufficient consumption and overinvestment result in the investment of excessive savings in foreign countries, causing huge trade surpluses and the accumulation of corresponding foreign assets, (e.g., US government debts), which are transformed from trade surpluses. China's decline in exports also underlines the crucial role of consumption in boosting short-term economic growth after the financial crisis. China's net export's contribution to GDP growth remains lower than 5% since 2008. China's annual growth rate of net export is close to 0 after the financial crisis, and is still in the trend of long-term decline. In this sense, China can no longer maintain sustainable economic growth through export expansion.

2.2 Consumption in Long-Term Growth

The long-term economic growth is determined by the productive capacity of a country, which depends on three elements: labor, capital, and technology. Improvement of the consumption level in China will not only stimulate the economic growth in the short term, but also promote healthy development of labor, capital, and technology, and contribute to the long-term growth of China's economy. Most importantly, promotion of consumption can effectively optimize China's capital efficiency and structure. In neoclassical growth theory, increasing consumption means a decline in savings, which reduces the output per capita and slows down economic growth before reaching a steady state. However, consumption in China plays an obviously different role in economic growth. China's overinvestment problem is closely related to the phenomenon that China's economic growth and investment are not consumption-oriented. Because of insufficient consumption, Chinese investors cannot find profitable investment opportunities, and hold large amount of unused savings and invest inefficiently. Therefore, promoting consumption does not hinder economic growth, but plays a crucial role in guiding the orientation of investment and improving investment efficiency. From the perspective of micro-enterprises, only enhancing the consumption development can motivate the enthusiasm of enterprises' production, and the investment will be consumption-led and

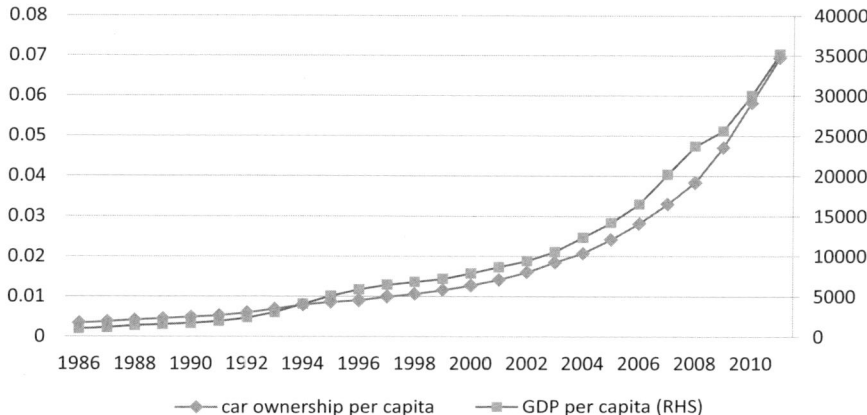

Figure 4-3: The numbers of car ownership and GDP per capita.
Source: Department of Transportation, NBS and CEIC databases.

avoid the overinvestment and overcapacity problem in contemporary China. Moreover, consumption promotion and consumption structure changes can speed up China's industrial upgrading process, and achieve the industrial goals that cannot be accomplished by the government's industrial policies. For example, China's government planned to develop automobile manufacturing into a pillar industry as early as 1986, but automobile consumption did not flourish in China until the 2000s, because automobile consumption requires a sufficiently high level of income (Figure 4-3). The automobile industry is not a special case. Government-led industrial policies always fail to accomplish their targets and waste resources. During the financial crisis, China's government proposed a revival plan for 10 industries, which was extremely ineffective and failed to promote the development of related industries. Therefore, change of consumption structure can induce adjustments of investment structure and industrial upgrading.

3. CHARACTERISTICS OF AND CHANGE IN CHINESE RESIDENTS' CONSUMPTION BEHAVIOR

To understand Chinese residents' consumption behavior, you must comprehend China's transition process of consumption pattern from a planned economy to a market economy first. We try to describe the change in consumer behavior from a planned to a market economy, and then analyze the characteristics of the current consumption pattern in China. Finally, we show the under-consumption problem in contemporary China.

3.1 Changes in Consumption Behavior During the Transition from a Planned Economy to a Market Economy[4]

The best starting point of studying consumer behavior changes from a planned economy to a market economy is the dynamics of Chinese residents' average propensity to consume (Figure 4-4). The stylized fact is, China had very high average propensity to consume in a planned economy and this value is increasingly lower with the development of the market economy. With the reform and opening up, Chinese urban residents' average propensity to consume has dropped from around 90% in the planned economy to 67.9% in 2012. In fact, as soon as we understand the mechanism behind the decline of Chinese residents' average propensity to consume, we will comprehend the transition of Chinese residents' consumption patterns from a planned economy to a market economy. China had given priority to the development of heavy industry since 1949. At that time, the whole country concentrated all the resources to develop heavy industries under a highly centralized planned economic system. Meanwhile, consumption and development of other industries were artificially suppressed. First, the state controlled sales and regulated the price of agricultural products through the planned system. Then, the relative low level of farmers' income and prices of raw materials was maintained in order to increase the profitability of industrial enterprises. Second, the state artificially suppressed manufacturing workers' wages, compared with the rise of labor productivity in the industrial sector. Wage growth was far below the growth rate of national income from 1953 to 1978. During this period, the annual growth rate of the worker's wage was only 1.4%, while the growth rate of national income was 6% (Yuan Zhigang, 2011).[5] Finally, China's government limited the production of consumer goods, and rationed consumer goods to residents

---

[4]A more detailed discussion on this issue is in Yuan Zhigang and Song Zhen (1999) and Yuan Zhigang (1996).
[5]Yuan Zhigang (2011). *A study of China's consumption frontier issues*. Fudan University Press.

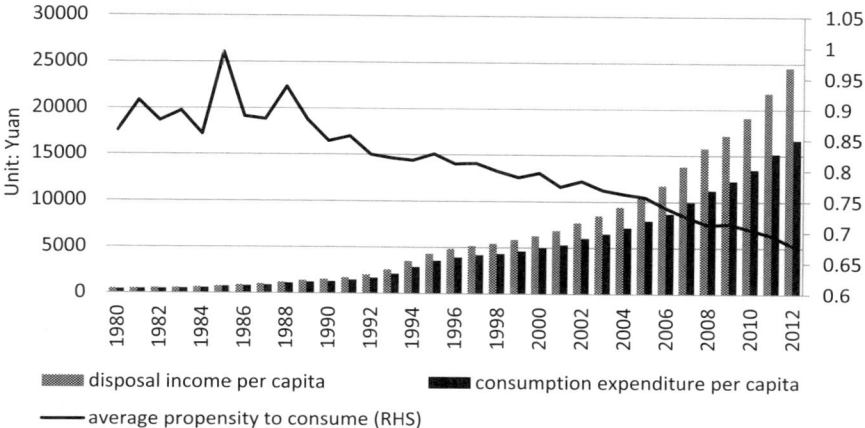

Figure 4-4: The change of average propensity to consume in urban area.
Source: NBS, CEIC databases.

under the planned economic system, which failed to promote residents' consumption. Overall, the planned economic system distributed resources to heavy industries, while keeping living standards as low as possible. Therefore, a high average propensity to consume is not surprising in China's planned economy due to the low level of income, which could only afford the necessities.

Based on the life cycle theory and the permanent income hypothesis, residents smooth consumption in each period to maximize their utility. In other words, the volatility of savings and consumption expenditure is less than income. However, fluctuations in income did not exist in the planned economy. Before the reform and opening up, Chinese residents' average annual wages had remained between 500 and 600 yuan, while the drop of income level caused by retirement was less than 3%. Therefore, Chinese residents had no need for consumption smoothing at that time, which also led to relatively higher average propensity to consume. Moreover, social security and medical expenditure were covered by the state and enterprises in the planned economy. It was not necessary to handle the risk and uncertainty by saving more. At the same time, the planned economic system had eliminated the possibility of systematic risk. Therefore, most of the residents' income was used for personal consumption without the requirement of precautionary savings.

Chinese residents' consumption decision can be explained by the classical consumption theory before 1978, and institutional factors had determined Chinese residents' relatively high average propensity to consume. Chinese residents could not accumulate savings in a planned economy. The main tool of "investment" in that period was raising children, because children could bring higher returns than savings in the future. Ye Wenzheng has shown that the cost of creating one unit of urban labor in 1979 was 2148.08 yuan, while the workers' annual average wage was 670 yuan. The present value of a worker's income was 5266.72 yuan (Ye Wenzheng 1998).[6] Therefore, investment through raising children became the optimal choice during the planned economy period, due to the extremely low interest rate. In 1949, China's population was 541.67 million and rose to 962.59 million by 1978, at an average annual growth rate of 2%.

China's government loosened the regulation of consumption since 1978. Then, Chinese residents' consumption pattern has changed dramatically, which is vividly demonstrated by the decline of average propensity to consume. With the progressive establishment of a market economic system, Chinese residents raise more and more savings, and continuously reduce consumption's share in personal income.

The share of workers' salary in total income is declining, while the pay-for-performance mechanism has increased the uncertainty level. Moreover, the pension is significantly less than the fully employed wage, while the extension of life expectancy highlights this gap. The gap strengthens the motivation for raising savings for consumption smoothing. Furthermore, due to the reform of the medical security system in China, there is a growing proportion of residents' healthcare expenditure to be borne by the individuals themselves. Meanwhile, a healthy social security system is not completed by market reforms, which leads to increasing uncertainties in the future. Therefore, the motivation of precautionary savings also increases after reform and opening up.

Furthermore, the increasingly high prices of housing and education are becoming Chinese residents' heavy burdens after market-oriented reform.

---

[6]Ye Wenzheng (1998). *The Theory of Children's Needs: The Cost and Utility of Chinese Children*. Fudan University Press.

The underdevelopment of the financial system causes liquidity constraints, which further raises the savings rate. According to a survey of residents in Shanghai, the share of residents who considered buying a house as the target of saving is as high as 55% (Yuan Zhigang 1999).[7] Meanwhile, in terms of demographic changes, the working-age population's share in total population is increasing constantly with the fall of average propensity to consume. The economically active population's share has risen from 2.26% in 1978 to 58.32% in 2011. Based on the life cycle theory, the rise of the labor force's share in the whole economy will increase savings. In this sense, the demographic transition process can also explain the drop in average propensity to consume.

3.2 Characteristics of Consumer Behavior in Contemporary China

Although the average propensity to consume of Chinese residents decreased in the transition from a planned economy to a market economy, Chinese residents' consumption level rose continuously and significantly.

The insufficient consumption problem does not appear until 1999, and the consumption level seems to be insufficient only when compared with the extremely high income growth in China. Residents' consumption in China has been in a continuous development process until 1999. In fact, sustainable development of consumption is embodied in both the growth of the total amount of consumption and the upgrading of the consumption structure. Now, we specify the main characteristics of the consumption pattern in contemporary China:

First, Chinese residents' total consumption rises continuously. Final consumption in 1978 was only 223.91 billion yuan, while final consumption has reached 22.856 trillion yuan in 2011, the average annual growth rate of which was 15.05%. The residents' final consumption was 175.91 billion yuan in 1978, and the residents' final consumption has risen to 16.495 trillion yuan in 2011, the average annual growth rate of which was 14.75% (Figure 4-5). Furthermore, the annual average growth rate of retail sales of consumer goods was 14.95% from 1993 to 2009. As two components of

---

[7]Yuan Zhigang and Song Zhen (1999). Urban Residents' Consumption Behavior Changes with China's Economic Growth. *Economic Research Journal*, 11: 20–28.

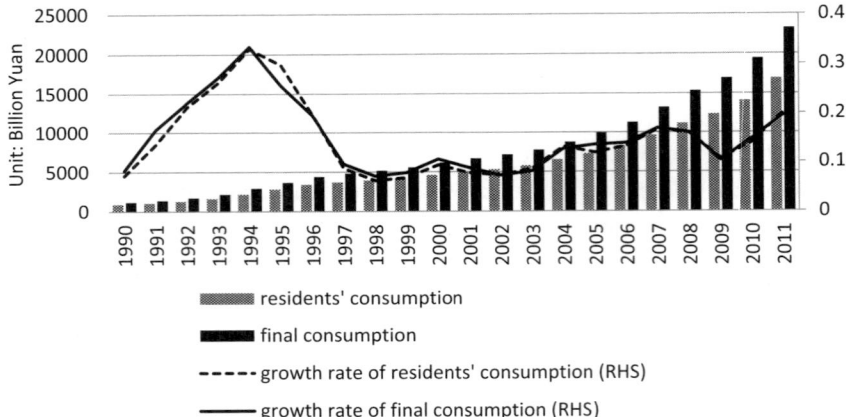

Figure 4-5: Final consumption and residents' consumption.
Source: NBS, CEIC databases.

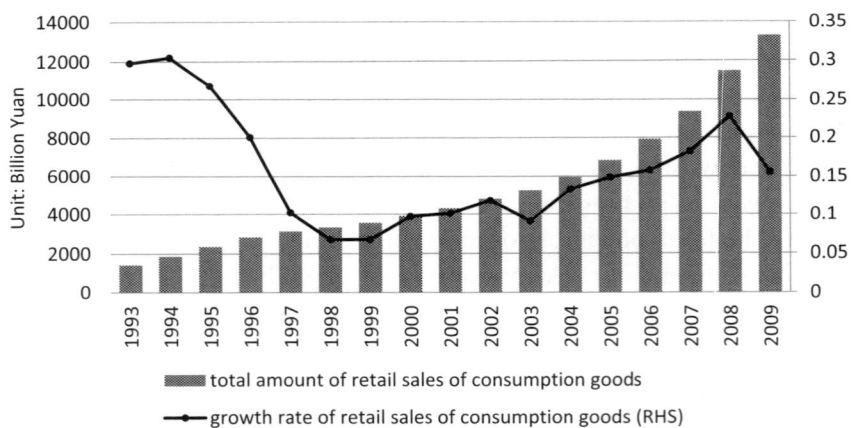

Figure 4-6-1: The amount and growth rate of retail sales of consumer goods.
Source: NBS, CEIC databases.

retail sales of consumer goods, the annual average growth rate of wholesale and retail was 15.24% and the annual average growth rate of accommodation and catering was 21.31% (Figures 4-6-1 and 4-6-2).

Second, Chinese residents' consumption structure has been upgraded and consumption diversification has been promoted. The Engel Index of urban residents has declined from 56.7% in 1981 to 35.8% in 2006, while

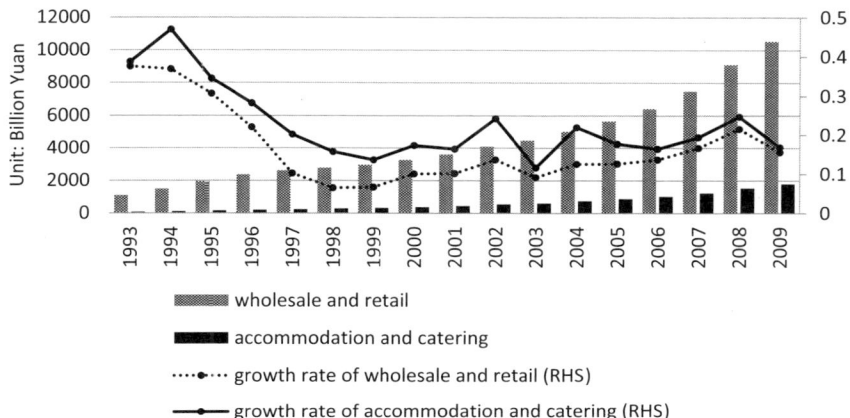

Figure 4-6-2: The monthly change of wholesale and retail & accommodation and catering.
Source: NBS, CEIC databases.

the Engel Index of rural residents has dropped from 67.7% in 1978 to 43.1% in 2007. In terms of the transition of urban residents' consumption structure, food, clothing and family equipment's shares have dropped from 53.3%, 15.3%, and 11.1% in 1985 to 36.3%, 11%, and 6.7% in 2011, and the share of medicine and health, traffic and communications tools, entertainment, and education and culture have increased from 0.7%, 1.3%, 10.3%, and 3.5% in 1985 to 6.4%, 14.2%, 12.2%, and 9.3% in 2011. In the meantime, rural residents have also reduced the proportion of expenditure on food and clothing, household equipment, and have raised the expenditure on medical products, means of transport and communication, entertainment, and education and cultural products (Figures 4-7-1 and 4-7-2). In terms of durable goods, the consumption of household electrical appliances is increasingly saturated. The number of refrigerators and color TVs per one hundred urban families were 42.33 and 59.04 units respectively in 1990, while the numbers have reached 97.23 and 135.15 in 2011. In terms of the automotive industry, the value of gross industrial output was 7.0472 billion yuan in 1981, which has risen to 3.32 trillion yuan in 2011. China's average growth rate of vehicle output was 15.45% during this period (Figure 4-8). China's automobile output has reached 19,271,808 units in 2012, but the car ownership per capita is only 0.0142. In this sense, China still has a

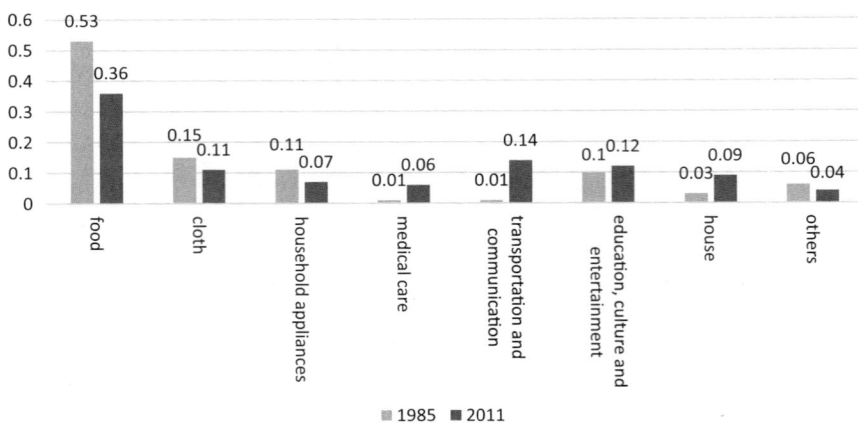

Figure 4-7-1: The change of consumption structure in urban area.
Source: NBS, CEIC databases.

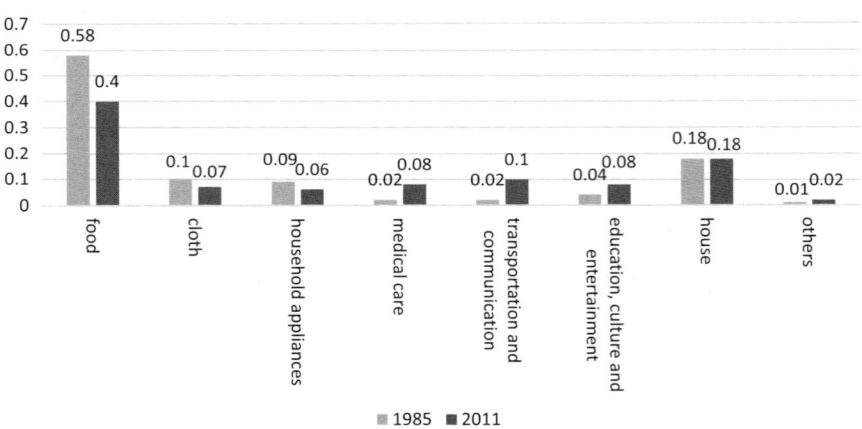

Figure 4-7-2: The change of consumption structure in rural area.
Source: NBS, CEIC databases.

great potential for the development of durable goods production, which is represented by the automobile industry.

Finally, Chinese consumers are increasingly concerned with quality, brand, and consumption environment. Along with the economic development and rise of income levels, consumers pay close attention to high-end

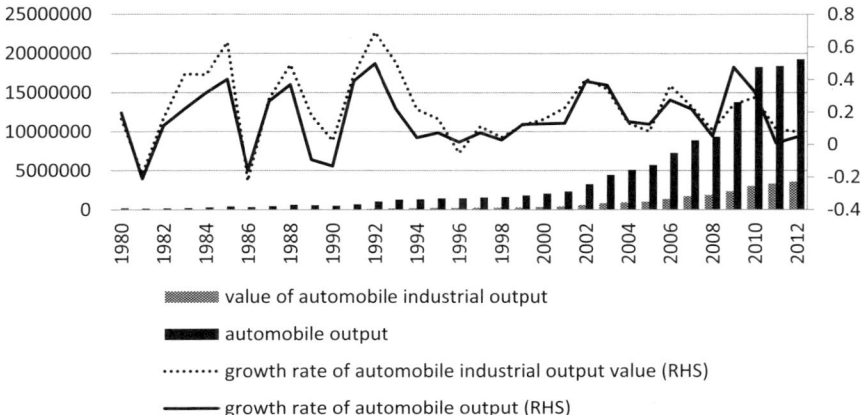

Figure 4-8: Annual change in the number and growth rate of car production.
Source: China Association of Automobile Manufacturers.
Note: The value of automobile industrial output is measured by million Yuan.

goods, which means that consumers are increasingly focusing on brand. In 2011, China's total advertising expenditure increased by 14.5% compared with 2010.[8] China's business environment is becoming increasingly consumer-oriented, which makes advertising crucial to profit. The total number of well-known trademarks in China has reached 1,359 in 2008, giving producers special legal protection in the specific industry. In some ways, all of the firms focus on brands. The phenomenon reflects the growing concern on quality of products. In fact, there are many quality problems of consumer goods in contemporary China's consumer markets, such as "substandard milk powder," "clenbuterol hydrochloride," "waste oils," and so on. The problems are serious threats to the quality of Chinese residents' consumption and living standards, which reflect both the government's poor regulation and the unhealthy consumption environment in China. However, China has been paying growing attention to the harmful impact of fake and shoddy goods on the market. Only mutual trust of market participators will enhance the development of the consumption market.

---

[8]CHRM (2012). *Report of China's Advertising and Media Markets in 2011*. Charm Communications.

Furthermore, a healthy consumption environment requires fair competition and consumers' awareness of market operation. China's consumption market is experiencing a painful improvement of the consumption environment.

Currently, residents' consumption in China has achieved the shift to a well-off society, and a well-off society means that the consumers have gradually changed the consumption pattern from dressing warmly and eating one's fill to valuing recreation and leisure, cultural activities, and so on. During the transition process, there are many problems in China's huge consumption market. But China's consumption market has been continuously developed. However, why do we underline the under-consumption problem in contemporary China? This is what we try to analyze in Section 3.3.

3.3 The Under-Consumption Problem in Contemporary China[9]

According to the preceding analysis, Chinese residents' average propensity to consume drops from a planned economy to a market economy. Meanwhile, Chinese residents' total amount of consumption increases and consumption structure is upgraded. The transition of consumption patterns in institutional changes is reflected in the decline of Chinese residents' average propensity to consume. However, when compared with other countries, China's under-consumption problem appears.

We start by cross-country comparison of consumption's share of GDP (Figure 4-9). From 1970 to 2010, the United States, Germany, France, and the UK's average consumption ratios were 72.78%, 68.83%, 70.48% and 74.45% respectively, while China's average consumption ratio was only 43.85% in the same period. Moreover, the United States' average consumption ratio maintains the increase trend in the past 40 years, rising from 70.29% in 1970 to 76.24% in 2010, while the average consumption ratios of Germany, France, and the UK have remained unchanged or increased. Only China's consumption ratio has declined from 47.69% in 1970 to 34.79% in 2010. In fact, the decline in average consumption ratio is

---

[9]A more detailed discussion on this issue is in Yuan Zhigang (2011).

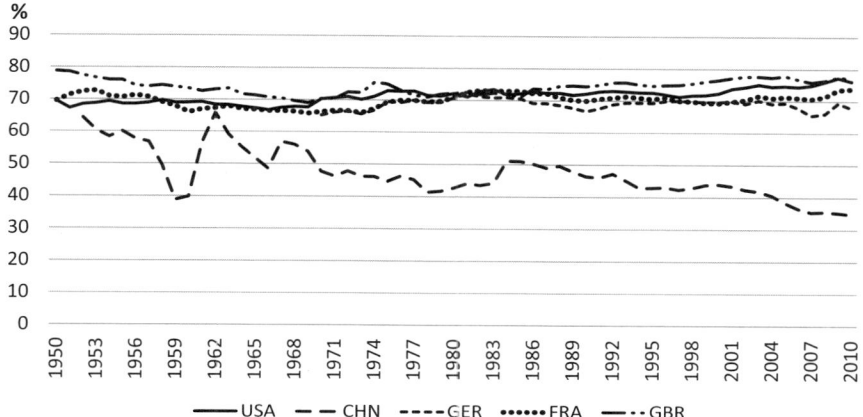

Figure 4-9: The comparison of China's consumption ratio with the developed countries.
Source: PWT 7.1.

not unique in China. The mean of all OECD countries' average consumption ratios has declined from 67.3% in 1950 to 60.6% in 2007. However, China's average consumption ratio is still far below the major developed countries in absolute terms.

Simple comparison between developed countries and China's consumption is unreasonable because it does not take the Oriental culture of savings and the takeoff stage of economic development into account. Because of these considerations, we compare China's average consumption ratio with major countries of East Asia (Figure 4-10). First, the average consumption ratio of East Asian countries is closer, obviously, compared with Western developed countries. The tradition of Confucian culture affects consumption patterns of the East Asian countries to some extent. Average consumption ratios of China and Singapore change in the same trend. Second, Japan and Korea during the rapid economic growth stage have shown a downward trend in average consumption ratio. The average consumption ratio of Japan declined from 70.19% in 1950 to 58.54% in 1970, and then gradually rose to the level of 60%. Korea's average consumption ratio also declined from 80.3% in 1953 to 51.24% in 1988. Therefore, Oriental culture and the necessary investment at the high-speed growth stage can partly explain the low average consumption ratio in China. However, putting Singapore, a city–state, aside, even the lowest consumption ratios

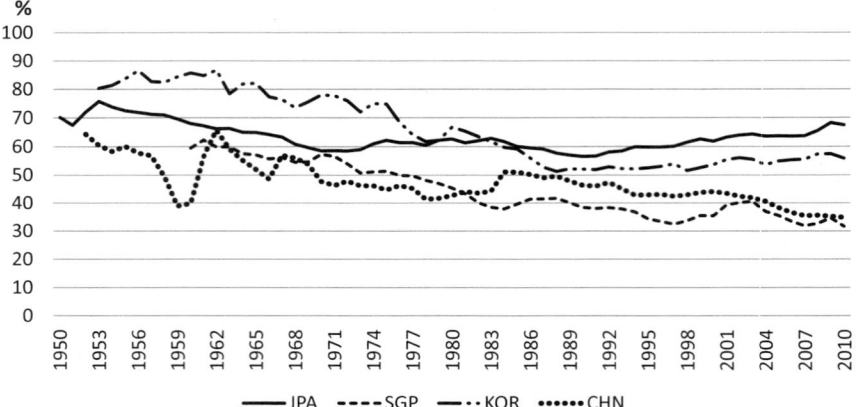

Figure 4-10: Comparison of China's consumption ratio with Asian countries.
Source: PWT 7.1.

in Japan and Korea are also higher than China's average consumption ratio. From 1960 to 2010, the average consumption ratio in China was 45.91%, and during the same period, the average consumption ratios of Japan and Korea were 61.88% and 63.46% respectively. During this period, the lowest average consumption ratio of Japan was 56.59%, while this value of Korea was 51.24%. After reform and opening up, China's highest average consumption ratio was 51.13% in 1984. Therefore, the extremely low average consumption ratio is hardly to be completely explained by culture and development stage.

In our previous study (Yuan Zhigang, 2011),[10] we have used 190 countries' data to estimate China's reasonable consumption ratio, and compare it with the actual data. We found China's average consumption ratio is too high before the reform and opening up, while in the first 20 years of reform and opening up, China's average consumption ratio was very close to the reasonable level. However, China has begun to deviate from the reasonable level of consumption ratio since 1998, and the underconsumption problem occurs. China's annual average consumption ratio in 1988 was 42.94%, which further reduced to 34.79% in 2010. This result

---

[10] Yuan Zhigang (2011). *A Study of China's Consumer Issues*. Fudan University Press.

is actually consistent with the comparison of consumption, investment, and output growth in Figure 4-2. The growth rate of final consumption since 1998 was significantly lower than the growth rate of output. In other words, the economic development is investment-led. Furthermore, we have decomposed the causes of the under-consumption problem into different factors. First, the residential income's share of GDP drops significantly. This factor's contribution to the decline of average consumption ratio was 78.9% from 2000 to 2007. Second, structural changes of urban and rural areas improve China's average consumption ratio. The factor's contribution to the decline of the average consumption ratio was −51.8%. Finally, the contribution of the decline of residents' average propensity to consume to the drop in the average consumption ratio was not high, only 18.1%. Therefore, although the change of Chinese residents' average propensity to consume is a reflection of changes in China's economic system, it is not the major cause of China's insufficient consumption. Insufficient consumption in China is closely related to residents' income and rural–urban structural change. At the same time, we should also take the absolute demographic changes in China into consideration. Changes in the demographic structure are becoming increasingly important in the China of the future. Therefore, as the main causes of insufficient consumption, urban and rural structure, income distribution, and demographic structure will be discussed in Section 4 in detail.

China's under-consumption problem is based on not only the comparison of consumption levels among different countries, but also the internal weakness of consumption related closely to investment-led economic growth since 1998. This problem can be explained clearly by income distribution and urban–rural and demographic structure, which will be discussed in Section 4.

4. THE CAUSES OF CHINA'S UNDER-CONSUMPTION PROBLEM

In Section 3.3, we pointed out that the main causes of China's under-consumption are the dual structure of urban–rural areas, unequal income distribution, and changes in demographic structures. In this section, we will elaborate on the factors.

4.1 The Impact of Dual Structure of Urban and Rural Areas on Consumption Behavior

China's society is characterized by dual structure of urban and rural areas. In the planned economy, rural wealth was transferred to cities through separation of urban and rural areas, supporting the development of heavy industries. Due to a rigid household registration system and lack of urbanization, China has not changed the reality of the urban–rural dual structure after the reform and opening up, which substantially hindered the development of Chinese residents' consumption.

Urban and rural residents' consumption level has been improved and consumption structure is constantly upgraded after the reform and opening up. The reform and opening up launched a comprehensive, market-oriented reform of state-owned enterprises in the city, and started family production responsibility contract system and township enterprises reform in rural areas since 1978. These reforms have increased the incomes of urban and rural residents, and promoted development of Chinese residents' consumption in terms of both total amount and structure. But dual structure of urban and rural areas has indeed caused enormous differences in urban and rural residents' consumption behavior and impeded the further development of consumption in China.

First of all, there are huge differences in the total amount of households' consumption expenditure in urban and rural areas. According to data from the National Bureau of Statistics, the total amount of Chinese residents' consumption was 16.49 trillion yuan in 2011. The amount of rural consumption was only 3.74 trillion yuan and 22.671% of the total amount, while the amount of urban consumption reached 12.76 trillion yuan and 77.329% of the total amount. In terms of growth of households' consumption expenditure, the average annual growth rate was 13.89% from 1998 to 2011. The average annual growth rate of urban households' consumption expenditure was 14.94%, while the value in rural areas was 10.55%. However, there was 48.73% of total population in the rural areas and 51.26% of total population in urban areas in 2011. In other words, 48.73% of total population in rural areas spent only 22.671% of total consumption expenditure in 2011. The growing gap between rural and urban consumption expenditures is highlighted since 1978 in Figure 4-11.

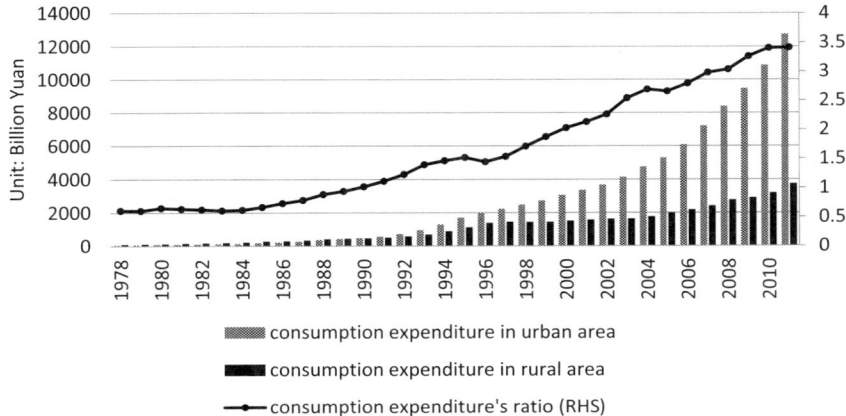

Figure 4-11: The gap of consumption expenditure between urban and rural areas.
Source: NBS, CEIC databases.

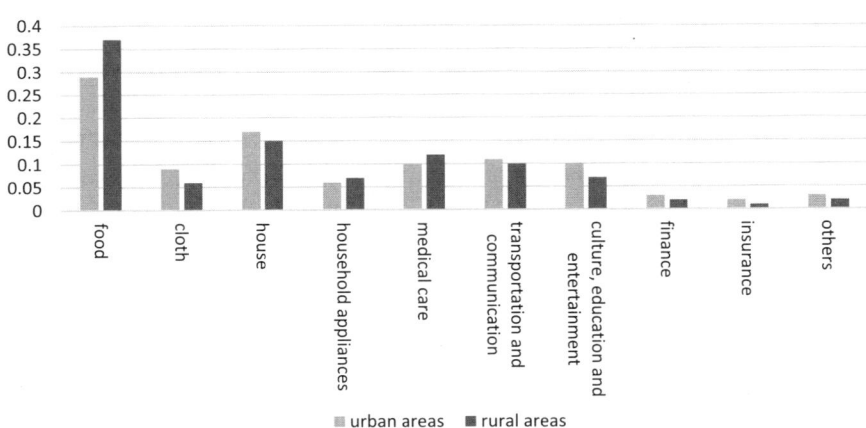

Figure 4-12: The comparison of consumption structure in urban and rural area.
Source: NBS, CEIC databases.

Second, China's urban and rural residents' consumption structures are different, and upgrading of rural residents' consumption structure lags behind the residents in urban areas. The structural differences in consumption expenditures of urban and rural residents remain significant and serious (Figure 4-12). In 2011, food and medical care's share of total consumption

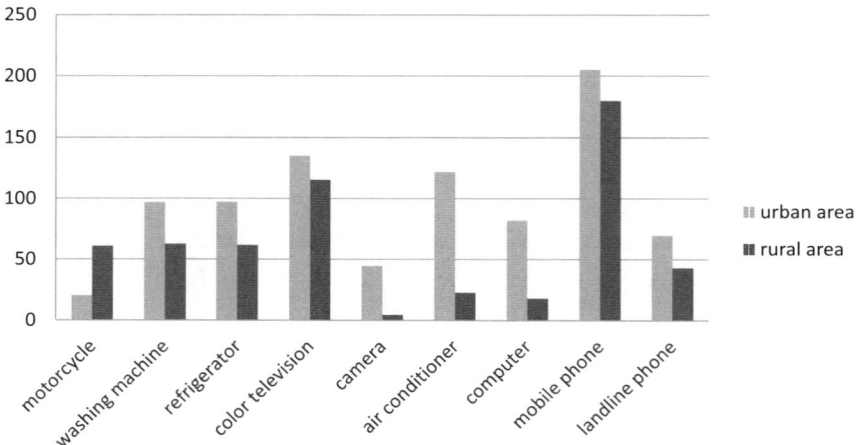

Figure 4-13: Number of major durable goods per hundred families in urban and rural areas.
Source: NBS, *China Statistics Yearbook*, CEIC databases.

expenditure in rural areas was higher than that of urban residents, while home electrical appliances, transport and communications, culture, entertainment expenditure's share was lower than urban residents. The structural differences between urban and rural consumption expenditure were also reflected by the gap of urban and rural consumption of durable goods in 2011 (Figure 4-13). Except the motorcycle, which has been phased out by urban life, the values of computer, telephone, and washing machine expenditures in urban areas were significantly greater than those by rural consumers.

By the above analysis, one of the most important factors of China's under-consumption problem is the dual structure of urban and rural of consumption behaviors. Rural residents' consumption in terms of both volume and structure significantly lags behind urban residents. Rural residents' consumption behavior is crucial to China's consumption development, because 49% of the total population is still in rural areas.

4.2 The Impact of Income Distribution on Consumption Behavior

In the earlier discussion of insufficient consumption, we have emphasized the fact that China's average consumption ratio is significantly lower than other countries. On a macro level, China's consumption's share of output declines. However, consumption behaviors vary greatly according to different income levels in China. Growing inequality in income distribution affects the consumption pattern significantly.

The urban lowest-income household consumption expenditure's share of disposable income was 93.54% in 2011, while the urban highest-income household consumption expenditure's share of disposable income was only 59.79%. Moreover, the gap of consumption's share of income between the lowest-income families and highest-income families was rising from 30.95% in 2001 to 33.75% in 2011. As Chinese residents' income increases, consumption's share of income decreases, and the gap of consumption between low-income and high-income household widens. The rich have relatively small average propensity to consume, while the consumption of the poor is constrained by low income. The growing inequality between the rich and the poor is continuously limiting consumption development in China. According to official statistics from the National Bureau of Statistics, although the Gini index in China has fallen for four consecutive years, the Gini index in 2012 has remained as high as 0.474 (Figure 4-14). According to the study of CHFS in Southwestern University of Finance

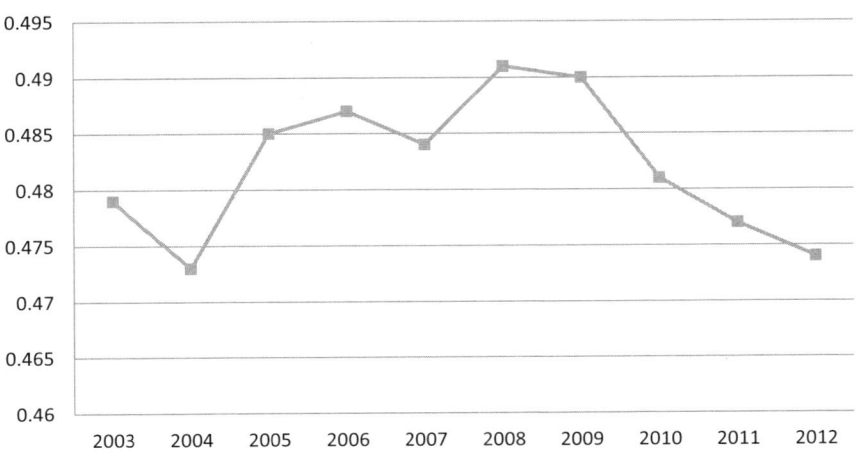

Figure 4-14: China's Gini index (2003–2012).

Source: NBS.

and Economics, China's Gini index reached 0.61 in 2010. However, the Gini index can only point out the unequal distribution of income in China on macro level. The structural analysis of unequal income distribution in China requires further discussion.

First, there is a wide gap between incomes of urban and rural residents in China. In 2011, China's urban residents' average disposable income was 21,809.8 yuan per capita, while the rural residents' average disposable income was only 6,977.3 yuan per capita. The average annual growth rate of urban residents' disposable income was 14.37% from 1991 to 2011, while this value was 12.79% in rural areas. Urban residents' disposable income remains 2 to 3 times that of the rural residents (Figure 4-15). Therefore, there are huge differences in total amounts and structure of consumptions in urban and rural areas.

Second, China's labor share of GDP is falling. According to *China Statistical Yearbook* labor's share of GDP, which was 52.79% in 1997, was 44.94% in 2011. Labor's share has dropped by 8%. Furthermore, according to ILO statistics, the average wage's share of output was 55.15% from 1995 to 2000, which has dropped to 51.95% in the period from 2001 to 2007. The decline in wage's share of GDP reduces the consumption demand and worsens the under-consumption problem further.

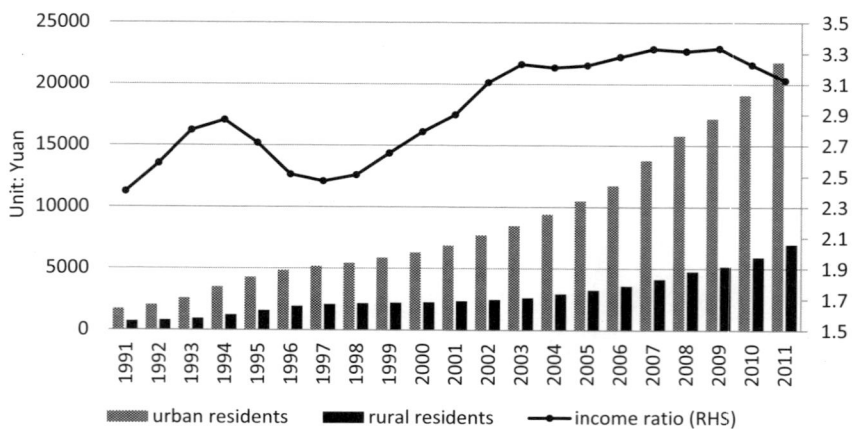

Figure 4-15: Comparison of the disposable income of urban and rural residents.
Source: NBS, CEIC databases.

Finally, the gap of income between state-owned sectors and private sectors is very large. The share of state-owned sectors in total wages in urban areas was 48.29% in 2011, while the share of state-owned sectors on employee number was only 18.67% in urban areas. Meanwhile, the decline of employment in state-owned sectors was faster than the drop of total wages from 1995 to 2011. The average annual decline rate of employment was 6.95%, while the average annual decline rate of total wages was only 2.84%. Furthermore, the income gap between the state-owned sectors and private sectors is incompletely reflected in wage differences, because many consumer goods are not distributed as tradable goods in state-owned sectors. State sectors raise workers' invisible income by additional welfare arrangements, which further aggravates the income gap between state-owned sectors and private sectors.

The seriously unequal income distribution in China is one of the most important causes of insufficient consumption. The rich in China own huge purchasing power. Luxury consumption in China has accounted for one-fourth of that of the world.[11] The Hurun rich list showed that 18% of the listed rich men were from China in 2012. However, average propensity to consume is low for the rich at the same time. Some scholars have estimated that 20% of Chinese residents hold 80% of the savings (Wang Jue, 1999).[12] When the majority of ordinary households with low incomes still worries about stubbornly high housing prices and expenditure on children's education and save a lot, China's under-consumption is reasonable.

4.3 The Effect of Demographic Structure on Consumption Behavior

Many phenomena in the economy can be explained by changes in demographic structure, which can also be used to analyze consumption behavior in contemporary China. China's change in demographic structure depends mainly on two factors: one is the baby boom after 1949 and the other is

---

[11] Bain (2013). *The Report of China's Luxury Market in 2012.* Bain & Company.
[12] Wang Jue (1999). The Reasons of Insufficient Domestic Demand and How to Expand Domestic Demand. *Commercial Economic Research*, 5: 4–6.

China's family planning policy introduced in the 1970s. These two factors have affected the current status and trend of the demographic structure and consumption behavior.

China has experienced a baby boom from 1949 to 1970. The average annual growth rate of China's population was 2.05% during the period. China's total population was 541.67 million in 1949, which had reached 829.92 million by 1970. After about 40 years, 300 million people are about 40–60 years old now, which is still working age. In fact, China's demographic structure is changing, and the working-age population's share was rising until 2012. In 1982, the working-age population's share of total population was 61.5%, while this proportion rose to 74.43% by 2010. Based on the life cycle theory, consumers will smooth consumption in order to maximize their utility. Save at work, consume in retirement. As the proportion of China's population aged 15 to 65 is continuously increasing, China's savings rate is on the rise.

China has adopted a family planning policy after the 1970s to limit the number of households' children. Therefore, China's population growth has slowed down significantly and the total dependency ratio declined, which is mainly caused by the decline in child dependency ratio. The influence of family planning policies on Chinese residents' consumption is mainly in two aspects: on the one hand, the population growth rate declines due to the family planning policy, which causes China's demographic structure to change from a mushroom shape to a spindle shape. The savings have increased and consumption has become weak because of the changes in the demographic structure, which we have described above; on the other hand, the family planning policy has changed consumers' behavior. China's residents value blood ties and the continuity of society. When the family cannot be continued through the increase in the number of children, most families will choose to improve children's qualities. Therefore, improvement of children's qualities changes household consumption patterns. The household's consumption plan is designed to match the long-term development for their children, which mainly includes expenditures on children's education and housing spending. In term of spending on housing, the average national house price was 1710 yuan per square meter in 1995, and has risen to 5,791 yuan per square meter in 2012. Due to fewer children in the family, the entire family, even grandma and grandpa, save their money

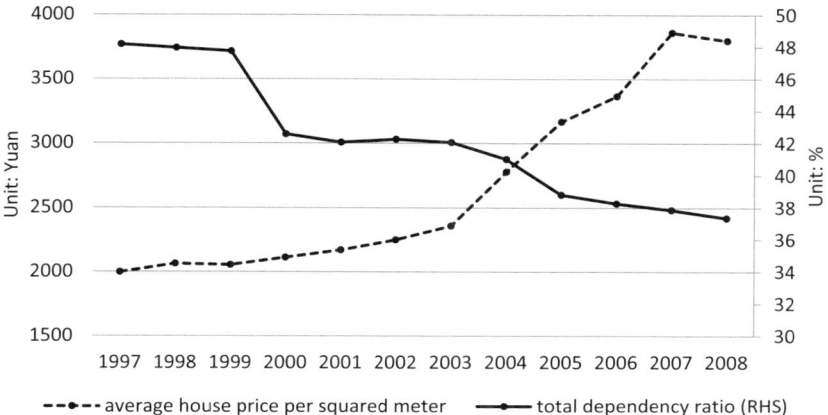

Figure 4-16: House price and family planning policy.
Source: NBS, *China Statistics Yearbook*, CEIC databases.

to buy a house for their children, the high demand of which pushes up house prices higher and higher (Figure 4-16). Moreover, Chinese residents' expenditure on education for their children is increasing. Research shows that one child's education will cost 250,000 yuan from 0 to 16 years old measured by the prices in 2003, and if receiving higher education, the costs would rise to 480,000 yuan (Xu Anqi, 2011).[13] One worker's average wage in urban areas was 41,799 yuan in 2011, which means raising a child costs one worker's 10 years' income. With China's soaring housing prices and education costs, the family planning policy has raised residents' growing concerns on house and education expenditure, further reducing the current level of consumption.

It is undeniable that China has a trend of an aging society, which will promote consumption in the future. China's working-age population of 15 to 59 years old decreased by 3.45 million in 2011, while the working-age people's share has declined for the first time since 2002. China gradually moves toward an aging society, which will raise consumption according to the

---

[13] Xu Anqi (2011). *The Economic Cost of Children: the Structural Changes and Optimization in the Transition Process*. Shanghai Academy of Social Sciences.

permanent income hypothesis and the life cycle theory. As a typical aging country, Japan's child dependency ratio was continuously declining from 1970 to 2011, while the old-age dependency ratio was rising. Meanwhile, Japan's final consumption's share of GDP was increasing from 59.95% in 1970 to 81.05% in 2011. However, whether the increase in the elderly population will cause the expansion of consumption is not clear in China. First, elderly people may choose to continue saving for bequest motivation. They do not only consider their own welfare, but also take their children's living standard into consideration. Oriental culture raises the children's importance for the elderly and accumulates wealth through saving for future generations. Second, the status of the only descendant is becoming more prominent in the family due to the family planning policy, and the uncertain environment enhances the elderly's concerns for the descendants' welfare. More and more Chinese families show a funnel-shaped structure, three generations of the family concentrate all of the wealth on young children to support their future development and improvement of life quality. Finally, the aging society that can really boost consumption in China is not coming, because baby boomers are still between 55 to 64 years old by 2012, while residents' savings in this age is still at a high level. As the retirement age is extended, Chinese residents will prepare more savings before retirement. Rise in savings causes low current consumption. Before the baby boomers retire, under-consumption remains a serious problem in China.

Therefore, China's current demographic structure is an important cause of the under-consumption problem. The baby boom and the family planning policy have direct impacts on current Chinese residents' consumption behavior.

5. CONSUMPTION IMPROVEMENT: FACTOR MARKET REFORM AND EQUAL PUBLIC GOODS SUPPLY

5.1 The Factor Market Reform

The key point of China's current market-oriented reforms is factor market reform. Factor market reform would both enhance the healthy development of the downstream market, and have a direct impact on residents' income. Moreover, production factors determine the long-term national economic development from the supply side. Among the factor markets, the labor, land, and capital markets have crucial impacts on residents' consumption in China, which are able to achieve the market-oriented reform of the dual structure of urban and rural areas, unequal income distribution, and changes in demographic structure, finally contributing to the sustainable development of Chinese residents' consumption.

As we described earlier, the artificial fragmentation of the labor market has negative impact on consumption, which is reflected in the dual structure of urban and rural areas and the unequal income distribution, while the population aging strengthens the constant trend. In fact, the process of China's reform in the labor market has not stopped since the early stage of reform. State-owned enterprises have addressed the hidden unemployment problem (Yuan Zhigang and Shao Ting, 2010)[14] and migrant workers appeared in the early 1990s, which continuously promoted competition in the labor market. However, China still has not achieved free movement of labor completely. In China, the main obstacle to free movement of labor is the household registration system, rooted in the planned economic system, which separates economic development, social security, and public service between the urban and rural areas. Such huge differences in fact form the urban–rural dual structures of consumption. On the one hand, the differences of economic development and consumption of rural and urban areas are strengthened by the household registration system. Rural residents' income is closely interrelated to agricultural production and they cannot move into cities permanently and benefit from urban development. Some scholars believe that the fragmentation of farming, caused by surplus farmers, wastes at least 19% of arable land in rural China (Li Jianlin *et al.*, 2006).[15] On the other hand, the household registration system widens the gap of social security and public services in urban and rural areas. Urban residents receive a relatively healthy social safety network. Pension spending of China's urban residents reached 1.28 trillion yuan in 2011, while the new rural social pension spending was only 58.77 billion yuan. Moreover, urban residents enjoy medical insurance

---

[14]Yuan Zhigang and Shao Ting (2010). Re-examining the Historical Status, Function and Solution of China's State-Owned Enterprises. *Academic Monthly*, 42(1): 55–66.

[15]Li Jianlin, Chen Yu Qi, Jiang Qingxia and Kuang Xiaoyu (2006). Reasons and Countermeasures of China's Arable Land Fragmentation. *Agricultural Economics*, 6: 21–23.

and unemployment insurance, which do not exist or have just started in rural areas. Social security and public service of rural residents is lagging far behind urban residents, and is still dominated by family insurance. Rural consumption cannot be promoted because of the difference in social security and public services between urban and rural areas. Furthermore, the urban household registration system causes a dual structure within urban areas, where local residents and migrant workers receive extremely different income, social security, and consumption. According to the National Bureau of Statistics, the number of migrant workers was 252.78 million in 2011. The majority of migrant workers concentrates on large and medium-sized cities, and widely engages in the manufacturing, construction, and service industries.[16] First of all, migrant workers' wages are significantly lower than those of urban residents. Average monthly wages of migrant workers were only 2,049 yuan in 2011, while urban residents' average monthly wage was 3,483 yuan. Second, migrant workers cannot receive enough social security. In 2011, pension insurance only covered 13.9% of all migrant workers and health insurance covered only 16.7% of them. Finally, there are differences of consumption environment between the migrant workers and urban residents. Based on the survey data of Shanghai in 2010 (Chu Rong Wei and Zhang Xiaodong, 2011),[17] more than half of migrant workers live in Shanghai farmers' buildings, while approximately 40% of migrant workers have never accessed the Internet. Their main leisure activities are watching television and listening to the radio. In other words, migrant workers are extremely disconnected from modern urban life. In some senses, China's migrant workers have neither the high income nor the complete social security of urban residents, while bearing similar economic pressures as urban residents. Therefore, migrant workers' spending power is greatly weakened.

Furthermore, China's land market is highly distorted, and the land is distributed without a competitive market. The state or collectives own lands, while rural residents only have rights to contract land. The transformation

---

[16]National Bureau of Statistics (2012). *The Report of China's Migrant Workers in 2011*.

[17]Chu Rong Wei and Zhang Xiaodong (2011). Interpretation of Chinese Migrant Workers in Consumer Market — the Bottom of Wealth's Pyramid. *Economic Theory and Business Management*, 7: 34–46.

of land from rural to urban management is completely monopolized by the state. The land non-marketization also distorts the labor market and deepens the problem of unequal income distribution. On the one hand, farmers cannot raise income significantly by selling their own land. Due to the lack of a rural land pricing mechanism, farmers have to transfer the land to the local government at extremely low prices, while local governments can gain tremendous benefits from land transfer. This wealth transfer from the farmers to local governments is actually hindering the increase of farmers' income, and widens the urban–rural income gap. On the other hand, the lack of a price mechanism means that land resources cannot be distributed to the most efficient places, which also results in the enormous waste of land resources. Cheap supply of industrial land and unreasonably high prices of residential land actually continue to push up the price level in urban areas. Farmers don't receive "the first pot of gold" from selling land to start their city life, which worsens the dual structure of rural and urban areas and obstructs the process of urbanization.

Meanwhile, China's capital market distortions, especially interest rate controls, limit the development of residents' consumption. First, China's government subsidizes investment of infrastructure projects through artificially maintaining low interest rates, resulting in excessive investment, which weakens consumption in China at the macro level. Second, low interest rates and the bad performance of the stock market have severely reduced consumption due to low capital income. Moreover, the gap between China's extremely low interest rates and high return of housing investment push up house prices. In a society without a healthy financial system and good investment opportunities, real estate is the only method to maintain the value of residents' wealth, causing strong demand for housing and extremely high prices. Meanwhile, China has no way to fully meet needs of inter-temporal borrowing. Therefore, Chinese residents are saving more and more in order to buy houses, resulting in the under-consumption problem. In other words, financial markets directly affect individuals' consumption decisions in China. Finally, financial resources are distributed to the state-owned enterprises through the banking system, which worsens the unequal income distribution problem. Currently, the good performances of state enterprises mainly rely on non-market-oriented allocation of financial resources, which cannot be distributed to the most efficient industries and enterprises, while the majority of private enterprises cannot borrow capital in the financial system, directly resulting in the rise of SMEs' outside financing with high risks in informal financial system. In this sense, the inefficiency of China's financial market is actually becoming a serious constraint on the economic development of China's capital allocation, which exacerbates the unequal income distribution in China.

Therefore, labor, land, and financial factor market distortion in China both limits the rise of residents' income from the demand side, and severely distorts market allocation of factors from the supply side, and finally hinders the future development of China's economy and living standards. The final solution of China's existing under-consumption problem starts from factor market reform. However, the fundamental driving forces actually come from complete transformation of China's government role.

5.2 The Equal Supply of Public Goods

We have emphasized the direct impact of factor market distortion on insufficient consumption in contemporary China, and this distortion is mainly caused by government intervention in the market. Meanwhile, the government fails to provide public goods equally, which exacerbates the problems of the dual structure of urban and rural areas and the unequal income distribution. These further worsen the situation of insufficient consumption in China.

The huge gap of public goods supply between rural and urban areas has been clarified in the preceding description. The differences worsen the problems of the dual structure of urban and rural areas and unequal income distribution. The unequal supply of public goods exists in many other fields, including medical care, pension, and social security. First, there are big regional differences among governments' educational spending. The expenditures on education per capita in Beijing and Shanghai, which were eastern regions, were 2,575.9 and 2,340.2 yuan respectively, while the expenditures on education per capita of Anhui and Guizhou, which are central and western regions, were only 946.2 yuan and 1,085.8 yuan in 2011. Moreover, the educational expenditures gap between rural and urban areas is huge. The educational spending on compulsory education in urban areas was 3.9 times that of the value in rural areas in 2006 (Liang Wenyan, 2008).[18] Second, China's housing security for low-income households is severely lagging behind, and has enormous regional differences. The planned supply of land area for affordable housing is 13,672 hectares in 2013, while the area for commercial housing is 109,217 hectares, which is 8 times that of the former. From the perspective of regional differences, in 2011, the government's expenditures on housing security in Shanghai and Beijing were only 8.25 billion yuan and 5.46 billion yuan respectively, while the government's spending on housing security in Inner Mongolia and Anhui, as central and western regions, has reached 14.04 billion yuan and 16.12 billion yuan. Third, the public service's level of employment training is low in contemporary China. Large numbers of migrant, unemployed workers and graduates cannot receive appropriate vocational and technical training, and thus are unable to meet specific requirements of jobs and adapt to the industrial transformation of China's economy. Eventually, many laborers cannot find appropriate jobs, while firms lack qualified workers. Finally, the public goods supply of environment management is also seriously unequal. The total outputs of water, environment, and public facilities management in Beijing and Shanghai were 14.88 billion yuan and 14.85 billion yuan in 2007, while the values in Anhui and Henan, as central and western provinces were only 7.15 billion yuan and 8.12 billion yuan. Furthermore, the public goods supply in the field of environment and resources is decreasing with the administrative ranking. For example, the wastewater treatment rate in cities was 75.25% in 2009, while the value in towns was only 41.64% (Li Hongxiang et al., 2012).[19] Therefore, there is seriously unequal public goods supply of medical care, pension, social security, education, housing security, employment training, and environment management in contemporary China.

On the one hand, unequal supply of public goods further exacerbates the dual structure of urban and rural areas. There are great differences in medical care, pension, social security, education, housing, job training, and

---

[18]Liang Wenyan (2008). The Analysis on Balanced Development of Compulsory Education and Scale of Fiscal Expenditures. *The Education Development Research*, 11: 50–54.

[19]Li Hongxiang, Cao Yin, Ge Chazhong, and Lu Yuantang (2012). How to Improve the Equality of Environmental Public Services Supply. *China Environment News*, March 27.

environment management between urban and rural areas. The low level of healthcare, pension, and social security raises rural households' uncertainty about the future, while lack of education opportunities, job training, and other public goods limit the further rise of rural households' income. The combination of low income and high uncertainty of income worsens the insufficient consumption problem in the rural areas. On the other hand, unequal public goods supply worsens the unequal income distribution problem. The income inequality is not only reflected by the income gap between urban and rural areas, but also includes the increasingly widening income gap between low-income earners and high-income earners. First, the dual structure inside urban areas means that the majority of migrant workers cannot get the same healthcare, pension, and social security as urban residents do. Second, the absence of housing security results in insufficient consumption by the low-income group, who suppress their consumption under high prices of housing. Meanwhile, the high-income group gains huge returns through housing investment. As a result, the wealth is transferred from the poor to the rich. Third, lack of job training has led to migrant workers and other low-skilled workers not being able to quickly find appropriate jobs through public training service, and further causes a decline of income level and rise of income uncertainty in the future. Finally, unequal distribution of education resources means there is no possibility of improving the low-income group's situation through self-actualization and high education level. The opportunity of equal competition is not accessible to each individual in the society. Then, the poor remain poor, and the rich become increasingly richer. Therefore, unequal public goods supply further worsens the insufficient consumption problem in modern China through the dual structure of rural and urban areas and unequal income distribution.

The adverse impacts of the urban–rural dual structure and unequal income distribution on households' consumption can be alleviated by equal public goods supply. On the one hand, the equal public goods supply will accelerate the urbanization process. The obstacle of household registration reform for urban residents can be effectively removed by equalizing the public goods supply. Meanwhile, labor resources will flow freely between urban and rural areas and within the cities and industries. Housing, social security, resources, environment, and other public services will accelerate the localization process of rural residents in the urban areas. And job training, education, and other public goods supply can promote the labor forces to meet the need of urban industrial development and structural upgrading process, and improve the income level and mitigate their income uncertainty. On the other hand, the equal public goods supply is crucial to the equality of opportunity in the whole society, which enhances economic vitality and boosts consumption. Every member of the society can receive the same social services and equal social environment for self-development. The equality of opportunity is not only promoting economic development and enhancing long-term consumption raise, but also maintaining social stability through improving the stable and equal environment of self-development, which creates a harmonized macro environment for improvement in consumption.

Therefore, with factor market reform, China should vigorously promote the equal supply of public goods, which will solve the insufficient consumption problem through changing the situation of the rural–urban dual structure, unequal income distribution, and demographic structure changes, and finally promote sustainable economic development in China.

REFERENCES

Bain (2013). *The Report of China's Luxury Market in 2012*. Bain & Company.
Chu, Rong Wei and Zhang Xiaodong (2011). Interpretation of Chinese migrant workers in the consumer market — the bottom of the pyramid of wealth. *Economic Theory and Business Management*, 7: 34–46.
CHRM (2012). *Report of China's Advertising and Media Markets in 2011*. Charm Communications.
Ezra, Feivel Vogel (2013). *Deng Xiaoping and the Transformation of China*. Life, Reading, Joint Publishing.
Hu's Report at the 18th National Congress of the Communist Party of China (2012). *March Firmly on the Path of Socialism with Chinese Characteristics and Strive to Complete the Construction of Well-off Society in all Respects*.
Huang, Renyu (2007). *China's Great History*. Life, Reading, Joint Publishing.
Il Houng Lee, Murtaza Syed and Liu Xueyan (2012). *Is China Over-Investment and Does it Matter?* IMF Working Paper No. wp12277.
Li, Hongxiang, Cao Yin, Ge Chazhong and Lu Yuantang (2012). *How to Improve the Equality of Environmental Public Services Supply?* China Environment News, March 27.

Li, Jianlin, Chen Yu Qi, Jiang Qingxia, Kuang Xiaoyu (2006). Reasons and countermeasures of China's arable land fragmentation. *Agricultural Economics*, 6: 21–23.

Liang, Wenyan (2008). The analysis on balanced development of compulsory education and scale of fiscal expenditures. *Education Development Research*, 11: 50–54.

National Bureau of Statistics (2012). *The Report of China's Migrant Workers in 2011*.

Wang, Jue (1999). The reasons of insufficient domestic demand and how to expand domestic demand. *Commercial Economic Research*, 5: 4–6.

Xu, Anqi (2011). *The Economic Cost of Children: Structural Changes and Optimization in the Transition Process*. Shanghai Academy of Social Sciences.

Ye, Wenzheng (1998). *The Theory of Children's Needs: the Cost and Utility of Chinese Children*. Fudan University Press.

Yuan, Zhigang (1996). Changes of households' consumption function in Chinese transitional economy. *Academic Monthly*, 9: 30–37.

Yuan, Zhigang (2011). *The Study of China's Consumption Frontier Issues*. Fudan University Press.

Yuan, Zhigang and Song Zhen (1999). Urban residents' consumption behavior changes with China's economic growth. *Economic Research Journal*, 11: 20–28.

Yuan, Zhigang and Shao Ting (2010). Re-examining the historical status, function and solution of China's state-owned enterprises. *Academic Monthly*, 42(1): 55–66.

Chapter 5
The Political Economy of Chinese Reform

Zhe Yang
School of Economics, Fudan University

1. INTRODUCTION

Chinese economic development has been an institutional transformation toward a more efficient market economic mechanism since the reform. This course has been promoted by both the top-level design and the local-level trial and error process. There is a specific attribute of decentralization in Chinese political regime, yet it is quite different from the federalism. Western institutional economics originates in the collective expression of individual preferences, which could hardly match the reality in China. In this chapter, the author will expand North's theory of three pillars, ideology-state-property rights, by introducing the idea of the "stationary bandit" and the "roving bandit" of Mancur Olsen (2005), with the intention of establishing a theoretical foundation to explain China's institutional evolution. The Chinese institution supply is provided by both the central and the local governments. The former decides the basic rules while the latter choose to obey or compromise these rules depending on which specific measures are apt to promote economic development and fiscal increase within their administrative regions. The large state-owned enterprises (SOEs) have been playing an active part in the institutional decision-making process and they create significant effects during the entire course of reform. Undoubtedly, long-term development must be enhanced by perfecting market economic institutions with low transaction cost and high efficiency, which is actually the concern of the local governments. However, the conditions for private economic development do not share the same speed as economic growth. Investment and export promoted growth is controversial with the long-term potential in its very nature. The private sector could only bring in more creativity and vigor when the monopolistic exploitation by the large SOEs eases up and the market could provide clearer expectations.

Coase and Wang (2013) defined the trial and error by the local government as "Reform in the Margins" with household responsibility, town–village enterprises, private economy, and development zones as representatives of locally promoted activities. These reforms kept the Chinese economy from declining while the SOEs failed to take on the economic growth as they were expected to. Nevertheless, the inefficiency and pursuit of market power of the SOEs forced down the economic potential. The determination of ideology guarantees that this institutional breakthrough would be too expensive for the local governments to accomplish without top-level institutional changes. Therefore, the subsequent reform still has to be carried out from both the top and the local levels.

Over 30 years of reform and opening-up, China has created a "miracle" of long-term economic growth. Behind the "miracle," the world's major economists did not see the improvements of the Chinese political system. Annual economic growth rate could reach a high speed of 10% per year for a long time in the absence of good system conditions, which many people find difficult to understand.

The essence of economic and social development is not a simple increase in the amount of economic indicators, but constantly improves various types of economic systems. China's reform and opening up is carried out in the absence of precedents for reference and involves ideological debate, a potential change of the political system, and gradual changes in the economic rules. The direction of the reform from a planned economy to a market economy is different from the Soviet Union or eastern Europe's "shock therapy" as decided from the start, but after a series of construction of "modern powerful socialist country," "socialism with Chinese characteristics," "planned commodity economy," and "socialist market economy with Chinese characteristics," which accompanied by a gradually ideological change. The penetration and replacement by the market economy of the planned economy have been pushed forward by the reforms in the margins and top-level design. In this period of more than 30 years, however, the bottom line of socialist production relations set up by ideology has been no breakthrough; the market eventually became a tool to build socialism.

2. REVIEW OF SYSTEM RESEARCHES ON CHINA'S REFORM

2.1 Method

From the view of historical process, China's reform and opening up is a starting point of China's modern economic development. Nevertheless, from the perspective of structural equilibrium and social and economic harmony, the reform has been far from achieving its desired goals. For seeking a right path to China's long-term economic development, we should have a clear cognition and summary of China's economic development process since the reform and opening up, and on this basis, find a reasonable development path of "path dependence."

Today, the problems of China's economic development do not only exist in the transformation of a planned economy to a market economy. The characteristics of transitional economy can summarize China's real economic system in terms of a fuzzy concept, but also in the urgent need of a clear path for China's economy from the viewpoint of a concrete analysis. The core of how to promote the sustainable and balanced development of China's economy in the long term relies on building a system environment that makes China get rid of the development pattern of an extensive economy, which helps find its way to solve issues such as improving the quality of economic development, the balanced development of people's living standards in both material and spiritual culture, and the status of Chinese products in the world market.

Mainstream economics analysis of the economy as a whole can be divided into two aspects of product market and factor market, and analyses of these two aspects in many cases lack consideration of the specific institutional environment. A so-called institutional environment is in fact a set of rules; primary rules can regulate the designation and standard of secondary rules and refined rules directly determine the revenue collection (payoff set) of economic subjects in the decision making. Operation laws at the collective level can be obtained via simple individual derivation in a perfect market economy, while deduced results based on the principle of self-interest to a large extent can fit the reality of events. But in an imperfect market economic system, solely analyzing the drawbacks cannot find the solution path on an overall level. Only when it discussed in the overall macroscopic perspective can we gain. For this kind of discussion, the specific national conditions are the primary environmental settings. On the problem of analysis of Britain or the United States directly applied to the issue of China's reform and opening up, in addition to the differences between international political and economic environments led by the different historical stages, geography, population, resources, and the previous system can make the same operation lead to two extremes of heaven and hell.

China is now in the transition from the planned economy of before the reform and opening up to a market economy, at the beginning of which the problems faced had great similarities with former socialist countries of the Soviet Union, but have China's own unique content in the political system, economic power and financial power, ethnic and cultural traditions, etc. China did not adopt countries such as Russia's "shock therapy," but gradually groped forward along the path "touch stone across the river" proposed by Deng Xiaoping and formed the early reform strategy called "one center, two basic points" in order to enhance China's economic strength as the basic starting point. In this process, although the color of "where politics goes, economy follows" gradually faded out, the dominant attributes of "plan" or "authority" in China's economic system haven't been completely eradicated; that is to say, the overall analysis of China's macro economy is not entirely carried out in accordance with mainstream neoclassical economics.

2.2 The Necessity of Political Economy and Institutional Research

A research approach that takes microscopic behavior analysis as its basis often needs to seek interaction of the macroeconomic operation and macroeconomic policy in the study of macro problems under the premise of microeconomic foundation, while not taking the differences of national conditions and traditional customs between different countries into account; therefore, when it is used to study the problems of China, it could make certain dogmatic mistakes. Perfect market economy should take perfect rules for its basis, these rules — explained according to Menger's theoretical starting point — appear for reducing the uncertainty of the economic and social life, which we call the "institution." "Institutions," divided into two kinds of formal institution and informal institution by Douglass C. North, respectively, affect individual decisions indifferent ways, whose basic characteristics are contained in the embedded of the informal institution and mandatory of the formal institution. Considering China's problems, the institutional environment composed of formal institution and informal institution determines that China's macroeconomic development cannot simply use the experience of the West, which might be used as a reference in concrete analysis, while when considering the root of China's economy, we should deem the realistic basic institutional framework as a primary object to study.

The development of the economy in general is regarded as the expansion of production activities; the intersection of actual demand and planned output determines the real output. However, output is merely an inevitable process in terms of overall economic development, while the distribution of interests eventually affects the economic development path. When the distribution has problems, any products market system that supports high yield in the short term is difficult to sustain. Marx found the defects of capitalism from the view of distribution when he discussed the inevitability of capitalist economic crisis; furthermore, when this thought is extended, the factor market of derived demand is the key to the long-term development of an economy. Trade in the factor market relates to both supplier and demander in the product market; crucially, it is directly related to the allocation problem.

Since Smith (1974), the growth of national wealth became the core issue of economics research. In terms of the explanation for China's economic development, there are two main types of analysis paths: one is the classical macroeconomic growth model, namely, the Solow growth model (Solow, 1956) and the endogenous growth model, where the economy growth is decomposed into the expansion of factor utilizing and the improvement of total factor productivity. On this basis, we can decompose the factors of China's "demographic dividend" release, accumulation of capital and foreign capital utilization; on the other hand, the other factors that cannot be quantified are attributed to the problems of total factor productivity; moreover, there is an analysis of combining technical progress with labor or capital. There is more empirical research on this basis of the analysis, while in theory, it will not be beyond the analysis framework of CD function or AK function. Nevertheless, we can only roughly estimate the mechanism of China's economic development, and can point out to what extent China's economic growth depends on the expansion of the factor of production inputs such as labor, capital and the extent to which it is driven by factors outside of production inputs, while the real development of factor market is totally neglected.

In the process of the Western world's rising, it is natural that labor and capital pursue interests; therefore, the classical models considering the growth of input factors and the change of the factor organization as the main power of economic growth is appropriate. But when the pursuit of interests is suppressed, factor prices will be inevitably distorted, leading to the relative price system being unable to match the needs of social development. Lack of supply of the formal institution is the key to price distortions, while political activity is the fundamental reason behind formal institutions' undersupply. Since the informal institution has some effect in reducing rent dissipation brought by market defects, artificial factor price system and rapid economic growth could be compatible with each other, but the problem of the disequilibrium of distribution will gradually deteriorate, posing a potential threat to long-term economic development.

2.3 Market and Decentralization

The "market" of factor market and product market means the rules of the exchange; the fundamental problem lies in the institution construction, rather than specific details of the market structure. Institution rules restrict the constraints, incentives, and motivation faced by the economic activity subject. China's economic reform is an evolution process changing from a planned price mechanism to a market price mechanism; this research begins with the comparative study of the economic system as well as consideration of the economic transformation (Kornai, 1986, 1992, etc.), which shows that "soft budget constraint" under the planned economy system is an important reason for low economic efficiency, which also provides an important theoretical tool for China's future fiscal reform and fiscal decentralization problem research.

Besides, Kornai also puts forward the important problems of the function division of the local government and the central government, and later studies even more directly consider the political system as an important factor of economic development for developing economies; the description of the political framework of the regionally decentralized authoritarianism (RDA) is especially important (Montinola et al., 1995). This framework describes the political basis on which the success of China's economic development depends; the core idea is that independent experiments in local government brought by the decentralization play a significant role in promoting institutional reform. The research is very rich, and through the modification and application of this framework produced a series of significant historic analysis literature (Cai and Treisman, 2004; Edin, 2000, 2003; Naughton, 2003; Qian et al., 1999). This series of research in applied economics adopted North's methods (North, 1981, 1990) of economic history analysis and new institutional economics, and combined with Coase and others' enterprise and market boundary problem (Coase, 1992), the research approach of the evolutionary economics (Nelson and Winter, 1982), and the research technique of evolutionary game theory, examined the evolution process of institutional change since China's reform and opening up and the corresponding incentive mechanism problem (Maskin et al., 2000; Pistor and Xu, 2004; Shen, 2005). However, from a practical perspective, to what extent China's RDA type of political and economic structure is established is questionable (Tsai, 2004); a decentralization of authoritarianism maintenance and stability for the market economic system requires the existence of uniformity of the factor and product markets as a prerequisite; segmentation of factor markets and the existence of local protectionism is a clear violation of the RDA framework.

3. THE THEORY CONSTRUCTION OF CHINESE CHARACTERISTIC MARKET ECONOMY

3.1 North and Olson

North's system analysis theory's starting point lies in the property rights arrangements. Clear property rights arrangement can reduce transaction costs, improve economic efficiency (Coase Ronald, 1937); property rights arrangement is determined by the state, the state's goal is to obtain rent maximization; the efficiency of the property rights arrangement can expand the tax base. Another important theoretical pillar of North is the collective expression of individual preference, that is, the ideology. The "ideology" that North envisioned is similar to Rousseau's "social contract," which is under the premise of social rules built based on scattered individuals' will. China is an authoritarian political society; ideology, or social contract does not come from the collective expression of most individuals' preferences, but shows the characteristics of apparent "path dependence," the core elements formed in the preferences expressed by minority of authority; the specific ideological change also lies in the change of these personal preferences, therefore, we can say that ideology and the government as a representative of the authority are unified in a certain extent.

The difference between politics based on the social contract and authority politics will not lead to change of the state's goals, but in terms of the latter, only with the impact of the external pressure could ideology possibly change. For every nation, social stability is far more important than economic growth, although a rising unemployment rate and falling economic growth often relate together, but when industrial layout and property rights arrangements undergo great changes, rising unemployment in the short term and increase of long-term potential economic growth both coexist, weighing scales tend to be more inclined to employment. On the other hand, when capital income and labor income gap is constantly widening, potential of long-term investment will inevitably be reduced; how to increase employment and improve labor income will become a problem that every nation must consider seriously. Successfully promoting the industrial structure is not only changing capital uses as written books said, but also to ensure adequate employment in the process. Preference change comes from competition of administration areas of the government, or say, a sense of crisis of stationary bandits (Olson, 2005). In a multi-party political system, the threats from the opposition to the ruling party guarantee that the ruling party must satisfy voters; under a one-party political system, the support of the people is fundamental to ensure its legitimacy and effectiveness. Stability, therefore, requires the direct determinants of party's decisions are inflation and unemployment, once price level and unemployment rate within the system rise to a certain degree, the political decision-making process will cause change in the rules, or create new rules to solve the problem. Starting from the reality, North's exogenous ideology assumption is no longer valid; in essence, in China's national construction, the real influence on the nation's ideology is endogenously determined.

3.2 Administrative Decentralization and Economic Decentralization

The model of 1930s' Soviet socialism used to be China's economic planning template. Nevertheless, in 1958 Mao Zedong's "On the Ten Major Relationships" clearly discussed the relationship between the central and local, expressed the necessity of decentralization in China. China's decentralization from the theoretical assumptions can be divided into two categories: administrative decentralization and economic decentralization. Administrative decentralization mainly existed in the planned economy period, when the power-sharing arrangements put most of the SOEs into the grasp of local government; however, due to the integration of government administration with enterprise, these enterprises essentially became the subordinate departments to local government, which made a "unified" huge central government become big decentralized local governments. Economic decentralization's outstanding performance is the enterprise reform, from the "decentralization of power and transfer of profits" to the contract system, to the reform of the company system. Brewed since 1993, the reform of the company system was formally implemented in 1997, aimed at solving incentive problems of enterprise management. Administrative decentralization and economic decentralization are decentralization arrangements carried out at the level of direct government intervention; the former is for the specific rules-making, and the latter is for the division of power in the control scope of anticipants and the degree.

3.3 Championship Competition and Reform on the Margins

When analyzing China's "economic miracle," many documents attribute China's rapid economic growth to the GDP "championship competition" system of local governments under the decentralization of political arrangements or similar institution arrangements (Xu, 2010), making a basic clear theory interpretation of the successful reason for the institutional arrangements in this analysis process. Deng Xiaoping, the chief designer of China's reform and opening up, proposed the theory of "touch stone across the river" at the beginning of reform and opening up, which essentially shows authigenic spontaneous fundamental characteristics of China's market economy order — "trial and error."

Although local governments no longer directly control all aspects of their administration's economy, their local development strategies highlight the competitions with other areas and extensive development pattern with great waste of resources becomes the main measure to grow for the reason that competition rules are too simple. We can make a simple deduction that under the economic growth mode that relies on resource development and investment, the areas with poor resources endowment tend to more easily break through the "poverty trap" via system innovation; Zhejiang Province as the most rapidly developed area in the early years of the reform and opening up is a sample of successful system innovation. The development of the central region is affected by the geographic location and historical heritage; with inconvenient transportation and tend to be conservative in the history of changes, these areas often have superior agricultural production conditions to Zhejiang, Jiangsu, and other places, while possessing a more backward industrial base inherited from the period of the Republic of China and the relatively weaker business culture — Henan is a representative area. The western part of China, besides the similar problems of the central region, is more important for the geopolitical considerations; it is difficult to form effective breakthrough from the system for their border position, that is, they have much higher system innovation costs. Guangdong's success has a lot to do with its geographical location. Hong Kong's system of high efficiency through attracting immigration forced Guangdong to become the window of the reform of China.

Coase and Wang (2013) name the non-top-level design reform created by this competition as "Reform on the Margins"; the outbreak of the economic activity from four aspects of agriculture, township enterprises, private enterprises, and special economic zones effectively prevented the failure of stagnation of system innovation at the beginning period of the reform. Under the so-called "adversity leads to prosperity," the poor and desperate lead the local government officials to make a choice of ideology conveyed by the central government, giving tacit permission or even support to activities that destroy current economic system limits when they face the pressure of stabilizing the social order.

4. CHINESE CHARACTERISTIC MARKET AND GOVERNMENT

The expression of economic changes appears to be the growth or drop of commodity production, the increase or decrease of choices people face, and the hoist or oppression of individual spiritual experiences. All these factors can be written in the economic history while these only cannot describe the truth about China's reform in the past 30 years. Economics used to focus on institutions and the school of institution used to prevail in United States for quite some time, yet the neo-institution school does not inherit this approach of research and pursues a way to plant institutions in the neoclassic economic researches with the help of "transaction cost." The Chinese reform was almost always about the changes in institutions. The innovation and application of technology are just a result of institutional changes and also one of the most important factors to determine the path of institutional reform.

4.1 The Political Arrangement-Decentralization

The reform of Chinese society continued in the way of decentralization, which is that authority and power was continuously distributed from the central government to the lower levels, SOEs, private families, and individuals. The efficiency can only be achieved when the utilization can bring about full satisfaction to the users, and it is in this definition that efficiency can be evaluated. The political economic structure of the Maoist administrative decentralization ended in failure due to its lack of incentive compatible institutions.

The reform in the past 30 years has been a rough cause and the speed of reform was relatively very slow. There are some internal factors for this. The discretionary power of the local governments grew in the process of decentralization and this allowed them to arrange their activities against the will of the central government. The distributed benefits urge the local government to protect their political interest. The cost of breaking down the *de facto* political interest arrangement can be very high. In this case, the mode of trial and error seems to be the most possible choice for economic reform. The political structure in China was not like in the former Soviet Union or East European countries. On the edge of reform and opening up, the central authority had already been weakened by a long history of decentralization. The reality of economic reform can tell us that in places where the strict regulations are scarce or the institutional environment forbids the people who have access to showing their wills from achieving their optimal goals, reforms are more likely to take place and the new ideology is more easily to turn into reality.

The shift from administrative decentralization to economic decentralization with the main concern about economic growth is actually about granting incentive and capacity to the local government to help promote local development. The so-called tournament or benchmark regional competition is based upon the performance evaluation institution on local government officers, which is aimed at economic growth or fiscal increase. This type of competition must be carried out in a socially stable environment and any competition that may endanger the central government's political legitimacy would not be tolerated. The individuals are weak facing the government, while they can be strong as a community as they can express their wishes and form the public voice. The public voice can be heard by the central and enforce supervision on local governments. However, this type of feedback institution is more inferior in either efficiency or stability compared to the legal system.

A local government is not a complete uniformity that can be compared to a person. All these administrations are dominated by all kinds of officers with a variety of political or economic interests. The will to promote local development is generally consistent with the officers, while what really matters is the validity and viability of their actions. Just before the Great Leap Forward in 1958, the central government put most of the SOEs under the authority of local governments. The local governments received more benefit from the enterprises while they were integrated with the enterprises and thus shared their financial burden. The extensive operation could not guarantee sufficient resources for the local infrastructure improvement. On the other hand, the local governments are only concerned about the local economy. Even if some of the information about the local economic structure could be sent to the central planner, the distortion and error of the information during transmission helped to create the imbalance of the entire economic structure, thus the long-term disequilibrium with agriculture subsidizing the heavy industries.

By the dawn of the reform and opening up, this mode still persisted. The soft budget of SOEs kept the fiscal income at a low level, yet due to the restraints of ideology, the development in the old institutions could only be achieved by expanded fiscal expenditure. Even before 1994, when the local fiscal revenue took a proportion of 70% of the entire country, the local governments still found it hard to collect enough resources. If we state it in the institutional way, there had been no new institutional supply for the local governments to promote development efficiently even in the decentralized context. When the institutional innovations became available to the local governments, agriculture and collective and private enterprises show great power partly because of the improvement of the local public services.

4.2 The Building of the Basic Market Principles

The essence of China's reform has been the shift from a planning economy to a market economy. A market economy is compatible with efficiency institutionally; therefore, it is an inevitable choice. The planning institutions are inferior to the market economy from the aspect of resource allocation due to their disadvantage in collecting and processing dispersed private information. When Karl Marx criticized the capitalist economy, the actual mechanism of economic crisis comes from the information loss, errors, and other distortions other than his description of the market failure. When the disequilibrium caused by information distortions mounted to a certain extent, the gap between supply and demand would no longer be sustainable and the debt would be cleared in an unorthodox way, the economic crisis. The critical source of economic crisis lies in the debt accumulation due to economic frictions (Minsky, 2010). In fact, the planning economy does not have the attributes to ensure the authenticity of information or to correct what has been done wrong. The reason there are no economic crises in the planning economy is just that there is no room for debt to be shown. The strict political oppression uses a rather tough way to clear the obligatory relationship rather than the debt itself. The debt exists between the country and itself rather than some other parties; therefore, there is no way for the debt to be defaulted. Anyway, the loss of value because of the default actually happens and the real effect does not disappear because of the clearing of the accounts.

The processing of the information is done by indexed expression about the dispersed information in the market economy. The private information would be collected and processed to ascertain level of data to help make economic decisions (Hayek, 2003), while the most important datum is price. The institution of price determination is the heart of economic institutions. There can be prices in the planning economy. Lange designed a planning economy that can create an efficient system of relative prices using some data on the demand and supply structure that would clear the entire economy. This system of price is quite close to the market price in the efficient market. However, no organization was capable of doing so.

In the beginning of reform, all kinds of prices including commodity prices, factor prices, or exchange rate were under the administration of the planner. The reform of prices started from the lift of the word "merchandise" (*shangpin*). There was a special institutional construction known as "dual-track" pricing. After the Moganshan conference in 1984, in order to make amends for the loss and imbalance of the industrial structure because of the price distortion, the dual-track pricing policy came to the front. The dual-track pricing is to tag the commodity in plan with a planned price, leaving the unplanned commodity production to the market to decide. This institution is good for increasing production and also for the rent-seeking activities. During the late 1980s, brokerage became a very promising job and corruption stung the nerves of the central government, as the consequences were inconsistent with the prevailing ideology. In the meantime, the progressive policies carried out in a few years brought about a constant increasing inflation. In order to solve these problems, the central government decided to launch the price "breakthrough," which means to turn to market prices once and for all. This movement proved to be a failure. The ensuing political turmoil in 1989 called for a pause in economic reform. In 1992 when Deng Xiaoping made an inspection trip in the south, the reform began to regain its vigor and deregulation on prices picked up its speed. By the end of 1994, most commodities were included in the market pricing system and only some of the most important goods that are vital to economic security were still under government administration.

4.3 Reform of SOEs

SOEs are considered to be the dominant force of socialist China and provided for the Chinese government solely during the planning economic era. In 1956 when the socialist transformation was finished, there were hardly any private sector and the SOEs took over the Chinese economy entirely. In 1956, the SOEs were held by and controlled by the central government. Then after the talk of Mao, *On Ten Major Relationships*, the SOEs started to be assigned to local governance. In 1958, most of the SOEs had been assigned to the local administration and it meant a large amount of resources that local governments could use, which helped worsen the catastrophic result of the Great Leap Forward. This consequence resulted in SOEs' governance being withdrawn back to the center; hence, the Chinese reform fell into a dilemma of chaos or centralization.

The principal–agent problem and the integration of the government and the enterprise regime decided that the SOEs do not have incentives to lower their costs and increase the productivity. The SOEs were the dominant source of revenue for the government, yet they lacked creating more values. The original operating environment easily pushed them to the state of constant loss, which means the local government must help balance the debt among most of the SOEs. The enterprises finally became a fiscal burden. The central government decided to take the "decentralization of power and transfer of profit" strategy after 1976. The concern was no longer about the allocation of the governance but the profitability of the enterprises, trying to improve operational efficiency by increasing the autonomy of enterprises. In the 1980s, the central government finally approved the household responsibility system and the status quo of the SOEs forced them to try a similar arrangement on the enterprise administration. The reforms of SOEs were carried out by the inducement of a monetary reward with the intention of forming a compatible institution of the workers, management, and enterprise. With a soft budget and the ambiguity of ownership, supervisors managed to retain the low productivity. The SOEs ended up with the tragedy of the commons. No significant management improvement succeeded during

Table 5-1: Profit and loss of the SOEs nationwide (1990–1998).

(billion yuan)

Year	Scale of Loss (%)	Total Loss of the Loss SOEs	Total Profit of all SOEs
1990	30.3	93.26	49.15
1991	28.0	92.59	74.45
1992	22.7	75.68	95.52
1993	29.8	47.94	166.73
1994	32.6	62.45	160.80
1995	33.3	80.21	147.02
1996	37.5	112.70	87.67
1997	43.9	142.09	53.98
1998	47.4	196.02	−7.80

Source: Wu, 2010.

this time and the loss continued to grow. In the 1990s, the loss was out of control and the SOEs appeared as a "three thirds"[1] situation (Table 5-1).

From 1992, many local governments developed the reform on SOEs secretly because of the fiscal burden. The nation-wide reform was launched from 1997 to 2004, invigorating large enterprises while relaxing control over small ones. This time the reform was no longer in the operation pattern but the ownership. The main goal of this reform was to extract the state-owned capital from the competitive industries and only the industries that concerned the economy and national security were left to the large SOEs. There were 113,800 SOEs in 1996, and the number went down to 98,600 in 1997 and 64,000 in 1998. As the reform progressed, there were only 17,100 SOEs in 2011.[2] As there was no pricing system to show the actual value of the state-owned assets, the privatization of the SOEs was accompanied by the loss of the state-owned fortune to the private sector. The SOEs were never good at profiting because of their internal attributes and the present value of the SOEs was certainly not very high. Yet when the

---

[1] "Three-thirds" means that one-third of the SOEs were loss, one-third false profit, and one-third profit.
[2] From the historic record of the SOEs, we would see that the number did not fall in 2004 but increased from 34,300 in 2003 to 35,600 in 2004. This is because in 2004 a discussion on reform was launched. The discussion was about the actual form of reform and the speed and extent of the reform, which mostly concerned the cost of reform of SOEs.

privatization was finished and the state-owned assets found their way in a market-oriented profiting pattern, the value of the assets would be increased in quite a large scale. In this case, we could argue that the privatization promoted the growth of the Chinese economy in two ways: on the one hand, it helped lower the entry barrier in many industries. The market shares that used to be occupied by the SOEs were transferred to the private sector. Most importantly, when the SOEs were no longer interested in the relative industries, the administrative power would have no reason to maintain the protective measures and the competition would take over. On the other hand, the so-called loss of state-owned assets can be counted as a subsidy toward the private enterprises. The more capital the private enterprises have, the more risk they would take in either investment or R&D activities.

Furthermore, the reform of SOEs also has some other fundamental effects. Before the reform, the SOEs had quite a lot of market share. Through the industry chain and intersection relations, the price distortion from the SOEs' production could be delivered to other goods and cause a distortion in the entire comparative price system. Moreover, the exit of SOEs means opportunities for private enterprises to get over the entry barrier or to implement multiple operations by merging with the SOEs from another industry.

4.4 Reform in the Margins

Coase and Wang (2013) focused on the non-government-dominated economic reform. They defined household responsibility, town and village enterprises (TVEs), private enterprises, and the industry park as the "reforms in the margins" critical to the economic reform and growth.

In a few years before the 1978 third plenary session, the collective community or household in the rural areas made some institutional experiments spontaneously on agricultural production, like Jiulongpo in Pengxi County, Sichuan Province, or Xiaogang village of Anhui Province. The household responsibility system was first forbidden by the central government and then recognized and popularized in the entire country. This system broke the originally rigid distribution mode and granted sufficient incentive to the rural household. The agricultural production increased significantly from then on. In 1984, the grain total output exceeded 400 million tons, 33.6%

more than that in 1978; the cotton total output was about 6.3 million tons, 2.9 times that in 1978; the total output of both oil plants and sugar crops more than doubled. The rapid growth of agriculture brought higher income. In 1978, the rural per capita net income was 133.6 yuan; it was 397.6 yuan in 1985 and 686 yuan in 1990.

The household responsibility system is an efficient way of organizing agricultural production and released quite a lot of rural labor. The labor surplus was later recognized as the "demographic dividend." The TVEs were the first to take advantage of the "demographic dividend" as there were few obstacles within the collective communities. The cheap labor and the "three-tier" enterprise organization of the TVEs made sure of the progressive development of the collective sector (Jin and Qian, 1998). The first TVEs came from the commune's or production team's collective enterprises. While the local government found out about the productive way of organization, they encouraged and aided the rural communities to establish quite a quantity of TVEs. In 1990, the TVEs had employed more than 80 million workers. With the marketization during the 1980s, the TVEs show great advantage over the SOEs as they have harder budget constraints and more specific property right and thus more incentive to pursue profit. The small scale of the TVEs also provided for more elastic operation patterns.

The private sector has been another promoting force in realizing the "Chinese economic miracle." The reforms happened first in the rural area for a reason. The rural areas were not covered by a systematic social insurance institution and the house-site and the unpaid acquirement of the plough land has been the dominant way of social insurance. When the rural reform took place, the excessive labor supply caused great pressure in the urban area, too. The relaxed market environment for private enterprises to develop was only a breach in the regulatory institutions, which means it was not constructed by the top-level politicians but only out of their negligence. Both the private firms and self-employed entrepreneurs developed rapidly. The self-employed labor in the urban areas increased from 150,000 in 1978 to 316,000 in 1979 and 814,000 in 1980. By the end of 1989, the registered private enterprises nationwide had reached 90,600, with employment of 1.64 million workers; by 2006, the registered private enterprises nationwide had reached 4.98 million, with employment of 65.86 million workers and total registered capital 7,603 billion yuan.

Before the reform of SOEs, the private sector took a lot of the fiscal burden of the local government. With the low productivity of the SOEs, local development through positive governmental activities could only be achieved by investment on infrastructure and redundant constructions, which required enormous fiscal expenditure. The fiscal demand and the revenue structure formed a great margin to collect more tax and fees from the private sector. In fact, what we would see in the 1980s without the development of the private sector would be a classic disaster.

Decentralization helps the local government to perform well in the construction of industry zones, high-tech zones, or some other development zones. Investment promotion plays a vital role in governmental activities to ensure local development. The local governments have sufficient incentive to provide a low-cost investment environment, cutting down the approval processes, tax exemption, free land for constructions, etc. These measures are not against the will of the central government; thus, no specific institutional restraint would be applied in this circumstance. As a matter of fact, the private sector needs to rely on the local administrations to create a more specific certainty, while the entire institutional system could hardly provide certain expectations because of the omission of powerful legal binding. The cooperation between the enterprises and the local authority can be used to save a lot of risk management cost and when it comes to the agglomeration economy in the industry zones, this cost-saving usually comprises a huge amount.

These four types of reform in the margin happened spontaneously with the central government — which is supposed to be the provider of specific institutions — as only an *ex post* endorser. The low production of agriculture led to a basic need of the peasants' survival, which challenged the legality of the relative government. In this case, we can extend the theory of ideology to the local government and call it a sub-level design process, which makes no difference to the Coase and Wang theory. The TVEs started as some private economic parts that were institutional rebels while the title of collective enterprises would save a lot of trouble. The local governments gained a lot from it and there was no need to be tough on them, as it was not called on by the top authorities. The development of the urban private economy was tolerated because there were no thoughts that they may pose any threat to the SOEs, which proved to be wrong in the marketization course. Anyhow, the private sector helped stabilize the economy while the SOEs provoked all kinds of possibility of recession due to the reforms. The industry zones, on the other hand, prospered in the 1990s, when the basic market principles had been established. After the SOEs reform, the initiative activities of the local governments fell into subservience assisting the market forces against the top-level policies.

5. THE PROSPECT OF THE REFORMS

The top-level design and the innovation in the grassroots like the reforms in the margins drove the establishment of the market rules compatible with the Chinese economic and social realities, which is the essential premise for the rapid growth in the past three decades. Yet, the moderate reforms bypass the sharp contradictions related to vested interests and the accumulation has brought darkness to future development. The vested interests create huge institutional obstacles that the spontaneous orders could not easily breach.

Two conditions are to be met for the spontaneous order to settle. One is that the orders are compatible with the majorities within the relative scope and are recognized by them. The second is that it does not violate the interest of the relative political group. The local governments usually contribute to this settlement of the spontaneous orders just because these orders are adequate to promote economic growth and do not challenge the political or economic interests of the members of the authorities.

In the perfect theoretical world, the prices are determined by the relative supply and demand or expectations of them, while in the real world, they almost always are not. The information the relative prices would express must include the will of the administrative authorities and some other people's preferences. The will of the authorities is not constantly consistent. In most countries, the policy adjustments happen very frequently. This is the exogenous uncertainty that the relative prices also must imply. The uncertainty is the core source of contractual cost. In every nearly complete contract, the negotiation and the reinforcement must refer to some extra cost to prevent the uncertainty that might follow.

A complete pricing system and a relatively free operating environment are necessary for the persistent development of the Chinese economy. It means that the government must provide an institution system with low transaction cost and low-cost certain expectations to the agents. The spontaneous orders might alleviate the pressure to some extent, but outside the grassroots world, essential institutional progress would only be found in the relative subjects that determine the top-level ideology.

5.1 Government and Enterprises

At present, there are large portions of power that are left to the administrative authorities, even after 30 years of reform. The relationship between the government and the enterprises comprises the hardcore of the Chinese characteristic of a market economy. The government's examination and approval system has been a historical institution and it reached a peak after the socialist transformation. The approval procedures have been reduced in the past years but still play a significant part in ordinary commercial activities. It helps the governments to retain their authority over average agents in the absence of legislation. The huge power of the administrations is consistent with the interest of either the local or the central government. The fees charged within the process could bring in more revenue and the approval process allows the authorities to correct the wrong done by the spontaneous market activities. There are different levels of examination and approval procedures according to different levels of governments. The total items including national and local levels of approval procedures reached over 50,000 in 2001. After six rounds of reform, the number has been significantly reduced to around 18,000, of which most are local level at around 17,200. The intention of the procedure is to prevent the tragedy of commons and to ensure the production quality, public environment, or citizens' security, etc. However, as it had been carried out according to the needs of the relative authorities, the approval procedures gradually became a measure for the government to exploit the private individuals and enterprises. Rent-seeking is equilibrium without proper administrative laws.

Corruption is not necessarily bad for economic development as it can be a substitute to reduce transaction costs when the market institutions are not complete. The enterprises need a stable and predictable environment to invest and operate. When the bureaucrats become the source of uncertainty, it is wise to pay the rent to establish a long-term relationship to avoid possible barrier and other costs. The bureaucrats control the power of not only the approval but every procedure that concerns the ordinary operation. Paid rents would guarantee that risk of R&D, channeling, or reinvestment would be acceptable. On the other hand, the long-term relationship is also beneficial for the local government rather than the bureaucrats. The investment on "*guanxi*" with the bureaucrats is sunk cost. The enterprises would rarely choose to change their registration locations because of tax preferences offered by another region. The long-time cooperation makes it easy for the government to collect relevant information in order to decide the direction of development on industries.

However, as long as the bureaucratic performance examination system remains, it is impossible for the local governments to let go of the administrative powers over direct regulation on the enterprises. The investment of the private and other sectors is required for the economic growth and the direct regulation and relative resources like land and fiscal revenue in-budget or off-budget are the main tools to fulfill their goals. Even though it is necessary to restrain the powers they could manipulate, it is not easy to accomplish in the process of political negotiation.

5.2 State-Owned vs. Private

In 1997, the financial crisis of Southeast Asia gave the Chinese economy an enormous shock. A lot of private companies went bankrupt. This was just the darkness before the dawn, as in just a few years, the private capital grew rapidly in the course of reform in SOEs. The third discussion on reform happened in 2004 and it went on in the next four years. The conclusion about state-owned capital calls upon the State-owned Assets Supervision and Administration Commission of the State Council (SASAC), which was founded in 2003, to carry on the reform. The dominant spirit of reform inherited the former era and the SOEs were encouraged to exit the competitive industries. In fact, the reform has ceased since then. In a lot of industries, we could see that the large SOEs exploit other companies through relationship among industries. Large SOEs control the key industries from upstream, like electricity, oil, coal, electric communications, etc. Monopolistic powers were formed, as the large SOEs could bargain with the central government directly and forced the administrative monopoly to compromise. The SOEs made a comeback.

In 2005, the state council issued a file on encouraging and supporting non-public development, trying to break down the upstream monopoly. Nevertheless, in 2006, the subordinate department of the state council, SASAC issued another file ordering that seven industries including telecommunication, energy, etc. should be controlled by the state-owned capital, which is in direct opposition to the 2005 file of the state council. Although it was when the discussion was still going on, it shows the political bargaining power the large SOEs were holding.

Therefore, it is necessary to add the state-owned capital related groups to the ideology determination process. Large SOEs could easily buy their way into the central government. The senior management is anointed by the central government and the agents they have in the top authorities could express their political willingness in the administrative policy-making.

The large SOEs are still not able to walk out of the dilemma that could not be solved in the 1980s and 1990s. The low efficiency and high cost must be transmitted downstream by higher markup and the cost would be finally afforded by the customers. This type of monopoly is the hardest to break and is beyond the power of the local authorities. The provincial authorities share the same administrative rank with the SASAC. It is difficult for them to challenge this great wall. All they could do is just to mediate within the institutional framework the top level has decided. The mediation cost is a great concern for them. When the mediation cost is surpassed by the potential revenue, they would offer some tacit consent and support to the partially institutional breakthrough, as in the case of reform in the margins, while when the cost is too high, the local government would certainly find another choice to support, which usually means that no conditions for private enterprises would be improved.

The private economy is the most powerful and vigorous force in economic growth and is vital to the long-term persistent development in every country in history. According to the statistics of the All-China Federation of Industry and Commerce, the number of employees in private enterprises was more than 170 million in 2012 and 80% of the newly increased posts were created by them. The SOEs may have a good balance sheet with a huge amount of profit, yet most profit comes from the exploitation of the private economy. The normal profit the monopolistic powers could have is far lower than what they actually achieved.

Although the support to private enterprises could cause larger competition pressure to the SOEs, the efficiency that could be achieved would redeem the cost fairly easily.

5.3 Breakthrough of Further Reform

The local governments and the large SOEs have shaped the Chinese economy in the past two decades as a so-called Chinese characteristic socialist market. While the pricing system might be functional to some extent, there are no complete compensatory and supportive institutions that could help it function. The large scale of investment driven by the local governments and distorted comparative prices and production structure has been creating more and more problems economically and socially. It is urgent to push forward another round of reform.

In the theoretical framework established in this chapter, vested interest gains more rights of political expression and plays the game of ideology with the governments. They could stand in a dominant position while the average individuals and NGOs have to compromise. The local governments and the large SOEs set up the barriers for further reform.

The only way to correct the direction of development is to cultivate the market institution. The problem with the local governments is the performance examination system that has been the fundamental structure for Chinese political operation. The cost of reform on the entire political organization is too high to pay. The large SOEs, on the other hand, have too many political relationships with the authorities and their reform would be a reform of the authorities.

As long as the reforms are constrained outside the scope of direct interests of the local governments and the large SOEs, the obstacles would not be too tough to breach. People always pay more attention to the things that are obvious and neglect the secondary issues that might cause some dramatic changes. The goods market is the main battlefield for the large SOEs and the results that the local governments care about is also related to the final production. No government officials would consider the detailed production procedure as their work. Thus, the factor markets, capital and labor, could be the breakthrough for further reform. However, this is not as simple as it seems in the theoretical analysis. It would require more research as well as practical experience to form such a systematic reform project.

REFERENCES

Acemoglu, Daron and Simon Johnson (2005). Unbundling institutions. *The Journal of Political Economy*, 113(5): 949–995.
Aghion, Philippe, Eve Caroli, E. and Cecilia Garcia-Penalosa (1999). Inequality and economic growth: The perspective of the new growth theories. *Journal of Economic Literature*, 37(4): 1615–1660.
Bai, Chong-En, Yingjuan Du, Zhigang Tao and Sarah Y. Tong (2004). Local protectionism and regional specialization: Evidence from China's industries. *Journal of International Economics*, 63(2): 397–417.
Berkowitz, Daniel and Wei Li (2000). Tax rights in transition economies: A tragedy of the commons? *Journal of Public Economics*, 76(3): 369–397
Bernstein, Thomas and Xiaobo Lü (2000). Taxation without representation: Peasants, the central and the local states in reform China. *The China Quarterly*, 163(1): 742–763.
Burns, John (1999). The People's Republic of China at 50: National political reform. *The China Quarterly*, 159: 580–594.
Che, Jiahua and Yingyi Qian (1998). Insecure property rights and government ownership of firms. *Quarterly Journal of Economics*, 113(2): 467–496.
Che, Jiahua and Giovanni Facchini (2007). Dual track reforms: With and without losers. *Journal of Public Economics*, 91(11–12): 2291–2306.
Coase, Ronald (1937). The nature of the firm. *Economica*, 4(16): 386–405.
Coase, R. and Wang, N. (2013). *How China Became Capitalist?* Beijing: China Citic Press.
Epple, Dennis and Allan Zelenitz (1981). The implications of competition among jurisdictions: Does Tiebout need politics? *Journal of Political Economy* 89: 1197–1217.
Fleisher, Belton M. and Jian Chen (1997). The coast-noncoast income gap, productivity, and regional economic policy in China. *Journal of Comparative Economics*, 25(2): 220–236.
Garnaut, Ross, Ligang Song and Yang Yao (2006). Impact and significance of state-owned enterprise restructuring in China. *The China Journal*, 55: 35–63.
Guo, Xiaolin (2001). Land expropriation and rural conflicts in China. *The China Quarterly*, 166: 422–439.
Hayek, Friedrich A. (2003). *Individualism and Economic Order*. Shanghai: Shanghai Joint Publishing Press.

Huang Haizhou and Chenggang Xu (1999). Institutions, innovations, and growth. *American Economic Review*, 89(2): 438–444.

Hurwicz, Leonid (2007). *But Who Will Guard the Guardians? Nobel Prize Lecture*, http://nobelprize.org/nobel_prizes/economics/laureates/2007/hurwicz-lecture.html.

Jin, Hehui and Yingyi Qian (1998). Public versus private ownership of firms: Evidence from rural China. *The Quarterly Journal of Economics*, 113(3): 773–808.

Kornai, Janos (1986). The soft budget constraint. *Kyklos*, 39(1): 3–30.

Kornai, Janos (1992). The postsocialist transition and the state: Reflections in the light of hungarian fiscal problems. *American Economic Review*, 82(2): 1–21.

Kornai, Janos, Eric Maskin and Gerard Roland (2003). Understanding the soft budget constraint. *Journal of Economic Literature*, 41(4): 1095–1136.

Lau, Lawrence (1999). *The Macroeconomy and Reform of the Banking Sector in China*. BIS Policy Papers.

Lau, Lawrence, Yingyi Qian and Gerard Roland (2000). Reform without losers: An interpretation of China's dual-track approach to transition. *Journal of Political Economy*, 108(1): 120–143.

Li, Wei (1997). The impact of economic reform on the performance of Chinese state enterprises: 1980–1989. *Journal of Political Economy*, 105(5): 1080–1106.

Lin Justin Yifu and Guofu Tan (1999). Policy burdens, accountability and soft budget constraint. *American Economic Review*, 89(2): 426–431.

Maskin, E., Qian, Y. and Xu, C. (2000). Incentives, information, and organizational form. *Review of Economic Studies*, 67(2): 359–378.

Minsky, H. (2010). *Stabilize an Unstable Economy*. Beijing: Tsinghua University Press.

Montinola G., Qian, Y. and Weingast, B. (1995). Federalism, Chinese style: The political basis for economic success. *World Politics*, 48(1): 50–81.

Naughton, Barry (2000). *How Much Can Regional Integration Do to Unify China's Markets?* Center for Research on Economic Development and Policy Reform, Working Paper No. 58.

Nelson, R. and Winter, S. (2002). Evolutionary theorizing in economics. *The Journal of Economic Perspectives*, 16(2): 23–46.

North, Douglass (1992). *Structure and Change in Economic History*. Beijing: Commercial Press.

North, Douglass (2008). *Understanding the Process of Economic Change*. Beijing: Renmin University of China Press.

Olsen, Mancur (2005). *Power and Prosperity*. Shanghai: Shanghai People's Publishing House.

Qian Yingyi (1994). A theory of shortage in socialist economies based on the 'soft budget constraint'. *American Economic Review*, 84(1): 145–156.

Qian, Yingyi and Gérard Roland (1998). Federalism and the soft budget constraint. *American Economic Review*, 88(5): 1143–1162.

Qian, Yingyi (1999). *The Institutional Foundations of China's Market Transition*. Paper prepared for the World Bank's Annual Conference on Development Economics, Washington, DC.

Qian, Yingyi, Roland, Gerard and Xu, Chenggang (1999). Why is China different from Eastern Europe? Perspectives from organization theory. *European Economic Review*, 43(4–6): 1085–1094.

Shleifer, Andrei and Robert Vishny (1994). Politicians and firms. *Quarterly Journal of Economics*, 109(4): 995–1025.

Solow, R. (1956). A contribution to the theory of economic growth. *The Quarterly Journal of Economics*, 70(1): 65–94.

Tiebout Charles (1956). A pure theory of local expenditure. *The Journal of Political Economy*, 64(5): 416–424.

Tsai Kellee (2004). Off balance: The unintended consequences of fiscal federalism in China. *Journal of Chinese Political Science*, 9(2): 1–26.

Watson, Andrew, Christopher Findlay and Yintang Du (1989). Who won the wool War?: A case study of rural product marketing in China. *The China Quarterly*, 118: 213–241.

Wu, Jinglian (2010). *Courses on Contemporary China's Economic Reform*. Shanghai: Shanghai Far East Publisher.

Xu, Chenggang (2010). The fundamental institutions of China's reforms and development. *Journal of Economic Literature*, 49(4): 1076–1151.

Young Alwyn (2000). The Razor's Edge: Distortions and incremental reform in the People's Republic of China. *Quarterly Journal of Economics*, 115(4): 1091–1135.

Chapter 6

Whither Federalism, Chinese Style

Yongqin Wang*
School of Economics, Fudan University

This chapter systematically presents the successes and the failures of Chinese style federalism, which is a combination of political centralization and economic decentralization that provides local governments with strong incentives to develop the local economy. Simultaneously, Chinese style federalism has led to market segmentation, widening interregional development gaps, and problems in provision of certain public goods, among other emerging costs. The costs are intrinsically related to the political centralization and limited factor mobility. Therefore, the successes of China's transition will depend on how China handles Chinese style federalism and gets it right in terms of both political accountability and factor mobility.

1. INTRODUCTION

The last three decades have witnessed China's history-making economic growth. Whether the fast growth is sustainable not only concerns the welfare of 1.3 billion people at home, but also has significant effects on the global economy. Recently China's economy has reached a crossroad where economic growth and social development face a host of difficulties such as

---

*Yongqin Wang, School of Economics, Fudan University. Email: yongqinwang@fudan.edu.cn. This chapter partly draws on Wang *et al.* (2007).

176 *Economic Transition in China*

the widening rural–urban and interregional income disparity, segmentation of domestic markets, and lack of equity in provision of public services.

To take stock of China's past accomplishments and look ahead into its future challenges in a concise way, some consistent analytical framework is essential. A key observation is that both China's phenomenal achievements at the previous stages of reform and the emerging problems can be attributed to Chinese style federalism in one way or another. We will first establish a theory of Chinese style federalism to analyze its pros and cons for development. To a large extent, economists have reached some consensus on the benefits of Chinese style federalism. The most remarkable contributions on this topic are the theory of federalism based on the soft budget constraint theory (Dewatripont and Maskin, 1995; Qian and Roland, 1998; Qian and Weingast, 1997) and the theory of Unitary Organizational Structure versus Multi-division Organizational Structure (Qian *et al.*, 1988, 1999). These theories argue that the economic structure (such as the extent of decentralization and the organizational structure of the entire economy) accounts for the significant gap in economic performance between China and Russia in terms of economic performance during transition. Although these theories can shed some light on how decentralization fostered economic growth through yardstick competition among jurisdictions in China, they are not yet a complete theory. A complete theory of decentralization should be able to analyze the key tradeoffs of decentralization, especially the positive incentives (benefits of decentralization) of local governments versus their perverse incentives (costs of decentralization). In recent years, the effects of such perverse incentives observed in China are becoming increasingly obvious, with the most important being the widening income gap between urban and rural areas and across regions. Since there has already been a well-established literature on the benefits of Chinese style federalism, our analysis will focus on its costs.[1,2]

In this chapter, we will systematically address the following questions: What is the nature of China's style federalism? What are its emerging

---

[1] Decentralization has become trendy in the developing world in recent decades. For more general discussion on decentralization and development, see Bardhan (2002).
[2] Xu (2011) is an excellent survey of the institutional foundations of federalism, Chinese style.

economic and social costs? How to mitigate the costs through institutional reforms? We will see that despite the miracle of China's economic growth, Chinese style federalism has also contributed to the internal and external imbalance in China's economy. Internal imbalance at the micro level includes a widening income gap both across space and among different social groups, as well as unequal access to public service, among other things. Imbalance at the macro level consists of insufficient domestic demand, continuing high-level savings and investment rates, economic growth mainly driven by investment and exports, and the resulting excess capacity and excess liquidity since the mid-1990s. Internal imbalance led to the external imbalance characterized by the high dependence on foreign trade, rendering China's economic development excessively dependent on external economies. The imbalance has posed a serious challenge for the sustainability of China's economic development.

The rest of this chapter is structured as follows: Section 2 briefly discusses the benefits of Chinese style federalism and its role in China's rapid economic growth since the reform and opening up in 1978; Section 3 provides a framework to account for the emerging costs of the decentralization reform; Section 4 presents further analysis of the costs discussed in Section 3; and Section 5 discusses how to reform Chinese style federalism toward a real federalism in the future.

2. INCENTIVES FACING LOCAL GOVERNMENTS IN THE CHINESE STYLE FEDERALISM

Since China has a large land area and population size, supervision of local governments is costly for the central government. Therefore, it is important for China to decentralize.

It is well accepted that the enormous gap of performance in transition between China and Russia can be attributed to the difference in the degree of decentralization and the organization structure of economy. The decentralization reform in China boosted inter-jurisdictional competition for mobile factors and hardened the budget constraint facing state-owned enterprises (SOEs) (Qian and Roland, 1998). The multi-division economic structure in China allowed for institutional experimentation in some areas, and yardstick competition between jurisdictions offered effective information on the performance of local governments for the central governments, which enabled the economy to withstand macroeconomic shock with greater ease. In contrast, the unitary economic structure in Russia did not enjoy the benefits of a multi-division structure (Qian et al., 1999).

In contrast with other transitional economies (i.e., Russia), China's decentralization was realized in the reform process during which central and local governments continually adjusted their fiscal relationships, leaving overall political structure unchanged. China's economic and political reforms focused on providing incentives to local governments by the appropriate allocation of power and financial benefits between the central and local governments. It began with the policy of devolution of authority and profit sharing in the 1970s, continued with local authorities taking full responsibility of their finances in the 1980s, to the revenue-sharing system starting in the mid-1990s. Traditional fiscal decentralization theory states that local governments have information advantages and residents choose to stay or to leave when they observe the quality of public goods provided by the local government. This so-called "voting by foot" mechanism pressures local governments to supply quality public goods (Tiebout, 1956). Devolution of authority of taxation and expenditure from the central to local governments proved to be more conducive to boosting economic efficiency, accelerating local economic development, and furthering national economic growth (Buchanan, 1965; Oates, 1972). From the perspective of soft budget constraint the fiscal decentralization system can provide market-preserving incentives to local governments (Weingast, 1995; McKinnon, 1997; Qian and Weingast, 1997).

Using panel data of provinces in China, Jin et al. (2005) empirically find that China's provincial government fiscal incentives prior to revenue-sharing reform promoted market development. With regard to the relationship between China's fiscal decentralization and economic growth before 1992, Lin and Liu (2000) and Zhang and Zou (1998) reached contradictory conclusions. In an extended sampling research from 1986 to 2002, however, Zhang and Gong (2005) find a significant positive effect on economic growth of China's fiscal decentralization following revenue-sharing reform and this effect varied over time and across regions.

Fiscal decentralization alone is not sufficient to afford full incentives for local government to develop the economy. Most literature since the late 1990s has begun to pay attention to the special decentralization practice of developing countries. Blanchard and Shleifer (2001) emphasize the link between China's fiscal decentralization and political centralization through comparison of China and Russia.[3] In Russia, the central government retains weak control over local governments, and local governments do not have an incentive to further economic development. In contrast, China's fiscal decentralization is intertwined with political centralization, and career prospects alone provide local government officials with very strong (political) incentives to promote economic development (Zhou, 2004). Li and Zhou (2005) empirically find that promotions of governmental officials in China are positively related with the GDP performance in their jurisdictions.

Inter-jurisdiction yardstick competition is the most important channel through which fiscal decentralization and political centralization influence local government. The term of yardstick competition is used to describe a political system in which officials are responsible for constituents. That is to say, residents and the central governments have less information about the behavior of local governments than local governments themselves. But constituents will evaluate by comparing the performance of local government with that of other jurisdictions as yardstick, and knowing this, local officials will adopt economy-spurring policies similar to what is applied elsewhere (Besley and Case, 1995; Baicker, 2005). This would be considered a form of bottom-up yardstick competition since it is motivated by local constituents. Because jurisdictions at the same level monitor and learn from each other, it leads to an improvement in the efficiency of governments, reduction of administrative costs, and prevention of authority abuse (Martinez-Vazquez and McNab, 2003). Interestingly, China's political system is characterized by local government officials answering to their superiors rather than to local constituents. Under China's centralized political system and GDP-based relative performance evaluation of local officials, local governments are engaged in "top-down yardstick competition" based on higher-level government evaluation. Competing for growth provides a strong incentive

---

[3] In their words, "In China, local governments have actively contributed to the growth of new firms. In Russia, local governments have typically stood in the way, be it through taxation, regulation, or corruption." (Blanchard and Shleifer, 2001).

for China's local governments to spur economic growth and has been conducive to economic growth.

3. COSTS OF CHINESE STYLE FEDERALISM: PERVERSE INCENTIVES

The achievements of China's decentralization reform can be explained through market-preserving federalism (Weingast, 1995; McKinnon, 1997; Qian and Weingast, 1997). However, it is important to stress that the benefits of China's decentralization reform came with heavy costs. To complete the theory of decentralization, both the benefits and costs of decentralization reform should be analyzed. In this section, we analyze the incentive structure facing politicians in China's political system, which gives rise to emerging costs of Chinese style federalism, which will be elaborated in Section 4.

One of the major differences between China's and Russia's economic transition is the role of central government. China's decentralization reform took the entire economy as a political organization in which the central government developed incentive mechanisms similar to those within an economic organization. Since governments still had enormous control on economic, political, and social resources, it is essential for economic growth to provide local government officials with appropriate incentives, in order to align their interests with local development. The identification of the cost of Chinese style federalism is equivalent to identifying the cost of introducing market-like incentives within the political system. We need to first identify the concrete differences between incentives in public sectors and private sectors before we can identify some pitfalls of market-like incentives created by the decentralization reform.

According to contract theory, incentives in political organizations are significantly different from those in economic organizations. First, each economic organization usually has a single well-defined target, such as profit maximization, while political organizations have heterogeneous preferences. On top of that, each interest group has its own preference and interests. Therefore, it is very difficult to define a standard for performance measure. Second, differing from corporations, whose primary pursuit is profit maximization, political organizations are multitasking since the preference is heterogeneous. Political organizations differ from economic organizations because in addition to efficiency and economic growth, a political organization also needs to pursue other objectives such as justice, equality, environmental protection, and public service quality among others. Thus, given that a political organization has to serve multiple objectives, it is very difficult for it to use high-powered incentive schemes on a single dimension (single-task) basis similar to piece rate incentive schemes that are prevalent in firms. Furthermore, GDP growth based performance evaluation tends to undermine other objectives. This problem is fully reflected in local governments ignoring issues relating to environment, income gap, education, and healthcare. It is more difficult for a political organization to design strong incentives, so they typically default to fixed wages, a weak-powered incentive.

Third, principal heterogeneity coupled with different external conditions results in the third discrepancy between a political organizations and economic organizations. Unlike corporate performance evaluation replete with organizations as benchmarks, it is very difficult to find a well-defined benchmark for the performance of a political organization. For instance, China's government could by no means be compared with the US government due to myriad inherent differences. China's local jurisdictions can be compared with each other, but vast differences in factors such as resources and population across regions make the comparison much less meaningful.

The above-mentioned three characteristics simply mean that it is very difficult to find sufficient statistics for the performance of government officials. Thus, we are led to the fourth difference between political organizations and economic organizations. The incentive scheme in a political organization is more likely to be based on relative performance rather than absolute performance. In the real world, a relative performance evaluation based incentive scheme frequently used in political organizations is promotion. An important mechanism of China's decentralization reform is to promote local government officials by evaluating their relative performance based on the economic growth (especially GDP growth) of their respective jurisdictions (Li and Zhou, 2005). However, without sufficient statistics, the relative GDP growth is likely to be a sub-optimal indicator in evaluating local government officials' performance. Also, such fiscal decentralization combined with the relative performance evaluation system has profound deficiencies. The first deficiency is that relative performance evaluation will lead to sabotaging competition among agents. Local governments employ various beggar-thy-neighbor tactics in rivalry for better GDP rankings. A case in point is local protectionism in various forms, leading to regional segmentation.[4] The most far-reaching effect on resource allocation is that such market segmentation will restrict the market size for products and services. Market restriction will in turn further limit the division of labor and specialization among jurisdictions, and undermine the long-term technological progress and institutional evolution, eventually damaging China's long-term economic development and ability to compete on an international platform.

Because the primary source of economic growth comes from urban secondary and tertiary industries, excessive dependence on GDP-based relative performance evaluation increases the existing urban biases. Local governments now pay much less attention to economic development in rural areas, as is evidenced by the substantial decline in the ratio of expenditures supporting agricultural production to total expenditures by local jurisdictions (Lu and Chen, 2006). Additionally, because all localities count on external investment to fuel economic growth, growth oriented local governments favor capital owners' interests at the expense of the general workforce.

A prerequisite for relative performance evaluation to work is that agents are faced with common shocks, so the ranking can reflect their real performance by filtering out the common shocks (noise).[5] In such a large country like China with significant variations among regions in terms of geography, history and economic development, relative performance is a noisy indicator. As a result, the relative performance evaluation based incentive scheme will be less effective than expected. This can be perceived as the second deficiency of relative performance incentives.

The third flaw can be implied by the second deficiency. Economic growth differences induced by increasing returns may occur because of the innate variations (e.g., in nature, geography, history, society, etc.) across regions or the differential preferential policies for different regions. Even

---

[4]For more detailed discussion, see Yan and Lu (2003).
[5]A shock here means anything that is out of the control of the agents.

without other external influences, poor regions become poorer, while rich areas become richer (Lu et al., 2004), thereby magnifying the noises in relative performance evaluation. It will be very difficult for the central government to see whether local economic growth performance is due to the increasing returns or as a result of local government effort.

The fourth deficiency of relative performance evaluation is that the relative performance evaluation based "tournament" always results in few winners and many losers. More importantly, since more affluent areas enjoy intrinsic advantages and increasing returns, officials in local governments in underprivileged economic areas begin at a disadvantage and are thus unable to be incentivized by relative performance evaluation based schemes.[6] Given the slim probability of advancement, officials might even have perverse incentive and seek alternative compensations such as defalcation and corruptible activities, or simply "throwing the handle after the blade." Polarization will follow with rich jurisdictions getting richer and poorer jurisdictions getting poorer.

4. COSTS OF THE CHINESE STYLE FEDERALISM

4.1 Unbalanced Development

Here, we briefly summarize the costs of unbalanced growth and gaps in income, access to public services, and market segmentation, based on the previous analysis.

4.1.1 Widening income gap

The most direct cost of transition and development since the beginning of China's reform and opening up is the widening of the income gap (Li and Sato, 2004). The income gap between urban and rural areas is the biggest component of overall income inequality, and it tends to reinforce itself. The cross-regional income gap has a great deal to do with urbanization. Areas with little urbanization tend to have lower per capita income. The

---

[6]Given the regional discrepancy, the competition for capital between regions has weak incentives for regions not endowed with innate advantages, according to Cai and Treisman (2005).

contribution of the urban–rural income gap to regional income inequality is as high as 70–80% (Chapters 3 and 4).

As we pointed out in Chapter 3, the divergence between the lives of urban and rural residents is closely related to the fiscal decentralization system. Because the fiscal decentralization system provides the incentive for local governments to develop the local economy and because the assessment system for local government officials is based on the amount of economic growth and investment attracted, the government has focused on urban-oriented economic policies. This has significantly decreased the amount of money available for rural production and local financial expenditures (Lu and Chen, 2006).

The widening cross-regional income gap is related to the decentralized fiscal system. Under this system, local governments must compete with each other in economic development. Eastern areas tend to perform better than other areas because of their history, advantageous location, and the government's previous policies. This advantage is self-reinforcing; development fosters more development, and it is hard for the backward areas to catch up. Differences formed during the process of competition manifested during the process of opening up. Generally, China has a large labor force but not much domestic capital. This capital shortage should be addressed. Winning over foreign investors may be key to widespread economic development (Zhang and Xia, 2006).

Competition among regions is also reflected in the grants made to different areas by the central government. Whether because economically developed areas have more bargaining power or because the central government pays more attention to overall economic growth than balanced development, economically developed areas receive more investment from the central government. Since tax revenue returns consider the 1993 census figures as base numbers, these payments have widened the regional income gap since the late 1990s (Raiser, 1998; Ma and Yu, 2003).

Interpersonal income gaps also widened the income gap between urban and rural areas and among regions.[7] With the existing urban–rural divide,

---

[7] China's interregional inequality may have declined in 2004 and the urban–rural income gap may have declined in 2010, but this is still not clear. The confusion comes from constraints on interregional and rural-to-urban labor mobility and on the inequality-reducing effects of subsidies for the poor, neither of which are sustainable.

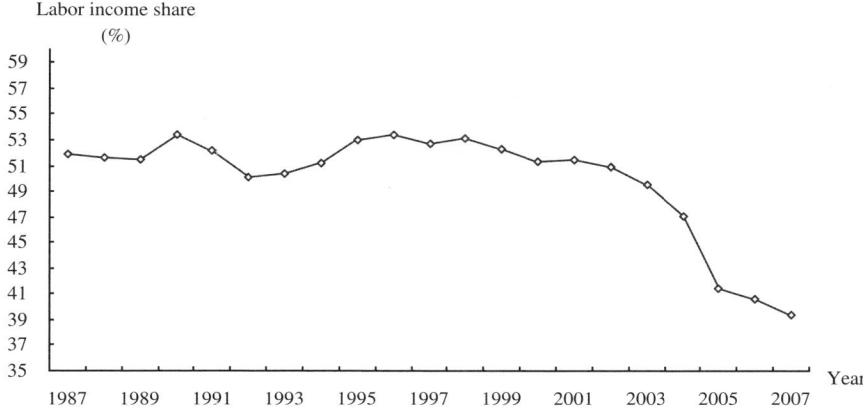

Figure 6-1: Proportion of national income made up by labor income.
Source: China Statistical Yearbook, China Statistics Press.
Note: In 2004, the sharp decline in the proportion of labor income was found to be related to the change in statistical criteria (Bai and Qian, 2009).

outflow of the rural labor force is restrained, and the marginal products of the rural labor force and the reservation wages of migrant workers have decreased due to the surplus rural labor force. This produces downward pressure on urban sector wages. Under the system of fiscal decentralization, local governments in China necessarily offer more protection to investors in order to attract more investment, especially because capital is rare. Laborers' rights are often neglected. Under this growth model, the income gap between capital owners and ordinary workers can widen. By 2007, the proportion of national income made up by labor income decreased from its peak in 1995 to less than 40% (Figure 6-1).

The widening of the income gap is also related to differences in social and political resources owned by different people. As discussed in Chapter 2, during marketization China's original social and political resources have been marketized and capitalized. Social relationships have not only improved the benefits of insiders, but also widened the income gap between insiders and outsiders. When the people with advantageous social relationships are also the ones with political and economic authority, income mobility may become limited as entrenched individuals monopolize opportunities.

4.1.2 Inequality and inefficiency of access to public service

In addition to the great differences in access to medical care, education, and social security between urban and rural areas, there is also a geographic problem. The locations of sources of public services are not themselves problematic. In many federal states, public services are provided by local governments. The short-term objectives pursued by local governments are often at odds with social objectives. Mechanisms that would inspire local governments to pursue long-term objectives are yet to be discovered. The development of education and medical care cannot promote economic growth in the short run, despite their far-reaching long-term significance. Local governments have been eager to shed the burden of education and medical care by carrying out marketization reform. Local government expenditures in these areas have decreased markedly, and central government expenditure fostering equal access to public services has become deficient. Only recently has the government paid more attention to improving people's livelihoods. Studies have found that fiscal decentralization discourages local governments from increasing expenditures in local public services (Fu and Zhang, 2007). As discussed in Chapter 5, the products and services surrounding medical care and education are sophisticated, and simple marketization reforms on the pattern of financing will exacerbate inequalities in access. This would not favor regions or individuals with low incomes as they attempt to develop human capital. Continued marketization of these fields creates both inequality and inefficiency.

Both public services and social security are linked to the household registration system, which impedes cross-regional labor mobility. The difficulty of cross-regional flow of factors promotes duplicate industrial structures and homogeneous competition among regions, which causes these regions to downplay their complementary strengths. If the laborers cannot move to developed areas freely, economies of scale cannot form. In this way, the existing public service system not only is in opposition to social equity but also works to the disadvantage of economic efficiency. The 17th National Congress of Communist Party of China (CPC) also pointed out that in order to narrow the cross-regional development gap, China must improve equal access to basic public services and promote reasonable factor mobility among regions.

4.1.3 Homogenous regional development strategies, market segmentation, and duplicate construction

When regions compete for economic growth and efficiency, local governments may turn to local protectionism and market segmentation. This has two causes:

First, the misallocation of resources and similar industrial infrastructure formed during the planned economy period. Industries and individual businesses that did not develop local advantages then continue to lack competitiveness under the market economy system (Lin, 2002). However, those industries and businesses still possessed great capacity for production, and they generated financial revenue for local governments. Protecting these local enterprises through market segmentation is, from the point of view of local officials, rational (Lin and Liu, 2004).

Second, increasing returns due to the process of learning-by-doing exist in many industries (especially growing industries with certain levels of technology). These industries have a certain first-mover advantage, and various regions are scrambling to develop so-called strategic industries, which leads to rounds of duplicated construction (Lu et al., 2004; Lu and Chen, 2006). When the issue of duplicate construction arises, market forces determine whether any given relevant enterprise will survive. When a region's strategic enterprises fail to compete, local governments turn to market segmentation and protectionism.

4.1.4 Increasing social costs of economic growth

Unbalanced growth also manifests in the sidelining of other development objectives, which increases high natural resource and environmental costs. The long-standing economic growth pattern adopted in China is highly dependent on exports. In China, labor is relatively inexpensive. This makes the country attractive to foreign investors, but it also makes China's growth dependent on low costs. A great many labor-intensive manufacturing industries consume resources and degrade the environment. Under

China's current system, local governments lack incentives to consider environmental and social costs.

Superficially, China's economic development exists on the basis of low cost. However, if implicit costs such as environmental and social costs are considered, then the price of China's economic development is much higher. China's aggregated emission of air pollutants remains high, and its carbon dioxide emissions are the highest in the world. Water quality is still far from satisfactory. On average 54% of the water in China's seven main rivers is not suitable for drinking. The estimated costs of premature deaths caused by environmental deterioration can reach 3.8% of GDP (World Bank, 2007).

Local governments also lack incentives to regulate labor and promote quality standards. Even if the country has national regulations, they cannot always be carried out at the local level. In recent years, accidents such as mine disasters and failures in product quality failures have been frequent. For example, according to the data from the State Administration of Work Safety, China produced 1.66 billion tons of coal in 2004, accounting for 33.2% of the worldwide total. However, deaths in mine disasters reached 6,027, accounting for 80% of the worldwide total. Local governments often skimp on safety regulations so that local businesses can reduce costs. Recent years have witnessed many food scandals, which caused national sensation and discontent among the people.

Pollution and overutilization of resources both reduce the benefits of China's GDP growth to the public and reduce the country's chances for sustainable development. If the pattern of economic growth is not adjusted in a timely manner, the constraints of the environment and finite resources may cause a bottleneck. China ranks 133 out of 144 on the international Environmental Sustainability Index. China's pattern of economic growth is dependent on the consumption of natural resources.

4.2 Macroeconomic Imbalances and the Dilemma of Economic Growth

China's economy experienced great highs and lows during the 1980s. After the mid-1990s, the macro economy tended to become stable, but structural conflicts became more and more evident. The structural imbalances in China's macro economy come from the imbalances discussed in Section 1.

Its ultimate origins can be traced back to the system factors relevant to the pattern of unbalanced growth.

Indicates that the reform of decentralization and other coordinated reforms initiated in 1994 increased the total output of the economy and eliminated the cyclical phenomenon of disorder without management and controlled stagnation,[8] which had troubled China for many years. This could be considered a positive result of decentralization reform. In this way, 1994 was a watershed year for China's macro economy. The pattern of government credit and money management and the mechanism of inflation (and deflation) changed markedly.

4.2.1 China's macro economy since 1978

If we divide the macro economy into two phases using the year of the implementation of the tax-sharing system, 1994, then the Chinese economy can be considered to have been under soft budget constraints from 1978 to 1994. This is common in traditional socialist planning (Kornai, 1986). This period featured expansion of both investment and consumption, but the economy still had many characteristics of a shortage economy, in which the macro economy experienced a cycle of disorder without management and controlled stagnation. As shown in Figure 6-2, there were huge changes in the relationship between economic growth and inflation before and after 1994, when the previous economic cycle disappeared.

Consumption and investment in GDP

Over the past 30 years, the proportion of China's GDP made up by domestic (resident) consumption has decreased, and the proportion made up of investment has increased. As shown in Figure 6-3, during the 10 years prior to economic reform, the investment rate was about 36%. This rose quickly after the 1990s, and in 2003, 2004, and 2005, it reached 43%. The long preceding period of high savings rates made this high investment rate sustainable. The savings rate in China was as high as 50% in 2005. From 2001 to 2005, investment made up over half of the GDP. This was

---

[8]This is a popular description of macroeconomic fluctuations in China in the 1980s and early 1990s.

190 *Economic Transition in China*

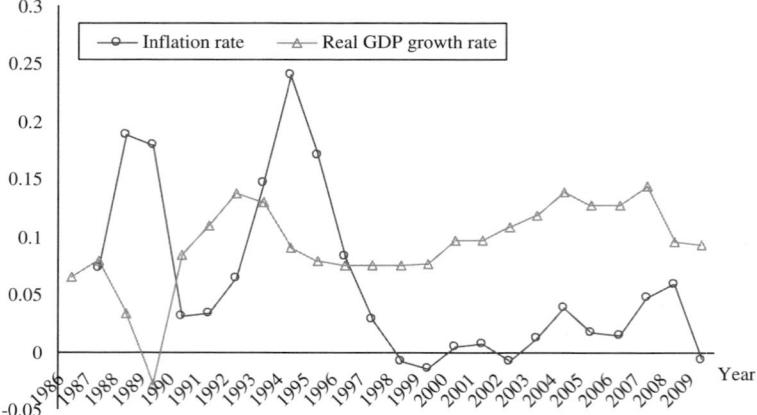

Figure 6-2: Growth of real GDP and inflation (1986–2009).
Source: *China Statistical Yearbook* (various years), China Statistics Press.

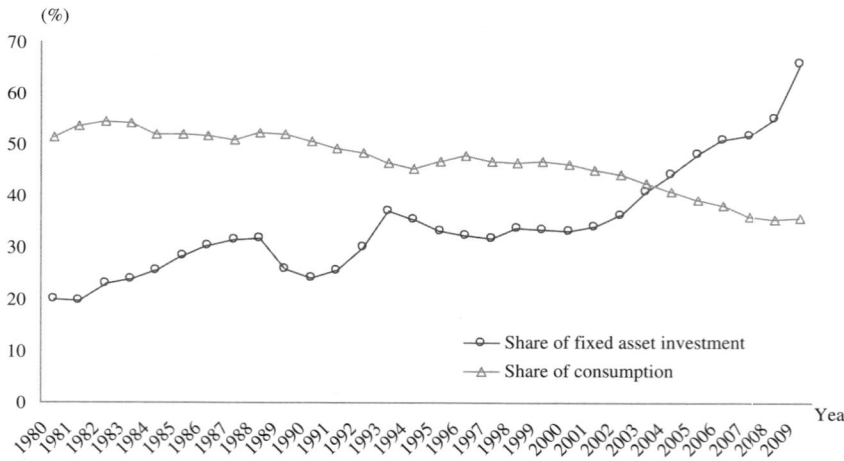

Figure 6-3: Proportion of fixed asset investment and household consumption in GDP (1970–2009).
Source: *China Statistical Yearbook* (various years), China Statistics Press.

remarkably higher than the rate of investment in other East Asian countries during the same development phase (Lardy, 2007). Due to the insufficiency of domestic consumption demand, China had to rely on exports to maintain economic growth, and the proportion of exports in GDP has increased

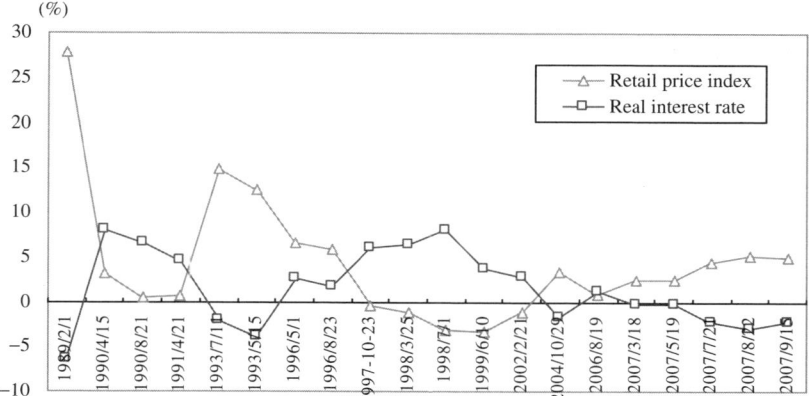

Figure 6-4: Retail price index and real interest rate for saving in China from Feb 1989 to Sep 2007.
Source: China Statistical Yearbook (various years), China Statistics Press.

yearly. Figure 6-3 shows the changes in fixed asset investment and household consumption during the past 30-plus years. Increases in the proportion of fixed asset investment clearly opposed that of consumption.

Excess liquidity since the mid-1990s

Many scholars measure excess liquidity from the perspective of the money supply (the ratio of M2 to GDP). However, excess liquidity is not solely a monetary phenomenon. Rather, it is the result of structural changes in the economy, domestic and foreign. One practical method of judging whether liquidity is excessive is to determine whether the real interest rate decreases over time. That can indicate equilibrium between the supply and demand of liquidity very precisely. From 1994 to just before the recent economic crisis, the real rate generally decreased (Figure 6-4).

4.2.2 Micromechanism of the imbalances of China's macro economy

One key to understanding the economic decentralization and macro economy that have existed in China since the reform and opening up is to understand how decentralization has changed the degree of governmental soft budget constraints on SOEs and the creation of liquidity. There are two other kinds of economic reform: marketization reform and fiscal decentralization reform. The first involves the gradual loosening of price controls and the introduction of market mechanism in which the decentralized allocation of resources renders more resources available to non-SOEs in an efficient manner. The latter involves the transfer of financial activities from the central government to local governments.

Effect of soft budget constraints on the macro economy before 1994

Soft budget constraints appeared in the planned economy whenever the central government had to rescue SOEs, usually when they suffered losses. Even when the government announced ahead of time that it would not bail out SOEs in the red, no one believed it (Kornai, 1986). In a highly centralized planned economy, the government is the only investor in SOEs. If one investment has problems, the government increases funding. This prevents the termination of projects that incur losses. It is even harder for the government to shut down operations that provide employment or social security services.

From 1978 to 1994, the reform of marketization and fiscal decentralization were carried out simultaneously. One characteristic of marketization reform is that the market share of the non-state-owned sector increases (both private and township-owned businesses). The deepening of marketization reform increased the amount of resources (including financial resources) allocated to the more efficient non-state-owned sector, which led to economic growth. During this period of incremental reform, the government neither loosened regulations nor privatized the state-owned sector. It only introduced non-state-owned economic entities in the margin. The government's soft budget constraints on the state-owned sector remained. Fiscal decentralization was indicated by the constant decline of the proportion of the central government's financial revenue and the continuous rise of the revenue of local governments (Chapter 2). During this period, there were no fundamental changes in the governmental soft budget constraints on state-owned entities, and the system of fiscal decentralization limited the financial strength of the central government. When the economy is in a depression, the government lacks sufficient financial resources to give aid to SOEs. The reform of the banking sector also prevents the government from directly interfering with the banks' credit habits. The only method remaining to the government is to pull the economy out of its depression by printing more money, which then causes inflation during periods of economic expansion. For this reason, growth and inflation have tended to occur simultaneously in China during this period (Brandt and Zhu, 2000). If the government withdraws power to award in financial field and directly controls the credit market, then economic depressions will be more frequent. That is the cause of the periodic fluctuation of disorder without management and controlled stagnation under control that occurred in the macro economy during this period.

Changes in the structure of the economy since 1994

The year 1994 was a watershed for economic reform in China. In 1994, the government announced the transition from the previous incremental system of reform to all-around reform. Along with the establishment of the modern enterprise system, reform of the tax-sharing system, and commercial bank reform, the problem of soft budget constraints that had originally limited SOEs was fundamentally changed. Reform of the tax-sharing system clearly defined the tax collection rights of the central and local governments. All previous attempts at separating tax revenue had failed, including those made from 1980 to 1987 and the fiscal contracting system implemented from 1988 to 1993. Under this contracting system, the fiscal retention rate between each region and the central government was set at a one-to-one discussion between local and central governments and based on historical statistics. This kind of arrangement did not clearly define the tax base and allowed interregional inequities to persist. The fiscal responsibility system also increased the financial revenue of the local governments. The central government's financial revenue continued to decrease. During the early 1990s, half of the central government's expenditures were sustained by debt (Wu, 2003).

The reforms in the tax-sharing system in 1994 clearly defined the tax base and the proportion of tax due to the central and local governments. The influence of these reforms had far-reaching impact. It promoted large-scale

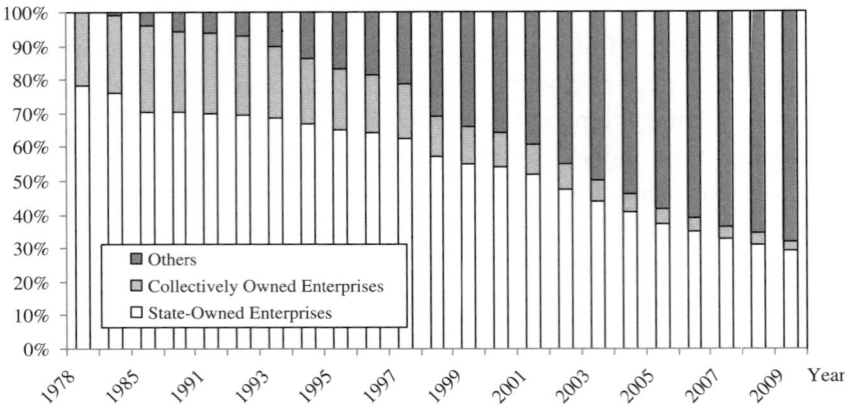

Figure 6-5: People employed by urban businesses according to ownership (1978–2009).
Source: China Statistical Yearbook 2010, China Statistics Press.

privatization of SOEs. Because most taxes went to the central government after the reform of the tax-sharing system on condition that the duties, responsibilities, and expenses of local governments would not decline, great pressure was brought to bear on local financial institutions. The privatization of inefficient SOEs was the usual strategy chosen of local governments (Zhang and Li, 1998; Li *et al.*, 2000). At the end of the 1990s, the non-state-owned economy made up the largest proportion of the national economy, becoming the fundamental power behind economic growth. Changes in China's urban ownership structure from 1978 to 2009 are shown in Figure 6-5. Changes in the ownership structure of the main economic indicators of industrial enterprises in 2009 are shown in Table 6-1. Both these figures show that the non-state-owned economy had become the absolute majority in each indicator.

Reform of the tax-sharing system diminished soft budget constraints. Privatization lessened government constraints on SOEs. However, there were still government constraints on some SOEs. The tax revenue of the central government increased after the reform of tax-sharing system, which made it unnecessary for the central government to invest in or protect SOEs to produce funds. These two effects both removed some of the motivation of central government to print more money. In this way, they decreased the pressure of inflation.

Table 6-1: Main indicators of all state-owned and non-state-owned industrial enterprises grossing more than 100 million yuan size in 2009.

Item	Number of enterprises (units)	Total volume of industry (price in relevant year)	Total capital	Revenue of the main business	Total profit	Annual average number of all employees (10 thousands)
Total	358,988	395,625	369.215	392,259	21,824	6,380.8
Stateowned enterprises	9,105	45,648	68,685	47,035	24,435	639.1
Proportion (%)	2.53	11.53	18.60	11.99	8.08	10.02
Collective enterprises	10,285	9,587	5,016	9,451	1,973	199.3
Proportion (%)	2.87	2.42	1.36	2.41	2.61	3.12
Others	339,598	340,389	295,514	335,773	21,824	5,542
Proportion (%)	94.60	86.04	80.04	85.60	89.31	86.86

Note: Non-SOEs grossing more than 5 million yuan per annum are listed.
Source: *China Statistical Yearbook 2010*, China Statistics Press.

Reform of the banking system solved the problem of government soft budget constraints on the state-owned sector. The establishment of China's commercial banking system had a late start and the system was under the administrative control of the central bank for a long time. This is in fact a characteristic of economic depression. The real official interest rate was generally negative. Since the beginning of China's reform and opening up, local banks have made annual plans to distribute credit. Each province also had a fixed investment share for SOEs and non-SOEs. This prevented capital from being allocated efficiently through the market. As China's economy developed, the right to distribute credit was gradually delegated to local banks. This tightened the relationship between local governments and banks, and it became capable of interfering with the distribution of credit from local governments, strengthening soft budget constraints. After the delegation, local governments were not willing to re-implement unified credit planning, but instead began to direct the capital under their control more efficiently, especially to non-SOEs. However, the central government still resorts to credit planning management, which it uses to control the loans made by state-owned banks, to limit the loans made out of the credit plans of state-owned banks, and emphasize the personal obligations of local leaders and state-owned bank leaders to complete their credit plans. From 1979 to 1993, 84% of the new loans went to SOEs, 33% of which were approved by the central bank. These "loans" were not usually expected to be paid back, creating an unhealthy situation for the banks.[9]

Banking system reform did not move toward marketization until 1994. Then the central bank shifted control of the money supply from a multi-level system to control by the central government. It also established an indirect controlling system. The object at this stage was also changed from a credit capital scale to a money supply system, and the application of various monetary policy tools became progressive. This weakened local governments' control of the banks, and it became difficult for local governments to allocate credit to banks. More loans then went to businesses that had shown better performance. The financial system was decoupled from the state-owned sector. This also tightened budget constraints.

The comprehensive reforms initiated in 1994 had three general macroeconomic results: First, the inflation cycle, which had been highly problematic from 1978 to 1994, disappeared. Second, production overcapacity gradually emerged. Third, excess liquidity began to appear and accumulate.

The reform of the tax-sharing system clarified the manner in which local taxes were to be distributed, making local governments compete fiercely to construct better infrastructure to attract investors and increase local GDP growth. Under the "small but comprehensive" industrial strategy of the period of the planned economy, investment was more or less equally distributed across regions, which intensified overinvestment and overcapacity. China's current development phase also causes the concentration of certain industries in certain places (Lin, 2007). In developed countries, private businesses tend to develop new technology. These businesses also absorb the risk and uncertainty of new ventures. In developing countries, private businesses are usually far from cutting edge. They usually select relatively mature and safe projects to invest in. Many businesses select the same industry or type of project to invest in, which leads to overinvestment and overcapacity.

---

[9] *Source*: *China Statistical Yearbook* (various years), China Statistics Press.

Overcapacity causes the total supply of many types of products to expand continuously. However, this can tighten the budget constraints of certain types of enterprises. The government no longer bails out SOEs by increasing the money supply. This creates a relatively stable amount of investment demand, but it also increases the gaps between urban and rural areas and among regions. The interpersonal income gap is also enlarged due to the reform of urban marketization. Because of this, consumer demand is relatively small. The slow increase in residents' consumption of Chinese-made goods and services is closely connected to the household registration system and the urban–rural divide. Large numbers of migrants relocating from rural to urban areas lack official urban registration. Because this makes many basic social services, such as education and pensions, more expensive and less accessible, they must cut back on their consumption of durable commodities and save much of their income for the future. They also face discrimination in the credit market. Migrants' marginal propensity to consume is an estimated 14.6% lower than that of official urban residents (Chen et al., 2010). The expansion of aggregate supply and the relative insufficiency of aggregate demand have caused increased production and declining prices. This is in consistent with the performance of China's macro economy after 1994 (Figure 6-6).

The phenomenon of excess liquidity was at first related to the development of the economy, urban marketization reforms, and the urban–rural division of the economy. Because of the way rural-to-urban migration is

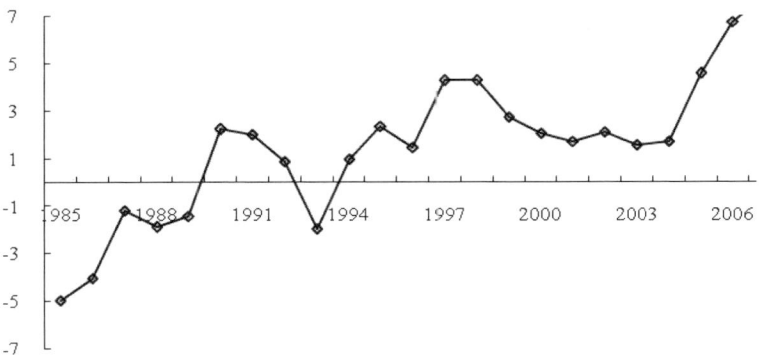

Figure 6-6: The proportion of China's trade surplus to GDP (1985–2008).
Source: *China Statistical Yearbook 2007* and the author's calculations.

regulated, the labor supply is greater in rural areas than it would be if China had free labor mobility. Considering rural land and capital resources, this lowers the marginal production of the rural labor force, which in turn determines the reservation wage of migrant workers. In the urban labor market, although the migrant workers face discrimination by the system, they are still able to compete with urban laborers. In this way, the low wages of migrant workers limit all wage growth in the urban sector. Slow increases in wages allow businesses to reap more profits. Savings and investments from the business sector increase rapidly. The reality of low wages and high profits makes up for the inefficiency of the domestic banking system by allowing businesses to rely more on internal financing through profits, decreasing their dependence on external financing and relieving the credit constraints brought on by China's inefficient financial system. Because it promotes high levels of investment, labor productivity increases much faster than wages (*The Economist*, 2007). A high level of investment increases China's production capacity, but sluggish wages limit increases in domestic demand. This leaves the economy heavily reliant on exports and further investment, and structural imbalances gradually grow more pronounced.

The comprehensive structural reform of the mid-1990s changed the nature of China's economic cycle. The tax-sharing system, among other important reforms, eliminated the phenomenon of soft budget constraints, the recruitment of SOEs through government increases in the money supply, and a great deal of the country's demand-pull inflation. However, the low wages caused by the surplus of rural labor and the minimal leverage of laborers throughout China has also greatly reduced eliminated cost-push (especially wage) inflation. Due to the reform of SOEs that took place in 1996, competition within the urban labor market has intensified, creating downward pressure on wages in cities. The widening income gap has limited the growth in demand. On the supply side, more intense regional competition and the rapid development of the non-state-owned economy have led to the rapid growth of production, creating deflation pressure.

Figure 6-6 summarizes the mechanism of the changes in China's macro structure after 1994. As shown in the figure, internal imbalances can become external imbalances. When there is insufficient domestic aggregate demand, China must depend on rapidly increasing amounts of exports to maintain the high speed of its economic growth. Increases in domestic wages have lagged behind increases in labor productivity, which have greatly increased the international competitiveness of China's products and has created conditions that facilitate increases in exports. After 1994, the long-undervalued RMB helped keep the prices of China's products low.

The rapid expansion of exports eliminated the trade deficit in the mid-1990s, which rapidly became an international trade surplus after 2005, creating an external imbalance. Since 1994, China's trade surplus has continued. Figure 6-6 depicts the proportion of foreign trade surplus to GDP, which is also soaring. Figure 6-7 portrays China's foreign trade dependence (i.e., proportion of imports and exports to GDP), which was as high as 70% in recent years. Such high trade dependence is rare in the world. While the existence of trade surplus shows the international competitiveness

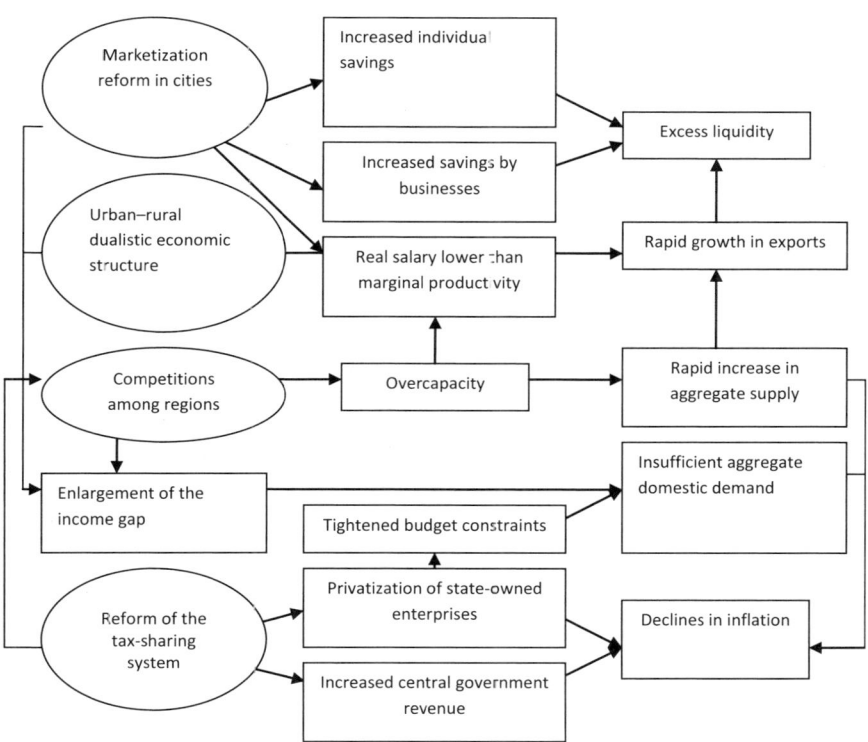

Figure 6-7: Micro-foundation of China's macro economy.

of Chinese goods, the proportion of trade surplus and the dependence on foreign trade is indeed too high for a large country like China. This shows a serious lack of domestic demand. As a result, China's economy is very sensitive to external economic fluctuations, increasing China's macroeconomic risk.

5. REFORMING FEDERALISM, CHINESE STYLE

Chinese style federalism, a combination of political centralization and economic decentralization, despite its growth effects, has been causing huge socioeconomic costs and has caused macroeconomic imbalances across the board. The evidence has shown that the system is not sustainable, given the increasing costs. And we believe that the success of China's transformation crucially depends on the reform of the current system.

5.1 Further Deregulation and Liberalizing the Factor Markets

In the earlier period of economic transformation, the economic structure of an economy is relatively simple and the production technology was far from the world technology frontier. What matters then is to mobilize resources and exploit the existing technologies. In this investment-based growth stage, rapid economic development can be achieved provided certain institutions (e.g., centralized system) to mobilize resources are in place (Acemoglu et al., 2006). However, with further economic development, such short cuts will be exhausted. Finally, the day will come when the economy has reached the world technology frontier and it will need innovation-based growth. This shift calls for a corresponding change in the role of government. In particular, the government should withdraw from the substantial interventions in economic activities to have a more arm's length relationship with business.

Meanwhile, the government should focus on the provision of public goods. As China is moving from a moral economy to a market economy, the traditional social networks for risk-sharing are dismantled, and the alternative public good provision by the government is yet to come, especially in terms of social security, healthcare, and education. Furthermore, the government should implement progressive reforms to narrow the income gap. The government should not only make proper redistribution through suitable taxes and transfer payments, but also create a fair and just environment for competition.

Economic resources controlled by local governments should be reduced through further deregulation. Given the special political and economic structure previously described under the Chinese style federalism, deregulation at the local level should be prioritized, to weaken the status as political entrepreneurs of local officials. A major objective of the deregulation is to reduce the central government's dependence on local governments and concurrently the role of the relative performance evaluation based incentive scheme, and hence reduce local protectionism among other costs associated with relative performance evaluation. Along with deregulation at the local level, measures should be taken to push domestic market integration toward a fully integrated national market, which will greatly boost specialization, endogenous technological progress, and economic growth.

In particular, factor markets such as land, labor, and financial markets still have a long way to go. Urban lands, nominally state-owned assets, were actually monopolized by local governments. Because of institutional factors such as the household registration system, the mobility of labor force between urban areas and rural areas was strictly limited and thus the freedom of labor force market was vastly limited. From the angle of production chain, Chinese manufacturers (mostly composed of private enterprises) of downstream industries (final products) were competitive, but upstream (factors or intermediate products) industries (mostly comprised of SOEs) were non-competitive (monopoly or oligopoly). Moreover, most Chinese downstream firms are labor-intensive industries characterized by low entry cost and near perfect competition, and the profit margin is extremely low. The market monopoly of upstream factors and intermediate products exacerbated the difficulties facing downstream industries and increased the input product price so that Chinese downstream manufacturers lost competitiveness in global markets prematurely. The delay of labor market liberalization seriously impeded the growth of downstream industries and aggravated the income gap between upstream and downstream industries. Therefore, the burning issue to be addressed for the next step of reform is to liberalize factor markets.

Liberalizing factor markets has important implications for local governance. Since China's local officials are appointed by the central government, they are not accountable to the local people. Enhanced factor mobility, in particular, labor market mobility will introduce the "exit" mechanism to local governance, which may enhance the competition of local governments for the provision of public service (like health and education) in the sense of Tiebout.

5.2 Getting the Decentralization of Public Good Provisions Right

A natural rationale for fiscal decentralization is to improve the efficiency of public goods provision through inter-jurisdiction competition. It is prohibitively costly for the central government to get perfect information to aggregate the preferences of local residents and efficiency of public goods provision by local governments. A theoretical insight is that if residents can move freely among jurisdictions, the voting by foot mechanism will lead to efficient provision of local public goods (Tiebout, 1956).

Take education for example: people will leave if they are not satisfied with the education provided by the local government. This in turn lowers market prices of real estate. Both factors influence human resources and economic growth in the jurisdiction. Hence, due to discretion of residents over where to live and reactions in local real estate markets, the investment in education and quality of education is "capitalized" through real estate markets. For instance, in the United States, residents vote on the rate of property tax to finance fiscal expenditure for public education. Parents choose the neighborhoods best satisfying their education demand. The tax base for education expenditure is property tax that depends on the value of real estate. Thus, through its influence on property values investment in education and quality of education is closely related to economic growth and revenue of local jurisdiction. Education expenditure based on property tax works as an efficient mechanism for local governments to provide quality education (Hoxby, 1995).

In China, although education expenditure is not financed by property tax, the mechanism by which people choose the best education service by changing their residences and, in turn, influence property values still exists. The price of real estate influences revenue from land lease and realty transfer tax and income of and education received by local residents. All these will have great impact on economic development and revenue of local jurisdictions in a direct or indirect way. Empirical evidence in the United States shows centralization in fiscal expenditure for public education is harmful to the efficiency of education provision (Hoxby, 1995; Peltzman, 1993, 1996).

In China, public services like education and medical service are provided by local governments, but there is widespread discontent among the public with the provided service.[10] This seems at odds with the efficiency result a la Tiebout we discussed. And why is that? Now we turn to the potential equity and efficiency loss in public service provision under Chinese style federalism.

Under the current system in which local officials get promoted based on local economic growth, local governments prefer those activities that will boost economic development in the very short run and neglect long-term objectives. For instance, provision of education and medical service has no immediate effect on economic growth, but it is very important in the long run. Moreover, it is difficult to design incentive schemes for local governments to pursue long-run social objectives. Local governments take education and medical service as a "hot potato" and have conducted large-scale marketization reform in this arena. Although there is no inherent flaw in fiscal decentralization for public goods provision, government investment is insufficient in public services such as education and medical service due to lack of an effective incentive mechanism.

Though the general inefficiency in the government organizing all economic activities in the era of planning economy is well known, the proper scope of government in a market economy needs further consideration. In this regard, Hart *et al.* (1997) show that the proper boundary between the government and the market depends on property of products. The private sector has an incentive to reduce cost, thus it is more efficient if products are supplied by markets when quality of products is easily monitored. But when quality of products is not observable and verifiable, private suppliers tend to reduce cost at the expense of quality, so provision or intervention by government is more efficient. Apparently, services like education and medical service fit into this category.

---

[10] A survey shows that 90% of the people are discontented with the reform of medical care (*China Youth Daily*, 2005).

Now we can see that provision of local public service by local governments under fiscal decentralization is more efficient. And local governments should take the responsibility of public goods provision instead of shirking their duty by complete marketization and privatization. Because the local officials' promotion system in China relies too heavily on economic growth, there is inefficiency in the provision of local public service. For local governments to provide public service efficiently, the central government needs to design effective incentive schemes and intervene wherever necessary. For the global public goods (bads) or the public goods (bads) with interregional externalities, like food security, social security, environmental protection, and judicial justice, the central government should take more responsibility, since the local government will not do a good job and quite to the contrary, they may "race to the bottom." In particular, considering China's undergoing urbanization, the *hukou* system, which ties people's social welfare programs to local governments, is harming labor mobility and the central government could centralize certain programs and make them portable to facilitate urbanization.

5.3 Reforming Local Government Finance

From a financial perspective, because local governments can still create excess liquidity and financial resources, local deregulation alone is not enough. Although decentralization reform hardened the local government's budget constraint, local governments can still create liquidity. Local governments can create liquidity through: (1) intervening in loans of local banks; (2) creating a large amount of off-budgetary revenues by arbitrary fee collection; and (3) creating a large amount of "capitalized" revenues through land leasing in the process of marketization and urbanization. In terms of a soft budget constraint, the effects of liquidity creation on resources allocation are equivalent to those under centralization (Dewatripont and Maskin, 1995). Therefore, although fiscal decentralization can harden the soft budget constraint facing local governments, the endogenous liquidity creation has a countervailing effect.

Left unbridled, such liquidity creation may have the following consequences: (1) budget constraint facing local governments will not be hardened and protection of inefficient state-owned sectors will continue (though such phenomena currently are not pervasive); (2) when the factor markets are imperfect, discretionary land leasing by local government to generate fiscal revenue will significantly distort the asset markets; (3) the liquidity creation capability varies greatly from region to region due to differences in natural condition, the scale of economy, and preferential policies, widening the interregional development gap and disparity in the provision of local public goods.[11]

In terms of the timing of the reform, given that local government has already finished the historical mission of marketization, privatization, and infrastructure construction at the local level, restricting their creation capability will at the current stage be less costly (liquidity creation was conducive to infrastructure construction at the early stage). Liquidity creation may be limited through reduction of the intervention in state banks by local government, reduction of the discretion of local government in land leasing, and improvement in the budgeting process of local governments to control their off-budget revenue.

The financing of urbanization and local public goods relies crucially upon the revenue from land lease and sale, which has created property bubbles in certain Chinese cities. Rising housing prices have become a severe social and political concern. A more sustainable way is to try to introduce local government bonds and property tax, as a substitute for the financing based on land leases and sales.

5.4 Improving Governance and Accountability of Local Governments toward Real Federalism

Last but not least, it is essential for China to reform the accountability and governance of the local government constitutionally. When it comes to "soft" public goods (such as education and medical care) provision by local governments, there is much room for improvement. Given the informational disadvantage on the part of the central government, it is necessary to keep the provision decentralized, but with more accountability of local governments. In the words of Hirschman (1970), if the previous reform mainly

---

[11] Given its limited space and subject matter, this chapter does not involve the macroeconomic implications of this point, despite its relevance to the macroeconomic behavior in China.

exploited the "exit" mechanism to engage local government in Tiebout competition for growth, the next round of reform should introduce more "voice" to improve the accountability of local governments. Otherwise, it is probable that local government behavior will change from "a helping hand" to "a grabbing hand." With the passing of time, local government will be more likely to collude with or be captured by local elites and interest groups.[12]

China's economic reform initiated in 1978 is great social engineering in human history. Chinese style federalism has given China a head start in performance relative to other transitional economies. To a large degree, the choice of decentralization versus centralization is a trade-off between incentives and coordination. The success of China's reform so far lies in getting local governments' incentives rights in the single task of economic growth (at the price of other dimensions), but as we have seen, emerging problems due to coordination failures are on the rise since economic development is a multidimensional process in nature. Therefore, now is a tipping point for China's future trajectory and China's sustainable growth to a large extent depends on whether it can get federalism right. As a big market economy with huge interregional heterogeneity, the feasible system is real federalism, where local government officials are elected by local people and they are constitutionally accountable to the local constituencies. Namely, for the long run, China should have the federalism commonly seen in the West, characterized by both economic decentralization and political decentralization, with totally free factor mobility.

REFERENCES

Acemoglu, D., Philippe Aghion and Fabrizio Zilibotti (2006). Distance to frontier, selection, and economic growth. *Journal of the European Economic Association*, 4(1): 37–74.

Bai, Chong-en, Yingjuan Du, Zhigang Tao and Yueting Tong (2004). Local protectionism and industrial concentration in China. *Economic Research Journal*, (4): 29–40.

---

[12]There have been some transitional mechanisms to improve the accountability of local officials. In particular, employing panel data from 1978 to 2004, Zhang and Gao (2007) show that term limits and rotation of provincial governors had positive effects on economic growth in China.

Bai, Chongen and Junjie Qian (2009). Factor distribution of national income: Stories underlying the statistics. *Economic Research Journal*, 3: 27–41.

Baicker, K. (2005). The spillover effects of state spending. *Journal of Public Economics*, 89(2): 529–544.

Bardhan, Pranab (2002). Decentralization of governance and development. *Journal of Economic Perspectives*, 16(4): 185–205.

Besley, T. and Case, A. (1995). Incumbent behavior: Vote-seeking, tax-setting, and yardstick competition. *American Economic Review*, 85(1): 25–45.

Blanchard, O. and Shleifer, A. (2001). *Federalism With and Without Political Centralization: China versus Russia*. IMF Staff Chapters, (48): 171–179.

Brandt, L. and Zhu, X. (2000). Redistribution in a decentralized economy: Growth and inflation in China under reform. *Journal of Political Economy*, 108(2): 422–439.

Buchanan, J. (1965). An economic theory of clubs. *Economica*, 32(125): 1–14.

Cai, H. and Treisman, D. (2005). Does competition for capital discipline governments? Decentralization, globalization and public policy. *American Economic Review*, 95(3): 817–830.

Chen, B., Lu, M. and Zhong, L. (2010). Household consumption constrained by *hukou* system. *Economic Research*, S1: 62–71.

China Youth Daily (Zhongguo Quingnian Bao) (2005). *Ninety Percent of People are Discontent with the Changes in China's Health Care System in the Last Ten Years*. August 22: 2.

Dewatripont, M. and Maskin, E. (1995). Credit and efficiency in centralized and decentralized economies. *Review of Economic Studies*, 62(4): 541–555.

The Economist (2007). *How Fit is the Panda*. The Issue of 29th, September.

Fu, Y. and Zhang, Y. (2007). Chinese style federalism and the bias in fiscal expenditure: The price of competition for growth. *Management World*, (3): 4–12.

Hart, O, Andrei Shleifer and Robert Vishny (1997). The proper scope of government: Theory and an application to prisons. *Quarterly Journal of Economics*, 112(4): 1127–1161.

Hirschman, A. (1970). *Exit, Voice, and Loyalty*. Boston: Harvard University Press.

Hoxby, C. (1995). *Is There an Equity-Efficiency Trade-Off in School Finance? Tiebout and a Theory of the Local Public Goods Producer*. NBER Working Chapter 5265.

Jin, H, Yingyi Qian and Barry Weignast (2005). Regional decentralization and fiscal incentives: Federalism, Chinese style. *Journal of Public Economics*, 89(9): 1719–1742.

Kornai, J. (1986). The soft budget constraint. *Kyklos*, 39(1): 3–30.

Lardy, N. (2007). China: Rebalancing Economic Growth. In: *China Balance Sheet and Beyond, Center for Strategic and International Studies and Peterson Institute for International Economics*.

Li, H. and Li-an Zhou (2005). Political turnover and economic performance: The incentive role of personnel control in China. *Journal of Public Economics*, 89(9): 1743–1762.

Lin, J. Y. (2002). Development strategy, viability and economic convergence. *China Economic Quarterly*, 1(2): 269–300.

Lin, J. Y. (2007). Wave phenomenon and the reconstruction of macroeconomic theories for developing countries. *Economic Research Journal*, (1): 126–131.

Lin, J. Y. and Liu, Z. (2000). Fiscal decentralization and economic growth in China. *Economic Development and Cultural Change*, 49(1): 1–21.

Li, Shaomin, Shuhe Li and Weiying Zhang (2000). The road to capitalism: Competition and institutional change in China. *Journal of Comparative Economics*, 28(2): 269–292.

Li, S. and Sato, H. (2004). *The Price of Economic Transition: An Empirical Analysis of Urban Unemployment, Poverty and Income Inequality in China.* China Finance and Economics Publishing Housing.

Lu, Ming, Zhao Chen and Ji Yan (2004). Increasing returns, development strategy and interregional economic segmentation. *Economic Research Journal*, (1): 54–63.

Lu, M. and Chen, Z. (2006). Urbanization, urban-biased policies and urban–rural inequality in China: 1987–2001. *Chinese Economy*, 39(3): 42–63.

Ma, S. and Yu, H. (2003). Fiscal transfer and interregional economic convergence. *Economic Research Journal*, (3): 26–33.

Martinez-Vazquez, J. and McNab, R. M. (2003). Fiscal decentralization and economic growth. *World Development*, 31(9): 1597–1616.

McKinnon, R. (1997). Market-Preserving Fiscal Federalism in the American Monetary Union. In B. Mairo and T. Ter-Minassian (Eds.), *Macroeconomic Dimensions of Public Finance*. London: Routledge, pp. 73–93.

Oates, W. (1972). *Fiscal Federalism*, New York: Harcourt Brace Jovanovich.

Peltzman, S. (1993). The political economy of the decline of American public education. *Journal of Law and Economics*, 36(1–2): 331–70.

Pelzman, S. (1996). Political economy of public education: Non-college bound students. *Journal of Law and Economics*, 39(1): 73–120.

Qian, Y. and Roland, G. (1998). Federalism and the soft budget constraint. *American Economic Review*, 88(5): 1143–1162.

Qian, Y., Roland, G. and Xu, C. (1988). *Coordinating Changes in M-Form and U-Form Organizations. Mimeo, European Centre for Advanced Research in Economics and Statistics, Université Libre de Bruxelles, Brussels.*

Qian, Y., Roland, G. and Xu, C. (1999). Why is China different from eastern Europe? Perspectives from organization theory. *European Economic Review*, 43(4): 1085–1094.

Qian, Y. and Weingast, B. (1997). Federalism as a commitment to preserving market incentives. *Journal of Economic Perspectives*, 11(4): 83–92.

Raiser, M. (1998). Subsidising inequality: Economic reforms, fiscal transfers and convergence across Chinese provinces. *Journal of Development Studies*, 34(3): 1–26.

Tiebout, C. (1956). A pure theory of local expenditures. *Journal of Political Economy*, 64(5): 416–424.

Wang, Y., Yan Zhang, Yuan Zhang, Zhao Chen and Ming Lu (2007). China's development path: The costs and benefits of decentralization reform. *Economic Research Journal*, (1): 4–16.

Weingast, B. (1995). The economic role of political institutions: Market-preserving federalism and economic development. *Journal of Law and Economic Organization*, 11(1): 1–31.

World Bank (1997). *Clear Water, Blue Skies: China's Environment in a New Century*. Washington, DC: World Bank.

Wu, Jinglian (2003). *Contemporary Chinese Economic Reform*. Shanghai Far East Publishing House.

Xu, C. (2011). The fundamental institutions of China's reforms and development. *Journal of Economic Literature*, 49(4): 1076–1151.

Yan, J. and Lu, M. (2003). Decentralization and regional development: Towards a theory of optimal decentralization. *World Economic Chapters*, (3): 55–66.

Zhang, J. and Gao, Y. (2007). Term limits and rotation of Chinese Governors: Do they matter to economic growth? *Economic Research Journal*, (11): 91–103.

Zhang, T. and Zou, H. (1998). Fiscal decentralization, public spending, and economic growth in China. *Journal of Public Economics*, 67(2): 221–240.

Zhang, W. and Li, S. (1998). Interregional competition and privatization of Chinese SOEs. *Economic Research Journal*, (12): 13–22.

Zhang, Yan and Jijun Xia (2006). A Review of Taxation Competition Theory, Working Paper, Fudan University.

Zhang, Yan and Liutang Gong (2005). Tax-sharing reform, fiscal decentralization and economic growth in China. *China Economic Quarterly*, (1): 75–108.

Zhou, Li-an (2004). The incentive and cooperation of government officials in the political tournaments: An interpretation of the prolonged local protectionism and duplicative investments in China. *Economic Research Journal*, (6): 33–40.

Chapter 7

Financial Reform: Opportunity and Challenge to China's Future Growth

Zhigang Yuan and Jingwen Yu
School of Economics, Fudan Univeristy

1. INTRODUCTION

In this chapter we examine the role played by the financial sector in supporting China's economic growth in the past, present, and future. Since 1978, China has achieved 9.9% economic growth, which is described as China's miracle (Lin *et al.*, 2003). During this time, even though China's financial system has made a lot of progress, the room left for further financial reform is still large. For example, the ratio of direct financing to indirect financing is small in China. Admittedly, both banks and markets are important for economic development; however, decentralized security markets are relatively more effective to finance more novel, longer-run, and higher-risk projects (Demirguc-Kunt *et al.*, 2011). This implies that as the economy grows, the optimal financial structure should become more market-based.

Furthermore, the role of the government in financial markets is highlighted. The interests and the credit channel are still under the control of the government, which represses financial development according to the theory of financial repression (McKinnon, 1973; Shaw, 1973). The price signal in the financial market could not show the true demand and the true supply, which distorts the resource allocation (Demirguc-Kunt *et al.*, 2011). Hence, resource allocation efficiency remains low in China.

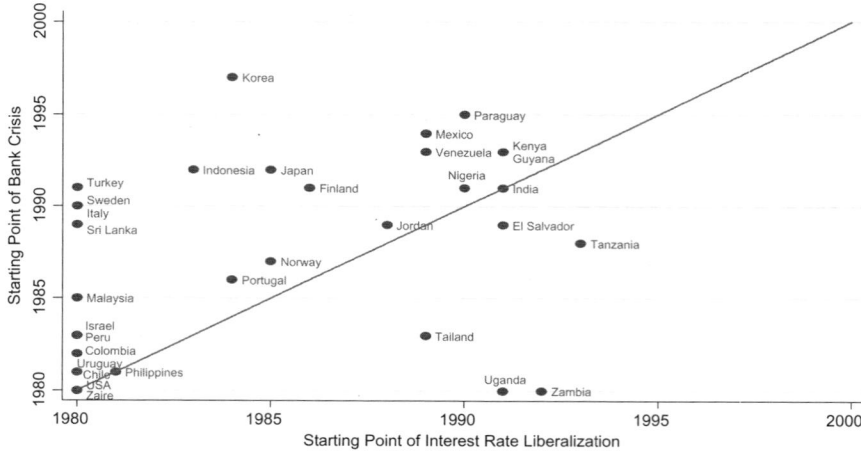

Figure 7-1: Sequence of interest rate liberalization and bank crisis.
Data Source: Demirguc-Kunt and Detragiache (1998).

At present, China has already entered the aging time. The cost for economic growth under strong financial control becomes larger than before. The extensive growth model is unsustainable in this circumstance. Enhancing resource allocation efficiency and transforming to the intensive growth model, which could be another driver for China's economic development, become more urgent. This is an opportunity faced by China. However, such financial reform will bring risk and fragility to China's financial system, and also China's economy. The emerging countries from both Asia and Latin America had experienced the banking crisis and even financial crisis after they carried out financial reform (Figure 7-1). The lessons from the Asian financial crisis in 1997 remind us of carrying on financial reform cautiously. How to make a suitable arrangement for financial reform with less risk and fragility is still a challenge to China.

This chapter proceeds as follows. In Section 2, the Chinese financial system in the past and the present will be introduced. In Section 3, the role of finance in Chinese economic growth will be investigated. In Section 4, we propose a hypothesis to explain Chinese economic growth in the last 30 years under the financial control. Moreover, the reasons for further financial reform are discussed. Section 5 provides the overall direction and the path of financial reform in China.

2. EVOLUTION OF CHINA'S FINANCIAL SYSTEM

2.1 Features of the Chinese Financial System Under a Planning Economy

After the People's Republic of China was founded, there were plenty of difficulties faced by the Chinese central government, such as economic collapse, hyperinflation, and social instability. Therefore, the principal target was to stimulate the economic development and get inflation under control. From 1949 to 1952, the national banking system was established. There was a unified monetary system, and bank branches on a national scale. The black market for foreign exchange was prohibited, and deposit and loan business was permitted. Since 1953, China imitated the Soviet model, and thus established a highly centralized and unified planned economic system, and a similar national banking system. The first Five-Year plan in 1953 focused on the construction of heavy industry, which was believed to be a precondition for industrialization. Correspondingly, the financial system was also dominated by the government as it had greater power in motivating the savings from the household. In a word, the government participated in the process of resource allocation directly at this time. The features of the financial system under the planning economy could be summarized as follows:

> First, the function of banks is limited. In fact, there is no modern banking system under a planning economy. The resource allocation is totally decided by the government. Therefore, the banking system serves a cashier role for the treasury department.

> Second, there is no actual central bank during this time. On the one hand, People's Bank of China could be nominally regarded as the central bank, because it has the function of maintaining the national financial order and managing and monitoring the currency issuance. On the other hand, People's Bank of China has the function of a commercial bank and non-bank financial institution.

> Third, the price of financial resource is distorted. The capital supply of the bank was totally passive. In order to achieve the goal of the government, the bank could provide the loan with zero interest rate or disequilibrium interest rate to state-owned enterprises (SOEs), which

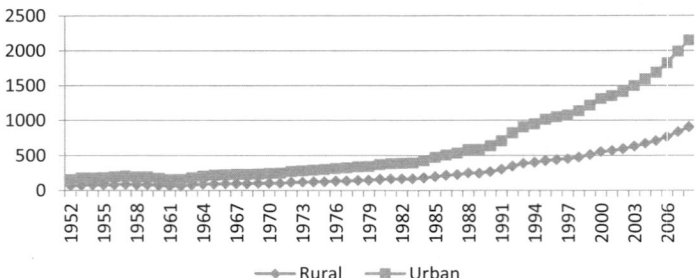

Figure 7-2: Consumption per capita in China (yuan).
Data Source: *China Statistical Yearbook*.

led to the soft budget of the SOEs and the deficiency in incentive and restraint mechanism of the bank.

However, the annual economic growth rate of China reached 6.1% from 1953 to 1978. This is also a miracle under a planning economy. There are abundant labor resources in China, while there are scarce capital resources. In order to solve this problem, the government represses the consumption of households mandatorily. In 1953, the consumption per capita was 72 yuan in rural areas and 188 yuan in urban areas. The former reached 138 yuan and the latter reached 405 yuan in 1978. The annual growth rate was 1.88% in rural areas and 2.22% in urban areas. However, the annual growth rate of consumption per capita jumped to 11.64% in rural areas and 12.41% in urban areas from 1978 to 2008 (Figure 7-2). The consumption of households was repressed before reform and opening up. Such repression policy generated great savings, and thus promoted the Chinese economic growth during this period.

2.2 Financial Reform After 1978

Since the adoption of reform and opening up policies, we have witnessed big changes in China and the financial system has experienced great reforms. The financial reform in China can be divided into three stages.

2.2.1 1978–1991: Establishment of central banking system and financial decentralization

The People's Bank of China was separated from the treasury department in 1978. In the 1980s, as one part of economic reform, the commercial banking function of the People's Bank of China was split into four independent but state-owned banks. Later, the State Council promulgated that from January 1, 1984, the People's Bank of China would perform the role of central bank specifically. Thereafter, a new financial system consisting of both a central bank and commercial banks was established. This was one of the most important steps in China's financial reform.

Moreover, the financial reform during this period was a kind of bottom-up reform that made it convenient for the local government to intervene in the allocation of financial resources. First of all, the Chinese economy has been organized mainly on geographical principles, which corresponds to an M-form organization rather than a U-form organization (Qian et al., 2006). The M-form organization is also known as a "regional organization," and thus could provide flexibility and allow for regional experiments without influencing the rest of the economy seriously. With an M-form organization, the local government has large power to intervene in the economy as well as financial markets. Second, the financial infrastructure was infertile in that time. The central financial management system was not established yet so that the local government could be involved in financial market more easily. The financial decentralization was formed gradually.

2.2.2 1992–2002: From financial decentralization to financial centralization

The market-oriented economic reforms were reinforced by Deng Xiaoping in 1992. The goal of China's socialist market economic reform was made clear. As a result, China's financial system began transforming to adapt to the socialist market economic reform. The financial reform during this period focused on the establishment of financial infrastructure. In order to establish an effective macroeconomic regulation and control system, financial legal system construction should be strengthened. At this stage, "Law of the People's Republic of China on the People's Bank of China," "Law of the People's Republic of China on Commercial Banks," "Law of the People's Republic of China on Negotiable Instruments," "The security law of the People's Republic of China," and "Decision of the Standing Committee of the National People's Congress on Punishment of Crimes of Disrupting Financial Order" were promulgated respectively, and the China Securities

Regulatory Commission (CSRC) was founded, which laid a primary legal foundation for further financial reform and provided juridical restrictions on the behavior of local government. The financial rights in local area were taken back by the central government, and thus, the financial restraint was strengthened.

The financial restraint system was established in 2002. First, even though interest rate control was deregulated gradually, the deposit interest ceiling and loan interest floor could be observed widespread. Second, the excessive competition was restricted not only in the banking industry but also in the capital market, which generated large room for rent seeking. Third, the central government placed a lot of restrictions on financial resource mobility in local areas.

2.2.3 2003–Present: Gradual improvement of financial system

In 2003, the China Banking Regulatory Commission was founded. Combined with the People's Bank of China, the CSRC, and the China Insurance Regulatory Commission, the specialized financial regulatory system had already been set up. Later on, financial reform focused on the banking system reform and opening up, especially state-owned bank reform. Such reform depended on the standardization and development of the capital market, innovation of the financial market, and establishment of a market mechanism. The specific policies on reform included reducing access restriction in the banking industry, introducing strategic investors, asset restructuring, and national capital injection. Hence, the Postal Savings Bank of China, Chinese Rural Credit Cooperatives, Village Bank, and micro-finance companies were established correspondingly. Foreign commercial banks were also allowed to conduct bank business with some restrictions. Consequently, the quantity and variety of financial service were improved significantly, which promoted the financial rights of the local government. The local government could take advantage of financial innovations to bypass the regulations of the financial management system. Therefore, the financial rights of local government were reinforced once again.

However, even though there is a lot of progress in financial development, the market power is still relatively weak. The visible hand of the government could be observed frequently in the financial market. The government still has great power in interest rate regulation and credit control. The financial institutions could absorb household savings with lower cost, and thus the interests of the savers were neglected. Moreover, the financial resources were largely allocated to SOEs to serve both economic and political purposes, which were called "Political Pecking Order" (Huang et al., 2008). As a result, the financing demand of non-SOEs could not be satisfied. Admittedly, the government-dominated financial system in China boosted the economic performance in the past, because the asymmetric information problem was common in the financial market and the national development strategy provided a reasonable reason for government intervention. The capital-intensive industry is in a primary position of national development strategy. Therefore, the repressed interest rate could stimulate the boom of investment in this industry.

In a word, such a financial model in China could be named "Development and Construction Financial Model," because the government-dominated financial system in China serves the purpose of economic development and economic construction, which has worked quite well in the last 30 years, as we could witness a 9.9% economic growth rate. More details will be discussed in the following sections.

3. CHINESE ECONOMIC GROWTH: ROLE OF FINANCE

3.1 Advantages of the Present Financial System

As mentioned before, the Chinese economy has experienced a rapid growth in the past years against the background of the repressed financial system. Objectively, there are some advantages of the Chinese financial system; otherwise, we could not explain both the rapid economic growth and the strong financial control. Specifically, the advantages of the financial system in China could be summarized as follows.

First, a factor-driven growth model is established. The repressed interest rate stimulates the investment and the investment boom facilitates the economic growth.

Second, the infrastructure investment is promoted by the state-owned sector. The political pecking order is a basic characteristic of the financial system in China. A large number of resources are transferred to the state-owned sector. The infrastructure investment with long-run cycle has positive externality. Consequently, the supply is insufficient if the resource is totally allocated by the market mechanism. In this case, the government could allocate the resource to the state-owned sector to support the infrastructure investment.

Third, the industrialization of China is supported by the financial system. As China is a developing country, capital is relatively scarce, which implies a relatively high price of capital. However, the government could repress the interest rate to lower the price of capital, and thus the development strategy in China could be supported and the goal of industrialization construction could be achieved.

Fourth, the problem of non-performing loans (NPL) is solved. The soft budget constraint is an essential feature of SOEs in the planning economy, which leads to a large number of NPL. This is a potential risk in the banking industry. However, the repressed interest rate, especially the deposit rate, led to a wide gap between the government-controlled deposit rate and the lending rate. As a result, the NPL could be reduced, which will make the banking industry more competitive.

3.2 Disadvantages of the Present Financial System

As the economy grows, the contribution of the "Development and Construction Financial Model" fades away gradually. Actually, the basic function of the financial system is financing the investment through absorbing the surplus of capital. This contains two aspects: First, the financial system has the function of allocating resource, satisfying the demand for investment, and thus supporting the development of the real economy. Second, the financial system has the function of providing various financial investment opportunities to the depositor. The financial investment demand of the depositor should also be satisfied. Therefore, the well-being of economic growth could be shared by all the people.

The present financial system in China mainly serves the purpose of the demand side with government intervention, sacrificing the benefit of the depositor through the controlled interest rate. This financial system is rooted in the fuzziness of demarcation criteria between the role of the market and the role of government in allocating resources.

The Fortune 500 list in 2012 had 69 Chinese enterprises, the number of which is steadily increasing on the list. It is the second largest number in the world after the United States, which coincides with being the world's second largest economy. Among these enterprises, there are 61 SOEs and 8 non-SOEs. This reflects the fact that the resources are mostly allocated to the state-owned sector in China. Furthermore, there are 11 financial enterprises with 19.0% profit rate. By contrast, the profit rate of non-financial enterprises is only 5.6% and that of financial enterprises except Chinese financial enterprises on the Fortune 500 list is 6.6% on average. The Chinese financial sector erodes the profit of the real economy, which is harmful to economic development in the long run. Specifically, the disadvantages of the present financial model could be reflected in four aspects.

3.2.1 Low efficiency of capital allocation

The Chinese financial system emphasizes the political purpose. The financial resources always flow to the state-owned sector, and thus the non-state-owned sector finds it hard to obtain the loan from the formal banking system. If the efficiency is higher in the state-owned sector than that in the other sector, such resource allocation is reasonable and acceptable, because the resource is allocated to the most efficient sector. However, the truth is just the opposite.

Theoretically, there are three reasons that could explain the low efficiency in the state-owned sector. First, the right and the responsibility are not defined clearly in the state-owned sector. This will lead to a series of principal–agent problems and the loss of efficiency (Zhang, 1999). Second, there are lots of policy burdens under the country's long-term development strategy, which causes the soft budget of state-owned sector (Lin and Liu, 2006). Third, there is an implicit contract between the state and the state-owned sector. The state could not quit this relationship. As a result, the state-owned sector with low efficiency could also obtain the resource or preferential policies from the government (Zhang, 1994).

Empirically, the technical efficiency of the non-SOEs is higher than that of SOEs through Stochastic Frontier Analysis (SFA) (Figure 7-3). Yao (1998) uses 14,670 enterprises from 12 industries to investigate the efficiency loss of SOEs. The results reveal that taking SOEs as benchmark, the technical efficiency of collectively owned enterprises, private enterprises, and foreign-funded enterprises is 22%, 57%, and 39% higher respectively.

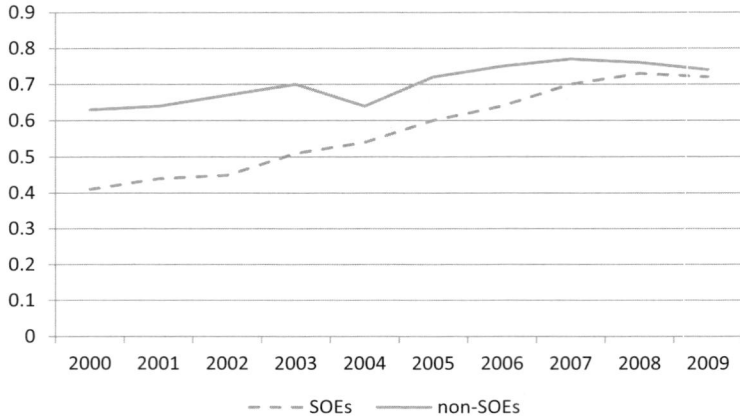

Figure 7-3: Technical efficiency between SOEs and non-SOEs.
Data Source: Wei and Nong (2012).

Liu and Shi (2010) propose a dual efficiency loss hypothesis. On the one hand, the low efficiency of SOEs implies more resources must flow to the SOEs to ensure their survival. This is one loss resulting from the low efficiency of SOEs. On the other hand, the non-SOEs, which have large demand for financing services, are subjected to a loss in this circumstance, because they are financially constrained. This is another loss. The provincial data in China has supported this hypothesis.

Therefore, an efficient financial market should allocate more resources to the non-state-owned sector. However, the present financial system does not achieve a more efficient resource allocation. The government plays an important role in the financial market, which represses the role of the market. The non-state-owned sector, which has experienced a rapid growth and contributed a lot to the Chinese economy in the last 30 years, is not preferred by the banking industry. This distorts the resource allocation, and thus leads to a lot of problems in China including external imbalance (Song *et al.*, 2011).

3.2.2 Low return on households' financial investment

One feature of the present financial system in China is financial repression. The repressed interest rate reduces the production cost of SOEs because SOEs have preferential policies to finance their projects. However, the repressed interest rate requires a limited financial investment channel. Otherwise, the savers could invest the money in other financial products rather than the deposit. As the Chinese economy grows at nearly 10% annually, the household wealth growth could be synchronized with economic growth on average, which means the return on financial product should be increased as much as the economic growth without restrictions on the financial market. The interest rate will increase eventually.

From 1980 to 2011, the GDP growth rate is 10% in China. However, the real deposit rate is −0.2% on average during this period. There are 14 years with negative real interest rate (Figure 7-4). The real deposit rate is not only lower than the GDP growth rate but also keeps negative, which implies that the growth of household wealth largely lagged behind the GDP growth rate, and furthermore the household subsidizes the banking institution. By contrast, from 1980 to 2011, the GDP growth rate in the United States is about 2.6% and the real deposit interest rate is 2.1%. They are quite close to each other (Figure 7-5).

Moreover, there are many immature, non-standard aspects in the stock market, which is another important investment channel for the household. Therefore, the stock market cannot protect the investor from encroaching. From 1992 to 2011, the ratio of dividend to market valuation is about

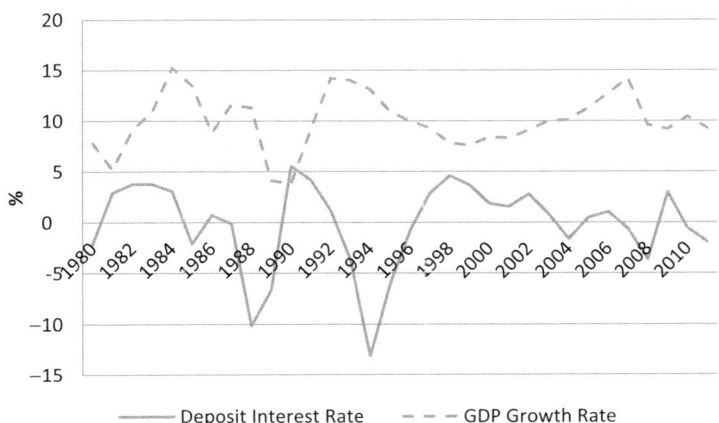

Figure 7-4: Deposit interest rate and GDP growth rate (China).
Data Source: CEIC.

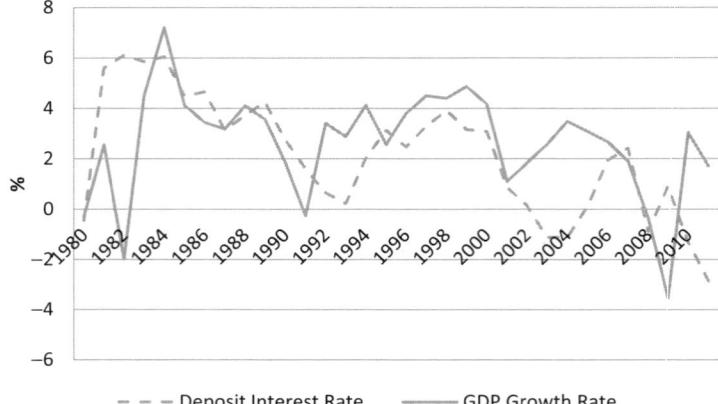

Figure 7-5: Deposit interest rate and GDP growth rate (US).
Data Source: CEIC.

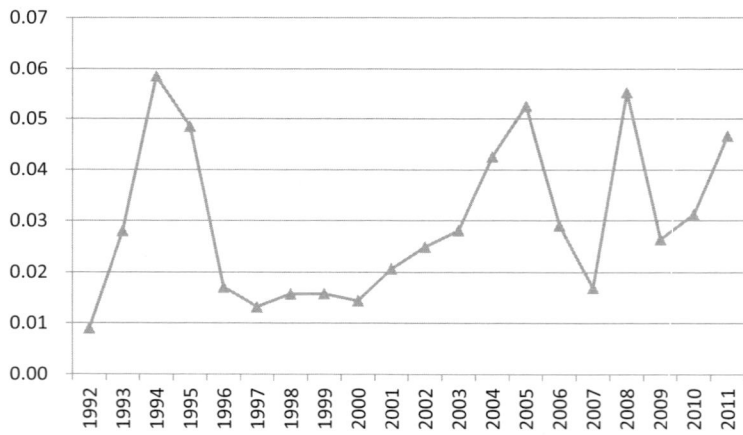

Figure 7-6: Ratio of dividend to market valuation.
Data Source: CSMAR.

3.0% on average, which is 1.5% lower than the deposit interest rate, and 1.9% lower than the inflation rate (Figure 7-6). The stock market has a more financing function for enterprises rather than optimizing allocation of resources function, which leads to a loss of investors' benefit.

3.2.3 Serious tunneling with "borrowing long and lending short"

Since the reform and opening up, China has adopted policies to conduct the reform gradually. The market mechanism begins to play a role in the resource allocation, and begins to be an incentive mechanism for the individual. Besides, the abundant labor resources combined with the capital over the world contribute a lot to the Chinese economy with the opening up policies.

Moreover, the global industrial chain is in a process of transfer. China has benefited a lot from such a process of globalization. The foreign trade dependence ([Export + Import]/GDP) grows from 9.8% in 1978 to 50.1% in 2011. The current account was US$114 billion deficit in 1978, and becomes US$15,490 billion surplus in 2011. The foreign exchange reserve grows from US$16.7 billion in 1978 to US$318,114.8 billion in 2011.

There are two facts behind these phenomena. The huge trade surplus implies the export of capital; the great foreign exchange reserve reflects not only the surge of trade surplus but also the inflow of foreign direct investment (FDI). In a word, China is exporting capital to other countries, while importing FDI.

The present financial system in China allocates the resources to the state-owned sector by a repressed interest rate. Consequently, the price of financial resources cannot reflect the resource scarcity. The financial system cannot screen the efficient enterprises and profitable projects. In response to this inefficient financial system, the capital flows to the United States and then returns to China through the developed financial system in the United States.

In other words, the financial system in China, which is efficient in absorbing the domestic savings, lacks efficiency in allocating the capital. Therefore, the foreign financial system becomes more important.

Specifically, China holds treasury bonds of the United States, while formulating lots of preferential policies to attract foreign investment. This seems to be self-contradictory. Actually, such a phenomenon is caused by the inefficiency of the financial system in China as explained above. Treasury bonds of the United States are a short-term investment with relatively low returns. In fact, the value depreciates gradually under the background of the Federal Reserve's quantitative easing (QE) policy. Generally, the annual return of Chinese foreign reserve is about 2.04% (Zhang *et al.*, 2010).

By contrast, FDI is a long-term investment with relative high returns. Especially, China has achieved nearly 10% GDP growth annually, which implies a remarkable return to invested capital. Bai *et al.* (2006) study the return to capital in China. The research results reveal a 20% return to capital in China approximately. The fact that the exporting capital becomes treasury bonds of the United States and the importing capital becomes FDI indicates serious tunneling from China to the United States (Tables 7-1 and 7-2). From this perspective, China is a loser under the present financial system.

Admittedly, the present financial system is a driving force for China's economic miracle. The benefits deriving from its advantages outweigh the costs incurred by its disadvantages. However, the cost of the present financial system steps into an increasing trend right now, which strengthens the motive for further financial reform. First of all, the non-state-owned

Table 7-1: External wealth of China (million US$).

Year	Portfolio equity assets	Portfolio equity liabilities	FDI assets	FDI liabilities	Debt assets	Debt liabilities
1990	44	2,132.903	6,443.879	12,574.48	41,776	55,301.41
1991	118	2,142.651	7,936.275	15,484.36	47,399	60,259.18
1992	216	2,334.666	14,644.75	23,734.96	51,116	72,427.95
1993	250	5,551.801	23,151.99	47,589.82	53,827	85,927.7
1994	270	7,161.495	20,311.32	64,941.19	59,953	100,456.9
1995	356	6,865.332	23,430.47	97,287.8	60,955	118,089.8
1996	662	10,750.06	25,423.8	130,540.2	66,544	128,817.1
1997	1,314	12,656.97	26,119	16,164.7	107,051	146,697
1998	1,776	7,815.23	30,745.88	189,520.6	145,922	143,982
1999	2,772	11,467.57	33,037.22	211,008.1	180,851	152,064.4
2000	5,570	14,738.41	32,051.72	235,175.1	236,022	145,710.5
2001	7,636	13,296.55	40,217.35	263,289.1	235,895	184,803.3
2002	5,610	16,473.27	45,235.79	292,411.6	251,066.2	186,114.1
2003	4,830	46,048.98	48,486.15	330,989.1	266,004.6	208,431.3
2004	5,678	57,256.2	52,704.05	368,970.1	257,538.5	247,679.3
2005	6,179.084	99,334.91	64,492.95	471,549.2	332,642.8	283,802.8
2006	8,924.904	261,987.6	90,630	614,383.5	473,460.6	325,076.5
2007	25,280.06	450,808.5	115,960.2	703,667.2	612,081.9	373,635.4

Data Source: Lane and Milesi-Ferretti (2007).

Table 7-2: External wealth of the United States (million US$).

Year	Portfolio equity assets	Portfolio equity liabilities	FDI assets	FDI liabilities	Debt assets	Debt liabilities
1990	197,596	243,789	616,655	505,346	1,190,067	1,653,248
1991	278,976	298,957	643,364	533,404	1,204,894	1,738,841
1992	314,266	328,988	663,830	540,270	1,206,167	1,866,722
1993	543,862	373,520	723,526	593,313	1,321,330	2,064,544
1994	626,762	397,720	786,565	617,982	1,410,401	2,262,721
1995	790,615	549,513	885,506	680,066	1,634,090	2,679,604
1996	1,006,135	672,397	989,810	745,619	1,875,621	3,070,584
1997	1,207,787	952,893	1,068,063	824,136	2,157,220	3,570,440
1998	1,474,983	1,250,342	1,196,021	920,044	2,278,536	3,776,624
1999	2,003,716	1,611,534	1,414,355	1,101,709	2,419,905	3,985,494
2000	1,852,842	1,643,205	1,531,607	1,421,017	2,725,936	4,505,193
2001	1,612,673	1,572,681	1,693,131	1,518,473	2,872,916	5,086,402
2002	1,373,980	1,335,792	1,867,043	1,499,952	3,249,454	5,851,305
2003	2,079,422	1,839,509	2,054,464	1,580,994	3,320,623	6,304,096
2004	2,560,418	2,123,258	2,498,494	1,742,716	4,092,131	7,720,077
2005	3,317,705	2,304,013	2,651,721	1,905,979	4,614,054	8,544,592
2006	4,328,960	2,791,892	2,948,172	2,154,062	5,692,157	10,487,306
2007	5,247,990	3,231,694	3,451,482	2,450,132	6,742,827	12,249,073

Data Source: Lane and Milesi-Ferretti (2007).

sector, experiencing a rapid growth, plays an increasingly important role in the Chinese economy. Furthermore, China faces an aging society, which will generate some unfavorable effects. The labor supply will shrink, and the savings will be reduced as the population ages. Hence, the factor-driven growth pattern cannot be maintained. If the growth is divided into two parts, factor inputs and resource allocation efficiency, then the former source of growth fades away. The improvement of allocation efficiency will become an important driving force for Chinese economic growth in the near future. This is a task of the financial system.

3.2.4 Structural imbalance under the present financial system

One distinguishing feature of the present financial system is the singleness of financial institutions' ownership structure. The state-owned commercial bank dominates the banking industry. Only by this financial control can the state exert influence on the capital allocation. There are five large-scale state-owned commercial banks in China including Bank of China (BOC), Industrial and Commercial Bank of China (ICBC), Agricultural Bank of China (ABC), Bank of Communications (BOCOM), and China Construction Bank (CCB). The total assets of these five banks reached 46 trillion yuan in 2011. By contrast, the total assets of small and medium-sized banks and the foreign banks were 14.9 trillion yuan and 1.74 trillion yuan in 2011, respectively. The five state-owned banks' assets take a large proportion (49.2%) of the total assets of the banking industry.

Moreover, the loan increment of the five state-owned banks is 50.1% of the total loan increment in 2011. The dominating role of state-owned banks in Chinese financial markets strengthens the financial stability, but also leads to the insufficiency of the financial innovations and the financial distress of medium-sized and small enterprises. Correspondingly, the local government and the SOEs are involved too much in Chinese financial system. A large abundance of financial resources are allocated to the local government-backed investment units and SOEs, which compresses the living space of the non-state-owned sector. As a result, we could observe both excessive financing in the state-owned sector and capital shortage in the non-state owned sector.

In 2010, the loan balance of the SOEs and collective enterprises is 61.63% of the total loan balance. This is two times higher than privately held enterprises. The loan balance of foreign invested enterprises is relatively small. In fact, the diversification of financial institutions will increase the competition in financial markets, and thus gives rise to innovation in both the organization of financial institutions and the financial products. The improvement of the competitive environment is conducive to the relief of financial constraints in medium-sized and small enterprises and also the market-based reform of interest rates.

Moreover, compared with the countries with a developed financial system, China presents a distinguishing feature of the financing mode that depends mostly on the indirect financing rather than the direct financing. In a word, the financial market is underdeveloped in China. For example, there were no stock options, stock futures, stock index options, ETF options in 2010, nor short-term/long-term interest rate options/futures, or currency options/futures. The market value/GDP of stock is 66.69% in China compared with 88.69% in the global economy (Table 7-3). In April 2012, the social financing scale was 0.96 trillion yuan, and the direct financing,

Table 7-3: China's financial development in 2010 (Billion US$).

	Global economy		Chinese economy	
	Market value	Market value/ GDP (%)	Market value	Market value/ GDP (%)
Stock	54,954	88.69	4,028	66.69
Stock Options	6,728	10.86	0	0.00
Stock Futures	2,966	4.79	0	0.00
Stock Index Options	123,288	198.97	0	0.00
Stock Index Futures	95,507	154.13	4.32	0.07
ETF Options	2,075	3.35	0	0.00
Bond	49,519	79.92	733	12.13
Short-Term Interest Rate Options	414,361	668.72	0	0.00
Short-Term Interest Rate Futures	994,109	1,604.35	0	0.00
Long-Term Interest Rate Options	55,358	89.34	0	0.00
Long-Term Interest Rate Futures	234,838	379.00	0	0.00
Currency Options	3,069	4.95	0	0.00
Currency Futures	35,680	57.58	0	0.00
Commodity Options	10	0.02	0	0.00
Commodity Futures	25,396	40.99	12,228	202.44
Total		3,385.64		269.20

such as issuing bonds and stocks, explains 11.27% of the total social financing scale. This number is 74.8%, 55.6%, and 43.1% in the United States, Germany, and Japan respectively. Demirguc-Kunt et al. (2011) finds that as the economy grows, the services provided by financial markets become comparatively more important than those provided by banks, which implies the crucial role of direct financing in economic development. It is suggested that China should pay more attention to financial development in order to achieve a rapid economic growth rate.

4. ECONOMIC GROWTH THROUGH FURTHER FINANCIAL REFORM

4.1 Explanation for Economic Growth with Financial Control in China

In the last 30 years, China has made great achievements in economic development with nearly 10% GDP growth rate. Such a success is made under the repressed financial system as described before. However, this is not consistent with the theory proposed by McKinnon (1973) and Shaw (1973).[1] There are lots of disadvantages for the present financial system in China, while there are also some advantages. The function of a repressed financial system with government intervention indeed depends on the development state as well as other factors.

According to the financial reform data provided by Abiad et al. (2009), financial repression in China is still serious and ranks it fifth among 91 countries in 2005. Only Ethiopia, Nepal, Uzbekistan, and Vietnam have more serious financial repression than China. However, China's economy grew rapidly in the last 30 years. Specifically, the degree of financial repression remains unchanged before 1995, but the economy makes great progress. When financial reform takes place after the middle of the 1990s, there is no significant change in economic performance in China (Figure 7-7). It seems

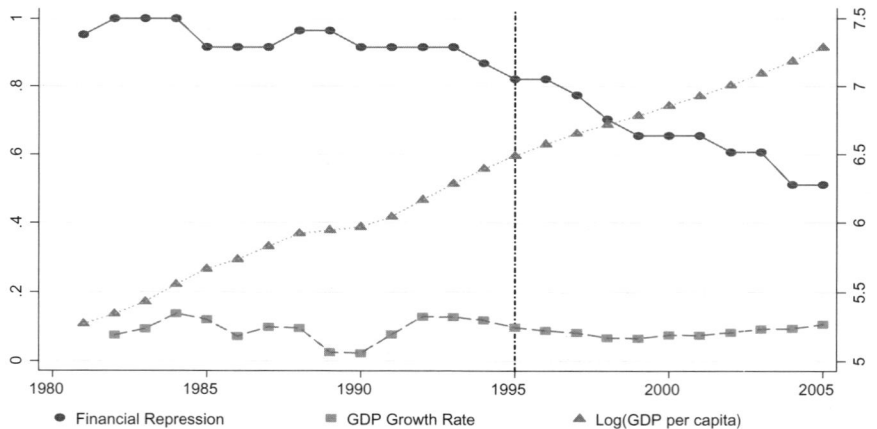

Figure 7-7: Financial repression and economic performance in China. *Data Source*: Abiad et al. (2009); WDI.

---

[1] McKinnon (1973) and Shaw (1973) argued that: (1) A repressed financial system led to a relatively low interest rate that weakened the saving motive. Therefore, the domestic savings stayed a low level, restricting the investment; (2) The financial market was segmented. Some sectors in the economy could not be fully developed. A marketed-based financial reform would promote the economic performance.

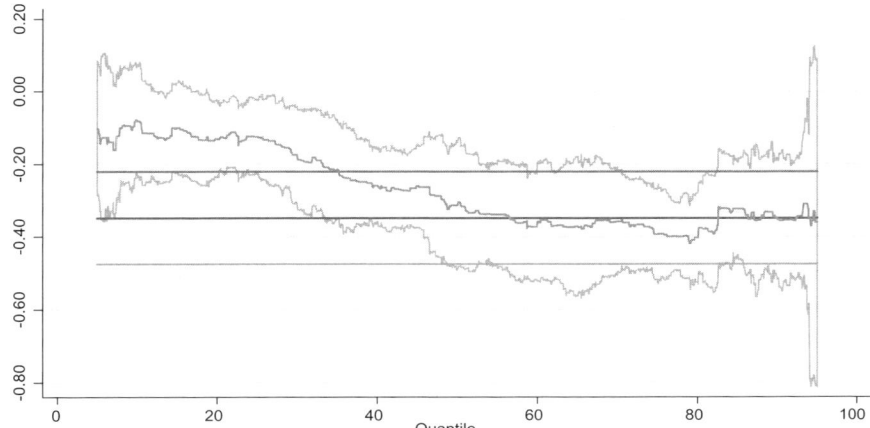

Figure 7-8: Quantile coefficients of financial repression for Log real GDP per capita.

Note: The econometric model will be introduced in the next part. The left axis provides the values of the coefficient estimates.

that the financial system plays no role in the Chinese economy, because we cannot use a changed variable to explain an unchanged variable.

From the cross-country data, we have observed that some countries with low GDP per capita benefit from financial repression, while some developed countries lose (Figure 7-8). How to explain the heterogeneous effect of financial repression is still a question faced by the theory proposed by McKinnon (1973) and Shaw (1973).

We propose a hypothesis of optimal financial repression to answer the above questions and conduct a case study through China to explain the economic growth under financial control. As discussed before, financial repression has both positive impacts and negative impacts on the Chinese economy. It is hard to deny the positive role played by financial repression in the last 30 years because of the great economic achievements made by China. Furthermore, financial reform generates both positive effects and negative effects. On the one hand, the positive effects include the efficiency improvement of resource allocation, financial development, and effective motivation for individuals. On the other hand, the negative effects are reflected in four aspects. Basically, these arguments provide reasonable grounds for government intervention in the financial market. First of all, the information asymmetry is widespread in the economy. For example, information about the solvency of financial institutions is hard to know for the public. Therefore, the supervision of financial institutions becomes a public good that will be undersupplied by the market mechanism. Market failure is a big obstacle for market-based reform (Stiglitz, 1993). Second, as for developing countries, the capital is scarce, which implies a relatively high price for capital. If the capital price is determined by the market, then the capital-intensive industry that is believed to be a precondition for industrialization is hard to develop (Wang, 2010). Third, financial reform requires high-quality financial supervision and an effective warning mechanism. The market-based reform provides an opportunity for capital to purchase high profit on a global scale, which will not only improve the efficiency of resource allocation, but also increase the fragility of the financial system (Broner and Rigobon, 2006). Fourth, the financial reform will intensify the competition in the banking industry, which will push down the profit of banks. As a response, the motive for investing in higher-risk projects of banks will be reinforced. The banking crisis is more likely to happen in this circumstance (Hellmann *et al.*, 2000).

However, in the early stage of economic development, the involvement of the government in the financial system is crucial for economic growth, because the market mechanism is too imperfect to generate correct signals about the market supply and demand, and thus, the behavior of the individual will be influenced adversely. Moreover, the infrastructure and industrialization, which have large externalities, are foundations for economic development. As a result, government intervention is helpful for the economic development in this circumstance.

As the economy develops, the sector affected by financial repression policies, such as non-SOEs in China, plays an increasing role. The improvement of the efficiency of resource allocation becomes urgent. Enterprises in the non-state-owned sector need more financial support from the formal financial sector, especially in the aging time. In other words, there is an optimal financial repression for each country. For developing countries, the financial repression might generate more positive effects rather than adverse effects, which implies financial repression could be an optimal choice. As the economy develops, the positive effect generated by financial repression diminishes, implying that financial reform could be an optimal choice. The optimal financial repression becomes low and the motive to reform is strengthened in this circumstance. In terms of optimal financial repression, it is the deviation of the actual financial repression from the optimal financial repression that affects the economic activity rather than the financial repression itself. Next, we will conduct empirical research to test this hypothesis through cross-country data.

4.2 Empirical Study

4.2.1 Data description

We take three steps to conduct our research. The optimal financial repression must be estimated first, and then we calculate the gap between the actual financial repression and the optimal extent of financial repression. Second, the cross-country data will be used to estimate the relationship between the gap calculated in the first step and the economic development. Third, the optimal financial repression in China will be calculated according to the results in the first step and the influence of financial repression in China will be estimated according to the results in the second step.

The key explanatory variable is the financial repression index, which comes from a new database of financial reform constructed by Abiad *et al.* (2009). The original data in Abiad *et al.* (2009) describes the financial reform covering 91 countries from 1973 to 2005. The index is constructed from seven dimensions: credit control and excessively high reserve requirement; interest rate controls; entry barriers; state ownership in the banking sector; capital account restrictions; prudential regulations and supervision of the banking sector; securities market policy. Each dimension has various sub-dimensions. Based on the score for each sub-dimension, each dimension receives a "raw score." When a "raw score" is assigned, it is normalized to a 0–3 scale. That is, fully liberalized = 3; partially liberalized = 2; partially repressed = 1; fully repressed = 0. The final scores are used to compute an aggregate index for each country/year by assigning equal weight to each dimension. The aggregate index is normalized to a 0–1 scale finally.[2] Because financial reform is just the opposite side of financial repression, we use one minus the financial reform index to get the financial repression index.

---

[2] See Appendix I "Coding Rules" in Abiad *et al.* (2009) for more details.

The financial repression index is the dependent variable in the first step. Economic development denoted by Log real GDP per capita is the dependent variable in the second step. Additionally, the key institutional, geographic, structural, and demographic traits are controlled in the econometric model. These control variables include openness to trade (Open), inflation, recession, human capital (Humancap), government consumption/GDP (Govcon), population (Pop), population density (Popden), youth dependent ratio (Youthdep), aged dependent ratio (Olddep), democracy (Polity), Legal origin, country's distance from the equator (Lat), and export of raw materials/total export (Rawex). There is a diffusion effect in each country (Simmons and Elkins, 2004). If one country in the region has adopted policies to conduct financial reform, then the other countries in this region will learn from this experience, and thus be inclined to proceed with financial reform. The regional financial repression, which refers to the minimum financial repression in this region, is denoted by Finrep_reg. Table 7-4 provides the specific definitions and sources of these data and Table 7-5 provides descriptive statistics.

Since the data about China begins from 1981, the data in the paper covers the period from 1981 to 2005. Some countries are dropped due to missing variables. Finally, the sample is divided into 5 regions including 63 countries.[3] All data are 5-year non-overlapping country averages.

4.2.2 Financial repression gap

To provide information on whether deviation of actual financial repression from optimal financial repression is associated with economic traits, as well as institutional, geographic, structural, demographic traits, we need to

---

[3]There are 5 regions including 63 countries: Advanced Countries (Australia, Austria, Belgium, the UK, Canada, Denmark, Finland, France, Germany, Greece, Ireland, Israel, Italy, Japan, Netherlands, New Zealand, Norway, Portugal, Spain, Sweden, Switzerland, and the United States); Emerging Asia (Bangladesh, China, India, Indonesia, Korea, Malaysia, Nepal, Philippines, Sri Lanka, and Thailand); Middle East and North Africa (Algeria, Egypt, Jordan, Morocco, Pakistan, Tunisia, and Turkey); Latin America (Argentina, Bolivia, Brazil, Chile, Columbia, Costa Rica, Dominican Rep, Ecuador, El Salvador, Guatemala, Mexico, Nicaragua, Paraguay, Peru, Uruguay, and Venezuela); Sub-Saharan Africa (Cameroon, Ghana, Kenya, Mozambique, Senegal, South Africa, Uganda, and Zimbabwe).

Table 7-4: Variable definitions and sources.

Name	Expression	Source	Definition
Financial repression	Finrep	Abiad et al. (2009)	1 — Original data
Real GDP per capita	Loggdp	WDI	Log real GDP per capita (Constant 2000 US$)
Recession	Recession	WDI	A dummy variable that refers to 1 if GDP growth rate < 0, otherwise 0.
Openness to trade	Open	WDI	(Export + Import)/GDP
Inflation	Inflation	WDI	Original data
Human Capital	Humancap	Barro and Lee (2010)	Log average years of schooling
Government size	Govcon	WDI	Government consumption/GDP
Raw material exports as % of total exports	Rawex	WDI	Raw material exports/total exports
Legal origin	English French German Nordic	Nation Master	A set of four dummy variables that refers to the legal origin of each country: British, French, German, and Scandinavian.
Distance from equator	Lat	Glaeser et al. (2004)	Latitude
Population size	Pop	WDI	Log population size (millions)
Population density	Popden	WDI	Log number of people per square km
Youth dependency ratio	Youthdep	WDI	Population aged 0–14/population aged 15–64
Aged dependency ratio	Olddep	WDI	Population aged above 65/population aged 15–64
Democracy	Polity	POLITY IV PROJECT	Original data

construct a measure of optimal financial repression for each country. We follow the guidance provided by Rajan and Zingales (1998) and Demirguc-Kunt et al. (2011) to construct an acceptable proxy of optimal financial repression.

In fact, we do not need a perfect estimate of optimal financial repression. An estimated result that is positively correlated with the true optimal financial repression could be acceptable because there will be no systematic bias in this circumstance.

Table 7-5: Descriptive statistics.

	Mean	Std. error	Observation
Financial repression	0.435	0.286	315
Real GDP per capita	8.081	1.567	315
Youth Dependency Ratio	0.541	0.228	315
Aged Dependency Ratio	0.123	0.071	315
Regional Financial Repression	0.199	0.171	315
Raw Material Exports	0.293	0.538	315
Democracy	4.841	6.181	315
Population Size	16.872	1.330	315
Population Density	4.092	1.236	315
Distance from Equator	0.319	0.193	315
Open to Trade	0.594	0.301	315
Government Size	0.152	0.057	315
Human Capital	7.323	2.648	315
Inflation	0.582	3.543	315
Financial Repression Gap	0.621	0.230	315
Legal Origin:			
English	0.302	0.460	315
French	0.540	0.499	315
German	0.095	0.294	315
Nordic	0.064	0.244	315

We use OECD countries in our sample to estimate the optimal financial repression.[4] We assume that OECD countries have optimal financial repression after controlling the key national traits because OECD countries have few interventions in financial markets, and few obstacles in reaching the optimal level of financial repression. This approach is similar to that adopted by Rajan and Zingales (1998) and Demirguc-Kunt *et al.* (2011). The former, use the United States and Canada as a benchmark for a perfect functioning financial system, while the latter uses OECD countries as a benchmark for an optimal financial structure. The financial repression is the dependent variable in this estimate. The key national traits are controlled. Table 7-6 provides the results. A high level of economic

---

[4]The OECD countries in this sample include: Australia, Austria, Belgium, Canada, the UK, Chile, Denmark, Finland, France, Germany, Greece, Israel, Italy, Japan, Korea, Netherlands, Mexico, Norway, Portugal, Spain, Sweden, Switzerland, Turkey, and the United States.

Table 7-6: Financial repression regression results (estimated on OECD sample).

	(1)	(2)
Real GDP per capita	−0.169***	−0.004
	(0.027)	(0.049)
Youth Dependency Ratio		0.447
		(0.275)
Aged Dependency Ratio		0.456
		(0.519)
Raw Material Exports		−0.101**
		(0.051)
Democracy		0.033***
		(0.009)
Population Size		−0.046***
		(0.014)
Population Density		−0.020
		(0.014)
Distance from Equator		−0.622***
		(0.197)
Recession		0.069
		(0.059)
Regional Financial Repression		2.102***
		(0.256)
Legal Origin (Benchmark: English)		
French		0.080
		(0.050)
German		0.073
		(0.055)
Nordic		0.035
		(0.056)
Constant	1.882***	0.407
	(0.257)	(0.515)
Observation	125	125
R^2	0.248	0.615

Notes: Standard error is in parentheses. ***denotes significance at the 1% level; **denotes significance at the 5% level; *denotes significance at the 10% level.

development is associated with a relatively low level of financial repression. The estimate results in column 2 will be used to predict the optimal financial repression for each country. The financial repression gap is the absolute value of the actual financial repression minus the optimal financial repression.

4.2.3 Relationship between financial repression gap and economic development

We proceed to the second step with a new econometric model. The dependent variable is Log real GDP per capital representing economic development. The key independent variable is the financial repression gap. The "standard controls" are used: Log real GDP per capita in 1981, government size, openness to trade, inflation, and human capital.

Table 7-7 reports both the OLS and quantile regression results of the financial repression gap on Log real GDP per capita. The OLS results show a negative relationship between the financial repression gap and economic development. Furthermore, the coefficients of the 25th, 50th, 75th, and 90th percentile of Log real GDP per capita are all negative, statistically significant at the 5% level. Only the coefficient of the 10th percentile of Log real GDP per capita is insignificant, but the sign is negative.

Table 7-7: Financial repression gap and economic development.

	(1) OLS	(2) Quantile_10	(3) Quantile_25	(4) Quantile_50	(5) Quantile_75	(6) Quantile_90
Financial Repression Gap	−0.348*** (0.065)	−0.081 (0.079)	−0.124** (0.051)	−0.314*** (0.090)	−0.394*** (0.063)	−0.346*** (0.084)
Openness to Trade	0.179*** (0.052)	0.026 (0.048)	0.084** (0.035)	0.207*** (0.072)	0.145** (0.065)	0.239** (0.099)
Government Size	−0.005* (0.003)	0.000 (0.004)	−0.001 (0.003)	−0.002 (0.004)	−0.006* (0.003)	−0.010** (0.005)
Human Capital	0.063*** (0.009)	0.013 (0.008)	0.015** (0.006)	0.040*** (0.012)	0.081*** (0.009)	0.122*** (0.018)
Inflation	−0.010** (0.004)	−0.007** (0.003)	−0.009*** (0.002)	−0.008* (0.004)	−0.008*** (0.002)	−0.009* (0.005)
Real GDP per capita in 1981	0.931*** (0.016)	1.033*** (0.016)	1.013*** (0.012)	0.966*** (0.021)	0.910*** (0.017)	0.823*** (0.036)
Constant	0.456*** (0.087)	−0.406*** (0.083)	−0.168*** (0.063)	0.234* (0.120)	0.686*** (0.101)	1.232*** (0.199)
Observation	315	315	315	315	315	315
R^2	0.975	0.876	0.875	0.868	0.848	0.798

Notes: Standard error is in parentheses. ***denotes significance at the 1% level; **denotes significance at the 5% level; *denotes significance at the 10% level.

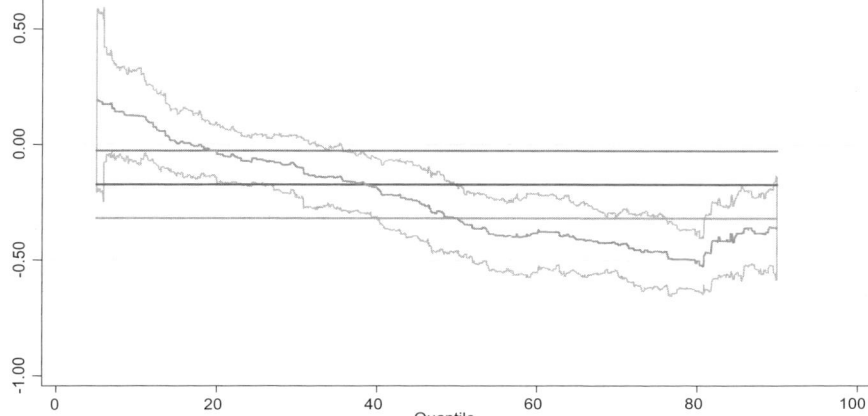

Figure 7-9: Quantile coefficients of financial repression gap for Log real GDP per capita.

Figure 7-9 presents the estimated coefficients from quantile regressions of the financial repression gap on Log real GDP per capita. The coefficients from the 5th through the 90th percentile of Log real GDP per capita are graphed. The left axis provides information on the values of the coefficient estimates, which gives two noteworthy results. First of all, the estimated coefficients are negative for each Log real GDP per capita percentile, which means an increase in the financial repression gap leads to a reduction in economic activity at each level of Log real GDP per capita. Second, the reduction in economic activity associated with an increase in the financial repression gap becomes large as the economy develops.

The results reveal that there is an optimal financial repression for each country. The optimal status depends on economic traits, such as economic development, as well as institutional, geographic, demographic, and structural traits. As the economy develops, the optimal financial repression diminishes, which implies financial repression could facilitate the economic performance of a developing country, but impede the economic growth of a developed country.

4.3 Chinese Case Study

Financial repression is a distinguishing feature of the Chinese financial system. However, China's economic miracle is realized under financial repression. Figure 7-10 gives an explanation. The figure tells that the financial

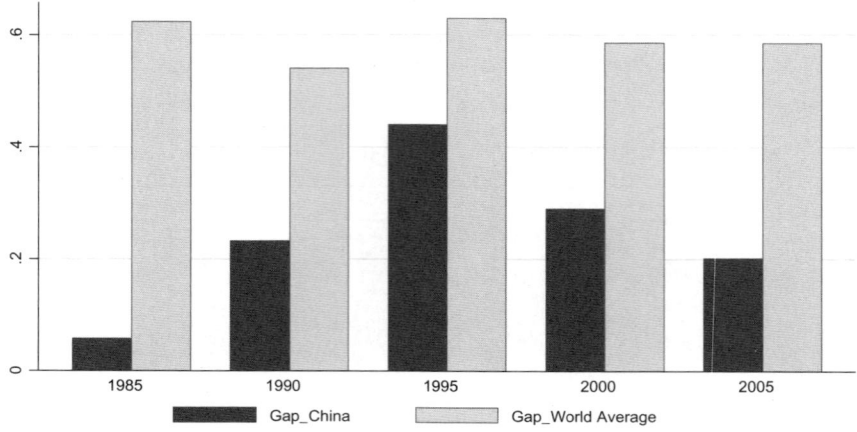

Figure 7-10: Financial repression gap (China vs. World Average).

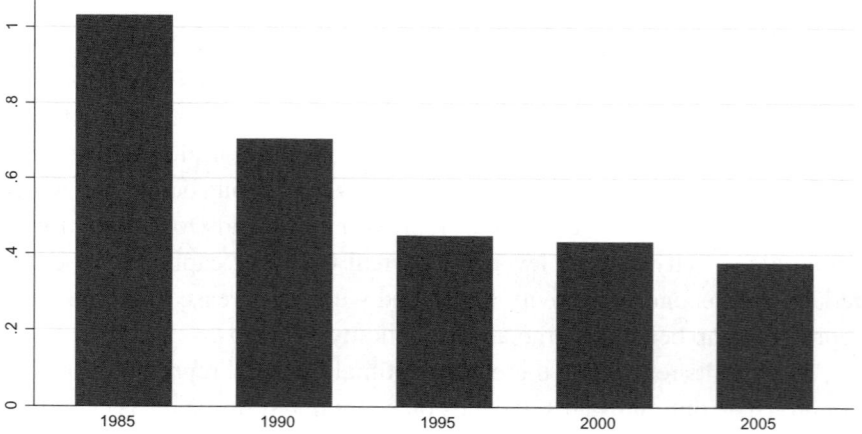

Figure 7-11: Optimal financial repression in China.

repression gap in China is relatively small compared with that of the world, which could explain the rapid economic growth in China quite well, because whether financial repression has a negative influence on the economy or not depends on the financial repression gap. Indeed, it is the financial repression gap affecting the economic development rather than the financial repression.

Figure 7-11 provides the information about the trend of optimal financial repression in China. The optimal financial repression becomes small overtime, even though the change diminishes. We could predict a decreasing trend of optimal financial repression, because the Chinese economy has the potential to continue to converge to the developed countries according to the experience of Japan and Korea, and the population aging becomes increasingly serious. These will raise the cost of financial repression, and thus lower the optimal financial repression.

Under the background of a decreasing trend in optimal financial repression, the Chinese economy is faced with two adverse impacts. First of all, as optimal financial repression decreases, the financial repression gap becomes large if there is no further financial reform. According to the results of both OLS and quantile regression in step two, an increase in the financial repression gap is associated with a reduction in economic activity, which produces a great loss for economic development. Furthermore, the results of quantile regression show that as Log real GDP per capita increases, the negative effect of the financial repression gap becomes even larger. This means Chinese economic development will give rise to a more negative effect of the financial repression gap to economic activity than before. In sum, the cost of financial repression is increasing with economic development. Therefore, financial reform at present becomes more important and more urgent than before. Admittedly, financial repression did not hold up economic growth in the last 30 years; however, the situation is changed as cost of financial repression increases, which will generate a harmful impact on the Chinese economy.

As the economy develops, the adverse influence produced by a segmented financial market will exacerbate. Financial repression implies one sector in the economy is supported by the government-oriented financial system, and another sector cannot obtain enough financial support. The allocation of financial resources does not depend on the efficiency principle. When the sector that is discriminated against by the financial system, which is the non-state-owned sector in China, becomes large as the economy grows, the demand for financial services will increase. Moreover, as demographics change, especially population aging approaches, the factor-driven growth model is faced with a huge challenge due to a reduction in labor, and also capital supply. The efficiency-driven growth model becomes more important for the future Chinese economy. This proposes an opportunity for financial reform in China. Besides, a feasible continuation of financial reform will be sufficient to compensate for a slowdown and decline in China's labor force. Tyers and Golley (2010) use a Global Trade Analysis Project (GTAP) to simulate Chinese economy growth in various scenarios. The labor force in China is projected to contract in the next decade, which will set the Chinese economy apart from other emerging Asia countries where relative labor abundance will increase, and thus the capital return goes up. If China's interest premium could be reduced by the gradual financial reform, then the GDP growth performance could be maintained with continued low fertility. Financial reform should be a priority in China's growth strategy.

5. FUTURE PATH OF FINANCIAL REFORM

The overall direction of financial reform in China could be summarized as two parts: globalization and marketization. Globalization means the Chinese financial system should move toward an opening process, in which the Chinese economy is integrated into the global economy and the Chinese financial system is integrated into the global financial system. This requires raising the ability of the domestic financial system to cope with external shocks. Marketization means the redefinition of the relationship between the government and the market. The market mechanism should play an increasingly important role in the financial market, which will reduce the degree of financial repression.

Both globalization and marketization imply that market-based financial reform is necessary for the future Chinese economy. The market-based financial reform means few interventions of the government in financial markets, and thus, the allocation of financial resources only depends on efficiency. The political pecking order should be abandoned. The price distortion will be corrected though financial reform, which will provide truthful information about supply and demand, and furthermore appropriate motivation for the individual. With an efficient financial system, the wealth of the household could be integrated with the highly efficient industry geographically and also could be combined with the youth population over the world inter-temporally.

The market-based financial reform will raise the competition in the banking industry, which will benefit the savers, because the interest rate will be raised to compete for savings. Additionally, interest rate liberalization will help the financial institutions to screen the best enterprises and the most efficient projects, and strengthen the motivation to supervise the operation of enterprises, which will reduce the moral hazard. As a result, the resource could be allocated by the efficiency principle, which could be helpful in satisfying the financial investment needs of households as the household wealth grows.

Moreover, when the aging time comes, the burden of providing for the aged becomes heavy, and the pension fund at present cannot fully meet the needs of aged people in the future. The demographic dividend is disappearing gradually and such a great transformation of demographic structure is irreversible. This implies that the demographic dividend provides a precious opportunity for economic development only once. Such a precious opportunity should be fully taken advantage of. At present, China possesses huge foreign exchange reserves, which correlate with the demographic dividend closely. However, the foreign exchange reserve is not fully utilized, and thus the return is relatively low, which will be a big problem for the burden of providing for the aged. Therefore, financial reform becomes more important, through which efficiency of resource allocation is improved. This will produce a correct signal and positive motivation for enterprises. The increase of enterprise efficiency will be helpful for the capital "walk out" strategy achieving the combination of foreign exchange reserves in China with the youth labor force in developing countries. A win–win situation emerges. On the one hand, the developing countries with relatively abundant labor force and relatively scarce capital resources could promote investment through importing capital. On the other hand, China's capital generated in the period of demographic dividend could share the demographic dividend of these developing countries.

Finally, even though financial reform becomes more important for the Chinese economy, dramatic financial reform is not desirable. It is the financial repression gap that determines the economic performance rather than financial repression itself. When adopting financial reform measures, economic traits, such as economic development level, as well as demographic traits, such as aged dependency ratio, and so forth should be taken into consideration, because the change of the actual financial repression should correspond with the change of the optimal financial repression. The deviation of the actual financial repression from the optimal financial repression could generate a harmful effect on the economy. Gradual financial reform seems more advisable.

REFERENCES

Abiad, A., Thierry Tressel and Enrica Detragiache (2009). *A New Database of Financial Reforms.* IMF Staff Papers, 57(2): 281–302.

Bai, Chong-En, Chang-Tai Hsieh and Yingyi Qian (2006). *The Return to Capital in China.* NBER Working Paper No. 12755.

Barro, R. and Lee, J.-W. (2010). *A New Data Set of Educational Attainment in the World, 1950–2010.* NBER Working Paper No. 15902.

Broner, F. and Rigobon, R. (2006). Why are Capital Flows So Much More Volatile in Emerging than in Developed Countries? In R. Caballero *et al.* (Eds.), *External Financial Vulnerability and Preventive Policies, Central Bank of Chile.*

Demirguc-Kunt, A. and Detragiache, E. (1998). *Financial Liberalization and Financial Fragility.* IMF Working Paper No. 98/83.

Demirguc-Kunt, A., Erik Feyen and Ross Levine (2011). *Optimal Financial Structures and Development: The Evolving Importance of Banks and Markets.* World Bank Mimeo.

Glaeser, E., Rafael LaPorta, Florencio López-de-Silanes and Andrei Shleifer (2004). Do Institutions cause growth? *Journal of Economic Growth*, 9(3): 271–303.

Hellmann, T., Kevin Murdock and Joseph Stiglitz (2000). Liberalization, moral hazard in banking, and prudential regulation: Are capital requirements enough? *American Economic Review*, 90(1): 147–165.

Huang, Y., Yue Ma, Zhi Yang and Yifan Zhang (2008). *A Fire Sale without Fire: An Explanation of Labor-Intensive FDI in China.* MIT Sloan Research Paper No. 4713-08.

Lane, P. and Milesi-Ferretti, G. M. (2007). The external wealth of nations Mark II: Revised and extended estimates of foreign assets and liabilities 1970–2004. *Journal of International Economics*, 73(2): 223–250.

Lin, Y., Fang Cai and Zhou Li (2003). *The China Miracle: Development Strategy and Economic Reform.* Chinese University Press.

Lin, Y. and Liu, P. (2006). *Economic Development Strategy, Openness and Rural Poverty: A Framework and China's Experiences.* UNU-WIDER Research Paper, United Nations University (UNU).

Liu, R. and Shi, L. (2010). Dual efficiency loss of state-owned enterprises and economic growth. *Economic Research* 1: 127–137.

McKinnon, R. (1973). *Money and Capital in Economic Development*, Brookings Institution Press.
Qian, Y., Gerard Roland and Chenggang Xu (2006). Coordination and experimentation in m-form and u-form organization. *Journal of Political Economy*, 114(2): 251–268.
Shaw, E. (1973). *Financial Deepening in Economic Development*. Oxford University Press.
Rajan, R. and Zingale, L. (1998). Financial dependence and growth. *American Economic Review*, 88(3): 559–586.
Song, Z., Kjetil Storesletten and Fabrizio Zilibotti (2011). Growing like China. *American Economic Review*, 101(1): 196–233.
Simmons, B. and Elkins, Z. (2004). The globalization of liberalization: Policy diffusion in the international political economy. *American Political Science Review*, 98(1): 171–189.
Stiglitz, J. (1993). *The Role of the State in Financial Markets*. Institute of Economics, Academia Sinica.
Tyers, R. and Golley, J. (2010). China's growth to 2030: The roles of demographic change and financial reform. *Review of Development Economics*, 14(3): 592–610.
Wang, S. (2010). *Financial Development Theory*. Beijing: China Development Press.
Wei, F. and Rong, Z. (2012). Comparison and analysis of the technical efficiency between SOEs and non-SOEs from 2000 to 2009. *Economic Review*, 3: 75–81.
Yao, Y. (1998). Effect of non-SOEs on industrial technical efficiency in China. *Economic Research*, 12: 16–21.
Zhang, J. (1994). Government and enterprise in socialist country. *Economic Research*, 4: 74–82.
Zhang, W. (1999). *Theory of Enterprise Entity and Chinese Enterprise Reform*. Peking University Press.
Zhang, B., Xun Wang and Xiuping Hua (2010). Nominal and real returns on China's foreign exchange reserves. *Economic Research*, 10: 115–128.

Chapter 8

China's Urbanization: Past, Present, and Future

Hao Zheng

School of Economics, Fudan Univeristy

Since the reform and opening up in 1978, the factor allocation efficiency of China has been improved greatly across both industry and space. Thousands of farmers migrated to cities and towns. As a result, hundreds of cities emerged, which stimulates the infrastructure investment and consumption. This is the largest-scale urbanization in history.

Of course, China's urbanization has some distinctive features. The administrative system has played an important role in the process of urbanization. This results in China's urban system and the division of urban population constantly changing with the adjustment of administrative systems. Cities at different administrative levels are expected to have different development potential. Another feature of Chinese urbanization is that industrialization has an important effect in promoting urbanization. Especially after China's accession to the WTO, population, capital, and many other resources quickly gathered together in the coastal cities for industrial production, vigorously promoting China's urbanization process. However, urbanization with lagged service industry has also been frequently questioned.

Because of the limitations of existing endowments, China will follow the urbanization pattern of Japan and South Korea, rather than Europe or the United States. Therefore, large cities' development and governance will be China's big issues. In fact, the policy maker has gradually shifted from constraint to reserved encouraging about the development of large cities, while in the past 10 years, China's large cities have indeed gained rapid growth.

Besides, the city location problem is particularly important; urban construction without population concentration may make it difficult to escape the fate of decay in the future. Hence, we should be cautious about the urban development in central and western China, especially some ecological reserve areas.

On the other hand, China's urbanization will face the constraints of land, capital, and environmental aspects. The red line of 18 million mu of land must be made flexible to adjust; however, because of the tight balance of China's grain supply, intensive use of the land is still important. The construction of high-density cities will induce a huge demand for rapid urban transport facilities. Energy and environmental constraints cannot be ignored, and the problem of water resources should receive more attention. To some extent, China's future urban distribution depends on the distribution of water resources in China.

1. THE BASIC FACTS OF CHINA'S URBANIZATION

1.1 China's Administrative Division

Before the discussion about China's urbanization, we need to explain the administrative division in China, because it is directly related to the definition of the urban population. Since ancient times, China's administrative divisions changed frequently. At first, Qin Dynasty set up the system of prefectures and counties, and then, the Han Dynasty added the province layer above the prefectures. The three-tier management system remained a long time, that is, provincial (state/*lu*)–city (county/*fu*)–county. While the first level and the second level have seen dramatic changes, the third level of the county remained broadly stable. Variability of the higher layers and stability of the county level is a basic feature throughout the history. After the founding of the PRC, China has established a new four-layer administrative system, which maintained the title of the province of the Ming and Qing dynasties in the first layer, and used the title of the "diqu" in the second layer. The third layer is still the county, and the township or town was established as the fourth layer of government agencies in the county.

After the reform and opening up, in order to meet the needs of economic development, the central government launched a nationwide reform of revocation of "diqu" and establishment of a prefecture layer. Many prefecture-level cities were created at that time, which helped prompt the urbanization of China. This reform initially completed around 2000. From 2005 to 2010, no prefecture-level city in China had been created. During this period China's administrative divisions were still four layers: the provinces (autonomous regions and municipalities directly under the central government) — prefecture-level cities (regions, autonomous prefectures) — county (county-level cities, municipal districts) — township. In fact, in some municipalities, there are only three layers because of the absence of the prefecture level.

Of course, there are still some other methods to establish the prefecture-level city. One is merging the counties into a city, which appeared after China's reform and opening up, such as the merging of Suo County and Pinglu County. Another style is multi-center combination, which included three sub-categories: the first category for distributed industrial and mining areas, and forest areas, such as Huainan City and Huaibei City; the second is some other cities merged into one city, such as Zhangjiakou; the third category appeared in recent years accompanied by the transfer of counties (cities) to municipal districts, such as Chongqing, Foshan, and Jiangmen.

There have been two reforms in the fourth layer: county to city and county (city) to district. The conversion from county to city occurred from 1980 to 1995; as is shown in Table 8-1, the number of county-level city

Table 8-1: China's administrative division (1980–2010).

Year	Prefecture level	#Prefecture city	County level	#Municipality	#County-level city	#Other
1980	311	102	2,766	511	118	2,137
1985	327	162	2,825	620	159	2,046
1990	316	185	2,833	651	279	1,903
1995	334	210	2,849	706	427	1,716
2000	333	259	2,861	787	400	1,674
2005	333	283	2,862	852	374	1,636
2010	333	283	2,856	853	370	1,633

Data Source: State Statistical Yearbook of China.

Table 8-2: Japan's county-level administrative division.

Year	City	Cho	Village	Total
1888	—		71,314	71,314
1889	39		15,820	15,859
1947	210	1,784	8,511	10,505
1956	495	1,870	2,303	4,668
1965	560	2,005	827	3,392
1995	663	1,994	577	3,234
2003	677	1,961	552	3,190
2005	739	1,317	339	2,395
2006	779	844	197	1,820
2008	783	812	193	1,788

Data Source: State Statistical Yearbook of Japan.

was growing dramatically. After the reform, the city's financial autonomy and urban image can be improved in a way that may promote economic development. In fact, as is shown in Table 8-2, in the progress of Japan's urbanization, reform of this division also happened. Changes from county to city in China are mainly reflected in the following points. After the county was converted to a city, its urban construction tax rate changed from 5% to 7%. Apparently, the reform can improve its fiscal revenue. However, studies have shown that the performance of the economy after the county converted to a city is not better than before (Fan et al, 2012). The county must meet some standards before converting to a city. Both the non-agricultural population and the non-farm income must reach a certain standard; however, it has also been pointed out that the economic growth performance is a more important indicator (Li, 2011). In 1997, the central government thought that the county converted to the city led to the heat of urban construction and misuse of cultivated land; therefore, this reform was forbidden from then on.

Although county conversion to cities was stopped, the county (city) conversion to district has been smoothly implemented. The main benefit of the county (city) converted to a municipality is that a prefecture-level city can directly dominate the subordinate municipalities' land plan and fiscal revenue. This is different from a county converted to the city. After the reform, many counties' administrative bodies were abolished and integrated into the prefecture-level city's government. In other words, the original block-based institutions become a compartmentalized integration and bar-based management approach. That is why there is often a certain amount of resentment among the counties while the prefecture-level cities are more satisfied with the result.

On the other hand, we have to note that many provinces in recent years attempt to implement the other two reforms: "provincial governing county" and "enhanced county."[1] These two reforms are intended to undermine the financial and jurisdiction power of the prefecture-level cities and intensify the direct control of the province on the county or expand the county-level administrative autonomy. Cai *et al.* (2011) found that the enhanced county policy improved the prefectural cities' fiscal revenue and curbed their fiscal expenditure. However, a "provincial governing county" had an opposite effect.

The enhanced county policy promoted the city's economic growth, but it was beneficial for the development of tertiary industry. However, a "provincial governing county" reduced the city's economic growth rate and increased the proportion of tertiary industry. Two reform measures have inhibited the expansion of the city, but would help to improve the environmental quality of the city. Therefore, we cannot generally conclude that "provincial governing county" reform will be detrimental to the interests of the prefecture-level city and hinder the process of urbanization. We should do an in-depth study of the advantages and disadvantages of various reform measures to guide the urbanization.

1.2 China's Cities and Urban Population

Based on the above depiction of China's administrative divisions, we can further define Chinese cities (towns) and the urban population. Based on the definition of a city's boundaries and scale, the definition of the urban population is obvious. Zhou (2006) have pointed out that the first scientific problem of urban studies is the basic validity of the concept. The article points out that there are three major measures for the division of the city. The first is a geographical entity (physical area of the city), that is, the

---

[1] "Provincial governing county" means that the province governments directly lead the county-level governments. "Enhanced county" means expanding the counties' powers to grant the county government greater autonomy.

built-up area of the city. This reflects the basic urban characteristics, which is an opposite geographical concept from the countryside. The second is a city administrative region (administrative area), in other words, the city government administration for a territory. The third is the functional area of the city, which is the urban population of daily social and economic activities. Woetzel *et al.* (2008) finds that city definitions can be divided into four definitions. The first is in accordance with the administrative division, such as Brazil. The second is in accordance with the administrative and scale, such as China. The third species is classified in accordance with the size of the population, such as the United States, which set the 天 threshold of density greater than 4,000 people per square kilometer and a total population of more than 50,000 people. The last is divided in accordance with the level of economic development and scale, such as Japan.

We also point out that China's official presentations tend to use "*chengzhenhua*" instead of "*chengshihua*."[2] This is mainly due to three considerations. First, China's urbanization process set off late; therefore, given the large rural population, the government is concerned about the big city disease. On the other hand, China's political representation is favorable about balancing strategy, which is including the balance between the eastern and western region and the balance between large cities and small towns. Therefore, the "city" and "town" are placed together. Until now, there is still not a mature city division measure.

The definition of the urban population is also changing all the time. At the first census in 1955, China's urban population included city, town, urban-type residential areas (including agriculture and non-agricultural). At the second census in 1964, the benchmark was non-agricultural population of the city and town. In 1982, the total population of the city and town were all included in the urban population, which meant that the period of urban population was overvalued. In 1986, the abolishment of rural towns and the creation of the city led to the rapid expansion of urban population. At the fourth census in 1990, a new standard was established, which included municipal district population and the core town of the county-level cities and counties' population. Of course, the definition of the urban population

---

[2] "*Chengzhenhua*" mean that urbanization will focus on both cities and towns. "*Chengshihua*" means that the urbanization will mainly focus on cities.

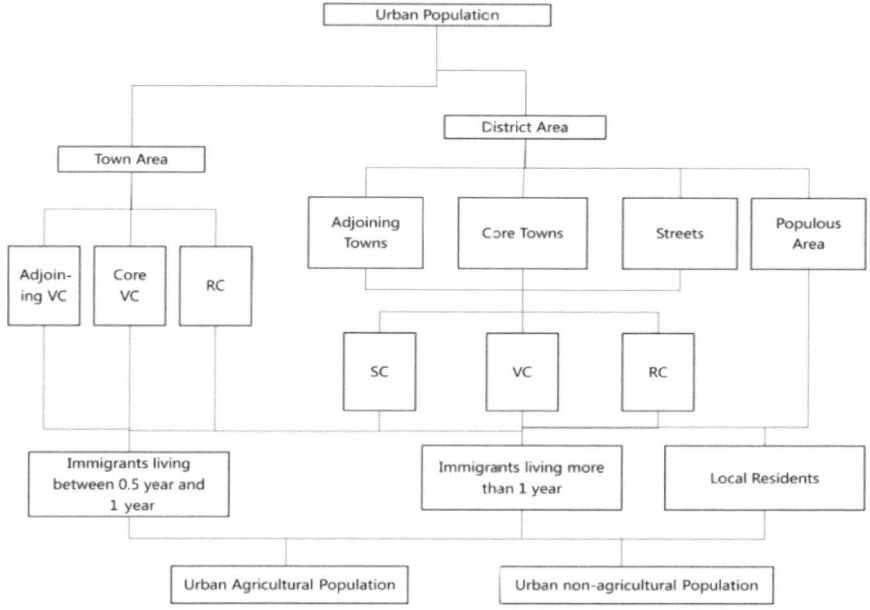

Figure 8-1: Definition of China's urban population in the fifth census.[3]

in the 2000 census conducted an adjustment, see Figure 8-1. The sixth population census follows the fifth census definition of urban population.

According to the above definition of urban population, we calculated two urbanization ratios according to different measures from 1970 to 2010. Before the reform and opening up, China's urbanization rate was maintained at less than 20%, see Table 8-3. After the reform and opening up, urban population increased a lot due to the return of 20 million educated youth. With the development of the township economic and private sector, local urbanization promoted the rapid rise of the urban population in the 1980s. In the 1990s, with the exchange rate regime reform and further opening up, China's coastal areas of export-oriented industries attracted a large number of migrant workers from inland provinces. At that time, inter-provincial population immigrants were the driving force for urbanization. After 2003,

---

[3]VC is the villagers' committee, RC is the residents' committee, SA is a special area with more than 3,000 people.

Table 8-3: China's urban population (1970–2010).

	Total million	Urban population		Urban population (*Hukou*)	
		million	%	million	%
1970	829.9	144.2	17.38	126.6	15.25
1975	924.2	160.3	17.34	142.8	15.45
1978	962.6	172.5	17.92	152.3	15.82
1980	987.1	191.4	19.39	168	17.02
1985	1,058.5	250.9	23.71	210.5	19.89
1990	1,143.3	302	26.41	235.7	20.62
1995	1,211.2	351.7	29.04	282.3	23.31
2000	1,267.4	459.1	36.22	322.5	25.45
2005	1,307.6	562.1	42.99	409	31.28
2010	1,339.7	665.6	49.68	459.6	34.32

Data Source: State Statistical Yearbook of China.

with the start of the real estate market reforms, a large number of suburban agricultural lands were transferred into non-agricultural land. Free transactions of the real estate market helped part of the floating population of the city to settle down in the cities. At this period, large and medium-sized cities became a mainstream of urbanization.

1.3 China's Urbanization and Industrialization

Many studies suggest that China's urbanization lags far behind the development of China's industrialization. As is shown in Figure 8-2, Brazil, Mexico, and many other developing countries' urbanization ratios are much higher than the level of China. Chenery and Syrquin (1975) drawn in the normal model of countries' development through a comprehensive analysis of more than 100 countries, including the average level of urbanization. According to the Chenery model predictions, the urbanization rate in the economies of the various stages of economic development is ahead of the rate of industrialization. However, the situation in China did not obey this law, see Table 8-4. When China's GDP per capita reached US$1,000, China's rate of industrialization was already 44.8%; however, the urbanization rate was only 39.09%. Many scholars try to explain this. Some scholars thought that China's lagged service industry caused the relatively low urbanization rate.

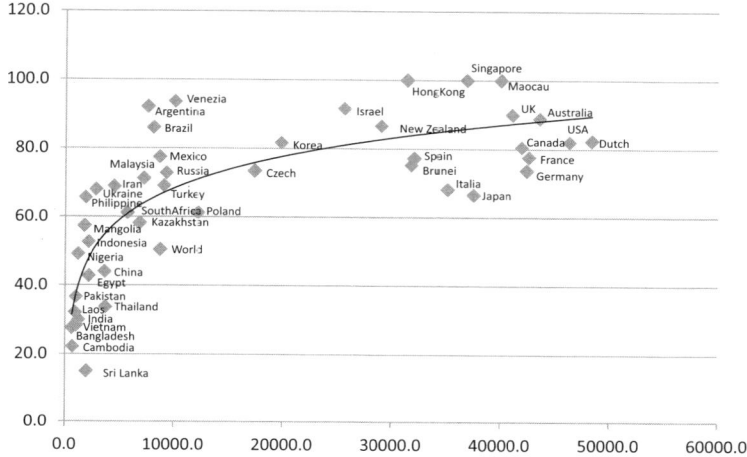

Figure 8-2: Countries' urbanization ratio and per capita GNI.
Data Source: World Bank WDI Database.

Table 8-4: Chenery model and China's facts.

	Chenery model			China's facts		
GDP per capita	Urbaniza-tion ratio	Industrializa-tion ratio	Gap	Urbaniza-tion ratio	Industrializa-tion ratio	Gap
100	22	14.9	7.1	17.78	36.8	−19.42
200	36.2	21.5	14.7	17.92	44.3	−26.38
300	43.9	25.1	18.8	24.52	38.9	−14.38
400	49	27.6	21.4	26.94	37.4	−10.06
500	52.7	29.4	23.3	27.99	40.8	−12.81
800	60.1	33.1	27	34.78	42.7	−7.92
1000	63.4	34.7	28.7	39.09	44.8	−5.71

Chang and Brada (2006) show that urbanization created a lot of employment opportunities through the expansion of the service sector. Self-sufficiency in the rural sector determines that its demand for services is limited. But the market orientation of the city means that residents have greater demand for transportation, retail, and other service industries; hence, urbanization can stimulate the services sector output and employment. However, due to the problems of income distribution, the development of the service sector is inhibited, resulting in a low urbanization rate.

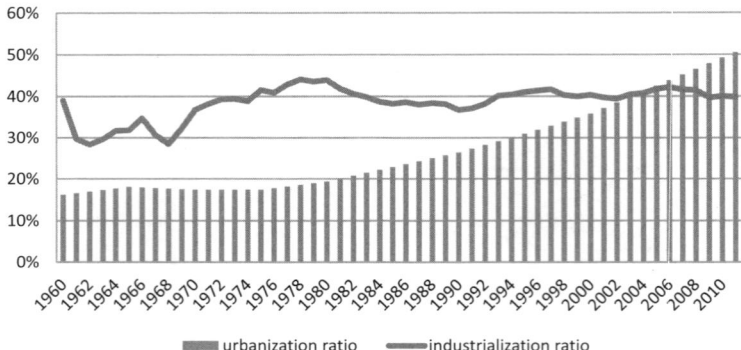

Figure 8-3: China's urbanization ratio and industrialization ratio (1960–2010). *Data Source*: World Bank database.

The second explanation is based on the analysis of the industrial chain. China's industrialization is accompanied by globalization. The growth of Chinese-made industry needs the help of the world's urban system. In the industrial system, China is responsible for the production, while some developed countries are responsible for research and development and sales and service in other countries. In fact, the latter have a greater influence on the service sector and urbanization rate.

Therefore, China maintains a low urbanization rate and a high rate of industrialization, see Figure 8-3.

A third explanation is that China's control of the land market and household registration system leads to a suppressed factor mobility, which also affected the process of urbanization. Jian and Huang (2010) pointed at China's long-standing heavy industry-oriented development strategy, and heavy industry is a capital-intensive industry that absorbs less labor. Furthermore, the household registration system and other systems limit the labor mobility from rural areas to urban areas, and the labor transfer to non-agricultural industries. Therefore, urbanization falls into chronic stagnation.

2. CHINA'S URBAN SYSTEM

2.1 The Classification of Urban System

Now there are three main urban systems in the world. The first one mainly consists of large cities, such as in the United States. Although the overall

Table 8-5: Cities more than 1 Million population taking up the countries' proportion (%).

	1960	1970	1980	1990	2000	2010	Density (2009) (per km^2)
Japan	32.1	40.0	43.2	46.2	47.3	49.5	350.0
Korea	21.0	31.4	42.2	50.8	49.3	47.4	503.0
US	38.7	41.3	40.7	41.6	43.1	44.7	33.6
Brazil	20.7	26.9	33.0	34.8	37.1	40.8	23.0
Argentina	38.2	40.6	40.5	39.2	38.8	39.1	14.7
Mexico	21.8	27.7	32.1	33.3	34.8	34.9	55.3
UK	31.4	28.3	27.2	26.0	26.2	25.6	255.6
France	21.6	22.2	22.0	22.1	22.1	22.2	114.3
EU	15.6	17.0	17.4	17.6	17.7	17.9	116.2
China	7.7	7.5	7.6	9.0	13.7	17.7	142.8
India	6.6	7.5	8.6	9.8	11.0	12.2	388.6
Germany	8.4	8.0	7.7	7.9	7.7	8.1	234.9

Data Source: World Bank database, *International Statistical Yearbook 2012*.

population density is low, the proportion of large urban population is high, while large cities mainly consist of the core city and adjacent areas, which is also named metropolis statistical area (MSA).

The other type is composed of small and medium-sized cities, such as Germany, Holland, Belgium, and other countries. The Randstad and Rhine–Ruhr region is a typical representative. In fact, within the EU, small and medium-sized cities are the majority. Of course, the EU's urban system may be related to its long time split situation. The third is the hub-and-spoke style, such as Japan and Korea with high population density (see Table 8-5). The Tokyo metropolitan area and the Seoul metropolitan area are distinctive examples; Japan and South Korea's high-density metropolitan development model has a greater association with high population density. Of course, we should also note that Japan and Korea have a high primacy ratio, which is related to the two countries' strong central government.

2.2 The Development of China's Urban System

The positioning of the urban system in China has been constantly adjusted. In the 1980s, we advocated a strategy of small towns, which is related to the idea of "small towns, grand strategy" put forward by Fei Xiaotong. During this period, bottom-up urbanization dominated the trend. The so-called bottom-up mode is related to the local township enterprises' development in southern Jiangsu in China's Jiangsu Province and the private sector development in Wenzhou of Zhejiang province. However, these types of urbanization end up with the fall of the two traditional development styles.

In 2001, the 10th Five-Year Plan indicated that we needed to implement a balanced urbanization model among large, medium, and small cities that is proper for our national condition. The urban system should be gradually formed. We should focus on the development of small cities and towns, and actively develop small and medium-sized cities, and improve the functions of the regional central cities. Meanwhile, big cities play a leading role, and provide the guidance for the towns to develop in order.

We should prevent blind expansion of city size. We must vigorously develop the urban economy and improve the ability of cities and towns to absorb employment. In fact, at that time city size was much smaller, therefore, the development is focused on the small and medium-sized cities. During this period, big cities got rich land premium from the real estate market reform, which also became a significant source of funding for major cities to improve their infrastructure. These further improved investment environment and livability of the capital city. Consequently, top-down urbanization started to become mainstream.

The 11th Five-Year Plan (2006) has proposed that we should adhere to coordinated development of big, medium, and small cities and small towns, enhance comprehensive urban bearing capacity, and actively and stably push forward urbanization according to the principle of land conservation and intensive development. The urban and rural dualistic structure will be gradually changed. This stage began to realize the large cities' power to promote the balanced development of medium and small cities and small towns. According to the 12th Five-Year Plan (2011), large cities should receive more attention.

Is our city system reasonable? How large is suitable for the city's scale? Many scholars have put forward their own views. Quigley thinks there are too many small cities in China, and the efficiency is too low. At first, the national policy was to encourage investment in large cities, but only allow the flow of migrants to surrounding cities. If rural labor is relocated to cities, the productivity will rise three times. If we increase the size of a small city, you can increase labor efficiency by 25% or even more. Henderson (2007) put forward a similar view. He finds that the administrative hierarchy of the city has restricted the development of small cities. Quality education, healthcare, and financial institutions are given priority in cities with higher administrative levels, mainly concentrated in the center of the city. Such a system caused unfair allocation of public resources, and thus led to the different development among cities. Au and Henderson (2006) use 285 Chinese cities' data to estimate the impact of urban agglomeration on productivity. As expected, the relationship between total productivity of the city and urban scale has an inverted U-shaped relation. From the estimated results, the urban agglomeration profits are high, which indicates that due to the implementation of migration control, most Chinese cities have not yet reached the scale of the effective size. However, this study has a problem, which is the underestimation of the population of major cities in China, because only the resident population in the census year data is accurate. Liu (2009) proves the existence of scale economies of China's cities, which also supports the expansion of big cities. Wang (2002) thinks limiting the development of the city in fact restricts the optimal allocation of resources, and limits the increase in productivity. Fu and Hong (2008), using manufacturing enterprises census data in 2004, test the benefit of different scale enterprises in cities of different sizes due to agglomeration economies. Of course, there are some different voices. Guan (2007) tends to consider the small cities as the buffer zone for the big cities, therefore, the development of small cities is also of great significance.

More specifically, Wang (2010) believes that at present, cities that have a population over 1 million are not too many, but still too few. Market regulation accompanied by the big cities' rational development will help improve the economic efficiency and the rational use of resources, especially conservation of land resources. But some symbiotic and complementary relationship exists between the different-sized cities and small towns. Medium-sized cities and small towns near the large city have better conditions for the development and they are conducive to the formation of reasonable urban agglomerations. Later in this chapter, we see that if some of the prefecture-level cities double the size, their unit labor real output can increase by 20–35%. This proportion is higher than that of Wang and Xia (1999), who estimated Chinese cities' optimal net returns to scale level of 17–19%. But the former is before deduction of the negative external effects of the city, while the latter refers to net income, net of negative external effects, so they are more consistent. Liu (2011) believes that there is no unified optimal city size. For part of the year and indicators of optimal city size, optimal size is a variable. On the whole, there do not currently exist over-sized cities, therefore, limiting big cities scale view basis.

2.3 The Present Situation of China's Urban System

Different scholars at different times come to different conclusions based on different data and analysis methods for the Chinese city. As a result, we need to sort out the present Chinese city size distribution. First of all, we should give the definition of the size of cities at all levels. City Planning Law of the People's Republic of China in 1989 points out that the mega-cities in China are those with non-agricultural population over one million. Then the large city has non-agricultural population over 500,000. A medium-sized city has non-agricultural population greater than 200,000 and lesser than 500,000. The small city has non-agricultural population of less than 200,000. But this plan was abolished on January 1, 2008, and at the same time the implementation of the People's Republic of China Town and Country Planning Act did not set the provisions of the city size. In other words, China has not yet defined the concept of city size from the legislative level. In 2010, a Green Paper was published on the scientific development of small and medium-sized cities by the China Summit Forum Organizing Committee, Committee for Economic Development of small and medium-sized cities and Social Sciences Documentation Publishing House jointly. The definitions are as follows: urban resident population of 50 million or less for small cities, 500,000–1,000,000 for the medium-sized cities, 1,000,000–3,000,000 for the city, 3–10 million for mega-cities, more than 10 million for huge city. In this analysis, we still stick to the City Planning Law of the People's Republic of China in 1989. We subdivided three levels for cities more than 1 million: mega-city above 4 million, extraordinary city 2–4 million, and giant city 1–2 million.

Table 8-6: The urban scale distribution of China (2000–2010).

Year	Mega city >4 million	Extraordinary city 2–4 million	Giant city 1–2 million	Big city 0.5–1 million	Medium city 0.2–0.5 million	Small city <0.2 million
2010 (6th census)	21	30	85	103	48	0
2010 (6th census, district[4])	15	26	37	102	90	17
2011	14	31	82	108	49	4
2010	14	30	81	109	49	4
2009	14	28	82	110	51	2
2005	13	25	75	108	61	4
2000 (5th census)	10	16	64	103	60	2
2000 (5th census, district)	8	14	33	78	107	15

Data Source: State Statistical Yearbook of China.

As is shown in Table 8-6, the number of large cities is rapidly increasing from 2000 to 2010. We define a city as "large city" if the city's population exceeds 1 million. At that period, the number of large cities grows from 90 to 134. Of course, this increase may be caused by many factors. The first is establishment of the new prefecture-level city, such as Huai'an, Hezhou, and Wuwei. The second reason is the expanding of districts' area. Many adjacent counties or small cities are merged into the core cities' districts at that time. The total population of these newly founded districts exceeds 4,000 million. The rest of the increase excluding the former two cases is the pure growth of the municipal districts. However, there exist some faked municipal districts in the Central and West China because of radical urban sprawl.

Of course, the urban population of the municipal districts is a better indicator to measure the size of the cities. This benchmark can be more effective excluding some low-density or undeveloped areas. According to the new standard, the number of large cities increases from 55 to 76. In 2010, more than 248 million citizens were living in the large city, forming

---

[4]These statistics include the urban population of the municipal districts, the others include all the population of the municipal districts.

18.1% of the total population. Besides, if we take the former standard, the result is more optimistic.

The calculation of the above measure of the urban population ignored some densely populated and economically developed county-level cities, such as Jiangyin, Kunshan City, Taicang, and Changshu City. Of course, the number of these cities is not large, mainly located in Jiangsu and Zhejiang Provinces. Therefore, little bias was caused by the above estimates. The rapid growth of the population of the city compared to the more than 1 million, 500,000–1,000,000 metropolitan growth is gentler according to two measures.

Most large cities are mainly located in the East China and South regions, see Table 8-7. Although there are a lot of big cities in Northeast China that have a scale between 500,000 and 1,000,000, Northeast China has far fewer giant cities. These big cities include the cities of Daqing, Anshan, Fushun, Jixi, and Hegang, which are mainly typical mining cities. These cities face a gloomy future for the depleting resources. During the past three decades, a number of large cities emerged in the Pearl River Delta, which has also become the largest urban agglomeration of the Chinese population density. However, the geographic scope of the Pearl River Delta is limited; therefore, the overall size of the population of the region will not continue

Table 8-7: The distribution of urban scale.

	Total	Groups					
		>4 million	2–4 million	1–2 million	0.5–1 million	0.2–0.5 million	<0.2 million
All	287	14	30	81	109	49	4
North	33	2	3	6	16	6	0
Northeast	34	2	2	5	21	3	1
Northwest	30	1	2	5	10	12	0
East	79	3	16	27	24	9	0
Middle-South	79	4	5	28	28	13	1
Southwest	32	2	2	10	10	6	2
East Area	101	10	15	22	36	18	0
Middle Area	101	2	6	10	44	37	2
West Area	85	3	5	5	22	35	15

Data Source: The Sixth Population Census of China.

to rise significantly. However, for the Yangtze River Delta, its density is relatively low, and the carrying capacity of resources is better; the cities are growing in parallel. There is further room for expansion. The city system in North China and Northeast region also showed the same trend, giant cities fewer than normal, and excessive population concentrated into the two mega-cities of Beijing and Tianjin, and this hinders the development of small and medium-sized cities around the development of mega-cities, which formed a pattern of centripetal development. In fact, in the surrounding cities in Hebei Province, there is the problem of salinization of the land, and the problem of water shortage has also plagued the Beijing–Tianjin–Tanggu Region. Even if the North Water Transfer Project were to be completed on schedule, the Beijing–Tianjin Region's water gap is still large, so not only does it not increase the size of the city of Beijing–Tianjin–Tanggu Region, there may be a risk of atrophy.

Where is the orientation of China city scale? The American urbanization model is clearly not applicable in our country. As a last large population of developing countries, our country cannot take this way with the consideration of land use curb or economic level or environmental protection. Europe formed a unique pattern dominated by small and medium-sized cities due to geopolitical segmentation and the development of cities and towns of the compact mode. However, the European model of development in China is also facing many difficulties. The EU's total population reached 503 million in 2012, and its area is 4.324 million km^2. Besides, the EU is rather flat with an average elevation of abundant water resources. However, only 12% of the land area in China is plain areas; population density is much higher than the European Union and the United States. It is more likely to select the Japanese and Korean models, which have more similarity in geographical structure, population density, and cultural background with China. In accordance with the Japanese and Korean model urbanization, China must follow the construction of high-density, intensive metropolis, and metropolitan area sites should be located in the eastern coastal areas, so you can better integrate into the international industrial division of labor. As an important indicator of industrial production growth in the period from 1995 to 2010, the region with the fastest growth in electricity demand is still the eastern region, the average annual growth rate is 11.7%; the Midwest is relatively slow. As is shown in Figure 8-4, none of China's regional

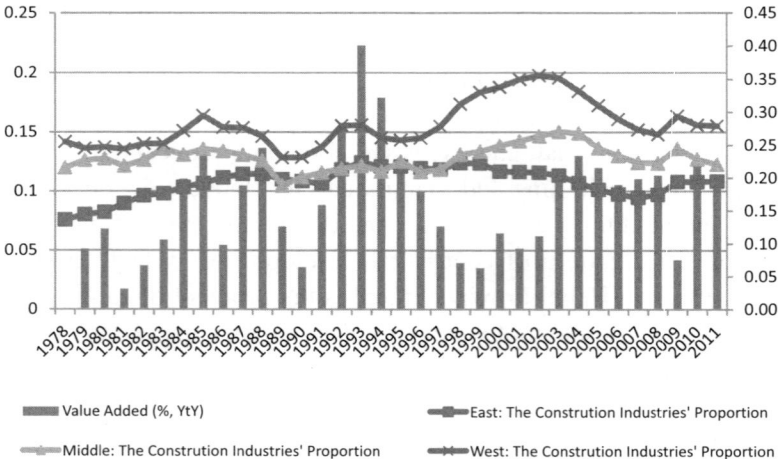

Figure 8-4: The proportion of construction industry taking up the secondary industry. *Data Source*: CEIC database.

development plans really promotes urbanization, including Great Western Development Strategy, the Rise of Central China Plan and the Northeast Area Revitalization Plan; and industrialization quality is also worrisome because there is only infrastructure construction without the upgrading of industries and the migration of population.

3. THE OPPORTUNITY AND CHALLENGE OF THE NEW URBANIZATION

After the 18th National Congress of the Communist Party of China (CPC), we advocated a new urbanization. We need to illustrate the definition of the new urbanization: the so-called new urbanization, adhering to the people-oriented. This could be a driving force for the new industrialization, promoting the modern city, urban cluster, urban ecology, and rural urbanization. The quality and level of urbanization will be enhanced, leading to the path of scientific development, intensive and efficient, functional, and environment-friendly, social harmony, distinctive, integrated urban and rural, medium and small cities and small towns coordinated development of urbanization road.

3.1 New Urbanization and Agriculture Sector's Modernization

The 18th National Congress of the CPC reported: "Adhere to the new industrialization of the Chinese characteristics, information technology, urbanization, agricultural modernization path, to promote the integration of information technology and industrialization depth, positive interaction of industrialization and urbanization, urbanization and agricultural modernization coordination, promote industrialization, simultaneous development of information technology, urbanization, agricultural modernization." Urbanization development is inseparable from the coordination of agricultural modernization; urbanization, land, labor, and other elements need to be imported from rural or agricultural areas which mean that it is necessary that we have a clear understanding about agricultural development, especially the food problem and arable land issues.

In 2006, the 4th Session of the 10th National People's Congress passed the National Economic and Social Development Five-Year Plan, which clearly confirmed the legal effect of 18 million mu of arable land that cannot be broken in the next five years. Then, the government reiterated on many occasions that we need to adhere to the 18 million mu of arable land red line. This is undoubtedly China's hard constraint of future urbanization, because the development of the city land and farming land has similar preferences. They all have certain requirements about water, climate, and the flatness of the land. The arable land red line in fact limits the spatial development patterns of urban development in China. Many scholars have questioned this arable land red line, while other scholars put forward cross-regional transfer of the land reform program to circumvent the red line.

3.1.1 The problem of the safety of food supply

The 18 million mu of arable land red line was originally proposed for food security. China's grain production achieved nine consecutive growths. As is shown in Figures 8-5–8-7, the production of rice, wheat, and corn acreage during this period increased significantly, while the beans planted area was reduced. Therefore, the beans supply gap is mainly filled by imports. From 2004 to 2012, China's grain area increased by 1.78 million hectares, with an increase of 11.9%, accounting for 32.3% growth of food production. In the meantime, grain yield increased 64.4 kg, with an increase of 22.3%,

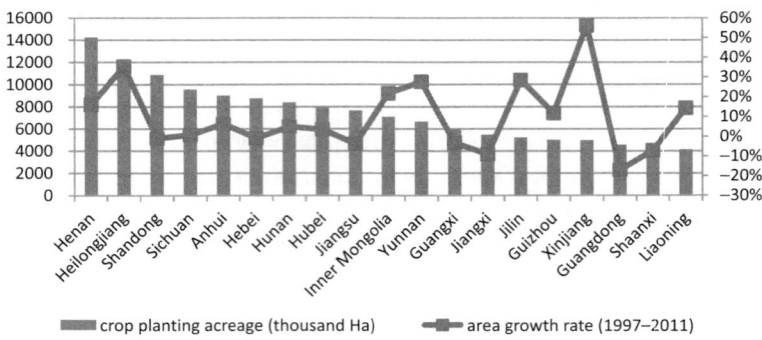

Figure 8-5: China's major provinces' crop acreage.

Data Source: CEIC database.

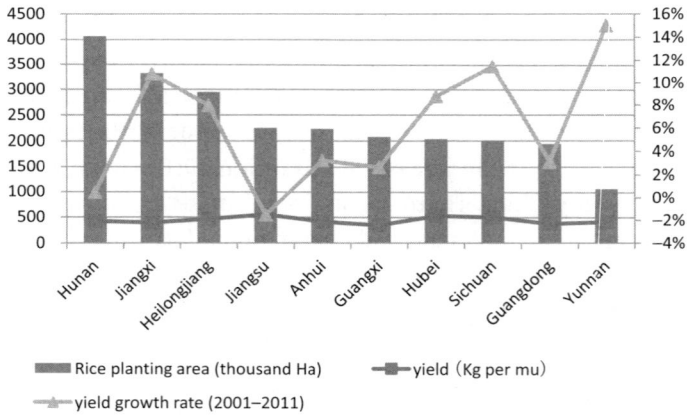

Figure 8-6: China's major provinces' rice acreage and yield.[5]

Data Source: CEIC database.

accounting for 67.7% growth of food production. In other words, one-third of the production growths rely on the expansion of the area, and two-third on increasing yields.

However, this structure of increase is complex. Although rice production has been increasing in the past nine years, its yield increases only a

---

[5]Mu is the traditional unit of land area in East Asia. One mu is approximately equal to 667 square meters.

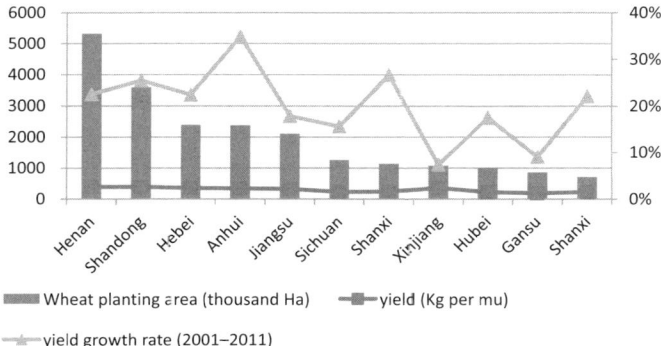

Figure 8-7: China's major provinces' wheat acreage and yield.
Data Source: CEIC database.

little. The yield of rice in 2004 was 420.7 kg per mu, while in 2011 it was only 445.82 kg per mu, increasing by only 6%. Besides, the corresponding increase in the total production of rice was only 12.2%. A similar phenomenon happened across provinces. As the major rice producing areas, the growth rate of the yields in Hunan and Jiangxi provinces are not significantly lagging behind the 20% growth rate of Henan and Shandong, which are acknowledged as the wheat-growing areas. This also shows that the rise of China's rice productivity encountered a bottleneck. The yield of 900 kg per mu is still restricted in the experimental fields. Besides, corn has the better performance with a 48% increase in yield, which mainly contributes to the planting area's growth rather than the yield's growth. Particularly, the growth of the crop acreage occurred mainly in the provinces of Heilongjiang, Henan, and Yunnan, while Guangdong, Jiangxi, and Shaanxi provinces' crop acreage dropped significantly.

On the other hand, from the international comparison, yields of two main foods, rice and wheat, have a high ranking in the main producing countries, namely, there is no room for improvement of China's major grain yield, see Figures 8-8 and 8-9. China indeed has comparative advantages in the production of rice and wheat. And rice is grown mainly in East Asia, South Asia, and Southeast Asia. Therefore, the supply of the main food cannot rely on international trade. In fact, with that huge amount of imports from the international agricultural market it is extremely easy to raise product prices. Regarding the stability of the future food supply, the

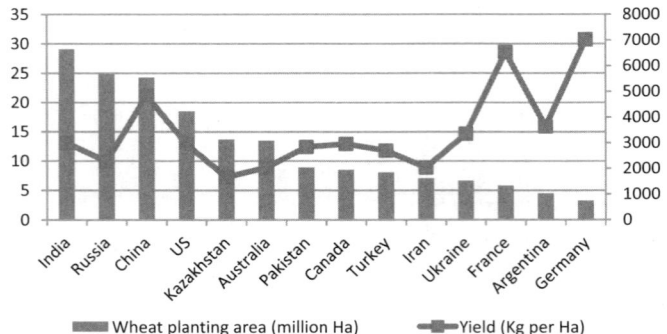

Figure 8-8: Major nations' rice acreage and yield.
Data Source: FAOSTAT database.

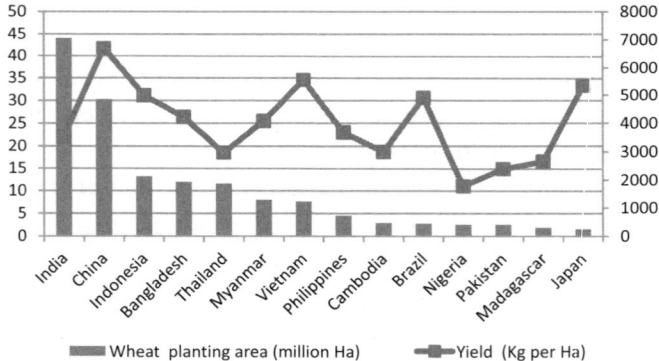

Figure 8-9: Major nations' wheat acreage and yield.
Data Source: FAOSTAT database.

current scale of arable land cannot be significantly reduced. Even if the red line is not a hard constraint, the scale of arable land will be maintained at around 18 million mu. Of course, the following inference is that the future of urbanization and agricultural modernization can release more agricultural labor to non-agricultural areas, but it is almost impossible to release a lot of transfer of agricultural land to non-agricultural land. So future agricultural development in China is unlikely to take the path of development of large farms, and the appropriate scale of operation of the family farm is a possible direction.

3.1.2 Family farm

Document No. 1 of CCCPC, released February 14, 2013, encourages and supports farmers to transfer to professional farm, family farm, and cooperative farm. As new agricultural business entities, the concept of "family farm" appears for the first time in the Central Document No. 1.

On April 3, 2013, Premier Li Keqiang chaired a State Council executive meeting to carry out the deployment of modern agricultural comprehensive reform pilot work. The meeting put forward an innovative agricultural production and management system. We should foster the growth of the stock cooperatives, cooperatives, leading enterprises, family farms, and other large new production and management, the development of various forms of appropriate scale operation. Leading enterprises and farmers are encouraged to stock cooperatives to establish a compact mechanism linking the interests.

For a long time, China's agricultural production faced more people and fewer lands, see Figure 8-10; the intensification of agricultural production is still low, although the per capita arable land area is approximately 0.215 hectares (equivalent to 3.2 mu). However, equilibrium allocation regarding the production of land further reduced the average area of a single piece of arable land, resulting in the improvement of agricultural productivity that relies on the application of fertilizers. And implementing appropriate scale of operation in agriculture and developing family farms will

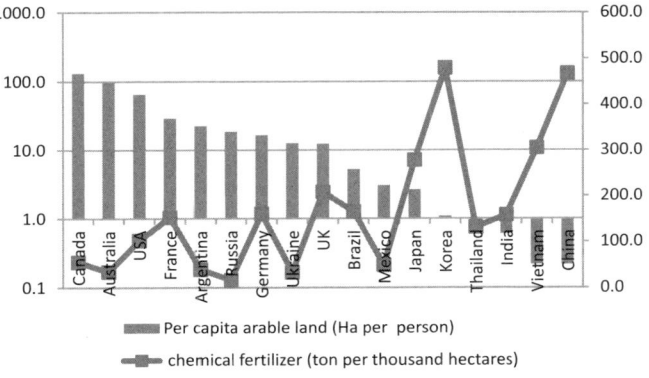

Figure 8-10: Major nations' per capita arable land and fertilizer usage.
Data Source: FAOSTAT database.

reduce the negative impact of the above factors and improve production efficiency.

However, we also need to recognize that many difficulties in the implementation of the agricultural scale management are mainly reflected in the following aspects:

First, the scale of operations must be modest. Chen and Dang[6] believe that a moderate expansion of the scale of agricultural production can improve operational efficiency, but it does not mean that the bigger, the better. Land resources' concentration also means that abundant farmers should withdraw from the traditional agricultural production and transfer to non-agricultural sector, and the transfer to non-agricultural sector should be progressive; on the other hand, the yield across provinces has certain differences, see Figure 8-11; therefore, the promotion of scale production should be gradual and keep in line with local conditions.

Second, clarification of land ownership is the premise and guarantee for the large-scale operation of agriculture, which means land resources' reallocation between farmers. Therefore, we must establish permanent farmers' contracted land use rights from the legal and institutional recognition

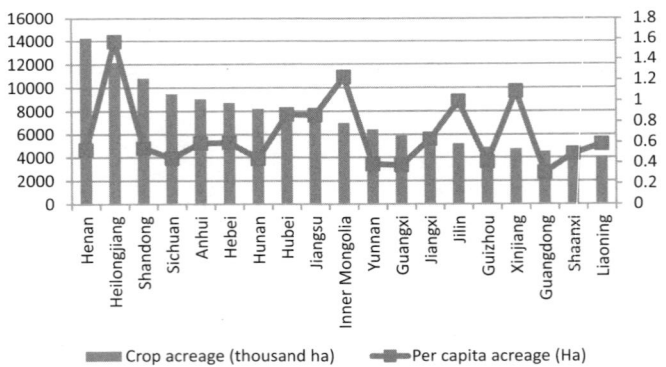

Figure 8-11: China's major provinces crop acreage.

Data Source: CEIC database.

---

[6]http://news.xinhuanet.com/politics/2013-02/28/c_114829814_2.htm; http://www.yangtse.com/system/2013/03/08/016491885.shtml.

and the opening of the mortgage and the elimination of agricultural land restrictions in order to protect the large-scale operation in advance.

Third, how to identify the family farm that is qualified for subsidies is also a major difficulty. The agro-processing factories and scale production have a greater difference in the form of registration. On the other hand, the source of subsidy funds will also be a major problem for local governments. At present, family farms only succeed in Songjiang District and a few other districts, which is associated with the financial strength of Shanghai.

In addition, the scale operation of agriculture also put forward higher standards for production technology and management of agriculture. Therefore, we are cautiously optimistic. On the other hand, we need to realize that, whether scale operation or raising the prices of agricultural products, there will be no qualitative change in the income of farmers, that is to say, narrowing the income gap between urban and rural areas in the future still relies mainly on agricultural workers' transferring to the town.

3.2 New Urbanization and the Infrastructure Construction

There is a gap between the level of China and the world's major economies in both road density and railway density, see Figure 8-12. China's railway network density is less than half of Japan, less than one-tenth of Germany; as for highway network, between China and Japan or South Korea, there is a significant gap. Even compared with the United States, China still has a gap

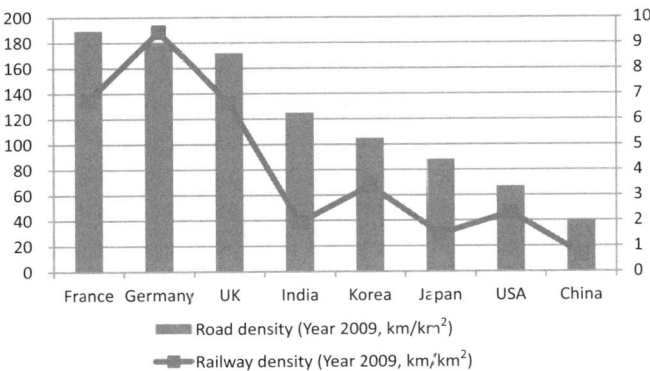

Figure 8-12: The world's major national road network and rail network density (2009). *Data Source*: CEIC database.

of one-third. Many studies have shown that the construction of infrastructure has a good role in promoting a country's economic development (Li and Liu, 1995; Guo and Jia, 2006; Liu and Hu, 2010). Thus, when talking about the future of China's new urbanization strategy, infrastructure will continue to be an important topic.

There exist a lot of differences in the level of infrastructure across cities. Most cities with low per capita GDP and low level of per capita road area need to complete the construction of the infrastructure by means of transfer payments (such as Bazhong and Longnan, etc.) But some exceptional cities with lower per capita GDP enjoy high-level per capita roads, which indicate a pace of construction of local infrastructure beyond the local level of economic development. This may lead to a local financial crisis. Another group of cities, such as Beijing, Shanghai, Guangzhou, Shenzhen, Foshan, and Ningbo City, with lower level of per capita roads and higher GDP per capita, are more suitable for the construction of rail transit to ease traffic pressure.

City rail transit construction greatly improves the city's traffic operational efficiency, improves the city's congestion, and reduces environmental pollution and carbon emissions. The most typical examples of the benefit of the subway construction are Barcelona and Atlanta, see Table 8-8. The two cities have many similarities. They held the Summer Olympics in 1992 and 1996 in succession, they both have a population between 2.5 and 2.8 million, but population density differences led to usage differences between the two cities, which also led to 10-fold difference in per capita carbon dioxide emissions. Therefore, the first requirement of subway development is the high-density, large-scale potential users.

Table 8-8: The comparison of Atlanta and Barcelona.

	Density (per km^2)	CO_2 emission (ton per person)	Subway length (km)	Subway covered population ratio	Public traffic ratio
Atlanta	6	400	74	4% (800 m Circle)	4.5%
Barcelona	176	38	99	60% (600 m Circle)	30%

Note: All data are the levels in 1990.

China has been more cautious for the development of the subway. China's first city subway was established in 1969; however, the popularity of the metro city in the country was in the 90 years after. Shanghai started running Metro Line 1, Line 2, and Line 3 in 1995, 1999, and 2000 respectively; Guangzhou opened Metro Line 1 in 1998; Shenzhen and Nanjing then also opened a city subway in 2004–2005. In 2012, Shanghai and Beijing own the two largest scale subway operations. At the same time, their utilization stays at a high level, which is close to the level of Moscow and Seoul and lower than Tokyo.

According to the document of the General Office of the State Council, the subway construction should meet the following basic conditions: the local general budget revenue reaches 10 billion yuan; GDP reaches 10 billion yuan; the urban population is more than 300 million; the traffic of planned routes should reach more than 30,000 passengers per hour. The urban rail transit projects will get priority support for mega-cities with better economic conditions or facing serious problem of traffic congestion.

After the financial crisis, with fiscal policy stimulating, the urban infrastructure construction gets more support. Shenyang, Chengdu, Foshan, Chongqing, Xi'an, Suzhou, Hangzhou, Wuhan, and other cities have started a large number of subway lines in the period 2010–2012, see Figure 8-13. Woetzel *et al.* (2008) thought that by 2025 there will be 170 cities meeting the requirements of the public transportation system of urban development,

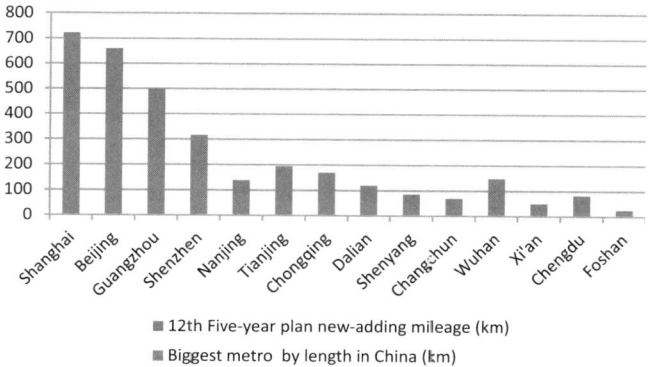

Figure 8-13: Major cities subway operator mileage and planning.
Data Source: The Cities' Government Working Report.

which is more than twice the number of the European. At the end of 2011, 12 Chinese cities have established the urban rail transit system, including Beijing, Shanghai, Shenzhen, and other cities. During the 12th Five-Year plan, 29 cities are expected to join the subway family.

However, we must also take high constructing costs and high operating costs into account.

It is a worldwide problem to maintain and operate the subway. Almost all the metro operations face deficits around the world. At present, China is constructing subway projects. The subway construction cost per kilometer is generally around 4–5 billion yuan, which greatly enhances the operational risks of the subway. Therefore, the weaker local governments may take heavy debt burden because of the subway. Therefore, subway planning must be a combination of factors including residential real estate and commercial development to reduce the high operating risks.

3.3 New Urbanization and Resource Constraints

Another challenge for new urbanization comes from the resources and environment. The new urbanization means lifestyle changes and improving of life quality. People living in the rural areas may rely on coal and wood for their energy consumption. Natural gas and liquefied petroleum gas gradually become the mainstream of urban life consumption, and household appliances will also increase the consumption of electricity. Besides, the per capita water consumption will increase with the increase in the size of the city.

However, China is short of water. Although the freshwater resources accounted for 6% of the world, less than Brazil, Russia, and Canada, ranking fourth in the world, the per capita level is only 2,200 cubic meters, which is only a quarter of the world average and one-fifth of that in the United States. China is also one of the 13 countries facing the most serious water shortage. On the other hand, China's water resource is highly uneven; the south has abundance, while the north has paucity. According to the sixth census data, China's northern provinces have a total population of 561 million, accounting for 41.9% of the country's total population, see Table 8-9. According to the 2011 Water Report, the northern rivers have 402.53 billion cubic meters water, accounting for only 17.3% of the country. The implementation of the

Table 8-9: Water resources of the first tier area in 2011(billion cubic meters).

	Total precipitation	Surface	Aquifer	Non-repetition	Water resource
Total	55,132.9	22,213.6	7,214.5	1,043.1	23,256.7
Songhua River	4,070.5	987.3	420.5	190.1	1,177.4
Liao River	1,481	332.1	179.8	77.9	410
Hai River	1,658.5	135.9	237.3	162	297.9
Yellow River	3,888.5	620.9	411.2	118.5	739.4
Huai River	2,672.8	643.3	399	249.3	892.6
Yangtze River	16,603.3	7,713.6	2,138	124	7,837.6
#Tai Lake Area	412.6	173.6	43.8	20.3	193.8
Southeast River Area	2,909.1	1,414.7	392.6	8.4	1,423
Pearl River	7,420	3,676.8	862.7	15.3	3,692.2
Southwest River Area	8,682.7	5,386	1,311.9	0	5,386
Northwest River Area	5,746.6	1,303	861.4	97.7	1,400.6

Data Source: 2011 Water Distribution Report of Ministry of Water Resources.

South-to-North Water Diversion Project to some extent alleviates the water shortage in the north; however, the high cost and the potential ecological impact of this project raise some doubts from the beginning of this project.

The promotion of urbanization can also lead to increased energy consumption. He *et al.* (2009) believe that the energy consumption of the urban population is about 3–4 times greater than that of the rural population. The process of urbanization promotes large-scale urban infrastructure and housing construction and needs a large quantity of cement and steel that can only be produced in the domestic sector, because there is no other country that could provide such amounts. In 2006, China accounted for about 5.5% of the world's total GDP, and consumed 30% of the total world steel and 54% of the total cement. The demand for energy-intensive industries during urbanization is rigid. From 2000 to 2007, the average annual growth rate of China's total electricity consumption is more than 11%, mainly due to the rapid growth of high energy-consuming industries. Urbanization is the main reason causing increasing demand for energy. China's per capita electricity consumption in 2020 will reach about 5000 kWh. Therefore, the average annual growth rate of per capita electricity consumption will be around 6% in the period 2007–2020. Sun and Cheng (2011) estimate that China's urbanization promotes rapid growth in energy demand. The higher the urbanization rate is, the greater the demand for energy. This paper estimates that by 2020, energy demand will reach 4.53 billion tons of standard coal. The faster the rate of economic growth is, the greater the demand for energy.

For a long time, China's energy consumption was dominated by coal. China's energy consumption in 2010 reached 3.25 billion tons of standard coal, and coal consumption accounted for nearly 70% of total energy consumption; while in 2000 China's energy consumption was less than 15 million tons, of which coal consumption accounted for 69.2%, that is to say, the proportion of coal consumption is stable and demand for energy consumption is surging. Most of China's coal reserves are located in the north. The coal reserves in Shanxi, Shaanxi, and Inner Mongolia account for 60% of the country's total reserves. The city cannot be operated normally without water and electricity, while China's 80% generating capacity relying on coal thermal power means that the operation of our city depends on water and coal. The south has more abundant water than the north, while the north has more abundant coal than the south. The choice of future urban locations is actually a choice between the north and the south and a trade-off between coal transportation and water reallocation. The cost of the South-to-North Water Diversion Project is estimated at about 350 billion yuan, which means the cost of southern water will reach about 8–12 yuan per cubic meter, higher than the desalination cost, which is about 4–6 yuan per ton. It is much higher than the average price of ordinary tap water, which is 2–4 yuan per ton. The transport of coal has a more mature system and supporting facilities. Therefore, coal reallocation is a better choice.

REFERENCES

Au, C. and Henderson, V. (2006). How migration restrictions limit agglomeration and productivity in China. *Journal of Development Economics*, 80(2): 350–388.

Cai, G., Zhang, X. and Deng, W. (2011). Does the reform of 'county directly administrated by province' damage the city's interests? *Economic Research*, (7): 65–77.

Chang, G. H. and Brada, J. C. (2006). The paradox of China's growing under-urbanization. *Economic Systems*, 30(1): 24–40.

Chenery, H. B. and Syrquin, M. (1975). Patterns of Development, 1950–1970. *London: Oxford University Press (for World Bank)*.

Fan, S., Li, L. and Zhang, X. (2012). Challenges of creating cities in China: Lessons from a short-lived county-to-city upgrading policy. *Journal of Comparative Economics*, (8): 476–491.

Fu, S. and Hong, J. (2008). Firm size, city size, and agglomeration economies — evidence from China manufacturing census. *Economic Research*, (11): 112–125.

Guan, Xiqiang (2007). The path selection of Guangxi Province's urbanization from the urbanization pattern of Taiwan. *Urban Studies*, (3): 20–25.

Guo, Q. and Jia, J. (2006). Infrastructure investment and economic growth. *Economic Theory and Management*, (3): 36–41.

He, X., Liu, X. and Lin, Y. (2009). China's electricity demand forecast under urbanization process. *Economic Research*, (1): 119–130.

Henderson, V. (2007). China's urbanization: Policy issues and options (In Chinese). *Urban Studies*, (4): 32–41.

Jian, X. and Huang, K. (2010). Empirical analysis and forecast of the level and speed of urbanization in China. *Economic Research*, (3): 28–38.

Li, B. and Liu, D. (1995). China's infrastructure and economic growth in regional comparative analysis. *Management World*, (2): 106–111.

Li, L. (2011). The incentive role of creating "cities" in China. *China Economic Review*, 22(1): 172–181.

Liu, S. and, Hu, A. (2010). Test of infrastructure externalities in China: 1988–2007. *Economic Research*, (3): 4–15.

Liu, Yongliang (2009). Dynamic analysis of Chinese urban scale economics. *Economic Dynamics*, (7): 69–72.

Liu, Yongliang (2011). Doubt of optimal city size in China. *Urban Design*, (5): 76–81.

Sun, H. and Cheng, J. (2011). Energy demand analysis and forecast in the China's industrialization and urbanization process. *China Population, Resources and Environment* (7): 7–12.

Wang, X. (2002). Urbanization and economic growth. *Comparative Economic and Social Systems*, (1): 23–32.

Wang, X. (2010). Urbanization path and city scale in China: An economic analysis. *Economic Research*, (10): 20–32.

Wang, X. and Xia, X. (1999). Optimize the urban scale, promote economic growth. *Economic Research*, (9): 22–29.

Woetzel, J., Devan, J., Jordan, L., Negri, S. and Farrell, D. (2008). *Preparing for China's Urban Billion*. New York: McKinsey Global Institute.

Zhou, Y. (2006). The first scientific question in urban studies is the correctness of the basic concepts. *Urban Design* (1): 1–5.

Chapter 9

China's Real Estate Market Development

Yuan Wang
School of Economics

1. INTRODUCTION

In the past decade, the Chinese real estate market has been a leading force of urbanization and economic growth. The prosperity of the real estate market not only improves the urban functions, but more importantly, brings a large sum of income to the local government in the form of real estate taxation and land revenue. In this way, the local government accumulates enough capital to manage the city (local government's "city management" incentives under current fiscal system will be discussed in Chapter 10). Most of this capital flows to urban infrastructure construction, with the purpose of promoting the city image and forming a brand effect, and further increasing the value of real estate projects and attracting more investment. In this cycle, the urban economy has realized rapid investment-oriented growth.

Recognizing the pillar role of the real estate sector in the Chinese economy, this chapter will take a closer look at China's real estate market, which has been reinstated since the economic system reform of 1979 and has been greatly promoted since the housing system reform of 1998. We will first discuss the development and characteristics of China's real estate market in Section 2 by looking at the problems of the land market, real estate development in different regions of China, the prospect of different submarkets, and the development of real estate finance. The relationship between the real estate market and economic growth in China will be discovered in Section 3.

Specifically, on the one hand, the thriving real estate market promotes the urban land market, which is monopolized by municipal governments. Benefiting from the considerable amount of land revenue, municipal governments can finance local public goods and promote urbanization. On the other hand, the real estate industry can have a spillover effect on upstream and downstream industries. Meanwhile, the fluctuating macro economy affects the development of the real estate market. The limited investment channel in China and the lagged finance market contributes to a serious real estate bubble in recent years. Section 4 will look at the real estate policies that provide a main source of uncertainty in China. As the industry becomes overheated since the year 2003, the central government's control policies over the real estate market have become more and more intensive. Different from market-oriented policies of the developed economies, the Chinese government relies on the command-and-control approach. In order to calm down the overheating housing prices in 2009, a new round of control policies have been adopted since 2010, with stringent restrictions on home purchase and real estate loans. However, in the long term, the effect of administrative policies is unstable; therefore, control policies in future should focus on building a public housing system and real estate tax reform. Moreover, due to different objectives, sometimes the stance of the central government is quite different from that of the local governments, where the latter are prone to rely on the local real estate sector to maintain government revenue and promote local economic development. This is compatible with local governments' fiscal and political promotion incentives under China's current fiscal system. We will discuss those issues in Chapter 10.

2. DEVELOPMENT AND TENDENCY: A CLOSER LOOK AT CHINA'S REAL ESTATE MARKET

China's real estate market was totally banned in 1958, with all urban property nationalized. The 1979 economic system reform has reinstated the real estate market and the 1980s saw the development of an urban land-use right leasehold system. Since then, the real estate sector has played a more and more prominent role in China's economic growth. According to the yearly change of the ratio of real estate sector added value to GDP, the development

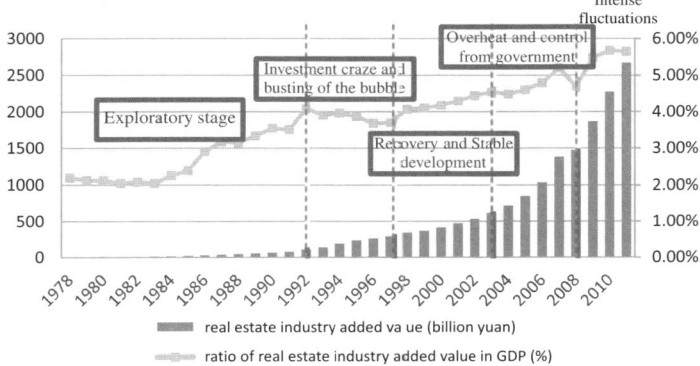

Figure 9-1: Real estate development and economic growth during 1978–2010. *Data Source: Statistical Yearbook of China.*

of China's real estate market can be divided into five stages (Figure 9-1 and Table 9-1):

Around 2000, the establishment of the urban land use right leasehold market began to drive the development of the real estate market, which at the same time linked local governments' revenue (land revenue accounts for a large part of it) with the real estate sector. The urban land market has been well developed since then; however, the land marketization still has a long way to go, one of the toughest tasks being government control on local land supply. Apart from generating other efficiency-loss problems, the government's allocation of land resource in place of the market is also responsible for the overheating real estate market. We will first discuss the problem of China's land market in the Section 2.1, and then turn to real estate development in different regions of China and the prospect of different submarkets. The development of the real estate market in different regions is unbalanced, especially between east China and mid-west China. Also, the relative importance of different submarkets is changing. In the past 20 decades, the housing market has been a leading force of growth and will continue to perform well in the next decade benefiting from China's continuing urbanization. However, in the presence of the intense policy uncertainty in the housing market, commercial real estate has shown great potential to hedge developers' investment risk and can be the next growth engine. Meanwhile, new business projects such as retirement estates and

Table 9-1: A retrospect on China's real estate market development since 1979.

Stage	Macroeconomic background	Real estate market development	Macro policies
Exploratory stage: 1978–1991	National economic level was low.	The real estate market was very immature, with a low degree of marketization and high volatility.	The housing system reform was started with two main targets: developing housing construction and fostering the housing market.
Investment craze and bursting of the bubble: 1991–1997	Domestic economic growth declined in 1990, while a more relaxed monetary policy in 1992 stimulated a new round of economic boom, with the emergence of serious inflation. Economic growth suffered from shocks of Asian financial crisis in 1997 and experienced a downturn.	High speculation in the real estate market has risen and the bubble begun bursting in 1995.	A more relaxed monetary policy was implemented in 1992 and the central government began rectifying and standardizing the real estate market after sensing the increasing speculation.
Recovery and Stable development: 1997–2002	The speed, quality, and efficiency of economic growth were apparently improved.	The real estate market experienced rapid development during this period.	The welfare-oriented allocation of housing was stopped in 1998 so that all residential housing was commercialized. The residential market was effectively promoted by the government.

(Continued)

Table 9-1: (Continued)

Stage	Macroeconomic background	Real estate market development	Macro policies
Macro-control from government and anti-control from market: 2003–2007	China has achieved rapid economic growth during this period, with the scale of investment in fixed assets becoming too large.	Housing prices kept going up. The real estate market was overheating with a deficient supply–demand structure of the residential market.	The central government began implementing regulations of the real estate sector, mainly through giving priority to the supply of small-sized residential housing, controlling real estate loans, and levying transaction taxes.
Intense market fluctuations: 2008 until now	The international financial crisis continued to spread, with a significant slowdown of the domestic macro economy. From 2009, the economic growth rate went far beyond market expectation, which in return led to inflation. In 2011, the European debt crisis and the United States' slow economic recovery has weakened the external demand, and slowed down domestic economic growth again.	The real estate market stepped into a downturn in 2008. However, it rapidly recovered since 2009. Hindered by government control policies from 2010, the market has experienced several ups and downs during the past few years.	Preferential policies were carried out for the recovery of the real estate sector in 2008 and 2009, while from 2010 till now, to cure the overheating housing prices, stringent measures of restriction in real estate sales and loans were taken nationally.

tourism estates are emerging in recent years. The last part of this section will describe the development of real estate finance in China, which still primarily consists of bank loans. The government in recent years has tightened bank credit toward the real estate sector, which gradually shifted fund demand of real estate enterprises to the trusts, funds, private equity, and other financing channels. In this way, real estate financing channels have been extended. However, the backward legislation and the regulated financial markets make real estate finance development in China face a lot of obstacles.

2.1 Urban Land Market in China

China adopts a rural–urban dual land system, which states that urban land belongs to the state, while rural land belongs to the rural collectives. As the state's actual representative, local government exercises administrative authority over urban and rural land. Using land expropriation power, local government can convert rural land at a low cost to urban land because the compensation is mainly calculated on the basis of past agriculture revenue and established through an administrative process. From the 1979 reform and opening up to the 1980s, the key institutional change is separating land ownership and land use rights, and building up a market for long-term lease for land use rights (Lichtenberg and Ding, 2009).[1] From the 1980s to 1990s, most of the allocations were done by negotiation between local officials and developers in a hidden process with the reported price being a tiny fraction of market value (Cai *et al.*, 2009). Lacking effective supervision, local officials as a monopolistic land supplier tended to control land price and the use pattern to achieve personal goals, which induced serious nationwide land corruption and inefficient land use. To solve these problems, another reform in 2002 banned such negotiated sales and required that all urban land leasehold sales be done through public auctions. Until 2010, public auctions accounted for 88.35% of the total land transactions volume (see Figure 9-2). Thanks to this reform, a market mechanism played a more decisive role in allocating land resources and as a result, land price,

---

[1] Lichtenberg, E. and C. Ding (2009). Local officials as land developers: Urban spatial expansion in China. *Journal of Urban Economics*, 66(1): 57–64.

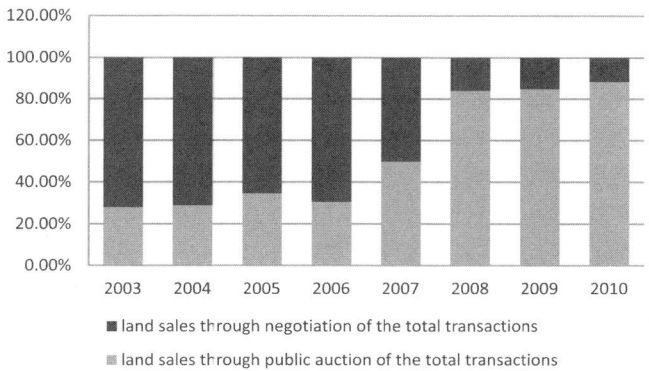

Figure 9-2: Land sales through public auction during 2003–2010.

Data Source: Statistical Yearbook of Land and Resources.

Figure 9-3: Price index of land and housing during 1998–2009 (compared to the previous year, which takes the value of 100).

Data Source: CSMAR.

which reflects the demand for properties, has rapidly increased as the real estate market prospers (see Figure 9-3). Land price per square meter of gross floor area in some cities even exceeds nearby housing prices at the same period. Expectations for housing price increases amplify the current evaluation of land parcels, which makes developers overbid in land leasehold auctions and drives land prices high. Although the central government clearly requires local governments to take measures to keep land price

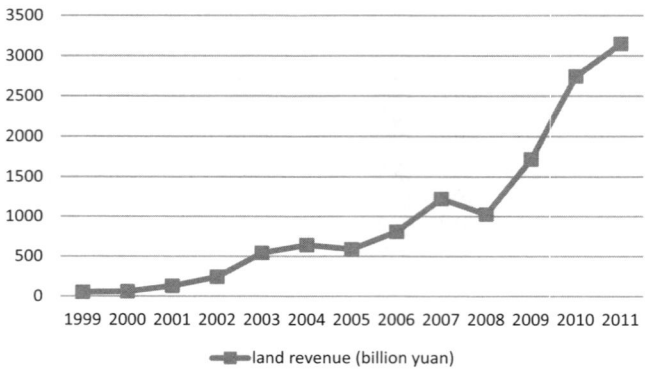

Figure 9-4: Land revenue during 2003–2010.

Data Source: *Statistical Yearbook of Land and Resources*.

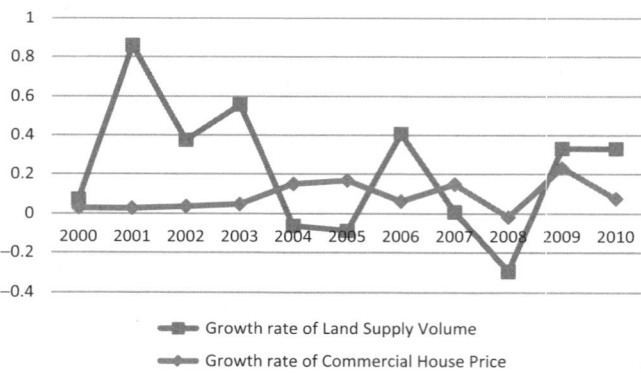

Figure 9-5: The growth rate of land supply volume and housing price during 2000–2010.

Data Source: CSMAR.

stable, this receives little effective responses from the locals, because the requirement is not compatible with local officials' incentives: leasehold sales have become major fiscal income for many cities since the 2000s. Figure 9-4 shows that from 1999 to 2011 the government's land lease revenue has went up by 6000%. In 2011, land lease revenue accounted for about 60% of on-the-book revenue of local governments. It can be read from Figure 9-5 that the growth rate of land supply volume and housing price has an inverse relationship, suggesting that local government could limit land supply to maintain a high-level development of the real estate sector.

Since 2010, the central government has determined to curb the abnormal land price growth by launching an Administrative Accountability system. Under this system, those cities whose land bid price hits an all-time high level will become accountability targets. In order to avoid the punishment, local officials begin to take all measures to bring down the land price, most of which are administrative interventions in the auction process. Those efforts indeed can control bid prices; however, they may also cause problems like corruption and misallocation of land resources. Besides, the administrative policies always work in the short term, which is no help to stabilize market expectations. The key to solve the problem is to decrease the government's high dependence on land revenue. In this case, fiscal and taxation system reform is imperative in future.

In China, land use planning lacks effective legal shelter, and local officials decide the land use pattern in their administrative regions. Figure 9-6 shows that more land resources are allocated to industrial use: industrial land supply accounts for around 55% of total land supply during 2003–2008, while residential and commercial land supply accounts for an average of 26% and 15% respectively. This can partly verify Henderson *et al.* (2009)'s perception: Chinese cities are often biased toward

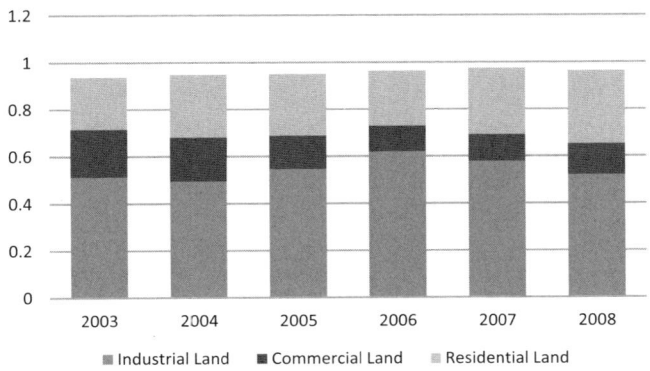

Figure 9-6: Land use pattern during 2003–2008 (land supply for free for specific use is excluded).

Data Source: *Statistical Yearbook of Land and Resources*.

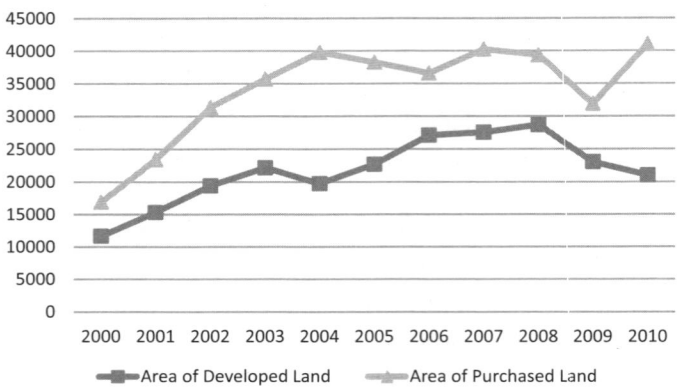

Figure 9-7: Land supply from government and land finished construction during 2003–2008.

Data Source: Statistical Yearbook of Land and Resources.

manufacturing, which generates a share of value added tax revenues for the city. Besides, developers usually take a long time to turn purchased land into effective housing supply. As shown in Figure 9-7, purchased land volume always exceeds developed land in a certain year. Between 2000 and 2010, the total area of land supply was 3.74 billion m^2, while total area of developed land was 2.38 billion m^2, leaving 1.36 billion m^2 land parcels vacant. Housing supply is reduced in this way, and prices are going up in response. The vacant land problem has two aspects: on the one hand, it is a kind of land speculation under the expectation of future price appreciation (Neutze, 1987); on the other hand, high uncertainty will also result in construction delay (Titman, 1985).

In the future, the following aspects will become key points of China's land market reform:

First of all, *reform the current fiscal and taxation system*. Recent fluctuation in the real estate market from 2008 has pushed some cities into a financial swamp where fiscal revenue largely relies on land revenue. Besides, lump sum payment for 40- or 70-year land leaseholds will erode cities' financial ability in the long run. Therefore, both central and municipal governments are actively exploring an effective land tax system that may take the form of property tax.

Second, *establish a rural land market*. Along with the development of an urban land leasehold market, a gray market of rural land has emerged and the scale has been getting larger in the past decade (current law bans rural land transactions). Since 2000, the attempts to establish a formal rural construction land market have been encouraged by the central government in limited plot cities (however, the agricultural land market is still banned). In future, the establishment and improvement of the land market in both urban and rural regions is the main focus of land system reform.

2.2 Real Estate Development in Different Regions

Due to the immobility and regional idiosyncrasy of housing, the development of the real estate industry has obvious regional characteristics (Liang and Gao, 2007). Especially in China, regional development is highly unbalanced. According to the National Bureau of Statistics, economic development in eastern, middle, and western China shows quite different patterns.[2] Table 9-2 lists main statistical characteristics of the real estate development in those three regions. As shown in the table, housing prices in the middle and western regions are generally lower than that in eastern region. However, suggested by the value of standard deviation, the housing price volatility in eastern regions is much higher than that in the middle and west. Figure 9-8 shows that in the year 2008 when China's real estate market suffered shocks from the global financial crisis, housing prices in eastern region fell for the first time, while the middle and western regions maintained an almost steady upward trend.

The annual average of the real estate investment volume in eastern regions is about three times that in the middle and western regions (as shown in Table 9-2); at the same time, the contribution of the real estate sector to GDP is greater in the east (as shown in Figure 9-8). However, Figure 9-9 shows that in most years, the middle and western regions have

---

[2] According to the National Bureau of Statistics, the eastern regions contain 11 provinces including Beijing, Tianjin, Hebei, Liaoning, Shanghai, Jiangsu, Zhejiang, Fujian, Shandong, Guangdong, and Hainan; the middle regions contain 8 provinces including Shanxi, Jilin, Heilongjiang, Anhui, Jiangxi, Henan, Hubei, and Hunan; the western regions contain 12 provinces including Inner Mongolia, Guangxi, Chongqing, Sichuan, Guizhou, Yunnan, Tibet, Shaanxi, Gansu, Qinghai, Ningxia, and Xinjiang.

Table 9-2: Statistical characteristics of real estate development in eastern, middle, and western China.

Index		East China 1998–2011	East China 2007–2011	Middle China 1998–2011	Middle China 2007–2011	West China 1998–2011	West China 2007–2011
House price (yuan/m^2)	Mean	4,112	5,937	2,090	3,119	2,196	2,551
	Std. Dev.	1,591	809	918	690	948	1,130
	Max	6,769	6,769	4,110	4,110	4,226	4,226
Real estate investment (billion yuan)	Mean	1,270	2,380	402	861	389	531
	Std. Dev.	1,010	807	410	337	382	459
	Max	3,570	3,570	1,330	1,330	1,280	1,280
Sales area (million m^2)	Mean	277	445	121	225	128	157
	Std. Dev.	154	81	92	55	94	114
	Max	510	510	295	295	295	295
No. of provinces		11	11	8	8	12	12

Data Source: CSMAR.

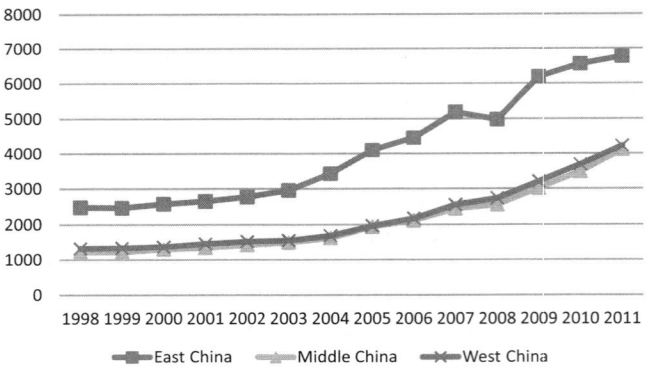

Figure 9-8: Housing prices in eastern, middle, and western China during 1998–2011.

Data Source: CSMAR.

a higher year-on-year growth rate of real estate investment than eastern regions, indicating a great growth potential in the middle and west. Since 2009, the change trend in three regions in Figure 9-10 is almost consistent, suggesting that in the post-crisis era, national markets show homogeneity by bearing consistent shocks from economic fundamentals.

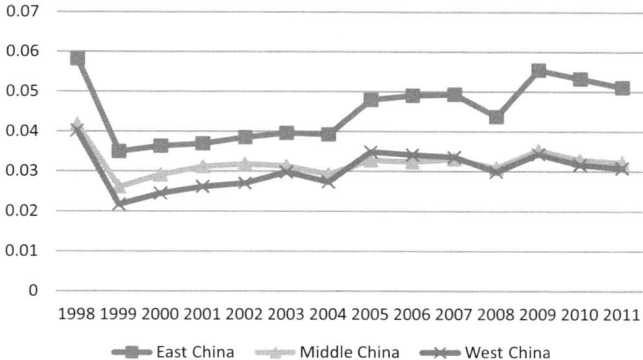

Figure 9-9: Contribution of real estate sector to GDP during 1998–2011 in different regions.

Data Source: CSMAR.

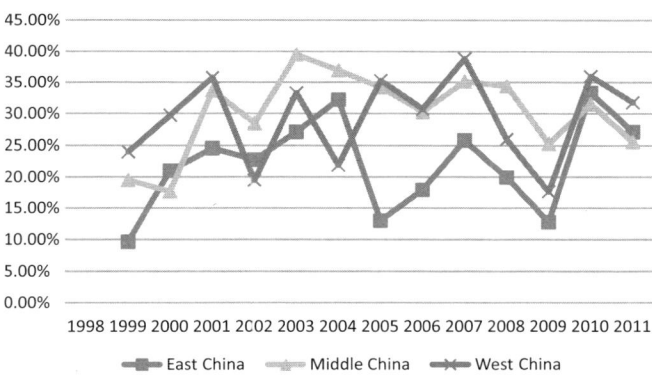

Figure 9-10: The year-in-year growth rate of real estate investment during 1998–2011 in different regions.

Data Source: CSMAR.

Real estate investment elasticity, defined by the growth rate of real estate investment divided by the growth rate of GDP, describes the real estate investment growth caused by an increase in GDP in a certain period of time. It can act as a measure of whether regional real estate industry is well coordinated with economic growth. Besides, it is also an important index to evaluate whether the regional real estate is overinvested. As shown in

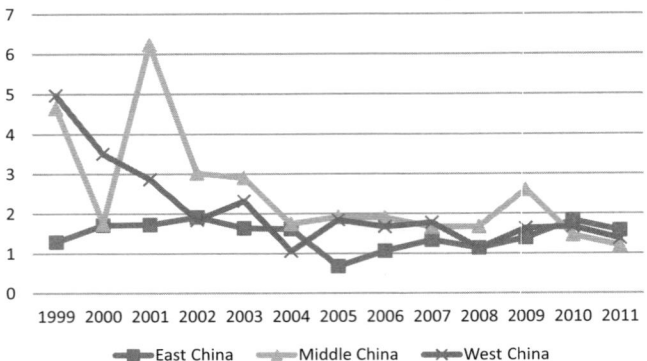

Figure 9-11: Real estate investment elasticity during 1999–2011 in different regions (Real estate investment elasticity = growth rate of real estate investment/growth rate of GDP).

Data Source: CSMAR.

Figure 9-11, except for the year 2005, the real estate investment elasticity across the three regions stays greater than 1, reflecting the fact that the Chinese real estate market has been the most important contributor to the national economy over the years. Prior to 2004, the real estate investment elasticity in the middle and west was experiencing drastic functions, the value of which was once more than 3, indicating the possible existence of an investment bubble. Since 2003, when the central government began a comprehensive macro control over real estate, the elasticity value is between 1 and 2 for most years across all the three regions with a relatively stable trend.

The real estate firm's self-financing ratio in the eastern region is significantly lower than that in the middle and west as shown in Figure 9-12. The middle region has the highest self-financing ratio, the annual mean being 42%. This suggests that eastern China has more effective financing channels, which promotes its development of the real estate market. However, eastern China's high dependence on loans also implies that the investment risk is highest in the east.

The ratio of sales area to built-up area of commercial housing acts as an index to reflect the market demand. As shown in Figure 9-13, the ratio remains larger than 1 over the years, suggesting active market demand in China's real estate market. The ratio is almost the same in eastern and middle

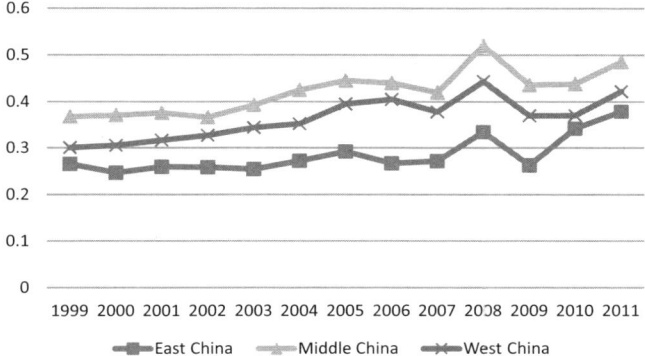

Figure 9-12: The real estate self-financing ratio during 1999–2011 in different regions.

Data Source: CSMAR.

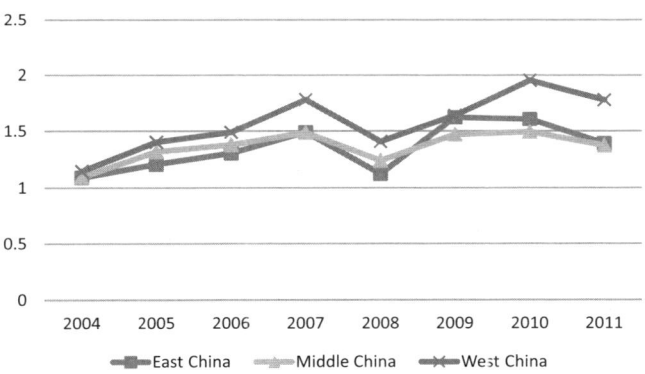

Figure 9-13: The ratio of sales area to built-up area of commercial housing during 2004–2011 in different regions.

Data Source: CSMAR.

regions, but is significantly higher in western China, which indicates market demand is relatively higher, and the western regions may have greater potential for real estate development. However, the ratio of purchased land area to developed land area suggests more serious land idling in western regions (in Figure 9-14), which caused a lack of effective housing supply and partly accounts for the high ratio of sales area to built-up area in the west.

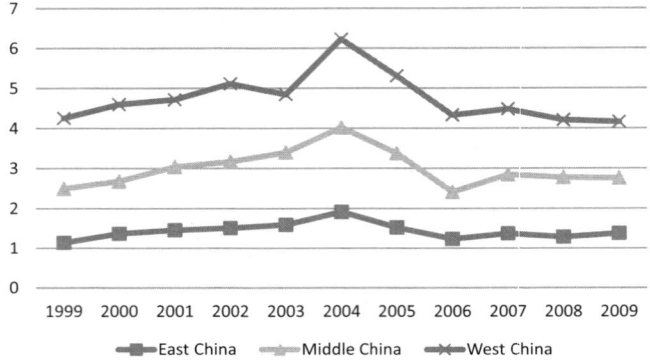

Figure 9-14: The ratio of purchased land area to developed land area during 1999–2009 in different regions.

Data Source: CSMAR.

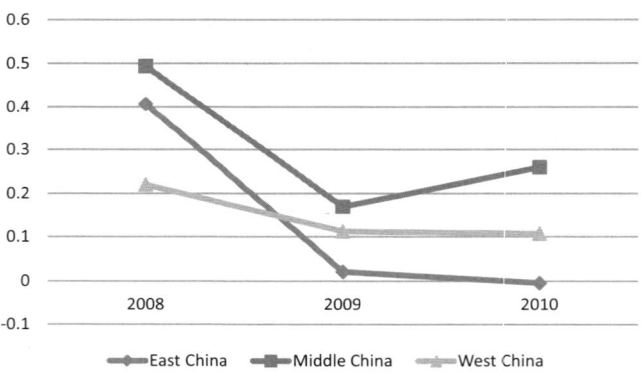

Figure 9-15: The growth rate of the areas of commercial housings for sale during 2008–2010 in different regions.

Data Source: CSMAR.

Recently, the National Bureau of Statistics reports areas of commercial housing for sale for all the real estate enterprises, where the larger the number is, the greater pressure real estate sales are facing, and the more likely the housing prices will drop. Figure 9-15 shows the growth rate of the areas of commercial buildings for sale during 2008–2010 in all the regions. It can be found that the number is large across regions in 2008 due to the financial crisis, and the middle regions were affected the most. Eastern China performed the best in the 2009 recovery, while the middle and western regions have also recovered drawn from the decrease of the number of the growth rate. In general, the growth rate of the for sale areas in the middle regions is significantly higher than the other two regions, suggesting that in recent years the real estate market situation shows less optimistic prospects in those regions.

2.3 Development of Submarkets

2.3.1 Residential estate

Since the 1998 housing system reform, the prosperity of China's real estate market is supported by the residential market. This is similar to the experience of South Korea: before the establishment of the housing market in 1998, the development of the real estate market lagged far behind the national economy; after the reform, people who accumulated considerable wealth became of marriageable age and became a leading force in residential purchase, resulting in the rise of housing prices. In China, the phenomenon that housing prices "catch up" with the national economy has been occurring during the last two decades. Up to now, the urbanization process has been far from complete, a lot of people will move from rural areas to cities in the future, which means that in the next few decades, demand for housing consumption is also very large. In contrast, newly built housing is still in short supply: according to statistics, up to 2009, China's urban housing was around 17 billion m^2, only 5 billion m^2 of which is built after the year 1998. Therefore, currently, the old shabby housing still accounts for a large part of existing housing, which makes people's demand for better housing continue for a relatively long period. In this sense, the residential market will still dominate China's real estate market for at least one decade, and on the other hand, investors and property buyers have formed a strong belief that housing prices will keep going up, which, in the end, contributes to the high rise of housing prices in the past two decades (as shown in Figure 9-16). China's rapidly rising housing price and the lagged construction of public housing have made the housing problem increasingly serious. At the same time, the real estate bubble in some cities has increased the risk of the whole industry. Since 2003, the central government began

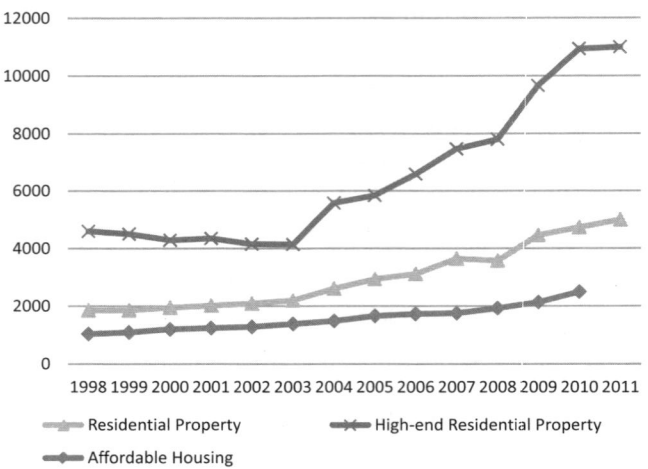

Figure 9-16: The housing price for residential estate during 1998–2011.
Data Source: CSMAR.

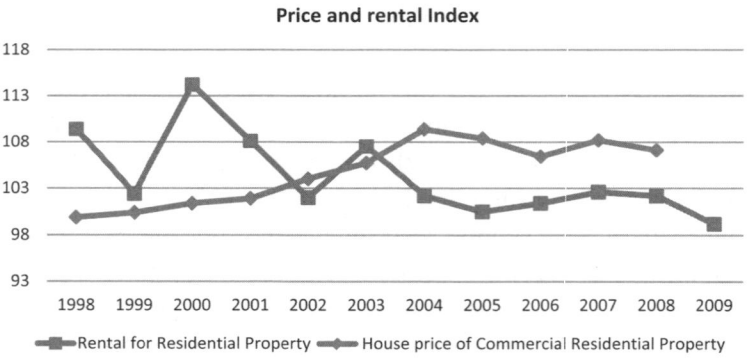

Figure 9-17: The housing price index and rent index for residential estate during 1998–2009 (compared to the previous year who takes the value of 100).
Data Source: CSMAR.

to exert consistent control over the real estate sector, trying to stabilize the housing prices. The market factors and policy factors contribute to the increasing volatility in the residential market (as shown in Figure 9-18). However, China's rental housing market is still quite immature. As shown in Figure 9-17, rents rose much more slowly than the housing prices. This

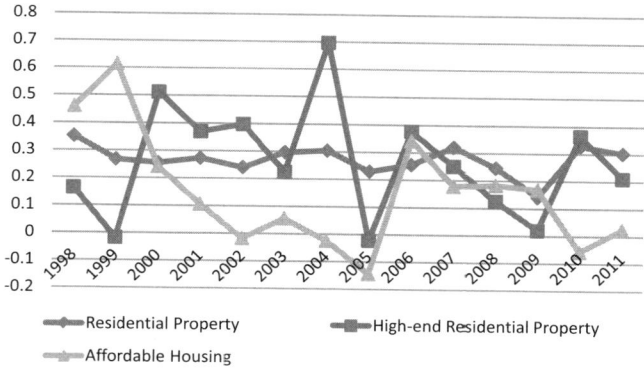

Figure 9-18: Investment growth rate of residential estate during 1998–2011.
Data Source: CSMAR.

partly relates to the Chinese preference of home ownership due to culture on the one hand, and to the existence of the housing investment bubble on the other.

High-end residential estates include villas and high-end condominiums, whose prices have risen rapidly since 2003 as shown in Figure 9-16. China's high-end residential market has been attracting a number of investors, leading to an imbalance of housing supply structure: the high-end condominiums and villas always have a high vacancy rate, while affordable commercial housing is generally short of supply. As a result, the high-end market has become a main target of the central government's control policy. When the macro economy goes through a downward fluctuation, the high-end market is the most vulnerable due to the lack of real consumer demand. Policy and market factors make high-end estate investment fluctuate quite dramatically (as shown in Figure 9-18). Investment growth rate of the affordable housing subsidized by the government also bares dramatic volatility, indicating China's public housing policy lacks consistency.

We use the ratio of sales area to built-up area of residential estate to evaluate market demand. As shown in Figure 9-19, the index is less than one before 2005, which means that the built-up area surpassed sales area each year and there was a problem of surplus. The situation was greatly improved after 2005 when the residential market was active and the index reaches more than one except in 2008. In 2010, the index reaches as high as 1.47,

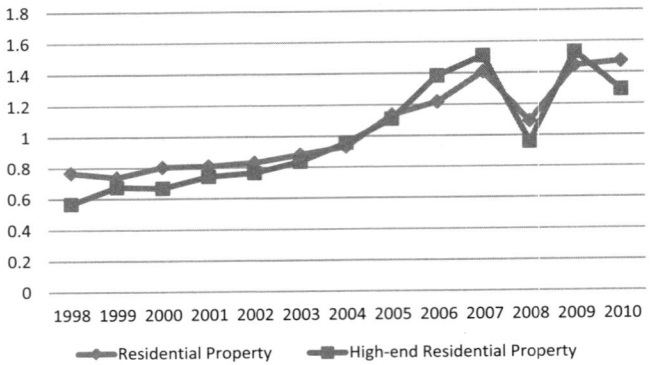

Figure 9-19: The ratio of sales area to built-up area of residential estate during 1998–2010. *Data Source*: CSMAR.

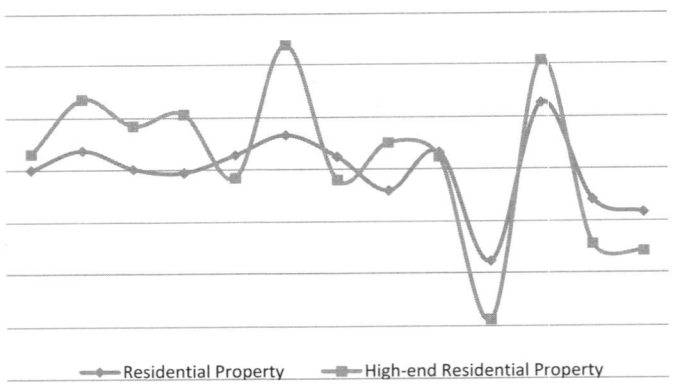

Figure 9-20: The growth rate of the areas of residential estate for sale during 2000–2010. *Data Source*: CSMAR.

which calls attention to inadequate supply in future. The index for high-end residential estate changes almost similarly to other residential estates.

The growth rate of the areas of residential estate for sale can also reflect the market situation. From Figure 9-20, the index has a slight increase during the period 2000–2003, while during the period 2003–2007 the index continued to show negative growth reflecting that residential estates were in great demand. However, the crisis in 2008 resulted in the sharp rise of developers' inventories, described by a peak in Figure 9-20. Then the housing market recovered quickly in 2009 and 2010 shown by the decrease of the index. But the recovery of the high end is much slower than that of the others. It can be inferred that market demand contributed to the recovery of the whole residential estate in 2009 and also drove the investment for the high-end to a high level in 2010.

To sum up, over the past 20 years, China's housing prices are rising firmly even under the control policies from the central government. However, the policy uncertainties together with market fluctuations have resulted in high volatility of residential market. At the same time, the government's investment for public housing is obviously insufficient, which aggravates the problem of housing. It can be expected that in the next decade, urbanization will continue to support consumer demand for ordinary residential housing, while at the same time, people's need for improvement of housing conditions makes the residential market full of potential. Due to the great restriction of high-end residential land supply, the high-end residential supply may become increasingly scarce. While the rapid growth of national wealth in recent years has formed real market demand for the high-end residential property, a further rise in its price could happen in future.

2.3.2 Commercial estate

Commercial estates include office buildings and other commercial buildings such as hotels and retail estates. According to other countries' experience, commercial real estate will play an increasingly important role in the development of the real estate market. In China, most developers were not familiar with the operating mode of commercial estate until 2002. Since then, with the rapid development of a modern service industry, commercial estates such as office buildings, shopping centers, hotels, and leisure entertainment centers have entered a rapid development period. As shown in Figure 9-21, investment growth rate of commercial estates has steadily increased since 2002. Since 2008, the Wanda Group's success in operating the symbolic "Wanda Plaza" across major cities has generated people's interest in the concept of an "Urban Complex." The "Urban Complex" combines the functions of shopping, office, residential, hotel, and entertainment

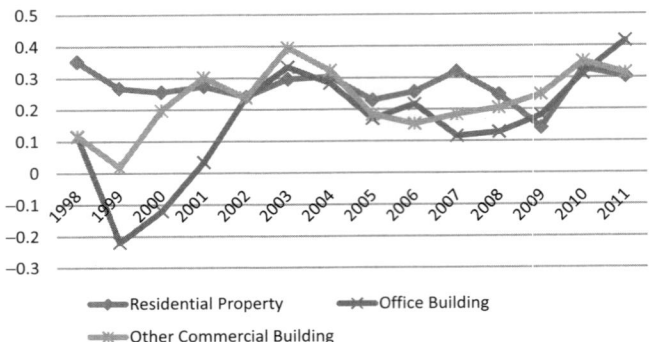

Figure 9-21: Investment growth rate of commercial estate during the period 1998–2011. *Data Source*: CSMAR.

and becomes the main mode of commercial estate development. Figure 9-21 shows that even in 2008, when investment in the residential market suffered severe tremors, the investment growth rate of commercial estates has maintained a slight increase, suggesting the great potential of China's commercial estate development. In the post-crisis era, the investment growth rate of commercial estates continues to exceed that of residential estates. This demonstrates the growth potential on the one hand, and on the other hand, as the control policies over residential estates are becoming intense in recent years commercial estates have acted as an effective tool to balance the investment risk in real estate enterprises.

Figure 9-22 describes the sales price of commercial estates, which has experienced sharp inflection in 2002 and 2008. The average growth rate of commercial property prices has surpassed that of residential property prices over the years. Moreover, the price of office buildings has increased faster than that of other commercial buildings. However, market demand for commercial estates is lower than that for residential estates, shown by the relatively low level of the ratio of sales area to built-up area of commercial estates (as shown in Figure 9-23). There may be another reason that some enterprises develop and own commercial estates, which drives the ratio low. Since 2008, market demand for commercial estates has highly increased in Figure 9-23, indicating great potential in future.

Overall, together with the rapid economic growth and development of the service industry, the commercial estate market has been gradually

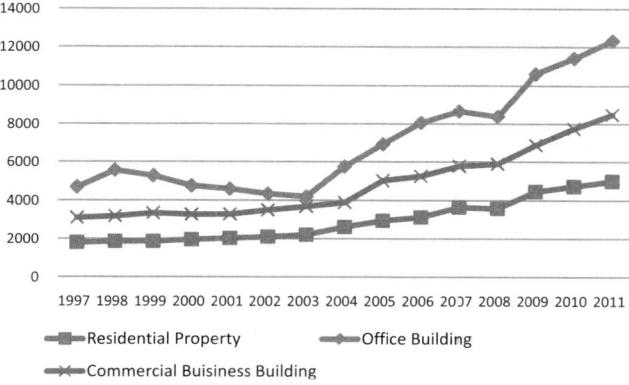

Figure 9-22: Commercial estate price during 1997–2011.

Data Source: CSMAR.

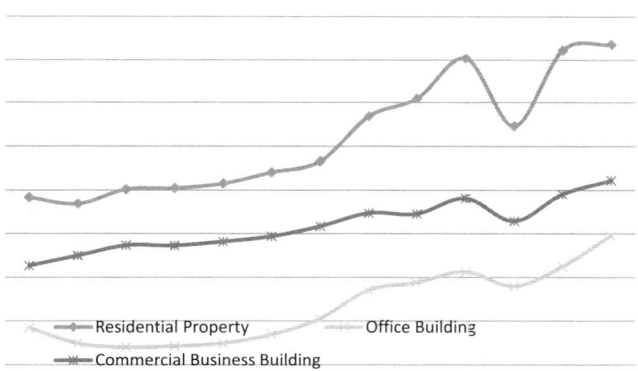

Figure 9-23: The ratio of sales area to built-up area of commercial estate during 1998–2010.

Data Source: CSMAR.

developed and a diversified development mode tends to appear. Since 2008, the investment growth rate of the commercial estates began to exceed that of the residential estates for the first time. It can be expected that in the long term, with the using-up of residential demand caused by urbanization, the commercial estates will replace the residential estates and become the leading force of real estate development.

2.4 Development of Real Estate Finance

2.4.1 A retrospect on China's real estate finance development since 1979

The development of China's real estate finance can be divided into three stages:

Exploratory stage: 1978–1997. In 1979, investment in infrastructure was first allowed to be funded by bank loans instead of financial allocation. This reform brought about the primary form of real estate finance. Since then, with the development of the real estate industry, real estate finance began to expand across the nation. In 1987, the Housing and Savings Bank was established in the city of Yantai and Bengbu and undertook the local housing finance business. They are China's first professional real estate financial institutions. Later in 1991, drawing on the experience of Singapore, Shanghai established a housing accumulation fund system. During this period, China's real estate financial development is mainly designed for the "housing system reform" and is basically policy-related.

Development stage: 1998–2003. In 1998, in conjunction with the State Council's decision of urban housing system reform, the People's Bank of China and the China Banking Regulatory Commission issued a series of supporting financial and monetary policies, and clarified the decision to support and promote commercial banks to develop housing finance. At the same time, the management of housing finance business of commercial banks was gradually standardized, and real estate finance has achieved great development in the diversified product types, expanded business scope, and normalized operation mode.

Innovation and expansion state: 2004–till now. Around the year 2004, the problem of the real estate investment bubble became worse. In order to calm down the overheated market, in 2004 and 2005, a series of policies was issued to tighten real estate loans from commercial banks. Real estate enterprises had to gradually turn to other financing channels such as trusts, funds, and private equity. In this way, the real estate financing methods have been largely expanded.

2.4.2 Real estate finance in China

The demand for China's real estate finance reform has been put forward for a long time, and financial institutions have explored various innovative financial products. When stringent regulation of real estate began in 2003, the industry discussed the market prospects and feasibility of developing real estate investment trusts (REITs) in China. However, up to now, the related legislative process is still in slow progress, and a prosperous and orderly financial market for real estate is still far away for China.

Therefore, in the short term, bank loans including development loans and mortgage loans will continue to provide important financial support for real estate enterprises. Real estate trusts, private placement, and equity investment can act as supplementary financing sources for large real estate enterprises, while small and medium-sized real estate enterprises that are facing huge financial pressure may need to raise funds by equity sale and other non-formal financial channels.

Data in Figure 9-24 shows that the "self-financing" ratio has increased from 25% in 1997 to 41% in 2011, while the "other funding" including deposits, advance payments, and personal mortgage loans account for 43% of the total funding in 2011 — which means currently Chinese developers obtain more than 80% of the funding from outside the banking system. In this sense, the trend of "disintermediation" in the real estate sector is quite

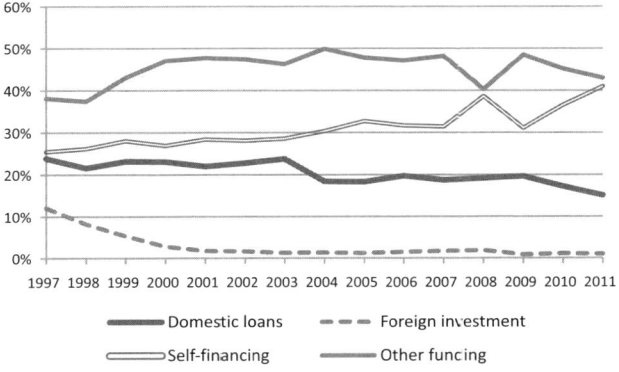

Figure 9-24: Funding sources of real estate enterprises during the period 1997–2011.
Data Source: CEIC.

obvious. Always facing the financial constraint, many real estate enterprises have been seeking effective informal financing channels; at the same time, their dependence on banks and other formal financial institutions continues to decline. Thus, the effect of the tight monetary and credit policy on taming the real estate market will probably be quite limited in future.

(1) Real Estate Trusts

China's new round of real estate control since 2010 has greatly tightened bank loans for the real estate sector. Thus, many real estate companies turn to non-bank financial institutions for financial support, which leads to the rapid development of real estate trusts. Data shows that the real estate collective capital trust reached 688.2 billion yuan in 2011, which accounts for 14.5% of the total collective capital trust of the year. Among the new collective and single capital trusts in 2011, real estate trusts account for 12%.

Figure 9-25 describes the average duration and annual return rate of collective capital trust since 2003. The average duration remains around 2 years with little change, while the average annual return rate substantially rose from 4.3% in 2003 to 9.1% in 2011, suggesting that with the monetary policy being gradually tightened, the capital cost of trust financing is also increasing.

As shown in Figure 9-26, the investment in real estate collective capital trust is expanding constantly, with an annual average growth rate of 34.3%

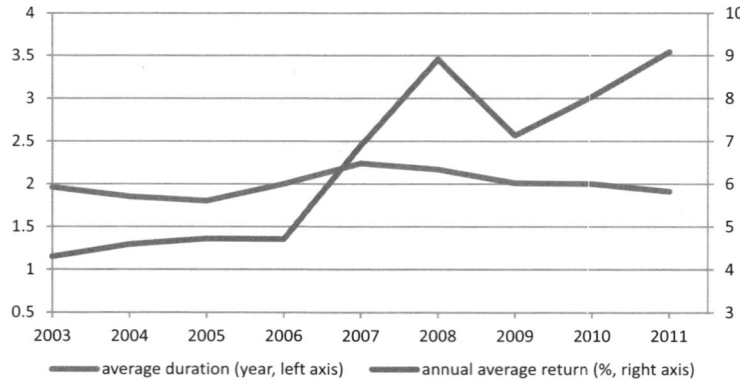

Figure 9-25: Average duration and return of the collective capital trust during 2003–2011. *Data Source*: http://www.use-trust.com.

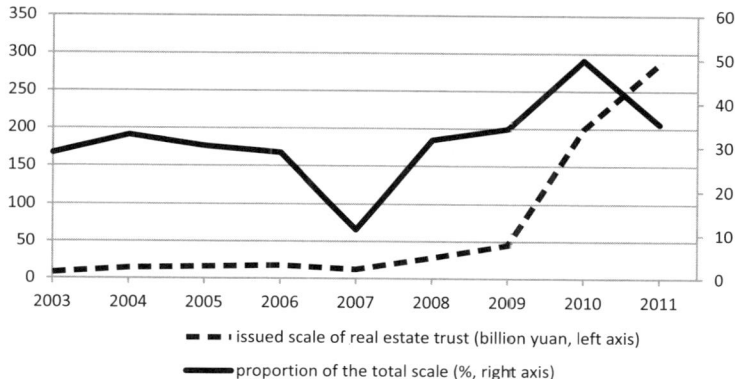

Figure 9-26: The issued scale of real estate collective capital trust during 2003–2011. *Data Source*: http://www.use-trust.com.

from 2003 to 2009. Since 2010, it has experienced an explosive growth, with an amount of 44.9 billion yuan in 2009 and the number rising to 199.3 billion and 286.8 billion in 2010 and 2011 respectively.

Overall, although currently the financing scale of real estate trusts only accounts for about 6% of that of the bank loans, their growth rate and future potential cannot be overlooked. If the tightened monetary policy and financial constraint of the real estate sector is maintained, the real estate trusts will continue to maintain a high growth rate, while financing costs will remain the current high level or rising.

(2) Real estate funds

At present, the development of China's real estate fund products is still at the starting stage (as shown in Table 9-3). The major products can be divided into two categories. One is called the "real estate trust funds" based on real estate trust loans, which amounts to 16.84 billion and 33.53 billion yuan in 2010 and 2011 respectively and only accounts for 0.6% and 0.7% of the total trust balance for the year. The other category is the "real estate equity fund" to raise public funds to invest in real estate stocks. It was developed by HSBC Bank, Holland Bank, and Deutsche Bank in 2007 and 2008; however, currently those attempts have stopped because of the negative effects of the 2008 financial crisis.

Table 9-3: General situation of the banks' real estate fund products.

Year	Issuer	Number of products	Currency	Investment project	Investment category
2007	HSBC Bank, Industrial Bank	3	RMB, US$	Hong Kong real estate stocks and mortgage	Stocks and credit assets
2008	Holland Bank, Deutsche Bank, Industrial Bank	10	Diversified foreign currency including euro and US$	Hong Kong real estate stocks and Asia Pacific Real Estate Securities Fund	Stocks
2010	China Construction Bank	2	RMB	Trust loans of public housing and resettlement building for urban renewal	Credit assets
2011	China Construction Bank	4	RMB	Trust loans of public housing and resettlement building for urban renewal	Credit assets

Data Source: Wind.

Table 9-4: Private equity investment (billion yuan).

Year	Private equity investment	Real estate private equity investment	Proportion of the total investment
2008	45.37	11.91	26.2%
2009	47.37	1.46	3.1%
2010	115.86	0.07	0.1%
2011	185.60	3.06	1.6%

Data Source: CEIC.

(3) Private equity

Private equity has been developed rapidly in recent years in China (see Table 9-4). From data in Section 2.4.2, 26.2% of the total private equity investment went to the real estate sector in 2008. However, due to the rising market risk and the macro control, real estate private equity decreased

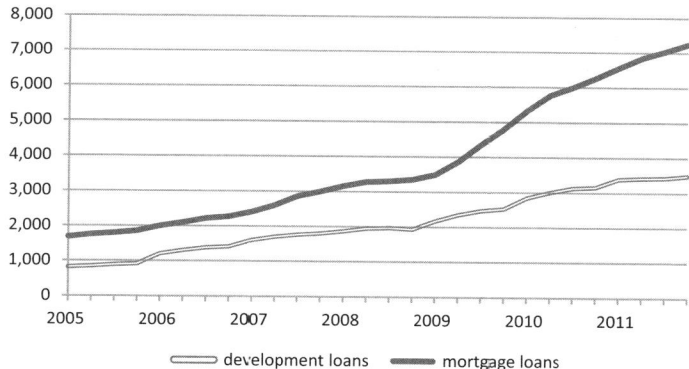

Figure 9-27: Real estate loans during 2005–2011 (billion yuan).

Data Source: CEIC.

significantly afterwards, the amount dropping to 3.06 billion yuan in 2011. Therefore, currently the real estate sector only gets a limited support from the financing method of private equity.

(4) Real estate loan

As a major financing channel, China's real estate loans have increased rapidly in recent years with the development of the real estate market. The development loans and mortgage loans amount to 914.1 billion and 1,855.9 billion yuan in 2005 and that number went to 3,488 billion and 7,242 billion in 2011, with an average annual growth rate of around 25% (see Figure 9-27). About 80% of development loans went to real estate development, and only a limited proportion went to the public housing construction supported by the central government's policy in recent years, while 98% of the mortgage loans are personal housing mortgage loans.

3. THE REAL ESTATE MARKET AND ECONOMIC GROWTH

In the past decade, the Chinese real estate market has been a leading force of economic growth. On the one hand, the thriving real estate market promotes an urban land market, which is monopolized by municipal governments. Benefiting from the considerable amount of land revenue, municipal governments can finance local public goods, and promote urbanization. On the other hand, the real estate industry can have a spillover effect on upstream and downstream industries. Meanwhile, the fluctuating macro economy affects the development of the real estate market. For example, the limited investment channel in China and the lagged finance market contributes to a serious real estate bubble in recent years. We will discuss the relationship between the real estate market and China's economic growth in the following Section 3.1.

3.1 The Real Estate Market and Economic Fluctuation

In the past decade, the real estate industry has made an important contribution to China's economic growth (Hui, 2012). According to the National Bureau of Statistics, its added value accounts for an average of 18% of GDP. Due to the prosperity of the real estate sector, that ratio reached as high as 33% in 2007, while in the following year, affected by the global financial crisis, the ratio fell to 6.7%. As shown in Figure 9-28, the growth rate of fixed asset investment moves ahead of that of GDP, reflecting China's investment-driven economic growth. In particular, in 1997 and 2008, when the global economy experienced widespread recession, China increased government investment (mainly the urban infrastructure investment) to stimulate economic growth, which makes the move of fixed assets investment in those years show a local peak in Figure 9-28. Moreover, investment in real estate

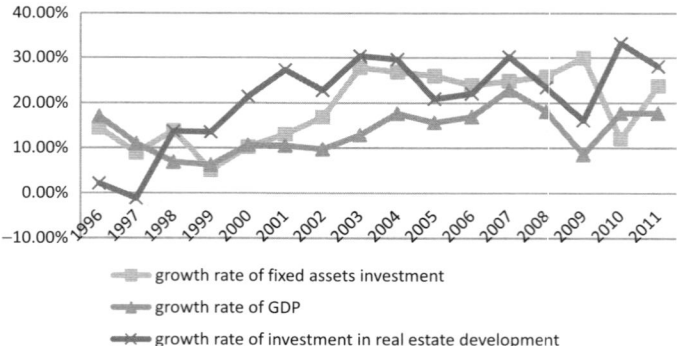

Figure 9-28: Real estate investment and economic fluctuation during the period 1996–2011 (Data in this table are calculated at current year).

Data Source: Statistical Yearbook of China.

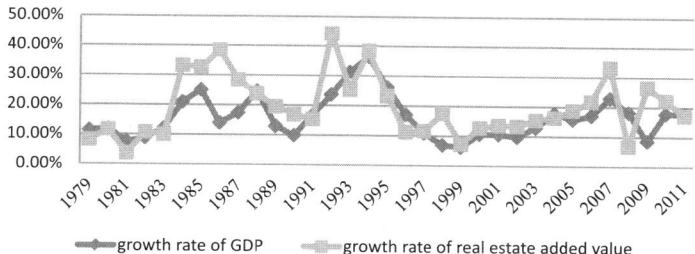

Figure 9-29: Real estate and economic growth during the period 1979–2011 (Data in this table are calculated at current year).
Data Source: Statistical Yearbook of China.

development moves almost consistently with the macro economy since 1998, reflecting the fact that real estate investment is affected by economic fundamentals to a large extent.

Figure 9-29 displays the moves of real estate added value. Before 1998, due to the immature real estate market, the growth rate of real estate added value is more volatile than that of GDP; while after the 1998 housing system reform, the former shows high consistency with the latter. Moreover, under external economic shocks, the real estate market reacted more sensitively: from Figure 9-29, the recession in 1997 and 2008 first caused shocks in the real estate market and then the macroeconomic growth reached bottom in the next year. Similarly, in the subsequent year, the real estate sector recovered in advance of the economic fundamentals. Consequently, in China, the fluctuation of real estate sector can be regarded as an important leading indicator of macroeconomic fluctuation.

3.2 Municipal Government, Real Estate Market, and Urbanization

In developed countries, urbanization is a spontaneous economic process with the economic development and industrial structure change. But in China with the "developmental state," "city management" is important content for the local government to achieve economic growth (Henderson *et al.*, 2009). Consequently, urbanization in China is different from that in developed countries: urbanization promoted by the government and high dependence on land resources are the prominent features. Figure 9-30

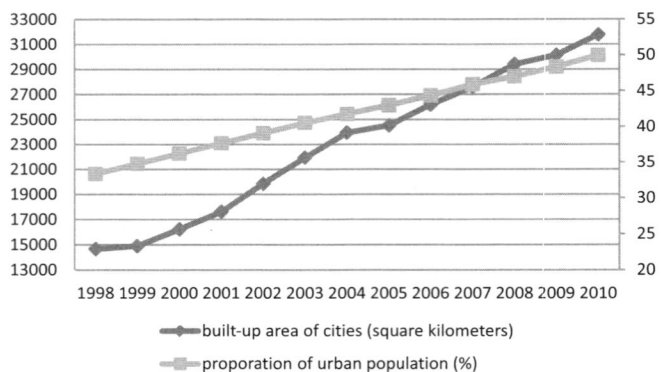

Figure 9-30: Urban expansion and urban population growth during the period 1998–2010.

Data Source: *Statistical Yearbook of China* and *Statistical Yearbook of China City*.

describes the fact that speed of urban expansion far exceeds that of people's migration from rural to urban areas.

From the 1979 reform and opening up to the late 1990s, in order to promote the development of local industry, China's local government worked hard to attract investment in the industry sector by suppressing the price of industrial land and subsidizing infrastructure and taxes. Industrialization has attracted a large number of rural workers to move into cities, accelerating urbanization in this way (Tao *et al.*, 2009). At the same time, industrialization promoted the development of the service sector. The population concentration, development of the service sector, and the well-served urban infrastructure all together provided the necessary condition for the prosperity of the real estate market.

Figures 9-31 and 9-32 describe the role of urbanization in the development of the real estate market. It is worth noting that the growth rate of real estate sales area and prices is much faster than that of urbanization measured by the increase of urban population, which implies large amounts of investment demand support the prosperity of the real estate market; thus, a problem of bubbles may exist. The prosperity of the real estate market not only further improves the urban functions, but more importantly, brings large sums of income to local government in forms of real estate taxation and land revenue (as shown in Figures 9-31 and 9-33). In this way, the local government accumulates enough capital to manage the city. Most of

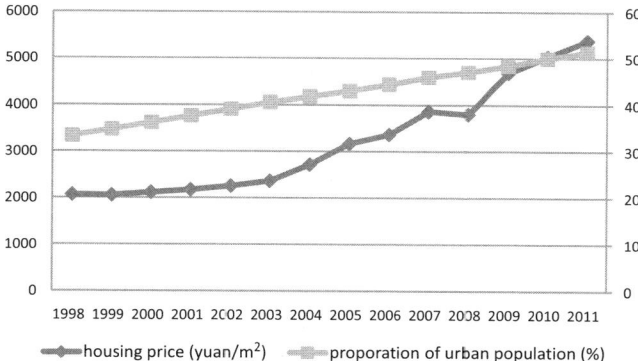

Figure 9-31: Urbanization and housing price during the period 1998–2011.
Data Source: Statistical Yearbook of China and *Statistical Yearbook of China City.*

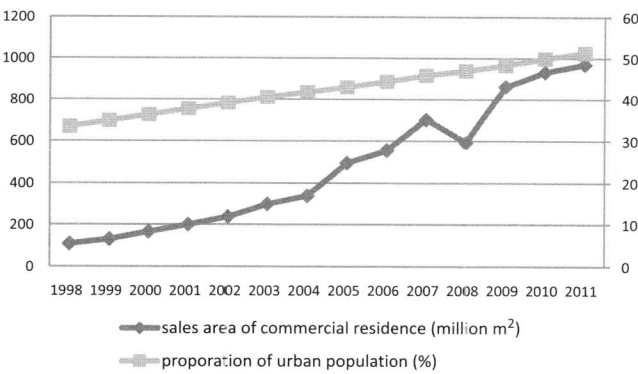

Figure 9-32: Urbanization and sales area of housing during the period 1998–2011.
Data Source: Statistical Yearbook of China and *Statistical Yearbook of China City.*

this capital flows to urban infrastructure construction, with the purpose of promoting the city image and forming a brand effect, and further increasing the value of real estate projects and attracting more investment. This cycle is compatible with local governments' fiscal and political promotion incentives (Henderson *et al.*, 2009). Under this interacting mechanism of urbanization and the real estate sector, the urban economy has realized rapid investment-oriented growth (Figure 9-34 shows this mechanism).

310 *Economic Transition in China*

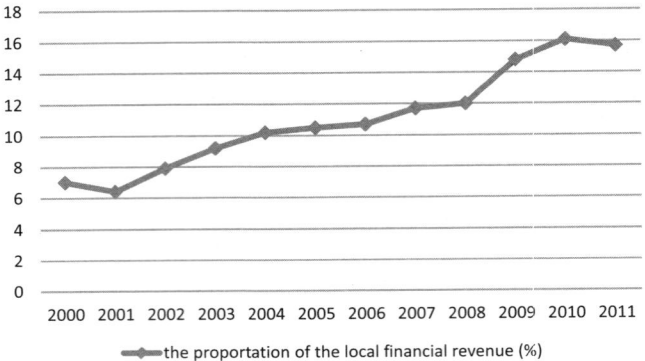

Figure 9-33: Real estate taxation during the period 2000–2011.

Data Source: http://www.mof.gov.cn/.

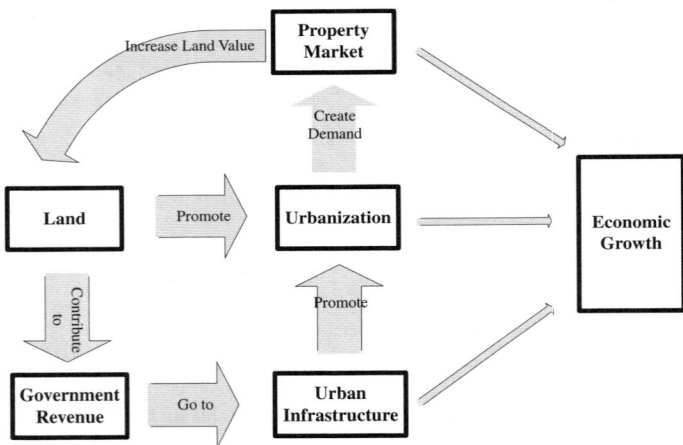

Figure 9-34: Relationship between land, urbanization, real estate market, and economic growth.

While the whole nation has experienced the rapid real estate price growth over the last two decades, the former mechanism of industrialization-promoted urbanization has gradually become the one promoted by people's expectation of land price increase since around 2000. Reports from the National Audit Office show that by the end of 2010 the number of cooperatives set up by local governments to raise funds for

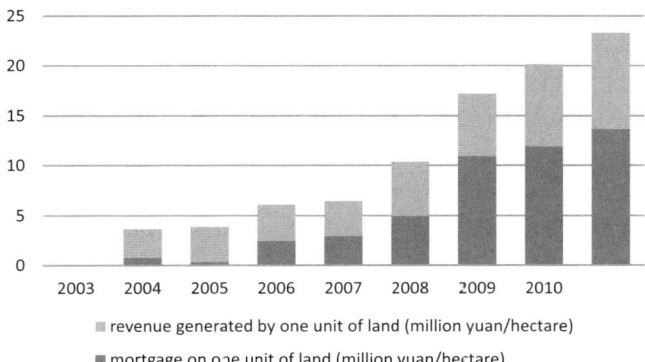

Figure 9-35: Mortgage on one unit of land and revenue generated by one unit of land during the period 2003–2010.

Data Source: Liu *et al.* (2012).

infrastructure amounted to 6,576. The main collateral of those government financing platforms is the land reserves and those platforms play the role of "land bank" (Liu *et al.*, 2012). In some cities, 60–70% of the infrastructure funding comes from those "land banks" (World Bank, 2005). Figure 9-35 shows that the government's mortgage on land is increasing year by year. Since 2008, with the increased government investment in infrastructure projects, mortgage on one unit of land has exceeded the corresponding revenue generated. In this context, since around 2000, urbanization in China was characterized by the government's promoting of "city construction" to attract investment funded by mortgage on land reserves. During that process, urban industry was reconstructed by the conversion of land use pattern and local agricultural population was converted into urban population with urban sprawl, while the central district was expanded to include suburbs promoted by the local government. All these attempts make the urbanization process deviate from the market orientation, which results in local financial overdraft, real estate bubbles, and the appearance of a "ghost city" in some cities. Moreover, this urbanization mode is closely tied to the real estate sector with the risk of "government bankruptcy" once the real estate industry has a downward shock.

According to the *Statistical Yearbook of China*, urban population with household registration accounts for 33.35% in 1998 and 51.3% in 2011 of the total population, with an average annual growth rate of 1.38%. Data from the World Bank shows that the global average urbanization rate is 52% in 2011, which means China's urbanization still has a long way to go. Consequently, the market demand for residence is still quite adequate in the next few years. The International Urban Development Report anticipates that by 2020, China's urbanization rate will reach 55%, during which 0.15 billion farmers will migrate to cities and become citizens. After the 1978 reform and opening up, China's urbanization mainly depended on the urban expansion or reclassification of "rural" areas as cities (Chan *et al.*, 2008), which made urban agglomerations relatively low. Data from the World Bank shows that in 2010, in the indicator of "Population in urban agglomerations of more than 1 million (% of total population)," China ranks in 77th place out of 132 countries. Therefore, in future a large part of population will concentrate in the central cities, which will bring pressure on the large-scale cities' capacity and also heat up the real estate market in large cities. From China's past experience, people's market demand for housing has a problem of irrationality and herd behavior caused by the stories of "overnight millionaires" due to housing wealth accumulation and supply falling short of demand. All this makes the future of China's real estate market full of uncertainty.

3.3 Real Estate Bubble

Since the establishment of the People's Republic of China in 1949, the basic objective of the financial system is to serve economic development, with great emphasis on national investment objectives and ignoring people's requirement of consumption and investment income. Implementing the long-term financial constraint policy, the government lowered the deposit interest rates through financial monopoly (as shown in Figure 9-36). The excessive government intervention also leads to great uncertainty in the capital market. At the same time, the rapid growth of housing prices over the past two decades forms a strong belief in the profitability of real estate investment. Under this circumstance, real estate has become the best investment choice. Around 2003, real estate investment fever has sprawled nationwide and different degrees of the real estate bubbles appeared in different regions.

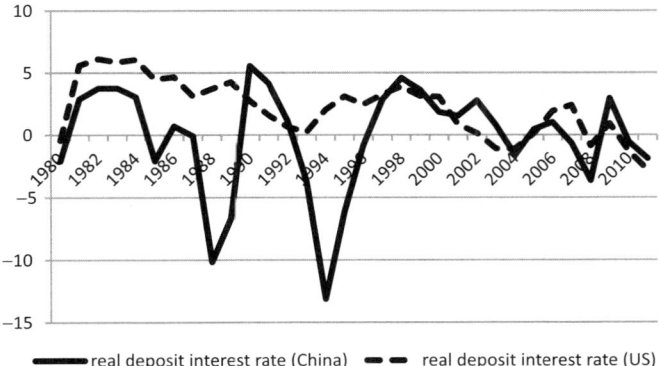

Figure 9-36: Real deposit interest rate of China vs. the United States during the period 1980–2010.

Data Source: CEIC.

According to the Charles Kindleberger (1989, 1992) definition of the "bubble," the continuous rise in the asset price in a continuous process confirms investors' optimistic expectations and attracts more new investors, some of whom are speculators and show no interest in the long-term profitability of the assets. As price continues to rise and speculative capital continues to add in, the asset price goes far beyond its long-term profitability. In this way, the "bubble" develops and expands. When it comes to the real estate sector, the existence of speculation will cause overconfidence of developers and consumers, resulting in excessive supply. The excessive expansion of the bubble can have serious consequences: the real estate industry and the whole economy will face high risk and finally experience a collapse as the bubble breaks.

Yuan and Fan (2003) point out China has the basic prerequisite to have rational bubbles, and the macro economy is likely to be dynamically inefficient with the return on capital being lower than the economic growth rate. However, studies have not reached a consistent conclusion on the level of China's real estate bubbles. Based on the available data, the index of housing price to income ratio can provide an intuitive measurement. According to Lv (2010)'s model, the reasonable upper bound of China's housing price to income ratio should lie between 4.38 and 6.78 according to the mortgage

314 *Economic Transition in China*

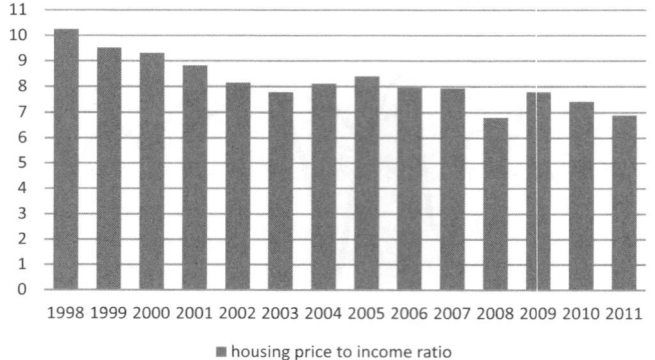

Figure 9-37: Housing price to income ratio during the period 1998–2011 (for a family of three people with the area of residence being 90 m^2).

Data Source: *Statistical Yearbook of China*.

interest rate over the past five years, and the minimum down payment. As shown in Figure 9-37, the ratio exceeds that upper bound for all the years except for 2008 and 2011.

More stringent measures on the real estate bubble include the method of statistical test and underlying price comparison (Gao *et al.*, 2012). The former method assumes that statistical data will fluctuate abnormally in a bubble market; therefore the existence of the bubble can be determined by monitoring the fluctuation of the real estate market (Hamilton, 1986; Diba and Grossman, 1988), while the latter method groups the housing price factors into economic fundamentals and bubble factors, then compares the underlying price to the transaction price through regression models and finally determines the measurement of the bubble. Kuang's (2010) empirical study on China's 35 large cities finds that expectation and speculation have a great influence on the housing price volatility, which provides empirical evidence for the existence of a bubble. Based on panel data of 30 large cities in China, Gao *et al.* (2012) find that bubbles in most studied cities have gone up. In 2010, the bubble degree lies between 20% and 30% in 13 cities, while only two cities have a bubble degree lower than 10%. They further shows that real estate bubble degree is significantly higher in eastern China than in the middle and west.

Generally speaking, using data from the Chinese real estate market, most studies have found evidence of the existence of a real estate bubble in some cities. To cure this problem, the new round of control policies since 2010 put emphasis on curbing real estate investment and speculation. Although market-oriented policies such as public housing construction and levying housing property tax are put forward, the command-and-control approach still plays the central role; for example, the policy of restriction in home purchase and mortgage, the administration accountability from above, and so on. Those restraints from the central government are short-term and volatile, which will do little to help stabilize the high-rising market expectations. In the long term, designing the right incentive compatible policy for local governments is the radical way out of the housing problem.

4. REAL ESTATE POLICIES

In order to cure the overheated real estate market, the central government's control policies in the real estate market have become more and more intensive. This policy risk exacerbates China's real estate market uncertainty. Different from macro control measures of the developed economies, China relies more on administrative intervention, such as the limit on home purchases and loans, censorship of real estate projects and so on. In order to calm the overheating housing prices in 2009, the new round of control policies have been adopted since 2010, with stringent restrictions on home purchase and real estate loans. However, in the long term, the effect of administrative policies is unstable; therefore, control policies in future should focus on building a public housing system and real estate tax reform.

4.1 A Retrospect on China's Real Estate Policies

China's economic system reform, started in 1978, turned on the recovery of the real estate industry. The cancelling of the welfare-oriented housing allocation in 1998 completely reinstated the real estate market. Since then, China's real estate market developed steadily and rapidly with a certain periodicity. In 2003, the real estate industry was regarded by central government as the backbone of domestic economy. At the same time, control

316   Economic Transition in China

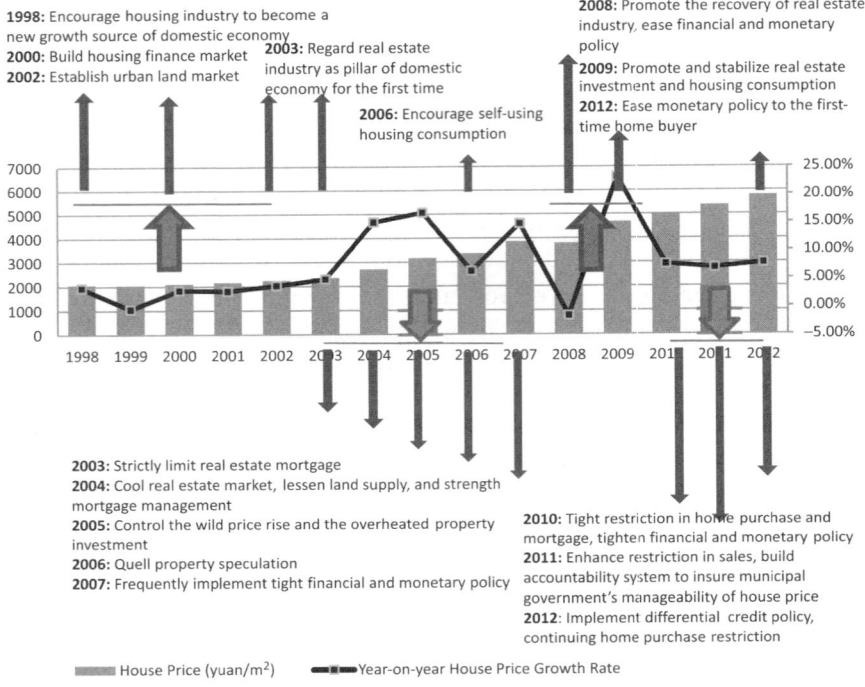

Figure 9-38: 1998–2012 House price and real estate policies.[3]

Source: Wang et al. (2012).

policies from the central government began to exert pressure on the market with great efforts to curb the soaring house price. In the recent decade, the game between policies and market has never ceased. Figure 9-38 illustrates the real estate policies in China since 1998, which shows great uncertainty and inconsistency.

The new round of control policies over real estate began in 2010 when housing price kept soaring from 2009 due to the supporting policies at the

---

[3] House price here refers to the nationwide average newly built commodity house price published by the State Statistics Bureau. Only the important nation-level policies are included. The upward arrows represent the favorable policies in the corresponding year, while the downward arrows represent the unfavorable policies; the bigger arrows refer to the general policy stance over the corresponding period; the length of the arrows denoting the intensity of the policies.

end of 2008. Real estate investment is firmly curbed and the center frequently issued new policies to calm down the overheated market. Affected by market situation and the government transition, control policies in this period are of the most stringent. The center put emphasis on the following points, including restricting investment demand, strengthening supervision, accelerating the construction of public housing, and tightening credit policy.

First of all, the restriction in home purchase and housing mortgage across cities has reduced the real estate sales volume to a great extent with the first-time buyers' consumption demand being encouraged and the demand for changing to a better residence as well as for investment being curbed. Second, since 2010 the center has strengthened the administration of developers' construction process in order to prevent idling of land purchased from the government and accelerate effective housing supply. Third, the center established an administration accountability system in which local officials will be punished if the housing price keeps soaring in their administration region. Fourth, municipal governments are required to accelerate the construction of public housing. In 2011, the center put forward the task of building 36 million sets of public housing by 2015, and the cities are under close supervision to guarantee the realization of this target. Fifth, monetary policy has been tightened since 2010 with the rising interest rate and deposit reserve ratio, while the real estate credit has been restricted and the approval for IPO and backdoor listing of real estate enterprises has been suspended. Sixth, property taxes are being tested in the cities of Shanghai and Chongqing, and other cities are likely to follow in the next few years.

The new round of control policies began to take effect in 2011 with housing price in major cities gradually going downwards and the land market cooling down as well. Since 2012, with the significant slowdown of the domestic macro economy, the center has implemented a relaxed monetary policy and at the same time, the municipal government began to ease the former control policies by reducing the interest rate of housing fund loans and subsidizing housing consumption. As a result, the real estate market is turning for the better recently. However, the home purchase restriction is still maintained and real estate investment remained to be curbed. The center is ready for more intensive control policies once housing prices keep rising in most major cities.

4.2 Policy Trend in Future

As an important part of the macro economy, the real estate sector's downturn will have a profoundly negative impact on investment and consumption of related industries, which generates a contradiction in the central government's target of "steady economic growth" and "curbing real estate investment." In 2012, the monetary and credit policies changed from being tight to loose and then tight again, reflecting the dilemma policymakers were facing. Although the center shows great resolution to curb the high-rise housing prices, local governments implement the instructions from above negatively, because government fiscal revenue relies much on the real estate sector. Generally speaking, in the short term the government transition in 2012 and 2013 will affect the control policies in that the center will do all it can to maintain the stability of housing prices and policy uncertainty will be greater during this period.

From a long-run point of view, the systematic reform of the real estate sector will be placed in a more important position. Alongside the evolution of control policies in recent years, it is expected that in the low-end market, the building of public housing system subsidized by the government will continue, in order to solve the housing needs for most low-income families. China's construction of public housing has entered a period of rapid development since 2007. According to the Ministry of Housing, from 2008 to 2011 the newly started public housing has accumulated to 23 million units, with 12 million units being completed and low-income households who benefit from public housing accounting for 11% of the total urban households. In the high-end market, real estate speculation and the rapid rise of housing prices will still be under intensive control before the establishment of an effective public housing system. In the long run, the administrative measures will gradually be weakened, while market-oriented measures such as property taxation and financial policies will become the major tools to prevent excessive investment and bubbles.

REFERENCES

Cai, H., Henderson J. Vernon and Zhang Qinghua (2009). *China's Land Market Auctions: Evidence of Corruption*. National Bureau of Economic Research.

Chan, K. W., Henderson J. Vernon and Tsui Kai Yuen (2008). Spatial Dimensions of Chinese Economic Development. In L. Brandt and T. Rawski (eds.), *China's Great Economic Transformation*, Cambridge University Press.

Diba, B. T. and Grossman, H. I. (1988). Rational inflationary bubbles. *Journal of Monetary Economics*, 21(1): 35–46.

Gao, B, Wang Huilong and Li Werijun (2012). *Real Estate Bubbles in 30 Large and Medium-sized Cities in China: Based on the Model of Expected Equilibrium Price*. School of business Nanjing University Working Paper.

Hamilton, J. D. (1986). On testing for self-fulfilling speculative price bubbles. *International Economic Review*, 27(3): 545–552.

Henderson, J. V., Quigley John and Lim Edwin (2009). *Urbanization in China: Policy Issues and Options*. China Economic Research and Advisory Programme, Center for International Development at Harvard University, Cambridge, MA.

Hui, Eddie Chi-Man, Lo Tony, K. K., Chen Jia and Wang Ziyou (2012). Housing and consumer markets in urban China. *Construction Management and Economics*, 30(2): 117–131.

Kindleberger, C. P. (1989). *Manias, Panics and Crashes: A History of Financial Crises*. New York: Basic Book.

Kindleberger, C. P. (1992). *Mariners and Markets*. New York: New York University Press.

Kuang, W. (2010). Expectation, speculation and urban housing price volatility in China. *Economic Research Journal*, (9): 67–78.

Liang, Y. and Gao, T. (2007). Empirical analysis on real estate price fluctuation in different provinces of China. *Economic Research Journal*, (8): 133–142.

Liu, S.-y., Fei-zhou Zhou and Ting Shao. (2012). *Reform of Land System and Transition of Development Pattern*. Beijing: China Development Press.

Lv, J. (2010). The measurement of the bubble of urban housing market in China. *Economic Research Journal*, (6): 28–41.

Neutze, M. (1987). The supply of land for a particular use. *Urban Studies*, 24(5): 379–388.

Tao, R, Lu Xi, Su Fu-bing and Wang Hui (2009). China's transition and development model under evolving regional competition patterns. *Economic Research Journal* (6): 21–33.

Titman, S. (1985). Urban land prices under uncertainty. *American Economic Review*, 75(3): 505–514.

Wang, Y., Tang Wei and Jia Shenghua (2012). *Uncertainty, Competition and Timing of Land Development: Theory and Empirical Evidence from Hang Zhou*. Asia-Pacific Real Estate Research Symposium, July.

World Bank (2005). *China: Land Policy Reform for Sustainable Economic and Social Development.* Washington D.C.

Yuan, Z. and Fan, X. (2003). A analysis of rational bubbles in the real asset market. *Economic Research Journal*, (3): 34–43.

Chapter 10
Fiscal System and Local Government Behavior

Shengyan Xu
School of Business Management, Hohai University

Wancong Li
School of Economics, Fudan University

This chapter describes the formation and development of local governments' land-based finance systems. We will discover the changes in the local governments' incentives in the institutional change in the fiscal system. Based on this, we will further show the mechanism and contribution to the economic development of this particular land-based finance. In conclusion, challenges and possible solutions will be discussed.

1. INTRODUCTION

China's economic structure consists of four main components: local residents, firms, local governments, and the central government. Under the control of the central government, local governments behave like entrepreneurs who promote local economic growth. Local governments' behavior is an important part of the study of both the long-term and short-term performance of China's economy.

The tax system reform in 1994 had a profound influence on the incentives of local governments. One outcome is that local government finance mainly relies on land and real estate related taxes, and local governments have a high degree of autonomy on land leaseholds, which means that local governments can determine which land is leasehold and the method of leasehold. Local governments' autonomy on land leaseholds stimulates these governments to increase fiscal revenue through city management to increase land and real estate related revenue.

Local governments' city management is inevitable due to the following reasons: (1) After the tax reform, local government enterprises' revenue decreases while risk increases. At the same time, local governments can decide land allocation while land leasehold revenue and land taxes are local revenues. Local governments have a financial incentive to manage cities for land-based finance. (2) Different from the long life cycle of nurturing industrial enterprises, land leasehold payments and real estate tax have short cycles and work quickly. (3) In the regional competition, local governments have no tax autonomy and thus cannot set their own tax rates or change the tax bases, nor can they introduce new taxes. What local government can control is land allocation. Consequently, local governments put emphasis on promoting local economic development and gaining competitive advantage in attracting private and foreign investment through city management.

City management by local governments leads to land-based finance. Chinese local governments monopolize urban and rural land supply markets under the dual land system, which provides a prerequisite for city management. The reform of the housing system in 1998 promoted the development of the real estate market and increased land price. With open market sales and urban land bank system, the local government set up a city management and land revenue maximization system. The scale of land-based finance is becoming larger and larger. In 1999, land leasehold revenue accounted for 9% of local independent fiscal income and 5% of the total local revenue (including the central refund), and in 2011, the numbers were 60% and 34%, respectively.

2. EVOLUTION OF CHINA'S FISCAL SYSTEM AND THE "TAX-SHARING" REFORM

A saying in ancient China is: "Finance is the country's lifeblood and the basis for everything." From the perspective of the fiscal system, it is possible to recognize the central–local relationship and explain the behavior of local governments.

2.1 Evolution of China's Fiscal System

Since 1949, the development of China's fiscal system can be divided into three stages. Prior to 1978, a centralized fiscal system was implemented with tax revenue and expenditure being controlled by the central government. In the second stage from 1978 to 1993, the central government gradually decentralized and implemented a tax sharing system with local governments being completely responsible for their own revenue and expenditure. Tax reform in 1994 further consolidated the decentralized tax sharing system in which taxes are divided into central taxes (federal tax), local taxes, and joint taxes. Central tax is collected by the central government for national spending, while local tax is collected by local governments, whose purpose is local economic development. Joint tax is taxed by both local and central governments and then split by a predetermined rule. State and local tax collection agencies are set up separately, and the duties and expenditure range of local and central governments are determined.

During the planned economy era prior to 1978, the tax revenue and fiscal expenditure was decided by the central government, called fiscal centralization. Although this system had promoted national economic growth by concentrating resources for national objectives, the inherent contradiction eroded the efficiency of the fiscal system and thus generated great fiscal pressure. In 1976, the economic crisis made the problem more serious, which made the fiscal system reform become a major issue for both the central and local governments.

Under the centralized fiscal system, local governments do not have to be responsible for their expenses, so they lack incentives to increase revenue. In order to mobilize local governments' incentive to increase fiscal revenue and ease the fiscal crisis, in 1977, the Ministry of Finance introduced the fiscal system that required local governments to be completely responsible for their own revenue and expenditure, also called "eating in separate kitchens." This meant the centralized tax collection system was changed to a decentralized one. The tax revenue distribution was signed as a contract between the central and local government. This system was first experimented in Jiangsu Province and extended nationwide in 1980. Later, the system was improved with minor adjustment. Before the "tax-sharing" reform in 1994, there were two major changes in 1985 and 1988, with the general trend being more and more decentralizated. In 1985, the tax system changed from a lump sum tax system to a proportional tax system; the term of "division of taxes, audit of the balance of payments, grading and fiscal responsibility system" had been formally introduced to replace the old terminology of "eating in separate kitchens." The tax revenue split between central and local governments was determined by the tax base and tax category. Different corporate affiliation led to different tax distribution schemes between the central and local governments, while local fiscal expenditure was still determined and financed by local government itself. In 1988, on the basis of the 1985 system, because economic development across provinces was quite different, the center made six different tax distribution schemes for 37 local finance units under its jurisdiction (including provinces, municipalities, autonomous regions, and municipalities with independent planning status). Each scheme had a different responsibility base, tax distribution ratio, turnover base, and incremental indicators. The center and local must repeatedly negotiate on those indicators according to the economic conditions in that year. Each local government tries hard to set a low distribution ratio and high expenditure indicators to internalize the achievements of local economic growth. Financial meetings of the time often said, "The key strategy of this year is to 'dispute' the fiscal indicators."

Another feature of the system of "eating in separate kitchens" is that it continues to use the traditional tax classification method introduced since 1949. Corporate income taxes are levied in accordance with corporate affiliation, while turnover taxes are levied according to the territory. Moreover, industrial and commercial taxes and local governments' revenue are combined tightly together. To a large extent, this arrangement encourages local governments to promote local enterprise development, especially the township enterprises' development (Zhou, 2006). Local governments cannot only gain the total tax revenue from the local businesses, since most firms at that time are owned by the government, but also a proportion of the firms' profit, which transfers to the local government and acts as its external budgetary revenue. By converting tax to profit, the local government's external budgetary revenue can be increased. Local governments prefer external budgetary revenue because it can be spent without reporting to the center and local government is not required to be audited on its external budgetary revenue. In this case, the central fiscal revenue is not growing with local economic development. In most years, the central tax revenue accounted for less than 30% of the national fiscal revenue, which gave the center a very hard time in tax collecting.

While the fiscal responsibility system does well in mobilizing the local governments in developing the local economy, it has obvious drawbacks. First, local governments place undue reliance on their own enterprises, and governments at all levels are interested in "enterprise management," distorting the development of enterprises and market competition. Second, this system strengthens the regionally segmented "vassal economy," contributing to redundant construction and government investment expansion and distorting the market price signals. Third, the complex and fickle fiscal responsibility contract leads to instability and normalization of the financial resources distribution between the center and local governments. Fourth, the central fiscal revenue does not grow with the development of the local economy. These problems eventually led to the tax sharing system reform in 1994. In accordance with the "Decision on the Implementation of the Tax-sharing Financial Management System" issued on December 15, 1993 by the State Council, this reform included three aspects: first, appropriate financial expenditure scope determined by the responsibility of the central and local governments; second, central and local fiscal revenue divided according to categories of taxes; third, implementation of a central to local tax return system. Besides, China has gradually built a VAT-dominated turnover tax system in the tax-sharing system reform.

2.2 The "Tax-Sharing" Reform

2.2.1 Theory

There has been controversy on the pros and cons of centralization and local decentralization in the study of the fiscal system and public decision making. Some scholars emphasize the necessity of decentralization, in that the local government has information superiority, which enables local governments to provide the same public goods more efficiently than the central government (Oates, 1972). Therefore, the transfer of fiscal revenue and expenditure power from the center to local governments will be more conducive to improving economic efficiency, thus promoting local and national economic growth (Zhang and Gong, 2005). Others insist on the advantages of centralization. First, public goods have a specific range of benefits. Local public goods are supplied more efficiently by the local government, while national public goods are supplied more efficiently by the central government. Second, the central government can create the external environment for regional competition. In order to promote competition between local governments, free relocation, no-cost population movements, and other conditions are needed in addition to decentralization. The existence of local barriers to migrants will go against the objective of regional competition. And the central government can play an important role in undoing those barriers. Third, the central government can help to eliminate the negative effects of local competition. Due to unbalanced economic development among regions, there is a great difference in local governments' ability to supply public goods. Thus, certain income and wealth redistribution is necessary, along with intervention and decision-making from the center. Fourth, the establishment of the fiscal system is conducive to macroeconomic stability. Fifth, taxation by the central government has a comparative advantage for certain taxes. For example, taxation by the central government can avoid income tax evasion by migrants.

Although there is debate in theoretical literatures on fiscal decentralization, in practice fiscal decentralization has become the mainstream of governance. Since the 20th century, a trend of fiscal decentralization has been developed in countries all over the world. Of 75 transition economies with a population of over five million, 84% commit to power decentralization to local governments (Dillinger, 1994; Zhang and Gong, 2005). As a big country, central and local power structure and financial governance is a common problem faced by governments of different periods. In 1977, the central government began to decentralize through the "eating in separate kitchens" fiscal system; further decentralization was adopted in 1994 through the tax sharing system reform.

2.2.2 Reform

Due to the problems of fiscal centralization, in 1977, the central government started "responsibility" reform, called "eating in separate kitchens." However, while the reform inspired local governments to develop the local economy and spare no effort in taxation, it also encouraged local governments to "hide wealth in enterprise," which caused the national fiscal

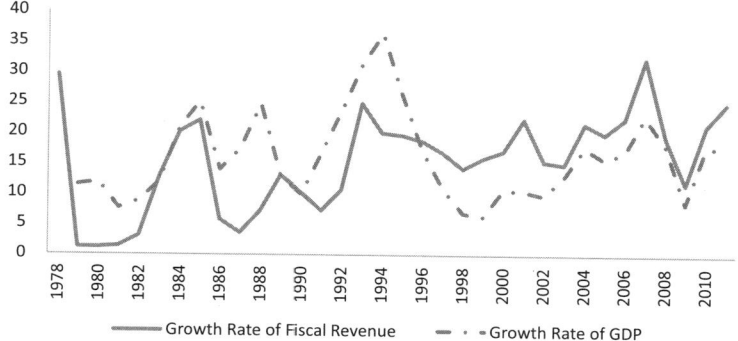

Figure 10-1: Growth rate of national fiscal revenue and GDP (%), 1978–2011.
Source: *China Statistical Yearbook (2012)*.

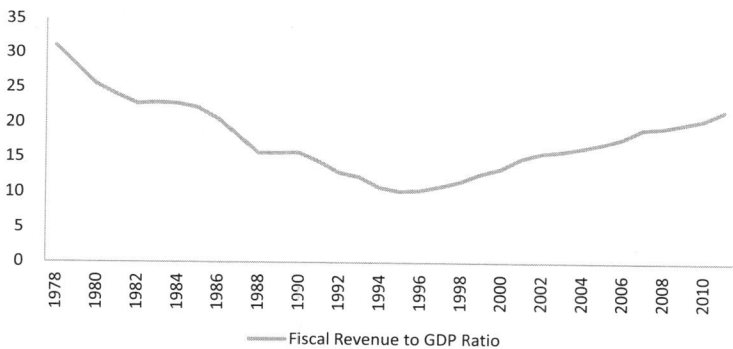

Figure 10-2: National fiscal revenue to GDP ratio (%), 1978–2011.
Source: *China Statistical Yearbook (2012)*.

revenue growth to be slower than GDP growth (as shown in Figure 10-1) and the share of fiscal revenue in GDP decreased gradually (as shown in Figure 10-2). The central financial difficulties force the center to implement further reforms of the fiscal system.

Under the perpendicular political system in China, the promotion of local officials is held by the central government, so the top-down fiscal decentralization reform can be carried out smoothly. The reform was promoted in provincial units, and the center and local governments divided fiscal revenue and expenditure. According to Zhou (2006), the 1994 reform mainly focused on the following aspects. First, the central and local budget income is divided by relatively fixed tax categories to avoid endless negotiations and bargaining. The categories include central taxes, local taxes, and shared taxes. Second, two relatively independent taxation authorities are set up for central and local authorities. Different from the former method of tax paid by corporate affiliation, all corporate taxes (mainly value-added tax and consumption tax) are included in the tax system and distributed by the tax-sharing rule. The income tax reform in 2002 further moved corporate income tax and personal income tax from local taxes to taxes shared by the central and local governments. Third, a tax return and transfer payment system is implemented. On the one hand, tax returns are decided according to the local tax revenue growth to maintain the enthusiasm of the developed regions in managing taxes. On the other hand, tax returns are transferred to underdeveloped areas to achieve regional equalization.

The "tax-sharing system" has achieved significant effects and greatly promotes the national fiscal revenue growth. It can be seen from Figure 10-1 that after the reform, the relationship between fiscal revenue and economic development has become much more coherent. The national fiscal revenue growth is positively correlated to GDP growth. After the reform, a VAT-dominated turnover tax system is built, which means the local authorities cannot change the gains of economic growth into local revenues to escape tax sharing. Since 1996, national fiscal revenue has been growing faster than GDP growth. The share of national fiscal revenue in GDP rose from 10.8% in 1994, and gradually to 22% in 2011 as shown in Figure 10-2.

2.3 Financial and Administrative Responsibilities Distributed between the Local and the Center After Tax Sharing Reform

2.3.1 Central and local tax structure

The tax-sharing system divides taxes into central taxes, local taxes, and central–local shared taxes. Central taxes include consumption tax, vehicle purchase tax, customs duties, and import value-added tax; local taxes include business tax, land use tax, farmland occupation tax, land value-added tax, property tax, urban maintenance and construction tax, travel tax, deed tax, and tobacco tax; central–local shared taxes include value-added tax, corporate income tax, and personal income tax. In addition, taxes paid by the railway sector, and head offices of banks and insurance companies are central tax.

After the reform, the central and local fiscal revenue sharing arrangement is as follows. According to *China Statistical Yearbook (2012)*, the central government's revenue includes: (1) Tariffs, imported goods VAT and consumption tax, export tax refund value-added tax, and consumption tax; (2) Consumption tax; (3) Business tax and urban maintenance and construction tax paid by railway departments, head offices of banks, head offices of insurance companies; (4) 75% of value-added tax, 60% of corporate income tax that is included in the shared part; (5) National corporate income tax and profits turned over by the central enterprises, which are not included in the shared part; (6) 60% of personal income tax, vehicle purchase tax, tonnage tax, 97% of stamp duty on securities transactions, offshore petroleum resources tax, and central non-tax revenue.

Local financial income includes: (1) Business tax (excluding centralized paid business tax of the railway sector, head offices of banks, and head offices of insurance companies), profits turned over by local enterprises; (2) City maintenance and construction tax (excluding the part paid by the railway sector, head offices of banks, and head offices of insurance companies), and property tax; (3) Urban land use tax, land value-added tax, travel tax, and farmland occupation tax; (4) Deed tax, tobacco tax, and stamp duty; (5) 25% of value-added tax, 40% of corporate income tax that is included in the shared range, 40% of personal income tax, 3% of stamp duty on securities transactions, other resource taxes excluding offshore petroleum resources tax, local non-tax revenue, etc. In local fiscal revenue in 2011, the general budget revenue was 5.25 trillion yuan, of which the tax revenue was 4.11 trillion yuan, accounting for 88.2%. In tax revenue, the composition of the main taxes was: sales tax, 32.9%; corporate income tax, 16.4%; value-added tax, 14.6%; personal income tax, 5.9%; deed tax, 6.7%; city maintenance and construction tax, 6.3%; land value-added tax, 5.0%; urban land use tax, 3.0%; farmland occupation tax, 2.6%; and real estate tax, 2.7%. Land-related direct taxes accounted for 26.4% of total tax; business tax and land tax together accounted for 59.2% of the total local tax revenues.

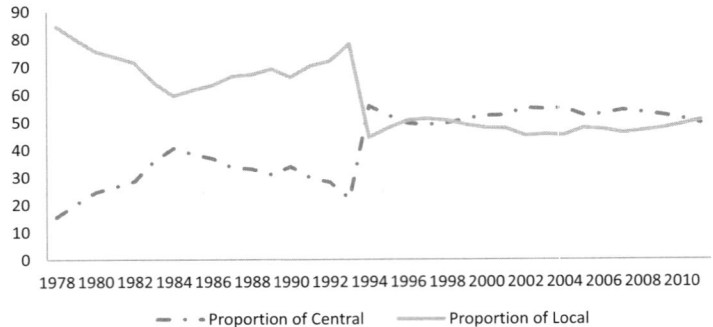

Figure 10-3: Central and local fiscal revenue structure (%), 1978–2011.
Source: Financial Statistics of New China's 50 years, China Statistical Yearbook.
Notes: 1. Central and local fiscal revenue are at the same level of income. 2. This table does not include domestic and foreign debts.

Through the tax system reform, the proportion of central fiscal revenue in the country's total fiscal revenue quickly rose from less than 30% to more than 50%, and then maintained at about 50%, as shown in Figure 10-3.

After the reform, value-added tax, which accounts for a large proportion of tax revenue, was re-designated as shared tax with 75% distributed to the center, while another major tax category, corporate consumption tax, is re-designated as a central tax. Due to the reform, the central fiscal revenue has increased rapidly with its control enhanced by the local economic growth. Business taxes and land-related taxes become major local taxes. In addition, as a compensation for decline in local taxes, revenue of land use right leasehold sales is re-designated to completely belong to the local government, rather than shared between the center and local authorities any more. Therefore, business tax, land-related taxes, and land leasehold revenue become the main sources of local government revenue. Business tax mainly comes from the service sector with the real estate industry acting as a major contributor. This had a direct impact on the incentive of the local government, resulting in a great dependence of local governments on land leasehold revenue and real estate industry.

2.3.2 Central and local fiscal expenditure structure

After the tax system reform, the central and local fiscal expenditure responsibilities basically continued to be the same as that in the

1980s. Government expenditures are determined in accordance with the distribution of responsibilities of the local and the center. Central government expenditures include general public services, diplomatic spending, defense spending, and public safety expenditures, as well as the expenditures on restructuring the national economy, coordination of regional development and implementation of macro control, and so on. Local government expenditures include general public services, public safety expenditures, social undertakings coordinated by local governments, and so on. This arrangement results in a significant decline in local government revenue without a corresponding decline in local expenditure responsibilities, as shown in Figure 10-4. Local fiscal expenditure in 1993 accounted for 71.7% of the national fiscal expenditure; reform of the tax system caused almost no decline in the proportion of fiscal expenditure. Since 2004, local fiscal expenditure accounts for more than 80% of the national fiscal expenditure in 2009, and in 2011 that proportion reached 84.9%. In the local financial expenditure, the proportion of infrastructure construction spending is relatively high, while spending on science, education, culture, and health is much lower. In recent years, the central government requires the local expenditure to be more focused on public services. The proportion of science, education, culture, and health spending in general

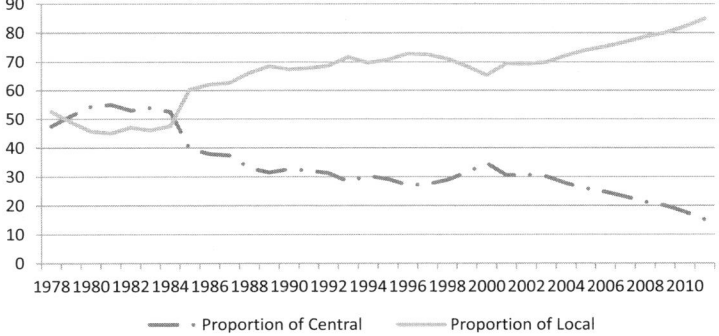

Figure 10-4: Central and local fiscal expenditure structure (%), 1978–2011.

Source: *Financial Statistics of New China's 50 years, China Statistical Yearbook.*
Notes: 1. Central and local fiscal expenditures are expenditures of the same level. 2. Figures in this table prior to 2000 do not include domestic and foreign debt service payments and the use of foreign loans for infrastructure construction expenditures. Since 2000, domestic and foreign debt interest payments are included in the national fiscal expenditure and central government spending.

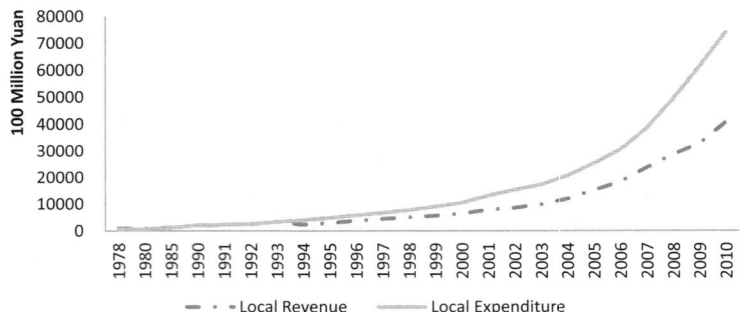

Figure 10-5: Local fiscal revenue and expenditure gap, 1978–2011.
Source: *China Statistics Yearbook (2012)*.

budget expenditures in 2011 rose to 27.4%. However, at the same time the central government requires the local government to set up corresponding funds to support related construction projects. As a result, pressure on local finance further increases.

After 1994's tax reform, the local government's fiscal balance has continued to expand, as shown in Figure 10-5. Since 2009, the expansion has become accelerated. In 2011, local fiscal revenue and expenditure gap was −4.02 trillion yuan, accounting for as much as −8.5% of national GDP. There are several possible reasons. On the one hand, the center requires local governments to increase the expenditure on people's livelihood and transform to a service-oriented expenditure structure. On the other hand, after the financial crisis, the central launched a 4-trillion yuan economic stimulus plan, which also requires local governments to spend more on infrastructure construction. The local fiscal gap forces local governments to look for extra-budgetary income. As a result, the local extra-budgetary revenue is rising rapidly after the tax system reform, and in recent years has accounted for more than 90% of the national extra-budgetary revenue.

2.3.3 Tax return from the central government

After the tax system reform, the central government implemented a tax return and subsidy system for regional development. In order to ensure the incentives in developing enterprises and take care of the vested interests, the tax return system takes the year 1993 as the base. The "two taxes"

(VAT and excise duty), which originally act as local governments' pillar financial resources, are returned to the local governments according to the net amount that the governments turn in after the tax reform. These taxes are further taken as tax return base to calculate the incremental returns to the local governments with 30% of the annual average growth rate. Two years later, the center further implements the "transitional-period transfer payment method." Considering the certain factors that directly impact local revenue and taking the local governments' effort into account, the center determines the amount of transfer payment subsidies, which is mainly used in solving particular problems in local finance. The transfer payment method is appropriately biased toward the minority areas. Figure 10-6 shows that the tax returns and subsidies from the center to the local governments account for more than 40% of total local fiscal revenue. Prior to 2009, even after including the financial return from the central government, local fiscal deficit still existed.

In addition, the existing financial return and subsidy system has some obvious problems. (1) The system only works in the transfer of the central and provincial finance, without a clear system for financial transfer below the provincial level. At county level, governments seldom implement the decentralized financial system with a clear division of fiscal revenue and expenditure by responsibility, which makes the county finance difficult. (2) The local tax system is far from perfect. Currently, except for business tax, local taxes are all micro tax, resulting in the lack of income stability at

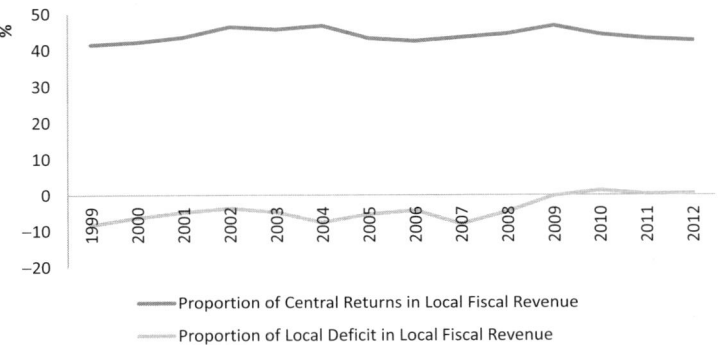

Figure 10-6: Central tax return and local fiscal deficit, 1999–2012.
Source: CEIC.

county and township level. (3) The management authority of local taxes is highly concentrated in the central government. (4) There are the following problems in the transfer payment system. Tax returns are based on base number, encouraging local governments' effort in economic development and taxation. However, there is no regulation on the procedures and management of the center to local subsidies. Besides, the local special subsidies lack certainty, and how to transfer payments between local governments is not clear. The result is that financial rights are concentrated in the upper government while expenditure responsibilities are transferred to the lower government. Facing great financial pressure and heavy expenditure responsibilities, county governments are forced to rely on extra-budget revenue.

3. CHANGES IN LOCAL GOVERNMENTS' INCENTIVES

The tax system reform in 1994 had a profound influence on the incentives of local governments. One outcome is that local government finance mainly relies on land and real estate related taxes, and local governments have a high degree of autonomy on land leasehold revenue, which stimulates local governments to increase fiscal revenue through city management to increase land and real estate related revenue.

3.1 From Enterprise Management to City Management

In the period of "eating in separate kitchens," except for the part to be turned in, taxes and the economic achievements of enterprise development belonged to local governments, so at that time local governments were keen to develop local businesses. Later, after the tax sharing reform in 1994, value-added tax and enterprise income tax became central–local shared tax with a large proportion distributed to the center, which made the risk of local government-run enterprises outweigh the benefits. Consequently, local governments began to restructure inefficient local enterprises to private enterprises. Besides, with autonomy in land allocation and land-related taxes being local taxes, one of the most significant changes is that local governments put much more emphasis on "city management" than "enterprise management."

The tax-sharing reform has significantly changed the relationship between local governments and enterprises, from a narrow local entrepreneurialism to private and foreign investment attraction. Before the tax-sharing reform, the corporate tax was levied according to corporate affiliation, keeping most benefits of local industrialization in the hands of local governments. Thus, we have seen that township enterprises all over the country flourished from the 1980s to the mid-1990s. Reform of the tax system re-designated all value-added tax and enterprises income tax to central–local shared taxes, and the tax system is independent of local governments, which led to a great reduction in local government revenue from enterprises. In the new tax system, local government business enterprises, regardless of whether they are making profits, are subject to value-added tax with 75% going to the center, leaving only 25% to the local government. Value-added taxes are levied directly by the tax department with little place for local government tax relief. Local governments must be directly responsible for the gains and losses of the enterprise, but the major benefits belong to the central government. This inevitably leads to a decline in local governments' enthusiasm in directly operating enterprises, so we can see the large-scale restructuring of township enterprises after the mid-1990s.

In a VAT-dominated tax system, local governments are indifferent to corporate affiliation; they are only interested in the scale of production. As long as there is production, there will be taxes and achievements. Consequently, the local governments work hard to attract private and foreign investment with large-scale foreign-funded enterprises being more favored. In the competition over investment, because the local government does not have tax autonomy, land as a key production factor becomes a bargaining chip. Under those circumstances, local governments compete over investment and capital through zero or even negative land price.

In the case of corporate tax revenue decrease, local governments began to seek new revenue growth in pursuit of local tax revenue growth. Since the housing system reform in 1998, with the establishment of land leasehold public auction and urban land bank system, local governments have found a way to increase government revenue, by increasing land value, promoting urban construction, attracting foreign investment, and finally developing local economy. On the one hand, local governments allocate cheap land to attract investment and promote local industry; on the other hand, the industrial development will promote the development of modern service industry, real estate, and other tertiary industries, which will increase sales tax revenue, land prices, and land related taxes. With the growth of fiscal revenue, local governments can further promote urban infrastructure construction and attract investments through industrial land subsidies, as discussed in Chapter 9.

3.2 Rise of Local Governments' Craze for "City Construction"

3.2.1 Relationship between local governments' land-based finance and large-scale "city construction"

"City construction" describes the phenomenon of local governments' constructing a new city. Prior to 2000, urban renewal plays a central role in governments' city management. To follow economic growth, local governments work hard on changing the worn appearance of the city, updating obsolete function facilities and improving the difficult living conditions of residents. The urban renewal even became a political task, such as the "365" dangerous building reconstruction plan that was put forward by Shanghai in 1992. The main problem plaguing local governments in this period is funding. The successful attempt is to utilize the increased added value for the reconstructed land parcel as self-finance for urban renewal.

Since around 2000, with the rapid development of the urban land leasehold market, local governments have been able to get capital support from mortgage on their land banks. At the same time, with China's accession to the WTO in 2001, the local governments' focus changed from mainly improving people's living conditions to emphasizing the city's image, and the concept of "city management" has been gradually formed. Revenue from land leasehold and mortgage on land banks has made large-scale city construction possible. The housing system reform in 1998 and urban land public auction system reform in 2002 contributed to the rapid increase in urban land price. By exercising land expropriation power and paying low land requisition compensation, local governments reallocate land to a more profitable use pattern by public auction or reserve land to land banks to get bank loans, which will consequently provide funding for infrastructure construction and subsidy for industrial development. Infrastructure construction and economic development will further raise land value, forming a virtuous development cycle. In this way, local governments' land-based finance drives city construction across the country in full swing. During this process, externality of infrastructure construction promotes economic development, but leads to high house prices and local government debt problems, which will hinder economic development if not properly resolved. The following example demonstrates the dominating role of local government in "city construction."

Case study: The influence of Chengdu's new administrative center moving to the new town on land price
http://news.hexun.com/2011-12-22/136555129.html

The city Chengdu's new administrative center, also known as "the new Yizhou City Plaza," is a new landmark building, located in the southern suburbs of Chengdu, about 7.8 km from the CBD. In 2003, corresponding to the "east and south development plan," the Chengdu Municipal Government decided to relocate part of the office to the undeveloped eastern and southern suburbs. Construction of the new administrative center began in 2004, with the total investment amounting to about 1.2 billion yuan, and more than 2.5 billion yuan if including the value of the land.

With a strong impetus from the relocation of the city's political center and subway construction in place, the undeveloped areas of southern Chengdu have attracted increasing investment since 2004, with the rapidly increasing land leasehold price. In 2004, Hutchison Whampoa purchased 69 hectares of land, at a price of only 309 million yuan per hectare, which was the highest of that time in southern Chengdu. However, four years later, the price rose to 1.90 trillion yuan per hectare when KWG Property purchased the number 28 lot in south Renhe Area.

3.2.2 The impact of large-scale "city construction"

Local governments utilize land-based finance to promote urban construction and expansion. The local government must first change the use pattern of the land. By urban sprawl, peri-urban agricultural land is converted to urban construction land; the city's construction land recycling is also carried on at the same time. Through the conversion of land use pattern, local governments can gain value-added benefits from land leasehold auction, as well as reconstruction of the city through planning.

The large-scale "city construction" has the following impacts:

(1) Real estate industry development is largely promoted. From 1991 to 2011, Chinese real estate enterprise sales have amounted to 29.59 trillion yuan with the total sales being 29 trillion yuan since 1997. At the same time, housing prices rose rapidly and have become the most vexing problem across the country. Since 2004, the central government continued to regulate the development of the real estate market, but the effect is very limited.
(2) Urban sprawl has become rapid, while the population agglomeration has lagged far behind. Local governments across the country are promoting construction of new towns. One of the most extreme examples is Kangbashi new town of Ordos in the desert. Because of the shortage of residents after completion, Kangbashi is known as the "ghost town." Those new towns are worried about being abandoned in future. However, in recent years, local governments' enthusiasm in building new cities is unabated; the scale is even increasing, especially in the recent rapidly developing central and western China. For example, in 2012, Lanzhou city bulldozed 700 barren hills to reconstruct Lanzhou City, while Xian city invested 100 billion yuan in bulldozing hills and building new towns. Financial support for these large-scale city constructions mainly comes from land-based financing.
(3) Large-scale infrastructure construction is carrying on. According to an estimation of China's capital stock in Jin Ge (2012), since 1994, the stock of infrastructure in China has been growing rapidly. The average growth rate calculated at constant prices is as high as 17% from 1994 to 2008, far beyond the GDP growth rate in the same period. Growth rate calculated at constant prices from 2003 to 2006 is more than 20%, which means the level of infrastructure is improved faster, as shown in Figure 10-7. According to the CEIC database, in 2011 China's highway mileage was 85,000 km, ranking second in the world. China has the

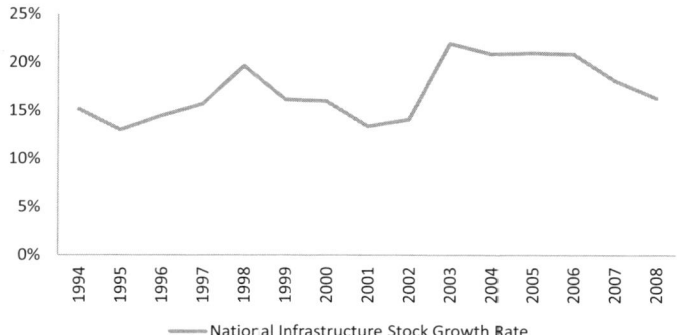

Figure 10-7: National infrastructure stock growth rate (in constant prices). *Source*: Jin Ge (2012).

world's fastest railway with a speed of 350 km per hour. Meanwhile, after fiscal decentralization reform, investment competition between local governments pushes local governments to promote local infrastructure (Zhang *et al.*, 2007), while land-based finance provides financial support for the construction.

3.3 The Local Governments' "Industrialization" and "Urbanization"

Local governments' large-scale investment in "city construction" has a significant contribution in maintaining China's rapid economic growth, but also affects the economic structure. The question of how local governments deal with the relationship between industrialization and urbanization has received great attention.

Local governments have no tax autonomy, and thus cannot set tax rates or change the tax bases, nor can they introduce new taxes. What local government can control is land allocation. Besides land management, do local governments still have a strong desire for industrial development? Because of the central and local tax system reform, the center gradually takes away the main part of the value-added tax and corporate income tax, while local governments have entire land leasehold revenue as compensation for revenue decreases. Han and Kung (2012) thought that this made local governments change from supporting "industrialization" to "urbanization." Local governments will vigorously develop real estate, and invest in infrastructure through land management, and care little for local industry. Tao *et al.* (2009) argued that after the reform of the tax system, the local government has not reduced enthusiasm in industrial development. The more developed the regional economy is, the higher the land revenue will be. With income from residential land acting as a subsidy to cost of industrial land (Tao and Wang, 2010), competing local governments often attract investment and promote local economic development through cheap industrial land (Zhang, 2008). Consequently local governments have strong incentives in industrial development. Even in cities with a higher proportion of the service sector like Beijing and Shanghai, the industrial land supply is much greater than the commercial and residential land. Other cities have even greater aspirations in industrial development, and the cities that are not suitable for industrial development have ambitious industrial development planning.

The order of urbanization and industrialization is a problem faced by local governments. The development process of cities in eastern China is that industrialization comes first and then urbanization. However, in recent years, the central and western cities put even more emphasis on urbanization than industrialization. Urbanization going ahead of industrialization has caused many concerns. Without industrial support, urbanization will have a crisis. However, others argue that urbanization can prepare good conditions for industrialization, and the size and distribution of cities will eventually be chosen with market participation.

Although the process of urbanization is speeding up in recent years, China's urbanization still lags behind industrialization. In 2010, China's urbanization rate was 51.3%, while the industrialization rate was 46.8%, making the ratio of urbanization rate to industrialization rate 1.09. Besides, the global average of that index was 1.95 in the same year, about twice that of China. That index of the developed countries, United States, France, Britain, Germany, and Japan, in 2010 was 4.10, 4.11, 4.09, 2.64, and 2.48 respectively, which shows the characteristics of urbanization rate higher than industrialization rate. The index of the "BRICS," Brazil, Russia, South Africa, and India, is 3.22, 1.97, 1.38, and 1.15, respectively, which is also higher than China. Therefore, China's urbanization has a larger potential to go higher.

4. FORMATION AND IMPACT OF LAND-BASED FINANCE

4.1 Conditions and Scale of Formation of Land-Based Finance

4.1.1 Formation of land-based finance

Formation of local governments' land-based finance is inevitable due to the following reasons. (1) After the tax reform, local government enterprises had decreased revenue and increased risk. At the same time, local governments can decide land allocation while land leasehold revenue and land taxes are local revenues. Local governments have the financial incentive to manage the city for land-based finance. (2) Different from the long life cycle of nurturing industrial enterprises, land leasehold payments and real estate tax have a short cycle and work quickly. (3) In the regional competition, local governments have no tax autonomy and thus cannot set their own tax rates or change the tax bases, nor can they introduce new taxes. What local government can control is land allocation. Consequently, local governments put emphasis on promoting local economic development through city management.

There are several conditions for the formation of land-based finance. (1) Chinese local governments monopolize urban and rural land supply market. (2) The reform of the housing system in 1998 released huge demand for housing of urban residents. At the same time, China is experiencing a rapid urbanization process. Every year, a large number of people migrate from rural to urban areas. The new urban population also has a huge demand for housing. With the maturity and development of the real estate market, a strong demand for land arises. (3) The public land transfer system enhances value of land. In the planned economy period, land supply is entirely through government allocation and is free of charge. After the reform and opening up, local governments gradually introduce compensated land supply. However, in the early stage, compensated land supply is mainly through land sell agreement. In land sale agreements, local governments have a relatively large right in determining land transferees and selling price, which result in corruption. In 2002, the central government required of local governments that transfer of business land must be open and market-oriented. After 2004, this provision is strictly enforced and an urban land bank system is gradually established all over the country. With open market sales and an urban land bank system, the local government set up a city management and land revenue maximization system.

4.1.2 Scale of land-based finance

The proportion of land-based finance in local revenue after 2003 is getting bigger and bigger with continuous growth of government revenue. Extra-budgetary revenue consists of land leasehold revenue and land mortgage financing, and budget revenue refers to the income of local governments from real estate and land taxes.

(1) Extra-budget revenue

From 1999 to 2011, national land leasehold revenue grew rapidly. In 1999, national land leasehold revenue was about 51.4 billion yuan, and in 2011, this number rose to 3.15 trillion yuan. The average annual growth rate is more than 50%, as shown in Figure 10-8. Proportion of land leasehold revenue in local fiscal revenue is becoming bigger and its impact on local finance is greater. In 1999, land leasehold revenue accounted for 9% of local independent fiscal income and 5% of the total local revenue (including the central refund), and in 2011, the numbers were 60% and 34% respectively (as shown in Figure 10-8).

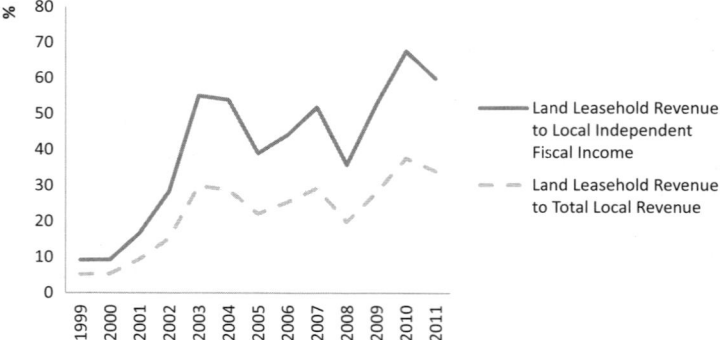

Figure 10-8: Land leasehold revenue and local fiscal revenue, 1999–2011.
Source: China Land and Resource Yearbook, China Statistical Yearbook.

The land leasehold revenue is even larger in developed cities. It is also influenced by the macro economy and has large fluctuations. For example, in 2009, land leasehold revenue in Hangzhou amounted to 103.8 billion yuan, ranking first in all kinds of cities across the country. Later, due to the macroeconomic environment and other factors, the revenue declined by more than 20% for two consecutive years. In 2012, with the land market in Hangzhou gradually rebounding, the amount of revenue stopped decreasing and rose slightly by 7%, reaching 61.1 billion yuan, which is still below the level of the same period in 2009 and 2010. In 2013, the market continues to rebound, and the main city of Hangzhou receives land leasehold revenue of more than 20 billion yuan in the first quarter, which is nearly one-third of last year's total revenue.

Mortgage on land is becoming far larger than the direct land leasehold revenue in recent years. The national land mortgage amounted to 182 billion yuan in 1999 and rose up to 2.5 trillion yuan in 2007. Due to the financial crisis in 2008, it declined slightly to 1.9 trillion yuan (as shown in Figure 10-9). It can be seen from the data that land mortgage is approximately twice land leasehold revenue. According to official data, at the end of 2011, mortgaged land in 84 major cities across the country is 300,800 hectares and mortgage loans are 4.8 trillion yuan, far exceeding the national total land leasehold revenue of 3.15 trillion yuan for the same period.

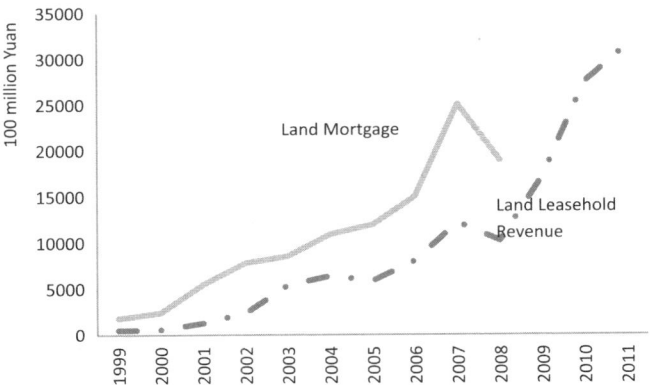

Figure 10-9: Land leasehold revenue and land mortgage loans.
Source: China Land and Resource Yearbook.

In fact, mortgage on land is far greater than the official data. The budget law established in 1994 states that local government cannot implement budget deficit and must achieve a balance of payment. Therefore, local governments have established a range of financing platforms. Land and other related assets are distributed into these platforms to raise money. According to the survey the author conducted in eastern coastal counties, annual increase of extra-budgetary financing is more than that of the fiscal revenue. The most common way is get mortgages on the government's land banks. Trust and other financing methods are also used. This process has been unregulated for a long time. Sometimes, the same land parcel is distributed into different financing platforms and repeatedly pledged.

Massive extra-budget financing of local governments has resulted in a huge amount of local government debt. According to data from the National Audit Office, at the end of 2010, the national local government debt balance is approximately 10 trillion yuan, including bank loans of 8.5 trillion yuan. This data is generally considered to be underestimated. The "2010 China's Regional Financial Operation Report" announced by the central bank pointed out that as of the end of 2010, the upper limit of the size of platform loans is 14.4 trillion yuan, higher than the data published by the Audit Commission. In fact, the scale of local government debt is far greater than these publicly announced data.[1]

(2) Growth of budget revenue

City management increases budget revenue in addition to extra-budgetary revenue growth. In the upswing of the real estate market, the taxes take only a short time to show effect and thus are preferred by local governments. According to sub-industry tax data from The *Chinese Tax Yearbook*, real estate tax contribution accounts for about 5% of the tertiary sector, while tax from the construction industry is four times that from the real estate

---

[1] The author visited a district financial staff of Changzhou. The interviewee said local government debt has risen to the extent that the government is unable to repay it. The local government's goal is to ensure continuity in the funding chain and it no longer considers the cost of financing. In some areas, because the Government has been unable to raise funds publicly, the financing task is issued to subordinates by the leadership. A part of the financing costs has even achieved the borrowing rate of small loan companies; the annual interest rate is more than 20%. Published data on public debt may be only one-tenth of the actual debt.

industry. In 2011, property tax, urban land use tax, land value-added tax, farmland occupation tax, and deed tax amounted to 828.8 billion yuan, accounting for 20% of the local fiscal income, which is about a quarter of the total land leasehold revenue of the same year.

Extra-budgetary revenue, especially the land leasehold revenue is concerned by the public. However, in recent years the cost of demolition of the land showed an accelerated upward trend, local governments gain less and less from direct land leasehold, while the land that can be mortgaged is becoming less and less. Because of the decline in land leasehold revenue and land related taxes, the budget revenue is becoming more important.

4.2 Operation Mode and Contribution of Land-Based Finance

4.2.1 Operation mode

Tax system reform in 1994 introduces local government financial pressure as well as fiscal revenue and GDP competition between regions, which results in the formation and development of land-based finance. The specific operational mode is as follows:

(1) Construction land allocation brings in direct land leasehold revenue. Land allocation has two ways. The first approach is to change rural land into urban construction land, which leads to the continuous outward expansion of urban area. Peri-urban suburbs are turned into urban areas first. When the expansion is limited, county or townships are often turned into urban areas through administrative division adjustment. The second approach is to update or transform existing urban construction land. Through the differential rent effect, residents in old residential areas of the city center are encouraged to move to the outskirts of the city, where living conditions of the residents can be improved while the city center can be reconstructed.

(2) Land mortgage loans through local financing platform. After the tax system reform, the central government limits the rights of local governments to take on public debt, so land mortgage is in a non-public status and progressed through some special local financing platform. Local governments establish cooperatives whose asset and cash flow meets

financing standards. These cooperatives are collectively referred to as the local financing platform. According to the 2010 Report on China's regional financial operation issued by the People's Bank of China in 2011, by the end of 2010, there were more than 10,000 local government financing platforms — an increase of more than 25% compared to the end of 2008. The proportion of the county level (including county-level cities) platforms is about 70%. In local government financing through local financing platforms, land is the most important collateral, and the annual increase of land mortgage loans is much larger than land leasehold revenue.

(3) Promote urban infrastructure construction with land-based finance. Land leasehold revenue and land mortgage bring liquidity for local governments. Aside from making up for budget deficits, they are mainly used in the construction of urban infrastructure. In the top-down assessment system, local governments bear a lot of transferred expenditure tasks from higher levels. In other words, policies from the center are often paid for by local governments. For example, China's basic education spending is the responsibility of the county government. When the education of migrant children became a big issue, the central government introduced a policy that requires local governments to provide equal education for the children of the floating population. This policy, although introduced by the central government, is funded by local governments. In construction of large national railways and highways, local governments are responsible for the demolition and corresponding construction fund. These funds mainly come from land-based financing. Aside from this, local officials need to strive for promotion. This leads to local government's investment in infrastructure construction, because infrastructure projects are prestigious and promote local economic development and revenue growth. Land-based finance provides financial support for the construction of local infrastructure while infrastructure improvements lead to increase in local land prices, which is a persistent cycle.

(4) Implement differentiated policies for commercial, residential, and industrial land use. Residential and commercial development mainly relies on the local market and thus can be monopolized by local governments. As a result, market-oriented high prices are set for

residential and commercial land uses. At the same time, regional investment competition is fierce and industrial development can bring constant tax revenue for local governments. Large-scale commercial development can enhance the image of the city. So, industrial and large commercial land is transferred in a low-cost, subsidized manner. High prices for the land bring land revenue and subsidies to industrial and large commercial land promote local economic development. Local economic development creates jobs and attracts population, improving the housing prices and value of the land, which expands the size of land-based finance.

4.2.2 Contributions of land-based finance

Although the land-based financial activities of local government in the past decade have been criticized, local governments did make positive contributions to local economic development through land management.

(1) Reduce the cost of resource allocation and promote the formation of Chinese manufacturing. Land allocation has very important influence on economic growth. Banerji and Ghatak (2009) pointed out that due to land allocation difficulties in India, industrialization is limited and increase in productivity and economic development is hindered. China's economic growth miracle, in addition to contribution of the "demographic dividend" (Cai, 2004), is also due to contribution of the "land dividend." Local governments provide convenient and efficient allocation of land for industrial development through the planning and construction of industrial parks. In order to attract foreign investment, local governments compete to provide services[2] and land leasehold revenue returns and subsidies to industrial enterprises. There is even zero or negative premium for industrial land. With large-scale introduction of foreign direct investment (FDI), a threshold effect of economic development is created, which promotes the formation of Chinese manufacturing industries. In order to put an end to the vicious competition between local governments, the Ministry of

---

[2] Industrial Park Management Committees are established and responsible for formalities of future projects and offer full service support in the process of production.

Land and Resources established that from January 1, 2007, the minimum price of industrial land would be implemented, and duty officers would be held liable for the subsidies and returns from the local government.[3]

(2) Improve the infrastructure and accelerate the process of urbanization. After the reform of the tax system, "investment" yardstick competition among local governments motivated local governments to substantially improve infrastructure. The primary purpose of Shanghai learning from Hong Kong's land transfer system was to raise funds for urban construction. The purpose of land use system reform in Shanghai was to implement separation of ownership and land use rights premised on public ownership of land, and gradually change free and indefinite use of land to compensated and limited use. Land use rights enter the market to optimize the allocation of land resources and gain financial support for city construction. In 1987, 43 enterprises in Shanghai paid land leasehold payment, totaling 5.7 million yuan. In 1995, the number of enterprises that were paying land leasehold payment increased to 1182, the land area was 10.6 million square meters; an amount of 0.11 billion yuan was levied. From 1986 to 1995, the total land leasehold payment amounted to 280 million yuan, which was reverted to financial funds for urban infrastructure construction.[4] Shenzhen is also exploring a land transfer system. On December 1, 1987, Shenzhen sounded the first auction hammer of Chinese state-owned land use right. A commercial and residential land located on the west side of Cuiyuan Village, Buxin Road, Luohu District, of 8,588 square meters was sold for 5.25 million yuan. Later, local governments all around the country learned from Shanghai and Shenzhen's compensated transfer practices. Although the specific practices of different regions are different, the vast majority of land leasehold revenue is used in construction of urban infrastructure and they have built good infrastructure.

---

[3]The Ministry of Land and Resources, 2006, No. 307.
[4]Annals of Shanghai, Shanghai Office of Local Chronicles, retrieved April 20, 2013. <http://www.shtong.gov.cn/node2/node2247/node4586/node79546/node79550/userobject1ai104001.html>.

(3) The land became a policy instrument used by local governments to intervene in economic development. Local governments construct industrial parks and attract investment through low-cost land acquisition, and promote infrastructure construction and urbanization through commercial and residential land leasehold revenue and land mortgage loans. In this process, the local government attracting investment often has a threshold effect on local economic development while infrastructure construction has significant externalities and reduces transaction costs. This city management mode starts industrialization and urbanization and provides a continuous driving force in the development of the eastern part (Liu, 2011). At present, local governments in the central and western part are also learning from this mode. The eastern coastal cities have advantages for industrial development. China experienced great development with the accession to the WTO. The population continued to gather in the eastern city, increasing the value of the land, so the above city management mode of local governments can be sustained. However, whether this pattern can continue the miracle of the eastern city in the central and western parts is a big question. Due to geographical reasons, the central and western parts lack advantages for the development of export trade. From the viewpoints of global markets, the future of China's export trade may not grow as rapidly as it did in the past, although the proportion of consumption in the Chinese economy has increased, and can bring some opportunities for industrial development in the central and western regions.

4.3 The Plight of the "Land-Based Finance" and the Future Direction of Reform

Over time, land acquisition causes social conflicts, high housing prices, economic virtualization, excessive expansion of cities, industrial hollowing and structural distortions, local debt, and other issues. With land acquisition and demolition costs rising, the cost of land allocation (Wan, 2006) is increasing and local debt continues to accumulate. The space for local governments to gain fiscal revenue growth and promote economic development through land allocation is getting smaller and smaller.

4.3.1 Rising costs of land acquisition and reduction in land leasehold revenue

In the early stage of land-based finance, land acquisition and demolition cost was relatively low. In recent years, the cost is increasing rapidly. For example, in Shanghai's Xuhui District, in 2003, the average minimum of house demolition compensation was 42% of the average price of a new house, and in 2006, this percentage rose to 92%.[5] According to a survey, in the Xuhui district, the demolition cost of most of the blocks has been higher than the open leasehold land prices, leaving almost no direct benefits from land leasehold. According to data from the State Council Development Research Center, in 2011, the nation's land leasehold revenue amounts to 3.3 trillion yuan, of which compensation for land acquisition, land development, and other costs accounts for as much as 74.6%, and the cost is still rising. On the other hand, the stability maintenance costs are also rising rapidly. According to the data of the Chinese Academy of Social Sciences, China had 187,000 "mass incidents" in 2010, 65% of which are related to land disputes. Moreover, according to the Letters and Visits office of the Ministry of Agriculture, in 2011, they received 5856 local land acquisition cases, accounting for 42.9% of all petitions, and the number of cases increased by 60% year-on-year. In 2012, the newly revised "Land Administration Law of People's Republic of China (Draft) Amendment," discussed raising the proportion of landless peasants in land value-added income allocation. This will help to reduce social conflicts caused by land acquisition, but will further increase the cost of land acquisition. Therefore, local governments' revenue from the land is declining and will further decline in the future.

4.3.2 Land-based financing leads to accumulation of local government debt risk

In 1994, when the reform of the fiscal and financial system started, the center prohibited local governments from debt financing on their own. However, the result today is local government debt. The reason is the transformation of government functions and fiscal reforms. On the one hand, since China's

---

[5]This is calculated by the author using data from the government's demolition compensation file.

1994 tax reform, fiscal powers are concentrated in the upper levels while administrative powers are distributed to the lower levels. The asymmetry of powers and responsibilities of local governments is very serious; a lot of investment in infrastructure is largely completed through local financing platforms. On the other hand, in 1994, the Budget Law was promulgated and implemented, but the government budget and final accounts were still incomplete, closed, and opaque, and the budget's "soft constraints" has been slow in fundamental improvements. Local government debt is separate from the budget. The public and the market have no way to know the facts of government debt, neither do the current government know about the scale, reasons, structure, and direction of debts of the previous government. It is the "soft constraint" of government budget and debt for many years that results in the loss of control of government borrowing and investment.

After the financial crisis in 2008, the central government launched a "four trillion" stimulus plan. The central government bears only 1.18 trillion yuan, and the remaining is funded by local governments and enterprises. In addition, according to the central "four trillion" plan, local governments arrange more than 20 trillion yuan, which causes rapid growth of local debt. At the end of 2012, according to the estimates of Fitch Ratings, the size of the local debt is 12.85 trillion yuan, accounting for 25.1% of GDP, which increases by 1.7% from 23.4% at the end of 2011. This does not include debt of local government related enterprises and other platforms. These debts are mainly repaid through land mortgage. With the central regulation of the real estate market and fluctuations of the real estate market, the value of land collateral fluctuates, bringing huge risk for the tight debt of local governments. In 2012, the local government land leasehold revenue declined significantly and contribution of the real estate industry to local fiscal revenue declined. The local debt is set to expire after 2013; if the land revenue continues to shrink local governments will face an unprecedented risk.

4.3.3 Abnormal and unsustainable development of cities

Under the existing land use system, due to cheap land acquisition, city construction by local governments is vigorous from the east to the west. In the past decade, through land-based finance, local governments raise large-scale construction funds for urban development and promote rapid urban expansion and infrastructure construction. But there are many hidden problems in this process. The first is the lack of motivation for industrial development of the city. In some areas, the new towns even become ghost towns because there is no industry and population. The second is the impact on urban land use efficiency. Local governments are actively and enthusiastically committed to building industrial parks of all sizes; the low level of industrial land intensive use leads to serious waste. Third, the mass constructive investment of governments accumulates debt risk as well as disturbing efficient allocation of resource. Factor allocation between regions is severely fragmented, hindering further flow of labor and capital to major cities. Other problems include highly isomorphic industry of different regions, excessive competition between cities, and waste of resources. This led to lack of major cities in China. Cities have not assembled to optimal efficiency scale.

4.3.4 High housing prices

In the process of land allocation, real estate prices are pushed upward rapidly. A redistribution process is formed and concentrates a considerable part of resources in the hands of local governments by means of market forces. The negative effects of high prices on the macro economy include the following points: (1) The real estate industry is related to many upstream and downstream industries. Excessive rise of prices accumulates asset bubbles. In the future, once the bubble bursts, prices will fall sharply, which will affect many existing industries while impacting employment and economic growth, even causing a crisis in the capital market and bringing macroeconomic risk. (2) The high prices suppress consumption and hinder China's transition from investment-driven to consumption-driven economic restructuring. (3) The high profits of the real estate sector exclude other real sector investment, leading to economic virtualization and reduction in incentives to innovate. (4) Although the real estate booms fueled the expansion of China's urbanization and infrastructure development, housing price growth will weaken people's needs and hinder the process of urbanization of the population. (5) High prices push up land and office rental costs, and labor costs. A rise in the cost of doing business has a greater impact on high-end modern service industry and finance, trade, and commerce industry, because the development of these industries must be positioned in the heart of the commercial plots. (6) Because of high prices, the residents cannot afford housing, which has worsened the problems of people's livelihood, and may even intensify social contradictions and affect social stability.

4.4 The Future Direction of Reform

Local power needs checks and balances, either from the central government or from the general public. The public vote for their own interests and China is a relationship-based society, which easily leads to society controlled by interest groups. The central government keeps restraint on local authorities through fiscal centralization and official assessment, and will continue for a long time in the future.

Land-based finance is a stage-specific phenomenon in the process of economic development in China. The United States, in the early stages of development, also increased revenue through land leasehold, but today it is gaining stable land related tax income from fiscal tax, inheritance tax, and gift tax (Wang *et al.*, 2011). Land-based finance has brought a rare bonus period for the construction of China's urbanization. On the one hand, the government should take advantage of this bonus. On the other hand, it should find an alternative way when land-based finance becomes unsustainable in the future. Future reforms can follow the following directions.

4.4.1 Fiscal system reform: Repartition of financial and administrative responsibility between the center and local

After the reform of the tax system, the center took the bulk of fiscal revenue, while main public spending is the responsibility of local governments. Financial expenditure gap forces local governments to solve the lack of funding by land-based finance. Therefore, to fundamentally solve the extra-budgetary funding problem of local governments, administrative powers should move upward or financial powers downward. At the same time, stable sources of income should be allocated to local governments. For example, less-developed areas can be encouraged to cover resource tax while developed areas can levy real estate tax. Also, revenue and expenditure responsibility at the city, district, county, and township levels should be clearly defined. Reform of the tax system did not provide fiscal decentralization provisions below the provincial level, resulting in upward move of government financial powers and downward move of administrative powers. Because of the revenue and expenditure gap, governments below the prefecture-level city are the main entities of land-based finance. Therefore, further implementation of fiscal decentralization reform is needed in the future.

4.4.2 The transformation of government functions: shift to service government

At present, the functions of the local government are not clearly defined; multi-objective assessment of local governments leads to too many tasks for local governments. In recent years, local governments are required to increase spending on people's welfare, such as the construction of security housing and increase in proportion of education expenditure to GDP. But requirements in the development of the local economy are not reduced, which further expanded the local government spending pressures. Under such conditions, the local government had to solve the spending problem by land-based finance. Therefore, the duties of the government need to be specified more clearly in the future, assessment criteria of officials should be determined, and local government functions should shift to a service-oriented government and change the local government from the "city management" into the city public service provider.

4.4.3 Land system reform: break local government monopoly and establish a diverse land market

Definition of rights and interests on land has a direct impact on income distribution. Over-protecting the interests of land users will push up land prices and house prices. Some residents become rich through demolition, such as the repeatedly appearing demolition billionaires in Shenzhen in recent years. This exacerbates the gap between the rich and the poor and increases the pressure of local government land acquisition. Local government can change from land leasehold revenue to land value-added tax. Collective land can also be allowed to directly enter the market to increase the efficiency of land allocation and break the monopoly of local government in land supply.

4.4.4 Open local government debt: local government bonds replace land-based financing

Since the local government has accumulated a huge amount of debt, the government should recognize the reality and fundamentally resolve the internal mechanism that causes the expansion of local debt. The budget law needs to be amended to step up into the orbit of rule of law of government borrowing as soon as possible. Developed countries are under strict constraints of the law, yet the government debt crisis is difficult to avoid. If China continues to ignore the local debt, the debt bubble may burst at any time, and its impact on the economy will be catastrophic. Under current conditions, there is still plenty of money squandered on prestigious projects. Therefore, by allowing local governments to issue bonds publicly, local borrowing activities and debt usages will be standardized. New debt can be used as one of the assessment indicators for officials to counter the present attitude of raising current debt regardless of the future repayment. Future local construction projects should be completed with local debt financing. Through the local debt market, the construction of the city is chosen — resolving the current problem of cities expanding everywhere — under the leadership of local governments, and promoting urban agglomeration.

REFERENCES

Banerji, S. and Ghatak, M. (2009). No way out of this plot, *Financial Express*, New Delhi, September 30.

Cai, F. (2004). Demographic transition, population dividend, and sustainability of economic growth: Minimum employment as a source of economic growth. *Population Research*, 28(2): 2–9.

Dillinger, W. (1994). Decentralization and its implications for urban service delivery, World Bank Publications.

Han, L. and Kung, J. K. (2012). *Fiscal incentives and policy choices of local governments: Evidence from China*. http://ihome.ust.hk/~sojk/Kung_files/fiscal%20incentives_JK.pdf.

Jin, Ge (2012). The estimation of China's infrastructure capital stock. *Economic Research Journal*, 4: 4–14.
Liu, S. (2011). Way out of land-related finance lies in the change of dynamic mechanism of urbanization. *Management and Administration on Rural Cooperative*, 5: 27.
Oates, W. E. (1972). *Fiscal Federalism*. New York: Harcourt Brace Jovanovich.
Tao, R., Xi Lu, Fubing Su and Hui Wang (2009). China's transition and development model under evolving regional competition patterns. *Economic Research Journal*, 7: 21–33.
Tao, R. and Wang, H. (2010). China's unfinished land system reform: Challenges and solutions. *International Economic Review*, 2: 93–123.
Wang, K., Hongmei Liu and Xuan Zhang (2011). Study on the evolution of the United States land related revenue. *Public Finance Research*, 2: 73–76.
Wan, Y. (2006). On the old city center of Shanghai settlements updated tuning mechanism, doctoral dissertation of Tongji University: 29–32.
Zhang, L. (2008). Dilemma and solution of agricultural land conversion: Analyses based on the economics literature. *World Economic Papers*, 6: 85–97.
Zhang, Y. and Gong, L. (2005). The Fenshuizhi reform, fiscal decentralization, and economic growth in China. *China Economic Quarterly*, 5(1): 75–108.
Zhang, J., Yuan Gao, Yong Fu and Hong Zhang (2007). Why does China enjoy so much better physical infrastructure? *Economic Research Journal*, 3: 4–19.
Zhou, Feizhou (2006). A decade of tax-sharing: The system and its evolution. *Social Sciences in China*, 6: 100–117.

Chapter 11

The Demographic Factors in the Chinese Economy

Qin Chen

School of Economics, Fudan University

1. INTRODUCTION

Over the last three decades, China's population demographic has changed from a country with high birth rate and young age structure, to a country with low birth rate, low mortality, and an aging population. Along with demographic changes, China's economy has experienced rapid growth. This chapter will analyze China's demographic changes in the past 30 years from multiple aspects.

The most significant change of China's demographic conditions is the rapid decline of the birth rate. Before the start of the mandatory family planning policy in 1968, China's total fertility rate was 7.025. With the implementation of the policy of "Late, Long, Few," China's fertility rate has declined in the late 1970s to about 3. In 2010, China's total fertility rate further declined to 1.18, which is far below the replacement level. The decline of fertility results in a lot of social and economic impact.

There are two main reasons for the rapidly declining fertility in China: (1) The implementation of the family planning policy, and (2) the development of society and economic growth. The chapter will begin with the discussion of the causes of fertility change, and the analysis of changes in fertility, and the prediction of future fertility change.

Next, this chapter analyzes and forecasts the future of China's population change. In addition to the age structure of the population, the spatial distribution of the population of China has also experienced a lot of changes.

In 1982, there were only 211 million people living in urban regions. The number increased to 666 million in 2010, which accounts for half of China's total population. The huge gap of income between urban and rural areas is one of the important driving forces of the rapid urbanization of rural population. But in the future, with the convergence of the urban–rural income, China's urbanization rate will have a range of possibility. This chapter will also forecast China's urban population changes.

Finally, this chapter will discuss the impact of changes of population on the Chinese economy. With the deepening of aging and the decreasing of China's demographic dividend, the ratio of workers to retired people who participated in the urban basic pension system fell from 5.4 in 1989 to 3.2 in 2010, which means the number of employees who support a retired person dropped by 40%. China's basic pension and the urban/rural residents' pension will be under greater pressure. We will predict the future operation of China's pension system.

Besides the impact on pension, Chinese population changes will affect some economic aspects, including the savings rate and international trade, etc. For instance, a series of papers by Wei found that the sex ratio in China affected the savings rate, economic growth, prices, and other aspects. We will summarize the relationship between the demographic change and economic development of China.

2. DEMOGRAPHIC CHANGE IN CHINA

The birth rate of China began to decline rapidly since 1949. As can be seen from Figure 11-1, China's birth rate exceeded 3% in the 1970s, but after the policy "Late, Long, Few" was implemented in the early 1970s, the birth rate gradually decreased to 2%. The strict one-child policy began to be implemented in the early 1980s. However, with the 1960s cohort entering their childbearing age, the birth rate rebounded in the early 1980s, and reached the highest in 40 years in 1987, about 2.33%. The birth rate began to drop afterward by about 50%, to only 11.9% in 2011. At the same time, the mortality rate in China remained between 0.6% and 0.7% from the late 1970s. Since 2003, China's mortality rate rose, which is the result of the serious aging situation.

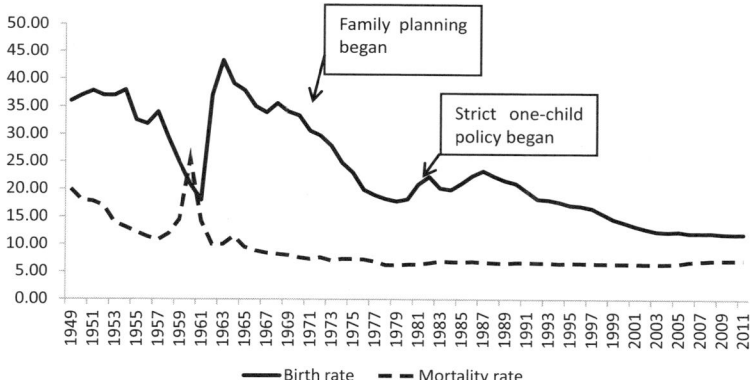

Figure 11-1: Birth rate and mortality rate of China (0.1%).
Source: Data for 1949 to 2005 are from the New China 60 years Statistics Assembly; 2006–2011 data are from the *China Statistical Yearbook 2012*.

The difference between births and deaths represents the natural growth rate of population. The highest growth rate in 40 years was in 1987, at approximately 16.6%. With the aging of the population and the increasing mortality rate, as well as the decrease of the share of women of childbearing age in total population and the declining birth rate resulting from the family planning policy, China's natural population growth rate has fallen to 4.79%, about 28.9% of the growth rate in 1987. With the further continuation of this trend, China's natural growth rate will become negative in the near future. China will enter the stage of negative population growth.

From the first census in 1964, China's population age structure began to evolve from pyramid-shaped to diamond-shaped. According to data from four censuses in 30 years (Figure 11-2), we find that China's population age structure has experienced large changes: the higher proportion of youth population (10–20) in 1982 goes to the right in the four censuses gradually, and in turn become a higher proportion of middle-aged population. In 2010, the older people in this part of population are about to reach their retirement age.

If we consider the population of 10- to 20-year-olds in 1982 as the first baby boomers, then the 10- to 12-year-old population in the 2000 census is the second lot of the crest of population brought by the last round of

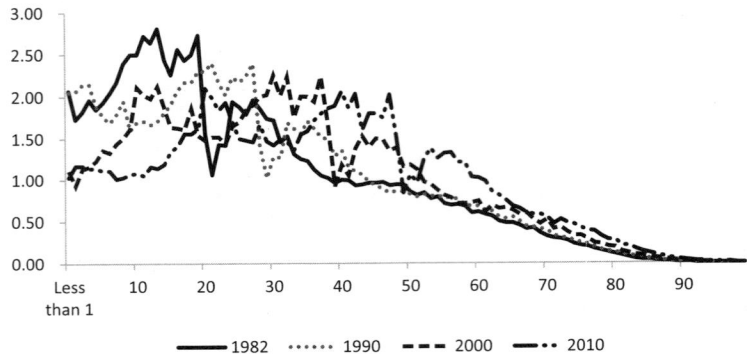

Figure 11-2: The population age structure of 4 censuses from 1982 to 2010.

the baby boom. Their interval is 23 years. Compared with the first round population crest, the second round population crest has a lower maximum and shorter duration. In the 2010 census, the third round of the population crest had not yet appeared, while the first and the second rounds of the population crest were still within the working age window. In this period, the proportion of children or the elderly population is relatively small, and China is now experiencing the most fruitful demographic dividend. But with the first lot of population crest reaching their retirement age, and the population entering working age is far less than the retirement speed of the population, the demographic dividend will quickly become a burden on the population.

2.1 The Cause of Fertility Changes

The root cause of the rapid aging of China is the decreasing birth rate. In 1982, women of childbearing age in China had a total fertility rate of 2.55. It meant 2.55 children in one woman's lifetime, which was still above replacement level. However, in 2010, the total fertility rate was only 1.19 children per woman, which is only half the replacement level. The decline in the total fertility rate in China has occurred in almost all ages, as shown in Figure 11-3.

We can find from Figure 11-3 that the fertility rate of women of childbearing age has declined in varying degrees. The peak of the fertility rate of women from the ages of 22 to 27 declined by about two-thirds compared

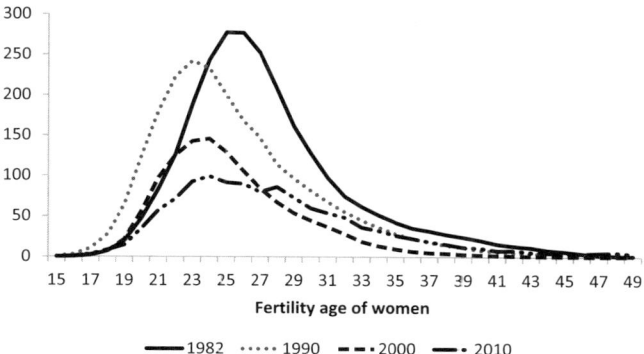

Figure 11-3: Fertility rate of women of childbearing age fertility rate of 4 censuses (number of births/1,000 persons).

Source: Data of 1990–2010 from the census summary, data of 1982 comes from the results of the micro data of 1982 census.

with the 1982 census. Another feature of the fertility change is that the peak of fertility rate was postponed. In the data of 1990, 2000, and 2010, the median childbearing age is 24, 25, and 27. The change of fertility rate of women in childbearing age results in the decline in the number of newborn population, and further contributed to the aging of the population. We will analyze the reason of the declining fertility from the aspects of family planning and other economic and social impacts below.

2.2 The Impact of Family Planning

One of the important reasons why fertility rate is declining is family planning. The existing literature tends to give a conservative result on the effect of family planning on fertility rate.

From 1970 to 1985, the fertility rate of the women in China of childbearing age declined from 6 to 2.6. Schultz and Zeng (1995) had investigated the in-depth fertility survey in 1985. They applied three sets of variables in the model of decreasing fertility rate: personal characteristics, community features, and family planning features. They find that the family planning could only explain a small share of the significant decline in fertility. Another similar study — Cai (2010) — believes that social and economic development has played a greater role in the process of the decline in fertility.

However, the above literature often only uses cross-sectional data, which might give a biased result of the effect of family planning on fertility. In economics literatures, researchers tend to use DID, Instrumental Variables to investigate the causal relationship between family planning and fertility decline.

McElroy and Yang (2000) use the family planning policy fine as the instrumental variable to discuss the effect of family planning on the decline of fertility. They find that the fertility of childbearing age women would have a 0.03 decrease as the fine increased by 10%. If the family planning were totally cancelled, the total fertility rate would increase by 0.33. It turns out that the effect of family planning is far lower than expected.

Li et al. (2005) use a different constraint on Han and ethnic minorities and the "Difference in Difference" method to implement a similar research. They find that Han women and minority women with similar characteristics born before 1945 had the same probability to have a second child. But under the implementation of family planning, the cohort of Han women born after 1945 had a significant decrease in the probability of second birth. The Han women born between 1955 and 1960 were lower by 20% to 25% in their second birth probability compared with their ethnic counterparts. Averagely speaking, the probability of second birth by Han women was decreased by 11% as a result of family planning.

Wang (2012) uses the policy difference of each stage as the variance of family planning to investigate the situation of lower fertility of women under different exposures of family planning policy. Wang (2012) also finds that the family planning policy can only explain a small share of the fertility decreasing. He also finds that women would postpone their marriage time under the effects of family planning.

The above literatures try to explain that the family planning policy only has a limited effect on the decreased fertility. In this chapter, we will follow the method used in Li et al. (2005) to analyze the effect of family planning using the difference of policy constraint between each women's group.

2.3 Family Planning in Ethnic Minorities

According to the discussion in Li et al. (2005), the minority ethnic and Han women face different policy constraints. Compared to the strict one-child

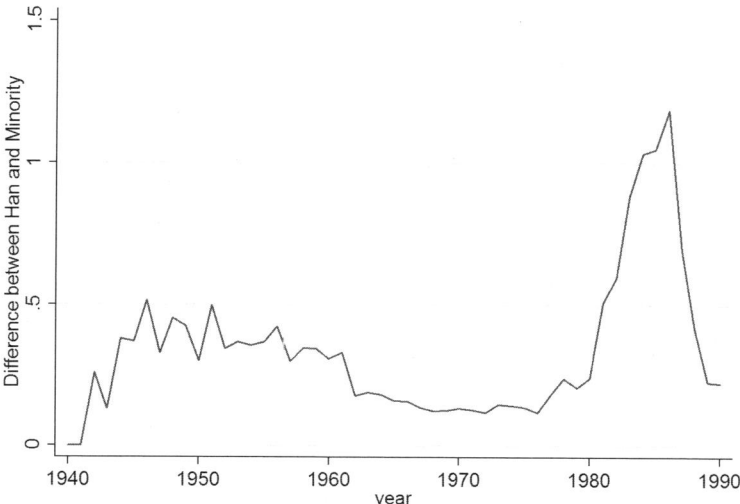

Figure 11-4: Difference in number of children between Han and Minority.

policy of the Han women, minority women generally can have two children, while some minorities in Xinjiang province can have four children, and minority women in Xizang has no limitation on the number of children. Zhuang minority and Manchu used to face family planning with less constraint. But as the populations of these two minorities reach 10 million, their privilege was eliminated in 1988 and 1990, respectively. The variance of family planning policy enables us to take a detailed look at its effect on fertility.

Using the 1% sample of 2005 mini-census, Figure 11-4 illustrates the difference in number of children between Han and minorities of different cohorts. We can see from Figure 11-4 that the difference was relatively large for the cohort born between 1940 and 1960. The gap shrank then, and rose again after the cohort born after 1975. For minority women born around 1985, the number of births is higher than Han by 1.2.

The above figure provides some interesting information for us. First, in the early 1980s, when the strict one-child policy began, the cohort that experienced the most serious exposure of family planning is the women born between from 1950 to 1960. If we consider the gap of fertility between Han and minority women as the result of family planning policy, it would be about 0.5. The rise of fertility of the cohort after the 1970s shows that people might choose to postpone their birth plan under a relatively strict policy.

However, Figure 11-4 shows that the fertility gap between Han and minorities can largely be explained by the low education attainment and low income of minority women. One possible reason is that the Han women born in the early 1980s experienced faster growth in years of schooling and income, which occurs simultaneously with the implementation of family planning, which brought about the gap in fertility between Han and minorities. Figure 11-4 separates the women with different schooling and checks the effect of family planning.

It can be seen from Figure 11-5 that the gap in fertility of Han and minorities was eliminated after we control their schooling. On the other hand, we can find heterogeneity in the effect of family planning on women born after the 1980s. For less educated people, strict birth constraint can postpone their childbearing age. But this effect disappears for the better educated women.

From the above analysis, it is not difficult to come to a conclusion. Although Han women and minority women face different family

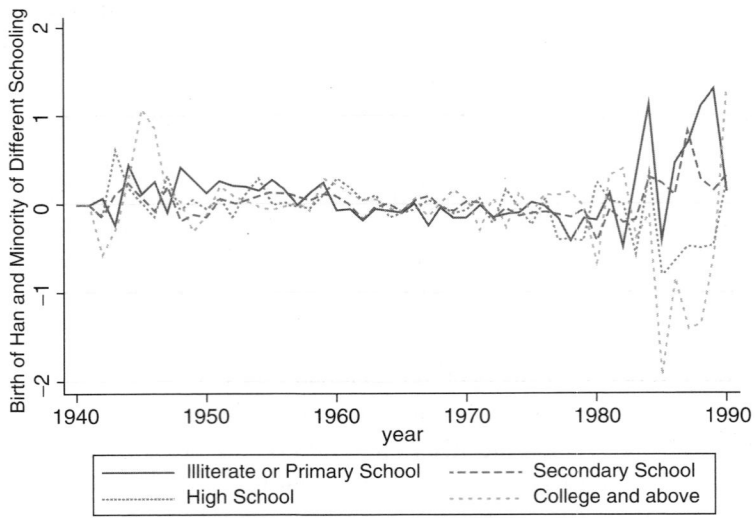

Figure 11-5: Fertility difference between Han and minorities by education and cohort.

planning constraints, we cannot find its effect on fertility after we control their schooling. The effect of family planning policy on childbearing age women gradually decreased when their schooling increased. In the highest schooling cohort, the effect becomes negative.

2.4 Difference between Non-Agricultural *Hukou* and Agricultural *Hukou*

Another variance of family planning policy occurs between non-agricultural *hukou* and agricultural *hukou*. In Yang (2004), we can find that the fertility constraint faced by agricultural *hukou* is more flexible than that faced by non-agricultural *hukou*. Families with agricultural *hukou* can have a second child if their first child is a daughter, and if there is a certain gap between two births. But in no case can an agricultural family have three children.

At the early stage of family planning policy, the fertility gap between urban and rural families is not as large as now. But the fertility decline in urban regions is far faster than that in rural regions. In 2010, the fertility rate in urban regions is less than 1, while the fertility rate in rural regions is about 1.5, see Table 11-1.

Similar to the practice of Figure 11-5, we show the fertility difference of rural and urban women with different education levels in Figure 11-6.

Table 11-1: Fertility difference between rural and urban areas.

Year	Urban	Rural	Year	Urban	Rural
1950	5.001	5.963	1982	1.580	3.320
1955	5.665	6.391	1985	1.210	2.480
1960	4.057	3.996	1990	1.548	2.537
1965	3.749	6.597	1995	1.124	1.556
1970	3.267	6.379	2000	0.936	1.430
1975	1.782	3.951	2005	1.056	1.638
1980	1.147	2.480	2010	0.983	1.438

Source: Data from 1955 to 1980 is collected from "*Population Yearbook of 1985*," data of 1985 is collected from "*China Population Statistics Yearbook 1989.*" Others are collected from each census.

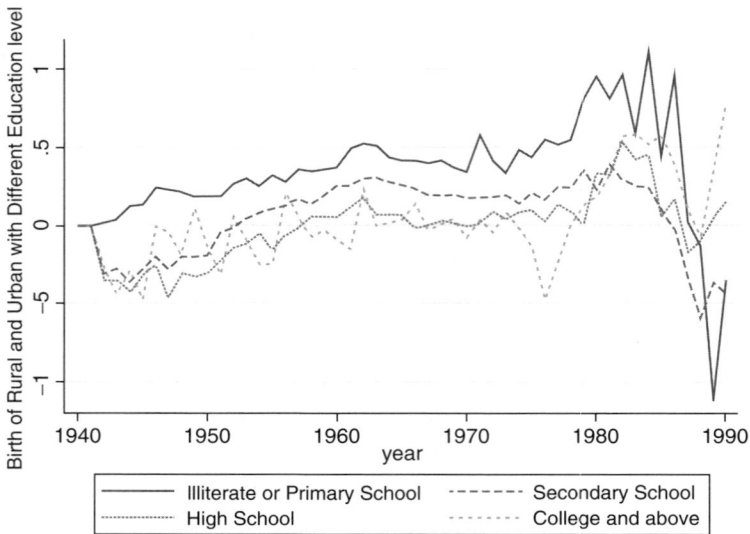

Figure 11-6: Fertility difference between rural and urban women by education and cohort.

We can find in Figure 11-6 that the effect of family planning was increasing over time. As the baby boom period is exposed to the family planning policy, the fertility of urban women born around 1960 is relatively large, about 0.5. On the other hand, when childbearing women's educational level increases, the effect on urban–rural fertility of family planning will decrease. Even if the rural women educated above college receive less constrained family planning policy, their fertility will not exceed that of urban women.

From the above analysis, we can see that although the family planning policy has a difference between Han and ethnic minorities, and non-agricultural *hukou* and agricultural *hukou*, the variation of policy does not greatly affect people's fertility choice. For childbearing age women with higher levels of education, the strict family planning policy did not have any impact. But for the less educated women of childbearing age, the family planning policy differences brought a number of 0.5 differences between rural and urban regions, and no significant fertility difference between Han and Minorities, except for an earlier fertility age. Overall, family planning for low-educated population has a limited effect — from the strict one-child to two-child policy, the fertility rate may rise about 0.5.

Moreover, the effect is mixed together with other effects, and 0.5 may be an overestimation. For highly educated population, family planning just does not work.

2.5 Impact from Other Aspects of the Economic and Social Impact — Education of Women

In Section 2.4, we find that the variation of family planning policy does not have a significant effect on the fertility rate. It means that a large share of decreasing of fertility should be attributed to factors other than family planning. In fact, family planning may no longer be the dominant cause of China's current low fertility. As per the interpretation in Zheng *et al.* (2009) and Xu Jing (2010), even if the family planning policy is canceled, the fertility rate will have no significant rise when the fertility desire is low. Cai (2010) believes that the force that makes fertility rate remain at low level is the socioeconomic factor and the transition of fertility desire. East Asian data can also corroborate the conclusions of this section. Although only China has a strict family planning policy, as we can see in Figure 11-7, the fertility of almost all the East Asian region declined significantly under the no family planning policy.

As can be seen from Figure 11-7, in South Korea and Taiwan, fertility has experienced an almost simultaneous downward trend with the Chinese mainland. As the East Asian countries and regions had experienced, China

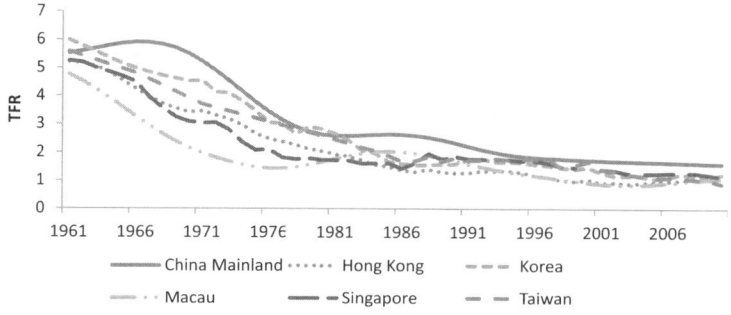

Figure 11-7: East Asian fertility levels over the years.

Data Source: World Bank; Taiwan data from the "Republic of China" Division of Household Registration Affairs.

may have shown the spontaneous fertility constraints brought about by the socioeconomic development. The reason for the decline in fertility is no longer the family planning policy. Other economic, social, and other factors on fertility may have occupied a more important position.

According to Zhang (1990), even after controlling for the woman's age, the timing of marriage, and child mortality, fertility is still subject to a variety of factors. One important factor is the level of women's education. A series of studies have analyzed the relationship between the level of women's education and fertility. In a theoretical study, Becker *et al.* (1960) finds that women's education level will increase women's income levels, and make them bear fewer children while providing a better education for each child. On the other hand, due to the positive selection effect in the marriage, highly educated women often marry highly educated males; this will increase the impact of education on fertility behavior (Behrman and Rosenzweig, 2002). Second, the higher level of education increased knowledge of contraception, and will also reduce the fertility level (Grossman, 1972). However, it is not easy to find empirical evidence on the causal relationship of the level of education and fertility. This is because the increased levels of education tend to occur simultaneously with the other factors that lower fertility, and the simple cross-sectional regression may overestimate the impact of education on fertility. Therefore, an important task of the study is to find instrumental variables which can affect the level of women's education, but do not affect other personal characteristics, to measure the impact of women's education on fertility. Currie and Moretti (2002) use the availability of college in the woman's county in her 17th year as an instrument for maternal education, and find that the number of their children will be decreased by 0.09 to 0.12 as the women's education increases by one year, and the results of the instrumental variables are less than the results of the linear regression, which is consistent with the former analysis. McCrary and Royer (2006) use an exogenous female enrollment policy change as the instrument for maternal education, and analyze the difference of fertility behavior of women who are exposed to the policy and the women who are not. The paper finds that the admission policy on women's fertility level was small. Zhang (2012) uses the colleges and universities shut down during the Cultural Revolution as an instrumental variable. It resulted in a rising dropout rate of college women, and is an exogenous variable. She used the same method as McCrary and

Royer (2006), and observed the fertility of women before and after a specific time of birth, and also did not find evidence of the level of education on fertility.

We must note that although a series of studies have begun to try to find the effect of the level of education of women on their reproductive behavior, people still did not get a unified conclusion. This series of studies, as well, are often only valid at a certain level of education, such as primary education or higher education, which weakens the universality of its conclusions. On the other hand, there is little literature giving an interactive description of fertility and women's education level. In addition, the level of female education is an excellent proxy variable for degree of social development, which represents not only the education levels, but also positively correlates with many other indicators of social development, such as the level of welfare protection, the level of economic development, health level, etc. To study the level of women's education on fertility, to some extent, is to study the impact of comprehensive social development indicators on fertility.

This chapter uses the 1990 census' 10% sampling data, as well as the 2000 and 2010 census county data to complete this study. 2010 county data in the census did not report the total fertility rate, and the chapter uses the following formula to approximate:

$$\text{TFR} = \text{Birth rate}(\%)/\text{Share of women of child-bearing age}(\%) \times 35$$

The formula means that the fertility level of women of childbearing age is equivalent to the average number of births by a woman multiplied by the number of childbearing women of 35 years. The approximation method can be verified in the 2000 statistics. The fertility generated by this approximation method is very close to the reported fertility, while the degree of correlation of these two fertilities is 0.824.

As can be seen in Figure 11-8, from 1990 to 2010, almost the entire region there has experienced substantial decline in total fertility rate. The northeast region, Shanxi, Qinghai, Anhui, Hubei, and Yunnan decline fastest. Based on the above analysis, family planning has relatively weak constraints on minorities and the rural population compared to Han and urban population, but as we can see in Figure 11-8, the distribution of fertility decline is irrelevant to the urban and ethnic characteristics.

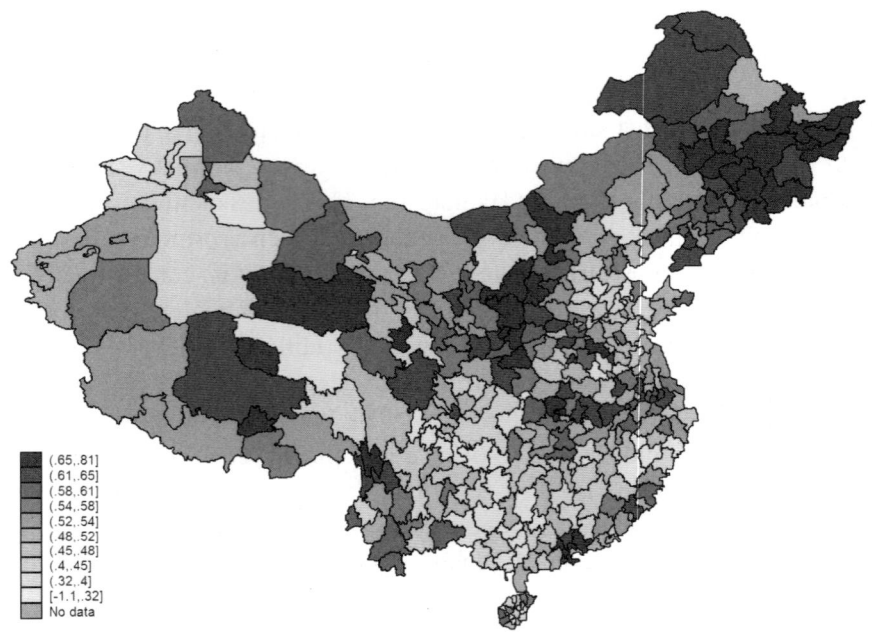

Figure 11-8: The percentage of reductions in fertility from 1990 to 2010.

Figure 11-9 is a scatter plot of the change of education level and fertility level from 1990 to 2010. We can find that there is a very significant negative correlation between the average level of education and total fertility rate in Figure 11-9. A one-year increase of average education of women results in a 0.41 drop in the total fertility rate, approximately four times of the result in Currie and Moretti (2002). Sub-regional levels of female education changes can explain 22% of the changes in fertility from 1990 to 2010. The effect of education on fertility is quite robust, 0.35 and 0.41 if we change the calculation interval to (1990, 2000) or (2000, 2010). We cannot deny that the effect may be a variety of mixed effects. As mentioned above, the level of women's education index is a composite indicator of the level of social protection, the level of economic development, and health level. But it is certain that it has little effect on the implementation of family planning — in the urban areas and ethnic minority areas where family planning policy implementation is most strict, the fertility decline is more moderate.

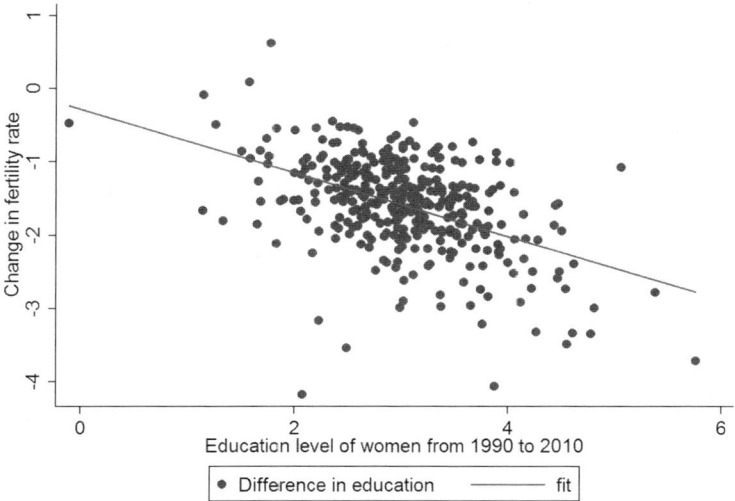

Figure 11-9: Average education level of women and change of fertility rate of 358 prefecture-level cities.

Then, a natural question is: Is it true that higher levels of women's education result in lower fertility? From the 1990 census, the female education in 35 cities (about 10% of the region) including Beijing, Shanghai, Guangzhou, Tianjin, and other developed cities is above 7 years. In 2010, the average level of women's education of these cities has risen to 9.7 years. On the one hand, the fertility rate in these cities has been at a lower level in 1990, about 1.86; Beijing and Shanghai have only 1.4 and 1.3, respectively. The constraint of family planning policy on these cities has been almost disappearing. The regression on these 35 cities provides stable results: as the level of education increases by 1, total fertility will fall 0.32. A three-year increase in the level of women's education in Beijing and Shanghai, results in a further decline of their fertility levels to about 0.6. On the other hand, the level of fertility has almost no decline in the area where there is no increase in the education level. In fact, the effect of rising education level on fertility decline is very stable; the quintile regression results show that the marginal effect on fertility of rising education is about 0.35 for the highest education group, see Figure 11-10.

We can make a general prediction on China's future fertility change on the former basis. In 2010, the average level of female education in 35 cities

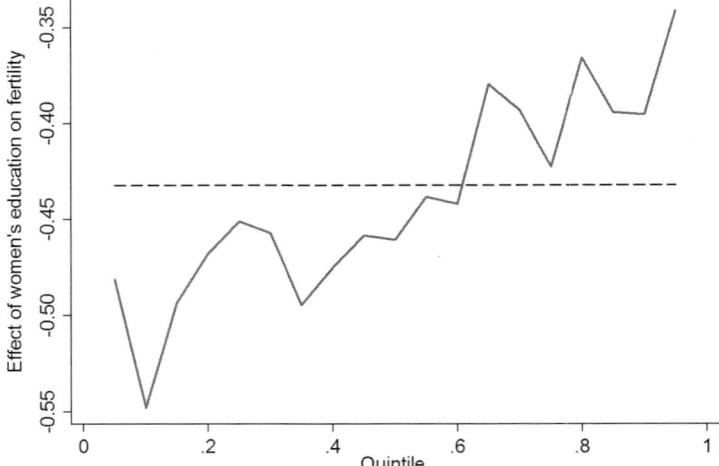

Figure 11-10: Effect of changes in years of education on fertility — quintile regression.

Table 11-2: Change of maternal education from 1990 to 2010.

Quintile	1990 maternal education	2010 maternal education	Change of maternal education 1990–2010
Lowest 10%	2.03	5.97	3.95
10–20%	3.94	7.38	3.44
20–30%	4.57	7.93	3.36
30–40%	5.01	8.08	3.07
40–50%	5.33	8.34	3.01
50–60%	5.57	8.48	2.91
60–70%	5.82	8.84	3.02
70–80%	6.20	8.93	2.73
80–90%	6.63	9.25	2.62
Highest 10%	7.52	9.75	2.22

with the highest level of education was 10.15 years, while 35 regions had the lowest level of only 5.81 years. When the females in the cities with lowest level of education reach an average level of education up to 10 years, their fertility rate will also be reduced by about 1.8.

As we can see in Table 11-2, the increase of maternal education shows a slowing trend. The level of maternal education in the region with lowest years of education was the fastest growing, while the level of maternal education in the region with relatively high education increased slowly. The relationship between the stock of the level of education and change of level of education can fit in the following formula:

$$\Delta edu = 4.5 - 0.3 \times edu.$$

The years of education of women will reach the maximum of 15 years in the above formula. If this trend persists for the next 20 years, we can predict a new set of distribution of years of education, and at the same time predicted changes in the level of fertility of the region based on changes in the level of education. The decreased fertility process will slow down; we assume that the effect of changes in the level of education on reductions in fertility will decline in the future, from the current 0.4 to 0.1 in Currie and Moretti (2002). Figure 11-11 shows the Total Fertility Rate change in 1990, 2010, and 2030. In 2030, the total fertility rate will drop to 0.73. Because we might expect a high level of education similar to the situation in Shanghai and Beijing at this time for those who have a lower level of education, we might also expect a further deepened aging situation in the future.

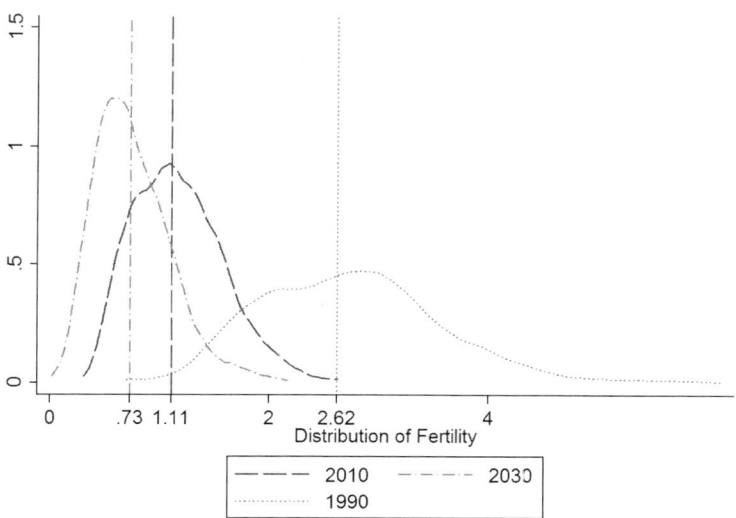

Figure 11-11: Changes of fertility of 2010 and 2030.

2.6 The Future of China's Population

This section will discuss the future population situation based on the fertility discussion above. After we verify the fertility rate and age-specific mortality, we can deduce future population changes.

Let us first introduce the following notations for expositional ease.

Superscript $i \in \{f, m\}$ and $j \in \{0, 1, 2, \ldots 100\}$ represent gender and age, respectively.

$p_t^{i,j}$ represents (adjusted) population in the period-t census/survey. For instance, $p_{2000}^{f,10}$ stands for population of urban females of age 10 in the 2000 census.

$\hat{p}_t^{h,i,j}$ represents simulated natural population in period t according to

$$\hat{p}_t^{i,0} = \sum_{j \in [15,49]} \theta_{t-1}^i b_{t-1}^{j-1} \hat{p}_{t-1}^{f,j-1}, \tag{11-1}$$

$$\hat{p}_t^{i,j} = \left(1 - m_{t-1}^{i,j-1}\right) \hat{p}_{t-1}^{i,j-1}, \ j > 0, \tag{11-2}$$

where b_t^j, $m_t^{i,j}$, and θ_t^i represent birth rates, mortality rates, and sex ratios at birth in the period-t survey, respectively.

$$\hat{p}_t^{h,i,0} = p_t^{h,i,0}.$$

The prediction of this section will use the population, fertility, and mortality data in the 2010 census. Based on the above analysis, we will make fertility and mortality predictions and analyze the population structure and total population under different fertility and mortality assumptions. First, we will simulate the 2010 population with the data in 2000 census, and compare it with the 2010 census data to test the reliability of the method.

Two remarks on the methodology should be made. From the comparison of fertility in two censuses, we found that the following: First, rural fertility is higher than urban fertility across ages. Second, the fertility in the 2000 census is very close to the fertility in 2010, showing its stability.

In addition, the fertility in 2000 and 2010 census may, to some extent, be underestimated. Using intercensal methods, Goodkind (2004) estimates 37 million children under age 9 missing in the 2000 census. A similar estimate of 30 million is obtained by Zhang and Cui (2003) who use primary school enrolments to back the actual child population. Retherford et al. (2005) and Zhang and Zhao (2006) use a similar methodology and find that the fertility of the 2005 mini-census should also be adjusted upward. We choose the adjustment coefficient of 1.2 because the 2000 census reveals a total fertility rate of 1.2 while the actual TFR is often believed to be above 1.4 in the literature (see e.g., Morgan *et al.*, 2009). In addition, using primary school enrollment data, the literature suggests that birth rates were under-reported by 16% in the 2000 census (Zhang and Cui, 2003). So 1:2 seems to be a reasonable number. The following results are robust to alternative values of the adjustment coefficient.

Further, we assume no misreporting in mortality rates and sex ratios at birth. A few studies cast doubt on the reliability of mortality rates, while sex ratios at birth are believed to be over-reported; that is, the births of females are under-reported (e.g., Goodkind, 2004). Nevertheless, none of the variables is quantitatively important for our main results presented below.

In the ideal case, the simulated total population and the age structure of 2010 should be identical to the number in 2010 surveys. Figure 11-12 shows that except for the 15- to 18-year-old population which is slightly lower than the 2010 census, the simulated population almost perfectly fit the 2010 census population. The disappearing children phenomenon found by Goodkind (2004) does not seem to appear in Figure 11-12, this is because we have adjusted the birth rate upward by 1.2 times. If there is no such adjustment, simulation of child stage population in 2010 will be less than the 2010 census.

After verifying the reliability of the method used in this chapter, we further use the 2010 census data to predict future population data. In the

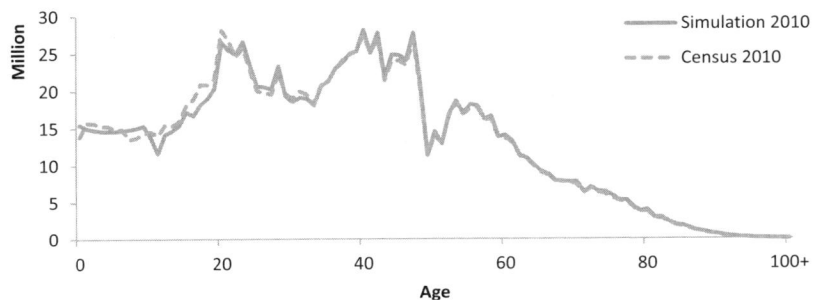

Figure 11-12: Simulation and census data of total population and age structure of 2010.

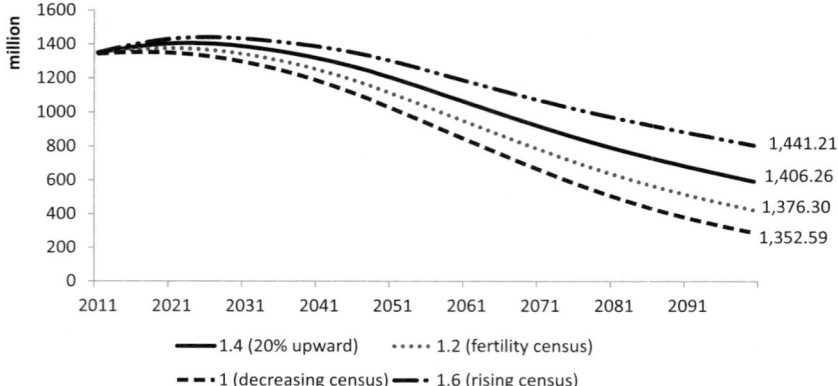

Figure 11-13: Total population change under various fertility rate scenarios.

simulation process in Figure 11-12, we assume a linear change of fertility and mortality in the last decade. We will use the fertility and mortality by age in the 2010 census as the benchmark for future population projections. Combined with the fertility analysis above and the changes in mortality and fertility from 2000 to 2010, we will make the population projection in different modes.

Figure 11-13 shows trends of the total population under different fertility scenarios. Under an optimistic assumption, the total fertility rate will rise to 1.6 in 20 years since 2010. In this assumption, China's total population in 2026 will reach a maximum value of 1.441 billion people. Given that China's rural fertility rate is only 1.44, the assumption that fertility rate will rise to 1.6 might be too optimistic. If the fertility rate remains at the same real level as 2010, and we assume that the fertility rate in the 2010 census is underestimated by 20%, China's population will reach its maximum in 2023 of 1.406 billion. According to the preceding analysis, the fertility in China might continue to decrease as the level of education of women enhances. If the fertility rate is 1.2, then China will reach the maximum value of 1.376 billion people in 2021, and will reach the maximum value of 1352 million people in 2018 if the fertility rate is 1. Therefore, a more optimistic estimate is that China's population will reach the highest value of about 1450 million people in 2025. If the low fertility phenomenon in Beijing, Shanghai, and other big cities spread to the country, then the highest amount of the total population in China will be around 1370 million in 2020.

After 2025, China's total population will begin to decline. Under the most optimistic assumptions of fertility, the total population will reduce to about 800 million people in 2100. When the fertility rate is only 1, the population in 2100 will be only 300 million people.

Table 11-3 lists the age structure in the range 2010–2100 under different fertility scenarios. In an optimistic fertility assumption, China's share of the population aged over 65 increases from 9.3% in 2010 to more than 20% in 2030, which is the current degree of aging in Japan. The aging situation began to stabilize at 30% in 2050. Under the low fertility assumption, the degree of aging in 2100 will reach 40–50%.

Compared with the proportion of the elderly population in China, China's share of working-age population and the share of youth population will decrease year by year. Under the assumption of a higher fertility rate, the population aged 15 to 64 can be stabilized at between 63% and 65%. And the fertility rate of 1.6 will yield an even higher adolescent population share. Under a low fertility assumption, China's working-age population can only be maintained at the level of 50% of all population, while the youth population share will rapidly reduce below 10% in 2100, about only 6–9%.

3. CHINA'S DEMOGRAPHIC CHANGES IMPACT ON THE ECONOMY

China's population change will have a profound impact on the economy, which contains the change of population age structures and sex structure. With the deepening of the aging, China's demographic dividend will gradually reduce, while the pressure on the current social security will gradually increase. But under the labor productivity increase brought about by the urbanization of the population as well as education, the negative impact of the aging of the population will be eliminated to some extent. Also, the gender imbalance in the population will also have a series of impacts. This section will summarize a series of literature, and discusses the impact of aging of the population, changes in the sex ratio on savings, investment, trade, and other aspects of the economy.

Table 11-3: Age structure in China from 2010 to 2100.

TFR	Age structure	2010	2020	2030	2040	2050	2060	2070	2080	2090	2100
1.6	Below 14	17.4%	18.7%	16.7%	14.2%	15.4%	14.1%	14.0%	14.8%	14.1%	14.2%
	15–59	73.3%	67.4%	63.7%	60.0%	56.6%	55.7%	58.4%	56.9%	56.4%	57.3%
	15–64	77.9%	72.8%	72.4%	66.8%	66.3%	61.7%	65.1%	65.4%	63.1%	64.7%
	65 and above	9.3%	13.9%	19.6%	25.8%	28.0%	30.1%	27.6%	28.3%	29.4%	28.5%
1.4	Below 14	17.4%	17.2%	14.8%	12.4%	12.8%	11.7%	11.6%	12.0%	11.5%	11.6%
	15–59	73.3%	68.7%	64.9%	60.4%	56.7%	54.5%	56.1%	54.8%	54.3%	54.9%
	15–64	77.9%	74.2%	73.9%	67.6%	67.2%	61.2%	63.9%	63.8%	61.7%	63.0%
	65 and above	9.3%	14.2%	20.2%	27.2%	30.4%	33.8%	32.4%	33.2%	34.1%	33.5%
1.2	Below 14	17.4%	15.6%	12.8%	10.6%	10.3%	9.2%	9.1%	9.1%	8.9%	8.9%
	15–59	73.3%	70.0%	66.2%	60.8%	56.5%	52.7%	52.6%	51.5%	51.2%	51.5%
	15–64	77.9%	75.7%	75.5%	68.3%	68.0%	60.3%	61.9%	60.8%	59.4%	60.2%
	65 and above	9.3%	14.4%	21.0%	28.7%	33.2%	38.1%	38.3%	39.4%	39.9%	39.6%
1	Below 14	17.4%	13.9%	10.6%	8.7%	7.8%	6.8%	6.6%	6.4%	6.3%	6.4%
	15–59	73.3%	71.4%	67.6%	61.0%	56.0%	50.2%	47.7%	46.6%	46.7%	46.6%
	15–64	77.9%	77.2%	77.3%	69.0%	68.5%	58.8%	58.7%	55.9%	55.6%	55.9%
	65 and above	9.3%	14.7%	21.8%	30.3%	36.2%	43.0%	45.7%	47.0%	47.0%	47.1%

3.1 The Impact of Population Aging on Demographic Dividend and Social Security

In 2012, the number of China's population aged from 15 to 59 was 93.727 million, 3.45 million less than that in 2011. This is the first decline in the working-age population. From this turning point, China will enter a long process in which demographic dividend is declining. In Table 11-1, China's working-age population share will begin to decrease from 73.3% in 2010 to about 56% in 2050. According to a different fertility assumption, the proportion of the working-age population may remain stable or further decline further to 50% in 2100. Under the labor force participation rate of 70%, every working-age person will have to support average two non-working people. According to the current pay as you go (PAYG) pension system and the replacement rate, the aging situation requires a social security tax rate of about 50% of the wage.

In this section, we will calculate the revenue and expense of the pension system under the changing population age structures. Due to the stagnation of insured labor force growth and the rapid increase in the retired population, there was no effective accumulation in the personal account, which brought about the serious phenomenon of "empty account" in the personal accounts of China's social pension insurance system. Therefore, China's social pension insurance system is still in a state of PAYG. Through the simulation of future population change and economic development, we are able to predict the future of the pension system evolution. The details of the simulation can be found in Chen Qin and Song Zheng (2013) and Song Zheng (2012).

3.2 Model and Assumptions

This section simulates the run of pension insurance using the method in Lee and Miller (2000), Auerbach and Oreopoulos (1999, 2000), and Storesletten (2003). Four parameters are required to calculate the revenue and expense of social insurance: the labor force participation rate, pension coverage, contributions rate, and replacement rate for retirees. Labor force participation rate is the share of urban workers in the working-age population of all cities and towns (population of working age is 18–54 for female and 18–59 for male); pension coverage is the share of participants of social pension insurance in total number of urban workers. Due to the household registration restrictions, most young migrants from rural areas to the city have not been covered by the urban pension insurance. The impact of rural–urban migrants on the budget of current urban pension insurance system is somehow limited. But we should notice that the pension coverage condition on migrants is gradually coming close to the standard of urban *hukou* residents. The coverage rate of new migrants is gradually increasing (Libo Hua and Song Yueping, 2010). From the Chinese households' income survey data (CHIP) in 2002, we find that the participation rate of urban pension system in migration was 4.7%. Migrants' participation rate in urban pension insurance has risen to 17.4% in 2007 CHIP. And the 2011 Chinese household financial data (CHFS) further shows that the participation rate of residents in urban areas with agricultural *hukou* in urban pension insurance rose to 29.3%, showing a rapid upward trend. But at this time, the participation rate of urban residents in the urban pension system is 80.6%, still higher than the participation rate of migrants. This section will divide the *hukou* residents and the migrants into two parts, and assign different participation rates to them. The contribution rate is the proportion of contributions to the total wage of the population who participate in the urban pension system. The replacement rate of the urban pension system is the proportion of pension to average wage of urban workers. Note that we have deducted the subsidies that account for about 15% of the income of the pension funds while calibrating the parameters (for instance, the financial subsidies of pension funds are 191.035 billion yuan, about 14% of the total pension revenue of 1.14908 trillion). A later simulation will also deduct the subsidy in calculation. Table 11-4 lists the data from 2006 to 2010 (National Bureau of Statistics of China, 2011).

Table 11-4: Model Parameters for pension simulation.

	2006	2007	2008	2009	2010
Labor force participation	75.1%	75.4%	75.2%	75.5%	76.6%
Contribution rate	18.2%	17.7%	17.3%	17.1%	16.1%
Replacement rate	50.7%	48.7%	48.2%	47.5%	45.8%
The number of pension beneficiaries (10,000)	4,635.4	4,953.7	5,303.6	5,806.9	6,305.0

We make the following assumptions for the future labor force participation rate and pension coverage. First, to compute social security balances, we need to know the product of employment rate and pension coverage rate, which represents the total number of pension contributors per hundred urban workers. So, we assume a constant employment rate of 76.6% (the 2010 employment rate) from 2011 onward.

Second, we calculate the pension coverage distribution in retirees and working populations. Pension coverage rate tends to be higher for old employees for the following two reasons. First, those who had worked for more than 15 years before the new pension system was implemented in 1997 are counted as pension participants and will receive pension benefits after retirement even if they have stopped contributing to the system. Second, rural migrants have a much younger age structure than urban residents but are less likely to be covered by the pension system. The high pension coverage rate for old workers can directly be seen from the sharp increase in the number of pension beneficiaries from 2005 to 2008. Therefore, we assume a high coverage rate for old employees above age 40 in 1997, which is constant over time, and a low coverage rate for the others, which is changing over time. The constant coverage rate for old employees is calibrated to match the average annual increase in the number of pension beneficiary from 2006 to 2010, yielding the rate of 97%. The time-varying low coverage rates for the others are calibrated to match aggregate pension coverage rates. The calibrated rate increases from 50% in 2010 to the steady state rate of 80% in 2030.

The 2011 CHFS data indicate a participation rate in the current pension system of urban household population rate of about 80%, while the rate of rural–urban migration is about 30%. According to the urbanization trend from 2000 to 2010, combined with the participation rate found in micro data (such as CHIPS, CHFS), we calibrated the participation rate of urban *hukou* residents and migrants from 2000 to 2010. The calibration results shows that if the participation rate of urban *hukou* residents is 70% in 2010, and the rate of urban migrants is 20% in 2010, then the simulation rate can well fit the real number in 2009 and 2010. The parameter set is also consistent with the difference of the participation rate between urban *hukou* residents and migrants. Taking into account that the participation rate of migrants rises rapidly these years, the benchmark assumption of this model is a linearly increasing pension coverage rate from 70% (20%) in 2010 to 80% in 2030 and then staying at that level afterwards. Note that if future employment rates fall, we need higher pension coverage rates to maintain the following results. In addition, due to the fact that the people who had contributed to the pension system for less than 15 years cannot get their retirees insurance benefits after retirement, the migrants who migrate to urban areas less than 15 years before their retirement cannot get their pension benefits after retirement. The model only includes the migrants who migrate to urban regions before 45 years for men and 40 years for women.

The contribution rate is another important parameter of the urban pension insurance. In 2010, the contribution rate of basic urban pension system was 28%, a relatively high level compared with the rest of the world. There are some difficulties to continue to increase the contribution rate. However, we can calculate from Table 11-4 that the real contribution rate is only 16.1%, about 57.5% of the policy contribution rate. There are a variety of reasons for the difference between the real contribution rates and policy contribution rate, such as informal employment or tax evasion. The ratio of real rate to policy rate ratio is named as "collection rate." We will use the "collection rate" to proxy the change of the real contribution rate. The benchmark assumption is that the collection rate will gradually increase after 2010, and reach 100% in 2030, resulting in a real contribution rate of 28%.

This chapter will also consider the framework of economic growth and the revenue and expenditure of the pension system, and calculate the urban pension insurance payments in the respect of gross domestic product (GDP). In this chapter, we will use World Bank (2012) data as the benchmark assumption of the increasing GDP and productivity (see Table 11-5).

Table 11-5: China's future trend in GDP and labor productivity.

	1995–2010	2011–2015	2016–2020	2021–2025	2026–2030
GDP growth (%)	9.9	8.6	7	5.9	5
Labor productivity growth (%)	8.9	8.3	7.1	6.2	5.5

Source: World Bank (2012).

After comparing the real average wage growth of China's urban population and the labor productivity growth between 1995 and 2010, we find that these two sets of numbers can substitute for one another to a large extent. In the simulation, the growth rate of wages of the urban population is replaced by labor productivity growth in Table 11-5. The discount rate is set to 5%.

3.3 Simulation Results

The effect of demographic parameters on the pension system comes mainly from aging and the retirement age. The fertility rate determines the ratio of intergenerational population, and the retirement age determines the ratio of the retirees and employees. Due to the below-replacement fertility, the contribution of migrants will shrink as their offspring grows up. In this situation, it will be difficult for the offspring's contributions to make up for their parents' pension expenditure. This reminds us that we must consider the fertility changing scenario in the PAYG pension system in the long run. Our next step is to predict the long-term balance of payments and contributions of the pension in different fertility assumptions.

The low fertility rates related to China's Family Planning Policy, is one of the causes of rapid aging in the current urban population. In 1968, before the constraint family planning policy was implemented, the fertility rate in China was 7.025. The fertility rate decreased quickly as the "Late, Long, Few" policy was implemented. At the end of the 1970s, the fertility in China was below 3. In the 2010 census, the total fertility rate is 1.18, far below the replacement level, only about 20% of the number in 1968. If China's fertility rate decreased with the implementation of the family planning policy, then the question is: Would the phasing out or relaxation of the family planning policy bring about a fertility re-increase, thus defer the process of aging and relieve the pressure on the expenditure of the urban pension system?

However, as we had discussed above, relaxing or even cancelling the policy of family planning would not necessarily bring about a substantial increase in fertility. In China's current low fertility phenomenon, the family planning policy might no longer be a dominant cause. Zheng (2004) and Xu Jing (2010) find that even if the family planning policy is canceled, the fertility rate will have no significant rise from the current low levels, let alone a return to the replacement level (2.1). Cai (2010) believes that while it is the family planning policy that makes the fertility in China decrease, the major force that makes the fertility remain at a low level is other socioeconomic factors. The data of East Asia can also corroborate the conclusions of this section. In the countries listed in Figure 11-7, all except Japan, which had a low fertility at the beginning, experience dramatic decrease in fertility without a constraint family planning policy. Similar to the experience in the East Asian countries and regions, China may have a self-constraint in fertility brought about by the social and economic development, and the reason for the decline in fertility is no longer the family planning policy. Therefore, even if the family planning policy is to be relaxed or even canceled, it is difficult to believe that the fertility in China will rise. On the contrary, under the previous forecast, the total fertility rate is likely to further decline with further improvement in the level of education of women. We will simulate the revenues and expenditure of urban pension system under the assumption that the fertility rate will remain unchanged or further decrease respectively.

Another method to help the balance of payments of the urban pension system reform is to postpone the retirement age. The postponement of the retirement age has become a more conventional approach in European countries to balance the pension funds. France extended the shortest working years required for a full pension by 2 years, from 60 to 62; Italy, Britain, and other countries also postponed the statutory retirement age. The female labor force experienced more impact in the retirement age postponement. The Italian government requires that the retirement age for female civil servants be postponed to 65 in 2012, which is the same as male civil servants. The postponement of the retirement age is implemented on the basis of the increase in life expectancy. The life expectancy in China had increased from 68 years in 1990 to 73.1 years in 2008; the average life expectancy of 60-year-olds also increased from 18.2 years in 1990 to 21.8 years in 2010. The pension benefits payment program before may have deviated from the balanced route. Postpone the retirement age or not? How would the postponement of the retirement age improve pension balance? This has become a problem for society in general. In the next step of the simulation, we will assume that the retirement age for men will be postponed

Table 11-6: Simulation scenarios.

	Fertility	Retirement age
Scenario 1	Remain at 2010 level	Current
Scenario 2	Decreased by 20%	Current
Scenario 3	Remain at 2010 level	Extend 5 years
Scenario 4	Decreased by 20%	Extend 5 years

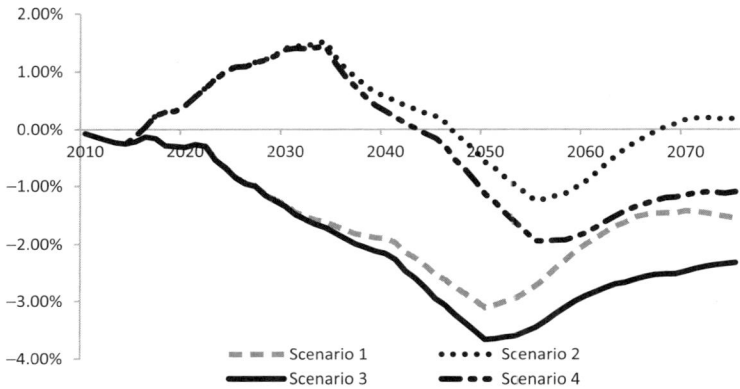

Figure 11-14: The ratio of balance gap to nominal GDP under four scenarios.

to 65 after a certain number of years, while the retirement age of women is postponed to 60, and analyze the urban pension system balance in the different postponement scenario.

The simulation contains four scenarios (see Table 11-6). Scenario 1 is the benchmark, while Scenarios 2 and 4 assume that fertility will further decrease by 20%, and Scenarios 3 and 4 would postpone the retirement age by 1 year every 4 years from 2014 to 2034. Simulation results will be illustrated in the form of ratio of the gap of pension funds to nominal GDP (see Figure 11-14).

Figure 11-14 illustrates the run of the urban pension system from 2010 to 2075. Under the benchmark scenario, with the deepening of aging, the gap between the revenues and payments of urban pension system will reach 3.1% of GDP in 2050. If the fertility rate further declines, the gap in 2050 will further deepen to 3.7%. The consequence of the fertility change on pension payments will appear in 2030, and will gradually increase.

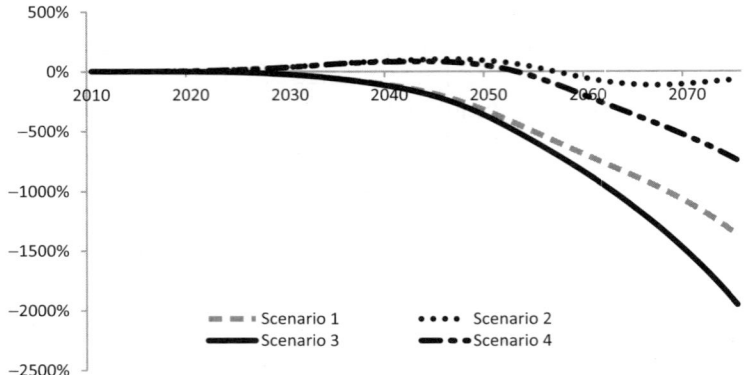

Figure 11-15: The ratio of accumulated deficit to GDP in 2010 under four scenarios.

Compared with the fertility change, the postponement of retirement age has a greater but narrowing effect on urban pension system. If the retirement age will be postponed to 65 for male and 60 for female, the balance of urban pension system will remain positive by 2045.

But under the assumption that fertility rate will further decrease, even if the retirement age were postponed, China's pension funds will enter a stage of deficit after 2045. In the last 30 years of the simulation, the annual pension deficit reached about 1% of GDP every year. However, if the fertility rate remains at the present level, the pension balance will get better in 2055, and will get rid of deficit in 2070.

Figure 11-15 is a cumulative value of the deficit of urban pension system under the four scenarios. In the case of a declining birth rate and non-postponement of the retirement age, the accumulated deficit is about 20 times the GDP of 2010 in 2075. If fertility has no further decrease, the accumulated deficit will be 1,366% of GDP in 2010. The further decrease of fertility will increase the accumulated deficit by a number about 6 times the 2010 GDP in a 65-year period. When the fertility rate remains unchanged, and the retirement age is postponed by 5 years in next 20 years, the accumulated pension deficit will reduce to 68% of GDP in 2010. Considering that China will maintain a relatively high level of real growth rate over the next three decades, 68% of the GDP in 2010 is a relatively low value of the liability.

Section 3.2 analyzes the run of the urban pension system. But another part of the larger pension system includes the rural population and urban residents who are not employed. Since a large number of rural–urban migrants are young adults, the rural population dependency ratio rises quickly. In 2050, the dependency ratio will rise to the highest value of 93%, which reflects the importance of improving the rural pension system. The new rural social pension system begun in 2009 is a two-pillar pension insurance, in which the first pillar provides the basic pensions to retirees, about 55 yuan per month, primarily sponsored by government subsidies; the second pillar is consistent with the individual contribution. Compared with the urban pension system, the rural pension system has more participants (about 50% higher than that in urban pension system) and less payment. In 2011, the payment of the rural pension system was 58.77 billion yuan, only 5% of the payment of the urban pension system in the same period, which is 1.27649 trillion yuan.

From 2012 onward, the new rural social pension system gradually began to transfer to the urban and rural residents' pension system. The participants of urban and rural residents' pension systems reached 484 million by the end of 2012, covering the rural population and the residents in urban areas who are not employed. Assuming that the basic pension will increase by 5% annually in accordance with the rate of inflation, we simulate the condition of subsidies on urban and rural pension systems from 2010 to 2030 on the basis of the urban and rural population migration forecasting and economic growth forecasting, the rural–urban migration assumptions, and labor force participation assumptions discussed above (see Figure 11-16). We found that with the decreasing of rural population, the subsidies to urban and rural pension systems gradually reduce in the future, from a proportion of about 0.15% in 2010 to about 0.25% in 2030. If we take the urban employee pension system and the urban and rural residents' pension system together, we find that China will face a huge deficit in the pension payments if there is no reform in the family planning policy and the retirement age. But on the other hand, if the fertility rate can be maintained at 2010 levels, and the retirement age can be postponed by 5 years in the next 20 years, the deficit of pension funds will be greatly reduced.

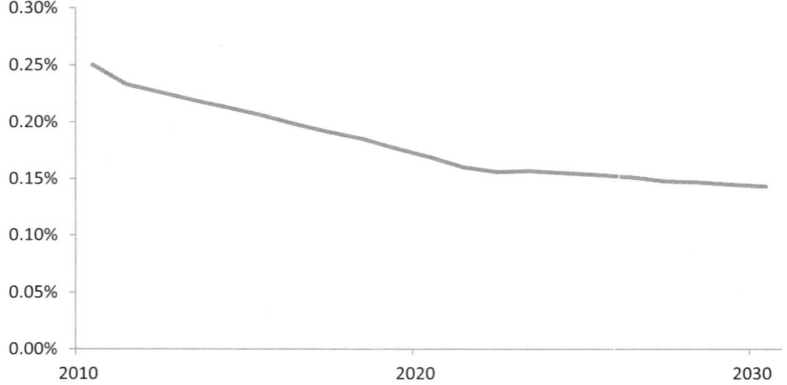

Figure 11-16: The subsidies of urban and rural residents pension system subsidies from 2010 to 2030.

4. THE IMPACT OF DEMOGRAPHIC CHANGES IN OTHER ASPECTS OF ECONOMIC DEVELOPMENT

In addition to the impact on the pension system, China's population change will affect the economy in many aspects.

4.1 The Impact on the Saving Rates

China's high savings phenomenon has aroused the attention of a large number of economists. Much literature tries to explain the phenomenon of China's high savings rate from multiple aspects, such as the rapid increase in health and education costs (Chamon and Prasad, 2010), the effect of construction reform and life cycle income (Song and Yang, 2010), as well as the constraints of the household registration system (Chen *et al.*, 2012). On these bases, Ge *et al.* (2012) studied the impact of demographic change on the household savings rate in China. Due to the impact of family planning, the average number of children in the Chinese family has been reduced. The effect of family planning policy differs by region and time because of the different enforcement of the policy, which enable the author to calculate the effect of age structure change on fertility. The result in

Ge *et al.* (2012) shows that changes in the age structure of the population have different impact on the saving rates of family members of different ages. Younger households save more because of the rising burden of parental care with fewer siblings. Middle-aged households save more as they have fewer dependent children to support. Older households with a reduced number of adult children save more because of old-age security concerns.

On the other hand, Wei and Zhang (2011) found that the change of the sex ratio of the population is also one of the reasons for the high savings rate in China. When the sex ratio rises, the marriage market becomes more competitive because the men are significantly more than women, which makes the son in the family save more to be more eligible in the marriage market. At the same time, although the family who has a daughter has an incentive to be a free-rider when men increase their savings, they will not decrease their saving rates, in order to keep their daughters' bargaining power after marriage. This upward saving rate caused by the above mechanism will overflow to other markets, which results in a rising house price in the region. The author uses the family planning fine as an instrument variable of sex ratios because the fine only affects the sex ratio through selective abortion channels and does not affect the saving rate directly, and finally gets a significant result. The author found that the sex ratio can explain China's current savings rate by 66%.

4.2 Impact on International Trade

Tian *et al.* (2012) explained the share and structure change of international trade from the aspects of the changing age structure of the population of each country. When a country has a higher proportion of labor force, it will have a higher total bilateral trade. This result is caused by two effects. (1) The scale effect: countries with a higher proportion of labor force will be able to produce more goods, thereby increasing exports. (2) The structure effect: the aggregate income is more than the aggregate consumption in the countries with higher proportion of the labor force. The combining of these two effects will increase the total bilateral trade. In this framework, the export-oriented industry might be a result of population structure in the countries with a larger share of young population like China.

On the other hand, Du and Wei (2011) found that the real exchange rate might be more underestimated in the region where sex ratio imbalance is serious. In the phenomenon of China's undervalued exchange rate, the gender imbalance may play a considerable role, resulting in an increase in China's exports.

5. CONCLUSION

This chapter discussed the population change and its impact on economy.

First, this chapter reviewed the demographic changes since the founding of the People's Republic of China, and discussed the relationship between family planning policies and the fertility. We find that the effect of family planning on China's current fertility rate is very small, but the effect of the average level of education of women on fertility remains stable. This chapter forecasted the average education level of women in the sub-region, and the fertility rate in these areas. We found that the fertility of the women of childbearing age may decline to 0.73 in 2030, and the relaxation of the existing family planning policy may only have a very limited effect on the slowdown of the declining trend in fertility.

We anticipate China's future population on the basis of different fertility projections. Even under the most optimistic assumptions, China's population will reach 1.44 billion in 2026 and then begin to decline. When there is further decline in fertility on the basis of the 2010 census, China's population peak will occur in 2018. Under an optimistic fertility assumption, the share of the population aged over 65 years will increase from 9.3% in 2010 and reach 20% in 2030, the same as the current degree of aging in Japan. The aging will begin to stabilize in 2050, at about 30%. Under the low fertility assumption, the share of the aging population in 2,100 will reach 40–50%. Compared with the proportion of the elderly population in China, the share of the labor force and the proportion of youth population decreased year by year. Under the assumption of a higher fertility rate, the population aged 15 to 64 can be stabilized between 63% and 65%. The share of adolescents is even higher if the fertility rate rises to 1.6. Under a low fertility assumption, China's working-age population can only be maintained at about half of the total population, while the share of youth population is rapidly reduced to only 6–9% in 2,100.

Population structure will change all aspects of the economy and produce a variety of effects, in which the most affected aspect is China's social security system. We simulated the revenues and payments of the pension system in China on the basis of the demographic change and pension system change forecasting. We find that the change of fertility will have an impact on the balance of payments of pensions after 2030, while the effect gradually expanded. Compared with the effect of fertility, the effect of retirement age postponement in urban pension system is much larger, but is gradually narrowing. When the retirement age is postponed to 65 years for males and 60 years for females in 2034, the pension fund will have positive balance until 2045. This chapter also calculated the run of urban and rural pension systems. Combining the basic pension insurance and the urban and rural pension systems together, we find that China will face a huge deficit in the pension payments if no reform is done on the fertility and retirement age. But on the other hand, if the fertility rate can be maintained at 2010 levels, and the retirement age can be postponed by 5 years in the next 20 years, the deficit of pension funds will be greatly reduced.

Finally, we summarized the effect of demographic change on economic growth and other aspects. The aspects that receive the impact of the changing population include savings rates and international trade. The study found that higher working-age share in the population and imbalanced gender ratio will result in high level of international trade and high savings rate in the channel of competitive savings, etc.

REFERENCES

Auerbach, A. J. and Oreopoulos, P. (1999). Analyzing the fiscal impact of US immigration. *American Economic Review*, 89(2): 176–180.

Auerbach, A. J. and Oreopoulos, P. (2000). The fiscal effects of US Immigration: A generational-accounting perspective. *Tax Policy and the Economy*, 14: 123–156.

Becker, G. S., Duesenberry James, S. and Okun Bernard (1960). *An Economic Analysis of Fertility: Demographic and Economic Change in Developed Countries*. Columbia University Press.

Behrman, J. R. and Rosenzweig, M. R. (2002). Does increasing women's schooling raise the schooling of the next generation? *American Economic Review*, 92(1): 323–334.

Cai, Y. (2010). China's below — replacement fertility: Government policy or socioeconomic development? *Population and Development Review*, 36(3): 419–440.

Chamon, M. D. and Prasad, E. S. (2010). Why are saving rates of urban households in China rising? *American Economic Journal: Macroeconomics*, 2(1): 93–130.

Chen, B., Lu, M. and Zhong, N. (2012). *Hukou and Consumption Heterogeneity: Migrants Expenditure is Depressed by Institutional Constraints in Urban China*. Available at SSRN 1989257.

Chen Qin and Song Zheng (2013). Will Urbanization help? — from rural–urban migration to the balanced pension fund [J]. *Financial Research*, (6): 1–15.

Currie, J. and Moretti, E. (2002). Mother's education and the intergenerational transmission of human capital: Evidence from college openings. *The Quarterly Journal of Economics*, 118(4): 1495–1532.

Du, Qingyuan and Wei Shang-Jin (2013). *A Theory of Competitive Saving Motive*. National Bureau of Economic Research.

Du, Q. and Wei, S.-J. (2011). *A Darwinian Perspective on Exchange Rate Undervaluation*. National Bureau of Economic Research.

Ge Sequin, Yang Dennis and Zhang Junsen (2012). Population policies, demographic structural changes, and the Chinese household saving puzzle [J].

Goodkind, D. M. (2004). China's missing children: The 2000 census underreporting surprise. *Population Studies*, 58(3): 281–295.

Grossman, M. (1972). On the concept of health capital and the demand for health. *Journal of Political Economy*, 80(2): 223–255.

Lee, R. and Miller, T. (2000). Immigration, social security, and broader fiscal impacts. *American Economic Review*, 90(2): 350–354.

Li, H., Zhang Junsen and Zhu Yi (2005). *The Effect of the One-child Policy on Fertility in China: Identification Based on the Differences-in-Differences*. Unpublished Working Paper.

Li, Bohua, Song Yuepin and Qi Jianan (2010). Current living situation of migrant population in China—A pilot survey of migrant population in five major cities [J]. *Population Research*, (1): 6–18.

McCrary, J. and Royer, H. (2006). *The Effect of Female Education on Fertility and Infant Health: Evidence from School Entry Policies Using Exact Date of Birth*. National Bureau of Economic Research.

McElroy, M. and Yang, D. T. (2000). Carrots and sticks: Fertility effects of China's population policies. *American Economic Review*, 90(2): 389–392.

Retherford, R. D., Choe, M. K. and Chen Jiajian (2005). How far has fertility in China really declined? *Population and Development Review*, 31(1): 57–84.

Schultz, T. P. and Zeng, Y. (1995). Fertility of rural China. Effects of Local Family Planning and Health Programs. *Journal of Population Economics*, 8(4): 329–350.

Song, Z. M. and Yang, D. T. (2010). *Life Cycle Earnings and Saving in a Fast-Growing Economy*. Unpublished paper, Chinese University of Hong Kong.

Song, Z. M., Storesletten, K. and Wang, Y. et al. (2012). Sharing High Growth Across Generations: Pensions and Demographic Transition in China. Mimeo, University of Zurich.

Storesletten, K. (2003). Fiscal implications of immigration — A net present value calculation. *Scandinavian Journal of Economics*, 105(3): 487–506.

Tian, Wei et al. (2013). Demographic and international trade [J]. *Economic Research*, (11): 87–99.

Wang, Fei (2012). Family Planning Policy in China: Measurement and Impact on Fertility, Working Paper.

Wei, S.-J. and Zhang, X. (2011). The competitive saving motive: Evidence from rising sex ratios and savings rates in China. *Journal of Political Economy*, 119(3): 511–564.

Wu (2010). Courses on Contemporary China's Economic Reform. Shanghai: Shanghai for East Publisher.

Xu, Jing (2010). Divergence between low fertility and desired fertility in China. *Population and Development*, (1): 27–37.

Yang Xiang (2004). Studies on family planning history of contemporary China [J]. Zhejiang University doctoral dissertation.

Zhang, G. and Zhao, Z. (2006). Reexamining China's fertility puzzle: Data collection and quality over the last two decades. *Population and Development Review*, 32(2): 293–321.

Zhang, J. (1990). Socioeconomic determinants of fertility in China. *Journal of Population Economics*, 3(2): 105–123.

Zhang, Shuang (2012). Mother's Education and Infant Health: Evidence from High School Closures in China, Working Paper.

Zheng, Z. (2004). Fertility desire of married women in China. *Population Science of China*, (5): 75–80.

Chapter 12
The Labor Market in China

Qin Chen

School of Economics, Fudan University

With the transformation of demographic conditions, the labor market in China has experienced tremendous change. We will discuss two main topics on the labor market of China.

The urbanization of labor featured the transformation of the labor market in the last 30 years. From 2000 to 2010, the share of urban population in China increased by 13.46%, to about 207 million people. Song *et al.* (2012) predict that the share of urban population will exceed 50% in 2050 at the current speed. The urbanization process provides the urban labor market with abundant labor supply, which enables enterprises to hire cheap, effective labor constantly. After China entered the WTO, export-oriented enterprises had increased China's exports dramatically, which helped China accumulate a huge amount of foreign reserves.

As the aging situation deepens in China, the overall constant labor supply will drain out shortly. In 2012, the amount of labor population began to decline. In the predictions of the previous chapter, we found that the share of labor in China will drop to 56% in 2050, which is now 73.3%. The decline of labor stock may result in a number of consequences, including the increasing cost of labor, less output, and decreasing aggregate saving.

However, the urbanization trend may help the supply of labor. In this paper, we will first discuss the contribution of urbanization of demographic conditions to the labor market. In 2012, there were about 262 million migrant workers who came from the rural region and were working off-farm, while in 2000, there were only 140 million migrant workers. The urbanization trend guaranteed a constant labor from rural to urban areas, thus slowing down the shrinking trend of labor. We will analyze the composition, speed, and structure of urbanization in the first section, forecasting the labor supply and labor structure, and test whether the Lewis Turning Point is approaching.

The second important issue in the labor market is the productivity of workers. The productivity of labor can be learned from two characteristics of labor. The first character is the education attainment. By analyzing the distribution and return of education, we can forecast productivity change. The second characteristic is the wage of labor. The inequality of wage is widening in China in the last 30 years. In this process, we can see a widening gap between urban and rural areas, between highly educated people and less educated people, and between urban residents and migrants. The inequality may indeed reflect the productivity of labor, but on the other hand, wrongly priced labor, that is, the distortion of labor wage, will be harmful for society to reach its frontier productivity. We will focus on the education and wage distribution of urban residents and migrants, and illustrate the big picture of the labor market change in China.

1. THE URBANIZATION OF LABOR

1.1 Literature Review

China is now experiencing a great urbanization process. However, although we can get some fragmented information from the data available, we still do not have a consistent opinion on the detailed process of urbanization in China, which is related to many important topics of China's economy.

The first issue in the urbanization in China is its speed and structure. The increment of urban population (207 million) can be divided into three parts: the natural increase in population of urban people during the 10 years; the people who did not move, but their residence experienced a reclassification from rural to urban; and the people who migrated from rural areas to urban areas. The third part of the urban population increment is defined as the real rural–urban migration, or the urbanization of population, while the second part is the urbanization of land. By calculating the three parts of increasing urban population, we can get the detailed process of urbanization in China.

Some literature had tackled just the same issues about the urbanization structure of China in the 1990s, but the results turn out to be significantly different. Wang (2004) use the 1990 and 2000 census and the 1995 mini-census to calculate the urban–rural migration of the periods 1990–1995 and 1995–2000, respectively. Combining the rural–urban migration during these two separate periods, she finds that there were 52 million rural–urban migrants between 1990 and 2000, which is about one-third of the total urban population increment in the 1990s. Subtracting the rural–urban migration and the natural increase population from the total urban population increase, she calculated the urban population increase generated by land urbanization, which is more than half of the urban population increment.

On the other hand, Chan and Hu (2003) use another approach to address exactly the same problem. They subtract the reclassification instead of migration from the total urban increase. Assuming that the increase generated by reclassification comes exclusively from the newly designated towns, the ratio of rural–urban migration in the total urban population increase rises to 60%, which doubles the 30% in Wang (2004).

While calculating the structure of urbanization, Chan *et al.* (1999) highlight the importance of *hukou* migrants who had changed their *hukou* to a new residence. Cai and Wang (2008) calculated the structure of *hukou* migrants and non-*hukou* migrants of 2000, and finds that in 2000, 34.9% migrants of the five-year flow belong to *hukou* migrants. But due to the unavailability of data regarding the *hukou* migrants in the 2010 census, we use other approaches to figure it out.

After identifying the real rural–urban migrants in the urbanization process, we calculate their scale. Several sources of the migrant data are used in former literatures (Chan, 2011), including the rural workers from Rural Household Survey (RHS), or the temporary population and *hukou* migrants from the Ministry of Public Security (MPS), to calculate the rural–urban migrants. As a complementary variable, some literatures also used micro data like China Urban Labor Survey (CULS), China Household Income Project (CHIP), Rural–Urban Migration in China and Indonesia (RUMiCI) Project, China National Rural Survey (CNRS), or other unique data sets. But these data sets become contradictory and misleading when we want to know the detailed facts of the urbanization of population.

Index	Literature	Time	Approach or Data	Data
Share of rural–urban migrant workers in urban labor force	Knight et al. (2011)	2007	132 million rural–urban migrants in 325 million urban labor force, rural–urban migrants data from RHS	40.6%
	Cai and Du (2011)	2009	39 million migrant workers over 310 million urban labor, migrant workers from urban employment data by NBS	12.5%*
Share of rural–urban migrant workers in rural labor force	Knight et al. (2011)	2006	RHS	26%
	Wang et al. (2011)	2008	CNRS	24%
	Kong et al. (2010)	2008	RUMiCI	25%
	Meng (2012)	2009	RHS	27%
	Meng (2012)	2009	RUMiCI	22%
Share of off-farm labor force in rural workforce	Rozelle et al. (2008)	2004	CNRS	51%
	Cai and Wang (2008)	2005	RHS	47.9%
	Rozelle et al. (2008)	2007	CNRS	60%
	Wang et al. (2011)	2008	CNRS	62%

*Cai and Du (2011) believe that the urban employment data by NBS do not adequately account for the migrant workers.

From the table above, we can find that the share of migrants varies by the sources of the data used in literatures. Knight, Deng and Li (2011) assume that the 132 million rural migrant workers are all rural–urban migrants. If the assumption is true, over 40% of urban labor force is composed of rural–urban migrants. But Cai and Du (2011) check the urban employment data by National Bureau of Statistics (NBS), and find that only 12.5% of the urban labor are migrant workers. A similar result appears while calculating the share of rural–urban migrant workers in the rural labor force. If RHS data is used, the share of rural–urban migrant workers would be significantly higher than the result estimated by micro data such as CNRS or RUMiCI. The RHS and other survey data have their own advantages and disadvantages. For the RHS data users, they only know that a migrant worker had moved out of his township border, but do not know whether the rural migrant worker goes to an urban region or a rural region. The assumption that the rural migrant workers all moved to urban regions will probably lead to an overestimated result. For the micro survey data users, although they can obtain more information from the respondents, the share of migrants might be an underestimation. In fact, the problem of underestimated migrants occurs in almost all micro survey data, including the China Family Panel Studies (CFPS), the China Household Finance Survey (CHFS), and the China General Social Survey (CGSS), in which the share of migrants is significantly lower than that in the 2010 census. To avoid their disadvantages, this section will combine the scale information from the RHS and the structure information from the micro survey data, and try to calculate accurate information.

1.2 Data Description

The 2000 and 2010 population censuses are the most important data sets in this section. There are some key definitions in these two data sets.

1.2.1 The definition of urban and rural

We have three types of regions in the census: the city, the town, and the township. The city and town are classified as urban, and the township is classified as rural. In the 2010 definition, the urban is the region that connected with the resident of the government of city, district, county, or town, along with the industrial and mining areas, development zones, research institutes, and universities which have more than 3,000 people. "Rural" is the region outside the urban. The only difference between the 2000 definition and the 2010 one is the region that does not connect to the resident of the government of city, but is still located in the municipal district, whose population density is above 1,500 people per square kilometer. It was classified as urban in the 2000 definition, but in the 2010 definition, it was changed to rural. Since in a high-density municipal district, we can hardly find a region that is disconnected, we believe that this difference will make little change to our estimation, and therefore, no corrective treatment is necessary.

1.2.2 The type of *hukou*

There are two types of *hukou*, agricultural and non-agricultural. In the 2000 census, 24.7% of people had non-agricultural *hukou*, and in the 2010 census, it was 29.1%. The changing composition of *hukou* can help us find the missing information about the real migration.

1.2.3 The types of domiciles and their urban–rural character

It is worth noting that there are six types of domiciles, which is the basic unit of China's administration. They are the Villagers' Committee or the Residents' Committee of Street, Town, or Township. The type of domiciles is determined by the original *hukou* composition, and they were directly linked with urban–rural classification before 1995: street and residents' Committee of town was the urban region, while the rest was rural. As the link faded after 2000, neither the types of domiciles or the urban–rural character are necessarily determined by the others. However, we can use the "Code to Distinguish Urban–Rural" from the NBS of China to estimate the urban–rural composition in each type of domicile (see Table 12-1).

There are 671,000 basic units in China, and about three quarters of them are classified as rural, and the rest are urban. From Table 12-1, we can see

Table 12-1: Types of domiciles and their urban–rural character.

	Street	Residents' Committee of town	Villagers' Committee of town	Township	Sum
Numbers	83,974	29,124	372,662	185,430	671,190
Urban	65,879	27,754	74,311	6,687	174,631
Rural	18,095	1,370	298,351	178,743	496,559
Urban (%)	78.5	95.3	19.9	3.6	26.0
Rural (%)	21.5	4.7	80.1	96.4	74.0

*Author's estimation.
Source: "Code to Distinguish Urban–Rural" from NBS.

that about 3.6% of the townships have been classified as urban and 20% of the villagers' Committee of town have been classified as rural. Taking into account the direct assumption that population is uniformly distributed in different types of basic units, we can adjust the share of urban population in the following calculation. The composition data in Table 12-1 can help us test whether the rural–urban share in total migrants is robust.

1.2.4 The definition of migration

In several censuses, migrants are defined as the people who had moved to another township/town/street in a given period. Another definition of migrants excludes the people who move within or between municipal districts in the same city. In this section we include all migrants. From the census data, we can find two parameters of migrants.

Table 12-2 can be found in the 2000 census; it was answered by the people who migrated to the place of residence in the last 5 years, wherever their domicile is. There is a similar table in the 1995 mini-census. They are the data source of Wang (2004).

But this table disappeared in the 2005 mini-census and the 2010 census, and the only data available in 2010 census for analyzing inner migration is presented in Table 12-3, which only includes the migrants out of their domicile, that is, non-*hukou* migrants. It is not difficult to find that the

Table 12-2: Population by types of resident and original location (migrated in last 5 years).

		Original Location			
Resident	All	Township	Resident's Committee of town	Villagers' Committee of town	Street
All	12,464,412	3,583,406	4,966,733	3,968,986	3,914,273
City	7,535,924	1,570,156	2,551,633	1,999,862	3,414,135
Town	2,168,359	806,405	1,123,832	851,960	238,122
Township	2,760,129	1,206,845	1,291,268	1,117,164	262,016

Source: Calculated by author from L-7-3a, L-7-3b, and L-7-3c in the "*China 2000 Population Census Assembly*".

Table 12-3: Population out of their domicile by types of resident and domicile.

Resident	All	Township	Domicile Resident's Committee of town	Villagers' Committee of town	Street
All	24,355,374	5,483,136	2,733,586	9,856,554	6,282,098
City	16,224,619	3,273,927	1,679,495	5,821,197	5,450,000
Town	5,000,740	1,355,337	767,106	2,389,724	488,573
Township	3,130,015	853,872	286,985	1,645,633	343,525

Source: Table 12-L-7-1 in the "*Tabulation on the 2010 Population Census of P.R.C.*"

migrants who change the domicile to their residence, that is, *hukou* migrants, are neglected in Table 12-3. We will handle this issue later.

1.2.5 The fertility and mortality

To calculate newborn people in urban areas, we should know the fertility and mortality in two censuses. The urban fertility in 2000 census is 0.86 in the city and 1.08 in the town; in 2010 the number becomes 0.88 and 1.15. A series of literature shows that the fertility in 2000 was an underestimation (see, e.g., Retherford *et al.*, 2005; Zhang and Zhao, 2006). Using intercensal methods, Goodkind (2004) estimated that 37 million children under age 9 were missing in the 2000 census. A similar estimate of 30 million is obtained by Zhang and Cui (2003) who use primary school enrolments to support the actual child population. Chen and Song (2013) simulate the demographic situation in 2010 using the 2000 census and an upward adjusted 2000 fertility, and find a consistent result with the 2010 census. We will adjust upward the reported fertility of the 2000 census in the following analysis.

A natural fertility and mortality rate occurs in the 2000s. To make the data in the two censuses comparable, we must adjust the data in the 2000 census by a series of fertility and mortality rates.

In this section, we hope to analyze the urbanization structure in the 2000s. It includes the real rural–urban migration, the natural increase in urban people, and the reclassified increase. We will address these three parts in the following sections.

2. THE SPEED OF RURAL–URBAN MIGRANTS, AND THE COMPOSITION OF URBANIZATION

2.1 Figure Out the Real Rural–Urban Migration in the 2000s

In this section, we will find the real rural–urban migration in the 2000s, those who lived in rural regions in 2000, experienced at least one move in the 2000s, and lived in urban regions in 2010.

We use the migrants listed in Table 12-3 as the calculation base. Table 12-3 is not consistent with the real rural–urban migration in 2000s in two ways. First, there is no 5-year limit in Table 12-3; all non-*hukou* migrants are included in the table no matter how long ago they left their domicile. Second, *hukou* migrants are not included in the table.

To figure out the real rural–urban migration in the 2000s, the non-*hukou* migrants who migrated before 2000 should be subtracted from Table 12-3, while the *hukou* migrants should be added. Let me make three important assumptions before continuing to the next step.

(1) We consider only the net migration; migration from urban to rural areas will be neglected. This means that the number of migrants we get is a lower bound estimation. Nevertheless, as the migrants from urban to rural areas only account for a small part in the total migrants, for example, 5.7% in the 2010 census, this assumption does not have a significant effect on the results.

(2) The migrants that move from rural to urban areas have agricultural *hukou* at the time of their migration. We can find support from the census data: only 4.7% rural people have non-agriculture *hukou* in 2000 (4.3% in 2010 census). We make a simplified assumption that the migrants with non-agricultural *hukou* are unlikely to move out from rural regions.

(3) The migrants will modify their *hukou* type from agricultural to non-agricultural when they change their domicile from rural to urban areas. This means that if a migrant changes his domicile to another place but maintains his agricultural *hukou*, he cannot be a rural–urban migrant.

A 2010 Urban Population composition analysis table (Table 12-4) can be created on the basis of the above three assumptions.

Table 12-4: The composition of 2010 urban population (10 and older).

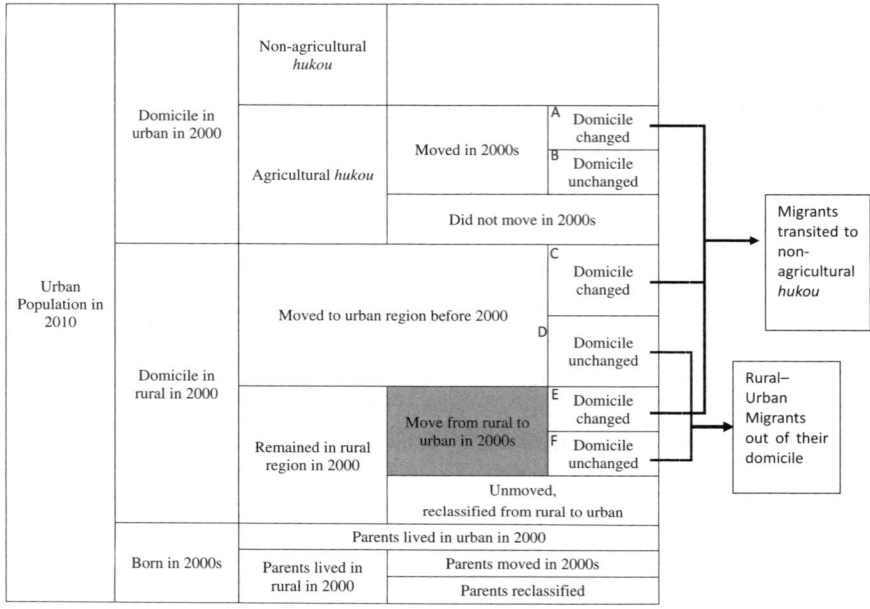

We will discuss the natural increase in urban people in the 2000s in Section 2.3. Notice that the grey cell displays the data we want, the real rural–urban migration in the 2000s, and it can be expressed by other cells in a simple identity.

$A + C + E =$ Migrants who have changed to non-agricultural hukou in 2000s (Check Assumption C)

$D + F =$ Rural–Urban Migrants out of their domicile in 2010

$E + F =$ The Real Rural–Urban Migration in 2000s

$=$ (Migrants who have changed to non-agricultural hukou in 2000s $- A - C$)

$+$ (Rural–Urban Migrants out of their domicile in 2010 $- D$)

$=$ Rural–Urban Migrants out of their domicile in 2010 $- (C + D) +$ (Migrants who have changed to non-agricultural hukou in 2000s $- A$)

= Rural–Urban Migrants out of their domicile in 2010
− Rural–Urban Migrants out of their domicile in 2000
+ Migrants from rural who have changed
to non-agricultural hukou in 2000s

In this way, the problem of calculating the real rural–urban migrants transforms to three independent problems: calculating the rural–urban migrants out of their domicile in 2000 and 2010, and figuring out the scale of *hukou* migrants from rural to urban regions in the 2000s.

1) Rural–urban migrants out of their domicile

From two censuses data, we can get Table 12-5.

Table 12-5 excludes the children younger than 10 years old in the 2010 census. The first estimated proportion of rural–urban migrants in total migrants is calculated directly by Table 12-3, in which the township/villagers' Committee of town are treated as rural outflow places, and the city/town as urban inflow places. The result turns out to be 58.2 million. After adjusting by the number in Table 12-1, the number of non-*hukou*

Table 12-5: Rural–Urban migrants out of their domicile in 2000 and 2010 (million).

Year	2000	With Death	2010	Difference
Total population	1,242	1,186	1,186	
Total migrants out of their domicile	144	142	242	
Proportion of migrants in total population	11.6%		20.4%	
Proportion of rural–urban migrants in total migrants	48.8%		52.7%	
Estimated rural–urban migrants	70.3	69.3	127.5	58.2
Proportion of rural–urban migrants in total migrants*	47.82%		51.04%	
Estimated rural–urban migrants*	68.9	67.9	123.5	55.6

Source: The data of migrants out of their domicile comes from Tables 12-1–12-4 in both censuses. The "Death" column shows the natural population in 2010 with the adjustment of 2000 population. The proportion of migrants in total population in 2010 can be directly calculated by Table 12-3. As of 2000, the people who had changed the domicile to their residence must be excluded in Table 12-2. We make it by using the 0.95% micro data of 2000 census. The proportion with asterisk (*) is the proportion modified by Table 12-1.

migrants becomes 55.6 million. The result does not differ much regardless of whether we use the information in Table 12-1.

2.2 *Hukou* Migrants in the 2000s

Cai and Wang (2008) calculates the non-*hukou* migrants and *hukou* migrants in 2000 using a 5-year flow measure. He finds that about four-fifths of the rural–urban migrants were non-*hukou* migrants, while others are *hukou* migrants. Given that the calculation is based on a 5-year flow measure, which is about half of the stock measure, the share of *hukou* migrants might be overestimated, because a *hukou* transition is more likely to occur in a long-term scope. In this section, we can calculate the migrants from rural areas who have transited to non-agricultural *hukou* in the 2000s in two steps.

First, figure out the people who transited their *hukou* from agricultural to non-agricultural.

From 2000 and 2010 censuses, the scale of non-agricultural people increased from 305 million to 384 million, about 80 million. We do not have the detailed age data for non-agricultural people, but following the method using in Song *et al.* (2012), we can roughly exclude the natural increase in people in the last 10 years, and find the net increase of people with non-agricultural *hukou*.

Using the fertility and mortality rate in 2000, we can simulate the non-agricultural population from 1 to 10. We find that a 10.26% increase occurs in the urban population in the 2000s. Assume that non-agricultural population have a similar fertility and mortality pattern as the urban population; the 305 million population would increase to 325 million in 2010. It implies 67 million *hukou* transited from agricultural to non-agricultural in 2000s.

Second, estimate the proportion of rural original migrants in the total of *hukou* migrants. We do not have these proportion statistics in the census, but it can be deduced from the CGSS data, which reports the respondents' *hukou* transition history. The *hukou* migrants can be divided into three parts: (1) the people who transit their *hukou* from agricultural to non-agricultural within their *hukou* border, and they are not migrants; (2) the rural original *hukou* migrants; (3) the urban original *hukou* migrants. We can see the *hukou* migrants' structure in Figure 12-1.

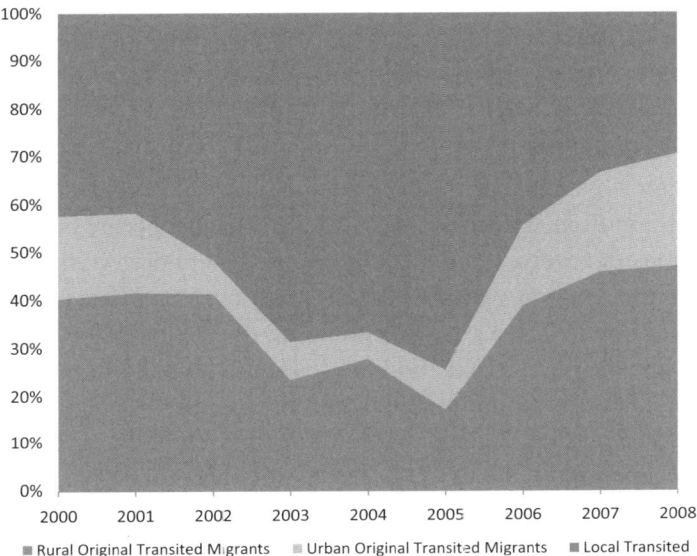

Figure 12-1: The structure of *hukou* migrants.

Figure 12-1 shows the three parts of *hukou* migrants. The rural original *hukou* migrants account for about 40% of the *hukou* migrants during the period 2000–2008. Given that the total *hukou* migrants in the 2000s is about 67 million, and assuming that the share of rural original *hukou* migrants in total *hukou* migrants remains constant in 2009 and 2010, we can infer that the rural original *hukou* migrants are about 26.9 million. Compared to the rural–urban non-*hukou* migrants ranged from 55.6 to 58.2 million, we have a share of rural–urban *hukou* migrants in all rural–urban migrants, a bit higher than the estimation in Cai and Wang (2008), which is caused by a long-term scope measure. Combined with rural–urban migrants out of their domicile, the total number of real rural–urban migrants is about 85 million.

2.3 The Natural Increase of Urban Population

In this section, we will address the natural increase in the urban population, which involves the number of newborn people in the 2000s. From

Table 12-4, we know that the newborn people in city regions during the 2000s can also be divided into three parts: the newborn children of original city people, by reclassification, and by migration. Following the method used in Song *et al.* (2012), we can calculate the urban population aged from 1 to 10 without considering the migrants and their children, about 50.7 million. Given that the real population in the 2010 census aged from 1 to 10 is 61.3 million, the difference of 10.6 million people are migrants from rural regions themselves in the 2000s, or are the children of migrants who live in the urban region. According to the analysis of migrants in Table 12-4, the 10.6 million children are also composed of two parts: the real migrant children, and the reclassified children. Assuming that the structure of these two parts is similar to the migrants and reclassified population structure discussed in Section 2.2, about 5.2 million children in the increased urban children are migrants or the children of migrants. We considered these children as the real migrants from rural region as well. Similarly, the rest of the children are considered as reclassified people.

2.4 The Composition of Increasing Urban Population

According to the discussion in Section 2.3, we can illustrate the structure of increasing urban population in Tables 12-6 and 12-7.

Table 12-6: The structure of increasing urban population.

Elements of increasing urban population	Total number	% of Total urban increase (lower bound of real migrants)	Result from Wang (2004)	Chan (2012)
Total urban population increasing	207	100	100%	100%
Real rural–urban migrants	90.3	43.6	30.82%	43%
Reclassified people	87.9	42.5	52.2%	42%
Natural increase of urban population	28.8	13.9	16.98%	15%

Source: The "real rural–urban migrants" are the sum of the real migrants discussed in Sections 2.1 and 2.2 and their children discussed in Section 2.3.

Table 12-7: Comparison of the age structure of migrants in urban areas with/without agricultural *hukou*.

Age	Urban migrants, 2000	Urban migrants with agri-*hukou*, 2000	Urban migrants, 2005	Urban migrants with agri-*hukou*, 2005	Urban migrants, 2010
0–15	12.38%	12.83%	14.00%	12.05%	12.10%
16–64	82.28%	84.55%	81.64%	85.66%	81.88%
65+	5.34%	2.62%	4.36%	2.29%	6.02%

Notes: 2000 and 2005 are from the micro data. 2010 is from the "*Tabulation on the 2000 Population Census of China*," 3-1a, 3-1b, 7-2a, 7-2b.

Table 12-6 illustrates a smaller amount of real rural–urban migrants than the reclassified people, which is somehow consistent with the result in Wang (2004). But the real rural–urban migrants still play a more important role in the 2010 census. The result is very close to the estimation in Chan (2012).

3. THE SCALE AND STRUCTURE OF RURAL–URBAN MIGRATION

The rural–urban migrants play an important role in the changing labor market in urban regions in China. In the last chapter, we find out the speed of migration: about 9 million people migrated from rural to urban every year in 2000s. In this section, we will address the total scale and the structure of rural–urban migrants and highlight some stylized facts of the migration process in China.

The scale of rural–urban migration is a big issue. From Chapter 11, we know that the scale of rural–urban non-*hukou* migrants lies within a wide range from 93.4 to 127.5 million. The scale of Migrant Workers Report by NBS may help us to find an accurate number. The 2010 migrant workers monitor reported that China has 242 million rural workers, in which 153 million are "migrant rural workers," while the rest are "local non-agricultural workers." The definition of migrant workers reported by NBS differs from the term "rural–urban migrants" used in this section in three major ways.

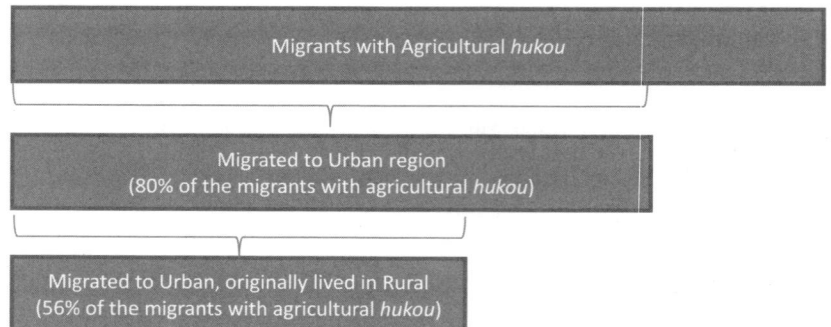

Figure 12-2: The structure of migrants with agricultural *hukou*.

(1) The migrant workers might move to rural regions instead of urban. From the 2000 census and 2005 mini-census, we find that 73% to 81% of migrants who have agricultural *hukou* move to urban regions, while the rest move to rural regions. We assume that 20% of the migrant workers move to rural regions in 2010, and they are not rural–urban migrants.

(2) Though the migrant workers have agricultural *hukou*, their original residence might be classified as urban. As we mentioned in Table 12-1, the urban–rural character of certain domiciles are not defined by their types. Assume that 30% of the people who have agricultural *hukou* are actually residents of urban regions, who cannot be rural–urban migrants. These two differences can be shown in Figure 12-2.

(3) The definition of migrant workers does not cover children below 15 and the elderly who report themselves as retired. From the 2000 and 2005 censuses, we find that children and the elderly above 60 account for 14–15% in total urban migrants with agricultural *hukou*. We do not have detailed data about their share in the 2010 census, but from the 2000 and 2005 censuses, we find that the share of children and the elderly in all urban migrants is about 4% higher than in urban migrants with agricultural *hukou* (see Table 12-7). We assume that the age structure will follow the pattern in the 2000 and 2005 census, so that the share of children and the elderly in urban migrants with agricultural *hukou* would be 14%, about 4% lower than that in all urban migrants. We can get the total rural–urban migrants by dividing the rural–urban migrant workers by 86%.

Based on the above three differences, we can calculate that in 2010, there are about 130 million rural–urban migrants in China based on the above three differences, lying within the range given in last part, about 19.5% of the total urban population, or 13.9% of the population with agricultural *hukou*. This number is lower than the estimation of Meng (2012), in which about 22% of rural labor force was working in cities in 2009. Figure 12-2 explains the difference. Notice that we had excluded the *hukou* migrants; the 99.6 million is a lower bound estimation of the total rural–urban migrants.

Besides the total scale, the age structure of rural–urban migrants is the second important information. The 99.6 million of migrants are not evenly distributed along the age in urban region, in which the younger generation may account for a larger scale relative to the older generation. Without the detailed census data, we cannot know the age structure of the rural–urban migrants, but we can infer the age structure of rural–urban migration from some survey data and the aggregated data in the census. Figure 12-3 illustrates the age profile curve in these surveys.

When we compare the age structure of migrants with agricultural *hukou* of 2008 CHIP and of all urban migrants in the 2010 census, we can also find a similar pattern in the comparison of the 2000 census. The age structure

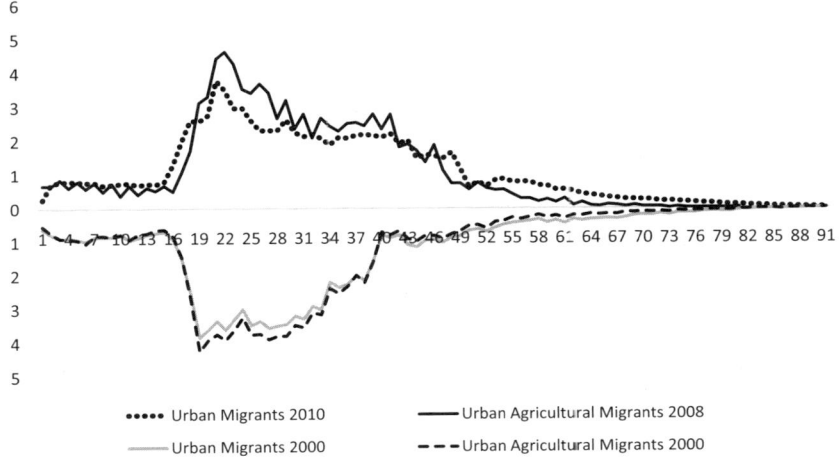

Figure 12-3: Age structure of migrants with agricultural *hukou* (%).

of migrants with agricultural *hukou* has less children and elderly, and is dense in the middle-aged population. Based on the above analysis, we will use the age structure in 2008 CHIP as the proxy of age structure of urban migrants with agricultural *hukou*.

3.1 Rural–Urban Migrants in Urban Regions

In urban regions, the migrants with agricultural *hukou* take a larger position than 2000. Table 12-8 and Figure 12-4 show an increasing share of the migrants with agricultural *hukou* in the total urban population.

Notice that in 2005 the share of rural–urban migrants is very close to that of 2000. It is because the 2005 mini-census had greatly underestimated the share of migrants in all population. After the publicity of the 2010 census, much migration data in 2005 had been modified to suit the new data. We find that the share of migrants doubled in almost every age group in the last 10 years. In the young age group from 15 to 39 years, the rural–urban migrants account for 20 to 30% of all urban population.

Table 12-8: Share of rural–urban migrants in urban region, by age group.

Age	2000 male	2005 male	2010 male	2000 female	2005 female	2010 female
0–4	7.93%	8.08%	11.20%	7.03%	7.81%	12.50%
5–9	7.12%	8.02%	10.10%	6.88%	7.45%	10.50%
10–14	5.21%	6.55%	10.20%	5.06%	6.08%	9.40%
15–19	13.76%	12.69%	20.60%	15.78%	15.56%	17.30%
20–24	16.21%	18.86%	30.50%	18.83%	20.48%	25.20%
25–29	15.94%	16.76%	30.10%	14.68%	15.83%	21.60%
30–34	12.99%	15.28%	24.50%	10.93%	13.54%	19.00%
35–39	9.10%	12.25%	21.40%	7.64%	10.38%	17.20%
40–44	6.00%	8.37%	16.40%	4.61%	7.02%	14.60%
45–49	5.06%	5.25%	10.70%	4.71%	4.34%	7.70%
50–54	4.05%	4.27%	9.20%	4.46%	4.18%	5.80%
55–59	3.44%	3.49%	5.10%	4.33%	4.14%	2.00%
60–64	3.35%	2.96%	3.50%	3.56%	3.65%	1.90%
65–69	2.53%	2.50%	2.70%	3.75%	3.22%	1.30%
70+	2.54%	2.35%	6.20%	4.18%	3.49%	5.00%

Notes: The 2000 and 2005 census data has been modified in Table 12-1, excluding the migrants with agricultural *hukou* who actually come from rural regions.

Figure 12-4: Share of rural–urban migrants in urban region, by age group.

3.2 Rural–Urban Migrants from Rural Region

How many people can be migrated from rural in the future? Li (2012) concludes that the probability of doing off-farm work for all rural laborers had reached 70% in 2007. For the age group of 16 to 20 years, the probability increased to 98% in 2007. It means that almost no rural workers can be transferred to off-farm work. We can find new evidence about this trend from the 2010 census.

On the one hand, Table 12-9 and Figure 12-5 shows the ratio of rural–urban migrants to all rural population of nearly every age group had doubled in the last 10 years. For the young age group from 20 to 35 years, the ratio of the population that had migrated from rural to urban areas increased from 10% to about 30%.

On the other hand, Table 12-10 below shows that the probability of population living in rural regions and working off-farm increased quickly. In 2010, about 30% to 40% young rural workers who have jobs are working off-farm, which also doubles the share of 2000.

Combined with the rural workers who had migrated to urban regions, if we look at all rural populations aged from 16 to 35, we will find that the probability of doing on-farm work had halved in the last 10 years. For the rural population aged from 16 to 19, the population dropped from 61 million to 46 million; only 20.3% are doing on-farm work, while the

Table 12-9: Share of rural–urban migrants out of rural region, by age group.

Age	2000 male	2005 male	2010 male	2000 female	2005 female	2010 female
0–4	3.9%	7.5%	7.2%	3.6%	7.2%	8.1%
5–9	3.0%	7.4%	7.1%	3.0%	6.9%	7.3%
10–14	2.1%	6.1%	7.3%	2.0%	5.7%	6.8%
15–19	8.4%	11.3%	18.8%	11.0%	13.5%	16.9%
20–24	11.4%	15.9%	28.1%	13.7%	17.0%	23.6%
25–29	10.4%	14.4%	28.4%	10.0%	13.7%	22.3%
30–34	8.1%	13.3%	24.7%	6.7%	11.9%	20.6%
35–39	6.4%	10.9%	20.8%	5.1%	9.4%	17.2%
40–44	4.3%	7.7%	14.8%	3.2%	6.6%	13.0%
45–49	3.0%	5.0%	10.2%	2.8%	4.2%	7.1%
50–54	2.3%	4.1%	8.3%	2.5%	4.0%	5.4%
55–59	1.9%	3.4%	4.1%	2.5%	4.0%	1.7%
60–64	1.9%	2.9%	2.6%	2.2%	3.5%	1.5%
65–69	1.5%	2.4%	2.0%	2.0%	3.1%	1.0%
70+	1.3%	2.3%	4.3%	1.9%	3.4%	3.4%

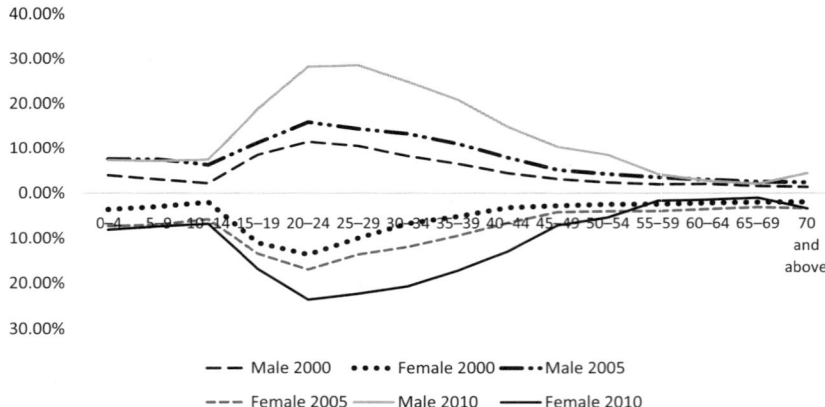

Figure 12-5: Share of rural–urban migrants out of rural region, by age group.

number was 41.3% ten years ago. From Figure 12-6, we can also find a decreasing curve in the probability of rural population doing on-farm work across age, which tells a truth of rapidly urbanization or "non-agriculturalization" trend for the younger generation in rural regions, and a diminishing cheap labor supply for future industrialization.

Table 12-10: Proportion of workers living in rural regions working off-farm.

Age	2000 male	2005 male	2010 male	2000 female	2005 female	2010 female
15–19	16.5%	27.9%	35.2%	19.8%	30.5%	34.7%
20–24	24.2%	31.5%	41.4%	20.4%	23.8%	34.1%
25–29	23.1%	30.6%	41.6%	14.2%	18.8%	31.0%
30–34	21.1%	27.5%	39.2%	11.4%	15.3%	28.0%
35–39	21.1%	24.8%	35.6%	10.7%	12.9%	24.3%
40–44	19.8%	23.2%	31.8%	9.3%	11.3%	20.5%
45–49	16.9%	20.1%	28.0%	6.5%	8.2%	16.1%
50–54	14.4%	15.6%	22.3%	4.2%	4.9%	10.1%
55–59	11.0%	11.7%	16.9%	2.8%	3.2%	6.4%
60–64	6.8%	7.4%	11.0%	2.2%	2.5%	4.7%

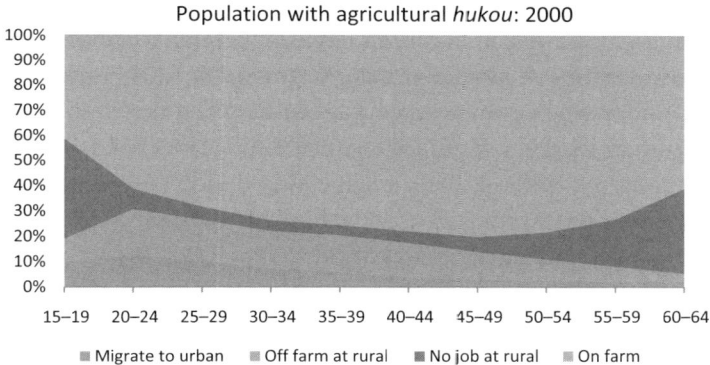

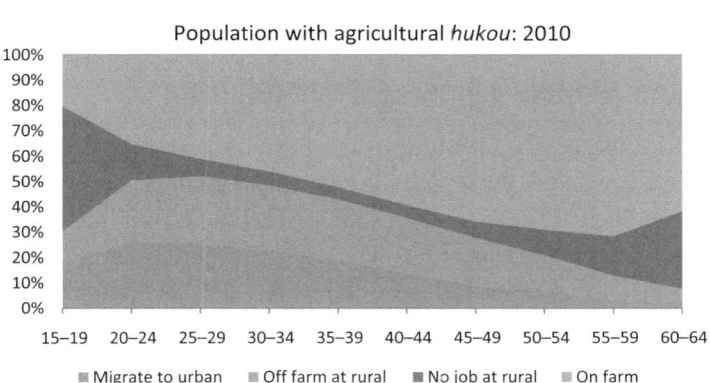

Figure 12-6: Population with agricultural *hukou*: 2000 and 2010.

4. THE EDUCATION AND WAGE IN THE LABOR MARKET

We will discuss the education profile and wage structure in the labor market in two parts.

First, we will analyze the education change in China within the last 30 years. The transformation of the education structure had resulted in tremendous change in the labor market in China. The most important topic in the labor market is the wage, and the relationship between wage and education, that is, returns of education. It reflects the productivity and the efficiency of the growth in productivity, which is the root motivation of the growth of China.

Second, we will focus on the education and wage structure of rural–urban migrants. Despite being an important part of the labor market in China, there is little research on the detail of migrants' labor market due to the unavailability of abundant data. Cai and Du (2011) use the CULS data, and find a wage convergence pattern between the migrant workers and local urban workers. But Golley and Meng (2011) and Meng (2012) present a contrary opinion that the education divide is widening between rural and urban areas, and the real wages of migrant workers may not have increased at all during the period 2000–2009. Here, we will first calculate the supply of rural–urban migrant workers of different education attainment, and then analyze the wage increase pattern of rural–urban migrants using a unique dataset of the migrants in Beijing, Shanghai, and Guangzhou.

4.1 Education Profile and Returns to Education

Figure 12-7 illustrates the education distribution geographically in 1990 and 2010. As we can see in these two figures, although the relative distribution of education does not seem to have changed much during the last 20 years, they all got an absolute increase. The education attainment in 1990 was 6.04 years in average. Twenty years later, the number increased by about 45% to 8.76 years. The region that gains the most education increase is the middle and west. The people in the Tibet Autonomous Region got the fastest education gain, about 3.7 years. On the other hand, the population in the northeastern provinces did not get a considerable education gain,

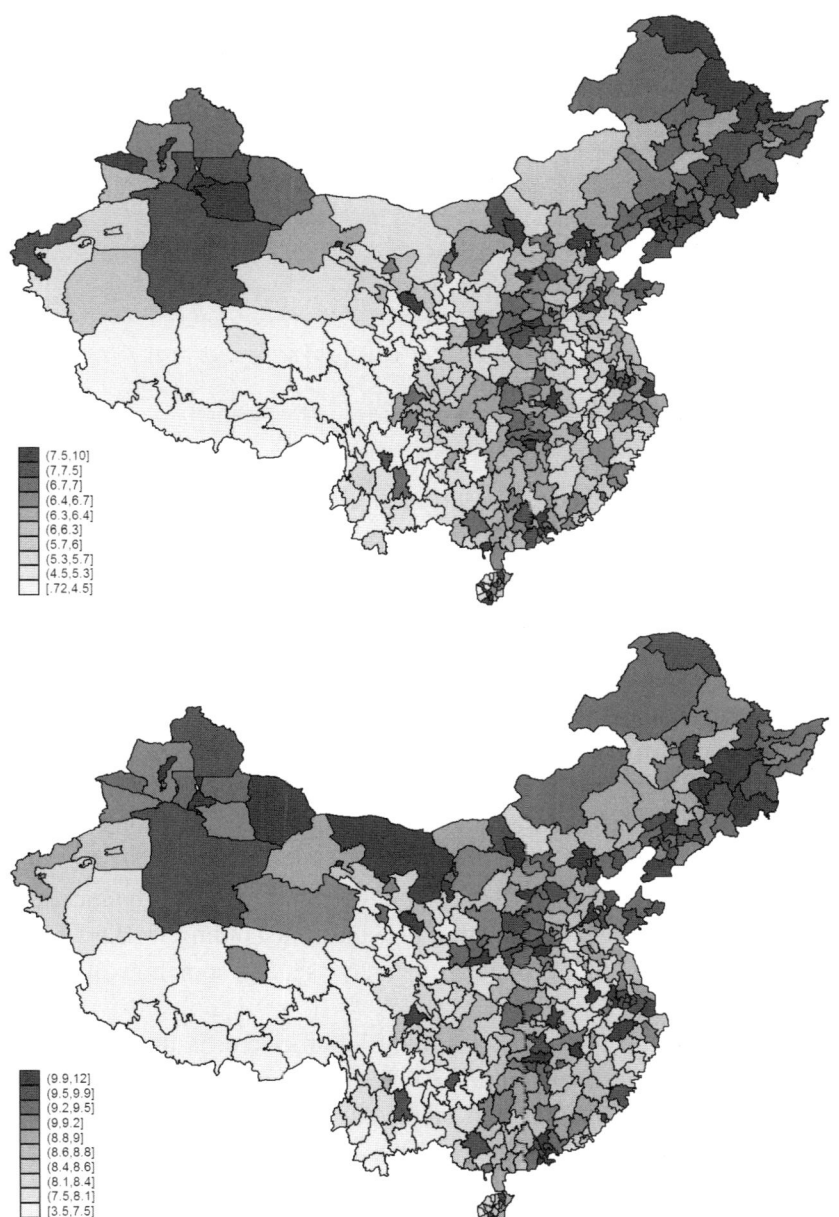

Figure 12-7: Education distributions in 1990 and 2010.

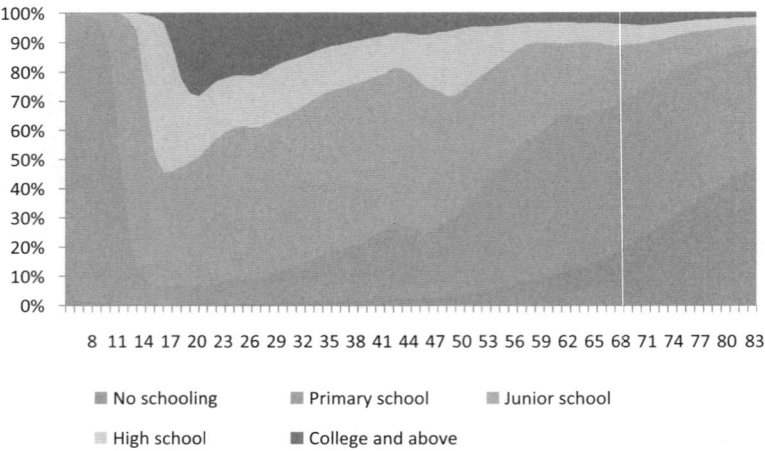

Figure 12-8: Education distribution across age (Census 2010).

only 2.1 to 2.4 years. The uneven gain of education attainment reflects the different productivity growth rate across China. Although, once provinces with strong heavy industries, Jilin, Liaoning, and Heilongjiang provinces had long experienced low growth rate in the last 20 years.

The education attainment distribution across age profile may provide more interesting information. From Figure 12-8, we find that the average education attainment increases quickly across age. In workers older than 38, those who have a college education or more is only 10%. But for the cohort who was 20 years old in 2010, the share increased to 27%. The increasing share of highly educated population provides outstanding workers for the growing demand of high productivity enterprise, and somehow offsets the shrinking labor trend.

Another feature of the transforming labor market is the changing of returns to education. Zhang *et al.* (2005) find an increasing return of education relative to low education labor. An additional year of schooling increased annual income by 4.0% in 1988 and by 10.2% in 2001. However, we found that the return of education began to stagnate. Using CHIP data, we find that an additional year of schooling increased annual income by 10.4% in 2002 and 10.2% in 2008. In 2011, the return to education further decreased to 9.4% (see Table 12-11).

Table 12-11: Returns to education, 1988 to 2011.

Year	Return to education	Year	Return to education
1988	4	1997	6.7
1989	4.6	1998	8.1
1990	4.7	1999	9.9
1991	4.3	2000	10.1
1992	4.7	2001	10.2
1993	5.2	2002	10.4*
1994	7.3	2007	10.2*
1995	6.7	2011	9.4**
1996	6.8		

*CHIPS 2002 and 2007.
**CHFS 2011, other from Zhang et al. (2005).

Table 12-11 somehow shows the fact that an expanding supply of highly educated labor will decrease the marginal return of highly educated labor relative to less educated labor when the output in China is mainly composed of labor-intensive industry rather than skill-intensive industry. A skill-biased technology change should be expected in China to sustain the high return of education.

4.2 Rural–Urban Migrants: Education and Wage

In the last 10 years, the wage and education structure of rural–urban migrants experienced large changes. We do not have the detailed education data of rural–urban migrants in the 2010 census, but we can use the education structure of non-*hukou* migrants from township or villagers' Committee of town as a similar proxy; see Table 12-12 to check the data in 2000 and 2005.

We find that the share of highly educated migrants is overestimated in the table of migrants from township or villager's Committee of Town. The degree of overestimation is lower in 2005 than in 2000, partly because the column of migrants from township or villager's Committee of Town only includes the migrants in a 5-year measure, and the average education attainment increased fast in 2000. This means if we use the education structure of migrants from township or villager's Committee of Town in 2010, we will get an overestimated number of highly educated people.

Table 12-12: Comparison of the education structure of rural–urban migrants or migrants from township/villager's committee of town.

	2000		2005		2010
	Rural–urban migrants	Migrants from township/villager's Committee of town	Rural–urban migrants	Migrants from township/villager's Committee of town	Migrants from township/villager's Committee of town
No schooling	5.85	4.69	4.86	4.96	2.47
Primary school	26.56	26.28	24.09	24.79	20.29
Junior high school	51.59	49.48	53.19	51.44	48.34
High school	15.17	16.27	15.59	15.82	19.78
College/ Undergraduate or above	0.81	3.24	2.27	2.99	9.13

From the table we find that in 2000, 84% of the rural–urban migrants' education is lower than junior high school, but in 2010 the share dropped to 71%. With the increasing of rural–urban migrants, the population of almost all levels of education had increased since 2000. But the highly educated migrants had increased much faster than the less educated. We can find in Figure 12-9 that the population of no schooling migrants increased 7%, almost no growth, while the population of high school increased by 232%, and the college/undergraduate or above share increased by 2800%.

Table 12-13 gives a direct impression on the population of rural–urban migrants and the residents in rural areas of each education level. We can find that as the education level increases, the migration rate increases. The growth of the migration rate is higher in highly educated population across time, too. The structure of education in rural areas changed a lot since 2000. Similar to the pattern of rural–urban migrants, the rural population with or under primary school decreased, while the population with college or higher diploma tripled.

The uneven growth of the rural–urban migrants of each education level comes along with a reverse growth mode of their wage. The highly educated rural–urban migrants endure a low wage growth rate in the last 10 years,

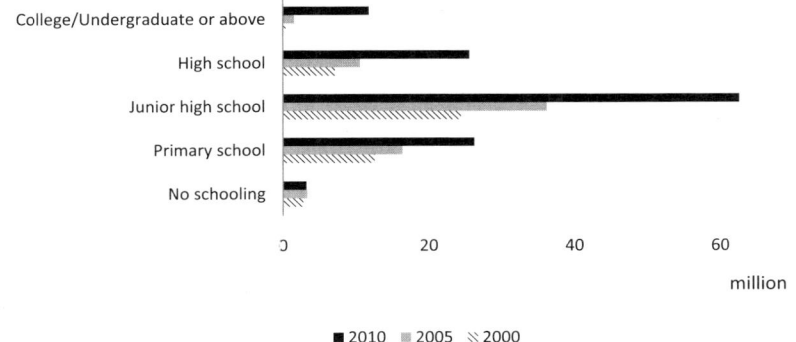

Figure 12-9: Rural–urban migrants by education level.

Table 12-13: Rural–urban migrants and rural residents by each education level (thousands).

	2000		2005		2010	
	Rural–urban migrants	Stay in rural	Rural–urban migrants	Stay in rural	Rural–urban migrants	Stay in rural
No schooling	2,281	85,987	2,722	91,315	2,458	44,175
Primary school	10,367	333,589	13,499	270,133	20,207	232,068
Junior high school	20,133	260,249	29,799	255,132	48,149	278,312
High school	5,919	41,561	8,736	41,856	19,696	47,100
College/ Undergraduate or above	312	3,792	1,273	5,032	9,090	12,553

Notes: The rural population by each education level in 2000 and 2010 data was directly drawn from Table 12-4-1c in each tabulation. The 2005 data was calculated from the Table 12-4-1c data and the sampling rate was 1.31%.

while the less educated migrants' wage increased fast. We have a unique dataset to illustrate this trend.

The National Population and Family Planning Commission of China conducted a survey called "Current Monitoring of Migrant Population" every year from 2009. The survey covered five provinces in 2009, and covered all 31 provinces from then on. The survey includes the personal information, the employment status, and some information on their family members. In 2012, 150,000 migrants aged from 15 to 59 were covered in this survey.

Some municipalities and prefectures receive more migrants than others. In the 2010 census, the migrants in Beijing/Shanghai/Guangzhou were 7.044 million, 8.977 million and 5.418 million about 40% of their all populations, and 12.5% of the out-of-county migrants of all country.

The survey has some more detailed questions in Beijing, Shanghai, and Guangzhou. In these three cities, the survey asks the migrants about their wage history. The wage history includes three questions.

(1) The monthly wage of the last job before the migrant inflows.
(2) The monthly wage of the first job after the migrant inflows.
(3) The monthly wage of the recent job.

From the monthly wage of the first job after the migrant inflows, we capture the wage growth history of the migrants in the last 10 years. Figures 12-10–12-12 illustrate the wage profile of Shanghai/Beijing and Guangzhou. In Figure 12-10, we can find a significant disparity between the wage growth rate of less educated migrants and highly educated migrants.

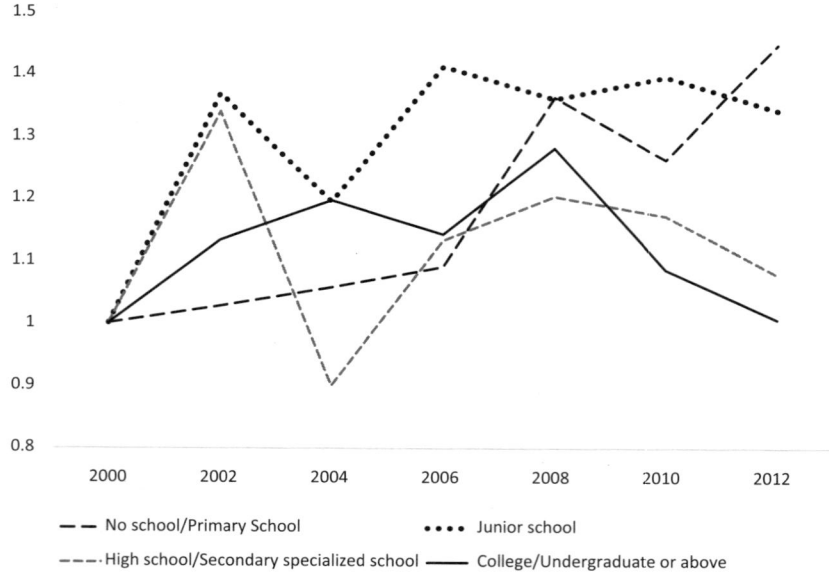

Figure 12-10: Monthly wage of first job in Shanghai, proportion relative to 2000.

The migrants who came to Shanghai in 2000 or 2001 without schooling or with primary school got their first job in Shanghai, they earned an average monthly wage of 1,302 yuan. But for the migrants who came to Shanghai in 2012, the monthly wage of their first job increased to 1,880 yuan, about 44% higher. But we cannot find a similar wage increase pattern in the highly educated migrants. The first job's monthly wage of college/undergraduate or above educated migrants increases much slower than the less educated migrants, and with more fluctuations. In 2001 to 2002, the first job's monthly wage of college/undergraduate or above educated migrants was 3,073 yuan. It increased to 3,900 yuan in the interval of 2007 to 2008, and then decreased to 3,090 yuan in 2012. It means that a fresh undergraduate migrant in Shanghai who gets his job in 2012 will earn as much as the seniors who graduated 12 years ago. Similar patterns can be found in Beijing.

In Guangzhou, the pattern differs; the high school/secondary specialized school migrants get the fastest first-job monthly wage growth, though the highest educated migrants still receives the lowest first-job monthly wage growth.

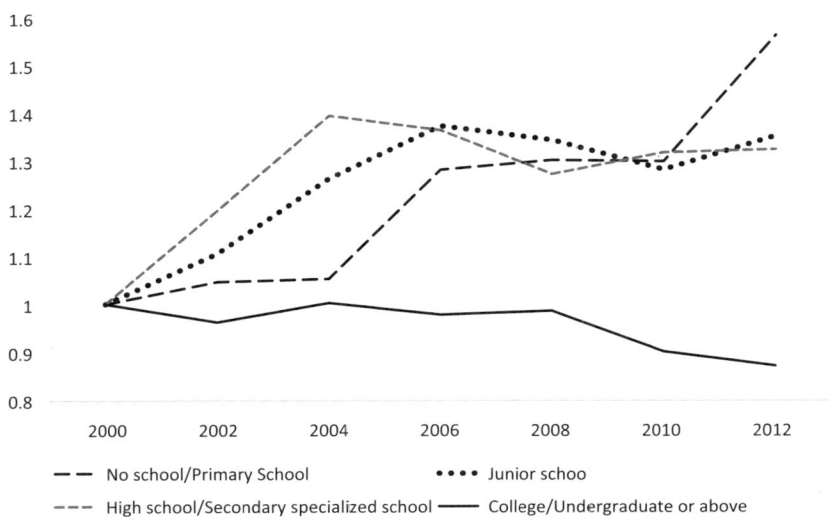

Figure 12-11: Monthly wage of first job in Beijing, proportion relative to 2000.

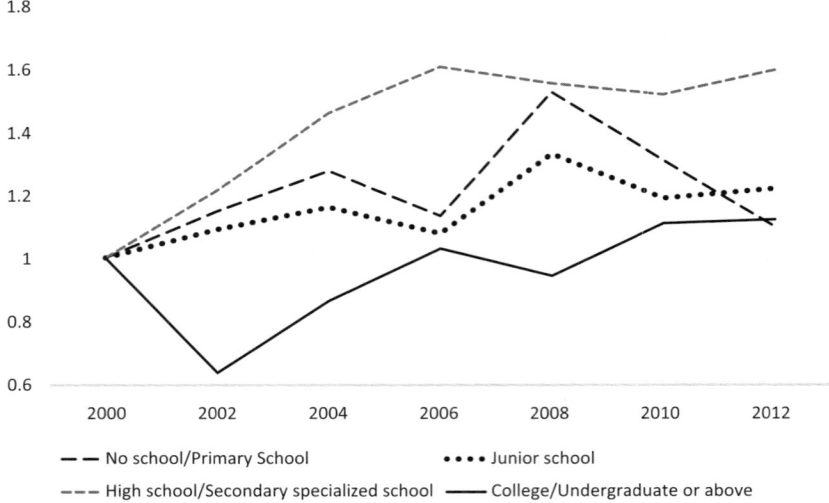

Figure 12-12: Monthly wage of first job in Guangzhou, proportion relative to 2000.

Combining the supply and wage growth rate of migrants of each education level, we can easily find some important facts:

1. As the less-educated rural population decreased and their migration rate increased slightly, the unexpected low growth rate of low skilled labor supply may partly lead to a high wage growth rate.
2. The expansion of high school may lead to a sharp growth of the supply in the highly educated population, along with the stagnation of their wage.

5. CONCLUSION

Using different data sources, this chapter focuses on the rural–urban migration issue, and tries to give a clear picture on the speed/structure/scale/education/wage of rural–urban migrants.

The complexity of definitions of migrants and the unavailability of *hukou* migrants make it impossible for the former literatures to calculate the speed of rural–urban migrants. Combined with the *hukou* migrants' information in CGSS data, this chapter analyzes the structure of migrants. We find that in the 2000s, about 90 million people had migrated from rural to urban regions, which accounted for 43.6% of the total increase in urban population. The reclassified people take about 42.5%, and the natural increase is 13.9%.

Second, using the reported number of rural workers by NBS and some assumptions from the last two censuses, this chapter gives an accurate scale of the rural–urban migrants in China. We also find that with the migration from rural to urban areas, about 30% of the young rural–urban migrants come from rural areas, and meanwhile nearly 30% of the population who once lived in rural regions had migrated to urban regions. The probability of working on-farm dropped quickly across age and time. The probability of population aged 16–19 who once lived in rural regions working on-farm was 9% in 2010, while in 2000 the number was 36%.

Finally, the chapter focuses on the education structure and the wage information of rural–urban migrants. Two facts were found in this analysis: (1) The shrinking of the less educated rural population and the low increase of their migration rate, contrary to the quick expansion of highly educated rural population whose migration rate increased from 7.6% to 42%. (2) Using a unique dataset that covers the most important inflow cities, stagnation can be found in the wages of highly educated migrants, while the wages of less educated migrants grew fast.

REFERENCES

Cai, F. and Du, Y. (2011). Wage increases, wage convergence, and the Lewis turning point in China. *China Economic Review*, 22(4): 601–610.

Cai, F. and Wang, M. (2008). A counterfactual analysis on unlimited surplus labor in rural China. *China & World Economy*, 16(1): 51–65.

Chan, K. W. (2011). *Internal Migration in China: Trends, Geography and Policies*. Population Distribution, Urbanization, Internal Migration and Development: An International Perspective.

Chan, K. W. (2012). Crossing the 50 percent population Rubicon: Can China urbanize to prosperity? *Eurasian Geography and Economics*, 53(1): 63–86.

Chan, K. W. and Hu, Y. (2003). Urbanization in China in the 1990s: New definition, different series, and revised trends. *The China Review*, 3(2): 49–71.

Chan, K. W., Liu, T. and Yang, Y. (1999). *Hukou* and non-*hukou* migrations in China: comparisons and contrasts. *International Journal of Population Geography*, 5(6): 425–435.

Chen, Q. and Song, Z. (2013). Facing Aging: Can Urbanization Help? *Financial Research*, 2013(6): 1–15.

Golley, Jane and Xin Meng (2011). Has China run out of surplus labour? *China Economic Review*, 22(4): 555–572.

Goodkind, D. M. (2004). China's missing children: The 2000 census underreporting surprise. *Population Studies*, 58(3): 281–295.

Knight, J., Deng, Q. and Li, S. (2011). The puzzle of migrant labour shortage and rural labour surplus in China. *China Economic Review*, 22(4): 585–600.

Kong, Sherry Tao, Meng, Xin and Zhang, Dandan (2010). The global financial crisis and rural–urban migration, Paper presented at the Beijing Forum.

Li, Hongbin, Lei, Li, Binzhen Wu and Yanyan Xiong (2012). The end of cheap Chinese labor. *The Journal of Economic Perspectives*, 26(4): 57–74.

Meng, X. (2012). Labor market outcomes and reforms in China. *Journal of Economic Perspectives*, 26(4): 75–101.

Retherford, R. D., Choe, M. K., Chen, J., Li, X. R. and Cui, H. Y. (2005). How far has fertility in China really declined? *Population and Development Review*, 31(1): 57–84.

Rozelle, S., Huang, J. and Zhang, L. (2008). China's labor transition and future educational challenges. Unpublished paper, Stanford University. http://scid.stanford.edu/group/siepr/cgi-bin/scid.

Song, Z., Storesletten, Kjetil, Wang, Yikai and Fabrizio, Zilibotti (2012). Sharing high growth across generations: Pensions and demographic transition in China. Biblioteca universitaria di Lugano (University Library of Lugano).

Wang, F. (2004). The composition of urban population growth between 4th census and 5th census. *Population Research*, 3: 60–67.

Wang, X., Huang, J. and Zhang, L. (2011). The rise of migration and the fall of self employment in rural China's labor market. *China Economic Review*, 22(4): 573–584.

Zhang, G. and Zhao, Z. (2006). Reexamining China's fertility puzzle: Data collection and quality over the last two decades. *Population and Development Review*, 32(2): 293–321.

Zhang, Junsen, Yaohui Zhao, Albert Park and Xiaoqing Song (2005). Economic returns to schooling in urban China, 1988 to 2001. *Journal of Comparative Economics*, 33: 730–752.

Zhang, W. M. and Cui, H. Y. (2003). Estimation on the accuracy of China's 2000 census. *Population Research (In Chinese)*, 27(4): 25–35.

Chapter 13
Social Justice and Intergenerational Income Mobility

Lin Chen*

Department of Social Sciences, Fudan University

1. INTRODUCTION

Intergenerational income mobility is the extent to which children's income depends on their father's. A moderate, intergenerational income mobility is important in promoting both social equality and economic development. On the one hand, it is a measure of equality as it reflects the dynamic income distribution and the opportunity inequality. On the other hand, with the growing importance of tertiary industry and environmental protection, human capital is becoming more and more crucial to economic development in the future. Higher intergenerational income mobility can promote the quality and quantity of a nation's human capital by helping poor children to achieve their full potential, improving the matching efficiency of the labor market, and providing an incentive for hard work and human capital investment.

Meanwhile, with the growing income gap and the social stability problem being more and more important, structural transition and change of the mode of economic growth is now becoming a pressing task of the China's economy. Higher intergenerational income mobility cannot only benefit economic growth but also alleviate the social pressure caused by the income inequality. The family planning policy and the extraordinary importance of

---

*The author gratefully acknowledges the support of the National Science Foundation of China (71203138).

children's welfare in Chinese traditional culture make intergenerational mobility more significant in China.

However, there are signs that the intergenerational mobility is showing a deteriorating turn recently. Both the public and governmental presses have joined in the hot discussion of intergenerational social and economic inheritance. This chapter is thus aimed at studying the intergenerational income mobility in China and providing possible policy recommendations. Compared with existing literature, we focus on the following work, which is still not perfectly solved in the current discussion.

First, we do a thorough literature review on intergenerational income mobility from the perspective of measurement, mechanism, influence, and policies. *The Handbook of Labor Economics* has done two well-organized reviews in 1999 and 2011, though all of them neglect the influences and policies. This paper is thus a more comprehensive review and the first of its kind in China.

Second, we concisely calculate the trend and extent of the intergenerational income mobility in China, which can contribute to the current debate on this issue. Using the labor income as the main statistic, and based on a careful selection of the effective sample, we find a rising mobility from 1988 to 1995 and a decreasing trend afterwards. The intergenerational income mobility will amount to above 0.6 after taking into consideration the measurement bias caused by using the single-year income instead of permanent income, which is relatively high in comparison with other countries.

Third, we decomposed the intergenerational income mobility in China using empirical and statistical methods. The results suggest that human capital, social capital, and wealth all have a big contribution in intergenerational income transmission in China, with housing assets and financial assets being the most important factors.

Finally, we suggest building a well-rounded policy system to improve the intergenerational mobility in China, including a sound public education system and a good family education atmosphere, well-provided basic public goods, as well as promoting education equality, eliminating the labor market segment, and deepening the market-oriented reform.

In all, we build a well-rounded economic research framework for intergenerational income mobility, and carry out empirical analysis using Chinese micro data. However, the exact causal mechanism of intergenerational mobility and the corresponding public policy still remains as a puzzle that is quite challenging and important for future research.

2. THE IMPORTANCE OF ENHANCING SOCIAL MOBILITY

2.1 Intergenerational Income Mobility and Justice

In his celebrated work *A Theory of Justice*, John Rawls begins with the sentence, "Justice is the first virtue of a social system, as is true of the first virtue of an ideological system." This book then laid the foundation for modern political philosophy of justice. Meanwhile, according to the research report by the Institute of the Nervous System and Human Behavior at UCLA, the area in the human brain that deals with equality is quite similar to the area dealing with food in the brain of laboratory mice, which shows justice and equality are basic needs of human beings.

Intergenerational income mobility is an index that measures justice and opportunity equality. On the one hand, it shows the domestic income distribution; on the other hand, it shows opportunity inequality from the perspective of family background, which is one of the most important parts of opportunities that influence a person's success and violates the principle of justice.

In April 2011, the UK government published its 86-page Report, *Opening Doors, Breaking Barriers: A Strategy for Social Mobility*, which is aimed at enhancing opportunity equality. It points out that justice can be best illustrated in the distribution of opportunity. Meanwhile, though solving the problem of fiscal deficit is the most urgent task for the government, their fundamental goal and value is to reduce the opportunity gap and opportunity deficit, and thus to build an open and liberal society.

2.2 Intergenerational Income Mobility and Economic Efficiency

The importance of human capital for economic growth makes intergenerational income mobility relevant to economic efficiency. Since the industrial revolution, energy and capital has been the core driving force for modern economic growth. However, with the increasing status of the service industry and the need for environmental protection, human capital is now becoming more and more important for future growth. Intergenerational income mobility can enhance both the quantity and quality of a society:

First, enhancing intergenerational income mobility can decrease the adverse effect of family background on poor children's development. Helping every child to fully explore their potential is the key to human capital accumulation. Research by developmental psychologists has shown that an individual's basic cognitive ability is formed at the age of 0 to 6, which make the early childhood period very important to a person's later development. However, children from poor families may be hindered from fully exploring their potential due to the lack of material support. All these make high intergenerational mobility relevant for enhancing the human capital accumulation.

Second, high intergenerational income mobility can provide the expectation that hard work will lead to success, which can serve as a good incentive for human capital accumulation and highly qualified human resources. On the contrary, a rigid social structure and a large influence of family background on success will lead to the negative feeling that neither hard work nor human capital accumulation can help one to succeed. This will, in turn, decrease the quality of human capital.

Finally, matching efficiency between job position and workers is an important premise of a well-functioning labor market. High intergenerational persistence may indicate that there is mismatch in the labor market and also for educational resources. Thus, improving intergenerational income mobility can greatly increase the efficient usage of human capital.

2.3 Intergenerational Income Mobility and the Economic Transition in China

China now faces the urgent task of economic and social transition. On the one hand, China has become one of the most influential economies after rapidly growing over the past 30 years. In 2010, China's GDP exceeded that of Japan and became the second largest economy in the world. Its GDP per capita reached 4,400 and it entered the rank of middle-income countries. However, on the other hand, the high growth driven by exports and public investment are also facing great challenges. Exports that rely on the lower-end manufactures are decreasing after the recent financial crisis, and public investment by the local government also brought the problem of environmental destruction and high local debt. Meanwhile, domestic consumption is difficult to enhance, given the low labor share and inadequate social welfare system.

Besides, due to the urban–rural inequality and the industrial monopoly in the factor markets, the income gap is becoming larger. According to Ravallion and Chen (2007), the Gini coefficient rose from 0.3 to 0.45 from 1981 to 2001, and further rose to 0.52 in the latest data released by the UN. Thus, the problem of income inequality has become more and more severe in China.

With this background, research on intergenerational income mobility is important for the future development of China. First, enhancing intergenerational income mobility can help the transition of economic growth mode and getting out of the middle-income trap. The main feature of China's economy is its large population. The high quality and quantity of human capital can transform this feature to a big advantage, which is exactly in accordance with the improvement of intergenerational income mobility.

Second, enhancing intergenerational income mobility can help to relieve the social pressure brought by the deepening income gap. Income gap only demonstrates the static income distribution in a society. Even if two societies have the same Gini coefficient, different intergenerational mobility will make them quite different in the meaning of efficiency and equality. Indeed, the income gap brought by differences of talent and working effort is not just a good incentive system, but also will not bring significant redistributive demand (Piketty, 1995; Benabou and Ok, 2001). It is the income gap brought by opportunity inequality that should be diminished by public policy. Enhancing intergenerational mobility is an important way to ensure opportunity equality.

Finally, the importance of offspring set by traditional Chinese culture makes the study of intergenerational mobility particularly important for China. And this culture is much more emphasized after the family planning policy is carried out. In fact, the altruism toward offspring is one of the driving forces for the development of human society. High intergenerational mobility indicates that children from less advantaged families can have high expectation of gaining success, as long as they invest in their human capital and work hard. This will make the parents more tolerant of the current income gap and increase their investment in their children's human capital. This will in turn help relieve the social pressure and benefit economic growth in the country.

However, the intergenerational mobility is under threat now in China. There has been a lot of talk about the phenomenon of the second generation of the rich and of the governors. Some data investigation has also proved the importance of family background in an individual's success. These factors make the problem of intergenerational income mobility important.

3. THE INTERGENERATIONAL INCOME MOBILITY IN CHINA

The economic research on intergenerational income mobility is built on the framework of family economics and human capital investment. Suppose a family has one parent and one child, its utility depends on the parental consumption and offspring income. The income of the family depends on the parent's income, which should be split between the parent's consumption and the investment in the child's human capital. Becker and Tomes use the following model to express this problem:

$$\begin{aligned} \max \ & U_i = (1-\alpha)\log C_{0i} + \alpha \log y_{1i} \\ s.t. \ & y_{0i} = C_{0i} + I_{0i} \\ & y_{1i} = (1+r)I_{0i} + E_{1i} \end{aligned} \quad (13\text{-}1)$$

The FOC solves,

$$y_{1i} = \tilde{\beta} y_{oi} + \alpha E_{1i}. \quad (13\text{-}2)$$

The coefficient $\tilde{\beta}$ is called the Intergenerational Income Elasticity (IIE) and measures the degree of intergenerational income mobility in a given society. This model is also called the Galton–Becker–Solon Equation, as Galton first put forward this method, Becker and Tomes (1979) first used it to study the intergenerational income mobility, and Solon (2004) gave a detailed analysis of the factors influencing the IIE. In this section, this model is used to demonstrate the trend and amount of the intergenerational income mobility in China. As there is no publicly available lifetime income data in China, we use annual data to calculate the benchmark IIE.

3.1 The Trend of Intergenerational Income Mobility in China

The data used in this study is from the Chinese Household Income Project Series (CHIPS, 1988, 1995, 2002), as well as the China General Social Survey (CGSS, 2006).

CHIPS is organized by the State Statistical Bureau and the Chinese Academy of Social Sciences with the purpose of measuring and estimating the distribution of income in both rural and urban areas of China. Every year, the data collection consists of two distinct samples of the urban and rural population that were selected from significantly larger samples drawn by the State Statistical Bureau. It is generally considered as the most comprehensive, publicly available, and strict micro data on Chinese income. The survey has now been carried out for four rounds, 1988, 1995, 2002, and 2007, with the data for the first three rounds being public and thus being the main data we used.

CGSS is organized by Renmin University of China and Hong Kong University of Science and Technology with the sample drawn from the fifth national population census in 2000 using a stratified sampling method. The survey has been carried out for three rounds, 2003, 2005, and 2006, with each round collecting data for the previous year. We use the last round as a complement to CHIPS because it is the latest publicly available micro income data in China and also the only one having information on both generation's income in the three rounds of CGSS.

The "income" in this study refers to the individual wage income including cash and item subsidies, as this is the most consistent and detailed data we can get from CHIPS. The sample is built in the following steps: First, to be in accordance with the relevant researches on OECD countries, we choose the father as the parent in the family, while sons and daughters are both included; second, we delete those individuals who are less than 20 years old or more than 65 years old, and also those who are not working, such as students and retirees; third, we choose the parent–child pairs who have all the information we need, and the age gap between the two generations is less than 10 years; finally, we delete those pairs whose parent or child is in the top or bottom 1% of the sample. This gives us the final sample used in the following estimation, with the main descriptive statistics shown in Table 13-1.

Table 13-1: Descriptive statistics for the time trend.

Mean (std. dev.)	1988	1995	2002	2005
Father				
Income	8.58	8.79	8.16	8.60
	(0.53)	(0.84)	(1.48)	(0.95)
Age	52.36	52.23	52.09	58.14
	(4.36)	(4.38)	(4.55)	(4.81)
Children				
=1 for son	0.53	0.57	0.62	0.46
	(0.50)	(0.49)	(0.48)	(0.50)
Income	7.94	8.31	8.32	9.34
	(0.60)	(0.76)	(0.99)	(0.68)
Age	23.36	23.22	24.39	32.13
	(2.93)	(2.54)	(3.52)	(5.37)
Observations	1891	944	1483	570

Note: All the income variables are the log values, and have been adjusted to the 2002 level by provincial CPI.

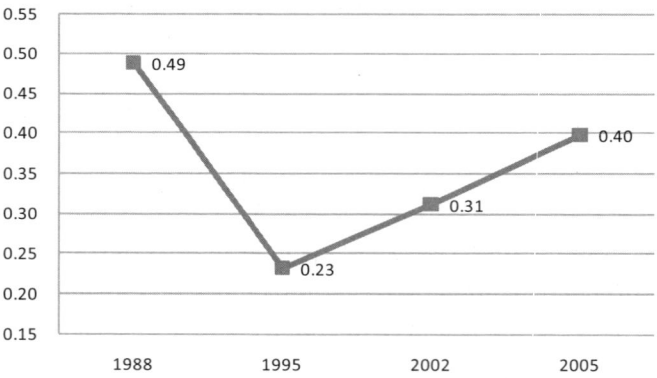

Figure 13-1: The trend of IIE in China (1988–2005, total).

Figure 13-1 shows the IIE calculated separately for the four years in the sample. It suggests a "V" shape of the IIE from 1988 to 2005. That is, the intergenerational income mobility is first enhanced and then decreased in this period.

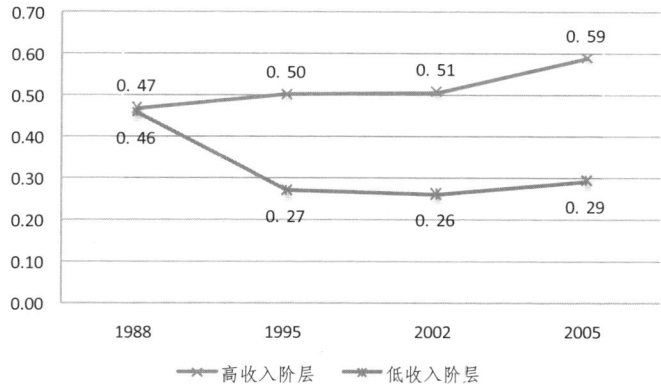

Figure 13-2: The trend of IIE in China (1988–2005, high- and low-income group).

3.2 The Intergenerational Income Mobility for High and Low Income Group

We then separate the total sample into high and low income group according to the median income in the rural and urban area. The separately calculated IIE is then shown in Figure 13-2. It can be seen that the IIE for different income groups has little difference in 1988, and then clearly diverges afterward. The IIE for high-income groups remains high and showed an increasing trend, while the IIE for low-income groups sees a significant drop and then stays low. This suggests the improvement for the intergenerational income mobility shown in Figure 13-1 is largely driven by the changes in the low-income group.

This result is not very surprising. In the last decade of the 20th century, the transition to a more market-oriented economy has provided much opportunity for the offspring from the low-income families. With the establishment of the compulsory education system and the flourishing manufacturing industry, many young people from the low-income families find a way to increase their income, which keeps the IIE low for this group. However, the reform and opening up process in China is also characteristic of the "dual-track" approach, which threatens little of the interest for the high-income group, which makes the IIE high for this group.

In the 21st century, the reform has been slowing down, which shrinks the opportunity for low-income children, and those from high-income families are more and more inclined to benefit from their parents' high income and social networks. All these make the IIE show an upward trend in the new century. Chen et al. (2010) built a theoretical model to show that it is a prerequisite for the peaceful transition in China to make the elites benefit from the reform, and letting their children inherit their status as elites is just one of this benefits.

4. THE ESTIMATION BIAS IN THE CALCULATION OF IIE IN CHINA

4.1 The Sources of the Bias

In the above sector, we use annual data to calculate the IIE, which will lead to an estimation bias as annual income ($y_{1,t}$ and $y_{0,t}$) will deviate from the lifetime income (y_1 and y_0) generally. This bias is determined by the nature of the parameters in the following model,

$$y_{1,t} = \gamma_{1,t} y_1 + v_{1,t}. \quad (13\text{-}3)$$

$$y_{0,t} = \gamma_{0,t} y_0 + v_{0,t}. \quad (13\text{-}4)$$

First, when $\gamma_{0,t} = \gamma_{1,t} = 1$, the bias is mainly caused by the transitory income ($v_{1,t}$ and $v_{0,t}$). Under this assumption, it can be proved that:

(1) The transitory shock to the children's income, and to the father's income, which is not correlated with the annual income observation, will not make the estimated IIE biased or inefficient.

(2) Under the Classical Error-in-Variables Assumption (CEV), the estimated IIE (β^{CEV}) will be biased downward,

$$p \lim \beta^{CEV} = \beta \lambda^{CEV} = \beta \frac{\sigma_{y_0}^2}{\sigma_{y_0}^2 + \sigma_{v_0}^2} < \beta. \quad (13\text{-}5)$$

(3) Under the CEV, if we use the average parental income from T years, the estimated IIE ($\beta^{CEV,T}$) will suffer less bias than β^{CEV}, as is shown

in Equation (13-6). λ is the reliability ratio. The larger λ is, the lower the bias will be.

$$p \lim \beta^{CEV,T} = \beta \lambda^{CEV,T} = \beta \frac{\sigma_{y_0}^2}{\sigma_{y_0}^2 + (\sigma_{v_0}^2/T)} < \beta, \text{ 且 } \lambda^{CEV,T} > \lambda^{CEV}. \tag{13-6}$$

(4) If the transitory income of father is not correlated to the lifetime income and follows the AR(1) process with the autoregressive coefficient δ, then the bias is more complicated,

$$p \lim \beta^{AR(1)} = \beta \lambda^{AR(1)} = \beta \frac{\sigma_{y_0}^2}{\sigma_{y_0}^2 + \alpha(\sigma_{v_0}^2/T)} < \beta. \tag{13-7a}$$

$$\alpha = 1 + 2\delta \frac{T - ((1 - \delta^T)/(1 - \delta))}{T(1 - \delta)}. \tag{13-7b}$$

Second, if the assumption that $\gamma_{0,t} = \gamma_{1,t} = 1$ does not hold, then the bias will vary with the age at which the income comes, and thus is called life cycle bias. Then,

(5) The measurement error in the children's income will also cause a bias in IIE, and the bias equals the regression coefficient of the children's lifetime income on the annual income, as is shown in Equation (13-8).

$$p \lim \beta^{LCY,CHILD} = \beta \lambda^{LCY,CHILD} = \beta \gamma_{1,t}. \tag{13-8}$$

(6) The measurement error in the parental income will also cause a bias in IIE, and this bias equals the regression coefficient of the parental annual income on the lifetime income, as is shown in Equation (13-9).

$$p \lim \beta^{LCY,FATHER} = \beta \lambda^{LCY,FATHER} = \beta \theta_{0,t}. \tag{13-9}$$

4.2 Correction of the Bias in the Estimation of IIE in China

We thus use the above method to check and correct the bias in the estimation of IIE in China. The data used in this section come from the retrospective income for the periods 1990–1995 and 1998–2002 in the urban area in CHIPS. All the other selection criteria are the same as those in Part 3.1. Table 13-2 reports the descriptive statistics.

Table 13-2: Descriptive statistics for the measurement error.

	1990–1995		1998–2002	
	Mean	Std. dev.	Mean	Std. dev.
Children				
Income in 1995 (2002)	8.264	0.765	8.790	0.819
Age in 1995 (2002)	23.334	2.693	24.854	3.080
Father				
Income in 1995 (2002)	9.033	0.487	9.351	0.573
Age in 1995 (2002)	52.902	4.427	53.071	3.736
Income in 1994 (2001)	8.936	0.489	9.249	0.613
Income in 1993 (2000)	8.968	0.489	9.224	0.538
Income in 1992 (1999)	8.940	0.513	9.149	0.565
Income in 1991 (1998)	8.880	0.513	9.088	0.529
Income in 1990 (1997)	8.797	0.514	—	—
Number of Observations	649		847	

Note: All the income variables are the log values, and have been adjusted to the 2002 level by provincial CPI.

We use this data to estimate the bias in Equation (13-7), with the results shown in Table 13-3.

The coefficient of reliability ranges from 0.739 to 0.933 when we use the 6-year average of 1990–1995, which means the IIE will be downwardly estimated by 6.7% to 26.1%. If we further assume the autocorrelation coefficient to be 0.5, then the real IIE should be 0.774 (0.663/0.857). Similarly, we can get the real IIE for 1998–2002 to be 0.539 (0.485/0.900).

Table 13-4 demonstrates our estimation for the coefficient of reliability when taking into account the life cycle bias in the father's income. As the average age in our sample is around 53, thus the reliability ratio in 1995 and 2002 should be 0.788 and 0.733 separately, which means the real IIE should be 0.841 and 0.662 respectively for the two periods.

Similarly, Table 13-5 demonstrates our estimation for the coefficient of reliability when taking into account the life cycle bias in the children's income. As the average age in our sample is around 23 and 25 for 1995 and 2002, the reliability ratio in 1995 and 2002 should be 0.777 and 0.812, respectively. This means the real IIE should be 0.853 and 0.597, respectively, for the two periods.

Table 13-3: Reliability ratio for the persistent transitory income bias ($\lambda^{AR(1)}$).

Number of years averaged	1995				
	$\delta = 0.0$	$\delta = 0.3$	$\delta = 0.5$	$\delta = 0.7$	$\delta = 0.9$
1	0.700	0.700	0.700	0.700	0.700
2	0.824	0.782	0.757	0.733	0.711
3	0.875	0.827	0.792	0.756	0.719
4	0.903	0.857	0.819	0.775	0.726
5	0.921	0.879	0.840	0.791	0.733
6	**0.933**	**0.894**	**0.857**	**0.806**	**0.739**
7	0.942	0.907	0.870	0.818	0.745
8	0.949	0.916	0.882	0.830	0.751
9	0.955	0.924	0.891	0.840	0.757
10	0.959	0.931	0.900	0.849	0.762

Number of years averaged	2002				
	$\delta = 0.0$	$\delta = 0.3$	$\delta = 0.5$	$\delta = 0.7$	$\delta = 0.9$
1	0.800	0.800	0.800	0.800	0.800
2	0.889	0.860	0.842	0.825	0.808
3	0.923	0.892	0.867	0.842	0.814
4	0.941	0.911	0.886	0.855	0.819
5	**0.952**	**0.925**	**0.900**	**0.867**	**0.824**
6	0.960	0.936	0.911	0.877	0.829
7	0.966	0.943	0.920	0.885	0.834
8	0.970	0.949	0.927	0.893	0.838
9	0.973	0.954	0.934	0.900	0.842
10	0.976	0.958	0.939	0.906	0.846

In all, if we take the largest estimation, the IIE for Urban China in the periods 1990–1995 and 1998–2002 should be 0.853 and 0.662. This is similar to the results by Gong *et al.* (2012), which use the administrative data from the Bureau of Statistics of China.

4.3 IIE in China Compared to Other Countries

Based on current IIE estimations in the research aimed at the international comparison, Table 13-6 collects the IIE for different countries. We can see that the IIE in China is among the highest group after correcting for the measurement error.

Table 13-4: Reliability ratio for the life cycle bias in father's income ($\lambda^{LCY,FATHER}$).

		1995			2002	
Age	Mean	Discount rate = 0.1	Discount rate = 0.9	Mean	Discount rate = 0.1	Discount rate = 0.9
45	0.724	0.726	0.596	0.712	0.711	0.737
46	0.754	0.756	0.647	0.712	0.711	0.737
47	0.752	0.754	0.650	0.610	0.611	0.669
48	0.717	0.718	0.645	0.860	0.859	0.871
49	0.712	0.713	0.661	0.813	0.813	0.817
50	0.797	0.798	0.735	0.707	0.707	0.705
51	0.786	0.786	0.726	0.766	0.765	0.797
52	0.691	0.692	0.662	0.826	0.822	0.824
53	**0.788**	**0.789**	**0.728**	**0.733**	**0.733**	**0.757**
54	0.741	0.742	0.683	0.732	0.729	0.751
55	0.693	0.695	0.588	0.757	0.752	0.803
56	0.799	0.799	0.787	0.766	0.764	0.796

Note: All the coefficients are significant at the level of 0.01.

Table 13-5: Reliability ratio for the life cycle bias in children's income ($\lambda^{LCY,CHILD}$).

		1995			2002	
Age	Mean	Discount rate = 0.1	Discount rate = 0.9	Mean	Discount rate = 0.1	Discount rate = 0.9
20	0.579	0.498	0.738	0.640	0.603	0.430
21	0.597	0.502	0.786	0.665	0.636	0.563
22	0.615	0.509	0.804	0.642	0.611	0.559
23	**0.777**	**0.575**	**0.858**	0.625	0.590	0.483
24	0.628	0.527	0.805	0.700	0.668	0.554
25	0.721	0.605	0.914	**0.812**	**0.778**	**0.701**
28	0.855	0.773	0.985	0.890	0.873	0.867

Note: All the coefficients are significant at the level of 0.01.

5. THE MECHANISM OF THE INTERGENERATIONAL INCOME MOBILITY IN CHINA

5.1 The Theoretical Problem in Finding the Causal Relationship

In order to discuss the mechanisms of intergenerational income mobility more clearly, we present here again the theoretical model of

Table 13-6: IIE estimation for different countries.

	Blanden (2011)	Nunez and Miranda (2010)	Corak (2006)	Solon (2002)	Lefranc et al. (2008)	Irene Ng (2007)	Jantti et al. (2006)	Mean
US	0.41	0.45–0.53	0.47	—	—	—	0.52	0.48
UK	0.37	0.39–0.59	0.5	0.42–0.57	—	—	0.31	0.45
Italy	0.33	0.48	—	—	—	—	—	0.41
France	0.32	—	0.41	—	0.47	—	—	0.40
Norway	0.25	—	0.17	—	—	—	0.16	0.19
Australia	0.25	—	—	—	—	—	—	0.25
Germany	0.24	0.34	0.32	0.11–0.34	—	—	—	0.27
Sweden	0.24	0.28	0.27	0.13–0.28	—	—	0.26	0.24
Canada	0.23	—	0.19	0.23	—	—	—	0.22
Finland	0.20	—	0.18	0.13–0.22	—	—	0.17	0.18
Denmark	0.14	—	0.15	—	—	—	0.07	0.12
Japan	—	—	—	—	0.22	—	—	0.22
Chile	0.52	—	—	—	—	—	—	0.52
Malaysia	0.54	—	—	0.26	—	—	—	0.40
Nepal	0.44	—	—	—	—	—	—	0.44
Pakistan	0.46	—	—	—	—	—	—	0.46
Singapore	—	—	—	—	0.28	0.58	—	0.43

intergenerational income mobility.

$$\max \ U_i = (1 - \alpha) \log C_{0i} + \alpha \log y_{1i}$$
$$s.t. \quad y_{0i} = C_{0i} + I_{0i} \quad (13\text{-}10)$$
$$y_{1i} = (1 + r)I_{0i} + E_{1i}$$

In this model, r is the return of the investment on children's human capital, and E_{1i} is what influences children's human capital besides parental investment. It can be decomposed to the following two parts,

$$E_{1i} = e_{1i} + \mu_{1i}. \quad (13\text{-}11)$$

In this equation, μ_{1i} is children's market luck, and e_{1i} is the endowment that will influence offspring's income in the labor market but is uncorrelated with human capital investment and luck. It includes many factors such as the ability and health inherited through genetic transmission, the reputation, network, habit, and preferences that are formed as a result of growing up in a particular family. We will then call it culture capital to distinguish it from the normal human capital that we gain through formal education. Part of this culture capital is inherited from the parents,

$$e_{1i} = \lambda e_{0i} + v_{1i}. \tag{13-12}$$

v_{1i} is endowment luck, and e_{0i} is parental endowment, λ is the degree of heritability. The FOC of the above model solves,

$$y_{1i} = \tilde{\beta} y_{0i} + \alpha \lambda e_{0i} + \alpha v_{1i} + \alpha \mu_{1i}. \tag{13-13}$$

In which $\tilde{\beta} = \alpha(1+r)$, and is the IIE calculated above. However, as the parental endowment, e_{0i} is hard to observe and is usually missing in our regression, the IIE calculated from Equation (13-13) cannot be explained causally. And due to the character of e_{0i}, it is quite difficult to get the causal explanation.

5.2 The Empirical Test to Find the Causal Relationship

The theoretical analysis gives a clear explanation of the different sources of intergenerational income mobility. However, the exact answer relies on empirical analysis. Though this is quite challenging, various attempts has been made by economists. We will make a review of current researches here.

5.2.1 Sibling (Neighborhood) effect and the importance of genes

In the early research, sibling and neighborhood effect is calculated to show the importance of the growing up environment for success, which is also used to find the reason for intergenerational mobility.

The initial studies have looked at the overall correlation between the siblings or those living in the same community. The basic idea is that if families and community upbringing have a great influence, then the income between the offspring of the same family and community will be greater compared with other randomly selected populations. Using the US data and the method of variance, researches find that coming from the same family can explain 50% of the income variance from the same family, and 10% of the income variance from the same community (Solon *et al.*, 1991; Oreopoulos, 2003).

However, sibling and neighborhood effect is just an omnibus measure representing the importance of family background and environment. Sibling effect includes not only the income of the parent, but also all the shared family factors influencing children's income. Neighborhood effect includes not only peer effect, but also the self-selection that parents made in order to choose the best environment for their children's growth. Therefore, they cannot serve as an effective way to identify the intergenerational income correlation inherent mechanism.

To further distinguish the importance of "genes" and "environment," economists have turned to study the income correlation of a variety of different types of brothers and sisters. Research in this area mainly draws on the study of "nature and nurture" disputes in psychology and behavioral genetics. The overall IQ variance is divided into three parts, namely, the genetic part, the family and environmental part, and the individual part. Based on the strict assumption of the degree of shared genetic and environmental factors for different types of brothers and sisters, the proportion of intergenerational correlation that these different parts can explain is then deduced on the sample IQ correlation of different types of brothers and sisters (Herrnstein and Murray, 1994).

In 1976, Behrman and Taubman first tried to use this method to study the mechanism for intergenerational income mobility. They suggest that genetic, environmental, and individual factors explain 52%, 5%, and 48% of the IIE respectively. More recently, Björklund *et al.* (2005) apply this method to extraordinary data in Sweden and decomposed the IIE in their sample. They got fairly similar results with the above conclusion in behavioral genetics. Genetic factors explain at least 10% (for female) to 20% (for male) of the intergenerational correlation, and individual factors at least 64%. The familial and neighborhood factors seem to be small.

Though this structural decomposition reached the ambitious goal of completely decomposing the genetic, environmental, and individual factors, it is quite hard to extend its usage due to the strict assumption and strong requirement for data. And its conclusion that environment does not matter is also greatly challenged (Sacerdote, 2008).

Later researches tried to extend these results. Björklund and Chardwick (2002) classify the child–parent pairs into six different kinds according to their biological relationship and whether they are living together. They then calculate the IIE for those different pairs. The results show that, for those children with their biological parents, the IIE falls significantly when they live a shorter time with their parents. It is 0.19 for those who are always living together, 0.16 for those who are not always and close to 0 for those who never live together. Meanwhile, the children with their non-biological parents have lower IIE, 0.07–0.13, which shows genetic factors also play an important part.

More research uses the data for adoptees. Under the assumption that adoption is a random process, there is no genetic relation between the child and the parent, and then the correlation between their incomes can be taken as the importance of environment. However, the research now has not gained consensus yet. Liu and Zeng (2009) use the PSID in the United States to show that they cannot find the importance of parental income on the adoptees' income, while Sacerdote (2002, 2007) finds the importance of genes and environment differ for different factors: Behavior such as drinking and smoking are more influenced by environment while physical characters such as overweight are more impacted by genes, and economic success like income is influenced by both. Björklund *et al.* (2006, 2007) further use the micro data with the information of both biological and non-biological parents, and find these two factors are both important and will also have an interaction between them.

In all, though much effort has been made by geneticists and economists, the exact decomposition of "nature" and "nurture" is far from being solved. More well-collected data and advanced techniques should be used to find a clear story.

5.2.2 External shocks and the importance of income

Different from the "nature" and "nurture" story, another branch of literature tries to find the relative importance of income compared to other factors. As lots of current public policies are aimed at helping the poor, the importance of material factors should be tested to gain insights of the assumptions of these policies.

The biggest difficulty lies in the endogeneity problem caused by the unobservability of parental ability shown in the above sector. Then, if we can find an external shock that is not correlated with parental ability, but influences parental income, then we can use this shock as an instrumental variable (IV). Then, the regression coefficient on parental income can be explained causally.

The key thus lies in finding the proper IV. Many early studies are criticized for using a poor IV. For example, Mayer (1997) uses the parental income from those years after observing children's income, and this relies on the assumption that human capital investment on the offspring will not be impacted by later parental income. Shea (2000) uses whether the parent belongs to the worker's union, their industry, and unemployment caused by shutting down of the factory as IV, but whether these factors are independent of parental income is still being questioned. Thus, though they both conclude that money itself does not matter that much, their results are not very convincing resulting in the poor IV.

More recent researches try to use more detailed macro data to build a more reasonable IV. For example, Oreopoulos *et al.* (2005) also use unemployment caused by shutting down of the factory as IV. However, the parents in their sample have similar characters and expectations for permanent income. They find the children whose parents are influenced by the shutting down tend to have a 8% lower income, and are more likely to apply for unemployment benefit.

Others try to find IV that is more independent of parental income. For example, Morris *et al.* (2004) use the income increase caused by public welfare and anti-poverty programs, and Dahl and Lochner (2008) uses the income change caused by Earned Income Tax Credit. All these shocks are less connected to parental income and thus can serve as a better IV. They all show income shock has an impact on child income that cannot be neglected.

5.2.3 The method of intermediate variables

While all the above literatures try to find the causal influence of either genes or income, there is another branch of literature that focuses on finding the impacts of different intermediate variables in the intergenerational transmission. One method is to add those intermediate variables as control variables and see the change of the IIE. Eriksson *et al.* (2005) use this method and find the IIE drops by 25% (female) to 28% (male) after controlling health. Another method is to use a more advanced statistical method to calculate the proportions that different intermediate variables can explain (Bowles and Gintis, 2002; Blanden *et al.*, 2007).

All these factors are influenced by the income, environment, and genes, and thus their result cannot be explained empirically. These methods provide us with the importance of different intermediate variables, which are usually the aim of public policies. Due to the lack of data available for China, we use this method below to see the mechanisms behind the intergenerational income mobility in China.

5.3 The Mechanism of the Intergenerational Income Mobility in China

We use the method suggested by Eriksson *et al.* (2005) to study the importance of different intermediate variables in the intergenerational income mobility in China. We focus on the importance of wealth, social capital, and human capital.

First, we calculate the Simple Intergenerational Income Mobility (SIGE) by the same method in Part 3.1,

$$y_{1i,t} = \alpha + \beta y_{0i,t} + bX_{i,t} + \varepsilon_{i,t}. \tag{13-17}$$

Then, by adding wealth, social capital, and human capital in Equation (13-17), we calculate the Conditional Intergenerational Income Mobility (CIGE),

$$y_{1i,t} = \hat{\alpha} + \hat{\beta} y_{0i,t} + r_{k,t} A_{k,t} + \hat{b} X_{i,t} + \hat{\varepsilon}_{i,t}. \tag{13-18}$$

In this equation, $t = 1995, 2002$, A represents different intermediate variables, $k = 1, 2, 3, 4, 5, 6$, representing housing assets, financial assets, land assets, social capital, and human capital. $r_{k,t}$ is the return of these assets on children's income.

Finally, we calculate the difference between CIGE and SIGE (($\hat{\beta} - \beta)/\beta$), which will be seen as the influence of the intermediate variables. The changes of the return (($r_{k,2002} - r_{k,1995})/r_{k,1995}$) are also calculated.

We use the data from CHIPS (1995 and 2002). Income is the wage income including cash and items. Human capital is measured by years of education, social capital is built as the principal component of four variables including Communist Party of China (CPC) membership, working units,

Table 13-7: Descriptive statistics for the mechanisms.

	Urban		Rural	
	1995	2002	1995	2002
Father				
Income	8.94	9.29	8.10	7.42
	(0.64)	(0.63)	(1.25)	(0.64)
Age	52.69	53.07	50.01	52.69
	(4.21)	(3.69)	(4.49)	(4.21)
Children				
=1 for son	0.57	0.55	0.57	0.68
	(0.49)	(0.50)	(0.50)	(0.47)
Income	8.29	8.83	8.39	7.99
	(0.72)	(0.74)	(0.93)	(0.99)
Age	23.29	24.78	22.90	24.13
	(2.54)	(3.05)	(2.53)	(3.77)
Years of education	11.63	12.78	8.60	8.91
	(2.41)	(2.42)	(2.48)	(2.18)
Social capital	0.07	0.82	-0.10	-0.56
	(0.99)	(1.29)	(1.31)	(1.00)
Family				
Housing assets	10.41	11.49	9.76	10.00
	(1.48)	(0.97)	(0.99)	(0.98)
Financial assets	9.27	10.30	8.67	8.27
	(1.19)	(1.20)	(1.18)	(1.58)
Land area	—	—	1.43	1.69
	—	—	(0.71)	(0.93)
Number of observations	781	585	164	898

Note: All the income and land area is the log value, and has been adjusted to the 2002 level by provincial CPI.

occupation, and industry. Wealth is measured by housing assets, financial assets, and land assets.

We select the individuals who have all the above information, and restrict it further to those aged 20 to 65, and the age difference between father and child not less than 10 years. The statistical description of the final sample is shown in Table 13-7.

Human capital is one of the most important factors for the determination of individual income. It is also an important candidate for the underlying channels that parental income influences children's income. In fact, the basic theoretical model for intergenerational income mobility is built on the framework of human capital (Becker and Tomes, 1979), and many public policies aiming at enhancing intergenerational mobility also start with the public educational system.

Does human capital and education have a big influence on the intergenerational income mobility in China? Our result supports this hypothesis. As shown in Table 13-8, the IIE drops by 6% and 2% for the urban and rural areas in 1995, and it further drops by 13% and 12% in 2002. This suggests education explains a significant part of the intergenerational income mobility in China, and its importance increases. If we look at the return of education from 1995 to 2002, it also rises by 75% and 74% for the urban and rural areas, which is similar to researches on this problem.

Social capital also influences individual income. Zhao and Lu (2009) find the contribution of social network on the rural income gap in China reaches 12.1–13.4%. This will encourage parents to invest in offspring's social capital, such as getting connections with influential people, and entering sectors and industries that have more political resources. One of the criticisms of the intergenerational income mobility in China is the corruption problem, which may work through the influence of social capital.

Does social capital and education have a big influence on the intergenerational income mobility in China? Our result supports this hypothesis. As shown in Table 13-9, the IIE drops by 5% and 4% for the urban and rural areas in 1995, and it further drops by 8% and 3% in 2002. This suggests social capital explains a significant part of the intergenerational income mobility in China, and its importance increases. If we look at the return of social capital from 1995 to 2002, it also rises by 51% and 23% for the urban and rural areas. Though the contribution of social capital is less than that of education, its importance cannot be neglected also.

An interesting find was that besides human capital and social capital, family wealth also plays an important part in the intergenerational income transmission in China.

First, as shown in Table 13-10, the IIE drops by 20% and 29% for the urban and rural areas in 1995, and it further drops by 21% and 31% in 2002. This suggests housing assets explain a larger part of the intergenerational income mobility in China than education and social capital, and their importance increases. If we look at the return of education from 1995 to

Table 13-8: Human capital and intergenerational income mobility.

	Urban (1995)		Urban (2002)		Rural (1995)		Rural (2002)	
Parental income	0.291***	0.274***	0.288***	0.252***	0.250***	0.246***	0.241***	0.212***
	[0.041]	[0.041]	[0.044]	[0.044]	[0.044]	[0.044]	[0.023]	[0.024]
Years of education	—	0.028***	—	0.049***	—	0.027	—	0.047***
		[0.010]		[0.012]		[0.017]		[0.012]
=1 for son	0.096*	0.098*	0.09	0.107*	0.190**	0.202**	0.027	0.03
	[0.051]	[0.050]	[0.056]	[0.055]	[0.080]	[0.080]	[0.055]	[0.054]
Age of son	0.119	0.106	0.500***	0.406**	−0.011	−0.088	0.103	0.097
	[0.099]	[0.099]	[0.137]	[0.137]	[0.213]	[0.218]	[0.071]	[0.071]
Age of son, square	−0.002	−0.002	−0.009***	−0.007**	0.000	0.002	−0.002	−0.001
	[0.002]	[0.002]	[0.003]	[0.003]	[0.004]	[0.004]	[0.001]	[0.001]
Age of father	−0.258**	−0.249**	0.188	0.188	0.179	0.108	−0.109	−0.133
	[0.102]	[0.102]	[0.166]	[0.164]	[0.184]	[0.189]	[0.090]	[0.089]
Age of father, square	0.003**	0.002**	−0.002	−0.002	−0.001	−0.001	0.001	0.001
	[0.001]	[0.001]	[0.002]	[0.002]	[0.002]	[0.002]	[0.001]	[0.001]
Constant	10.516***	10.313***	−6.083	−5.108	1.32	3.923	7.387***	7.844***
	[2.593]	[2.584]	[4.013]	[3.964]	[4.879]	[5.121]	[2.170]	[2.155]
R^2_adj	0.068	0.076	0.158	0.182	0.219	0.227	0.117	0.132
Prob > F	0.000	0.000	0.000	0.000	0.000	0.000	0.000	0.000
Number of observations	781	781	585	585	164	164	898	898
Change in IIE		−6%		−13%		−2%		−12%
Change in r_k				75%				74%

Notes: (1) *, **, *** for $p < 10\%$, $p < 5\%$, $p < 1\%$;
(2) robust standard deviation in brackets;
(3) the change in IIE is the change between before and after controlling education, for example, −6% = (0.274 − 0.291)/0.291; the change of r_k 的 is the change of the coefficient on education from 1995 to 2002, for example, 75% = (0.049 − 0.028)/0.028;
(4) Similar for Tables 13-9–13-11.

Table 13-9: Social capital and intergenerational income mobility.

	Urban (1995)		Urban (2002)		Rural (1995)		Rural (2002)	
Parental income	0.291***	0.277***	0.288***	0.266***	0.250***	0.239***	0.241***	0.234***
	[0.041]	[0.041]	[0.044]	[0.044]	[0.044]	[0.045]	[0.023]	[0.024]
Social capital	—	0.100***	—	0.151***	—	0.031	—	0.038
		[0.025]		[0.021]		[0.031]		[0.025]
=1 for son	0.096*	0.110**	0.09	0.09	0.190**	0.198**	0.027	0.033
	[0.051]	[0.050]	[0.056]	[0.055]	[0.080]	[0.081]	[0.055]	[0.055]
Age of son	0.119	0.099	0.500***	0.469***	−0.011	−0.037	0.103	0.1
	[0.099]	[0.099]	[0.137]	[0.136]	[0.213]	[0.215]	[0.071]	[0.071]
Age of son, square	−0.002	−0.002	−0.009***	−0.009***	0.000	0.001	−0.002	−0.002
	[0.002]	[0.002]	[0.003]	[0.003]	[0.004]	[0.004]	[0.001]	[0.001]
Age of father	−0.258**	−0.248**	0.188	0.213	0.179	0.171	−0.109	−0.123
	[0.102]	[0.101]	[0.166]	[0.165]	[0.184]	[0.184]	[0.090]	[0.090]
Age of father, square	0.003**	0.002**	−0.002	−0.002	−0.001	−0.001	0.001	0.001
	[0.001]	[0.001]	[0.002]	[0.002]	[0.002]	[0.002]	[0.001]	[0.001]
Constant	10.516***	10.682***	−6.083	−6.141	1.32	1.926	7.387***	7.855***
	[2.593]	[2.570]	[4.013]	[3.979]	[4.879]	[4.915]	[2.170]	[2.190]
R^2_adj	0.068	0.085	0.158	0.173	0.219	0.219	0.117	0.118
Prob > F	0.000	0.000	0.000	0.000	0.000	0.000	0.000	0.000
Number of observations	781	781	585	585	164	164	898	898
Change in IIE		−5%		−8%		−4%		−3%
Change in r_k				51%				23%

Table 13-10: Housing assets and intergenerational income mobility.

	Urban (1995)		Urban (2002)		Rural (1995)		Rural (2002)	
Parental income	0.291***	0.232***	0.288***	0.228***	0.250***	0.177***	0.241***	0.167***
	[0.041]	[0.064]	[0.044]	[0.046]	[0.044]	[0.045]	[0.023]	[0.025]
Housing assets	—	0.107***	—	0.147***	—	0.188***	—	0.181***
		[0.027]		[0.030]		[0.041]		[0.028]
=1 for son	0.096*	0.176*	0.09	0.07	0.190**	0.182*	0.027	0.018
	[0.051]	[0.081]	[0.056]	[0.057]	[0.080]	[0.075]	[0.055]	[0.054]
Age of son	0.119	0.332	0.500***	0.501***	−0.011	0.042	0.103	0.066
	[0.099]	[0.179]	[0.137]	[0.142]	[0.213]	[0.199]	[0.071]	[0.070]
Age of son, square	−0.002	−0.006	−0.009***	−0.009***	0.000	−0.001	−0.002	−0.001
	[0.002]	[0.004]	[0.003]	[0.003]	[0.004]	[0.004]	[0.001]	[0.001]
Age of father	−0.258**	−0.386**	0.188	0.057	0.179	0.13	−0.109	−0.116
	[0.102]	[0.146]	[0.166]	[0.176]	[0.184]	[0.170]	[0.090]	[0.088]
Age of father, square	0.003**	0.004**	−0.002	0	−0.001	−0.001	0.001	0.001
	[0.001]	[0.001]	[0.002]	[0.002]	[0.002]	[0.002]	[0.001]	[0.001]
Constant	10.516***	9.336*	−6.083	−4.013	1.32	0.874	7.387***	6.808**
	[2.593]	[4.151]	[4.013]	[4.222]	[4.879]	[4.525]	[2.170]	[2.123]
R^2_adj	0.068	0.163	0.158	0.213	0.219	0.331	0.117	0.157
Prob > F	0.000	0.000	0.000	0.000	0.000	0.000	0.000	0.000
Number of observations	781	781	585	585	164	164	898	898
Change in IIE		**−20%**		**−21%**		**−29%**		**−31%**
Change in r_k				**37%**				**−4%**

Table 13-11: Living area and offspring income in urban areas.

	1995	2002
City center	\multicolumn{2}{c}{Reference group}	
City area	0.039	−0.117 **
	[0.050]	[0.059]
Suburbs	0.121	0.017
	[0.083]	[0.089]
Outer suburbs	0.202	−0.355 **
	[0.152]	[0.144]
=1 for son	0.087	0.119 *
	[0.048]	[0.053]
Age of son	0.075	0.533 ***
	[0.091]	[0.116]
Age of son, square	−0.001	−0.010 ***
	[0.002]	[0.002]
Years of education	0.014	0.045 ***
	[0.010]	[0.012]
Unit of work	controlled	controlled
Occupation	controlled	controlled
Industry	controlled	controlled
Constant	7.412 ***	1.094
	[1.235]	[1.564]
R^2_adj	0.072	0.149
Prob > F	0.000	0.000
Number of observations	781	585

Note: *, **, *** for $p < 10\%$, $p < 5\%$, $p < 1\%$.

2002, it also rises by 37% for the urban area, while reducing by 4% for the rural area.

Table 13-11 further proves the relationship between housing assets and offspring income. After controlling the usual demographical characters of the offspring, their income is still influenced significantly by the area where they live. Using the city center as the reference group, living in the city and suburbs all have an insignificant positive impact on the children's income in 1995, and change to a negative impact in 2002. The explaining power of this regression also rises from 7.2% to 14.9%.

Second, as is shown in Table 13-12, the IIE drops by 36% and 14% for the urban and rural areas in 1995, and it further drops by 41% and 51% in 2002. This suggests financial assets also explain a much larger part of

Table 13-12: Financial assets and intergenerational income mobility.

	Urban (1995)		Urban (2002)		Rural (1995)		Rural (2002)	
	(25)	(26)	(27)	(28)	(29)	(30)	(31)	(32)
Parental income	0.291***	0.186***	0.288***	0.169***	0.250***	0.216***	0.241***	0.118***
	[0.041]	[0.044]	[0.044]	[0.046]	[0.044]	[0.046]	[0.023]	[0.026]
Social capital	—	0.164***	—	0.169***	—	0.101**	—	0.141***
		[0.022]		[0.024]		[0.035]		[0.017]
=1 for son	0.096*	0.084	0.09	0.115*	0.190**	0.194*	0.027	0.074
	[0.051]	[0.052]	[0.056]	[0.055]	[0.080]	[0.078]	[0.055]	[0.056]
Age of son	0.119	0.093	0.500***	0.397**	−0.011	−0.036	0.103	0.104
	[0.099]	[0.100]	[0.137]	[0.135]	[0.213]	[0.205]	[0.071]	[0.074]
Age of son, square	−0.002	−0.001	−0.009***	−0.007**	0.000	0.001	−0.002	−0.002
	[0.002]	[0.002]	[0.003]	[0.003]	[0.004]	[0.004]	[0.001]	[0.001]
Age of father	−0.258**	−0.208*	0.188	0.217	0.179	0.21	−0.109	−0.05
	[0.102]	[0.104]	[0.166]	[0.163]	[0.184]	[0.177]	[0.090]	[0.093]
Age of father, square	0.003**	0.002*	−0.002	−0.002	−0.001	−0.002	0.001	0
	[0.001]	[0.001]	[0.002]	[0.002]	[0.002]	[0.002]	[0.001]	[0.001]
Constant	10.516***	9.047***	−6.083	−6.036	1.32	0.346	7.387***	5.637*
	[2.593]	[2.626]	[4.013]	[3.937]	[4.879]	[4.726]	[2.170]	[2.279]
R^2_adj	0.068	0.13	0.158	0.216	0.219	0.279	0.117	0.142
Prob > F	0.000	0.000	0.000	0.000	0.000	0.000	0.000	0.000
Number of observations	781	781	585	585	164	164	898	898
Change in IIE		−36%		−41%		−14%		−51%
Change in r_k				3%				40%

Note: *, **, *** for $p < 10\%$, $p < 5\%$, $p < 1\%$.

Table 13-13: Land assets and intergenerational income mobility.

	Rural (1995)		Rural (2002)	
	(33)	(34)	(35)	(36)
Parental income	0.250 ***	0.241 ***	0.241 ***	0.198 ***
	[0.044]	[0.047]	[0.023]	[0.026]
Land area	—	0.044	—	−0.108 ***
	—	[0.059]	—	[0.030]
=1 for son	0.190 **	0.242 **	0.027	0.015
	[0.080]	[0.085]	[0.055]	[0.057]
Age of son	−0.011	−0.025	0.103	0.104
	[0.213]	[0.218]	[0.071]	[0.073]
Age of son, square	0.000	0	−0.002	−0.002
	[0.004]	[0.004]	[0.001]	[0.001]
Age of father	0.179	0.005	−0.109	−0.121
	[0.184]	[0.203]	[0.090]	[0.092]
Age of father, square	−0.001	0	0.001	0.001
	[0.002]	[0.002]	[0.001]	[0.001]
constant	1.32	5.863	7.387 ***	8.216 ***
	[4.879]	[5.306]	[2.170]	[2.254]
R^2_adj	0.219	0.208	0.117	0.126
Prob > F	0.000	0.000	0.000	0.000
Number of observations	164	164	898	898
Change in IIE		−4%		−18%
Change in r_k				−345%

Note: *, **, *** for $p < 10\%$, $p < 5\%$, $p < 1\%$.

the intergenerational income mobility in China than education and social capital, and its importance increases. If we look at the return of education from 1995 to 2002, it also rises by 3% for the urban area, while rising by 40% for the rural area.

Third, as shown in Table 13-13, for the rural families, the IIE drops by 4% and 18% in 1995 and 2002. This suggests land assets also play a role in the intergenerational income mobility in China.

In fact, the importance of wealth differs in the urban and rural areas. First, though the contribution of housing assets in rural areas is also high, it declined a little from 1995 to 2002. Second, the contribution of financial assets stays stable in the urban area, while it increases a lot in the rural area.

Third, the land area has an unexpected negative impact on the offspring's income.

This phenomenon is closely related to the social and economic transition in the country. Financial income is becoming more and more important for the rural family as more and more farmers are going to the cities to earn non-agricultural income. In the meantime, as the land and house in rural areas cannot be easily transmitted to cash as in the urban area, this makes it difficult for the rural families to benefit their children's human capital from land, along with the low price of agricultural products.

Table 13-14 proves the above supposition by testing the impact of different income sources on children's income in the rural area. Agricultural income has an insignificant positive impact on children's income in 1995,

Table 13-14: Different income sources and children's income in rural areas.

	1995	2002
Agricultural income	0.122	−0.146 **
	[0.240]	[0.058]
Industry & sideline income	0.027	0.002
	[0.150]	[0.027]
Other income	0.051	0.071 **
	[0.112]	[0.033]
=1 for son	0.372	−0.122
	[0.399]	[0.115]
Age of son	0.471	0.016
	[1.598]	[0.127]
Age of son, square	−0.011	0.000
	[0.034]	[0.002]
Years of education	0.008	0.120 ***
	[0.099]	[0.025]
Unit of work	controlled	controlled
Occupation	controlled	controlled
Industry	controlled	controlled
Constant	1.138	7.034 **
	[17.678]	[2.127]
R^2_adj	0.087	0.157
Prob > F	0.000	0.000
Number of observation	164	898

Note: *, **, *** for $p < 10\%$, $p < 5\%$, $p < 1\%$.

while this changes to a significant negative impact in 2002. The positive impact of industry and other income increases at both the statistical and economical standards.

6. THE PUBLIC POLICIES FOR ENHANCING INTERGENERATIONAL INCOME MOBILITY

In order to further study the influence of public policies on intergenerational income mobility, we use the provincial data from China. We go back to the provincial IIE on the corresponding public expenditures to see the impact of different public expenditures. Table 13-15 gives the results.

Table 13-15: Public expenditures and intergenerational income mobility.

Dependent variable: provincial IIE (10,000 RMB)	
Infrastructure construction expenditures	−0.068
	[0.126]
Cultural expenditures	−13.124***
	[2.911]
Educational expenditures	−1.758***
	[0.491]
Healthy expenditures	−1.852**
	[0.916]
Public security expenditures	−0.948**
	[0.437]
Social security expenditures	−0.583*
	[0.258]
Social welfare expenditures	3.192**
	[1.218]
Administrative expenditures	1.389**
	[0.534]
Average housing price (yuan per square meters)	1.838**
	[0.884]
Constant	0.145
	[0.151]
Number of observations	40
R^2_adj	0.298

Notes: 1. IIE is calculated using CHIPS and CGSS, fiscal data is collected from the *Chinese Statistical Yearbook*. 2. We only use the data from 2002 and 2005 to keep coherence in the measurement of expenditures.

Table 13-15 shows that infrastructure construction expenditures, cultural expenditure, educational expenditures, health expenditures, and public security expenditures are negatively correlated with the IIE, while other expenditures are positively correlated with the elasticity. We thus suggest the following method to improve the intergenerational income mobility in China.

6.1 Build a Sound Educational System for the Young

We suggest improving the infant healthcare and education system, and to attach due importance to family education and a good social atmosphere for the growth of the young. As mentioned earlier, the growth of infants and young children in the early period have important influence on personal achievement. This early period of growth is also completely out of individual control. Therefore, providing a better growth environment for infants and young children, especially providing adequate supply of basic public goods for children from different families, is the most efficient way to achieve the goal of equal opportunity. The sound system for the growth of infants and children not only includes childcare and healthcare system for infants and young children, but also includes a system that helps young mothers to balance their role at work and in the family. It also includes creating a good social atmosphere for family education.

6.2 Provide Adequate and Balanced Public Goods

We suggest that public goods should be adequately provided for the whole population, including education, healthcare, infrastructure, cultural facilities and social security. Growing environment has a big influence on adult success. The social and human capital gains from living in an affluent neighborhood can greatly benefit the children. If we can provide adequate public goods for the children from the poor families, then their disadvantages may be offset. Education and healthcare are the most basic supplies in this system.

It should be noted that a sound social security system can also help to enhance intergenerational mobility. On the one hand, it will release the pension pressure on the parents and thus give them more money to invest in children's human capital. On the other hand, it will also release the pressure on young people to support their old parents, which will, in turn, give them greater ability to invest in their human capital after entering the labor market.

6.3 Diminish the Discriminations in the Labor Market

The discrimination in the labor market should be diminished, such as *hukou* and regional discrimination. If the cultural inheritance is in some degree reasonable, then the social discrimination on certain groups of people directly violates the rule of equality. In China, due to the wide gap between rural and urban areas and the unbalanced regional development, children from different areas face quite different opportunities, which make the elimination of discrimination quite important for enhancing intergenerational income mobility.

6.4 Deepen the Market-Oriented Reform

Though the product market in China now is quite competitive, the factor market, including the financial and resource market is still not built up yet. Monopoly in these industries makes it quite difficult for the children from disadvantaged families to enter. The big monopoly profit they earn is proved to be one of the important factors contributing to the large income gap in China. Thus, deepening the market-oriented reform is suggested to help enhance the intergenerational income mobility in the country.

6.5 Build a More Sound Legal System

Under a sound legal system, corruption can be reduced and make it more difficult for the advantaged parents to help their children illegally. This is not only important for enhancing the intergenerational income mobility in the country, but also a prerequisite for stable development in China.

REFERENCES

Becker, G. S. and Tomes, N. (1979). An equilibrium theory of the distribution of income and intergenerational mobility. *The Journal of Political Economy*, 87(6): 1153–1189.

Benabou, R. and Ok, E. A. (2001). Social mobility and the demand for redistribution: The POUM hypothesis. *The Quarterly Journal of Economics*, 116(2): 447–487.

Blanden, J., Paul Gregg and Lindsey Macmillan (2007). Accounting for intergenerational persistence. *Economic Journal*, 117: C43–C60.

Bladen, Jo (2011). Cross-country rankings in intergenerational mobility: A comparison of approaches from economic and sociology. *Journal of Economic Surveys*, June. DOI: 10.1111/j.1467-6419.2011.00690.x.

Björklund, A. and Chadwick, L. (2002). *Intergenerational Income Mobility in Permanent and Separated Families*. Paper to be presented at the 2002 ESPE Meeting in Bilbao, June 13–15.

Björklund, A., Jantti, M. and Solon, G. (2005). Influences of Nature and Nurture on Earnings Variation: A Report on a Study of Various Sibling Types in Sweden. In: Bowles, Samuel, Gintis, Herbert, Osborne Groves, Melissa, eds., Unequal Chances: Family Background and Economic Success [M]. Princeton University Press, Princeton, pp. 145–164.

Björklund, A., Lindahl, M. and Plug, E. (2006). The origins of intergenerational associations: Lessons from Swedish adoption data. *Quarterly Journal of Economics*, 121: 999–1028.

Björklund, A., Jantti, M. and Solon, G. (2007). *Nature and Nurture in the Intergenerational Transmission of Socioeconomic Status: Evidence from Swedish Children and their Biological and Rearing Parents*. IZA Discussion Paper No. 2665.

Bowles, Samuel and Herbert Gintis (2002). The inheritance of inequality. *The Journal of Economic Perspectives*, 16(3): 3–30.

Chen, Y., Naidu, S. and Yuchtman, N. (2010). Intergenerational mobility and institutional change in 20th century China [R]. UC Berkeley Working Paper.

Corak, Miles (2006). Do Poor Children Become Poor Adults? Lessons from a Cross Country Comparison of Generational Earnings Mobility. IZA DP No. 1993.

Dahl, G. and Lochner, L. (2008). *The Impact of Family Income on Child Achievement: Evidence from the Earned Income Tax Credit*. NBER Working Paper 14599.

Eriksson, T., Bernt Bratsberg and Oddbjorn Raaum (2005). *Earnings Persistence Across Generations: Transmission Through Health*. Memorandum 35/2005 (University of Oslo, Norway).

Gong, H., Leigh, A. and Meng, X. (2012). Intergenerational Income Mobility in Urban China. *Review of Income and Wealth*, 58(3): 481–503.

Herbert, Osborne Groves, Melissa, eds. (2005). *Unequal Chances: Family Background and Economic Success*. Princeton: Princeton University Press.

Herrnstein, R. J. and Murray, C. (1994). *The Bell Curve: Intelligence and Class Structure in American Life* [M]. Simon and Schuster, 2010.

Jantti, Markus, Bratsberg, Bernt, Røed, Knut, Raaum, Oddbjørn, Naylor, Robin, Eva, Osterbacka, Anders, Björklund and Eriksson, Tor (2006). American Exceptionalism in a New Light: A Comparison of Intergenerational Earnings Mobility in the Nordic Countries, the United Kingdom and the United States. Discussion Paper No. 1938 Institute for the Study of Labor (IZA) Bonn.

Irene, Ng (2007). Intergenerational income mobility in Singapore [J], *The B.E. Journal of Economic Analysis & Policy*, 7(2), Article 3.

Lefranc, Arnaud, Fumiaki, Ojima and Takashi, Yoshida. The Intergenerational Transmission of Income and Education: A Comparison of Japan and France. RSCAS Working Papers with number 2008/25.

Liu, Haoming and Zeng, Jinli (2009). Genetic ability and intergenerational earnings mobility [J]. *Journal of Population Economics*, 22, 75–95.

Mayer, S. E. (1997). What Money Can't Buy: Family Income and Children's Life Chances [M]. Cambridge, MA: Harvard University Press.

Morris, P., Duncan, G. J. and Chirstopher Rodrigues (2004). *Does Money Really Matter? Estimating Impacts of Family Income on Children's Achievement with Data from Random-Assignment Experiments*. Chicago Workshop on Black–White Inequality.

Nunez, Javier I. and Leslie, Miranda (2010). Intergenerational income mobility in a less-developed, high-inequality context: The case of Chile [J]. *The B.E. Journal of Economic Analysis & Policy*, 10(1), Article 33.

Oreopoulos, P. (2003). The long-run consequences of living in a poor neighborhood. *The Quarterly Journal of Economics*, 118(4): 1533–1575.

Oreopoulos, P., Page Marianne and Ann Huff Stevens (2005). *The Intergenerational Effects of Worker Displacement*. UCDAVIS Working Paper.

Piketty, T. (1995). Social mobility and redistributive politics. *The Quarterly Journal of Economics*, 110(3): 551–584.

Ravallion, M. and Chen, S. (2007). China's (uneven) progress against poverty. *Journal of Development Economics*, 82(1): 1–42.

Sacerdote, B. (2002). The nature and nurture of economic outcomes. *The American Economic Review*, 92(2): 344–348.

Sacerdote, B. (2007). How large are the effects from changes in family environment? A study of Korean American adoptees [J]. *The Quarterly Journal of Economics*, 122(1): 119–157.

Sacerdote, B. (2008). *Nature and Nurture Effects on Children's Outcomes: What Have We Learned from Studies of Twins and Adoptees?* Dartmouth College and NBER, Working Paper.

Solon, Gary (2002). Cross-country differences in intergenerational earnings mobility [J]. *The Journal of Economic Perspectives*, 16(3): 59–66.

Solon, G. (2004). A Model of Intergenerational Mobility Variation Over Time and Place. In: Miles Corak, ed., *Generational Income Mobility in North America and Europe*. Cambridge: Cambridge University Press, pp. 38–47.

Shea, John (2000). Does parents' money matter? *Journal of Public Economics*, 77(2): 155–184.

Solon, G., Mary Corcoran, Roger Gordon and Deborah Laren (1991). A longitudinal analysis of sibling correlations in economic status. *Journal of Human Resources*, 26(3): 509–534.

Yao Xianguo and Zhao Liqiu (2006). *Intergenerational Income Mobility and the Transmission Path in China: 1989–2000*, the Sixth China Economics Annual Conference Selected Papers [D], 2006.

Zhao, J. and Lu, M. (2009). The contribution of Guanxi to income inequality in rural China and a cross regional comparison: A regression based decomposition. *China Economic Quarterly*, 19(11): 363–390.

Chapter 14

Further Development of Urbanization and the Policy Research on the Rural Migrant Workers Granted Urban Citizenship

Jing Tan
School of Economics, Fudan University

> Something momentous was happening in the society and culture that released the aspirations and energies of common people as never before...
>
> — American historian Gordon Wood, 1994[1]

1. INTRODUCTION

With the perspective of economic development, the citizenization[2] of Chinese migrant workers is mentioned here because China is now facing economic restructuring. This economic restructuring mainly results from the shrinking external demand and the need to boost domestic demand. Also, China will continue to walk on the path of reform and opening up; thus, there are numerous things for the Chinese to do in accordance with resource endowment and comparative advantage. For example, accumulating human capital for the non/low-skill labor force, facilitating the

---

[1] De Soto, Hernando (2000). *The Mystery of Capital*. London: Bantam Press, Transworld Publishers. p. 11.
[2] Citizenization in China is a part of urbanization. It means granting urban residency and urban citizenship to rural migrants, including rural migrant workers and their family members living with them. And as for the urban residency and urban citizenship, they include the same rights of rural migrants as local inhabitants in urban areas, such as permanent living rights, permanent jobs, regular housing, public schooling, and entitlement of social insurance. (See Chun-Chung Au and J. Vernon Henderson, 2006, for a detailed description.)

transition of rural workers into modernized industrial workers by means of migration and citizenization, promoting the transformation of Chinese society from a large-scale-population country to a country rich in human capital, and finally, sharing the economic growth with all the Chinese people. As De Soto (2000) said in his book, the rapid development in the United States originated in squatter rights to its citizens and extending the rights to property ownership. For now, China is facing the challenges to increase the civil rights of rural migrants, that is, citizenization. Thus, in order to get 1.3 billion Chinese people together across the "middle-income trap," the reform of factor markets including the labor market, the financial market, and the land market, and the construction of relevant institutions are urgently needed.

This chapter will continue as follows: First, it introduces the basic background and history of citizenization, that is, China's "two-step urbanization"; second, it outlines the basic characteristics of rural migrant workers and their migration patterns; and third, the chapter investigates the cost of citizenization of rural migrant workers, as well as the sharing mechanisms of enterprises, individuals, and governments. Throughout the research, we find that it is a certain kind of distortion for the lack of social security of rural migrant workers. Precisely because of the lack of urban civil rights, the enterprises save 30% of the wages from rural migrant workers' costs. In accordance with current institutions, enterprises and individuals will bear most of the costs in citizenization, while the government's role is weakened. Therefore, it is urgently needed to change this to a cost-sharing pattern. In addition, the establishment of the rural land ownership system will help to strengthen the wealth accumulation of the rural migrations, thus rendering an important support for citizenization. Overall, citizenization of rural migrant workers not only incurs costs, but also contributes to human capital accumulation and urbanization development, so a comprehensive consideration is needed.

2. CHINA'S "TWO STEPS OF URBANIZATION" AND ITS HISTORY

Most countries have experienced the process of non-agricultural transition and accelerated urbanization, such as OECD countries and "Asia's Four

Little Dragons." For example, urbanization in Britain begins in the mandatory migration patterns of the Enclosure Movement, urbanization in the United States is characterized by a liberal style, and Japan's urbanization is a rural to urban migration process caused by both increasing productivity and governmental guidance. Despite these processes and patterns, the common feature of urbanization among these countries is that once rural workers make decisions to work and live in the cities, they are urban residents. This means workers are free to choose labor markets and patterns of labor supply in accordance with the principles of market factor allocation. So, if it works like this, there is no institutional suppression of labor productivity and distortion of labor price, and rural migrant workers enjoy the same social welfares and benefits as the local inhabitants.

However, in China, the story is quite different. Generally, people are divided into two groups with different "citizenship" and legal residency, that is, the urban "citizenship" and residency, as well as the rural "citizenship" and residency. Two types of people have different housing, employment, public healthcare, and so on, according to their local entitlement (the urban or rural sector).

Therefore, citizenization is essential just for the reason that people move from rural to urban areas, bringing with them their legal "citizenship" and residency from rural areas, and they come into the city either illegally or legally as temporary workers.

The development background consists of the institutional discrimination between urban and rural areas in their development process, the household registration system tied up with the welfare system, as well as the dominant position of the urban sector in the development (Chen Zhao and Lu Ming, 2008). These combine to result in the two-step urbanization process in China. The first step that has been achieved is to facilitate the transition from rural farmers to rural workers in urban areas, and the second step, which is not yet achieved, is the transformation of rural migrant workers into local inhabitants. The completion of the two steps would be the so-called "realized urbanization" or "thorough urbanization" (Liu Chuanjiang, 2005). It is thus clear that citizenization of rural workers means not only non-agricultural employment, but also the same lifestyle and civil rights as local inhabitants. In addition, citizenization of rural labor force is the most important part for development and social harmony in both urban and rural areas, while it is part of the story in further development of urbanization and citizenization. Besides, there are the challenges of citizenization of landless farmers, citizenization of farmers not in labor force, and so on.

Historically, directly related to the national industrialization strategies and economic development strategies, the process of urbanization in China mainly goes through three stages.

I. *Period of Excessive Control with Incorrect Orientation* (1949–1978). This period is characterized by government-led overtaking strategy and scissors difference[3] between urban and rural areas. The main features and events of this period are: (1) Top-down patterns of development in defiance of comparative advantages, and the overtaking strategy of giving priority development to heavy industry (Lin Yifu, 2003); (2) Emphasis on the development of big cities, and taking the nationalization and collectivization approach; (3) Establishment of urban and rural scissors difference system, such as binary household registration system, the price distortions of urban and rural products, rigid labor mobility, slow process of urbanization, extreme scarcity of human and physical capital in rural areas, and huge differences in development between urban and rural areas. The main policies relating to the restriction on rural migration into urban areas are, *Provisions on Process Hukou Immigration (Draft) In 1964*,[4] cancellation of the clause in the Constitution relating to free migration in 1975 and restrictions on *hukou* (the Household Registration) system (migration from rural to urban areas) in 1977, issued by the Ministry of Public Security (Liu Chuanjiang, 2008).

II. *Period of Marketization* (1979–2000). This is a period of decentralization, market-oriented transformation, and gradual reform. Its main features are:

1) The start of emphasis on market mechanisms, gradual liberalization of commodity markets with dual-track approach and limited

---

[3] Scissors difference in prices was sustained by the government.
[4] In Chinese,《公安部关于处理户口迁移的规定（草案）》.

opening to the outside. The main events are:
   a. Paying taxes instead of profits by the state-owned enterprises (SOEs) from 1983 to 1984;
   b. Gradual liberalization of the grain, oil, and non-staple food prices from 1988;
   c. Cancellation of the grain and oil ration system based on the *hukou* system in the early 1990s;
   d. Starting the stage of SOEs restructuring for establishing a socialist market economic system;
   e. Establishing a modern enterprise system in SOEs proposed in the 14th National Congress of the Communist Party of China (CPC) in 1992.
2) The 1994 tax-sharing reform, which promotes initiatives of the local governments.
3) Urbanization strategy is "giving priority to the development of small and medium-sized towns" and the scale effect is neglected.
4) The rural industrialization acts as part of the Chinese industrialization strategy. And the events are the full implementation of the Household Responsibility System[5] in rural areas in the early 1980s, which greatly improves the productivity in rural areas, and releases a large number of surplus workers.
5) The rural labor forces involved in non-agricultural employment takes the approach of shifting to other sectors within rural areas (Wei Houkai, 1994), and the restrictions on rural migration to urban area are released in 1984.

III. *Period of Accelerated Industrialization and Further Reform* (2001–Now). This is a period of gradual reform of factor markets and further development of urbanization. Its main features are:
   1) Acceleration of the process of marketization and opening to the outside world, with the events of China's entering into the WTO in 2001 and the establishment of the socialist market economic system framework in the 16th National Congress of CPC in 2002;

---

[5] "The Household Responsibility System is a practice in China, first adopted in agriculture in 1981 and later extended to other sectors of the economy, by which local managers are held responsible for the profits and losses of an enterprise." From *Wikipedia*.

2) Adjustment of the urbanization strategy to "promoting the balanced development of large, medium, and small cities and small towns" in the 16th National Congress of CPC in 2002 and the 17th National Congress of CPC in 2007;
3) City construction and expansion campaign in local governments and land-based finance overused;
4) Serious price distortion in land market and financial market resulting from imperfection institution;
5) Development in accordance with comparative advantages, and further improving labor market to facilitate the movement of rural labor to urban areas. And with increase in agricultural productivity, economic growth, and institutional improvement, the first step of urbanization has completed already, that is, farmers become rural migrant workers in urban areas.

During the process of urbanization and industrialization, the dual-track approach and gradual reform in China becomes a successful counterexample to the mainstream economic development theory represented by the "Washington Consensus" in 1989. However, the *hukou* system founded in 1963 characterized by discrimination is still active with some changes — the goods allocation function has been removed in the early 1990s, and the function of welfare benefit allocation still works. Now the *hukou* system, from the perspective of welfare and civil rights, hinders the citizenization and labor market development, and distorts the decision process of rural labor supply. This means that the rural migration workers are the *de facto* population but not the *de jure* population living in cities, so that the urban sector would use the *hukou* system to sustain the comparative advantage for low-cost labor and to make capital accumulation and social welfare for their household population (*de jure* population) (Chen Zhao and Lu Ming, 2008). Therefore, the migrant workers actually have significant differences in availabilities of welfare and public goods in urban areas compared to *de jure* population, such as employment security, social insurance, the education of their children, and housing security.

The 2012 Central Economic Working Conference puts forward the proposal that China should take a new road of urbanization. One of the most important contents in that proposal is to promote further development of urbanization and to achieve "thorough urbanization" though citizenization of rural migrant workers. Citizenization is due to lack of relevant institutional reform, but it is also an opportunity and a challenge to strengthen the human capital accumulation of the migrant workers. In 2010, China's urbanization rate was close to 50%. At the same time, the proportion of non-agricultural *hukou* (Household Registration in urban areas) was only 34% (Figure 14-1). This means more than half of the people work and live in urban areas, and in every 10 of them, about 3 people identified as farmers need to be residencized,[6] or they will not act as stable labor supplies and general consumers for urban sector.[7]

Since the 30 years of economic development and industrialization after the reform and opening up, the proportion of industrial sector output value has remained around 40%. In accordance with the theory of Chenery

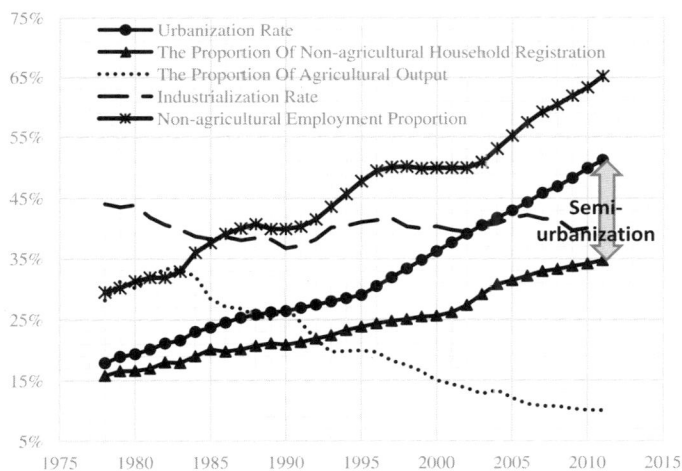

Figure 14-1: Urbanization rate, the proportion of non-agricultural household registration, the proportion of agricultural output, non-agricultural employment proportion, and industrialization rate over the years.

Data Sources: China Statistical Yearbook in 2012, China Health Statistical Yearbook in 2012.

---

[6] Residencize means to go through the process of urban citizenship.
[7] Chinese scholars call this kind of temporary labor supply with low level of consumption in urban areas "migratory bird pattern" migration.

industrialization stage, China will go into the late stage of industrialization. The extensive use of non-skill/low-skill labor cannot meet the demand for a higher level of human capital, and for now, this "migratory bird pattern" of migrant workers undoubtedly hinders their human capital accumulation and transition to modern industrial workers. In short, the basic situation of urbanization in China can be summarized as follows: "Institutional reform, social welfare division, and civil rights entitlement do not meet the demand of migration and development." So, it is important to stimulate the workers' initiatives, to help non-skilled/low-skilled workers improve productivity, and to facilitate human capital accumulation by promoting migration and further construction of the labor market.

The ultimate goal of citizenization is to improve people's living standards. Calculation of the arc elasticity of GDP per capita to urban population scale (UPE) and the arc elasticity of GDP per capita to non-agricultural *hukou* population scale (NHE) shows that after 2000 these two kinds of elasticity have an increasing trend. It means that urbanization and non-agriculturalization bring about an increase in GDP per capita, while NHE is higher than UPE (Figure 14-2), since non-agriculturalization of *hukou* means having urban *hukou*, that is, citizenization to some

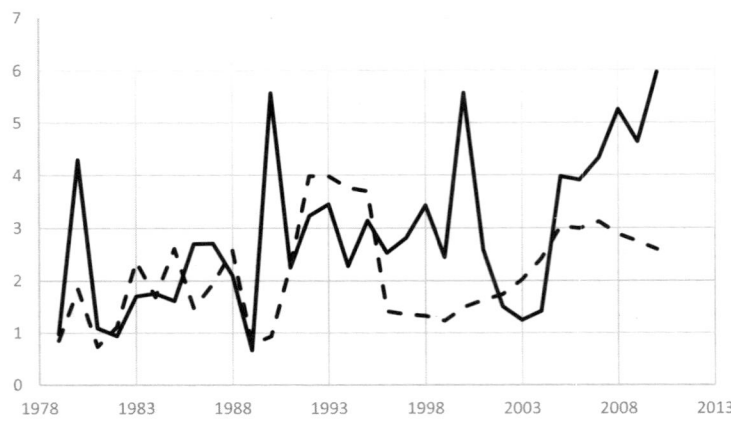

Figure 14-2: The arc elasticity of GDP per capita to UPE and the arc elasticity of GDP per capita to NHE over the years.

Data Sources: *China Statistical Yearbook.*

Note: In the figure, GDP per capita is calculated with the 1970 constant prices.

extent. So citizenization will bring more economic development than the current semi-urbanization. This may be because citizenization contributes to increasing productivity of migrant workers, changing non/low-skilled workers into modern industrial workers, and continuously accumulating human capital through learning by doing and migration.

According to the standpoint of New Structural Economics, in order to obtain sustained economic growth, China needs to continue improving the labor endowment structure and enhance the human capital accumulation. Citizenization is a part of urbanization, and in China, it is urbanization in the late stage, which needs to be carried on according to the comparative advantages following the market principles. For China, the comparative advantage is abundant labor. In this chapter, we will discuss the issue of citizenization based on the following views:

1) To establish an open and unified labor market without migrant friction;[8]
2) To form an orderly and stable labor supply;
3) To make good use of the comparative advantage of China's abundant labor force at the present stage and to try to enhance this endowment structure;
4) To maintain the competitiveness of the economy, and in the process of urbanization and citizenization, to avoid the rising cost of the enterprises;
5) To establish a unified and standardized social security system according to Beveridge's principles[9] such as universalism and a minimum level of welfare.

3. THE CHARACTERISTICS OF RURAL LABOR FORCE MIGRATION IN CHINA

3.1 The Scale of Rural Workers

"Rural workers in urban areas" play a special role in the two-step urbanization, and is the result of lack of reform in the *hukou* system while the minimum requirement to receive social welfare benefit is set too high.

---

[8]Migrant friction generally means that people have free movement and enjoy the same civil rights and social benefits as local inhabitants.
[9]From The Report of the Inter-Departmental Committee on Social Insurance and Allied Services, known as Beveridge's 1942 Report.

In this chapter, the rural workers in urban areas are the groups that engaged in non-agricultural economic activities with rural *hukou*. These workers can be divided into two groups, local rural workers employed in local township and village enterprises and rural migrant workers with inter-town and intercity[10] migration.

By the end of 2012, the number of Chinese rural workers reached 262.61 million, of which there are 99.25 million local rural workers, accounting for 37.8% of all rural workers. There were 163.36 million rural migrant workers, accounting for 62.2% of all rural workers.[11] Since 2008, despite an upward growth trend in the number of rural workers, the proportion of the rural migrant workers declined slightly (Figure 14-3).

Policies and relevant institutions affect the migration decision-making process. With the influence of the policy orientation about regional development and urbanization development, the scale of rural workers and their migration modes has changed with the relationship between supply and

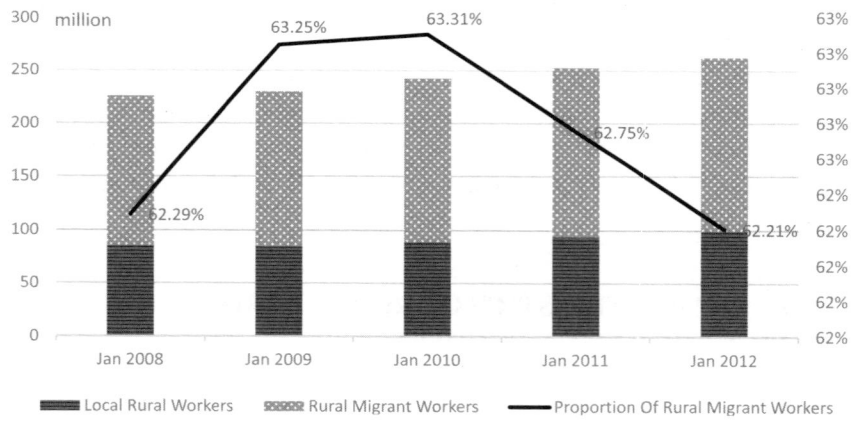

Figure 14-3: The scale of rural migrant workers and local rural workers from 2008. *Data Sources*: CEIC.

---

[10] In this chapter, the two kinds of workers are called "local rural workers" and "rural migrant workers," respectively, for short. And "rural workers" is the shorter form for the rural workers in urban areas.

[11] *Data Sources*: CEIC, Database of Chinese Economy.

demand in the labor market. These changes can be categorized by three main stages:

1) *Local Transfer Period* (1980s). Since 1984 and the gradual lifting of migration restrictions, township and village enterprises have become the main channel for non-agricultural employment of farmers. Under the influence of national urbanization strategies, that is, *"giving priority to development of small and medium-sized towns,"* the number of rural migrant workers increased from 2 million in the early 1980s to 30 million in 1989.

2) *Regional Transfer Period* (1990s). Various policy restrictions on labor mobility were lifted in this period, and the rural workers were mainly employed in urban industrial sectors and service sectors.[12] Further, there were some other significantly different treatments of local *hukou* workers[13] and rural migrant workers in the urban labor market. For example, Shanghai, Guangzhou, and Beijing have issued rules to limit the migrants employed in certain sectors, and even imposed additional costs or fees on use of migrant workers by the enterprises. During this period, the number of rural migrant workers reached from 60 million to 100 million, of which there were 22 million inter-provincial rural migrant workers in 1993.

3) *Period of Civil Rights Improvement* (Since 2000s). In this period, the total number of rural workers increased with structural shortages and new features in spatial dispersal. The main event at this stage is the enactment of *"Some opinions on resolving the problems faced by migrant workers"*[14] by the State Council. In 2006, the institutional discrimination within the urban labor market began to disappear. The growth rate of rural workers decreased, and overall population of rural migrant workers saw an average annual increase of 5.95 million from 2000 to 2008. Although the share of rural workers is still large, a structural shortage began to appear in 2004. The small towns and cities absorbed most of the

---

[12] In China, the agricultural sectors are generally called the primary industry, the industrial sectors generally mean the secondary industry, and the service sectors roughly refer to the tertiary industry.
[13] Local *hukou* workers means the *de jure* workers or the local inhabitants in labor force.
[14] In Chinese,《国务院关于解决农民工问题的若干意见》.

rural workers, so employment in towns and village enterprises (including local rural workers and rural migrant workers in towns) acted as the main channel to absorb rural workers with the proportion of 60%. As for rural migrant workers, they mainly migrated to the large- and medium-sized cities, accounting for 63.3% of all the rural migrant workers. In the meantime, the proportion of inter-provincial migration declined. As for the spatial dispersal, the eastern region is still the major "receiving" place[15] for rural migrant workers, while the share proportion in this region decreased from 75.4% in 2005 to 62.5% in 2009. In the central and western regions, the share proportion of rural migrant workers gradually increased (Research Group of Development Research Center of The State Council, 2011).

3.2 Major Characteristics of Rural Workers

With the increase in agricultural labor productivity and scarcity of land resources, rural workers in the urban labor market emigrate as the rural surplus labor forces. On the other hand, they are usually the "elites" in rural areas with physical fitness and relatively high level of human capital. Rural workers have features that distinguish them from other groups. For example, rural workers are often young or middle aged, their level of education is generally higher than others in "sending" places and lower than local inhabitants' in "receiving" places, they intend to migrate to the southeast coast region of China and gradually spread to the central and western small towns or cities, they are more likely employed in manufacturing and construction industries, the longer they stay in the cities, the more they prefer to permanently stay there, in recent years, they show the characteristics of family migration (Jian Xinhua and Huang Kun, 2007; Research Group on Strategic Issues of China's Rural Workers, 2009), social networks tend to be an important factor for rural workers integrated into the urban labor market (Zhang Yuan and Lu Ming, 2009), and the scale of rural workers will continue to increase (Han Changfu, 2006).

---

[15]The "receiving places" mean "current residential locations", and the "sending places" mean the "former residential locations" or the place where one's *hukou* is registered.

Compared with local urban workers, rural workers' human capital (measured by education level) and their social capital are less than the local urban inhabitants, and their social support and social network in urban areas are insufficient (Li Shuzhuo et al., 2006). Thus, they tend to enter the urban informal sector or be involved in informal activities. Despite the increase in income of recent years, their wage level is still lower than the local urban labor with high work intensity, harsh working environment, low level of social security, and low social benefit coverage (Li Peilin and Li Wei, 2010). Most of their income is spent in housing and food in urban areas, and they have very strong willingness to save. Because of the high living costs in urban areas and agricultural land left behind in their hometown, the rural workers become a group of migrants with "migratory bird pattern" for the cities, and do not act as a stable part of urban labor market.

With the increasing migration from rural to urban areas, the rural workers are divided into two groups. Chinese scholars always use the birth year 1980 as the cutoff point. People born before 1980 are the first generation of rural workers and those born in or after 1980 are the second or new generation of rural workers.[16] New generation rural workers already have a large scale with a proportion of 34.6% to total rural workers according to the 2005 National Population Sample Survey. The migrants' dynamics monitoring survey data in 2010 by National Population and Family Planning Commission shows that new generation rural workers account for 47% of total rural workers. Different from the first generation rural workers, there is a higher proportion of females in new generation rural workers; the new generation's average years of education are higher than the first generation — more than 5% of them have a college degree or above; new generation rural workers are more likely to be involved in inter-provincial migration; new generation rural workers are currently of marriage and childbearing age; the employment of new generation rural workers is mainly in manufacturing, and their employment expectation changes especially in terms of the employment environment; the proportion of new generation without labor contract is less than the first generation, yet still high at 31.1%;

---

[16]The second generation of rural workers in urban is different from the filial generation of rural workers in urban. The filial generation of rural workers refers to the children of rural workers.

new generation rural workers are faced with a severe lack of social security; and finally, the new generation is more likely to get permanent residency in cities than the first generation.

On the other hand, low level of employment, thrift, and hard work remain the common features of the two generations of rural workers in urban areas (Wang Zongping and Duan Chengrong, 2010; Liu Chuanjiang, 2010; Duan Chengrong and Ma Xueyang, 2011).

4. THE INSTITUTIONAL BARRIERS AND COSTS FOR CITIZENIZATION OF RURAL MIGRANT WORKERS

The dominant barrier between rural and urban areas from the *hukou* system in China is gradually disappearing, and most rural surplus workers are making optimal choice for labor supply through migration. The real difference between rural migrant workers and local residents is reflected in the complementary or substitute relationship of the employment structure. With the influence of the "hidden barrier" between rural and urban areas from the *hukou* system, rural migrant workers are not real urban residents with urban citizenship, and their migration is characterized by "semi-freedom and limited mobility." The inequality of rural migrant workers is mainly in the following respects: employment opportunities, employment stability, social welfare, social benefits, education and training of themselves and their children, and housing security (Liu Chuanjiang, 2009). Nowadays, the "hidden barrier" of migration the *hukou* system is the institutional tool used by the urban areas to lower the labor cost in order to attract investment and reduce the pressure of public resources. That is why the process of urbanization in China is split into two steps. This section will discuss the core issues of citizenization of rural migrant workers, that is, the social security issues, as well as the major cost involved in the process of citizenization.

4.1 Social Insurance of the Labor Force and Labor Costs

Germany issued a Sickness Insurance Act in 1883, an Accident Insurance Act in 1884, and an Invalidity and Old-Age Act in 1889, and established the world's most comprehensive workers' social security schemes at that time. After the Beveridge Report in 1942, the welfare states were established, which became important references for other countries in the world to establish a social security system. China's social security system for workers is built by the government, employers, and the social members jointly. The existing social security system for urban workers can be summed up as "Five Social Insurances and Urban Housing Fund," including urban employees' basic endowment insurance, urban employees' unemployment insurance, urban employees' basic medical insurance, urban employees' maternity insurance, urban employees' occupational injury insurance, and housing fund. The current social security system for urban employees is a relatively large expense for both enterprises and individuals. There are different insurances for different social groups as we shall describe briefly in the following.

1) *The Endowment Insurance System.* At present, China's urban and rural endowment insurance includes three types: First, the urban employees' basic endowment insurance, with the payment rate of 20% for enterprises and 8% for individuals and the wages as the payment base. Second, social endowment insurance for urban residents, with 10 levels of payment standard that will make differences in pension received and monthly government subsidies of 55 yuan; third, the new rural social endowment insurance, with five levels of payment standard that will make differences in the pension received and monthly government subsidies of 55 yuan.
2) *Unemployment Insurance.* There is only one kind of insurance in this regard, urban employees' unemployment insurance. According to the provisions of *Regulations on Unemployment Insurance*, wages of stuffs is used as the payment base, and 2% of the premium rate is paid by urban enterprises for their workers while 1% of the premium rate is paid by individuals.
3) *The Medical Insurance System.* The Chinese urban and rural medical insurance system consists of three types: First, the urban employees' basic medical insurance system introduced in 1998, and the total proportion of 8% of wages is paid for the insurance by enterprises and individuals. Second, the new rural cooperative medical scheme; this insurance is mainly for the rural population, and they are always involved with the household as the enrollment unit. Third, urban residents' basic medical

insurance started with a pilot construction in 2007, and this insurance is mainly for individuals not in the labor force or not employed.

4) *Maternity Insurance.* There is only one kind of insurance in this regard, urban employees' maternity insurance. This insurance should be paid by employers. The payment base is wages in the enterprises, and the payment rates are typically between 0.4% and 2.4%.

5) *Occupational Injury Insurance.* In accordance with the decision of the State Council on Amending the *Occupational Injury Insurance Regulations*, this insurance should be paid by employers. The payment base is wages in the enterprises, and the payment rates are typically between 0.5% and 2.0%.

6) *Urban Housing Fund.* According to the *Regulations on Housing Fund Management*, individuals and enterprises monthly deposit shall be no less than 5% of the workers' monthly wage in the previous year. The cities that could afford it can increase this proportion of deposit appropriately.

In accordance with the above regulations and systems, it can be briefly calculated that an enterprise in urban area rendering "Five Social Insurances and Urban Housing Fund" to all its employees will have an additional cost. And this cost will account for about 35% of the employees' wages, and individuals need to spend about 16% of their wages for these insurances (Table 14-1).

Table 14-1: The payment rate of urban employees' basic Social Insurance and Urban Housing Fund in China.

Types of insurances	By enterprises (%)	By individuals (%)
Urban employees' basic endowment insurance	20	8
Urban employees' unemployment insurance	2	1
Urban employees' basic medical insurance	6	2
Urban employees' maternity insurance	0.4–2.4	0
Urban employees' occupational injury insurance	1	0
Total of Social Insurance	29.4–31.4	11
Urban Housing Fund	5	5
Total	34.4–36.4	16

Therefore, the phenomenon of temporary employment with no or less social insurances nor labor contact for rural migrant workers not only results from the local governments' discriminant treatments, but also has its cause in the insurance system's design, because it is an important means for enterprises to compress the labor cost in competition. However, what we want to know is whether the welfare burden of the enterprises and the governments result from the huge size of labor, or high welfare spending level for certain social members. Consider the differences of urban employees' basic endowment insurance between SOEs and non-state enterprises (NSEs) as examples (Figure 14-4). During the period 1999–2010, the pension fund received per person increased in both SOEs and NSEs. In terms of pension fund received per person, the ratio of SOEs to NSEs is about 1.04, with no significant difference between the two. However, in terms of pension fund spent per person, the ratio of SOEs to NSEs is about 1.54, and the annual average growth rate of SOEs pension fund spent per person reaches 14.67%, which is much higher than the 8.64% of growth rate in NSEs. That

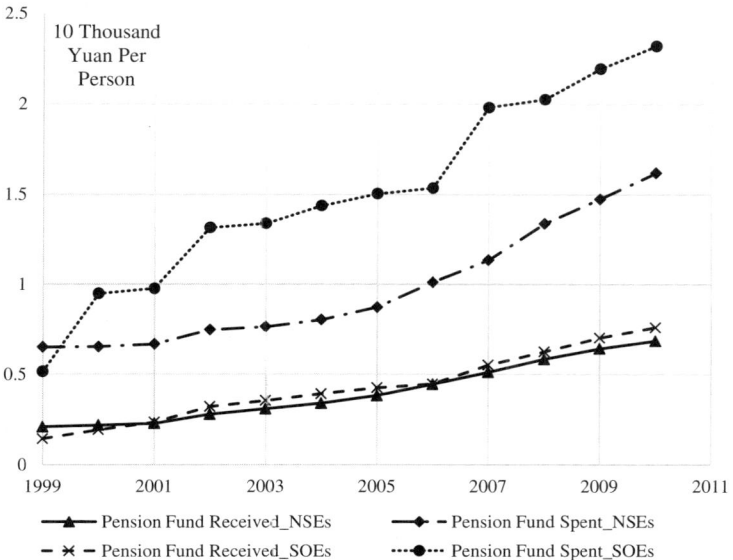

Figure 14-4: The differences of pension fund received per capita and spent per capita of urban employees' basic endowment insurance between SOEs and NSEs (1999–2010).
Data Sources: *China Labor Statistical Yearbook in 2011*.

is, the problem of increasing insurance spending and heavy social welfare burden for enterprises and governments is not just the too-big coverage, but serious inequality in welfare and security products, and the employees' welfare level in SOEs is generally too high.

There is not only the staff privilege of SOEs in social welfare issues, but local governments in urban areas also provide more welfare for local *hukou* workers than for migrant workers. Consider urban employees' social insurances in Shanghai as an example; for employees with Shanghai *hukou* in the urban labor market, enterprises need to pay "Five social insurances," and for migrant workers without Shanghai *hukou* in the urban labor market, enterprises only need to pay "Three social insurances," including the endowment insurance, medical insurance, and occupational injury insurance. Therefore, insurances paid for local workers and migrant workers respectively increase the cost of enterprises by 37% and 28.5% of the employees' wages (Table 14-2).

Comparing the basic social insurances conditions across nations Table 14-3 shows that the proportion of social insurances paid by Chinese urban enterprises is relatively high; especially the employers' contribution ratio is significantly higher than the personal contribution ratio.

In short, in the process of further development of urbanization and citizenization, as for the issues of regulating the labor market and standardizing

Table 14-2: The social welfare differences between workers with and without Shanghai *Hukou* in the urban labor market.

Types of Insurance	Workers with Shanghai *Hukou* in urban labor market		Migrant worker without Shanghai *Hukou* in urban labor market	
	By enterprises (%)	By individuals (%)	By enterprises (%)	By individuals (%)
Endowment Insurance	22	8	22	8
Medical Insurance	12	2	6	1
Occupational Injury Insurance	1	0	1	0
Maternity Insurance	1	0		/
Unemployment Insurance	2	1		/
Total	37	11	29	9

Table 14-3: The basic labor social insurances conditions across nations.

Nations	Payment rate		
	By enterprises (in %)	By individuals (in %)	Total (in %)
Australia	0.00	9.00	9.00
Belgium	13.07	24.80	37.87
Brazil	8.00	21.00	29.00
Canada	6.73	7.44	14.17
China	11.00	29.00	40.00
France	9.90	32.68	42.58
Germany	20.43	20.85	41.28
India	13.75	22.36	36.11
Indonesia	2.00	7.24	9.24
Italy	9.19	31.78	40.97
Japan	13.12	13.77	26.89
Mexico	2.00	8.60	10.60
Poland	22.71	17.38	40.09
Russia	0.00	30.20	30.20
South Africa	1.00	1.00	2.00
South Korea	7.79	8.74	16.53
Spain	6.25	31.08	37.33
Sweden	7.00	20.92	27.92
Thailand	5.00	5.20	10.20
The United States	7.65	9.70	17.35

Data Sources: *People's Daily*, http://finance.ce.cn/rolling/201209/11/t20120911_16944527.shtml.

Notes: The social insurances of Chinese workers in rural areas are not included in the table.

the workers' social insurances, enterprises and local governments both are facing rising labor costs given the current social security system. In fact, compared to most other countries in the world, the level of social insurances for China's urban employees is relatively higher. Rising labor costs due to social insurances are largely related to the fact that certain groups of labor forces enjoy a much higher level of social welfare. In other words, the existing social security system is not only contrary to the principle of low or minimum level, but also is contrary to the principle of unity and full coverage. Liu Xiaofeng et al. (2010) pointed out that even in the absence of wage discrimination in China's labor market, unequal public services can also cause discord, and this discord will intensify with the growth of the urban economy. Therefore, as for the labor social insurance system reform, more groups including rural migrant workers are needed to be brought into the unified social security system. Moreover, the reform of welfare distribution caused by the current social insurance system is needed to be carried out.

4.2 The Social Security Status of the Rural Migrant Workers and Their Insured Will

Most Chinese rural migrant workers have lower incomes and a large part of their income needs to be sent back home for other family members. Rural migrant workers therefore in the urban areas consume less and save more. According to the FAO[17] of the United Nations, the Engel coefficient adjusted shows that families of rural migrant workers are only just entering the subsistence phase (Table 14-4). Therefore, 10% or even higher of their wages spent on insurances is a relatively heavy burden for rural migrant workers, thus greatly weakening their insurance willingness.

Besides, the conversion of social security across regions and insurances' categories will also affect the insured willingness of rural migrant workers. At present, migration of rural migrant workers has relative instability. According to the dynamic monitoring database of migrants in Beijing, Shanghai, and Guangzhou in 2012, the number of rural migrant workers who have migrated at least three times in their migration history accounts

Table 14-4: The economic situation of rural migrant workers' families in Beijing, Shanghai, and Guangzhou in 2012.

	Beijing	Shanghai	Guangzhou
Engel coefficient	0.424	0.475	0.436
Engel coefficient adjusted*	0.556	0.601	0.553
The ratio of remittances to income	13.13%	12.73%	14.31%

Data Sources: Sample survey database of migrants' dynamic monitoring in Beijing, Shanghai, and Guangzhou in 2012.
Note: *The denominator equals the family expenditure minus the rental costs.

---

[17]Food and Agriculture Organization.

for 61%. But in China maternity insurance, unemployment insurance, and occupational injury insurance could not transfer with migration. And because of China's social insurances taking the method of "combination of social pooling and individual account," according to *Social Insurance Law*[18] in 2010, *The Interim method of Urban Employees' Basic Endowment Insurance Transfer*[19] in 2010 and *The Interim method of Medical Insurance Transfer For Migrant Workers*[20] in 2010, the medical insurance and endowment insurance can be partly transferred across regions. And employees' endowment insurance can be only transferred with personal account and 12% of the pooling accounts; employees' medical insurance can be only transferred with personal account; employees' urban housing fund can be applied for full extraction. In addition, different types of endowment insurances for rural migrant workers still do not have the practical transfer measures. (In 2012, the Ministry of Human Resources And Social Security issued the *Interim Measures Between Urban And Rural Endowment Insurance System (Draft)*,[21] and it is expected that the conversion methods between different types of endowment insurance will be carried out in 2013.)

The heavy burden of social insurance payment rate for migrant workers and lack of efficient methods for interregional transfer and cross-categories transfer of social insurances jointly reduce the insured willingness of rural migrant workers. According to the survey conducted by the Development Research Center of State Council in 2010, there are 30.4% of rural migrant workers who do not participate in any insurances in the "receiving" place; the proportion of rural migrant workers who participate in endowment insurance and occupational injury insurance is relatively high, both more than 50%. In another report of *Annual Statistical Bulletin of Human Resources and Social Security Development* issued by the Chinese Ministry of Human Resources and Social Security, at the end of 2011, the proportion of migrant workers who participate in urban employees' basic endowment insurance is only 16.4% (Table 14-5).

---

[18] In Chinese,《社会保险法》.
[19] In Chinese,《城镇企业职工基本养老保险关系转移接续暂行办法》.
[20] In Chinese,《流动就业人员医保转移接续暂行办法》.
[21] In Chinese,《城乡养老保险制度衔接暂行办法（征求意见稿）》.

Table 14-5: The ratio of rural migrant workers who participate in the "Five Social Insurances And Urban Housing Fund" in several investigations.

Year	Sources		Urban housing fund	Basic endowment insurance	Basic medical insurance	Unemployment insurance	Occupational injury insurance	Maternity insurance	Uninsured ratio
2005	The Ministry of Labour and Social Security		—	33.70%	21.60%	10.30%	31%	5.50%	—
2006	Services Survey Center of the National Bureau of Statistics		4.76%	26.63%	26.23%	15.35%	32.54%	—	—
2010	Development Research Center of State Council	Receiving Place	—	50.60%	41.60%	29.20%	50.20%	22.40%	26.90%
		Sending Place	—	11.80%	65%	—	—	—	30.40%

4.3 Training of Rural Migrant Workers and Their Living Capabilities in Urban Areas

Rural migrant workers have strong homogeneity, which undermines their competence in the labor market. Borjas (1987) pointed out that although there may be substitute or complementary effects of immigration to different groups in the labor market, the increase of immigrants has a significant negative impact on their own wages. Therefore, in addition to social security and the endowment of urban civil rights, it can be another important aspect of citizenization to improve the heterogeneity of rural migrant workers, that is, to enhance their human capital accumulation, to increase their labor productivity, and finally, to facilitate the transformation of rural migrant workers into modern industrial workers. After two years of *Rural Migrant Workers' Training Plan (2003–2010)* issued by the General Office of the State Council, a survey on the quality of rural migrant workers' life conducted by Services Survey Center of the National Bureau of Statistics shows that the proportion of rural migrant workers involved in vocational training is 47.23%. As for the training situation in vocational schools, since 2006 the proportion of students with rural *hukou* in vocational schools has gone through a trend of increase, and this proportion is higher than students with urban *hukou*. By 2011 the proportion rises more than 10 percentage points, and students with rural *hukou* have an annual increase rate of 9.8%, faster than the overall students' growth rate of 6% in vocational schools (Table 14-6).

Table 14-6: The scale and proportion of students with urban *hukou* in vocational schools.

Year	The number of students in vocational schools (person)	Students with urban *hukou* (person)	Proportion of students with urban *hukou*
2006	3,208,150	1,925,786	60.03%
2007	3,671,475	2,523,705	68.74%
2009	4,142,578	3,034,340	73.25%
2010	4,209,752	3,149,865	74.82%
2011	4,293,723	3,073,155	71.57%

Data Sources: China Labor Statistical Yearbook.

Looking at the financial sources of vocational schools, since 1990, the absolute amount of funding from government education expenditure is increasing, yet the government funding proportion to total funding is decreasing. Funding from enterprise support only accounts for a small portion of total funding; furthermore, in 1990 it accounted for 14.75% of total funding, and in 2006 it only accounted for 2.10%, while in the same year, 30.68% funding was from the government. Therefore, the government plays a very important role in supporting vocational training, yet not only is enterprise support decreasing tremendously, it never plays an important part in supporting vocational education (Table 14-7).

4.4 Housing Projects of Rural Migrant Workers and Citizenization

The longer their stay in urban areas, the more migrants want to stay, and the possibility of continuing to live in urban areas will see a significant increase (Zhu Baoshu, 1999; Ren Yuan, 2006). Particularly with the

Table 14-7: The scale and sources of fund of vocational schools.

Year	Total (100 million yuan)	Sources of funding			
		Undertaking expenditure fund (100 million yuan)		Company expenses fund (100 million yuan)	
			Proportion (%)		Proportion (%)
1990	15.60	6.10	39	2.30	14.74
1995	53.70	13.18	25	4.44	8.28
2000	56.94	21.91	38	3.22	5.66
2001	68.15	23.61	35	3.24	4.75
2002	67.37	28.18	42	2.80	4.15
2003	81.40	30.50	37	2.80	3.44
2004	112.50	37.40	33	5.20	4.62
2005	123.40	37.80	31	3.80	3.08
2006	143.10	43.90	31	3.00	2.10
2007	198.20	—	—	—	—
2008	204.43	—	—	—	—
2009	237.30	—	—	—	—
2010	260.42	—	—	—	—
2011	271.53	—	—	—	—

Data Sources: China Labor Statistical Yearbook.

rapid development of urbanization, the rural migrant workers experience an intergenerational differentiation that divides the rural migrant workers into the first generation and the new generation. And the significant differences between the two are that the new generation in the lifestyle is much closer to the local urban population, with more willingness to stay in the city and their level of human capital is also relatively higher. However, the high cost of living has become the main factor with regard to China's citizenization of rural migrant workers (Chen Guanggui, 2004), not to mention buying their own houses to settle down in urban areas. According to the 2012 sample survey of migrants' dynamic monitoring in Beijing, Shanghai, and Guangzhou, private rental housing is the main occupation choice for rural migrant workers. Of the total rural migrant workers in Beijing, Shanghai, and Guangzhou, renters account for 58.42%, 73.36%, and 60.59%, respectively. The rural migrant workers families that have rent expenditures account for 63.95%, 80.45%, and 70.23%, respectively, in Beijing, Shanghai, and Guangzhou. Furthermore, in the rural migrant workers' families that have rent expenditures, 10% of their household income goes toward rental expenditure, and 20% of their household spending goes toward rental expenditure (Table 14-8).

Housing has become a key threshold to the citizenization of rural migrant workers in China. Some local governments have attempted to provide housing for migrant workers, including public rental housing and low-income housing only for release. For example, Hangzhou of Zhejiang province provides rental apartments for migrant workers, and the size is 10 square meters one person, and the apartments' rent is controlled by the Municipal Price Bureau; Chongqing establishes the "blue-collar apartment" mainly in small size as low-income housing for migrant workers in

Table 14-8: The situation of average rent in the rural migrant workers' families in Beijing Shanghai and Guangzhou in 2012.

Regions	The monthly average rent (yuan)	The proportion of rent to household expenditures	The proportion of rent to household income
Beijing	588.51	20.35%	11.94%
Shanghai	482.28	18.88%	9.62%
Guangzhou	408.25	18.50%	10.18%

the industrial park areas, and the project is undertaken by the enterprises and the local government. There are also housing arrangements in the form of affordable housing, such as Ganjiang of Jiangxi province provides the "new citizen apartment" for rural migrant workers.

Overall, low income and high housing prices jointly make it quite difficult for rural migrant workers to buy a house in the resettlement areas. So, for facilitating stable migration, it is very important to accelerate the low-income housing or public rental housing construction and avoid welfare-oriented migration and reduce the opportunity cost of land.

4.5 The Cost of Citizenization of Rural Migrant Workers

4.5.1 The existing research on the cost of rural migrant workers' citizenization

Most of the rural migrant workers intend to live permanently in urban areas. According to the sample survey of migrants' dynamic monitoring in Beijing, Shanghai, and Guangzhou in 2012, about 78% of the labor migration has rural *hukou*, while more than 73% of these people (rural migrant workers) plan to stay in Beijing, Shanghai, and Guangzhou in the next 5 years or even longer. The stable residence of these rural labor forces greatly enriches the urban sector labor supply in both size and species. So to provide the necessary social insurances and public services for the rural migrant workers is of great significance for urbanization development. In accordance with the above, citizenization is a process of sharing the urban civil rights with the rural migrant workers. Inevitably, some public costs and private costs will occur, which requires the establishment of a reasonable and effective sharing mechanism among the governments, enterprises, and rural migrant workers themselves.

Most of the research divides the costs of citizenization of rural migrant workers into public costs and private costs (Zhang Guosheng, 2009; Zhou Xiaogang, 2010). Public costs include the cost of investment in infrastructure and public management, and private costs are the lifestyle shifting costs from rural to urban, the cost of housing, the cost of children's education, and social security costs. Nevertheless, there are huge differences in studies on the costs of citizenization of rural migrant workers since 2004. For example, in 2005 the Chinese Academy of Sciences' Report shows that the average cost of citizenization of rural migrant workers is 25,000 yuan per person, and since 2009, the average cost per person calculated by studies has reached from 80,000 yuan to 100,000 yuan (Table 14-9).

4.5.2 A brief calculation of the citizenization cost of rural migrant workers

I. Some basic assumptions

In this chapter, a brief calculation of the citizenization cost of rural migrant workers will be conducted. And we will focus on only the expenses that are more pressing and directly contribute to the citizenization of rural migrant workers. Here, the following assumptions will be made:

1) The cost will be calculated in 2010 prices and generally using 2010 as the basic situation;
2) According to the sample survey of migrants' dynamic monitoring in Beijing, Shanghai, and Guangzhou in 2012, it is assumed that first migration age of rural migrant workers is 24.21 years;
3) The citizenization cost of rural migrant workers will take the individual migrant worker as a unit. To avoid double counting, the calculation will start with the following situation: A representative immigrant first enters the urban labor market in his 24th year, and the major events in his life cycle will be involved, such as vocational training, his children's entrance to school, and retirement (after retirement the worker will live relying on his own pension and therefore, the costs of the elderly living with their migrant worker child are not involved in the citizenization cost of their child);
4) In accordance with the life expectancy of the country's population in 2010, a 72.5-year life expectancy of the rural migrant worker is assumed. This rural migrant worker's retirement age is assumed to be 60 years. Therefore, this rural migrant worker is expected to live 48.5 years in the urban areas, and pays the insurance and participates in labor force for 36 years and receives the pension for 12.5 years;
5) According to the sample survey of migrants' dynamic monitoring in Beijing, Shanghai, and Guangzhou in 2012, it can be assumed that each of the migrant workers' families has 1.51 children (statistically) on average, and the migration probability for a child is 0.5. Since most of the

Table 14-9: Different studies relating to the citizenization costs of rural migrant workers.

Year	Citizenization cost (yuan/person)	Scope	Contents	Sources
2004	5,000	Small towns	Citizenization of rural population	Chen Guanggui
	10,000	Large and medium-sized cities	Citizenization of rural population	
	20,000	Megacities	Citizenization of rural population	China Sustainable Development Strategy Report by Chinese Academy of Sciences
2005	25,000		Citizenization of rural population	
2006	20,000	Small cities	Supporting municipal public facilities	The New Requirements of the Migrant Workers to Urban Construction by The Research Group of the Ministry of Construction
	30,000	Medium-sized cities	Supporting municipal public facilities	
	60,000	Large cities	Supporting municipal public facilities	
	100,000	Megacities	Supporting municipal public facilities (excluding operation and management costs)	
2009	80,000		Government spending, including education and affordable housing for short-term expenses as one third of the total cost, the old-age insurance subsidies for the long-term costs as 40% to 50% of the total cost	Development Research Center of the State Council

(Continued)

Table 14-9: *(Continued)*

Year	Citizenization cost (yuan/person)	Scope	Contents	Sources
2009	100,000	Southeast coast areas	The first generation of rural migrant workers	Social Costs of citizenization of Rural Migrant Workers: The Perspective and Policy Options of the Big Developing Countries in Transition by Zhang Guosheng
	90,000	Southeast coast areas	The new generation of rural migrant workers	
	60,000	Inland	The first generation of rural migrant workers	
	50,000	Inland	The new generation of rural migrant workers	
2009	98,000		Public costs of 73,500 and private costs of 24,700	China Urban Development Report 2009
2010	100,000			China Development Report 2010: China's new-approach urbanization strategy to promote the development of human beings by China Development Research Foundation

spouses migrate with the migrant workers into urban areas according to the dynamic monitoring, it is assumed that the rural migrant worker in the city has about 0.755 children, and 0.3775 children will migrate with the worker;

6) The citizenization costs mainly include: the establishment of a social security system for rural migrant workers, the costs of education for migrant children, vocational training costs of the migrant workers, and urban housing costs;
7) This representative migrant worker does not participate in any other form of social insurances;
8) Ignoring the future discount rate.

II. The social security costs for the rural migrant worker

We suppose that social security for the rural migrant worker will take the same method of "Five Social Insurances and Urban Housing Fund" as local workers (Table 14-10), and use the average wage of 36,500 yuan of employees in urban areas in 2010 as the payment base and this wage remains unchanged. In accordance with the Convention on the Minimum Standards of Social Security by ILO,[22] the minimum wage substitute rate

Table 14-10: The social security costs for the rural migrant worker.

	By individuals	By enterprises	
Basic endowment insurance	8.0%	20.0%	**Allocated to each**
Basic medical insurance	1.0%	2.0%	**year of the stay**
Occupational injury insurance	2.0%	6.0%	**in urban areas**
Maternity insurance	0.0%	1.0%	**of every migrant**
Unemployment insurance	0.0%	0.4%	**worker**
Urban housing fund	5.0%	5.0%	
Total	16.0%	34.4%	
(yuan)	**Annual Payment**	**Total Payment**	
Total for enterprises	12,569.42	452,498.98	9,329.88
Total for individuals	5,846.24	210,464.64	4,339.48
Total for governments	2,265.42	28,317.73	583.87

[22] International Labor Organization.

of pension is 55%. Suppose that except for the endowment insurance, other types of insurances do not need an additional spending from the governments to meet the budget. Then, it can be calculated that if the costs are divided into the rural migrant worker's 48.5 years stay in urban areas, the annual expenditures are 9330 yuan, 4339 yuan, and 583.87 yuan for the enterprises, individuals, and the governments, respectively.

III. The education costs for the migrant children

The education costs for the rural migrant worker's mainly include the costs in pre-school, primary, and secondary education, that is, the migrant children's education spending from kindergarten, elementary, middle, and high school. In accordance with the current relevant policies and regulations, the migrant children will receive 9-year compulsory education in the place where their parents work and mainly enter the public schools.

There is a huge expenditure gap between rural and urban education. Since migrant children migrate into cities with their parents, they face an additional education expenditure. Part of the issue can be solved through central government redistribution and local education transfer payments. Table 14-11 is based on the basic fact of education fund per student in both urban and rural areas in 2010. Since it has been assumed that each migrant worker has 0.3775 children with her or him, the children's education costs are paid by governments and individuals (parents). Then, it can be found that for this representative migrant worker, her or his migrant children will increase the annual personal spend by about 114.55 yuan, and increase the annual governmental spend by about 131.76 yuan.

IV. The vocational training costs of the rural migrant worker

We postulate that the rural migrant workers receive job training in vocational schools, and *ceteris paribus*, the migrant receives the same amount of education as others. According to the *China Labor Statistical Yearbook 2012*, in 2010, vocational schools trained 4.68 million person*times the number of graduated students is 3.71 million. If the training period is 1 year, then each student has accepted about 1.26 times job training. Therefore, it is assumed that the representative migrant worker participates in 1.26 times vocational training within his 48.5 years life in the city. In addition, because the revenue and expenditures of training funds of vocational schools are close to

Table 14-11: The education costs for the migrant children.

Costs (yuan)	Nursery	Primary school	Middle school	Senior middle school	Total	Allocated to each year of the stay in urban areas of every migrant worker
Individual costs in urban	1,726.51	1,008.66	1,263.93	3,386.71		
Government costs in urban	1,875.34	4,355.64	5,596.38	4,844.84		
Individual costs in rural	—	684.07	812.72	2,459.03		
Government costs in rural	—	3,876.24	5,061.33	3,821.46		
Net increasing costs for individuals	1,726.51	324.59	451.21	927.68		
Net increase in costs for governments	1,875.34	479.40	535.05	1,023.38		
Total net increase in costs for individuals during the school period	8,632.55	1,947.52	1,353.64	2,783.04	14,716.75	114.55
Total net increase in costs for governments during the school period	9,376.70	2,876.39	1,605.15	3,070.14	16,928.39	131.76

Data Sources: Funding for the National Education Statistical Yearbook 2011.

each other, we use the funding revenue and its structure to proximate funding expenditure and its structure. In 2006, enterprises funding accounted for 2.1%, assuming the ratio remains unchanged. Therefore, according to the situation in 2010, for 1.26 times training of the migrant worker, the enterprise needed to pay 160.49 yuan and the government needed to pay 9468.70 yuan. Therefore, the migrant annually receives 3.31 yuan payment from the enterprise and 195.23 yuan payment from the government.

V. Temporary housing support costs of rural migrant workers during transition period

As mentioned earlier, the migrant worker needs temporary low-income housing support when just entering the city. And this temporary social security is different from urban housing fund, because the latter aims at providing help for permanent settlement. Allocation of low-income housing is mainly in the form of rent subsidies, with rent control houses and rent relief as the supplement.

According to the relevant policies and regulations in 2003, the low-rental housing requires living space less than seven square meters per person. Take Yangzhou for example. From January to March 2013, the average housing price is around 7,378 yuan/m^2. According to property law, property rights of estate are limited to 70 years. Then the annual spending on temporary housing is about 105.4 yuan/m^2. On the other hand, the low-income housing costs only 10 yuan/m^2 per month and the government subsidizes 9.25 yuan/m^2. This also means that the government needs to pay a monthly subsidy of 8.033 yuan for the representative rural migrant worker. If a low-rent housing contract is valid for 8 years, the migrant worker living for 8 years in space of seven square meters needs to pay a total amount of 504 yuan or 10.39 per year. And at the meantime, the government needs to pay 5,398.4 yuan for this migrant worker totally or 111 per year.

VI. Total cost of citizenization of the rural migrant worker

According to the above calculations, Table 14-12 lists the four main costs involved in the process of citizenization of rural migrant workers. Different from other studies, the costs in this chapter also include the cost of

Table 14-12: Total costs of citizenization of the rural migrant worker.

(Yuan)	By enterprises	By governments	By individuals	Total
The social security costs	9,329.88	583.87	4,339.48	14,253.23
The education costs for migrant children	0	131.76	114.55	246.31
The training costs	3.31	195.23	0	198.54
Temporary housing costs	0	111.31	10.39	121.7
Total	9,333.19	1,022.17	4,464.42	14,819.78

vocational training and temporary housing support from the perspective of a representative rural migrant worker.

The data shows that for the representative rural migrant worker, her or his one year in the city will incur 14,800 yuan costs for social insurances, children's education, vocational training, temporary housing support, and so on. If she or he stays in the city for the rest of her or his life (for 48.5 years), the total costs are expected to reach 718,800 yuan. In accordance with the above sharing costs of citizenization, the enterprises will undertake nearly 63% of the total costs, and the individuals will undertake 30% of the total costs while the governments will undertake only 7% of the total costs. Therefore, the labor costs for enterprises will undoubtedly rise since citizenization in the current institution.

If we change certain assumptions and *ceteris paribus*, the amount of the costs and sharing proportions for enterprises, individuals, and the governments are subject to change.

First condition: Improving the level of pension received. Change the wage substitute rate of pension for rural migrant workers to 100% and *ceteris paribus*. Then it can be calculated that the annual costs of citizenization for the migrant worker are increased to 18,500 yuan. The enterprises, governments, and individuals share the proportion of 49%, 28%, and 23% respectively.

Second condition: Reducing the burden of pension fund payment. Reduce the enterprises' payment rate of the basic endowment insurance from 20% to 8% and *ceteris paribus*. Then it can be calculated that the annual costs of citizenization for the migrant worker are reduced to 12,100 yuan. The enterprises, governments, and individuals share the proportion of 48%, 17%, and 35% respectively.

For the current condition, enterprises and individuals share most of the costs of citizenization. And both improving the level of pension received and reducing pension fund payment by enterprises will cause a change from the current situation, and the governments will play a more important role in the process of citizenization after change. Finally, it is needed to be cautious about the above conclusion, because:

First, the above costs of citizenization of rural migrant worker are based on 2010 prices and conditions, and do not take into account the discount rate of future costs, so there would be an inevitable deviation in the time-series in designation of costs' sharing mechanisms.

Second, the above social security system is constructed in accordance with the current social insurance system for urban workers, and the results do show that the enterprises in the process of citizenization take on too much responsibility.

Third, in this section, we postulate homogeneity among workers, so we discuss the citizenization condition of a representative rural migrant worker, especially her or his annual costs in citizenization. In this regard, our contribution to current literature is that annual cost will make it more rational for the "migratory bird pattern." And another contribution is that we pay more attention to the sharing proportions of enterprises, individuals, and the government. Most other researches on this topic are concerned with the overall cost of citizenization of all migrant workers. However, the overall costs of citizenization depend on the migration scale, migration time, migration age, the different civil rights between rural and urban areas, as well as some specific cases. For example, a considerable portion of the migrant workers already have social insurance, and the problem for them is the transfer cost across categories and regions; also a considerable portion of the migrant workers' children have been incorporated into the urban compulsory education system. Thus the aggregation is much more likely to overrate the total direct costs of citizenization, and makes it more difficult to figure out how much the cost is. And these researches always impressed us with the huge cost of citizenization, and lead us to tend to ignore the contribution of rural migrant workers in the urban areas.

Fourth, as for the problem of education of migrant children, it is needed to make the redistribution of the educational resources between the "receiving" places and "sending" places, or increase the central government's overall fund allocation to the region. For the migrant workers who have already social insurances, lower transfer costs of social insurances among regions and categories are very important, that is, to enhance the flexibility of the social security system is an important task during citizenization.

Fifth, the citizenization of rural migrant workers not only incurs costs, but also, it contributes to the urbanization process and development, as citizenization can facilitate the human capital accumulation and increase the labor productivities. So we should not just consider the cost, we also need to think much bigger and brighter of the social benefit from the citizenization of rural migrant workers.

Sixth, we need to make a clear definition of the existing civil rights in both rural and urban areas. In rural areas, clarification of the civil rights means clarification of the wealth the rural population possesses. At present, due to the absence of a sound system of rural land ownership, rural migrant workers lack wealth support for their citizenization and have much higher opportunity cost to leave their hometown. Thus, under the condition of limited capacity of government and enterprises, increasing the rural productivity and establishing the land exit mechanism should be an important means for promoting citizenization.

REFERENCES

Borjas. G. J. (1987). Immigrants, minorities, and labor market competition. *Industrial and Labor Relations Review*, 40(3): 382–392.

Chen, Guanggui (2004). Housing price, the costs of citizenization of rural population and China's urbanization. *Chinese Rural Economy*, (3): 43–47.

Chen, Zhao and Lu Ming (2008). From segmentation to integration: The political economy of urban–rural economic growth and social harmony. *Economic Research Journal*, (1): 21–32.

Development Research Center of State Council (2011). *Civilianizing the Rural Migrants: Institutional Innovation and Top-level Policy Design*. Beijing: China Development Press.

Duan, Chengrong and Ma Xueyang (2011). A study on the new situation of the younger generation of farmer-turned migrant workers in China. *Population and Economics*, (4): 16–22.

Han, Changfu (2006). The trend and perspective of rural migrant workers in China. *Economic Research Journal*, (12): 4–12.

Huang, Ningyang (2012). *Studies on Chinese Rural Labor Transfer during the New Period*. Beijing: Science Press.

Jian, Xinhua and Huang Kun (2007). Up-to-date situation of rural migrant workers in China: A survey of 765 rural migrant workers. *Population Research*, (6): 37–44.

Li, Peilin and Li Wei (2010). The economic situation and social attitudes of rural migrant workers in recent years. *Social Science in China*, (1): 119–131.

Li, Shuzhuo, Ren, Yike and Yang, Xusong (2006). Analysis of whole social network properties of rural–urban migrants in China. *Chinese Journal of Population Science*, (3): 19–29.
Lin, Yifu (2003). *New Structural Economics*. Beijing: Peking University Press.
Liu, Chuanjiang (2005). Citizenization of rural migrant workers in the urban and rural development. *Population Research*, (4): 48–51.
Liu, Chuanjiang (2008). *Studies on the Citizenization of Chinese Rural Migrant Workers*. Beijing: People's Publishing House.
Liu, Chuanjiang (2009). The impact of double "*Hukou*" wall" on citizenization of rural migrant workers. *Economist*, (10): 66–72.
Liu, Chuanjiang (2010). China's new generation of migrant workers: Characteristics, problems and countermeasures. *Population Research*, (2): 34–39.
Liu Xiaofeng, Chen, Zhao and Lu, Ming (2010). Social integration and economic growth: endogenous policy change of urbanization and urban development. *Journal of World Economy*, (6): 60–80.
Research Group on Strategic Issues of China's Rural Workers (2009). General Report on Chinese Migrant Workers Status and Their Development Trends. *Reform*, (2): 5–27.
Ren, Yuan (2006). Gradual precipitation and residence — induced long term residence: Analysis on floating population's residence pattern in urban China. *Chinese Journal of Population Science*, (3): 67–72.
Research Group on Strategic Issues of China's Rural Workers. (2009). *General Report on Chinese Migrant Workers Status and Their Development Trends. Reform*, (2): 5–27.
Wei, Houkai (1994). Discussion on the issue of China's rural industrialization. *Economist*, (5): 75–82.
Wang, Zongping and Duan Chengrong (2010). Analysis on the characteristics of the second generation peasant-workers. *Population Research*, (2): 39–44.
Zhang, Guosheng (2009). A study on transformation of peasant workers into urban residents in the perspective of social cost. *China Soft Science Magazine*, (4): 56–69.
Zhang, Yuan and Lu Ming (2009). Does the social network help to increase the wages of migrant peasant-workers? *Management World*, (3): 45–54.
Zhou, Xiaogang (2010). Research on the Problem of Rural Workers' Citizenization During Urbanization in Central Region: Taking the Example of Jiangxi Province. Master Dissertation, Nanchang University, p. 486.
Zhu Baoshu (1999). Analysis of immigrants' residence situation in Shanghai. *Chinese Journal of Population Science*, (3): 38–45.

Index

age structure, 357, 359, 360, 375, 377–379, 381, 388, 389
aging, 357–361, 373, 377, 379, 383, 385, 390

championship competition, 155
Chinese style federalism, 175–177, 180, 183, 200, 201, 203, 206
citizenization, 463–466, 468–471, 476, 480, 485–492, 495–498
consumption behavior, 112, 113, 117, 118, 121, 130, 132, 133, 135, 136, 138

demographic, 357, 358, 360, 377, 379, 383, 388, 390, 391
demographic dividend, 358, 360, 377, 379

economic development, 1, 2, 4, 5, 7, 9, 16–21, 26–32, 37–39, 211–213. 217, 219, 227, 230–232, 235–239, 241
external imbalance, 177, 198, 199

financial repression, 211, 220, 228–242
fiscal system, 321–323, 325–327, 353

globalization, 1, 2, 4, 11, 18, 19, 28, 33–35, 38
growth strategy, 17

industrialization, 245, 252, 254, 262, 263, 335, 339, 340, 347, 349

intergenerational income mobility, 427–435, 440–443, 446, 448–451, 453, 454, 456–458
internal imbalance, 177, 198

land-based finance (ing), 321, 322, 336–339, 341, 342, 345–347, 349–351, 353–355
local governments' behavior, 321

mechanisms of intergenerational income mobility, 440
migrant workers, 463–465, 468–474, 476, 479, 480, 482–498

new urbanization, 262, 263, 269, 270, 272

potential economic growth, 41–43, 45, 46, 51, 60, 66
productivity, 396, 416, 418

real estate market, 277–281, 283, 286, 287, 290, 293, 297, 302, 305–308, 310, 312, 314, 315, 317
reform in the margin, 148, 155, 156, 163, 165, 166, 169
return of education, 396, 416, 418, 419
rural migrant workers, 463–465, 468, 469, 472–474, 476, 479, 482–493, 495–498
rural workers, 464, 465, 471–476

total fertility rate, 357, 360, 362, 369, 370,
    373, 375, 376, 383, 384
trade in value added, 71, 74
transaction cost, 147, 154, 157, 167

under-consumption, 112, 113, 118, 126,
    128, 129, 132, 134, 135, 138, 141, 142

urban system, 245, 254–256, 258
urbanization, 339–341, 348, 349, 352, 353,
    358, 377, 381, 395–397, 402, 403, 414,
    463–473, 476, 480, 487, 488, 491, 497